Psychology

Psychology

An Introduction

Fifth Edition

Charles G. Morris

University of Michigan

Prentice-Hall, Inc.
Englewood Cliffs, New Jersey 07632

Library of Congress Cataloging in Publication Data

Morris, Charles G.
    Psychology : an introduction.

    Bibliography.
    Includes indexes.
    1. Psychology.   I. Prentice-Hall, Inc.   II. Title
BF121.M598 1984   150   84-22304
ISBN 0-13-734385-X

Printed in the United States of America.

10 9 8 7 6 5 4 3 2

PRENTICE-HALL INTERNATIONAL, INC., *London*
PRENTICE-HALL OF AUSTRALIA, PTY. LIMITED, *Sydney*
PRENTICE-HALL OF CANADA, LTD., *Toronto*
PRENTICE-HALL HISPANO AMERICANA, S.A. *Mexico*
PRENTICE-HALL OF INDIA PRIVATE LIMITED, *New Delhi*
PRENTICE-HALL OF JAPAN, INC., *Tokyo*
PRENTICE-HALL OF SOUTHEAST ASIA PTE. LTD., *Singapore*
WHITEHALL BOOKS LIMITED, *Wellington, New Zealand*

Credits:
Art Director: Florence Dara Silverman
Production Editor: Jeanne Hoeting
Book Designer: Joan Greenfield
Page Layout: Joan Greenfield
Cover Designer: Florence Dara Silverman/Joan Greenfield
Cover Photo: Fred Burrell
Line Art: Danmark and Michaels, Inc.
Photo Researcher: Ilene Cherna
Manufacturing Buyer: Ray Keating

ISBN 0-13-734385-X

Overview

Contents

vii

6: Learning   185

7: Memory   219

Preface

A year ago Prentice-Hall asked teachers of introductory psychology to describe the "ideal" introductory psychology text. Their response was that it should be (1) clearly written, (2) interesting to students, (3) easy to study from, (4) balanced in coverage, and (5) up-to-date. On these five dimensions the Fourth Edition of *Psychology: An Introduction* was rated favorably by users. But in all five areas there were suggestions for improvement. Closing these gaps has been a major goal of the Fifth Edition.

Features of the Fifth Edition

Clarity

I have been through the book sentence by sentence at various stages of the revision process, reworking language that seemed in any way unclear, uneven, or unsatisfactory. In the process, the chapters on memory (Chapter 7) and cognition (Chapter 8) were essentially rewritten from scratch and fortified with numerous tactical examples. There is now no comparison between these chapters in the Fifth Edition and the corresponding chapters in the previous edition.

Other areas of improvement in clarity are: the discussion of sensory thresholds (Chapter 3); the sections on response acquisition, aversive conditioning, and social learning theory (Chapter 6); and the discussion of Carl Rogers' personality theory (Chapter 12). The sections on pure and applied research (Chapter 1); Gestalt principles (Chapter 4); primary drives and theories of emotions (Chapter 5); physical and motor development (Chapter 11); trait theory and Freudian theory (Chapter 12); stress and ways of coping (Chapter 13); affective disorders and substance abuse (Chapter 14); and attitudes and cognitive consistency (Chapter 16) were also substantially reworked for clarity and concision.

Student Interest

Student interest has always been a characteristic of this text, but the Fifth Edition contains much new material that is both interesting and at the same time helps illustrate important concepts. For example, new case studies have been added throughout the book, though they figure most prominently in the personality, adjustment, abnormal, and therapies chapters. In fact, the personality chapter (Chapter 12) has been completely reorganized and rewritten around an in-depth case study that graphically illustrates the differences between theoretical viewpoints.

Gender differences, mental retardation and giftedness, brain tissue transplants, hearing disorders, job opportunities using psychology, drugs, daycare, medical decision making, effects of unemployment—these are some of the new topic areas that are both stimulating and conceptually informative.

A concerted effort has also been made to use more real-life examples of psychological processes. For example, reading is used to illustrate visual information processing (Chapter 3); anger is used to show the effect of emotions on behavior (Chapter 5); migraine headaches are used to explain biofeedback and conditioning (Chapter 6); and divorce, unemployment, and bereavement are used to illustrate the effects of extreme stress (Chapter 13).

Easy to Study From

One comment from faculty members who have used previous editions has been "My students can understand your book without my help." But studying should be even easier with the Fifth Edition. Each chapter begins with an outline of the major headings and closes with a numbered summary. Within each chapter, the text stops periodically to review previous topics and to put forthcoming material into context. These "bridges" should help students grasp more readily the flow of ideas in the chapter. The chapter summaries have also been extensively revised to include more useful information and to correspond more closely with the organization of the chapter. These summaries now provide a brief but comprehensive overview of the major topics covered in each chapter.

Boxed inserts now appear throughout the book, ranging from in-depth coverage of issues raised in the text, to recent research and controversies, to clinical case histories. Review questions are provided with every chapter to spotlight the key terms and ideas. Drawings, charts, and graphs are used where needed to help clarify important concepts, experimental designs, and research data.

An added feature of this edition is the running glossary in the margin of the text, which eliminates the need to look in the back of the book for definitions of technical terms.

Balanced Coverage

Previous editions have always attempted to strike a balance between natural science and social science coverage. In retrospect, it seemed to me that the Fourth Edition was weighted slightly on the social science side. So, for the Fifth Edition, social psychology has been streamlined to just one chapter and sensation/perception expanded into two separate chapters. The result is that exactly half of the chapters are now devoted to social science topics.

There has also been some shifting of organization so that the natural science material comes at the beginning of the text and the social science material comes at the end. But I have continued to assure that the chapters are independent of one another and can be read and assigned in any order.

Up to Date

In every chapter I have sought the most recent information available to assure that the Fifth Edition would be up-to-date and current. Close to half of the references are new to this edition and about two-thirds of the references are dated in the last five years, including a number from 1984.

Another gauge of currency is the inclusion of several topic areas that have been unusually active in recent years. Certainly cognitive psychology is one example. The memory and cognition chapters, written entirely from the most recent sources, reflect this currency. Cognition has also been given increased attention in the learning chapter (contingency theory, social learning theory), the intelligence chapter (which now emphasizes the nature of mental processes and abilities more than IQ tests), the developmental chapter (social cognition, language, and meta-memory), the adolescence and adulthood chapter (new section on cognitive development) and the social psychology chapter (social cognition and attitudes).

The social psychology chapter has also been extensively updated to reflect recent work in that field. The discussion of social perception is almost entirely new and includes material on schemas as well as self-fulfilling prophecies. The section on attitudes and behavior is all new, and reflects the renewed interest in this area in the past five years. Similarly, the section on group processes is new and includes the most recent work on group decision making and effectiveness.

Elsewhere in the book there is increased emphasis on such topics as the ethics of using animals in research, psychology and public policy, behavior genetics, human sexuality, expression of emotion, constraints on learning, gender differences, capacities of neonates, posttraumatic stress disorder, and short-term therapies.

General Comments

Here, as in previous editions, I have written the text in a way that keeps the reader reading. A conversational style is used throughout the book to set a tone of familiarity, to ease the flow, and to arouse curiosity and interest. The Fifth Edition aims at capturing and holding the reader's visual interest as well. Color is now found throughout the book, but is used to particular advantage in the natural science chapters to illustrate physiological, sensory and perceptual processes.

Supplementary Aids for the Student

The *Study Guide and Workbook* by Jay-Garfield Watkins offers for each chapter an annotated table of contents, study objectives, key terms and concepts, a programmed review, and two practice multiple-choice tests.

The *Interactive Study Guide* offers self-scoring review quizzes for each chapter for students who have access to the Apple II computer.

Supplementary Aids for the Instructor

The *Instructor's Manual* by Robert W. Wildblood is based on this edition and provides detailed chapter outlines and chapter objectives; lecture, discussion, and demonstration ideas; lists of recent references; and annotated film lists.

The updated and expanded *Test Item File* by Mary Segal contains approximately 2500 multiple-choice questions. Questions are provided in parallel form and test conceptual understanding as well as factual recall. Test preparation and typing can be obtained within 24 hours through the Prentice-Hall phone-in testing service. A computer version of the *Test Item File* is available for many mainframe and personal computers.

Finally, approximately 100 transparencies, many of which are in full color, are available to instructors. These include illustrations from the text as well as other non-text material.

Acknowledgments

The fifth edition of a textbook naturally involves the present and past contributions of numerous people. With the publication of this edition I wish to acknowledge all those associated with the former editions. The book continues to reflect their ideas and expertise.

For this edition, I would like particularly to thank Matthew Leeds for his valuable research.

The Fifth Edition has also benefitted from extensive critical reviews by interested and knowledgeable professionals. I am indebted to the following for their invaluable assistance:

Robert Bauer
Fairmont State College
Lucy Butler Bell
Daytona Beach Community
  College

Cynthia Benedictson
Daytona Beach Community
  College
Thomas E. Billimek
San Antonio College

Douglas Bors
Duquesne University

Donald Bowers
Community College of
Philadelphia

D. Bruce Carter
Syracuse University

Patricia Crane
San Antonio College

Norman Culbertson
Yakima Valley College

Winifred Curtis
Community College of
Rhode Island

Glenn Davidson
Ball State University

Kathleen M. Dillon
Western New England
College

Donald Elman
Kent State University

Stephen Farra
Northwestern College

A. Paxton Ferguson III
Eastern Connecticut State
University

Chet Fischer
Radford University

Bernard Gorman
Nassau Community College

Joseph Gratto
De Vry Institute of Technology

Michael J. Green
North Harris County College

Andrew Hansson
Grand Rapids Jr. College

Harold H. Hartstein
Hillsborough Community
College

Barbara Hermann
Gainesville Junior College

Larry Hjelle
State University College at
Brockport

John H. Hovancik
Seton Hall University

Wayne L. Hren
Los Angeles Pierce College

Javel Jackson Bell
McLennan Community
College

V. Susan Jones
North Lake College

Paul Kaplan
Suffolk County Community
College

Svenn Lindskold
Ohio University

Anne Maganzini
Bergen Community College

Barry Mallinger
Radford University

Martin Marino
Atlantic Community College

Raymond Martinetti
Marywood College

Angela McGlynn
Mercer County Community
College

Peter Nachtwey
Clarion University of
Pennsylvania

William Noseworthy
University of Newfoundland

Valerie R. Padgett
Mississippi State University

Wendy Palmquist
Plymouth State College

Randy Potter
Clarion University of
Pennsylvania

Donna Raymer
College of Lake Country

Ed Reid
Shelby State Community
College

Robert Seaton
College of DuPage

Joseph A. Sidera
Kings College

Mary J. Thomsen
Los Angeles Pierce College

Vivian K. Travis
Winthrop College

Lynn Yankowski
Maui Community College

Various members of the Prentice-Hall staff also deserve special thanks and recognition. Psychology editor John Isley and his assistant Marilyn Coco; Art Director Florence Dara Silverman; Manufacturing Buyer Ray Keating; Director of the Photo Archives Anita Duncan; Director of Book Project Susanna Lesan—all have contributed immeasurably to this and to previous editions. I would also like to mention Marketing Manager Paul Rosengaard, who has put special effort into this edition.

The production of the Fifth Edition was carefully supervised by Jeanne Hoeting, to whom I am indebted for her hard work and high degree of professionalism.

Particular acknowledgment is due to photo researcher Ilene Cherna, and to writers David Crook, David Merrill, Betty Gatewood, Virginia Adams, and Saralynn Esh. Their collective skills have truly helped make the book what it is.

Finally, I wish to thank my editor, Maggie Murray, for her continued hard work and commitment to the book and for making it feel like a shared experience.

Psychology

Outline

The Science
of Psychology

1

Why are you taking a psychology course? What would you like to learn from it? What questions would you like to have answered?

When students like you were asked these questions, they mentioned things like:

What is motivation? Why do some people have more than others? Why does it sometimes disappear?

How much of a person's behavior (if any) is inherited?

How valid are IQ tests? Do IQ tests and tests like SATs and ACTs really tell us how well we are likely to do in school or college?

What is the best and most effective way to learn?

What effects do different types of punishment have on children's behavior?

What influence do parents have on their children's personalities?

How does the brain function and affect our behavior?

Does ESP exist?

Who determines what is classified as "abnormal behavior"? Is any type of behavior truly abnormal?

How successful is psychotherapy in curing psychological problems?

How do you explain the similarities between twins who have grown up in different environments?

Are humans naturally aggressive?

Does the person shape behavior or does behavior shape the person?

Why major in psychology? Does it have practical uses? How does psychology relate to other fields?

Of what use is psychology to the average person in today's society?

As you can see, psychology students have a surprising number and variety of interests. Surely you share some of them. Like most people you are probably curious about such things as intelligence testing and how heredity affects behavior; about the development of personality; about "abnormal behavior" and how psychologists treat it. And like most students, you are probably wondering what exactly psychology is and whether it is a practical field of study.

It is also likely that you have begun to develop your own answers to these kinds of questions. We all like to observe ourselves and others. We exchange our various experiences, philosophies, and advice with friends.

Scientific method Approach to
knowledge characterized by collecting data, formulating a hypothesis, and testing the hypothesis empirically.

We speculate on why people sometimes act as they do and think about
how they might act in other situations. And over time we each begin to
develop our own ideas about human psychology.

Psychologists share your interest in behavior and the unseen mental
processes that shape behavior. But they approach these topics in a somewhat different way. Psychology is a science, and psychologists use techniques based on the **scientific method** when they seek answers to questions such as these. The scientific method seeks to answer a question by
collecting data through careful observation, formulating a hypothesis
about the significance of those data, and testing the hypothesis empirically. Later on in this chapter we'll look at some of the techniques
psychologists use, but first it is worth noting that psychology wasn't
always based on the scientific method. In fact, the scientific method has
only been applied to psychological issues for about the last 100 years.
Before that time psychology was not a formal discipline at all but a branch
of the general field of philosophy. Let's begin with an overview of the
growth of the science of psychology.

The Growth of Psychology

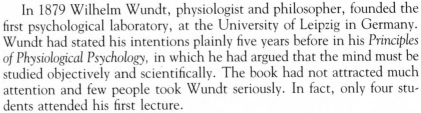

Wundt and Titchener: Structuralism

Wilhelm Wundt

In 1879 Wilhelm Wundt, physiologist and philosopher, founded the
first psychological laboratory, at the University of Leipzig in Germany.
Wundt had stated his intentions plainly five years before in his *Principles
of Physiological Psychology,* in which he had argued that the mind must be
studied objectively and scientifically. The book had not attracted much
attention and few people took Wundt seriously. In fact, only four students attended his first lecture.

Considering how radical Wundt's views actually were, it is surprising
that they went unchallenged at the time. For centuries people had regarded their mental processes with awe. Plato, for example, had divided
the world into two realms, with mind being pure and abstract, and all else
physical and mundane. Yet Wundt argued that thinking is a natural
event like any other—like wind in a storm or the beating of a heart. Why
did this radical view go unchallenged? For one thing, British philosophers
like Hobbes and Locke had already asserted that physical sensations are
the basis of thought. Moreover, by 1879 the scientific method com-
manded great respect in the academic community. And then, perhaps
most important of all, there was Charles Darwin. The traditionalists of
the day had their hands full fighting evolution. Compared to that,
Wundt's scientific psychology seemed tame.

By the mid-1880s, however, Wundt's new psychological lab had attracted many students. Wundt's main concern at this point was with
techniques for uncovering the natural laws of the human mind. To find
the basic units of thought, he began by looking at the process by which
we create meaningful patterns out of sensory stimuli. When we look at a
banana, for example, we immediately think, Here is a fruit, something to

peel and eat. But these are associations based on past experience. All we *see* is a long yellow object.

Wundt and his co-workers wanted to strip perception of its associations in order to find the very *atoms* of thought. To do this, they trained themselves in the art of objective introspection, observing and recording their perceptions and feelings. Some days, for example, were spent listening to the ticking of a metronome. Which rhythms are most pleasant? Does a fast tempo excite, a slow beat relax? They recorded their reactions in minute detail, including measures of their heartbeat and respiration. However crude and irrelevant all this may seem to us today, it did introduce measurement and experiment into psychology and thus marked the beginning of psychology as a science.

Perhaps the most important product of the Leipzig lab was its students; they took the new science to universities around the world. Among them was Edward Bradford Titchener. British by birth, Titchener became the leader of American psychology soon after he was appointed professor of psychology at Cornell University, a post he held until his death in 1927.

Psychology, Titchener wrote, is the science of consciousness—physics with the observer kept in. In physics an hour or a mile is an exact measure. To the observer, however, an hour may seem to pass in seconds, a mile may seem endless. According to Titchener, psychology is the study of such experiences. Titchener broke experience down into three basic elements: physical sensations (including sights and sounds); affections or feelings (which are like sensations, but less clear); and images (such as memories and dreams). When we recognize a banana, according to Titchener's scheme, we combine a physical sensation (what we see) with feelings (liking or disliking bananas) and with images (memories of other bananas). Even the most complex thoughts and feelings, Titchener argued, can be reduced to these simple elements. Psychology's role is to identify these elements and show how they are combined. Because it stresses the basic units of experience and the combinations in which they occur, this school of psychology is called **structuralism.**

Structuralism School of psychology that stresses the basic units of experience and the combinations in which they occur.

Edward Bradford Titchener

Sir Francis Galton: Individual Differences

Meanwhile, in England, Francis Galton, Darwin's half-cousin, was dabbling in medicine,* experimenting with electricity, charting weather, and poring over the biographies of famous people. He also found time to explore the Sudan and Southwest Africa. Born into a rich and eminent family, Galton never had to work for a living. Throughout his life he remained an intellectual adventurer—to the great gain of psychology and several other fields! Galton was a pioneer in the development of mental tests and the study of characteristics that distinguish one person from another. Impressed by the number of exceptional people in his own family, Galton set out to study other eminent families in England, and in the process he discovered that genius might be hereditary. Intrigued, he invented tests to measure individual capacities and worked out ways of comparing the scores. He found a wide range of abilities and complex

*Galton and the faculty at Trinity College did not agree on how to study medicine. Galton thought his idea of sampling each potion in the pharmacy, starting with the A's, was quite ingenious. The faculty did not!

Sir Francis Galton

Functionalist theory Theory of
mental life and behavior that is
concerned with how an organism
uses its perceptual abilities to
function in its environment.

relations between one ability and another. Later he became interested in mental imagery and word associations. With himself as subject, he wrote down the first two things called to mind by each of 75 words. He then tried to explain his reactions in terms of his past experiences. Madness also fascinated Galton. He decided that the best way to study madness was to become mad himself. He thus began to pretend that everyone he saw on his walks through the park was out to get him—including the dogs.

William James: Functionalism

William James

William James, the first American-born psychologist, was as versatile and innovative as Galton. In his youth he studied chemistry, physiology, anatomy, biology, and medicine. Then, in 1872, he accepted an offer to teach physiology at Harvard. There James read philosophy in his spare time and began to see a link between it and physiology. The two seemed to converge in psychology.

In 1875 James began a class in psychology at Harvard (he later commented that the first lecture he ever heard on the subject was his own). He set aside part of his laboratory for psychological experiments. He also began work on a text, *The Principles of Psychology*, which was published in 1890.

In preparing his lectures and his textbook, James studied structuralist writings thoroughly and decided that something in Wundt's and Titchener's approach was wrong. He concluded that the atoms of experience— pure sensations without associations—simply did not exist. Our minds are constantly weaving associations, revising experience, starting, stopping, jumping back and forth in time. Consciousness, James argued, is a continuous flow. Perceptions and associations, sensations and emotions, cannot be separated. When we look at a banana, we see a banana, not a long yellow object.

Still focusing on everyday experience, James turned to the study of habit. We do not have to think about how to get up in the morning, get dressed, open a door, or walk down the street. James suggested that when we repeat something several times, our nervous systems are changed so that each time we open a door, it is easier to open than the last time.

This was the link he needed. The biologist in him firmly believed that all activity—from the beating of the heart to the perception of objects— is functional. If we could not recognize a banana, we would have to figure out what it was each time we saw one. Thus mental associations allow us to benefit from previous experience.

With this insight, James arrived at a **functionalist theory** of mental life and behavior. Functionalist theory is concerned not just with learning or sensation or perception, but rather with how an organism uses its learning or perceptual abilities to function in its environment. James also argued for the value of subjective (untrained) introspection and insisted that psychology should focus on everyday, true-to-life experiences.

In 1894 one of James's students, James R. Angell, became the head of the new Department of Psychology at the University of Chicago. John Dewey, who had studied structuralist psychology at Johns Hopkins, became professor of philosophy at Chicago that same year. Together they made Chicago the center of the functionalist school of psychology. Both Angell and Dewey pioneered the application of functional psychology to education.

John B. Watson: Behaviorism

Conditioning The acquiring of fairly specific patterns of behavior in the presence of well-defined stimuli.

John B. Watson was the first student to receive a doctorate in psychology from the University of Chicago. His dissertation was on learning in rats. One of the department's requirements was that he speculate on the kind of consciousness that produced the behavior he observed in his rats. Watson found this absurd. He doubted that rats had any consciousness at all. Nevertheless, he complied with the regulations, received his degree, and returned to his laboratory to think about consciousness.

Ten years and many experiments later, Watson was ready to confront both the structuralist and functionalist schools. In "Psychology as the Behaviorist Views It" (1913) he argued that the whole idea of consciousness, of mental life, is superstition, a relic from the Middle Ages. You cannot define consciousness any more than you can define a soul, Watson argued. You cannot locate it or measure it, and therefore it cannot be the object of scientific study. For Watson, psychology was the study of observable, measurable behavior—and nothing more.

John B. Watson

The view Watson adopted was based largely on Ivan Pavlov's famous experiments. Some years before Watson's article appeared, this Russian physiologist had noticed that the dogs in his laboratory began to drool as soon as they heard their feeder coming—even before they could see their dinner. Pavlov had always thought that salivation was a natural response to the presence of food, so he found the dogs' anticipatory response odd. He decided to see if he could teach them to drool at the sound of a ringing bell, even when no food was in the room. He explained his successful results as follows: All behavior is a response to some stimulus or agent in the environment. In ordinary life, food makes dogs salivate. All Pavlov did was to train his animals to expect food when they heard a certain sound. He called this training **conditioning.**

In a famous experiment with an 11-month-old child, Watson showed that people can also be conditioned. Little Albert was a secure, happy baby who had no reason to fear soft, furry white rats. But each time Albert reached out to pet the rat Watson offered him, Watson made a loud noise that frightened Albert. Very soon Albert was afraid of white rats. (Watson & Rayner, 1920). Thus conditioning changed the child's behavior radically.[*]

Watson saw no reason to refer to consciousness or mental life to explain this change. Little Albert simply responded to the environment—in this case, the coincidence of the loud noises and white, furry objects. Watson felt the same was true for everyone—that all behavior could be explained with the stimulus-response formula. Psychology, he felt, must be purged of "mentalism."

[*]Watson had planned to work further with Albert—to take away the fears he had caused the boy to develop—but, unfortunately, Albert's mother took the boy away before Watson had the chance (Watson & Rayner, 1920).

Gestalt psychology School of psychology that studies how people perceive and experience objects as whole patterns.

Behaviorism School of psychology that studies only observable and measurable behavior.

Reinforcement Anything that follows a response, making that response more likely to recur.

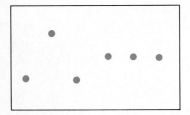

Figure 1-1

In the 1920s, when Watson's behaviorist theory was first published, American psychologists had all but exhausted the structuralist approach. Wundtian experiments had lost their novelty and attraction. So Watson's orthodox scientific approach (if you cannot see it and measure it, forget it) found a warm audience. Moreover, Watson launched two new fields of study: learning and child development.

Gestalt Psychology

Meanwhile, in Germany, a group of psychologists were attacking structuralism from another angle. Wertheimer, Köhler, and Koffka were all interested in perception, but particularly in certain tricks that the mind plays on itself. Why, they asked, when we are shown a series of still pictures flashed at a constant rate do they seem to move (for example, movies or "moving" neon signs)? The eye sees only a series of still pictures. What makes us perceive motion?

The structuralists, as you will recall, wanted to break perception down into its elements. A trained Wundtian introspectionist, for example, would see nothing but six dots in Figure 1-1. But Wertheimer and his colleagues argued that anyone else looking at such a figure would see a triangle and a line formed by the dots.

Phenomena like these were the force behind a new school of thought, **Gestalt psychology.** Roughly translated from the German, *gestalt* means "whole" or "form." When applied to perception, it refers to our tendency to see patterns, to distinguish an object from its background, to complete pictures from a few cues. Like James, the Gestalt psychologists thought that the attempt to break perception and thought down into their elements was misguided. When we look at a tree, we see just that, a tree, not a series of branches.

In the 1930s Nazism was on the rise, and the Gestalt school broke up. Wertheimer, Köhler, and Koffka all eventually settled in America.

B. F. Skinner: Behaviorism Revisited

Behaviorism was already thriving when the Gestalt psychologists reached America. B. F. Skinner was one of the leaders of behaviorism. Like Watson, Skinner believed that psychology should only study observable and measurable behavior. He too was primarily interested in changing behavior through conditioning—and discovering natural laws of behavior in the process. But his approach was subtly different from that of his predecessor.

Watson had changed Little Albert's behavior gradually by changing the stimulus. For Albert to learn a fear of white rats, Watson had had to repeat the same experience over and over, making a loud noise every time Albert saw a rat. Skinner added a new element—**reinforcement.** He rewarded his subjects for behaving the way he wanted them to behave. For example, an animal (rats and pigeons are Skinner's favorite subjects) is put in a special cage and allowed to explore. Eventually the animal will reach up and press a lever or peck at a disk on the wall. A food pellet drops into the box. Gradually the animal learns that pressing the bar or

B. F. Skinner

pecking at the disk always brings food. Why does the animal learn this? Because it has been reinforced, or rewarded. Skinner thus made the animal an active agent in its own conditioning.

Sigmund Freud: Psychoanalytic Psychology

It is hard to believe that **psychoanalysis** was once the dark horse of psychology. Sigmund Freud, who practiced in Vienna, was largely unknown in the United States until the late 1920s. By then Freud had worked his clinical discoveries into a comprehensive theory of mental life that differed radically from the views of American psychologists.

Freud believed that much of our behavior is governed by hidden motives and unconscious desires. He proposed a series of critical stages that we must pass through in the first years of life. We must successfully resolve the conflicts we meet at each stage in order to avoid psychological problems later on. Unfortunately it is possible to become "fixated" at any one of these stages and carry related feelings of anxiety or exaggerated fears with us into adulthood.

Freud not only emphasized childhood experiences, he also maintained that many unconscious desires are sexual. A little boy at age 5, Freud argued, desires his mother and wishes to destroy his father, who is his rival. Of all Freud's concepts, his emphasis on the sexual drive in the formation of personality has been the most controversial. Many of his colleagues rejected his viewpoint. Alfred Adler felt that it was the child's struggle to overcome a sense of inferiority that was central to forming personality. Carl Jung looked to the individual's impetus to self-realization in the context of the racial history and religious impulse of the human species.

Nonetheless, Freudian theory has had a huge impact on academic psychology (particularly on the study of personality and abnormal behavior) and it is still influential, as we shall see. Freud also founded **psychotherapy,** which uses psychological techniques to treat personality and behavior disorders.

Existential and Humanistic Psychology

Existential psychology, as the name suggests, draws on the existential philosophy made popular in the 1940s by, among others, Jean-Paul Sartre. Existential psychologists are concerned with meaninglessness and alienation in modern life. These feelings lead to apathy and psychological problems, and to alcoholism and addiction to drugs. Psychoanalyst Rollo May, for example, argues that modern Americans are lost souls—a people without myths and heroes. R. D. Laing, another existentialist, believes that we must reevaluate our attitude toward psychotic behavior. Such behavior, according to Laing, is not abnormal, but is rather a reasonable, normal response to an abnormal world. Existential psychology seeks to help people find an inner sense of identity so that they can achieve freedom and take responsibility for their actions.

Humanistic psychology is closely related to existential psychology. Both argue that people must learn how to realize their potential. But

Psychoanalysis Both Freud's personality theory and his form of therapy.

Psychotherapy Use of psychological techniques to treat personality and behavior disorders.

Existential psychology School of psychology that sees the meaninglessness and alienation of modern life as leading to apathy and psychological problems.

Humanistic psychology School of psychology that emphasizes nonverbal experience and altered states of consciousness as a means of realizing one's full human potential.

Sigmund Freud

Rollo May

Cognitive psychology School of
psychology devoted to the study
of mental processes generally.

Psychology The scientific study of
behavior and mental processes.

where existential psychology emphasizes restoring an inner sense of identity and willpower, humanistic psychology focuses on the possibilities of nonverbal experience, the unity of mind, altered states of consciousness, and letting go.

Existential and humanistic viewpoints have never predominated in American psychology, but they continue to be influential, particularly in the understanding of personality and abnormal behavior, as we shall see.

Cognitive Psychology

In the past decade or two a new perspective has begun to emerge and shape the field of psychology. **Cognitive psychology** is the study of our mental processes in the broadest sense—thinking, feeling, learning, remembering, and so on. According to cognitive psychologists, there is more to our behavior than just simple responses to stimuli. For example, once we see what happens when we respond to a stimulus, our understanding of that stimulus changes, and it is this cognitive understanding that guides our future behavior. Thus cognitive psychologists are especially interested in the ways in which people perceive, interpret, store, and retrieve information.

In contrast to the behaviorists, cognitive psychologists believe that mental processes can and should be studied scientifically. Although we cannot observe cognitive processes directly, we can observe behavior and make inferences about the kinds of cognitive processes that underlie the behavior. For example, we can read a lengthy story to people and then observe the kinds of things they remember, the ways in which their recollections change over time, and the sorts of errors that occur. On the basis of systematic research of this kind, it is possible to gain insight into the cognitive processes that underlie human memory, for example.

Although cognitive psychology is relatively young, it has already had an enormous impact on almost every area of psychology. Even the definition of psychology has changed as a result. Ten years ago most introductory psychology texts defined psychology simply as "the scientific study of behavior." Now many of those same texts point out that "behavior" includes thoughts, feelings, experiences, and so on. Other texts, including this one, now define **psychology** as "the scientific study of behavior and mental processes." Although you will see the influence of cognitive psychology throughout this book, it is most evident in the chapters on learning, memory, sensation/perception, and motivation/emotion.

Areas Within Psychology Today

You now have some idea about the major theoretical viewpoints in psychology. Another way to view the field is to look at the kinds of interests and concerns that psychologists have. Like so many other professionals in society these days—from doctors to professional football players—psychologists have become specialists. As they study problems, they come across new questions that require examination, which raises further questions, and on and on. And so new areas of research continually emerge, and psychologists tend to become even more specialized. The American Psychological Association, for example, is made up of 40 divisions (see Table 1-1), each of which represents an area of special interest to contemporary psychologists.

A good way to appreciate the concerns of the various specialties of psychology is to take a single issue and see what questions each specialist might ask about it. For example, are there sex differences in behavior, and if so, what causes those differences?

DEVELOPMENTAL PSYCHOLOGY. The developmental psychologist studies mental and physical growth in humans from the prenatal period through childhood, adolescence, adulthood, and old age. The "child psychologist" is a developmental psychologist who specializes in the study of children. Developmental psychologists would be especially interested in the age at which various gender differences in behavior begin to emerge, whether the differences increase or decrease as men and women grow older, and what causes the differences.

PHYSIOLOGICAL PSYCHOLOGY. Physiological psychologists investigate the extent to which behavior is caused by physical conditions in the body. They particularly concentrate on the brain, the nervous system, and the body's biochemistry. They would be especially interested in whether differences in behavior between men and women are due to differences in their nervous systems or in their biochemistry.

Table 1-1 1984 American Psychological Association Divisions

Division

1. General Psychology	23. Consumer Psychology
2. Teaching of Psychology	24. Theoretical and Philosophical Psychology
3. Experimental Psychology	25. Experimental Analysis of Behavior
5. Evaluation and Measurement	26. History of Psychology
6. Physiological and Comparative	27. Community Psychology
7. Developmental Psychology	28. Psychopharmacology
8. Personality and Social	29. Psychotherapy
9. Society for the Psychological Study of Social Issues	30. Psychological Hypnosis
10. Psychology and the Arts	31. State Psychological Association Affairs
12. Clinical Psychology	32. Humanistic Psychology
13. Consulting Psychology	33. Mental Retardation
14. Industrial and Organizational	34. Population and Environmental Psychology
15. Educational Psychology	35. Psychology of Women
16. School Psychology	36. Psychologists Interested in Religious Issues
17. Counseling Psychology	37. Child, Youth, and Family Services
18. Psychologists in Public Service	38. Health Psychology
19. Military Psychology	39. Psychoanalysis
20. Adult Development and Aging	40. Clinical Neuropsychology
21. Applied Experimental and Engineering Psychologists	41. Psychology and Law
22. Rehabilitation Psychology	42. Psychologists in Independent Practice

EXPERIMENTAL PSYCHOLOGY. Experimental psychologists investigate such basic processes as learning, memory, sensation, perception, cognition, motivation, and emotion. They would be particularly interested in any differences in the way men and women store and retrieve information from memory, the way they process sensory information, and the way they go about solving complex problems.

PERSONALITY PSYCHOLOGY. Personality psychologists study the differences in traits among people, such as anxiety, sociability, self-esteem, the need for achievement, and aggressiveness. They would be interested in whether men and women differ on traits such as these, as well as on other characteristics such as intelligence and self-concept.

CLINICAL AND COUNSELING PSYCHOLOGY. Almost half of all psychologists specialize in clinical or counseling psychology. Clinical psychologists are interested in the diagnosis, causes, and treatment of abnormal behavior. Counseling psychologists are concerned with "normal" problems of adjustment that most of us face sooner or later, such as choosing a career or coping with marital problems. Clinical psychologists would be interested in whether men experience certain kinds of behavior disorders more or less often than women, the causes of such differences, and whether men and women differ in their responsiveness to various kinds of psychotherapy. Counseling psychologists would be more interested in gender differences in the kinds of personal day-to-day problems men and women must face, as well as differences in the way they cope with those problems.

About half of all psychologists specialize in clinical or counseling psychology. Career counseling in schools and universities is one aspect of counseling psychology.

SOCIAL PSYCHOLOGY. Social psychologists investigate the influence of people on one another. How are people influenced by those around them? Why do we like some people and dislike others? Do opposites really attract? Do people behave differently in groups from the way they behave when they are alone? Social psychologists would be interested in whether men and women differ in their responses to persuasive messages, and the kinds of roles they tend to play when in groups.

INDUSTRIAL/ORGANIZATIONAL PSYCHOLOGY. Industrial and organizational psychologists address the problems of training personnel, improving working conditions, and studying the effects of automation on humans. They would be interested in whether organizations tend to operate differently under the leadership of women as opposed to men, as well as the effect of male and female administrators on morale and productivity.

The Goals and Methods of Psychology

To this point you've read about the major viewpoints in psychology, and about many of the specialty areas in psychology today. By now you may be wondering whether there is any common thread to it all. What is there that draws these different viewpoints and interests together under the single heading "psychology"? One answer is that psychologists, regardless of their theoretical viewpoint or area of interest, share common goals and methods. Like all scientists, psychologists seek to *describe, explain, predict,* and *control* what they study.

Let's see what this means by looking at how psychologists would approach the question of whether there are sex differences in aggressiveness. Some people believe that males are naturally more aggressive than females. Others say this may be only a stereotype, or at least that it is not always true. Psychologists would want to know first: Do men and women actually differ in aggressive behavior? A number of research studies have addressed this question and the evidence seems unequivocal—males do behave more aggressively than females, particularly when we consider physical aggression (Frieze et al., 1978). Having established that sex differences in aggression do exist, and having *described* those differences, psychologists then seek to *explain* the differences. Psychobiologists might seek to explain them on the basis of anatomy or body chemistry; developmental psychologists might look to early experience and the way children are taught to behave "like a boy" or "like a girl"; social psychologists might explain the differences as being due to societal constraints against aggressive behavior in women.

If any of these explanations is correct, then it should allow us both to *predict* and to *control* aggressive behavior. For example, if sex differences in aggression arise because males have a greater amount of the male hormone testosterone, then we would predict that reducing the level of testosterone would reduce aggressive behavior in men. If, on the other hand, sex differences in aggression are due to early training, then we would predict that the sex differences would be less in families where parents did not stress gender differences in behavior. Finally, if sex differences in aggressive behavior are due to societal constraints against women expressing aggression, we would predict that removing or at least reducing those constraints would result in higher levels of aggressive behavior among women.

You can see how if any (or all) of these explanations for sex differences in aggressiveness turns out to be correct—that is, if the predictions are supported by research—it becomes possible to control aggressive behavior to a greater degree than was possible before. Each of these predictions could be tested through research and the results used to indicate which of the various explanations seems to be the most successful.

Psychology is not alone in trying to describe, explain, predict, and control behavior. The behavioral sciences—anthropology, sociology, political science, and psychology—are so closely related that it is often hard to tell where one ends and the next begins. For example, all of them would regard a campus protest as a good subject for study. But how would their approaches differ?

An anthropologist might see the day's activities in terms of cultural patterns and rituals. He or she would note that making speeches from a soapbox is a long and honored American tradition; that linking arms to form a human barricade resembles the snake dance of Japanese protesters; that in political movements, as in primitive societies, people often call others who are not related to them "brother" and "sister."

A sociologist might be most interested in the interactions of the

Naturalistic observation Research method involving the systematic study of animal or human behavior in natural settings rather than in the laboratory.

groups that were formed and in the bonds forged among people. Crowds, the sociologist would note, behave differently from individuals and from small groups. The crowd develops an organizational structure and a status system. It makes and enforces its own codes of correct and incorrect behavior.

A political scientist might focus on the distribution of power and authority among leaders and groups. An economist, being concerned mainly with the distribution of goods, would note that the students have a different attitude toward property than do most Americans. A historian would try to compare this event to others in the past and would seek its causes.

A psychologist surveying the same situation would be most interested in how individuals in the crowd behave and why they behave that way. Does their participation grow out of their political attitudes and values? Is there some underlying motive for attending the protest? Do people at this particular protest tend also to go to other protests, and if so, why?

In order to get answers to these and other questions about people and their thoughts, feelings, and behavior, psychologists use several kinds of research methods.

The Naturalistic-Observation Method

We have all heard about the virtue of "telling it like it is." Psychologists use this method to study animal or human behavior in its natural context instead of in the laboratory under imposed conditions. Most of us use this method in everyday life without realizing it. When you watch dogs play in the park, or observe how your professors conduct their classes, you are using a form of **naturalistic observation.** A psychologist with this real-life orientation might observe behavior in a school or a factory. Another might actually join a family to study the behavior of its members. Still another might observe animals in nature, not in cages. The primary advantage of this method is that the observed behavior will be more natural, spontaneous, and varied than in a laboratory.

For example, W. H. Whyte (1956) wanted to see how people living in a suburban community chose their friends. He kept tabs on his subjects by reading the local newspaper. The social column told him when parties were given and who was invited. After collecting such data for some time, Whyte noticed that there were definite friendship patterns in the community. *Proximity*—people's nearness to one another—was the critical factor in determining which people became friends. Whyte concluded that all things being equal, people are more apt to make friends with those who live nearby. He might have been able to learn this by asking people, but he could not have found it out in a laboratory.

Whyte restricted his observations to one specific behavior—going to parties. It is not always possible, however, to make such restrictions. Because naturalistic observation does not interfere with people's behavior in any way, the psychologist using it has to take people's behavior as it comes. A naturalistic observer cannot suddenly yell "Freeze!" when he or she wants to study what is going on in more detail. Nor can he or she tell people to stop what they are doing because it is not what the psychologist wants to study.

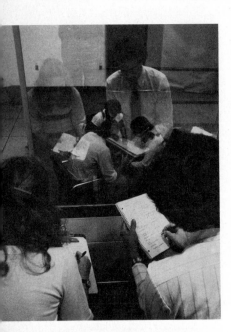

When people are unaware that they are being watched, they act more naturally. A one-way mirror is sometimes used for naturalistic observation.

There are both advantages and disadvantages to naturalistic observation. One of the central problems is observer bias. Any police officer will tell you how unreliable eyewitnesses can be. Even psychologists who are trained observers may subtly distort what they see to conform to what they hope to see. Also, in their detailed notes of the observation, psychologists may not record behavior that they think is not relevant. When using this method, it may be desirable to rely on a team of trained observers who pool their notes. This often results in a more complete picture than one observer could draw alone.

Another problem is that the behavior observed depends on the particular time, place, and group of people involved. Unlike laboratory experiments that can be repeated again and again, each natural situation is a one-time-only occurrence. Because of this, psychologists prefer not to make general statements based on information from naturalistic studies. They would rather test the information under controlled conditions in the laboratory before they apply it to situations other than the original.

Despite these disadvantages, naturalistic observation is a valuable tool for psychologists. After all, real-life behavior is what psychology is about. Although the complexity of behavior may present problems, naturalistic observation is a boon to psychologists. It gives them new ideas and suggestions for research. Researchers can then study these ideas more systematically and in more detail in their laboratories than can researchers in the field. It also helps researchers to keep their perspective by reminding them of the larger world outside the lab.

The Experimental Method

As we have noted, psychologists want to get at the root causes of phenomena; they want to explain thoughts, feelings, and behavior. Perhaps a psychologist has noticed that most students in her Monday morning class are unusually quiet and do not respond to her questions. She suspects this is because they stay up late on Sunday nights. Thus the psychologist begins with a hunch or **hypothesis:** Students who do not get enough sleep find it difficult to remember facts and ideas. But this commonsense explanation is not enough. The psychologist wants proof—facts that are unbiased. She wants to know that all other possible explanations have been ruled out. To test her hypothesis, she decides to conduct an experiment on the relationship between sleep and learning.

Her first step is to pick **subjects,** people she can observe, to see whether her hypothesis is right. She decides to use student volunteers. To keep her results from being influenced by sex differences or intelligence levels, she chooses a group made up of equal numbers of men and women who scored between 520 and 550 on their College Boards.

Next she designs a learning task. She needs something that none of her subjects will know in advance. If she chooses a chapter in a history book, for example, she runs the risk that some of her subjects may be history buffs. Considering various possibilities, the psychologist decides to print a page of geometric forms, each labeled with a nonsense word. Circles are "glucks," triangles "pogs," and so on. She will give the students one-half hour to learn the names, then take away the study sheets and ask them to label a new page of geometric forms.

Hypothesis Tentative assumption that is tested empirically.

Subjects Individuals whose reactions or responses are observed in an experiment.

Psychology students conducting a laboratory listening experiment to investigate brain specialization. Subjects' responses to various sounds are being recorded.

Independent variable In an experiment, the variable that is manipulated to test its effects on the other, dependent variables.

Dependent variable In an experiment, the variable that is measured to see how it is changed by manipulations in the independent variable.

Experimental group In a controlled experiment, the group subjected to a change in the independent variable.

Control group In a controlled experiment, the group not subjected to a change in the independent variable; used for comparison with the experimental group.

Experimenter bias Expectations by the experimenter that might influence the results of an experiment or their interpretation.

Now the psychologist is ready to consider procedures. Asking people if they have slept well is not a reliable measure. Some may say "no" to have an excuse for doing poorly on the test. Others will say "yes" because they do not want a psychologist to think they are unstable and cannot sleep. Then there are subjective differences: Two people who both say they slept well may not mean the same thing. So the researcher decides to intervene—to control the situation a little more closely. Everyone in the experiment, she decides, will spend the night in the same dormitory. They will be kept awake until 4:00 A.M., and then they will be awakened at 7:00 A.M. sharp. She and her colleagues will patrol the halls to make sure that no one falls asleep ahead of schedule. They will check to see who is sleeping soundly between 4:00 and 7:00 A.M. By determining the amount of sleep the subjects get, the psychologist is introducing and controlling an essential element of the experimental method—an **independent variable.** The psychologist believes that the students' ability to learn her labels for geometric forms will depend on their having had a good night's sleep. Performance on the learning task (number of correct answers) thus becomes the **dependent variable.** Changing the independent variable (the amount of sleep), should also change the dependent variable (performance on the learning task) should also be changed, according to the hypothesis. In particular, this group of subjects who get only 3 hours of sleep should do quite poorly on the test.

At this point the experimenter begins looking for loopholes in her experimental design. How can she be sure that poor test results mean that the subjects did less well than they would have done if they had had more sleep? Their poor performance could be the result of knowing that they were participating in an experiment and therefore were being closely observed. To be sure that her experiment measures only the effects of inadequate sleep, the experimenter divides the subjects into two groups. The two groups contain equal numbers of males and females of the same ages and with the same College Board scores. One of the groups, the **experimental group,** will be kept awake, as we have described, until 4:00 A.M. That is, they will be subjected to the experimenter's manipulation of the independent variable—amount of sleep. The other, the **control group,** will be allowed to go to sleep whenever they please. Because the only consistent difference between the two groups should be the amount of sleep they get, the experimenter can be much more confident that if the groups differ in their test performance, the difference is due to the amount of sleep they got the night before.

Finally, the psychologist questions her own objectivity. She is inclined to think that lack of sleep inhibits students' learning, but she does not want to prejudice the results of her experiment. That is, she wants to avoid **experimenter bias.** So she decides to ask a third person, someone who does not know which subject did or did not sleep all night, to score the tests.

The psychologist will interpret even the most definitive findings with some caution. Only after other researchers in other laboratories with other subjects have repeated an experiment and found the same results does the psychologist really consider the original conclusion reliable. (Psychology, like all science, is a communal enterprise.)

For some studies, a laboratory may be less suitable than a naturalistic setting. Ellsworth (1977) has noted that the laboratory is not the best setting for testing variables such as fear, conflict, grief, or love. It may be hard for subjects to express these feelings except in a limited way in the laboratory. Also, the strange and unfamiliar environment of the laboratory may affect these feelings and reactions. For example, behavior patterns between parents and children are very different in the laboratory and in the home. In the laboratory young children are more anxious and parents behave more positively toward them than they do at home (Bronfenbrenner, 1977). Finally, since in the laboratory the subjects *know* that they are being observed by psychologists, they may try to appear healthy, normal, tolerant, and intelligent (Ellsworth, 1977). This increases the problem of testing people's true responses to situations.

The Correlational Method

An experiment is one of the most powerful ways to investigate many behaviors, but it is not always the most practical way. Suppose a psychologist wants to find out what makes a good pilot. Perhaps the Air Force has asked him to study this question because it costs thousands of dollars to train a single pilot, and each year many trainees quit. The psychologist could conduct an experiment—he might raise 10 children in playrooms filled with toy planes, cars, baseballs, and stuffed animals. This method, which studies the same group of subjects over time, is called the *longitudinal method.* It would probably tell the psychologist what he wanted to know, but both he and the Air Force would have to wait years for the result.

The **correlational method** provides a shortcut. The psychologist could begin by choosing 100 proven pilots and 100 unsuccessful ones. To gather information, he could give his pilots a variety of aptitude and personality tests. Suppose he found that all the successful pilots score higher than the unsuccessful pilots on mechanical aptitude tests, and that all the successful pilots are cautious people who do not like to take chances. There would then seem to be some **correlation,** or degree of relation, between these traits and success as a pilot. The psychologist could therefore recommend that the Air Force use certain tests to choose the next group of trainees. Suppose he also found that all the successful pilots played golf, came from large cities, and liked pecan pie. There is no logical reason why these facts should go with piloting a plane; they just do. Puzzled, the psychologist might test another group of successful pilots for these characteristics. If he found that these pilots, too, played golf, came from large cities, and liked pecan pie, he could conclude that a correlation existed, even though he probably could not explain it.

Through correlational studies psychologists can thus identify relations between two or more variables without needing to understand exactly why these relations exist. This method has been extremely useful in making standardized tests. Intelligence tests, College Boards, tests for clerical and mechanical aptitude—all are based on extensive correlational studies. A person's performance on a test of clerical aptitude, for example, may be compared to success or failure in an office job.

Most psychologists use several methods to study a single problem. For example, a researcher interested in creativity might begin by giving a group of college students a creativity test that she invented to measure

Correlational method Research technique based on the naturally occurring relationship between two or more variables.

Correlation Degree of relationship between two or more variables.

their capacity to discover or produce something new. She compares the students' scores with their scores on intelligence tests and with their grades to see if there is a correlation between them. Then she spends several weeks observing a college class and interviewing teachers, students, and parents to correlate classroom behavior and the adults' evaluations with the students' scores on the creativity test. She decides to test some of her ideas with an experiment and uses a group of the students as subjects. Her findings might cause her to revise the test, or they might give the teachers and parents new insight about a particular student.

Ethics in Research

It is likely that you will have the chance to be a subject in an experiment in your psychology department. You will probably be offered a small sum of money or class credit to participate. But it is possible that your participation may puzzle you and that you will learn the true purpose of the experiment only after it is over. Is this deception necessary to psychology experiments? And what if the experiment should cause you discomfort?

Most psychologists agree that these questions raise ethical issues. And so, more than 30 years ago the American Psychological Association drew up a code for treating experimental subjects (APA, 1953). But in 1963 the issue of ethics was raised again when Stanley Milgram published the results of several experiments.

The apparatus used by Milgram in his "learning experiment." This experiment raised serious ethical questions.

Milgram hired people to help him with a learning experiment and told them that they were to teach other people, the "learners," by giving them electric shocks when they gave wrong answers. The shocks could be given in various intensities from "slight shock" to "severe shock." The people were told to increase the intensity of the shock each time the learner made a mistake. As the shocks increased in intensity, the learners began to protest that they were being hurt. They cried out in pain and became increasingly upset as the shocking continued. The people giving the shocks often became concerned and frightened and asked if they could stop. But the experimenter politely but firmly pointed out that they were expected to continue.

This was the crux of the experiment. Milgram was investigating obedience, not learning. He wanted to find out whether anyone in the situation just described would actually go all the way and give the highest level of shock. Would they follow their consciences, or would they obey the experimenter? Incredibly, 65 percent of Milgram's subjects did go all the way, even though the learner stopped answering toward the end and many subjects worried that the shocks might have done serious damage.

So Milgram found out what he wanted to know. But to do it, he had to deceive his subjects. The stated purpose of the experiment, to test learning, was a lie. The shock machines were fake. The learners received no shocks at all. And the learners themselves were Milgram's accomplices who had been trained to act as though they were being hurt (Milgram, 1963).

Although the design of this experiment is not typical of the vast majority of psychological experiments, it caused such a public uproar that the profession began to reevaluate its ethical health. In the wake of the controversy, a new code of ethics on psychological experimentation was approved and has recently been revised (APA, 1982). Each year this code of ethics is reviewed to be sure that it is up-to-date and that it is fully adequate to protect the subjects of research. Moreover, the federal government recently amended its Code of Federal Regulations to include an extensive set of regulations concerning the protection of human subjects. Failure to abide by these regulations can result in the termination of federal funding for the investigator and penalties for his or her institution.

But controversy about the ethics of research continues. Those favoring strict ethical controls feel that the rights of the subject are of prime importance. They believe that procedures should never be emotionally or physically distressing, and that the experimenter should first tell the potential subject what can be expected to happen. Some psychologists have described deliberately misleading experiments as "trickery," "fakery," and "clownery" deserving of condemnation (Rubin, 1983). They suggest, instead, the use of role-playing methods, in which subjects are asked to act "as if" they were engaged in particular behaviors for the purpose of the experiment.

Other psychologists insist that strict ethical rules could damage the scientific validity of an experiment and cripple future research. "Absolute moral values corrupt absolutely" (Gergen, 1973, p. 908). These psychologists also point out that few subjects—by their own admission—have been appreciably harmed by deceptive experiments. Even in Milgram's manipulative experiment, only 1.3 percent of the subjects reported negative feelings about their experience.

Still other psychologists suggest that the effect of experimental procedures on subjects is itself something that is deserving of research. They point out that as a science, psychology should base its ethical code on demonstrated facts, not conjecture. For example, the latest revision of the APA ethical code requires that "After the data are collected, the investigator should provide the participant with information about the nature of the study and attempt to remove any misconceptions that may have arisen" (APA, 1982, p. 6). Presumably this is intended to eliminate misconceptions and harmful after-effects. But Holmes (1976b) notes that when the APA originally adopted its code, there was little or no evidence that this procedure would actually have the desired effect, although subsequent research indicates that debriefing does in fact work as intended (Holmes, 1976a, 1976b).

Often the debate on ethical issues has focused on laboratory experiments. But questions have also been raised about the ethics of conducting naturalistic research studies. Is it ethical to study and collect data on people who are parking their cars or shopping in a store without first telling them that they are subjects of research? One study found that many people would indeed feel harassed, or that their privacy had been invaded, if they were unknowingly observed and studied (Wilson & Donnerstein, 1976). In fact, 38 percent of the people questioned stated that the public should protest against such methods of research.

In the long run, psychology can only benefit from the ethical-standards controversy. Although unanimous acceptance of a formal code of ethics is a long way off, most experimenters find the APA ethical code a useful step in the right direction.

The Social Relevance of Psychology

Pure research Research for its own sake, usually done to test a theory or to follow up on other research rather than to solve practical problems.

Applied psychology Direct study of social problems, often with the intent to change human behavior.

Pure Versus Applied Psychology

We have described the goals of psychology as: describe, explain, predict, and control. But not all research is directed equally at each of these goals. **Pure research,** or research for its own sake, is more concerned with description, explanation, and prediction. Usually pure research is carried out to test a theory or to follow up on other research. It is only rarely a response to a pressing practical problem. Pure research may or may not eventually have practical application to social problems. **Applied psychology,** however, is the direct study of the problems of the teacher, the worker, the spouse, or perhaps of the wider social effects of racism or militarism. Applied research is often more concerned with prediction and control than with description and explanation; it is usually intended eventually to change human behavior, though it may have major theoretical importance as well.

The distinction between scholarly theory and practical use is an old one. It dates back to the different models of science proposed in the 17th century by René Descartes and Francis Bacon. Descartes considered all scientific endeavor intrinsically worthwhile (pure research). For Bacon, science was to be used to promote human welfare (applied research) (Fishman & Neigher, 1982).

Psychologists themselves have mixed views about social relevance. In a survey of some 2,500 graduate students and faculty in the psychology departments of over 100 American universities, nearly half of those polled chose social relevance as "the most important issue confronting contemporary psychology" (Lipsey, 1974, p. 542). When asked where they would like to work, however, many of the respondents rated institutions stressing "help with social problems" as their least favorite choice. Most preferred scholarly, pure-research-oriented universities (Lipsey, 1974).

In spite of this preference of psychologists for pure research, psychology as a discipline has dramatically increased its attention to applications in the last few years. This has come about largely in response to major federal funding cuts in areas that were seen to have little practical impact. Moreover, this trend toward increased applied research is likely to continue as psychology competes with other social sciences for limited funds to maintain its research and service programs. Hatch (1982), for example, points out that psychology simply must give increased attention to such real-life problems as pollution, urban decay, alcoholism, smoking, and drug abuse. Not surprisingly, this proposal has caused considerable controversy within the profession of psychology as well as outside it.

Some have called for psychology to play a more active role in improving public understanding of the importance of pure science while at the same time helping people to solve difficult social problems (Bazelon, 1982). One interesting suggestion is to create partnerships between scientists and citizens on community-based research projects that can not only improve the quality of both pure and applied research but also encourage public support for research that is helping people to help themselves (Chavis et al., 1983).

Psychology and Common Sense

To many people, including quite a few introductory psychology students, psychology seems to be based on nothing more than common sense, lightly disguised by fancy jargon. If you believe that psychological research is just a complicated process of confirming what most people already know, you may be right—sometimes.

Walter and Harriet Mischel (1982) recently investigated the possibility that even children could accurately predict the findings of some psychology experiments. The Mischels described 12 psychology experiments to fourth- and sixth-graders and asked them to predict the outcomes. On average, fourth-graders were able to correctly guess outcomes for 7 of the 12 experiments. Sixth-graders did even better, correctly guessing 9 out of 12 outcomes.

Does this mean that psychologists are wasting a lot of time and effort in "discovering" what even a sixth-grader could tell them? Not really. A number of studies have shown that much "commonsense" psychological knowledge is simply incorrect when put to the test. For example, Eva Vaughan (1977) gave students in an introductory

psychology course a list of 23 commonly held beliefs in several areas of psychology. All 23 statements were false. However, a remarkably high percentage of the students believed many of these statements to be true. For instance, 85 percent of Vaughan's students agreed that "the basis of the baby's love for [the] mother is the fact that [the] mother fills physiological needs for food, etc." But research has shown that the infant's love for the mother is based primarily on the comfort the infant receives from physical contact with her. Also, 80 percent of the students believed that "the best way to ensure that a desired behavior will persist after training is to reward that behavior every single time it occurs." Actually, rewarding a desired behavior only some of the time increases the likelihood that it will persist.

Studying psychology will reinforce some of your commonsense beliefs because some of what you know on the basis of your own experiences and what others have told you is quite correct. On the other hand, this course will show you that some of what you—and most people—think of as common sense is actually quite wrong.

Fishman and Neigher (1982) also believe that the social-relevance issue has become critical. The challenge, as they see it, is to improve the quality of both pure and applied research and to tie all research more directly to such social goals as public service, social policy consultation, and education and training. Unless psychology can meet these kinds of challenges, its very future as a discipline may be at stake.

Using Animals in Psychological Research

The breach between pure and applied research has raised questions about the use of animal subjects in research. Some psychologists believe that since psychology is, in part at least, the science of behavior, animal behavior is just as interesting and important as human behavior. But however interesting animal behavior may be, what possible relevance does the behavior of a 7-inch-long laboratory rat have to everyday human problems? Immediately, none perhaps. But many experiments—systematic brain surgery, for example—simply cannot be performed on human beings and so must be done with animals if anything at all is to be learned. Psychologists also use animal subjects because their behavior is simpler than human behavior and their genetic histories and immediate environments can be controlled more easily. The short life spans of some animals also make it possible to study behavior over many generations, which

Guinea Pigs (and Rats, Pigeons, Monkeys, Dogs, etc.) in Psychological Research

For the past two centuries there has been an almost continual controversy over the use of animals in medical and psychological research. In 1876 a movement in England protesting experimental surgery on animals resulted in the British Cruelty to Animals Act, which requires that researchers acquire licenses to use living animals in their work. Today the debate about research on animals is still raging.

Several groups in this country, including Mobilization for Animals and Psychologists for the Ethical Treatment of Animals (PsyETA), are calling for more restrictive legislation regarding the use of animals in research. These groups believe that causing animal suffering is inhumane. Just as researchers would rule out harmful experimentation on human subjects, they should put an end to experimentation that causes animal suffering. Many scientists and their supporters hold an opposing view. They contend that the goals of their research—to reduce or eliminate human suffering, to enrich human life, and to deepen understanding of life forms in general—morally justify some animal suffering in order to meet those objectives (Gallistel, 1981).

The American Psychological Association has established guidelines concerning the use of animals in psychological research. Under these guidelines the investigator is responsible for making "every effort to minimize discomfort, illness, and pain of animals"; and animals should be killed "rapidly and painlessly" when they are no longer needed.

But for many animal protection activists, the APA guidelines are not enough. The activists claim that the misuse of research animals occurs despite organizational guidelines and protective legislation. Moreover, they believe that psychological researchers unnecessarily repeat many experiments on animals and that there is little evidence that any human benefits come from this work. Also, these critics maintain that psychologists and others involved in animal research make few efforts to find alternative means of gathering data.

One target of recent criticism is physiological psychologist Edward Taub, who in 1983 received a Guggenheim Fellowship to support his research on monkeys' sensory mechanisms. The award angered activists because Taub had been convicted of animal cruelty in some prior research on monkeys. PsyETA also formally protested Taub's receipt of several additional awards from the APA itself (Cunningham, 1983).

One important organization, although it opposes the protectionists' views, has nonetheless instituted new, more stringent policies regarding animal research. The National Institutes of Health (NIH) supports almost 40 percent of American biomedical research, much of which involves animal subjects. Henceforth a project will not receive NIH funding unless it has first been approved by an animal research committee, including someone not affiliated with the institution doing the research; the institution's attending veterinarian; and a scientist experienced in lab animal medicine. The NIH hopes that its more restrictive policies will prevent the passage of even more limiting legislation supported by animal protectionists (Miller, 1984). Whether it also succeeds in reducing the controversy over animal research ethics remains to be seen.

would be highly impractical or even impossible with humans. Moreover, with animals there are no "social" complications between experimenter and subject.

The trained psychologist must reflect carefully on the limitations inherent in comparisons of animal and human behavior. Without analysis, there is a danger that animal studies may lead to grandiose and faulty conclusions about human social behavior (Mason & Lott, 1976). Certainly "mental illness" in a rat is different from that in a human. But if we are careful not to simply equate animal behavior with human behavior, research using animals can add much to our understanding of behavior, including human behavior.

In recent times the use of animals in psychological research has become controversial in other ways as well. Several groups have protested experimentation that causes animal suffering. In response, the APA and other organizations have established stricter guidelines concerning the use of animals in psychological research. Despite these measures, however, the debate surrounding the ethical use of animals in research continues (see the box on p. 20).

Application

Psychology and Careers

Within the past 15 years psychology has become one of the most popular majors in the college curriculum. In 1970–1971, 37,000 students were awarded BAs in psychology. By 1983–1984, that figure had doubled. What happens to these people? Do they all go on to careers in psychology as clinicians, researchers, and the like? What kinds of jobs do they look for and what kinds of jobs do they find once they are equipped with their hard-earned degrees?

Surveys show that between one-third and two-thirds of those who receive bachelor's degrees in psychology do not go on to graduate school in psychology. Many use their undergraduate study of psychology as a general preparation for life—an informative and worthwhile course of study that indirectly relates to and prepares them for careers in other fields. Others, however, go directly into careers that relate to psychology.

One possibility is teaching psychology at the high-school level. Nearly 1 million students are currently enrolled in high-school psychology courses across the nation. Although full-time high-school psychology teachers are rare—many double as teachers of other subjects or as counselors—opportunities do exist. Most high schools require their teachers to have a bachelor's degree and teacher certification, although a master's degree is preferable; in some states the MA is specifically required after a certain number of years.

Recently several community colleges have started offering associate degree programs in psychology. Graduates of these training programs are well qualified for paraprofessional jobs in state hospitals, mental health centers, and other human service settings. Job responsibilities may include the screening and evaluation of new patients,

record keeping, other direct patient-contact activities, and assistance in community consultation.

Many other careers outside of psychology also draw upon one's knowledge of psychology without requiring postgraduate study. A sample: (1) Community relations officers are involved in promoting good relations with the local community. (2) Affirmative action officers specialize in recruitment and equal opportunities for minorities. (3) Recre-

Many other careers outside psychology draw upon a knowledge of human behavior. Personnel administrators are involved in the testing, hiring, and training of employees and deal with employee relations.

Studying psychology is valuable preparation for careers in fields like urban planning and architecture.

ation workers plan community recreation facilities. (4) Urban planning officers are responsible for city planning and renewal. (5) Personnel administrators deal with employee relations. (6) Health educators provide public information about health and disease. (7) Vocational rehabilitation counselors assist handicapped persons with employment. (8) Directors of volunteer service recruit and train volunteers. (9) Probation and parole officers work with parolees. (10) Day-care center supervisors supervise preschool children of working parents. (11) Research assistants assist with psychological research in large hospitals, businesses, and government. (12) Laboratory assistants are involved with animal behavior research.

For those who do pursue advanced degrees, the opportunities for a career in psychology are widespread and varied. Colleges and universities currently employ about 40 percent of the people who hold advanced degrees in psychology (Stapp & Fulcher, 1983). For many of them, teaching is a secondary activity; they devote most of their time to counseling or research. Outside of the universities, holders of advanced degrees work in many places: in the public schools, in prisons, in hospitals and mental health clinics, in government agencies, in the military, and in business. Only a small percentage of psychologists are primarily employed in private practice, though that number is increasing.

Recently the American Psychological Association (APA) developed standards that were later written into many state licensing laws. These standards require people in psychological settings and in private practice to be supervised by a doctoral-level psychologist. Such regulations limit the opportunities for those with master's degrees to move into higher positions. Although there are jobs available to people with master's degrees, most of them are in business, government, schools, and, to a lesser extent, hospitals and clinics.

In discussing careers in psychology it is important to distinguish among psychiatrists, psychoanalysts, and psychologists. Although they may provide overlapping services, their main functions differ. A *psychiatrist* is a medical doctor who has completed three years of residency training in psychiatry. He or she specializes in the diagnosis and treatment of abnormal behavior. Besides giving psychotherapy, the psychiatrist also takes medical responsibility for the patient. As a physician, he or she may prescribe drugs and use other medical procedures to help a patient. A *psychoanalyst* is a psychiatrist who has received additional specialized training in psychoanalytic theory and practice.

Most, but not all, *psychologists* hold PhD degrees in psychology—the result of 4 to 6 years of study in a graduate program in psychology. The PhD program for all psychologists includes broad exposure to the theories and findings of psychology, a special focus on a subdiscipline—such as clinical or social psychology—and extensive training in research methods. Certain subdisciplines, such as clinical and counseling psychology, require additional training in diagnosis and psychotherapy; these programs also require at least 1 year of training in psychotherapy in an internship program that is accredited by the APA.

Years ago, when competition for jobs was less intense than it is today, graduate students in psychology specialized in a single area, or subdiscipline, such as clinical, developmental, or educational psychology. Current employment conditions, however, require students to branch out. Psychology students on the graduate level now often specialize in two fields, such as a major in experimental psychology and a minor in industrial psychology, or school/clinical psychology, or developmental/aging, and so on. Such training provides breadth in a traditional area and depth in an applied specialty.

If you want further information on careers in psychology, the APA will send a free copy of its booklet *Careers in Psychology* upon request. Write to: Public Sales Department, APA, 1200 17th Street, NW, Washington, D.C. 20036. The booklet contains not only a wealth of information about careers but also a current list of books and articles that provide even more information on careers.

Summary

1. *Psychology* is a science that studies behavior and the mental processes that shape behavior. Psychology has been a formal discipline based on the *scientific method* for about the last 100 years.

2. Wilhelm Wundt established the first psychological laboratory, at the University of Leipzig in 1879, where he intended to study the mind in an objective and scientific manner. He introduced measurement and experiment into psychology, which until then had been a branch of philosophy.

3. One of Wundt's students, Edward Bradford Titchener, became professor of psychology at Cornell University and the leader of American psychology. Wundt and Titchener both believed that psychology's role is to identify the basic elements of experience and to show how they are combined. This school of psychology is known as *structuralism.*

4. Sir Francis Galton pioneered the study of individual differences and the development of mental tests.

5. William James, the first native American psychologist, believed that sensations cannot be separated from associations. Mental associations, he claimed, allow us to benefit from previous experience. James firmly believed that all activity is functional, and by applying biological principles to the mind, he arrived at the *functionalist theory* of mental life and behavior.

6. John B. Watson confronted both the structuralist and the functionalist schools, stating that we can no more define "consciousness" than we can define the "soul." Psychology, he maintained, should concern itself only with observable, measurable behavior. Watson's theory is part of the behaviorist school of psychology. Watson based much of his work on Pavlov's conditioning experiments and thought that all behavior could be explained by stimulus and response.

7. While Watson was working in America, a new school of thought, *Gestalt psychology*, was being developed in Germany. Roughly translated, *gestalt* means "whole" or "form." Gestalt psychologists suggested that perception depends on our tendency to see patterns, to distinguish an object from its background, to complete pictures from a few cues.

8. *Behaviorism* was thriving in America when B. F. Skinner replaced Watson as its leader.

Skinner's beliefs were similar to Watson's, but he made the animal an active agent in the conditioning process by adding *reinforcement* to stimulate learning.

9. *Psychoanalysis* was not seen as a part of psychology until the late 1920s, after Freud had worked out his theories on the effects of underlying motives and unconscious desires on behavior. His emphasis on the sexual drive in the formation of personality remains the most controversial aspect of his theories. Freud also founded *psychotherapy* with his famous "talking cure."

10. *Existential psychology* is concerned with feelings of meaninglessness and alienation in modern life and how they contribute to apathy and other problems such as alcoholism and drug abuse. *Humanistic psychology* is related to existential psychology and emphasizes communication through the senses in order to achieve the realization of one's potential.

11. *Cognitive psychology* is the study of our mental processes in the broadest sense. It is concerned with how people perceive, interpret, store, and retrieve information. Cognitive psychologists believe that mental processes can be studied scientifically.

12. Psychologists today practice within many specialized areas. The American Psychological Association, for example, is made up of 42 separate divisions, each of which represents an area of specialized interest. Some of the major areas within psychology are developmental psychology, physiological psychology, experimental psychology, personality psychology, clinical and counseling psychology, social psychology, and industrial/organizational psychology.

13. The common goal of all psychologists is to *describe, explain, predict,* and *control* human behavior. Psychologists use several different kinds of research methods to study human behavior.

14. The *naturalistic-observation* method is used to study animal and human behavior in natural settings, instead of in the laboratory. The *experimental method* begins with an idea or *hypothesis* about the relationship between two or more variables. To find out if they are related, the experimenter manipulates the *independent variable* to see how it affects the *dependent variable*. The experimenter uses precautionary *control groups* to help ensure that he or she is observing only the effects of one independent variable.

15. The *correlational method* is a means of investigating the relation between certain characteristics and behavior variables without needing to manipulate or change any variables.

16. More than 25 years ago the American Psychological Association (APA) drew up a code of ethics on psychological experimentation. Each year the code is reviewed and updated to be sure that it is fully adequate to protect the subjects of research. Although many psychologists feel this is a step in the right direction, controversy over the ethics of research continues.

17. Psychology has common goals, but not all research is directed equally at each of these goals. *Pure research,* or research for its own sake, is more concerned with description, explanation, and prediction. *Applied research* directly studies real social problems and is more often concerned with prediction and control. More attention has gone to applied areas in the last few years as a direct result of cuts in the federal budget for pure research. Psychology faces the difficult challenge of maintaining high standards in pure and applied research and directing both kinds of research to the solution of important social problems.

18. Psychologists use animals in research because some types of experiments cannot be done on humans. Animals also have shorter life spans, which lets a researcher study behavior over several generations, and animals' genetic history and immediate environment can be better controlled. Psychologists are careful about generalizing from animal to human behavior. They do find, however, that animal research makes a large contribution to their knowledge of behavior. The use of animals in psychological research has become a growing ethical issue. The APA and other organizations that sponsor research have issued more stringent guidelines covering the use of animals in experimentation.

1. Psychology has been a formal discipline based on the _____ method for about the last 100 years.
2. Match the following terms with their appropriate descriptions:

____ structuralism
____ functionalism
____ behaviorism
____ psychoanalysis
____ existential psychology
____ humanistic psychology
____ Gestalt psychology
____ cognitive psychology

A. concerned with how an organism uses its perceptual abilities to function in its environment.
B. stresses the whole character of perception.
C. concerned with alienation and meaninglessness in modern life and resulting psychological problems.
D. studies only observable and measurable behavior.
E. stresses the basic elements of experience and the combinations in which they occur.
F. emphasizes non-verbal experience and altered states of consciousness in realizing one's potential.
G. studies mental processes in the broadest sense.
H. maintains that hidden motives and unconscious desires govern much of our behavior.

3. The technique of objective introspection is associated with which of the following:
   a. James and Angell   c. Freud
   b. Wundt and Tichener   d. Laing and May
4. _____ pioneered the use of tests to measure human abilities.
5. B. F. Skinner added the new element of _____ to conditioning.

6. As a result of the influence of the cognitive school, psychology is now defined as the study of _____ and _____ _____ .
7. The four goals common to all psychologists are to _____ , _____ , _____ , and _____ human behavior.
8. A method of research known as _____ _____ allows psychologists to see how behavior operates in real-life situations.
9. Testing done in the _____ can be repeated and information can be collected under controlled conditions.
10. The independent/dependent variable in an experiment is manipulated to see how it affects a second variable; the independent/dependent variable is the one observed for any possible effects.
11. The experimental method makes use of all the following EXCEPT:
    a. hypotheses   c. experimenter bias
    b. variables   d. subjects
12. The _____ method of research is used to identify naturally occurring relationships among variables without having to manipulate any variable.
13. _____ research is research done for its own sake; _____ research, by contrast, is directed at the resolution of practical problems.
14. Which of the following is a TRUE statement about ethics in research:
    a. controversy over ethical standards has almost disappeared
    b. the APA code of ethics in use today dates from 1953
    c. ethical questions only apply to laboratory experiments
    d. failure to follow federal regulations can result in penalties
15. Which of the following is a TRUE statement about using animals in research:
    a. it is difficult to control an animal's immediate environment
    b. results can add to our understanding of human behavior
    c. the APA has not yet issued guidelines in this area
    d. there is little danger of making faulty comparisons between animal and human behavior

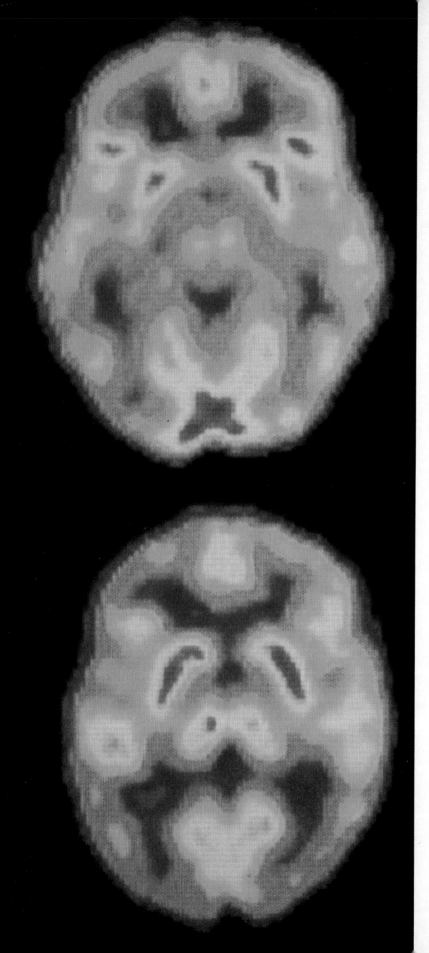

Outline

Physiology and Behavior

2

The radio says it is 9:00 A.M. but your new watch reads 9:05, so you set it back 5 minutes. Later in the day, you look at your watch and see that it says 3:15 P.M., but according to the clock in the library it is only 3:00. A little annoyed, you go to a watchmaker and explain your problem. He opens the watch case and examines the maze of tiny gears and levers inside. He discovers the difficulty, replaces the mainspring, and you are back on time.

In this chapter we are going to take our cue from the watchmaker. Psychology is the study of behavior. But often we cannot understand behavior unless we know a little about what goes on inside the human body, what makes us tick. Most of the time—when the watch is running perfectly or when the body is functioning normally—we tend to forget about the very complex activities that are constantly going on. But nonetheless they continue: the cells keep functioning and reproducing themselves; the organs and glands keep regulating such diverse activities as digestion and growth; and the nervous system keeps receiving, interpreting, and sending messages. And without these continuing and coordinated activities, there could be no life—certainly no psychological life—as we now know it.

The body possesses two major systems for coordinating and integrating behavior. One is the **endocrine system,** which consists of a number of glands that secrete chemical messages into the bloodstream. These chemicals perform a variety of functions, including preparation of nerves and muscles to act, control of metabolism, and regulation and development of secondary sexual traits. The second system is the **nervous system,** which relays messages in the form of nerve impulses throughout the body. The more we learn about the nervous system and the endocrine system, the more we understand how they work together to integrate the body's extraordinarily complex activities.

To understand how intricate these activities are, consider what happens when you burn your finger on a match. What happens next? "It's simple," you might say. "I automatically snatch my hand away from the heat." But, in fact, your body's response to a burn is not simple at all. It involves a highly complex set of activities. First, special sensory neurons pick up the message that your finger is burned. They pass this information along to the spinal cord, which triggers a quick withdrawal of your hand. Meanwhile the message is being sent to other parts of your nervous

Endocrine system Internal network of glands that release hormones directly into the bloodstream to regulate such important body functions as metabolism.

Nervous system The brain, the spinal cord, and the network of neurons that transmit messages throughout the body.

Neuron Individual cell that is the smallest unit of the nervous system.

Cell body Part of the neuron that contains the nucleus, and is the site where metabolism and respiration take place.

Dendrites Short fibers that branch out from the cell body and pick up incoming messages.

Axon Single long fiber extending from the cell body that carries outgoing messages.

system. Your body goes on "emergency alert": You breathe faster; your heart pounds; your entire body mobilizes itself against the wound. At the same time, the endocrine system gets involved: Hormones such as epinephrine are released into the bloodstream and carried throughout the body to supplement and reinforce the effects of nervous system activity. Meanwhile your brain continues to interpret the messages being sent to it: You experience pain; perhaps you turn your hand over to examine the burn; then you might walk over to the sink and run cold water over your hand. In other words, even a simple event such as burning your finger results in an extremely complex, coordinated sequence of activities that involves the body's nervous system working hand in hand with its endocrine system.

In our effort to understand how physiology affects psychological processes, we will first look at the nervous system. Then we will take a look at the endocrine system. Finally, we will consider the extent to which genes influence our behavior.

The Nervous System

The nervous system has a number of parts that all work together. These parts are various and complex, and in some cases their functions are still a mystery. Before considering the larger parts of the nervous system, we will examine its smallest unit, the individual nerve cell or neuron. This important cell underlies the activity of the entire nervous system.

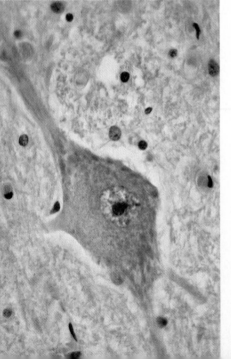

A photomicrograph of a single neuron, showing the cell body, dendrites, and axon.

The Neuron

There are more than 100 billion nerve cells, or **neurons,** in the brain of an average human being. That is more than 20 times the number of people living on the earth! And there are billions more neurons in other parts of the nervous system. Like all other cells, each neuron has a **cell body,** which contains a nucleus where metabolism and respiration take place; the cell body is enclosed by a cell membrane. Unlike other cells, however, neurons have tiny fibers extending from the cell body (see Figure 2-1) that enable the neuron to receive messages from surrounding cells and pass them on to other cells. No other cells in the body are equipped to do this.

The short fibers branching out from the cell body are called **dendrites.** The dendrites pick up messages coming in from surrounding areas and carry them to the cell body. Also extending from the cell body of the neuron is a single long fiber called an **axon.** The axon is very thin and usually much longer than the dendrites. For example, in adults the axons that run from the brain to the base of the spinal cord, or from the spinal cord to the tip of the thumb, may be as long as 3 feet; but most axons are only 1 or 2 inches long. The axon carries outgoing messages from the cell and either relays them to neighboring neurons or directs a muscle or gland to take action. A group of axons bundled together like parallel wires in

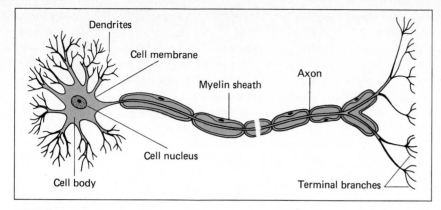

Figure 2-1

A typical myelinated neuron.

Nerve Group of axons bundled together.

Myelin sheath Fatty covering found on some axons.

Sensory or **afferent neurons** Neurons that carry messages from sense organs to the spinal cord or brain.

Motor or **efferent neurons** Neurons that carry messages from the spinal cord or brain to the muscles and glands.

Interneurons or **association neurons** Neurons that carry messages from one neuron to another and do most of the work of the nervous system.

Ions Electrically charged particles found in the semiliquid solutions inside and outside the neuron.

Polarization Condition of a neuron at rest when most positive ions are on the outside and most negative ions are on the inside of the cell membrane.

an electric cable is called a **nerve.** Since there may be hundreds of dendrites on a single neuron, and since the axon itself may branch out in numerous directions, one neuron can be in touch with hundreds of others at both its input end (dendrites) and its output end (axon).

Look at the neuron in Figure 2-1. Its axon is surrounded by a fatty covering called a **myelin sheath.** The sheath is pinched at intervals, which makes the axon resemble a string of microscopic sausages. Not all axons are covered by myelin sheaths, but myelinated axons are found throughout the body. As we will soon see, the sheaths help neurons act with greater efficiency, as well as providing insulation to the neuron.

Although all neurons relay messages, the kind of information they collect and the places to which they carry it help to distinguish among different types of neurons. For example, neurons that collect messages from sense organs and carry those messages to the spinal cord or to the brain are called **sensory** (or **afferent**) **neurons.** Neurons that carry messages from the spinal cord or the brain to the muscles and glands are called **motor** (or **efferent**) **neurons.** And neurons that carry messages from one neuron to another are called **interneurons** (or **association neurons**). Interneurons account for 99.98 percent of all the neurons in the central nervous system (Nauta & Feirtag, 1979), and they perform most of the work of the nervous system.

The Neural Impulse

We've referred several times to the fact that neurons carry messages. How do these messages get started? When a neuron is resting, its cell membrane forms a partial barrier between semiliquid solutions that are inside and outside the neuron. Both solutions contain electrically charged particles, or **ions.** The charged particles outside the neuron are mostly positive ions such as sodium, while those inside the neuron are mostly negatively charged ions. Since there are more negative ions inside the neuron than outside, the electrical charge inside the neuron is said to be negative relative to the outside and the neuron is said to be in a state of **polarization.**

"I realize that those of you who are planning to go into psychiatry may find this dull."
(Drawing by Ed Fisher; © 1962 the *New Yorker Magazine, Inc.*)

Action potential or **neural impulse** The firing of a nerve cell caused by depolarization of the neuron.

Graded potential A shift in the electrical charge in a tiny area of the neuron caused by an incoming message too weak to stimulate the neuron to fire.

While the neuron is in a resting state, the cell membrane lets many substances pass freely in and out. It refuses, however, to let positive sodium ions come into the neuron. In this way, the cell membrane keeps the neuron in a polarized state. But when a point on the cell membrane is adequately stimulated by an incoming message, the cell membrane suddenly opens at that point, allowing the sodium ions to rush in. When enough sodium has entered the neuron to make the inside positively charged relative to the outside, the cell membrane closes and no more sodium ions can enter.

The breakdown of the cell membrane does not occur at just one point. In fact, as soon as the cell membrane allows sodium to enter the cell at one point, the next point on the membrane also opens. More sodium ions flow into the neuron at the second spot and depolarize this part of the neuron. The process is repeated along the length of the neural membrane, creating a **neural impulse** or **action potential** that travels down the axon, much like a fuse burning from one end to the other (Hodgkin & Huxley, 1952) (see Figure 2-2). When this happens, we say the neuron has fired.

The neuron does not fire in response to every impulse it receives. If the incoming message is not strong enough, it may simply cause a shift in the electrical charge in a tiny area of the neuron. This **graded potential** then simply fades away, leaving the neuron in its normal polarized state. In other words, the incoming message must be above a certain *threshold* to cause a neuron to fire, just as you must pull the trigger on a gun hard enough to make it fire.

Figure 2-2

When a point on the neural membrane is adequately stimulated by an incoming message, the membrane opens at that point and positively charged sodium ions flow in, depolarizing the neuron. This process is repeated along the length of the membrane, creating the neural impulse that travels down the axon, causing the neuron to fire.

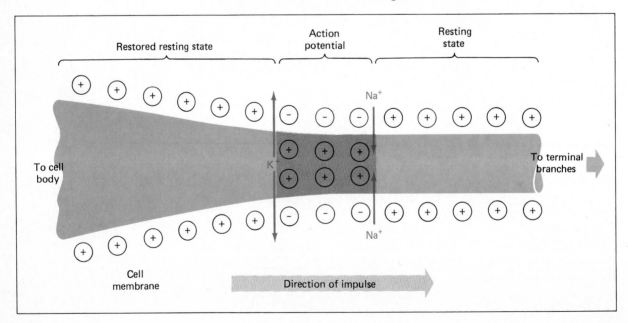

For a period of about .001 second after firing (the **absolute refractory period**), the neuron will not fire again no matter how strong the incoming messages may be. This is not surprising if we remember that the neuron has stopped letting sodium in and is depolarized. But then, in what is called the **relative refractory period,** the cell starts to pump positive ions out again until the inside of the neuron returns to a negative charge relative to the outside. During this phase, which lasts for only a few thousandths of a second, the neuron will fire, but only if the incoming message is considerably stronger than normal. Finally equilibrium is restored and the neuron is returned to its resting state, ready to fire again (see Figure 2-3).

This whole process occurs very quickly, but there is a wide range in the speed with which individual neurons conduct impulses. In some of the largest myelinated axons the fastest impulses may travel at speeds of nearly 400 feet per second. Axons with myelin sheaths can conduct impulses very rapidly because the impulses leapfrog along the string of pinched intervals, or **nodes,** that lie along the sheaths. Neurons without myelin sheaths tend to be slower. Their impulses are conducted in a steady flow, like a fuse. Impulses in the slowest of these unmyelinated neurons poke along at little more than 3 feet per second.

Absolute refractory period A period after firing when the neuron will not fire again no matter how strong the incoming messages may be.

Relative refractory period A period when the neuron is returning to its normal polarized state and may refire if the incoming message is much stronger than usual.

Nodes Pinched intervals on the myelin sheaths of some axons that help speed the passage of neural impulses.

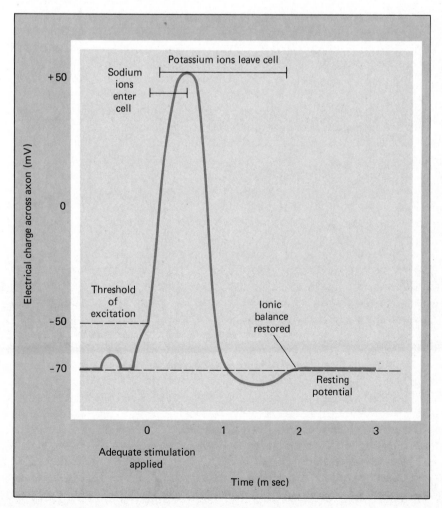

Figure 2-3

The incoming message must be above a certain threshold to cause a neuron to fire. After it fires, the cell body begins to pump potassium ions out of the neuron until a state of ionic equilibrium is restored. This process happens very quickly and within a few thousandths of a second the neuron is ready to fire again.
(Adapted from Carlson, 1977)

Axon terminal or **synaptic knob**
Knob that forms the end of an axon.

Synaptic space or **synaptic cleft**
Tiny gap between the axon terminal of one neuron and the dendrites or cell body of the next neuron.

Synapse Area composed of the axon terminal of one neuron, the synaptic space, and the dendrite or cell body of the next neuron.

Synaptic vesicles Tiny sacs at the end of an axon that release chemicals into the synapse.

Neurotransmitters Chemicals released by the synaptic vesicles that travel across the synaptic space and affect the next neuron.

Receptor site A site on the other side of the synaptic space that matches a neurotransmitter, which locks into it.

Acetylcholine (ACh) An excitatory neurotransmitter often found where neurons meet skeletal muscles.

At any instant a neuron is either firing (on) or resting (off), just as a gun is either being fired or not. This simple on-off switching code is all the neuron can use to pass along the messages it receives. But how can such a simple on-off code communicate very complex information? Think once more about the gun. Pulling even harder on the gun's trigger will not cause the bullet to travel any faster or any farther. Either it fires because you pulled hard enough, or it does not fire because you did not pull hard enough. But if you pull the trigger again and again, and if other people around you are firing their guns at the same time, there will be a volley of shots. This will convey very different information than a single shot to someone who hears it.

The same is true of neurons. Strong incoming signals do not cause a stronger neural impulse: Each neuron fires just as strongly as before. But the neuron is likely to fire more often when stimulated by a strong signal, and neighboring neurons are also more likely to fire. The result is rapid and widespread neural firing that communicates the message, "There's a very strong stimulus out here."

The Synapse

We have been discussing the operation of a single neuron. But the billions of neurons in the nervous system work together to coordinate the body's activities. How do they interact? How does a message get from one neuron to another?

Imagine a single neuron that receives its messages from just one other neuron and transmits messages to just one neuron. The dendrites or cell body of the neuron pick up a signal; then, as we have seen, if the signal is strong enough the neuron fires, and an impulse starts down the axon until it reaches the end. At the end of the axon is a tiny knob called an **axon terminal** or **synaptic knob.** In most cases, there is a tiny gap between this axon terminal and the dendrite or cell body of the next neuron. This tiny gap is called a **synaptic space** (or **synaptic cleft**). The entire area composed of the axon terminal of one neuron, the synaptic space, and the dendrite or cell body of the next neuron is called the **synapse** (see Figure 2-4).

If the neural impulse is to travel on to the next neuron, it must somehow travel across the synaptic space. It is tempting to imagine that the neural impulse simply leaps across the gap like an electric spark, but in reality the transfer is made by chemicals. What happens is this: Most axon terminals contain a number of tiny oval sacs called **synaptic vesicles** (see Figure 2-4). When the neural impulse reaches the end of the axon, it causes these vesicles to release varying amounts of chemicals called **neurotransmitters.** These chemical substances travel across the synaptic space and affect the next neuron.

There are dozens of known neurotransmitters, and their functions are still being investigated. For each such substance there are matching hookup or **receptor sites** on the other side of the synaptic space. The neurotransmitter fits into the proper receptor site just as a key fits into a lock. Some neurotransmitters "excite" the next neuron, making it, in turn, more likely to fire. **Acetylcholine** (ACh) is one such excitatory transmitter and is often found where neurons meet skeletal muscles.

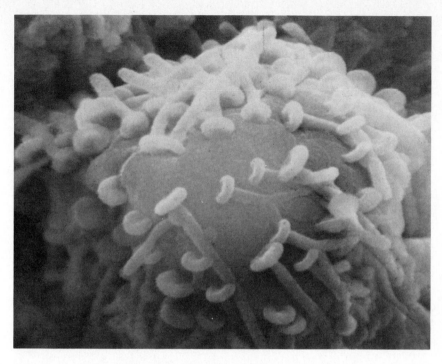

Dopamine A prevalent inhibitory neurotransmitter.

Enkephalins and **endorphins** Neurotransmitters involved with the reduction of pain.

A photograph taken with a scanning electron micrograph, showing the synaptic knobs at the ends of axons. Inside the knobs are the vesicles that contain neurotransmitters.

Other transmitter substances "inhibit" the next neuron, making it less likely to fire. **Dopamine** is one prevalent inhibitory transmitter. Recently another group of inhibitory transmitters has been linked to the body's own relief of pain. Both **enkephalins** and **endorphins** appear to reduce pain by inhibiting the neurons that transmit pain messages in the brain. Endorphins are chains of amino acids that act like neurotransmitters. One endorphin was found to be 48 times more potent than morphine when injected into the brain, and 3 times more potent when injected into the bloodstream (Snyder, 1977) (see the box on p. 34). Enkephalins also occur naturally in the brain, but seem to have smaller and shorter-term pain-relieving effects (Bolles & Fanselow, 1982). We will see shortly, when we look at the action of drugs, just how these various neurotransmitters can control a number of everyday psychological processes.

Once a chemical transmitter has been released into the synaptic space and performed its job, what happens to it? If it remains loose, or if it continues to occupy receptor sites, it will continue to affect the next neuron indefinitely, long after the initial message or signal is over. Some neurotransmitters (such as ACh) are simply destroyed by other chemicals in the synapse. Others (such as dopamine) are recycled—they are taken back into the vesicles to be used again. In either case, the synapse is cleared up and returned to its normal state.

Figure 2-4

A highly simplified drawing of the synapse, showing the synaptic vesicles and the tiny synaptic space that separates most neurons from one another.

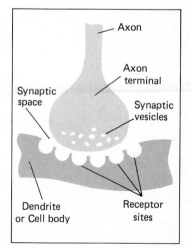

Synapses and Drugs

Most drugs that affect psychological functions alter the way synapses work. Some drugs impede the release of transmitter chemicals from neurons into the synaptic space. For example, the toxin produced by the

Endorphins

Endorphins are a group of neurotransmitters involved in the natural relief of pain. In fact, they are often called the body's own narcotic (Rosenzweig & Leiman, 1982). The word *endorphin* is a contraction of "endogenous morphine," meaning morphine produced within the body itself.

The discovery of endorphins took place very rapidly and in a different manner from that of other known neurotransmitters. In most cases, a transmitter substance has been identified first and its receptor sites found later. With the endorphins it was the other way around. In the early 1970s scientists found receptor sites in certain parts of the brain and spinal cord that bind external narcotics like morphine. Further work showed that these receptor sites are especially numerous in areas of the brain known to control the experience of pain. Investigators reasoned that such receptor sites would not exist unless the body produced narcotics that could stimulate them. The intensive search for such substances ended in 1975, when endorphins were finally isolated in brain tissue.

The exact role of endorphins in reducing pain is not yet clear. Some evidence suggests that they contribute to joggers' heightened ability to withstand pain after running: Running appears to lower sensitivity to pain by increasing the amount of endorphins in the central nervous system. After running a mile, one group of joggers could withstand the pain of a 3-pound weight on their index finger about 70 percent longer than they could before running. Endorphins were similarly found to affect moods, possibly contributing to the "runner's high" that many people feel at the end of a good run (Haier et al., 1982). Experimental research with animals indicates that various kinds of stimulation, such as electrical shocks, raises the amount of endorphins in the brain. The same research suggests that endorphins may play a part in other processes besides pain inhibition. For instance, they may hinder certain aspects of memory in animals, as well as contribute to pleasurable sensations. And there seem to be endorphin-related effects on body temperature, breathing, and the circulatory system (Bolles & Faneslow, 1982).

The discovery of these natural painkilling substances raised the hope that if scientists could produce them artificially in the laboratory, they would not be as addictive as the opiates. Unfortunately the synthetic endorphins did not live up to expectations. Repeated administration of these substances has resulted in tolerance and dependence symptoms similar to those of drug addiction (Olson et al., 1979).

The question remains as to just why the synthetic endorphins are addictive while the natural ones are not. One explanation is that the synthetic substances are not exactly the same chemically as the real thing. The altered structure, which is necessary in order to permit the drug to penetrate the barrier between the bloodstream and the brain, may make the synthetic endorphins addictive. Then, too, synthetic endorphins are designed to retain their anesthetic effect over a longer period of time than the natural substance, which breaks down rapidly. The chemical changes necessary to achieve this may have made the synthetic substance addictive. Researchers are still looking for a nonaddictive "natural" painkiller, but so far they have been unsuccessful.

microorganism that causes botulism prevents the release of the transmitter ACh. The result is paralysis and sometimes a rapid death. Other drugs such as reserpine cause transmitter chemicals to leak out of the synaptic vesicles and be rapidly broken down by enzymes. The result is a shortage of transmitters and decreased activity at the synapse. Reserpine is often prescribed to reduce blood pressure because it decreases the activity of neurons that excite the circulatory system. Lysergic acid diethylamide (LSD) reduces the activity of serotonin, an inhibitory transmitter, and it may also affect dopamine, though as yet it is not known exactly how. You may be wondering how suppression of activity could produce the spectacular sensations of an LSD "trip." The drug provokes these effects by suppressing activity in neurons that normally inhibit other neurons in the brain. In response, impulses in the brain increase in frequency, generating hallucinations.

In contrast to drugs that reduce the amount of neurotransmitters, some, such as the venom of the black widow spider and amphetamines, speed up the release of transmitter chemicals into the synaptic space. The spider's poison causes ACh to be poured into the synapses of the nervous system. As a result, neurons fire repeatedly, causing spasms and tremors.

We have seen that some drugs have their effect by increasing or decreasing the amount of neurotransmitters in the synapse. Other drugs work directly on the receptor sites at the other side of the synaptic gap. Morphine and other opiates are able to lock into the receptors for endorphins, the body's natural painkillers, because they have similar chemical structures. Atropine, a poison derived from belladonna and other plants, blocks receptor sites, preventing transmitter substances from having their effect. When morphine or atropine occupy the receptor sites, chemical transmitters cannot attach themselves to the neuron, and this tends to shut down the nervous system. Curare, the poison with which some South American Indians tip their arrows, works in the same way.

Still other drugs interfere with the destruction of neurotransmitters after they have done their job. Once transmitter chemicals have bonded to receptor sites and stimulated or inhibited the neuron, they normally are either deactivated by enzymes or reabsorbed by the vesicles they came from. A number of stimulant drugs interfere with this process. Caffeine, for example, inhibits the action of the enzymes that break down a neurotransmitter, thus prolonging its effect. As a result, the neurons keep firing, causing a state of high arousal in the nervous system and sometimes a case of "coffee nerves." Cocaine affects the synapses in much the same way, only it prevents transmitter chemicals from being reabsorbed. Again, the effect is continued stimulation of the receptor sites and a generalized arousal of the nervous system (Carlson, 1980).

Amphetamines work in several ways: They not only increase the release of the chemical transmitters norepinephrine and dopamine, but they also inhibit reabsorption of these substances into the original axon after they have locked into receptor sites on the next neuron. As a result, the next neuron continues to fire while the overall supply of norepinephrine drops. The nervous system responds with a state of alertness or arousal—a "high."

One fascinating recent finding is that neurotransmitters in some cases may be the cause of certain kinds of mental illness. Schizophrenia, for example, seems to be associated with an overabundance of the chemical transmitter dopamine. Some drugs that have been developed to treat schizophrenia (chlorpromazine is an example) seem to reduce the symptoms of this disorder by blocking dopamine receptors. We will explore these interesting discoveries more fully in the chapters on abnormal behavior and therapy.

Divisions of the Nervous System

If the brain alone has more than 100 billion neurons, and each neuron can be "in touch" with hundreds or even thousands of other neurons (Stevens, 1979), then our bodies must contain hundreds of trillions of synapses through which each neuron is indirectly linked to every other neuron in the nervous system. Though it is impossible to comprehend

Central nervous system Division of the nervous system that consists of the brain and the spinal cord.

Peripheral nervous system Division of the nervous system that connects the central nervous system to the rest of the body.

Hindbrain Brain area containing the medulla, pons, and cerebellum.

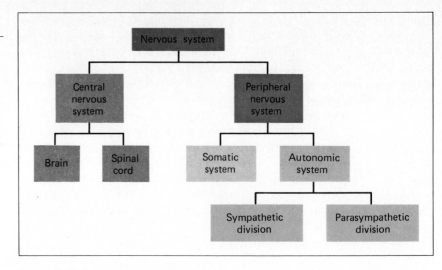

Figure 2-5
A schematic diagram of the divisions of the nervous system and their various subparts.

such an immense system of interconnected neurons, there really is some structure, some organization, to it all.

The nervous system is usually divided into two major parts: the **central nervous system** and the **peripheral nervous system.** The central nervous system consists of the brain and spinal cord. The peripheral nervous system connects the brain and spinal cord to everything else in the body: sense organs, muscles, glands, and so on (see Figure 2-5). Obviously, without the peripheral nervous system the central nervous system could not do its job. What would it be like if the brain and the spinal cord were isolated from the rest of the body? To answer this question, we first have to understand what the central nervous system normally does.

The Central Nervous System

The brain is surely the most fascinating part of the whole nervous system. Containing more than 90 percent of the body's neurons, the brain is the seat of awareness and reason, the place where learning, memory, and emotions are centered. It is the part of us that decides what to do and whether that decision was right or wrong. And it imagines how things might have turned out if we had acted differently.

THE BRAIN. As soon as the brain begins to take shape in the human embryo, we can detect three distinct parts: the hindbrain, midbrain, and forebrain (see Figure 2-6). These three parts are still present in the fully developed adult brain, though they are not so easily distinguished one from another. We will use these three basic divisions to describe the parts of the brain, what they do, and how they interact to influence our behavior.

Since the **hindbrain** is found in even the most primitive vertebrates, it is believed to have been the earliest part of the brain to evolve. The part of the hindbrain nearest to the spinal cord is the **medulla,** a narrow structure about 1.5 inches long. The medulla controls such things as breathing, heart rate, and blood pressure. The medulla is also the point at which many of the nerves from the body cross over on their way to the higher brain centers; the nerves from the left part of the body cross to the right side of the brain and vice versa.

Above the medulla lies the **pons,** which connects the cerebral cortex at the top of the brain to the topmost section of the hindbrain, the **cerebellum.** The cerebellum is composed of two hemispheres. It performs a wide range of functions. It handles certain reflexes, especially those that have to do with balance and breathing, and it coordinates the body's actions to ensure that movements go together in efficient sequences. Damage to the cerebellum causes severe problems in movement, such as jerky motions, loss of balance, and lack of coordination.

Above the pons and cerebellum the **brain stem** widens to form the **midbrain.** As its name implies, the midbrain is in the middle of the brain, between the hindbrain at the base and the forebrain at the top. The midbrain is especially important to hearing and sight. It is also one of several places in the brain where pain is registered.

Supported by the brain stem, budding out above it and drooping over somewhat to fit into the skull, is the **forebrain.** In the center of the forebrain, and more or less directly over the brain stem, are the two egg-shaped structures that make up the **thalamus.** The thalamus relays and translates incoming messages from sense receptors (except those for smell) throughout the body. Many of the messages that travel from one part of the brain to another also pass through the thalamus. Some of the neurons in the thalamus seem to be important in regulating the activity of higher brain centers. Others control the activities of those parts of the nervous system outside the brain and spinal cord.

Medulla Part of the hindbrain that controls such functions as breathing, heart rate, and blood pressure.

Pons Connects the cerebral cortex at the top of the brain to the cerebellum.

Cerebellum Two hemispheres at the topmost part of the hindbrain that control certain reflexes and coordinate the body's movements.

Brain stem The top end of the spinal column that widens out to form the lower part of the brain.

Midbrain Region between the hindbrain and the forebrain; it is important for hearing and sight and is one of several places in the brain where pain is registered.

Forebrain Top part of the brain, including the thalamus, hypothalamus, and cerebral cortex.

Thalamus Area of the forebrain that relays and translates incoming messages from the sense receptors, except those for smell.

Figure 2-6

A cross section of the brain, showing the hindbrain, midbrain, and forebrain.

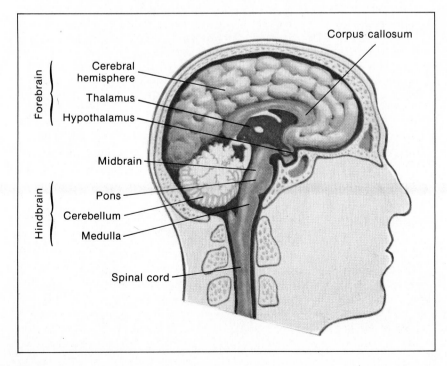

Forebrain
Hindbrain

Corpus callosum
Cerebral hemisphere
Thalamus
Hypothalamus
Midbrain
Pons
Cerebellum
Medulla
Spinal cord

Hypothalamus Forebrain region that governs motivation and emotional responses.

Cerebral cortex The two hemispheres of the forebrain that regulate most complex behavior.

Below the thalamus is a smaller structure called the **hypothalamus.** This part of the forebrain exerts an enormous influence on many kinds of motivation. Centers in the hypothalamus govern eating, drinking, sexual behavior, sleeping, and temperature control. The hypothalamus is also directly involved in emotional behavior. Centers in the hypothalamus are responsible for such emotions as rage, terror, and pleasure. Also, in times of stress the hypothalamus appears to play a central role, coordinating and integrating the activity of the nervous system.

At the top of the brain stem are the two cerebral hemispheres commonly called the **cerebral cortex.** These are what most people think of

Brain Waves

As large numbers of neurons fire in the brain, they generate sequences of rhythmic variations in electrical activity known as *brain waves.* The shape and pattern of these waves vary depending on what you happen to be doing at the time. Using electrodes placed directly on the scalp, psychologists can record brain-wave activity on an *electroencephalograph,* or *EEG.* By means of this device, investigators have uncovered a number of different types of brain waves. *Alpha waves* are present when a person is sitting or lying awake with eyes closed. These waves are commonly associated with a state of relaxation. Alphas change to higher-frequency *beta waves* when a person is awake and still, but with eyes open. High-frequency *gamma waves* are characteristic of being awake and in a highly excited state. At the other extreme are the low-frequency *delta waves* that occur during deepest sleep. Also, the site of origin in the brain varies with the type of wave. Alpha waves, for instance, are usually recorded in the occipital and parietal lobes. Delta waves are much more variable in location.

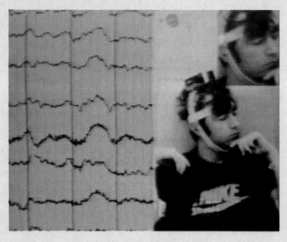

Other patterns of waves arise when the brain is exposed to stimuli such as sound or light or when it enters certain psychological states. Researchers have discovered an EEG pattern that appears in the interval between some type of warning signal and a response, such as pressing a button. This seems to suggest that subtle psychological processes, such as a state of expectancy, can affect brain waves (Rosenzweig & Leiman, 1982).

Recently medical researchers have discovered that epilepsy is associated with highly unusual patterns of electrical activity in the brain. When undergoing a seizure, the brain is swept by sudden and dramatic changes that have been compared to electrical storms. During these disruptions, the height of the EEG can reach 5 to 20 times that of normal brain waves (Rosenzweig & Leiman, 1982). In grand mal seizures the EEG pattern in large areas of the brain reflects bursts of unusually rapid firing by individual neurons. The effect of these abnormalities on the behavior of the victim is striking. The person loses consciousness and the body stiffens for 1 or 2 minutes, then enters a phase marked by a sequence of sudden jerks and relaxation.

Psychologists do not yet understand what causes these uncontrolled bursts of firing. It is known that head injuries, exposure to chemicals, and problems with metabolism can bring about seizures, but just why this happens remains a mystery. Nonetheless, researchers have developed a number of drugs that inhibit transmission of the nerve impulses that mark epilepsy and as a result the number and severity of attacks can be reduced. In extreme cases, it is also possible to reduce epileptic seizures through brain surgery. Later in this chapter we will discuss some fascinating discoveries that have been made as a result of this kind of "split-brain" surgery.

The two cerebral hemispheres sit on top of the brainstem and take up most of the area inside the skull.

Convolutions Folds in the cerebral cortex that allow its mass to fit inside the skull.

Sensory projection areas Areas of the cerebral cortex where messages from the sense receptors are registered.

Motor projection areas Areas of the cerebral cortex where response messages from the brain to the muscles and glands begin.

Association areas Areas in the cerebral cortex where incoming messages from the separate senses are combined into meaningful impressions and outgoing messages from the motor areas are integrated.

Frontal lobes Largest of the association areas; the site of such uniquely human activities as self-awareness, initiative, and planning.

first when they talk about "the brain," and as the above photo shows, they take up most of the room inside the skull. They balloon out over the brain stem, fold down over it, and actually hide most of it from view. The cerebral cortex is the most recently evolved part of the nervous system and is more highly developed in humans than in any other animal. It accounts for about 80 percent of the human brain's weight and contains 70 percent of the neurons in the central nervous system. If it were spread out, it would cover 2–3 square feet, so in order to fit inside the skull, the cerebral cortex has developed an intricate pattern of folds—hills and valleys called **convolutions.** These convolutions form a pattern in every brain that is as unique as a fingerprint.

The areas of the cerebral cortex where messages from the sense receptors are registered are called **sensory projection areas.** Response messages from the brain start their return trip in the **motor projection areas,** and from there they go to the various muscles and glands in the body. There are also large areas throughout the cerebral cortex that are neither completely sensory nor completely motor. These are called **association areas,** and they make up most of the cerebral cortex. It is in the association areas that messages coming in from separate senses are combined into meaningful impressions, and where motor messages going out are integrated so the body can make coordinated movements. The association areas are involved in all of the activities we commonly attribute to the brain: learning, thinking, remembering, talking.

The largest of the association areas is located in the **frontal lobes** of the brain, just behind the forehead. Accounting for about half the volume of the cerebral cortex, the frontal lobes appear to be the site of mental processes that are unique to humans—self-awareness, initiative, and the ability to plan. However, the exact functions of these lobes are

New Tools for Looking at the Brain

The pace of scientific discovery has long been connected to the invention of instruments that improve our powers of observation. The invention of the telescope, for example, allowed Galileo to challenge existing ideas about the solar system. The development of the microscope made possible the detailed study of cells, the existence of which had been suspected but not proved. In recent years a number of devices designed to map various structures and operations of the brain promise to revolutionize our understanding of how the human brain works.

A CAT scan of a normal human brain.

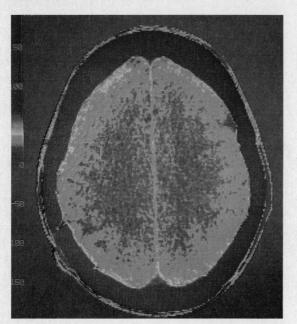

About 20 years ago the invention of computerized axial tomography (CAT) scanning gave us our first sectional images of body structures, including parts of the brain. This specialized x-ray technology photographs the brain from many points around the circumference of the skull and produces images like that shown below left. Even more successful at producing pictures of the inner regions of the brain—its ridges, folds, and fissures—is a brand-new imaging technique called nuclear magnetic resonance (NMR). An image created by NMR is shown below. Both these techniques permit unparalleled mapping of the brain's structures.

An NMR image of a human head.

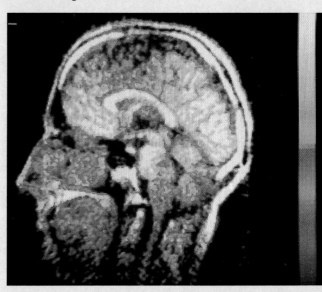

still obscure. In part, this is because much of our knowledge about brain function comes from research on animals, whose frontal lobes are relatively undeveloped. Therefore, in studying the frontal lobes, we have had to rely on the relatively rare cases of people with some kind of frontal lobe damage. One such famous case became public in 1848. It involved a bizarre accident that happened to a man named Phineas Gage.

Gage, who was foreman of a road construction gang, made a careless mistake while using some blasting powder and a tamping iron. As a result, the tamping iron tore through his cheek and severely damaged both frontal lobes. Gage remained conscious, walked to a doctor, and, to the amazement of those who saw the accident, suffered few major aftereffects. There was no physical impairment, and his memory and skills seemed to be as good as ever. He did, however, undergo major personality changes. Once a steady worker, he lost interest in work and drifted from

Neither CAT scanning nor NMR, however, can provide a moving picture of the brain in action. Two techniques allow researchers to do just that—to observe the brain as it actually reacts to sensory stimuli such as pain, tones, and words. One technique is a kind of electroencephalography or EEG (you read about this in the box on p. 38) that measures the electrical activity the brain produces as it responds to stimuli. The second technique is positron emission tomography (PET) scanning. As neurons in a given part of the brain fire, that part of the brain replenishes its energy supply by absorb-

ing sugar from the blood. PET maps the location in the brain of radioactive sugar molecules that are released into the bloodstream.

This technology will permit the matching of anatomical structures (from CAT and NMR) with sites of energy use (PET) and areas of electrical activity in the brain (EEGs). When all four techniques are combined, scientists may finally be able to study the impact of drugs on the brain, track the formation of memories, and map the location of other mental activities in unprecedented detail (Buchsbaum, 1983).

A PET scanner.

An EEG machine and printout.

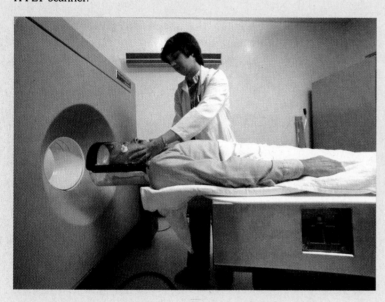

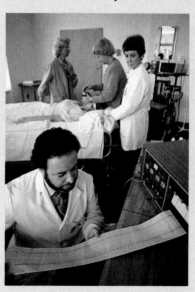

job to job. Other personality changes were so great that, in the view of his friends, Gage was no longer the same man.

Since Gage's time, careful observation of brain-damaged people has refined these early impressions of the functions of the frontal lobes. This part of the brain seems to permit goal-directed behavior. Patients with damage to the frontal lobes have trouble completing tasks that involve following complex directions or performing tasks in which the directions change during the course of the job. The frontal lobes also appear necessary to a normal emotional life. People whose frontal lobes have been severed often seem apathetic and capable of only shallow emotions, though this apathy may be interrupted by periods of boastfulness and silliness (Rosenzweig & Leiman, 1982). The frontal lobes also seem to play a role in the ability to keep track of previous and future movements of the body. Much more research needs to be done before psychologists can understand how this part of the cortex contributes to such a wide and subtle range of mental activities.

Besides their other functions, the frontal lobes receive and coordinate messages from the three other lobes of the cortex. Each of these other lobes is responsible for a different sense. The **occipital lobe,** located at the very back of the brain, receives and interprets visual information from both eyes. Next to the occipital lobe is the **temporal lobe,** which controls hearing and does some additional processing of visual information. The temporal lobe may also be the area of the brain where memories are permanently stored. The **parietal lobe** sits on top of the temporal and occipital lobes (see Figure 2-7). This lobe receives sensations of touch and bodily position and informs the brain of events worthy of special attention. Injury to any of these lobes will directly affect the sense area involved. We will look more closely at the connections between the senses and the brain areas where sensations are registered in the next chapter.

HEMISPHERIC SPECIALIZATION. We have been talking about the cerebral cortex as if it were all one piece. But if you look closely at the photos on p. 43, you will notice in the top and bottom views what appears to be a split down the middle of the cortex, running from front to back. In this case, appearance is reality: The cerebral cortex is made up of two separate hemispheres. In a sense there is a "right half-brain" and a "left half-brain," and the only place they are directly connected is through a thick ribbonlike band across the bottom called the **corpus callosum** (see Figure 2-6). In general, the left half of the brain receives messages from and sends messages to the right side of the body. The right half of the brain does this for the left side of the body.

Under normal conditions the two hemispheres are in close communication through the corpus callosum and work together as a coordinated

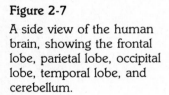

Figure 2-7

A side view of the human brain, showing the frontal lobe, parietal lobe, occipital lobe, temporal lobe, and cerebellum.

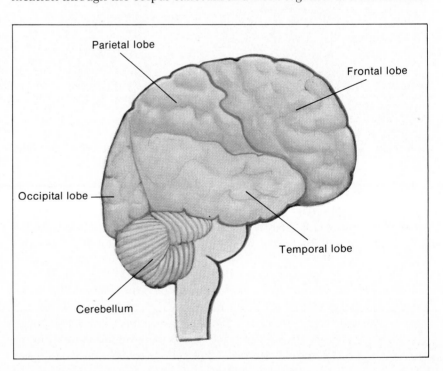

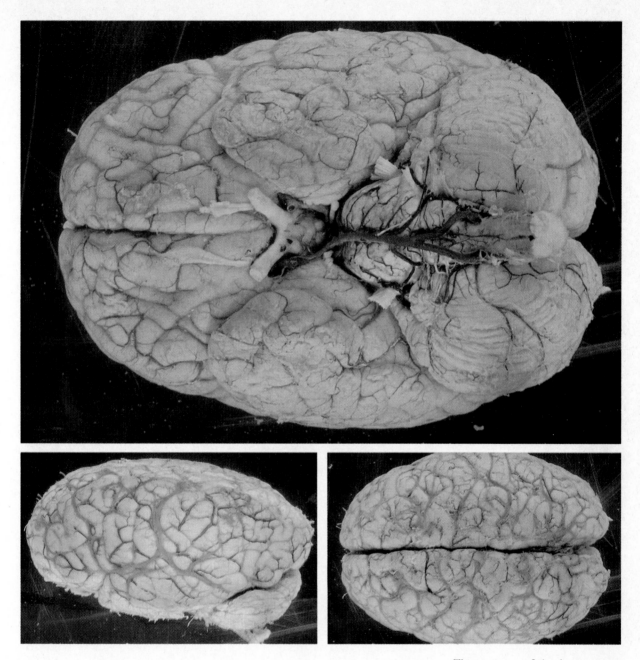

Three views of the brain. Visible in the top and bottom right photos is the split down the middle of the brain. The photo at bottom left is of the blood vessels found in the brain.

unit. Nonetheless, some evidence began to collect early in this century that the cerebral hemispheres are not really equivalent. For example, damage to the left hemisphere often seems to result in severe language problems, while similar damage to the right hemisphere seldom has that effect. Then, in the early 1960s, Sperry and his colleagues at the California Institute of Technology started treating epileptics by cutting the corpus callosum (Rosenzweig & Leiman, 1982). The intent was to stop the spread of seizures from one hemisphere to the other, but the operations also cut the only direct communication link between the two hemispheres and thus made it possible to watch each hemisphere work on its own. The results were startling.

Electrical Stimulation of the Brain

Electrical stimulation of the brain, or ESB, can be used to see how the brain controls actions, thoughts, and emotions. It can also be used to try to control those very behaviors or emotions. Stimulating part of the brain with electrical current produces a "counterfeit" nerve impulse: The brain is fooled into thinking that it has received a real impulse from one of its sensory receptors. It thinks something really is going on "out there" and makes a person behave accordingly.

For example, in a much publicized demonstration, José Delgado (1969) implanted a radio-controlled electrode in the brain of a bull bred especially for bullfighting, one that will charge any human being. He went into the arena with the bull, armed only with a radio transmitter. When the bull charged him, Delgado pressed a button on the transmitter, sending an impulse to the electrode in the bull's brain, and the bull stopped in his tracks. The experiment seems to suggest that the stimulation had a direct effect on the bull's aggressive tendencies, or, according to Delgado, "The result seemed to be a combination of motor effect . . . plus behavioral inhibition of the aggressive drive." The social implications are provocative: Should we be concerned about the use of such "behavioral inhibition" in humans?

Although brain stimulation is now being used for therapeutic purposes in many parts of the world, visions of a Big Brother controlling our behavior seem to be premature. According to psychobiologist Elliot Valenstein (1973), we are a long way from practical manipulation of human behavior through brain control. The Delgado experiment raises many questions. For example, did Delgado really find the precise location in the bull's skull that controls aggression? Valenstein contends that the electric shock to the bull's brain interfered with movement and made it impossible for the bull to continue its charge. Valenstein also suggests that rather than being pacified after repeated shocks, as Delgado claimed, the bull was simply confused and frustrated and just gave up.

The use of brain stimulation to control behavior, while interesting as a research technique, has very limited practical value. There are several reasons for this. First, no single area of the brain is likely to be the sole source of any given emotion or behavior. As Valenstein (1973) states, "Unfortunately, the nervous system is not organized in a way that makes it possible to separate functions in terms of their social implication" (p. 352). Second, the effects of brain stimulation depend on many other factors. Valenstein and others have shown that electrical brain stimulation in animals does not produce a consistent motivational state or behavior (Valenstein, 1977). Environmental changes, for example, often produce different responses to the same stimulation in the same subjects. Not surprisingly, human subjects show an even wider difference in their responses: The same person will exhibit different behavioral responses to identical brain stimulation given at different times. Thus, although stimulation of the brain can produce effects that help us understand the working of the central nervous system, "brain control" such as that described by Michael Crichton in his novel *The Terminal Man* simply is not possible.

The two hemispheres do indeed appear to have different functions and to store different information. The left hemisphere is dominant in verbal tasks, such as identifying spoken and printed words, while the right side is superior in geometric reasoning and analysis of spatial information (see Figure 2-8). But more recent evidence shows that the right brain may not be completely without verbal skills. Most of the split-brain patients studied so far have had no real language ability in the right hemisphere, but some could recognize simple words with their right hemisphere, and at least a few displayed quite sophisticated verbal skills there (Gazzaniga, 1983; Zaidel, 1983). Moreover, the right hemisphere may be responsible for certain other abilities. It appears to be vital to some aspects of concept formation, as in being able to understand how the parts of a story fit together and what a story is all about. For example, split-brain patients studied by Gardner (1981) listened to stories and were asked to retell them. These patients could recall the main details of the stories quite well. But they tended to confuse the order of sentences, leave out parts of the story, and misinterpret the point of the story.

Although the differences between the two hemispheres are intriguing, remember that under normal conditions the right and left halves are in close communication through the corpus callosum and thus work together in a coordinated, integrated way.

THE RETICULAR FORMATION. We separated the brain into forebrain, midbrain, and hindbrain to simplify our discussion. But the brain itself often ignores such distinctions and sets up systems that jump across these boundaries, drawing together different parts of the brain to perform certain functions. One such system is the **reticular formation** (see Figure 2-9).

The reticular formation (or RF) is made up of a netlike bundle of neurons running through the hindbrain, midbrain, and part of the forebrain. Its main job seems to be to send "Alert!" signals to the higher parts of the brain when an incoming message is important. The RF apparently also decides which of several incoming messages is most urgent. Some messages seem to be toned down by the RF; others never reach the higher centers of the brain at all. Because of the RF, we can concentrate our attention on one message and ignore distracting messages from other sense receptors. We can read an interesting book, for example, while the

Reticular formation (RF) Network of neurons in the hindbrain, midbrain, and part of the forebrain whose primary function is to filter incoming messages and alert the higher parts of the brain to those that are important.

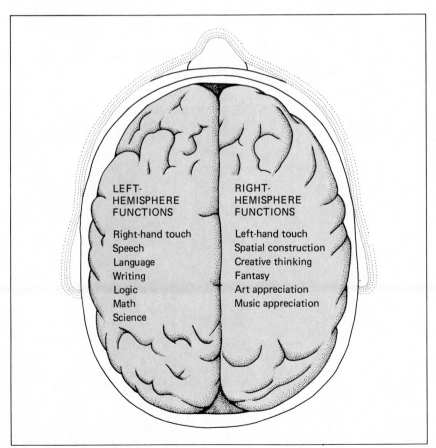

Figure 2-8

The two hemispheres of the cerebral cortex. The left hemisphere controls movements of the right hand and the right hemisphere controls the left hand. The left hemisphere is dominant in verbal tasks, while the right hemisphere is dominant in spatial construction.

LEFT-
HEMISPHERE
FUNCTIONS

Right-hand touch
Speech
Language
Writing
Logic
Math
Science

RIGHT-
HEMISPHERE
FUNCTIONS

Left-hand touch
Spatial construction
Creative thinking
Fantasy
Art appreciation
Music appreciation

Limbic system Ring of structures around the thalamus that plays a role in learning and emotional behavior.

Hippocampus Part of the limbic system that is vital to memory formation.

Spinal cord Complex cable of nerves that runs down the spine, connecting the brain to most of the rest of the body.

television is blaring, telephones are ringing, and people are talking in other parts of the room. The RF can also be shut down. An anesthetic, for example, works largely by shutting down this system. Permanent damage to the RF can cause a coma.

THE LIMBIC SYSTEM. Another example of the interconnected nature of parts of the central nervous system is the **limbic system,** a ring of structures around the thalamus in the center of each cerebral hemisphere (see Figure 2-10). The limbic system includes the hypothalamus, part of the thalamus, and several other forebrain structures. It also contains nerve fibers that connect it to the cerebral cortex and to the brain stem.

Although much of how the limbic system functions remains a mystery, it is believed to affect or control learning and emotional behavior. For example, one of its parts, the **hippocampus,** plays an important part in memory. Patients with damage to the hippocampus cannot form new memories. They can remember things that happened years ago but will forget completely the recent death of a near relative.

THE SPINAL CORD. The complex cable of nerves that connects the brain to most of the rest of the body is known as the **spinal cord.** We talk of the brain and the spinal cord as two distinct structures, but there is no clear boundary between them since, at its upper end, the spinal cord enlarges and merges into the hindbrain. Moreover, although the spinal cord tends to receive less attention than the brain, without it we would be severely crippled. People who have accidentally severed their spinal cords by breaking their necks provide tragic evidence of the importance of the spinal cord to normal functioning.

The spinal cord is made up of bundles of long nerve fibers. The spinal cord has two basic functions: to permit some reflex movements and to carry messages to and from the brain. To take the example we gave at the

Figure 2-9

A cross section of the brain showing the location of the reticular formation, which involves parts of the hindbrain, midbrain, and forebrain.

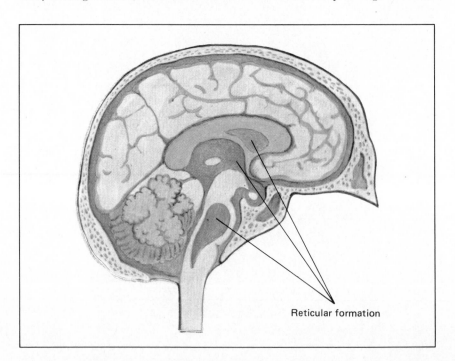

Reticular formation

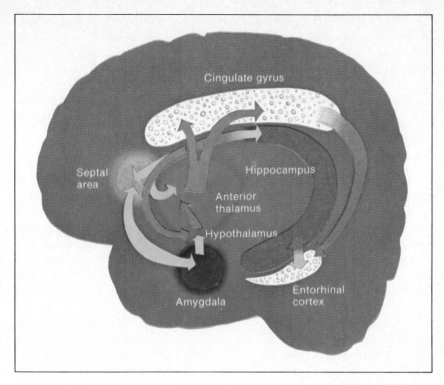

Figure 2-10

A stylized picture of the limbic system, showing how different areas of the limbic system interact during emotional stress.
(From C. Levinthal, 1979.)

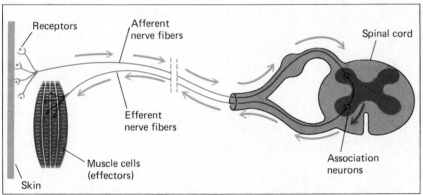

Figure 2-11

Simple reflexes are controlled by the spinal cord. The message travels from the sense receptors near the skin through the afferent nerve fibers to the spinal cord. In the spinal cord, the messages are relayed through association neurons to the efferent nerve fibers, which carry them to the muscle cells that cause the reflex movement.

beginning of this chapter, when you burn your finger on a match, a message signaling pain comes into your spinal cord and this causes the almost instantaneous reaction of pulling your hand away (see Figure 2-11). The pain message also travels up the spinal cord to your brain, but before it even gets there, your hand is being pulled out of the flame. Most of these spinal reflexes are protective; they enable the body to avoid serious damage and maintain muscle tone and position.

The Peripheral Nervous System

We saw earlier that the nervous system is made up of two major parts: the central nervous system (the brain and spinal cord) and the peripheral nervous system. The peripheral nervous system carries messages to and

Somatic nervous system The part of the peripheral nervous system that carries messages from the senses to the central nervous system and between the central nervous system and the skeletal muscles.

Autonomic nervous system The part of the peripheral nervous system that carries messages between the central nervous system and the internal organs.

Sympathetic division Branch of the autonomic nervous system that prepares the body for quick action in an emergency.

Parasympathetic division The branch of the autonomic nervous system that calms the body after stress.

from the central nervous system. Without the peripheral nervous system, no information could get to your spinal cord and your brain, and your brain could not give directions to the muscles and glands in your body. Even the simple reflex of pulling your hand away from a flaming match would not work: The peripheral nervous system carries the pain message to your spinal cord and carries the instructions from the spinal cord to your hand. The peripheral nervous system is made up of two major parts: the **somatic** and the **autonomic nervous systems.**

THE SOMATIC NERVOUS SYSTEM. The somatic nervous system is composed of all the afferent or sensory neurons that carry information to the central nervous system and all the efferent or motor neurons that carry messages from the central nervous system to the skeletal muscles of the body. All the things we can sense—sights, sounds, smells, temperature, pressure, and so on—have their origins in the somatic part of the peripheral nervous system. In later chapters we will see how the somatic nervous system affects our experience of the world both inside and outside our bodies.

THE AUTONOMIC NERVOUS SYSTEM. The autonomic portion of the peripheral nervous system is composed of all the neurons that carry messages between the central nervous system and the internal organs of the body (the glands and the smooth muscles such as the heart and digestive system). The autonomic nervous system obviously is necessary to such body functions as breathing and assuring a proper flow of blood. But it is also important in the experience of various emotions, which is why it is of special interest to psychologists.

To understand the autonomic nervous system we must make one more distinction. The autonomic nervous system consists of two branches: the **sympathetic** and **parasympathetic divisions** (see Figure 2-12). These two divisions act in almost total opposition to each other, but both are directly involved in controlling and integrating the actions of the glands and the smooth muscles within the body.

THE SYMPATHETIC DIVISION. The nerve fibers of the sympathetic division are busiest when you are frightened or angry. They carry messages that tell the body to prepare for an emergency and to get ready to act quickly or strenuously. In response to messages from the sympathetic division, your heart pounds, you breathe faster, your pupils enlarge, and digestion stops. As we will see shortly, the sympathetic nervous system also tells the endocrine system to start pumping chemicals into the bloodstream to further strengthen these reactions. Sympathetic nerve fibers connect to every internal organ in the body, which explains why the body's reaction to sudden stress is so widespread. However, the sympathetic division can also act selectively on a single organ.

THE PARASYMPATHETIC DIVISION. Parasympathetic nerve fibers connect to the same organs as the sympathetic nerve fibers, but they cause just the opposite effects. The parasympathetic division says, in effect, "Okay, the heat's off, back to normal." The heart then goes back to beating at its normal rate, the stomach muscles relax, digestion starts again, breathing slows down, and the pupils of the eyes get smaller. Thus

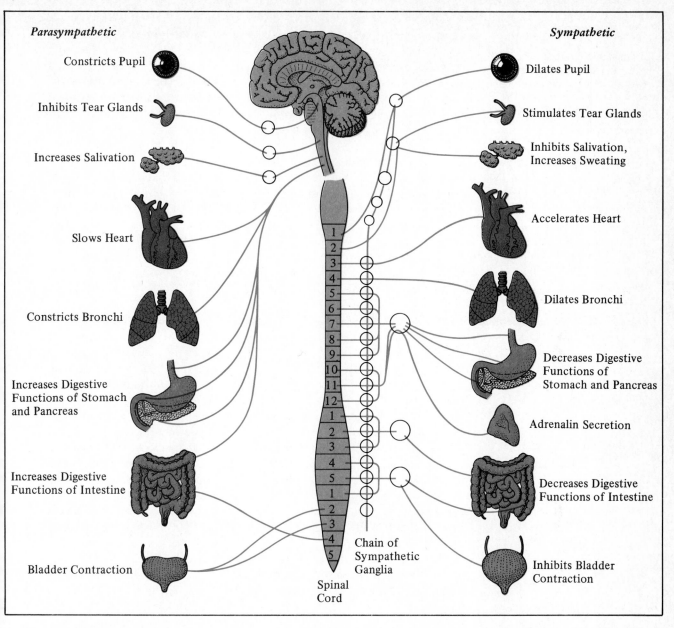

Parasympathetic

Constricts Pupil

Inhibits Tear Glands

Increases Salivation

Slows Heart

Constricts Bronchi

Increases Digestive
Functions of Stomach
and Pancreas

Increases Digestive
Functions of Intestine

Bladder Contraction

Sympathetic

Dilates Pupil

Stimulates Tear Glands

Inhibits Salivation,
Increases Sweating

Accelerates Heart

Dilates Bronchi

Decreases Digestive
Functions of
Stomach and Pancreas

Adrenalin Secretion

Decreases Digestive
Functions of Intestine

Inhibits Bladder
Contraction

Chain of
Sympathetic
Ganglia

Spinal
Cord

the parasympathetic division compensates for the sympathetic division and lets the body rest after stress.

Usually these two systems work together: After the sympathetic division has aroused the body, the parasympathetic division follows with messages to relax. In most people, however, one division or the other tends to dominate. In ulcer patients, for example, the parasympathetic divison tends to dominate: They salivate heavily, their hearts beat rather slowly, and their digestive systems are often overactive. People whose sympathetic division dominates show the opposite symptoms: Their mouths are dry, their palms moist, and their hearts beat quickly even when they are resting.

The autonomic nervous system was traditionally regarded as the "au-

Figure 2-12

The sympathetic and parasympathetic divisions of the autonomic nervous system. The sympathetic division generally acts to arouse the body, while the parasympathetic follows with messages to relax.

Hormones Chemical substances released by the endocrine glands that help regulate bodily activities.

Endocrine glands Glands of the endocrine system that release hormones into the bloodstream.

Thyroid gland Endocrine gland located below the voice box that produces the hormone thyroxin.

Thyroxin Hormone that regulates the rate of metabolism.

tomatic" part of the body's response mechanism. You could not, it was believed, tell your own autonomic nervous system when to speed up or slow down your heart's beating or when to stop or start your digestive processes. These things were thought to run as automatically as a thermostat controlling the temperature of a room. The latest evidence, however, suggests that we have more control over the autonomic nervous system than we think. Many studies seem to show that people (and animals) can indeed manipulate this so-called automatic part of the nervous system. For example, it is possible to learn to control such things as high blood pressure, migraine headaches, and even ulcers. Some people have even learned to control their own heart rate and brain waves. These are all cases in which the autonomic nervous system is brought under a person's deliberate control; and we will look more closely at these possibilities when we discuss biofeedback in Chapter 6.

The Endocrine System

Figure 2-13

The glands of the endocrine system.

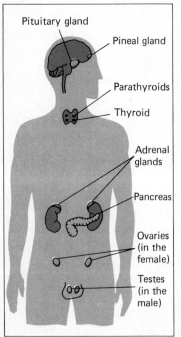

The nervous system is not the only mechanism that regulates the functioning of our bodies. To return to our earlier example, when you burn your finger on a match, you quickly withdraw it from the heat. But your response to the burn does not end with the nervous system. In addition, chemical substances called **hormones** are released into your bloodstream by internal organs called **endocrine glands.** These hormones are carried throughout your body, where they have widespread effects on a variety of organs. Under less dramatic circumstances, hormones, acting either singly or together, are responsible for such things as differences in vitality among people; for the readiness of nerves and muscles to react; for the rates of metabolism, growth, and sexual development; for the body's preparations for pregnancy and childbirth; and for emotional balance in general.

The locations of the endocrine glands are shown in Figure 2-13. Our discussion will focus on those glands whose functions are best understood and those whose effects are most closely related to the way we behave.

The Thyroid Gland

The **thyroid gland** is located just below the larynx, or voice box. It produces one primary hormone—**thyroxin,** which regulates the body's rate of metabolism. That is, it determines how fast or how slowly the foods we eat are transformed into the energy we need to function normally. Differences in the metabolic rate determine how alert and energetic people are, and how fat or thin they tend to be.

If your thyroid gland produces too much thyroxin, your appetite will be huge: You will eat everything in sight, though you may stay very much underweight. Your reactions may also be speeded up and extremely intense, especially your reactions to stress. Too little thyroxin leads to the other extreme: You will want to sleep and sleep and still feel constantly tired. Without enough thyroxin your body is unable to maintain normal temperature, muscle tone is reduced, and metabolism is sluggish.

The Parathyroid Glands

Embedded in the thyroid gland are the **parathyroids**—four tiny pea-shaped organs. They secrete **parathormone,** which controls and balances the level of calcium and phosphate in the blood and tissue fluids. The level of calcium in the blood has a direct effect on the excitability of the nervous system. A person with too little parathormone will be hypersensitive and may suffer from twitches or muscle spasms. Too much parathormone, on the other hand, can lead to lethargy and poor physical coordination.

The Pancreas

The **pancreas** lies in a curve between the stomach and the small intestine. The pancreas controls the level of sugar in the blood by secreting two regulating hormones—**insulin** and **glucagon.** The two hormones work against each other to keep the blood-sugar level properly balanced.

When the pancreas secretes too little insulin so that there is too much sugar in the blood, the kidneys attempt to get rid of the excess sugar by excreting a great deal more water than usual. The tissues get dehydrated and poisonous wastes accumulate in the blood. The person has *diabetes mellitus* and needs insulin and a special diet to keep blood-sugar level normal. Oversecretion of insulin, on the other hand, leads to too little sugar in the blood and the chronic fatigue of *hypoglycemia.*

The Pituitary Gland

The endocrine gland that produces the largest number of different hormones and thus has the widest range of effects on the body's functions is the **pituitary gland.** This gland is located on the underside of the brain, connected to the hypothalamus. The pituitary gland has two parts that function quite separately.

The **posterior pituitary** (toward the back of the gland) is controlled by the nervous system. It secretes two hormones that signal the uterus to contract during childbirth, alert the mammary glands to start producing milk, cause the blood pressure to rise, and regulate the amount of water in the body's cells.

The **anterior pituitary** (toward the front of the pituitary gland) is controlled by chemical messages from the bloodstream and is often called the "master gland." It produces numerous hormones that trigger the action of other endocrine glands. Among the functions of the anterior pituitary is the production of the body's growth hormone, through which it controls the amount and timing of body growth. Dwarfism and giantism are the result of too little and too much growth hormone, respectively.

The functioning of the anterior pituitary provides a good example of the interaction between the endocrine system and the nervous system.

Parathyroids Four tiny glands embedded in the thyroid that secrete parathormone.

Parathormone Hormone that controls the levels of calcium and phosphate in the blood and tissue fluids.

Pancreas Organ lying between the stomach and small intestine that secretes insulin and glucagon.

Insulin and **glucagon** Hormones that work in opposite ways to regulate the level of sugar in the blood.

Pituitary gland Gland located on the underside of the brain that produces the largest number of the body's hormones; composed of the posterior and anterior pituitary.

Posterior pituitary Separately functioning part of the pituitary that is controlled by the nervous system.

Anterior pituitary Part of the pituitary known as the "master gland" because it produces numerous hormones that trigger the action of other glands; one of these hormones regulates body growth.

Gonads The reproductive glands—testes in males and ovaries in females.

Adrenal glands Two endocrine glands located just above the kidneys.

Adrenal cortex Outer covering of the two adrenal glands that releases hormones important for dealing with stress.

Adrenal medulla Inner core of the adrenal glands that also releases hormones to deal with stress.

Beta endorphin One of the endorphins, a natural painkiller released by the body.

ACTH Hormone released by the anterior pituitary that stimulates hormone production of the adrenal cortex.

Epinephrine Adrenal hormone that is released mainly in response to fear and causes the heart to beat faster.

Norepinephrine An adrenal hormone that causes blood pressure to rise; also, an excitatory neurotransmitter that carries nerve impulses across the synaptic gaps.

The operation of the anterior pituitary is partly controlled by hormones that are released by the hypothalamus—part of the nervous system (Schally, Kastin, & Arimura, 1977). Hormones released from the anterior pituitary cause the gonads to produce still other hormones, which in turn affect the hypothalamus to produce changes in behavior or feeling. Thus the hypothalamus affects the anterior pituitary, which indirectly affects the hypothalamus. This circular route of influence gives some idea of the two-way interaction that often takes place between the nervous system and the endocrine system.

The Gonads

The **gonads**—the *testes* in males and the *ovaries* in females—work with the adrenal glands to stimulate the reproductive organs to become mature. They also account for the appearance of what are called secondary sex characteristics—breasts, beards, pubic hair, change of voice, and distribution of body fat appropriate to males or females. As we will see in Chapter 5, hormones from the gonads play an important role in controlling the sex drive, particularly among animals.

The Adrenal Glands

The two **adrenal glands** are located just above the kidneys. Each adrenal gland has two parts—an outer covering called the **adrenal cortex** and an inner core called the **adrenal medulla.** Both the adrenal cortex and the adrenal medulla are important in the body's reaction to stress. Imagine that you are walking down the street when you see a professor to whom you owe an overdue paper. As you approach each other, you realize that there is no graceful escape. You begin to experience stress. The hypothalamus secretes a hormone that causes the anterior pituitary gland to release two more hormones. One is **beta endorphin,** one of the body's natural painkillers (see the box on p. 34). The other is **ACTH,** a messenger hormone that goes to the adrenal cortex. Alerted by ACTH from the pituitary, the adrenal cortex in turn secretes hormones that increase the level of blood sugar, help to break down proteins, and help the body respond to injury. Meanwhile the adrenal medulla is stimulated by the autonomic nervous system so that it also pours several hormones into the bloodstream: **Epinephrine** activates the sympathetic nervous system, which makes the heart beat faster; digestion stops; the pupils of the eyes enlarge; more sugar flows into the bloodstream; and the blood is prepared to clot fast if necessary. Another hormone, **norepinephrine** (which also acts as a neurotransmitter), not only raises the blood pressure by causing the blood vessels to become constricted; it is also carried by the bloodstream to the anterior pituitary, where it triggers the release of still more ACTH, thus prolonging the response to stress. The result is that your body is well prepared to deal with threat.

The complicated details of all these hormonal processes are much less important for our purposes than an understanding that the endocrine system plays a major role in helping to coordinate and integrate complex psychological reactions. In fact, as we have said before, the nervous system and the endocrine system work hand in hand. We will see other examples of this in Chapter 5, where we talk about motivation.

We have seen in our overview of the nervous system and endocrine system a very close connection between biology and psychology. There are still other connections: Even the genes that we inherit from our parents can affect important psychological processes, as we will now discover.

Behavior genetics Study of the relationship between heredity and behavior.

Behavior Genetics

Charles Darwin (1809–1882) was one of the first to recognize the impact of heredity on such psychological characteristics as intelligence, personality, and mental illness. For example, in a discussion of gestures, he described the following case:

> A gentleman of considerable position was found by his wife to have the curious trick, when he lay fast asleep on his back in bed, of raising his right arm slowly in front of his face, up to his forehead, and then dropping it with a jerk so that the wrist fell heavily on the bridge of his nose. The trick did not occur every night, but occasionally. (Darwin, 1872, p. 34)

To protect the gentleman's nose, it was necessary to remove the buttons from the cuff of his nightgown. Years after the man's death, his son married a woman who observed precisely the same behavior in him. And their daughter exhibited the same gesture as well.

Darwin heard about this case from his half cousin, Francis Galton (1822–1911), who was the first person to try to demonstrate systematically how behavior characteristics can be transmitted genetically. Galton was especially interested in the transmission of mental traits. To show that high mental ability is inherited, he identified about 1,000 men of eminence in Great Britain—judges, political leaders, scholars, scientists, artists, and so on—and found that they belonged to only 300 families. Because only one in 4,000 people in the population was "eminent," Galton concluded that eminence must be an inherited trait.

Galton's findings were challenged by others who claimed that environmental factors such as educational and social advantages could have accounted for the concentration of eminence in just a few hundred families. In the early 20th century Galton's assumptions about the inherited nature of behavioral traits came under more fundamental attack from the behaviorists. The founder of behaviorism, J. B. Watson, argued that

> we have no real evidence of the inheritance of traits. I would feel perfectly confident in the ultimately favorable outcome of careful upbringing of a *healthy, well-formed* baby born of a long line of crooks, murderers and thieves, and prostitutes. Who has any evidence to the contrary? (Watson, 1930, p. 103)

The question of how much influence heredity has on various behaviors is at the heart of modern **behavior genetics** and, as we will see, psychologists still disagree on the answer to the question.

To begin to appreciate the "nature-nurture controversy," we need to become familiar with some of the basic mechanisms of inheritance.

Genetics

Genetics Study of how traits are passed from one generation to the next.

Genes Elements found on the chromosomes that control the transmission of traits.

Chromosomes Pairs of threadlike bodies within the cell nucleus that contain the genes.

Genetics is the study of how plants, animals, and people pass traits from one generation to the next. In this context a trait is the characteristic that is being expressed: curly hair, a crooked little finger, the inability of the blood to clot, or an allergy to poison ivy.

Gregor Mendel (1822–1884), a Moravian abbot, gave modern genetics its beginning in 1867 when he reported the results of his research on many years of systematically breeding peas. Mendel believed that every trait was controlled by elements that were transmitted from one generation to the next. He called these elements **genes.**

Much more is known today about genes and how they work. We know, for example, that within a cell nucleus genes are lined up on tiny threadlike bodies called **chromosomes,** which are visible under a micro-

A photomicrograph of a single gene, showing the twisting strands of DNA. Magnified 100,000X.

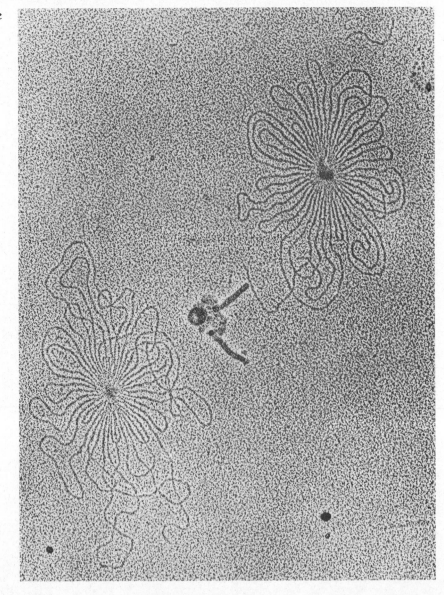

The 23 pairs of human chromosomes found in every normal cell. Twenty-two of the 23 pairs of chromosomes look exactly alike. The members of the 23rd pair, the sex chromosomes, may or may not look alike. Females have equivalent X chromosomes, while males have only one X and one Y chromosome, named for their distinctive appearance. The presence of an additional number-21 chromosome will result in Down's Syndrome, as in the inset at right.

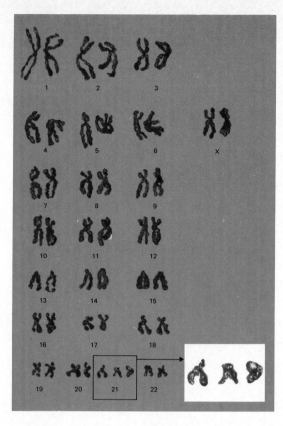

Deoxyribonucleic acid (DNA) Complex molecule that is the main ingredient of chromosomes and genes and forms the code for all genetic information.

Dominant gene Member of a gene pair that controls the appearance of a certain physical trait.

Recessive gene Member of a gene pair that can control the appearance of a certain physical trait only if it is paired with another recessive gene.

scope. The chromosomes are arranged in pairs, and each species has a constant number of pairs. Mice have 20 pairs; monkeys have 27; peas have 7. Human beings have 23 pairs of chromosomes in every normal cell.

The main ingredient of the chromosomes and genes is **deoxyribonucleic acid (DNA),** a complex molecule that looks like two chains twisted around each other. The order of this twisting DNA forms a code that carries all our genetic information. The individual genes, which are the smallest message units of the DNA, carry instructions for a particular process or trait. It is now understood that the nucleus of every cell contains DNA with enough genetic coding to direct the development of one single cell into a fully grown adult with billions of cells!

Chromosomes, as we said, are arranged in pairs, and each pair carries a complete set of genes. Because each pair provides the coding for the same kinds of traits, a gene for a given trait may therefore exist in two alternate forms. We can think of a gene for eye color, for example, as having one form, B, which will result in brown eyes; and another form, b, which will result in blue eyes. If a boy receives b genes from both parents, his eyes will be blue. But if he inherits a b gene from one parent and a B gene from the other, his eyes will be brown (see Figure 2-14). The B form is thus said to be the **dominant gene,** while the b form is **recessive.** Although the boy with one B gene and one b gene has brown eyes, the recessive b gene is still present and can be passed on to offspring if it is paired with a recessive b gene from the other parent.

We have been talking about characteristics such as eye color that are

Polygenic inheritance Process in which several genes interact to produce a certain trait; responsible for our most important traits.

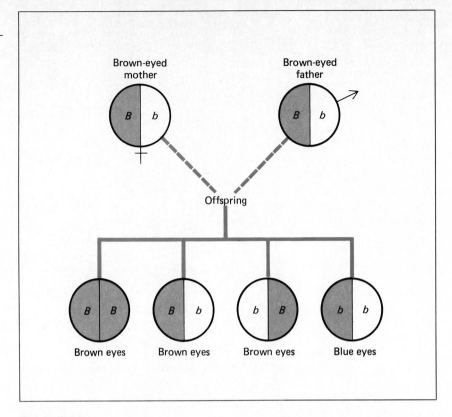

Brown-eyed mother

Brown-eyed father

Offspring

Brown eyes   Brown eyes   Brown eyes   Blue eyes

Figure 2-14

Transmission of eye color by dominant (B) and recessive (b) genes. This figure represents the four possible mixtures of eye-color genes in these parents' offspring. Because three out of the four combinations result in brown-eyed children, the chance that any child will have brown eyes is 75 percent.

controlled by single genes. In fact, though, most of our important characteristics, such as intelligence, height, and weight, cannot be traced back to a single gene. Rather, a number of genes make a small contribution to the trait in question in a process known as **polygenic inheritance.** Like the instruments in a symphony orchestra, each contributing separate notes to the sound that reaches the audience, the genes in a polygenic system contribute separately to the total effect.

It is also known that the effects of heredity need not be immediately or fully apparent. In some cases, expression of a trait is delayed until later in life. For example, many men inherit "male pattern baldness" that does not become apparent until middle age. In other cases, genes predispose a person to develop a particular trait, but environmental factors can alter or suppress expression of the trait. Having the proper genes provides a person with the potential for a trait, but that trait may not appear unless the environment cooperates. A person with an inherited tendency to gain weight may or may not be obese depending on diet, exercise program, and overall health. With these general principles in mind, let's look at how psychologists study the relation between genetics and behavior and see what they have learned so far.

Genetics and Behavior

Psychologists have devised several methods to approach the problem of determining the heritability of behavioral traits (Henderson, 1982; Plomin, DeFries, & McClearn, 1980; Parke & Asher, 1983). **Strain studies** involve intensive inbreeding of close relatives such as brothers and sisters over many generations to create strains of animals that are genetically very similar to one another and different from other strains. Obviously strain studies cannot be carried out on humans. But mice are often used because they breed so quickly and yet have relatively complex behavior patterns. When animals from different strains are raised together in the same environment, differences between them largely reflect genetic differences in the strains. Using this method, for example, it has been shown that in mice the sense of smell, susceptibility to seizures, and performance on a number of learning tasks are all affected by heredity.

Selection studies can also be used with animals to estimate heritability. If a trait is closely regulated by genes, then when animals having the trait are bred with one another, more of their offspring should have the trait than one would normally find in the general population. By measuring changes in the proportion of successive generations that have the trait, an estimate of its heritability can be made.

Artificial selection has been used for thousands of years to create breeds of dogs and many other animals that have desirable traits. Terriers, for example, were originally bred to crawl into burrows and chase out small animals living there. In France dogs have been bred for specialized aspects of farm work, while in the United Kingdom dogs have been bred for centuries to point to hidden prey or retrieve downed birds. The fact that dog breeds differ greatly in many respects, including the development of social relationships, excitability, and trainability, suggests that these psychological characteristics are at least to some extent genetically controlled (Plomin, DeFries, & McClearn, 1980).

Strain studies Studies of the heritability of behavioral traits using animals that have been inbred to produce strains that are genetically very similar to one another.

Selection studies Studies that estimate the heritability of a trait by looking at successive generations of animals bred with one another.

Artificial selection has been used to create breeds of dogs and many other animals that have desirable traits. Differences in trainability for example, make some breeds of dogs better candidates at dog shows.

Family studies Studies of heritability in humans based on the assumption that if genes influence a certain trait, close relatives should be more similar on that trait than distant relatives.

Twin studies Studies of identical and fraternal twins to determine the separate influences of heredity and environment on human behavior.

Identical twins Twins developed from a single fertilized ovum, and therefore identical in genetic makeup.

Fraternal twins Twins developed from two separate fertilized ova, and therefore different in genetic makeup.

Adoption studies Research carried out on children adopted at birth by parents not related to them with the object of determining environmental effects on human behavior.

Of course, for the purpose of studying the genetic basis of human behavior, both strain and selection studies are out of the question. A number of techniques have been developed, however, to study heritability in humans by analyzing the behavioral similarities of members of the same family. **Family studies** are based on the assumption that if genes influence a trait, close relatives should be more similar on the trait than distant relatives because close relatives share more genes. So far, family studies have uncovered strong evidence that heredity plays a role in some forms of mental illness. Siblings of schizophrenics, for example, are about 8 times more likely to be schizophrenic than someone chosen randomly from the general population. And children of schizophrenic parents are about 10 times more likely to be schizophrenic than other children. Such findings, however, do not completely rule out the role of environment. Growing up in a household in which both parents are schizophrenic might cause a child to become schizophrenic, even if that child does not have the genetic potential for that disorder (Plomin, DeFries, & Mc-Clearn, 1980).

In an effort to separate more clearly the influence of heredity and that of environment on human behavior, psychologists often use **twin studies.** There are two kinds of twins. **Identical twins** develop from a single fertilized ovum and are therefore identical in genetic makeup. Any differences between them should, therefore, be due to environmental differences. **Fraternal twins,** however, develop from two separate fertilized egg cells and have no more in common genetically than other brothers and sisters. The differences between fraternal twins are thus due to both heredity and environment. Now, if identical twins are no more alike on some characteristics than fraternal twins, then heredity cannot be very important in that trait (assuming the various pairs of twins have similar environments).

Twins studies have provided evidence for the heritability of a number of behaviors. For example, if one identical twin is schizophrenic, about half the time the other twin will become schizophrenic. For fraternal twins, the chances are only about one in six that this second twin will become schizophrenic (Gottesman & Shields, 1982; Rao et al., 1981). The much greater similarity between identical twins suggests strongly that heredity plays an important role in schizophrenia.

Mental abilities also seem to be affected by heredity. According to one summary of many twin studies, about half of the differences between people in general intelligence can be explained by heredity (Loehlin & Nichols, 1976). In Chapter 9 we will examine this relationship much more closely. Genetic differences also play a major role in specific cognitive abilities such as verbal and spatial skills and memory. Evidence has also been found in twin studies for genetic influences on temperament and personality, mannerisms such as the strength of handshake, smoking and drinking habits, and even tastes in food (Farber, 1981).

Recently researchers have become interested in **adoption studies** as well. Adoption studies focus on children who were adopted at birth and brought up by parents not genetically related to them. Thus unusual similarities between adopted children and their adoptive parents are likely to be due to their shared environments, not heredity.

Adoption studies provide additional strong evidence for the heritability of intelligence and some forms of mental illness. For example,

one study located 47 people who had schizophrenic mothers but who had been adopted at birth and reared by normal parents. Of these 47, 5 became schizophrenic. In another group of people who had been adopted at birth but did not have a schizophrenic parent, there was no schizophrenia (Heston, 1966). Studies of biological and adoptive families have also suggested that chronic alcoholism and suicide—two phenomena that would at first appear to be tightly tied to environmental influences—have a strong genetic basis. This might help to explain why everyone who drinks does not become an alcoholic, and why only a few people turn to suicide when they despair (Kety, 1979).

Identical twins develop from a single fertilized ovum and are identical in genetic makeup. Notice that each twin wears glasses and shows just about the same amount of hair loss.

Social Implications of Behavior Genetics

Science is not simply a process that takes place in a laboratory; it can have widespread effects on society at large. To the extent that we can trace human traits such as intelligence, temperament, and mental illness to their origins in chromosomes and genes, we increase the extent to which we can control human lives. And because this control permits choices that were previously not available, we face new ethical dilemmas.

Advances in genetics, for example, have improved the ability to predict birth defects in babies not yet even conceived. Genetic counselors using family histories can spell out the likelihood that the children of a given marriage will inherit genetic problems. Before deciding to have a child, a high-risk couple must weigh some very serious ethical questions.

Amniocentesis Technique that involves collecting cells cast off by the fetus into the fluid of the womb and testing them for genetic abnormalities.

Once conception has occurred, a technique called **amniocentesis** permits detection of many genetic problems before the baby is born. Amniocentesis involves collecting some of the cells that the fetus has cast off into fluid surrounding it in the womb and testing them for chromosomal or genetic abnormalities. In about 2 percent of the cases genetic problems are found. Does the child nonetheless have a right to life? Do the parents have a right to abort the fetus? Should society protect all life, no matter how imperfect it is in the eyes of some? If not, which defects are so unacceptable that abortion is justified? Most of these questions have a long history, but recent progress in behavior genetics and in medicine has given them a special urgency.

Progress in behavior genetics has also provoked debates about social equality in the United States. In 1969 psychologist Arthur Jensen published an article in which he argued that since intelligence is largely inherited, and since blacks on average have lower scores on IQ tests than whites at comparable socioeconomic levels, the racial differences in intel-

The Basis of Sex Differences: Genes, Hormones, and Neurons

We have discussed the nervous system, the endocrine system, and genetics in three distinct sections of this chapter. In real life the influence of these systems on particular kinds of behaviors cannot be separated so easily. For example, on average men have been found to be more aggressive and to score better on tests of quantitative and spatial abilities. On average women tend to score higher on tests of verbal ability. Some evidence suggests that women are also slightly more compliant and less dominant than men (Maccoby & Jacklin, 1974). Are these differences due to heredity or are they learned? Do they reflect some basic difference in the nervous systems of men and women? Are they due in part to hormonal differences? As you might suspect, the answers to these questions are the subject of hot debate.

Clearly genes determine one's sex. But hormones are important in determining the result of this genetic difference. Anke Ehrhardt and her colleagues studied a group of women who had been exposed before birth to large doses of the male sex hormone testosterone. At age 10, these girls were psychologically different from other girls. They were tomboyish—relatively uninterested in playing with dolls—and showed less desire to eventually marry and have children. Other investigators, using different samples, have found very similar results (Konner, 1982).

Some researchers believe that sex differences in brain structure may underlie some psychological differences. In male rats, for example, tes-

tosterone seems to increase the density of synapses in the front of the hypothalamus, a part of the brain that regulates some sex-specific behavior. Whether this increased density actually causes sex differences in behavior remains unclear. In any event, no sex differences have been found to date in human brains, although they may in fact exist.

Certainly some sex differences in behavior are due to differences in hormones after birth. Testosterone seems to contribute to, if not directly cause, increases in aggressive behavior. One study reported by Konner (1982) found that among male prison inmates, the higher the levels of testosterone, the earlier the age of first arrest. Other evidence suggests that sex hormones tend to concentrate in areas of the brain that play a role in courtship, sex, maternal behavior, and violence (Konner, 1982). Thus behavioral differences between men and women in these areas may be due in part to differences in hormones.

Many psychologists, however, stress the role of learning as the basis for sex differences in behavior. According to Michael Lewis, "As early as you can show me a sex difference, I can show you the culture at work" (Gelman et al., 1981, p. 72). During the course of development children learn how to behave like boys and girls. In Chapter 10 we will discuss this process of sex role development more fully. For our present purposes, it is enough to note that genes, hormones, and the nervous system all contribute to differences in the ways in which males and females behave.

ligence must be due to genetic inequalities. Jensen went on to argue that compensatory education programs such as Head Start that were designed to enrich the environment of black children were of limited value. Jensen's article sparked an explosive debate on the heritability of intelligence and alternative reasons for race differences in IQ test scores, as well as on the implications of these data for public policy. We will examine this debate in detail in Chapter 9, but for our present purposes the Jensen controversy demonstrates the uneasy relationship between scientific evidence and social values. With progress in understanding how heredity can affect human behavior, psychologists must increasingly be concerned about how others might make use of their findings (Plomin, DeFries, & McClearn, 1980).

Application

Brain Transplants

In this age of technology most people are no longer taken aback by the idea of tissue or even organ transplants. Grafts of skin and bone removed from elsewhere in the patient's body are fairly routine. Transplants of kidneys, livers, and hearts have received a great deal of attention from the popular as well as the medical press. But to the general public transplanting brains or even parts of the brain still belongs to the realm of horror or comedy films—or science fiction. Such things can happen to Frankenstein's monster or to characters in the films of Steve Martin and Woody Allen, but not to people in real life. Though there is no likelihood that it will ever be possible to transplant entire brains, recent advances in brain research have made transplants of live brain tissue a possibility for the future. The ability to graft tissue onto the brain is especially promising as a treatment for diseases involving the degeneration of nerve cells, such as Parkinson's disease, Huntington's chorea, and even Alzheimer's disease.

So far most of the research on brain-tissue transplants has used rats. In the late 1970s, after experiments showed that heart tissue could be grafted to nerve fibers behind a rat's eye, researchers began to try to graft brain tissue to neurons in the brain. Psychiatrist Richard J. Wyatt and neuroscientist William J. Freed, of the National Institute of Mental Health, in particular have explored the possibility of curing Parkinson's disease by

means of brain transplants (Young, 1983). Victims of this disease lose a tiny number of cells—2,000–3,000—in a particular location on each side of the brain. The loss of these cells results in a deficit of the chemical transmitter dopamine, which in turn causes those stricken to lose normal control over their muscles.

Wyatt and Freed sought to learn whether dopamine-producing neurons could be transplanted into rat brains. To answer this question, the two investigators damaged one side of rats' brains to imitate the damage associated with Parkinson's disease. When these rats were later given a stimulant, they just walked around and around in circles. Next Freed took dopamine-producing cells from rat embryos and injected them into the damaged area of the brain through a small hole in the skull. Several months later many of the rats no longer engaged in the circling behavior. The implanted neurons were flourishing and apparently could fire normally. Still, the symptoms of the disease did not completely disappear in all the rats.

Later research with rats showed that cells from embryos are not the only choice for transplants. The adrenal glands of adult animals also produce dopamine, and experiments with implanting an adrenal gland in the parts of the brain affected by Parkinson's disease also succeeded in rats. The circling behavior ceased as the adrenal cells took hold and produced new supplies of dopamine.

Rejection of implanted brain tissues by the

body's defenses is not as great a threat as with other kinds of transplants. The brain normally prevents foreign molecules from passing through the walls of blood vessels. This same barrier also keeps out elements of the body's immune system that are responsible for tissue rejection. However, this blood-brain barrier is not uniformly effective throughout the brain, which means there is some danger that implanted tissues will be rejected.

Unfortunately a number of more serious problems remain to be solved. Experiments with rhesus monkeys have dramatized one of the major difficulties. Some time after they had injected tissue into monkeys' brains, Wyatt and his colleagues could not find the grafted tissue in many of the animals. This may have been partly because of the size of the monkey brains, or it may have been that the tissue had washed away from the implantation site rather than clinging there and growing. Still another problem is how to spread the implanted tissue throughout the target area beyond the point where it is inserted. This is essential to treating widespread degeneration, as in Alzheimer's disease and Huntington's chorea. Techniques for grafting tissues obviously must be perfected before they can be applied to humans.

If these and other obstacles can be overcome, the payoff could be quite high. Degenerative brain diseases may become curable. Patients who have suffered spinal cord damage may also be helped by tissue transplants. Research on brain-tissue transplants may also lead to new knowledge about the ability of the nervous system to heal itself after injury. The use of grafts will test the limits of this ability and extend it. The same work may also provide information about the biological basis for learning and memory.

Summary

1. The body has two major systems that coordinate behavior. The *nervous system* conducts messages throughout the body in the form of neural impulses; the *endocrine system* sends chemical messages through the bloodstream. These two systems function together in coordinating our activities.

2. The nervous system is made up of *neurons* that are specialized to send and receive information. Neurons have tiny fibers called *dendrites* and a single long fiber called an *axon* extending out from the *cell body*. By means of its dendrites and axon, one neuron can be in touch with hundreds of others. A group of axons bundled together is called a *nerve*.

3. *Sensory* (or *afferent*) neurons carry information to the spinal cord or to the brain. *Motor* (or *efferent*) neurons carry messages from the spinal cord or the brain to the muscles and glands. *Interneurons* (*association* neurons) make the connections between incoming and outgoing messages. Interneurons perform most of the work of the nervous system.

4. When a neuron is resting, its cell membrane keeps it in a state of *polarization*, with positive *ions* on the outside and negative ions on the inside. When sodium ions flow into the neuron and depolarize it, the process will cause the neuron to fire. The incoming message must be above a certain threshold to cause a *neural impulse* or *action potential*; otherwise the *graded potential* will fade away. During the *absolute refractory period* after firing, the neuron will not refire no matter how strong the incoming messages may be. The number of neurons firing at any given moment and the number of times they fire affect the complexity of the message.

5. Axons with *myelin sheaths* conduct impulses more rapidly than those that do not have these sheaths. The impulses are speeded by leaping along the intervals of *nodes* on the myelin sheaths.

6. The axon of every neuron ends in an *axon terminal* or *synaptic knob*. A tiny gap, called a *synaptic space* or *synaptic cleft*, separates the end of each terminal from the next neuron. A *synapse* consists of the axon terminal, synaptic

cleft, and dendrite of the next neuron. When a neural impulse reaches the end of an axon, it causes tiny sacs called *synaptic vesicles* to release some amounts of chemicals. These chemicals, called *neurotransmitters*, travel across the synapse, where they affect the next neuron.

7. There are dozens of known neurotransmitters with various functions. Neurotransmitters work by fitting into matching *receptor sites* on the other side of the synaptic space just as a key fits into a lock. Some transmitters "excite" the next neuron and make it more likely to fire. Other transmitters "inhibit" the next neuron from firing. *Endorphins* and *enkephalins* inhibit the transmission of pain messages in the brain. After release, neurotransmitters are destroyed chemically within the synapse or cycled back into the vesicles, and the synapse returns to its normal state.

8. Drugs that affect psychological processes interfere with chemical activity at the synapse. Some drugs cause an increase or decrease in the amounts of neurotransmitters in the synapse. Others block receptor sites for neurotransmitters across the synapse. Still others work by preventing the destruction or reabsorption of neurotransmitters once they have done their job.

9. The brain, the most significant element of the nervous system, has three distinct parts: the hindbrain, midbrain, and forebrain. The *hindbrain* consists of the *medulla*, which controls breathing and many other reflexes and is the place where many nerves from other parts of the body cross on the way to the higher brain centers; the *pons* connects the forebrain to the *cerebellum*, which handles certain reflexes and coordinates the body's movements.

10. Above the pons and cerebellum, the *brain stem* widens to form the *midbrain*. The midbrain is especially important to hearing and sight.

11. The *forebrain* is composed of the *thalamus*, which relays messages from the sense receptors and messages from one part of the brain to another; the *hypothalamus*, which influences many kinds of motivation and emotional behavior; and the two cerebral hemispheres known as the *cerebral cortex*.

12. Areas of the cortex where messages from the sense receptors are registered are called *sensory projection areas*; response messages begin in the *motor projection areas* and travel from there to the various muscles and glands; messages from the separate senses are combined into meaningful patterns in the *association areas*. The association areas are involved in all higher mental processes like thinking, learning, remembering, and talking.

13. The largest of the association areas are in the *frontal lobes*. The frontal lobes are the site of uniquely human mental activities, and they contribute to a balanced emotional life. Damage to the frontal lobes can result in major personality changes. The other lobes of the cortex are each responsible for a different sense. The *occipital lobe* controls vision; the *temporal lobe* controls hearing; and the *parietal lobe* receives sensations of touch and body position.

14. The cerebral cortex is separated into two distinct hemispheres. In general, the left hemisphere controls the right side of the body, while the right hemisphere controls the left. The two hemispheres control different skills as well. The left hemisphere is dominant in verbal abilities; the right hemisphere is superior in spatial abilities and geometric reasoning. The right hemisphere is not completely without verbal abilities, however. Though the hemispheres are specialized, they are in close communication through the *corpus callosum* and normally work together.

15. The *reticular formation* consists of neurons that run through the hindbrain, midbrain, and part of the forebrain. Its primary function is to filter incoming messages and alert higher parts of the brain when a message is important.

16. The *limbic system*, a ring of structures around the thalamus, is thought to play a major role in learning and emotional behavior. One of its parts, the *hippocampus*, is vital to memory formation.

17. The *spinal cord* is a complex cable of nerves that connects the brain to most of the rest of the body. The brain cannot function normally if the spinal cord is severed. The spinal cord sends messages to and from the brain and controls certain reflex motions.

18. The *peripheral nervous system* carries messages to and from the central nervous system and without it the central nervous system could not work. The peripheral nervous system consists of the *somatic nervous system*, which carries messages to the central nervous system from the senses, and from the central nervous system to the skeletal muscles; and the *autonomic nervous system*, which carries messages between the central nervous system and the body's internal organs.

19. The two divisions of the autonomic nervous system work in opposite ways. The *sympathetic division* readies the body for action and triggers the release of activating chemicals into the bloodstream. The *parasympathetic division* acts to calm the body after stress. The autonomic nervous system is what controls "automatic" responses like breathing, heart rate, and digestion. It is possible to control such responses voluntarily through techniques like biofeedback.

20. The endocrine system is made up of *glands* that secrete chemical substances called *hormones* into the bloodstream. Hormones affect such processes as metabolism, growth, and sex development, and are involved in regulating emotional life.

21. The *thyroid* gland produces *thyroxin*, which regulates the body's metabolism. The *parathyroid* glands secrete *parathormone*, which controls levels of calcium and phosphate. The *pancreas* regulates the level of blood sugar by secreting *insulin* and *glucagon*.

22. The two parts of the *pituitary gland*, which is located in the brain, have a wide range of effects. Hormones from the *posterior pituitary* direct preparation for childbirth; the *anterior pituitary* produces growth hormones and other hormones that trigger action of other endocrine glands. The anterior pituitary is known as the "master gland."

23. The *gonads* work with the *adrenal glands* to stimulate sex development. The two adrenal glands are important in the body's response to stress. Both the *adrenal cortex* and *adrenal medulla* release hormones that prepare the body to deal with threats.

24. Psychological processes are also influenced by genes. *Behavior genetics* explores the relationships between heredity and behavior. Some issues examined by behavior geneticists are the inheritance of sex characteristics, mental abilities, and forms of mental illness.

25. *Genetics* is the study of how traits are passed on from one generation to the next. *Genes* are lined up on *chromosomes* that are arranged in pairs within the nucleus of every cell. The chemical base of genes is the molecule *deoxyribonucleic acid,* or *DNA*. The order of the DNA molecule forms the code for all genetic information. Individual genes carry information for particular processes or characteristics.

26. Most of our major traits, like intelligence and height, are transmitted by *polygenic inheritance*. Several genes interact to produce the trait, each one making a small contribution.

27. The effects of heredity may not be immediately or fully apparent. The expression of a trait may be delayed until a later time in life. Environmental factors can also alter, suppress, or induce the expression of a trait.

28. A number of methods are used to study heritability of behavioral traits in animals and humans. *Strain studies* employ inbreeding to create genetically similar strains of animals. *Selection studies* look at successive generations of offspring to estimate heritability. *Family studies* are based on the assumption that if genes influence a trait, close relatives should be similar on the trait.

29. Psychologists use *twin studies* and *adoption studies* to separate out the influences of heredity and environment on various traits. Twin studies compare differences seen in sets of both *fraternal* and *identical twins*. Adoption studies look at children adopted at birth by parents who are not genetically related to them. Twin studies and adoption studies, along with family studies, show evidence of the role of heredity in intelligence, some forms of mental illness, and certain aspects of personality and temperament.

30. Progress in behavior genetics raises important social issues. With more power to control aspects of heredity and behavior, we face major new ethical dilemmas. Greater awareness of the implications and potential use of scientific findings will be needed.

1. Match the following terms with the correct definition.

   ____ neuron
   ____ nerve
   ____ axon
   ____ dendrite

   A. group of axons bundled together.
   B. receives incoming messages from surrounding neurons.
   C. carries outgoing messages away from the nerve cell.
   D. single nerve cell.

2. When a neuron is in a polarized state, there are mostly _____ ions on the outside of the cell membrane and mostly _____ ions on the inside.

3. During the absolute refractory relative refractory period the neuron will fire only if the incoming message is considerably stronger than usual.

4. A very strong incoming signal will cause a neuron to fire more strongly than before and in turn cause neighboring neurons to fire more strongly.   T/F

5. When a neural impulse reaches the end of the axon it is transferred to the next neuron chemically through the release of _____ .

6. The _____ _____ _____ connects the central nervous system to all parts of the body beyond the brain and spinal cord.

7. Which of the following is NOT part of the brain's structure:
   a. hypothalamus   c. limbic system
   b. corpus callosum   d. parathyroid

8. The two cerebral hemispheres are known as the _____ _____ .

9. Match the following terms and their definitions:

   ____ sensory projection areas
   ____ association areas
   ____ motor projection areas

   A. areas in the brain where response messages originate and then travel to muscles and glands

10. The limbic system/reticular formation alerts higher parts of the brain to important incoming messages.

11. The left hemisphere of the brain receives messages from the left side of the body while the right hemisphere does this for the right side of the body.   T/F

12. Match the following terms and their definitions:

    ____ pancreas
    ____ gonads
    ____ thyroid
    ____ anterior pituitary

    A. known as the "master gland" because it triggers the action of other endocrine glands
    B. releases a hormone that regulates the body's metabolism
    C. regulates the level of blood sugar
    D. helps to stimulate sex development

13. Communication in the endocrine system is dependent upon _____ , chemicals secreted directly into the bloodstream.

14. The parts of the endocrine system that play a major role in preparing the body to deal with threats are:
    a. the thyroid and parathyroid
    b. the thyroid and the pituitary gland
    c. the adrenal cortex and the adrenal medulla
    d. the posterior pituitary and the anterior pituitary

15. A recessive gene can control the appearance of a certain physical trait only if it is paired with a dominant/recessive gene.

16. Match the following terms with the correct definition:

    ____ strain studies
    ____ family studies
    ____ selection studies

    A. looks at successive generations of offspring to estimate heritability.
    B. employs inbreeding to create genetically similar strains of animals.
    C. based on the assumption that if genes influence a trait, close relatives should be similar on the trait.

Outline

Sensory Processes

3

How do we know when it is raining?

This simple question may have several answers, depending on what sense we are using to experience the rain at the time. We may look out the window and see the falling raindrops. Lying in bed at night, we may hear the rain pounding on the roof. If we are outside, we may feel the rain hitting our skin. Some people might even say that they can smell the rain or "sense" from the atmosphere that it is coming.

We use all our senses continually, but usually we are not aware of them all. Walking to the dentist, we may be so conscious of the sensation of throbbing pain from a toothache that the sounds of traffic or the smell from a bakery we pass on the way may not even register with us.

Much of the time we take our sensory experiences for granted. We accept that a rose smells sweet and a lemon tastes sour without asking why. We do not wonder why being whirled around on a roller coaster ride makes us dizzy, or why we are "blind" for a few moments when we come from the bright sunlight into a darkened movie theater. We really begin to understand just how much we depend on our senses and how much pleasure we get from them only when we lose one of them temporarily. Losing your balance on an uphill climb can be quite unnerving! Eating gourmet food when you have a heavy cold is generally a very disappointing experience!

When psychologists study sensation, they want to learn how information from the outside world—and from our own bodies—gets through to us. The psychologist studying sensation wants to learn how light bouncing off the objects around us results in vision, how sound waves become sounds, pinpricks become pain, and so on. In this chapter we will discuss **sensation,** the experience of stimulation of the senses, with reference to all of the body's senses: sight, hearing, balance, smell, taste, touch, and pain. In the following chapter we will consider the closely related process of *perception,* the interpretation of sensations by the brain.

Sensation Experience of sensory stimulation.

67

The Nature of Sensory Processes

Absolute threshold The least amount of energy that can be detected as a stimulation 50 percent of the time.

The General Character of Sensation

Described in general terms, the sequence of events that produce a sensation seems quite simple. First, some form of energy, either from an external source or from within the body, stimulates a receptor cell in one of the sense organs, such as the eye or the ear. A receptor cell is specialized to respond to one particular form of energy—light waves, for instance, or air pressure. The energy must be intense enough, or the receptor cell will not react to it. But given sufficient energy, the receptor responds by sending out a coded electrochemical signal. The signal varies with the characteristics of the stimulus. For instance, a very bright light might be coded by rapid firing of a set of nerve cells, while a dim light would set off much slower firing. As the neural signal passes along the sensory nerves to the central nervous system, it is coded still further, so that by the time it reaches the brain, the message is quite precise and detailed. Thus the coded signal that the brain receives from a flashing red light is very different from that signaling a soft yellow haze. And both these signals differ from the code for a loud, piercing noise.

From these various signals the brain creates sensory experiences. In a way, every sensory experience is an illusion created by the brain. The brain sits isolated within our skull, listening to the "clicking" of coded neural signals coming in over millions of nerve fibers. The clicks on an optical nerve are not any more "visual" than the clicks on an auditory nerve. But the brain interprets the clicks on the optic nerve as "visual nerve energy," and thus they give rise to visual experience instead of to sounds, tastes, or smells. Even if the clicks are caused by something other than light, the brain still responds with a visual experience. Gentle pressure on an eye, for instance, results in signals from the optic nerve that the brain interprets as visual patterns (see the box on Phosphenes on page 69). In the same way, both a symphonic recording and a stream of water trickling into the ear stimulate the auditory nerve, and both will cause us to hear something.

Sensory Thresholds

We have seen that the energy reaching a receptor must be sufficiently intense or it will have no noticeable effect. The minimum intensity of physical energy that is required to produce any sensation at all in a person is called the **absolute threshold.** Any stimulation below the absolute threshold will not be experienced.

How much sensory stimulation is needed to produce a sensation? How intense does a sound have to be, for example, for a person to hear it? How bright does a "blip" on a radar screen have to be for the operator to see it? In order to answer this kind of question, psychologists present a stimulus at different intensities and ask people whether they sense anything. You might expect that there would come a point where people would suddenly say, "Now I see the flash," or "Now I hear a sound." But

Phosphenes: Colorful Effects Without Light

A bang on the head and pressure on the eyes—the two have something in common: Both can make you see phosphenes. Phosphenes are the luminous patterns and blobs that you've probably seen float and swirl about your closed eyes. They can come in many colors—including purple, red, yellow, and blue—and geometric shapes—circles, triangles, hexagons, and squares. You can produce a phosphene easily. Close your left eye. Then, keeping your right eye open, lightly press on the eyelid on the outside of your right eye. (Be careful to touch lightly. If your eye begins to hurt, stop.) A dark spot should appear in your right visual field near your nose. You may also see a second, brighter spot nearby.

Other types of pressure on the eyes can generate vivid, highly complex phosphenes. By pressing moderately with both palms against your eyelids, you might see a pattern of red triangles against a black background. With deeper pressure, the results can be truly kaleidoscopic—wavy lines, colored triangles, and even checkerboardlike squares that appear and disappear in quick succession. Other kinds of phosphenes occur in flickering light as well as in darkness. In total darkness, as in a cave, they can give the impression of real lights blinking just out of reach (Walker, 1981). At very high frequencies, flashing lights like those used in discos can evoke dizzying arrays of phosphenes, all in full color.

As bright as they are, phosphenes have nothing to do with light. Various forms of eye activity can trigger phosphenes. Some result from stretching or compression of the optic nerve. Others are generated as pressure to the eyes hinders the flow of blood, reducing the oxygen supply to the retina. Even the sudden relaxation of muscles of the eye, which can happen when the eye switches focus, can cause pressure variations that trigger phosphenes. It is not yet clear whether these phosphenes are produced by the rods and cones or by the bipolar and ganglion cells. But at least some types of phosphenes appear to originate beyond the eyes, in the visual cortex of the brain. In all these cases, pressure on the eyes stimulates cells in the visual cortex of the brain that are designed to recognize geometric patterns, causing those patterns to seem to hang in space before you (Walker, 1981).

An artist's rendering of phosphenes, which can appear in various colors and geometric shapes as well as wavy lines.

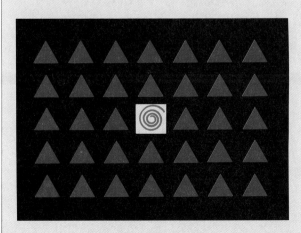

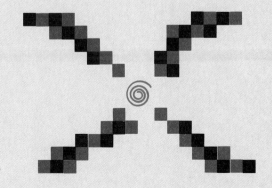

Difference threshold or **just noticeable difference (jnd)** The smallest change in stimulation that can be detected 50 percent of the time.

actually, there is a range of intensities over which a person sometimes, but not always, can sense the stimulus. For a variety of reasons, psychologists have agreed to set the absolute threshold at the point where the person can detect the stimulus 50 percent of the time that it is presented (see Figure 3-1).

Although there are differences between people and even differences from day to day for the same person, the absolute threshold for each of our senses is remarkably low. According to McBurney and Collings (1977), the approximate thresholds are as follows:

Taste: 1 gram (.0356 ounce) of table salt in 500 liters (529 quarts) of water.
Smell: One drop of perfume diffused throughout a three-room apartment.
Touch: The wing of a bee falling on your cheek from a height of 1 centimeter (.39 inch).
Hearing: The tick of a watch from 6 meters (20 feet) in very quiet conditions.
Vision: A candle flame seen from 50 kilometers (30 miles) on a clear, dark night.

Imagine now that you can hear a particular sound. How much stronger does the sound have to be before you notice that it has become louder? The smallest change in stimulation that you can detect 50 percent of the time is called the **difference threshold.** This is also called the **just noticeable difference,** or **jnd.** Like the absolute threshold, the difference threshold will vary from person to person and from time to time in the same person. But difference thresholds also vary with the absolute level

Figure 3-1

Determining a sensory threshold. The red line represents an ideal case—at all intensities below the threshold the subject reports no sensation or no change in intensity; at all intensities above the threshold the subject does report a sensation or a change in intensity. In actual practice the ideal of the red line is never realized. The blue line shows the actual responses of a typical subject. The threshold is taken at the point where the subject reports a sensation or a change in intensity 50 percent of the time.

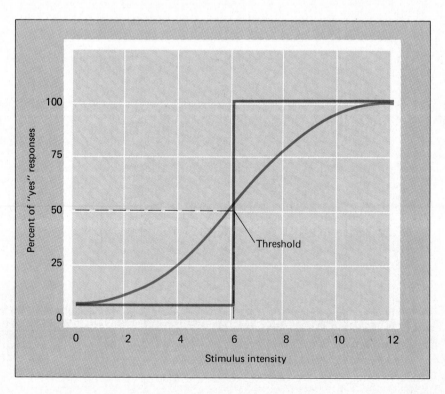

of stimulation. Generally, the stronger the stimulation, the bigger the difference must be in order for you to sense it. Turning on a light at sunset is more noticeable than turning on the same light at noon on a sunny day. Adding 1 pound to a 5-pound load will certainly be noticed; adding that same pound to a 100-pound load probably will not make a noticeable difference. And finally, some of our senses are more sensitive than others to changes in stimulation: We are very good at detecting changes in the pitch of a note or the brightness of a light, but much less sensitive to changes in the loudness of a sound or in pressure on the surface of our skin.

So far we have been talking about some general characteristics of sensation, but each of the body's sensory systems works a little differently. Each one contains receptor cells that specialize in converting a particular kind of energy into neural signals. The threshold at which this conversion occurs varies with the system. So do the mechanisms by which sensory input is processed and coded and sent to the brain for still more processing. In the following pages we'll discuss the unique features of each of the sensory systems in turn.

Cornea The transparent protective coating over the front part of the eye.

Pupil Small opening in the iris through which light enters the eye.

Iris Colored part of the eye.

Lens Transparent part of the eye that focuses light onto the retina.

Retina Lining of the eye containing receptor cells that are sensitive to light.

Fovea Area of the retina that is the center of the visual field.

Vision

Animals vary in their relative dependence on the different senses. Dogs rely heavily on the sense of smell, bats on hearing, some fish on taste. But for humans, vision is probably the most important sense, and therefore it has received the most attention from psychologists. To begin to understand vision, we need to look first at the parts of the visual system beginning with the structure of the eye.

The Visual System

The structure of the human eye is shown in Figure 3-2. Light enters the eye through the **cornea,** the transparent protective coating over the front part of the eye. Then it passes through the **pupil,** the opening in the center of the **iris,** the colored part of the eye. In very bright light the muscles in the iris contract to make the pupil smaller and protect the eye from damage. This also helps us to see better in bright light. In dim light the muscles extend to open the pupil wider and let in as much light as possible.

Inside the pupil the light passes through the **lens,** which focuses it onto the **retina,** the inner lining of the back of the eyeball that is sensitive to light. The lens changes shape to focus on objects that are closer or farther away. Normally, the lens is focused on a middle distance, at a point neither very near nor very far away. To focus on an object that is very close to the eyes, tiny muscles around the lens contract and make the lens rounder. To focus on an object that is far away, the muscles work to make the lens flatter.

On the retina, directly behind the lens, is a depressed spot called the **fovea** (see Figure 3-3). The fovea occupies the center of the visual field.

The images that pass through the lens are in sharpest focus here. Thus the words that you are now reading are hitting the fovea, while the rest of what you see—a desk, walls, or whatever—is hitting other areas of the retina.

THE RECEPTOR CELLS. The retina of each eye contains the receptor cells responsible for vision. These cells are sensitive to only one small part of the spectrum of electromagnetic energy, which includes light along

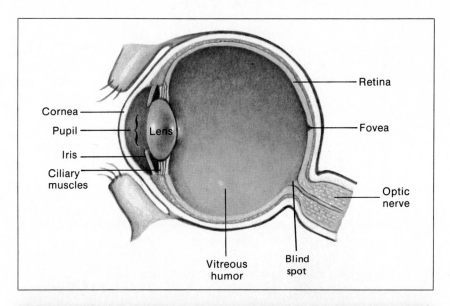

Figure 3-2

A cross section of the human eye.

Figure 3-3

A view of the retina through an ophthalmoscope, an instrument often used to inspect the blood vessels in patients' eyes. The dark area in the center is the fovea. The bright yellow circle marks the blind spot, the place where the optic nerve leaves the eye.

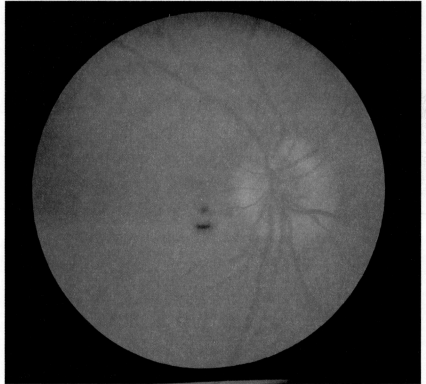

with other energies (see Figures 3-4 and 3-5). There are two kinds of receptor cells in the retina—**rods** and **cones**—named for their characteristic shapes. The retina of each eye contains about 120 million rods and 8 million cones. Rods respond only to varying degrees of light and dark, and not to colors. They are chiefly responsible for night vision. Cones, on the other hand, respond both to light and dark and to colors. They operate chiefly in daylight. Cones are less sensitive to light than rods are (MacLeod, 1978). In this regard, cones, like color film, work best in

Rods Receptor cells in the retina responsible for night vision and not specialized to receive color.

Cones Receptor cells in the retina responsible for color vision.

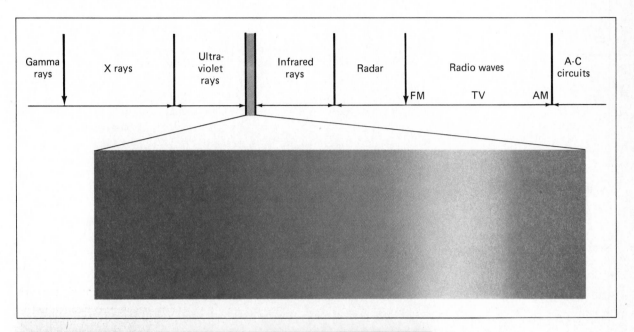

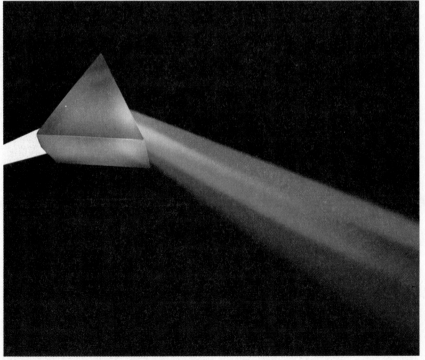

Figure 3-4

The electromagnetic spectrum. The eye is sensitive to only a very small segment of the spectrum, known as visible light.

Figure 3-5

Sunlight contains the wavelengths for all the colors we can see. When sunlight is passed through a prism, the wavelengths are bent at different angles and the light is separated into a color spectrum. A natural spectrum, a rainbow, occurs when sunlight is bent by the atmosphere.

relatively bright light. The more sensitive rods, like black-and-white film, respond to much lower levels of illumination.

Rods and cones differ in other ways as well. Cones are found mainly, but not exclusively, in the fovea, which contains no rods. Nearly 100,000 cones are packed into the fovea, which, as you recall, is situated where images are projected onto the retina in sharpest focus. Rods predominate just outside of the fovea. As we move outward from the fovea toward the edges of the retina, both rods and cones get sparser. At the extreme edges of the retina, there are no cones and only a few rods.

Rods and cones also differ in how they connect to the nerve cells leading to the brain. Both rods and cones connect to what are called **bipolar neurons,** which are neurons with only one axon and one dendrite (see Figure 3-6). In the fovea cones generally connect with only one bipolar neuron—a sort of "private line" arrangement. Rods are usually on a "party line"—several of them may share a single bipolar neuron.

Knowing these facts about rods and cones can help you understand some of the more common experiences in seeing. For example, you may have noticed that at night you can see a dimly lit object better if you look slightly to one side of it rather than directly at it. This has to do with the location of the rods and cones. When you look directly at an object, its image falls on the fovea, which consists only of relatively light-insensitive cones. However, when you look slightly to one side of the object, its image falls next to the fovea and onto the highly light-sensitive rods. Moreover, such a weak stimulus will cause only a weak response in the cones, and this probably will not be sufficient to fire its bipolar neurons. But because many rods converge on a single bipolar neuron, that neuron is much more likely to fire and thereby start a sensory message to the brain.

At other times, vision is improved when more cones are stimulated. Have you ever tried to examine something but could not make out the details? You probably found that by increasing the amount of light on the object—perhaps by moving it into direct sunlight or under a lamp—you could see it better. This is because the better the illumination, the greater

Bipolar neurons Neurons that have only one axon and one dendrite; in the eye these neurons connect the receptors on the retina to the ganglion cells.

Figure 3-6

The layers of the retina. Light must pass through the ganglion cells and the bipolar neurons to reach the rods and cones. The sensory messages then travel back out again from the receptor cells, through the bipolar neurons, to the ganglion cells. The axons of the ganglion cells gather together to form the optic nerve, which carries the messages from both eyes to the brain. (From Hubel, 1963).

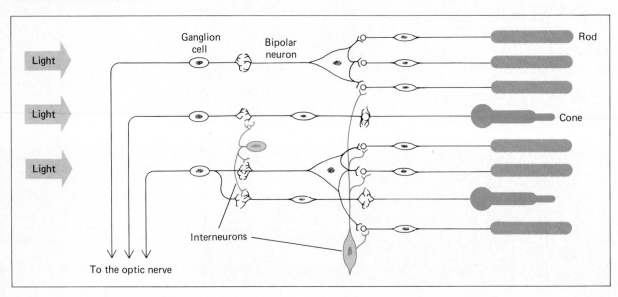

the number of cones stimulated, and the greater the number of cones stimulated, the more likely they are to stimulate the bipolar cells, starting a message on the way to the brain. Our ability to see increases, almost without limit, as light intensity increases. So for "close" activities like reading, sewing, and writing, the more light the better (McBurney & Collings, 1977).

For related reasons, vision is sharpest—even in normal light—whenever you look directly at an object and its image falls on the fovea. Here in the fovea the one-to-one connection between cones and bipolar neurons allows for maximum **visual acuity,** the ability to distinguish fine details. You can easily demonstrate acuity to yourself by doing the following: Hold the book about 18 inches from your eyes and look at the "X" in the center of the line below. Notice how your vision drops off for words and letters toward the left or right end of the line:

This is a test to show how visual**X**acuity varies across the retina.

Your fovea picks up the "X" and about four letters to either side. This is the area of greatest visual acuity. The letters at the left and right ends of the line fall well outside the fovea, where there are many more rods than cones. Rods, as you remember, tend to "pool" their signals on the way to

Visual acuity The ability to distinguish fine details.

Reading: There Is More Than Meets the Eye

Basketball fans often admire the subtle muscular coordination that it takes for a player to snatch a pass out of midair and in one motion stuff the ball through the hoop. But just watching the game, each fan engages in one of the subtlest muscular movements the human body can perform: eye movement. Keeping track of the various players requires thousands of tiny jumps of the eye, called *saccades*. The muscles that control saccadic motion are among the fastest in the body. On the other hand, following a moving target like the ball requires slower, smoother eye movements that must match the speed of the ball.

Both kinds of eye movement are also essential to reading, which is probably the most sophisticated visual activity imaginable. As you move your eyes along a line of text, you move them in a series of fixations. The eye comes to rest on a part of the line for about 1/4 of a second and then skips rapidly (about 1/20 of a second per skip) to the next resting point. Good readers scan a line of text using fewer and faster fixations than poor readers do; slower readers tend to move their eyes back to sections of text that they have already covered.

Not surprisingly, most speed-reading courses concentrate on improving eye movement to increase reading efficiency, but there is more to reading than moving your eyes over type. You must also compare the patterns of type in your visual field with letters and words stored in your memory. The area of greatest visual acuity falls about 4 letters on either side of the fixation point. But research shows that you can get information about the shapes of *words* over an area that extends about 15 letters on each side. This ability translates into a maximum reading rate of about 200 words per minute, approximately the average rate at which words are spoken. Therefore readers who can recognize not just individual letters but whole words or phrases at a glance can decode print much faster than readers who cannot.

Rapid reading also depends on familiarity with the material being read and the ability to exploit the repetition that exists in all written material. Very rapid readers learn to decode the meanings on the page without processing every letter or word. The secret to this ability is to build expectations about upcoming text on the basis of what has already been read. Thus the reader may be able to complete a sentence after reading only isolated words at the beginning (Hochberg, 1978). This ability permits reading speeds well over 200 words per minute. Of course, if you happen to be studying a calculus text, where much less skipping and anticipation are possible, this skill is not likely to be very useful!

Adaptation Adjustment of the senses to stimulation such as light.

Dark adaptation Increased sensitivity of rods and cones in darkness.

Light adaptation Decreased sensitivity of rods and cones in bright light.

Afterimage Sense experience that occurs after a stimulus has been removed.

Figure 3-7

First stare continuously at the center of the top circle for about 20 seconds. Then shift your gaze to the dot in the lower circle. Within a moment, a gray-and-white afterimage should appear inside the lower circle.

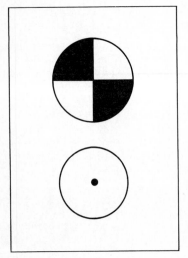

the bipolar neurons; and while this increases sensitivity, it cuts down on the fine details in the signal that goes to the brain. Outside the fovea acuity drops by as much as 50 percent!

ADAPTATION. The sensitivity of rods and cones changes depending on how much light is available. This process is known as **adaptation.** When you go from bright sunlight into a dimly lit theater, your cones at first are fairly insensitive to light: You can see little or nothing as you look for a seat. But during the first 5 or 10 minutes in the dark, the cones become more and more sensitive to whatever light is around. After about 10 minutes, you will be able to see things directly ahead of you about as well as you are going to: The cones do not get any more sensitive after this point. But the rods, which have been adapting also, continue to become more sensitive to light for another 20 minutes or so. They reach maximum sensitivity about 30 minutes after you have entered the darkened room. This process in which the rods and cones become more sensitive to light in response to lowered levels of illumination is called **dark adaptation.** But even with dark adaptation there is not enough energy in very dim light to stimulate the cones to respond to colors. So when your eyes are dark-adapted, you see only a black-and-white-and-gray world of different brightnesses.

In the reverse process, which is **light adaptation,** the rods and cones become less sensitive to light. By the time you leave a movie theater, your rods and cones have become very sensitive, and the bright outdoor light sometimes hurts as a result. In the bright light all the neurons fire at once, overwhelming you. You squint and shield your eyes and each iris contracts, all of which helps to reduce the amount of light entering your pupils and striking each retina. As light adaptation begins, the rods and cones become less sensitive to stimulation by light, and within about a minute both rods and cones are fully adapted to the light. At this point squinting and shielding your eyes are no longer necessary.

You can observe the effects of dark and light adaptation by staring continuously at the center of the top circle in Figure 3-7 for about 20 seconds. Then shift your gaze to the dot in the lower circle. A gray-and-white pattern should appear inside the lower circle (if you blink your eyes, this illusion will be even stronger). When you look at the lower circle, the areas that were black in the upper circle will now seem to be light, and the areas that were white in the upper circle will now appear gray. The reason for this **afterimage** is that the part of the retina that was exposed to the dark areas of the upper circle became more sensitive (it dark-adapted), while the area exposed to the white part of the inner circle became less sensitive (it light-adapted). When you shifted your eyes to the blank circle, the less sensitive parts of the retina produced the sensation of gray rather than white. This afterimage fades within a minute as the retina adapts again, this time to the solid white circle.

You can see from these examples that visual adaptation is a partial, back-and-forth kind of process. The eyes adjust—from no stimulation to stimulation, from less stimulation to more, and vice versa—but they never adapt completely. Consider what would happen if stimulation somehow remained constant and the eyes adapted completely. Gradually all the receptors would become wholly insensitive and we would not be able to see anything at all. If you were to stare at the circle in Figure 3-7 for a long time, and if its image on your retina could be held perfectly still, the circle would slowly fade and finally disappear altogether. This would be true for all objects we tried to look at. If you want to see a normal occurrence of full adaptation, go into a dark room with a penlight and shine the light into one of your eyes from above and to the side of your head. You will see something that looks like the branches of a tree. These are the blood vessels that run across your retina in front of the rods and cones. Normally these vessels are invisible because their shadows are held perfectly still on the retina where they fall on the same rods and cones. But when you shine the light from a very unusual direction, as suggested here, the shadows stimulate different rods and cones, which allows you to see them.

Obviously it is important that our eyes not adapt this way when we are trying to see objects in the real world. And they don't usually, because light stimulation is rarely focused on the same rods and cones long enough for them to become wholly insensitive. One reason for this is that small involuntary eye movements cause an image on the retina to drift slightly, and then snap it back in place again with a tiny flick. At the same time, the eyes continually show a slight, extremely rapid tremor—a tremor so minute that it goes completely unnoticed. All these movements together keep an image moving slightly on the retina, so the receptors never have time to adapt completely.

FROM EYE TO BRAIN. Up to now we have been focusing on the eye itself and the beginnings of visual processing in the retina. But messages from the eye must eventually reach the brain in order for a visual experience to occur. As you can imagine from Figure 3-6, the series of connections between eye and brain is quite intricate. To begin with, rods and cones are connected with bipolar neurons in many different numbers and combinations. In addition, sets of neurons called *interneurons* link receptor cells to one another and bipolar cells to one another. Eventually these bipolar neurons connect with the **ganglion cells,** leading out of the eye. The axons of the ganglion cells are what join to form the **optic nerve,** which carries messages from each eye to the brain. The optic nerve itself consists of only about 1 million axons. This means that in each eye the signals from many million rods and cones have been combined and reduced to fit just 1 million wires that lead to the brain!

The place on the retina where the axons of all the ganglion cells join to leave the eye is called the **blind spot**—it contains no receptors. We are not normally aware of the blind spot. When light from a small object is focused directly on it, however, the object will not be seen (See Figure 3-8).

After they leave the eyes, the fibers that make up the optic nerves separate, and some of them cross to the other side. The nerve fibers from

Ganglion cells Neurons that connect the bipolar neurons in the eyes to the brain.

Optic nerve The bundle of axons of ganglion cells that carries neural messages from each eye to the brain.

Blind spot Place on the retina where the axons of all the ganglion cells leave the eye and where there are no receptors.

Figure 3-8

To locate your blind spot, hold the book about a foot away from your eyes. Then close your right eye, stare at the dot, and slowly move the book toward you and away from you until the X disappears.

Optic chiasm Point near the base of the brain where some fibers in the optic nerve from each eye cross to the other side of the brain.

Hue The aspect of color that corresponds to names such as red, green, blue.

Figure 3-9

The neural connections of the visual system. Messages from the left visual field of each eye travel to the right occipital lobe. Those from the right visual field of each eye go to the left occipital lobe. The crossover point is the optic chiasm.

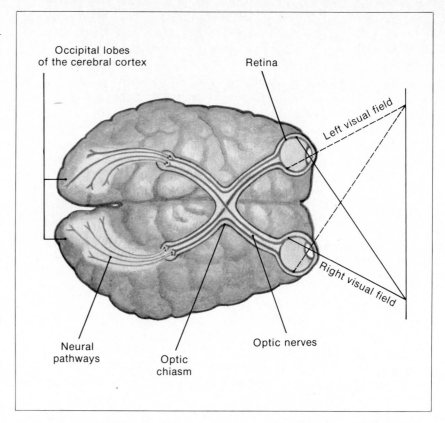

the right side of each eye travel to the right hemisphere of the brain; those from the left side of each eye travel to the left hemisphere. The place where some of these fibers cross over is called the **optic chiasm** (see Figure 3-9). This crossing enables the fibers of the optic nerves to carry their messages to several different parts of the brain. Some of the messages reach the part of the brain that controls the reflex movements that adjust the size of the pupil. Others reach the part of the brain that directs the eye muscles to change the shape of the lens. But the main destinations for the messages from the retina are the visual projection areas of the cerebral cortex, where the pattern of stimulated and unstimulated receptor cells is registered and interpreted.

Color Vision

Unlike many other animal species such as dogs and cats (see the box on page 79), humans can see an extensive range of colors. In the following pages we will first discuss some characteristics of color vision and then consider how the eyes convert light energy into sensations of color.

COLOR PROPERTIES. Look at Figure 3-10. What do you see? Most people say they see a number of different colors—some greens, some yellows, some reds, and so forth. Psychologists call these different colors **hues;** and to a great extent, what hues you see depends on the wavelength of the light reaching your eyes (see Figure 3-4).

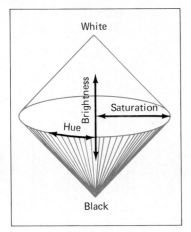

Figure 3-10
The color solid. The dimension of hue is represented around the circumference. Saturation ranges along the radius from the inside to the outside of the solid. Brightness varies along the vertical axis. The drawing on the left illustrates this schematically.

Species Differences in Color Vision

When you and your cat look at the same things— the cat food you are opening, the rug he is sharpening his claws on, the dangerous dog next door—the two of you do not see the same things. Your cat's ability to see colors is much less developed than your own. Cats can see some colors, but only when the colored surfaces are large. Thus your cat may be able to see the color of your carpet, but you probably appreciate the multicolored label on his Nine Lives can more than he does.

In fact, compared to most other mammals, humans have unusually good color vision. The ability to see colors is nonexistent in rodents: rats are completely color-blind. Color vision among the carnivores—dogs and cats, for example—is limited, while some primitive primates, including tree shrews, can see colors moderately well. Monkeys and apes, the members of the primate order most closely related to humans, can see colors very well. It is possible that this ability evolved partly because it gave the tree-dwelling common ancestors of monkeys, apes, and humans advantages in foraging for brightly colored fruits. Color vision is not limited to a few mammals, however. Some reptiles, fish, insects, and shellfish can also distinguish colors (Rosenzweig & Leiman, 1982).

But even among animals that can see colors,

there are differences in what colors they can see. For example, bees can see ultraviolet light, but they cannot see red. Pigeons cannot see indigo and violet, monkeys cannot see some blue, indigo, and violet, and human infants are insensitive to violet. And even if an animal is sensitive to light of a certain wavelength, we do not know how that light is experienced. We experience light with a wavelength of 600 nm as "yellow," but to a bird this same light may produce a different experience entirely.

Animals differ not only in terms of the parts of the spectrum that they can see but also in the way they divide up the spectrum into color categories. Researchers have discovered that bees lump together wavelengths that we distinguish as yellow and green. Bees that have been fed sugar water from a dish with a yellow bottom tend to return to dishes with green as well as yellow bottoms. Apparently bees perceive the two hues as the same. Monkeys, on the other hand, perceive as quite separate colors what we see as simply shades of the same color. Such differences among animal species suggest that the receptor cells in their eyes, and the neurons to which the cells are connected, process light in somewhat different ways, though we are just beginning to discover what those differences are (Bornstein & Marks, 1982).

Saturation The purity of a color.

Brightness The nearness of a color to white as opposed to black.

Additive color mixing The process of mixing lights of different wave lengths to create new hues.

Complementary colors Two hues, far apart on the spectrum, that when added together in equal intensities produce a neutral gray rather than a third hue.

Now look again at Figure 3-10. You will notice that although each color patch on the triangle is the same overall hue, the color is deepest at the left edge and tends to get paler, or more washed out, toward the man's hand. This paleness occurs when light of other wavelengths dilutes the purity of a hue. Psychologists refer to the purity of a hue as its **saturation.** A pure color is one that is high in saturation. An impure or washed-out color is low in saturation.

Look back at the color solid in Figure 3-10 and squint your eyes so that you can barely see the colors, or turn off some of the lights in the room to make it almost dark. The colors appear darker; in fact, the purples may begin to look black. You have just reduced the **brightness** of the colors. Brightness depends mainly on the strength of the light entering your eye. The brighter the color, the whiter it seems. In the purple wedge from the color solid, the colors near the top are very bright and may appear almost white; those near the bottom appear almost black.

Hue, saturation, and brightness are three separate aspects of our experience of color. While people can distinguish only about 150 hues, different levels of saturation and brightness combine to give us more than 300,000 different color experiences (Hochberg, 1978; Kaufman, 1979). Some of this variety is captured in a slice from the color solid in Figure 3-10. The slice is all one hue (reddish purple), but the patches vary in saturation (from left to right) and in brightness (from top to bottom).

COLOR MIXING. For centuries scientists have known that it is possible to produce all 150 hues simply by mixing together a few lights of different colors (see Figure 3-11). In the 17th century the English physicist Isaac Newton found that combining lights of two different colors produced a new color that generally could be found at a place on the spectrum between the two original lights. Red and green lights combine to give yellow. This process of mixing lights of different wavelengths is called **additive color mixing.**

Newton also discovered that some lights combine to produce a neutral gray rather than a new hue. Such colors are termed **complementary colors.** In the color circle in Figure 3-12 colors on opposite sides of the circle are complementary. Red and blue-green are examples of complementary colors, as are blue and yellow. Other colors, such as red and blue, combine to form a hue (purple) that is not found in the spectrum—

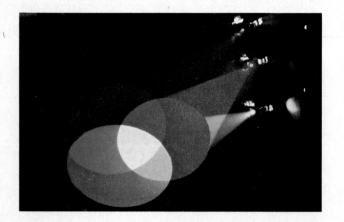

Figure 3-11

Mixing light waves is an additive process. When red and green lights are combined, the resulting hue is yellow. All three lights together result in white light.

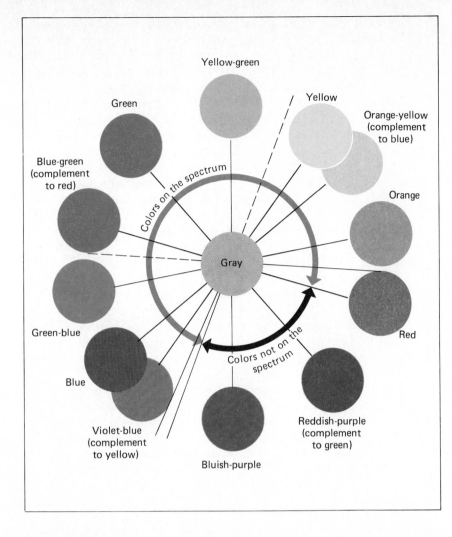

Figure 3-12 (left)

The color circle. The circle includes the colors found on the spectrum as well as some nonspectral colors. Colors on opposite sides of the circle are complementary; when mixed together, they produce a neutral gray.

Nonspectral color A hue, such as purple, that is not found in the spectrum.

Primary colors A set of three colors, such as red, green, and blue, that when mixed in unequal amounts can produce any visible hue.

Subtractive color mixing The process of mixing pigments, each of which absorbs some wavelengths of light and reflects others.

a **nonspectral color.** If you compare the color circle in Figure 3-12 with the spectrum in Figure 3-4, you will notice some colors in the circle that do not appear on the spectrum. If all the colors of the spectrum are combined, the result is white light.

Newton's work was refined in the 19th century. Early in that century the English physicist Thomas Young proposed that if red, green, and blue lights were mixed in the right intensities, they could produce any hue that the human eye can detect. James Maxwell, a Scottish physicist, confirmed that red, green, and blue are indeed **primary colors:** If mixed together in equal amounts, they produce gray; but if mixed in unequal amounts, they can be made to produce any visible hue. Maxwell discovered many other sets of primary colors exist as well.

Most people have more experience with mixing pigments such as paints than with mixing lights. The process of mixing pigments, called **subtractive color mixing,** produces very different results from those obtained by combining lights. This is because each of an artist's pigments absorbs a different part of the spectrum, so some wavelengths are subtracted while others are reflected (see Figure 3-13). Blue paint, for instance, reflects blue light as well as some green light (which is close to

Figure 3-13 (below)

The process of mixing paint pigments rather than lights is subtractive, because pigments absorb some wavelengths and reflect others. A mixture of the three primary pigments absorbs all wavelengths, producing black.

Trichromatic theory Theory of color vision that holds that all color perception derives from three different color receptors in the retina (usually red, green, and blue receptors).

Opponent-process theory Theory of color vision that holds that three sets of color receptors (yellow-blue, red-green, black-white) respond in an either/or fashion to determine the color you experience.

Color blindness Partial or total inability to perceive colors.

Trichromats People who have normal color vision.

Monochromats Persons who are totally color-blind.

Dichromats People who are blind to either red-green or yellow-blue.

blue on the spectrum), but it absorbs all other light waves. Yellow paint reflects yellow light as well as some nearby green light. When blue and yellow paints are mixed, the combined pigment reflects only green light and absorbs everything else. Thus blue and yellow pigments absorb everything except green light, which they both reflect.

THEORIES OF COLOR VISION. We have seen so far that cones in the retina are responsible for our color vision. Somehow the cones in the eye send a unique message to the brain in response to each of the colors that we can distinguish. But the question of how this takes place is still much debated. Consider the fact that in the fovea there are only 100,000 cones, yet we can distinguish 300,000 different kinds of colors. Obviously there are not enough cones in the fovea to have one for every color! Somehow relatively few kinds of cones must combine to provide both the full range of color and the clear, sharp images that we perceive when we look right at colored objects.

A German physiologist named Hermann von Helmholtz remembered that Thomas Young was able to produce all the various hues by mixing just three kinds of light: red, green, and blue. Helmholtz suggested that the eye contains some cones that are most sensitive to red, others that are most sensitive to green, and others that respond most strongly to blue-violet. By mixing the signals from the three receptors, then, you should be able to create any color. Yellow light, for example, would produce the sensation of yellow by stimulating the red and green receptors fairly strongly and the blue-violet receptors weakly. Helmholtz's explanation of color vision is known as the **trichromatic theory.**

In 1878 another German physiologist, Ewald Hering, proposed an alternative to this theory. He took into account the fact that we never see yellowish-blue light or reddish-green light. A mixture of red and green produces a reddish or greenish hue if the intensities of the two lights are unequal, or a neutral gray light if the two intensities are equal. However, it is possible to see yellowish reds and greenish blues. To explain these and other observations, Hering proposed the existence of three pairs of color receptors: a yellow-blue pair, a red-green pair, and a black-white pair. The members of each pair work in opposition to each other. The yellow-blue pair cannot relay messages about yellow and blue light at the same time, nor can the red-green pair send both red and green messages at the same time. The red-green and blue-yellow pairs determine the hue that you see, while the black-white pair determines brightness. Hering's theory is now known as the **opponent-process theory.**

Each of these two theories accounts for certain visual phenomena especially well. Trichromatic theory explains most efficiently the fact that three primary colors can be combined to produce any other hue. It also provides a convincing explanation for various kinds of **color blindness,** the partial or total inability to perceive hues. About 10 percent of men and 1 percent of women are color-blind. People with normal color vision are **trichromats:** they can match any given hue by combining three primary colors. At the other extreme are **monochromats**—the rare people who see no color at all but respond only to shades of light and dark. More common than monochromats are **dichromats**—people who are blind to either red-green or blue-yellow. Red-green color blindness, for example, can result from a deficiency in either the red or the green

Seeing Red

Red fire engines are gradually going out of style, thanks to what scientists have learned about how well the eye sees red compared to other colors. The rods, which are primarily responsible for night vision, are not equally sensitive to light from all parts of the spectrum.

A look at the figure below reveals that the rods are most sensitive to colors in the blue and green range and about a thousand times less sensitive to the red end of the spectrum. This means that at night, blue and green lights are much more visible than red lights. Red objects actually look black at night!

Cones, which dominate during day vision, also do not respond to all colors equally well. The figure shows that the cones are most sensitive to green and yellow; like the rods, they are not very sensitive to red. During daylight yellowish green is over 100 times more visible than red. These considerations have prompted many fire departments to switch from red paint for their engines to lime yellow, which is much more visible day *and* night.

Fire companies are not the only organizations changing their use of colors. Traditionally the Coast Guard has used red-and-black buoys to guide ships through dangerous waters. Because both colors look black at night, the Coast Guard has recently shifted from black to green, the color that the dark-adapted eye sees best. Green buoys are more visible than either red or black buoys, day and night. The Coast Guard, as well as many police departments, uses bright blue emergency lights, which are much more visible than red lights, especially at night.

A graph showing the greater sensitivity of rods to colors in the blue and green range, and of cones to the green and yellow range. Neither are very sensitive to the red end of the spectrum. (Based on Shiffman, 1976)

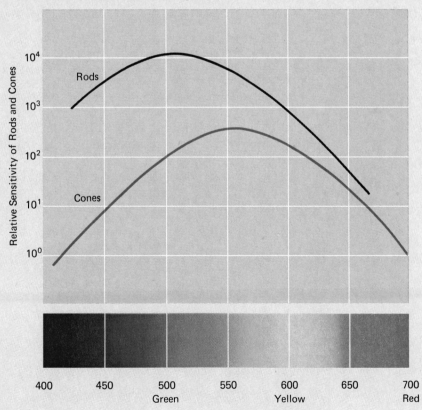

Figure 3-14

People who are color blind have a partial or total inability to perceive hue. To show what this means in everyday life, we have printed a photo of boats both in normal color (left) and as someone with red-green color blindness would see it (right).

receptors. In both cases, the person confuses red and green, since both red and green appear to be a desaturated yellow (see Figure 3-14).

Opponent-process theory tends to explain other phenomena better than trichromatic theory. For example, if you look at the flag in Figure 3-15 for about 30 seconds and then look at a sheet of white paper, you will see an afterimage. Where the picture is green, you will see a red afterimage. And where the picture is yellow-orange, you will see a bright blue afterimage. And where the picture is black, you will see a bright white afterimage. The afterimage is always in the complementary color. Hering's explanation for afterimages is that the receptor pairs have adapted to the stimulation. While you were looking at the green bars in the flag, the red-green receptors were sending "green" messages; but they were also adapting to the stimulation by becoming less sensitive to green light. When you later looked at the white page (made up of light from all parts of the spectrum), the red-green receptors responded much more to wavelengths in the red portion of the spectrum, and so you saw a red bar. Can you predict in advance what kind of afterimage you will experience after you stare at the dot in the center of Figure 3-16 for about 30 seconds?

The two theories of color vision—trichromatic and opponent-

Figure 3-15

Stare at the white spot in the center of the flag for about 30 seconds. Then look at a blank piece of white paper and you will see an afterimage.

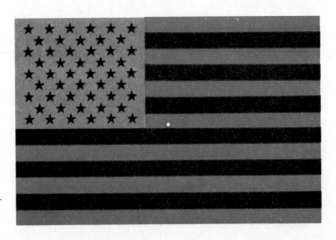

process—have coexisted for over a century. Neither has succeeded in ousting the other. The reason seems to be that both theories are valid, but for two different stages in the visual process. We now know for certain that there are three kinds of receptors for color, just as trichromatic theory holds. But while these receptors have peaks of sensitivity at blue, green, and yellow-green, all are responsive to a broad range of colors. Moreover, contrary to the Helmholtz theory, there is no "red" receptor in the retina (Rosenzweig & Leiman, 1982). We also have evidence that either the bipolar neurons or the ganglion cells in the retina code colors in an opponent-process way. The team of DeValois and DeValois (1975) have discovered three types of ganglion cells. One type responds only to brightness and not to color. As the intensity of light increases, so does the rate at which these neurons fire. A second set of ganglion cells increases its rate of firing when red light strikes the cones and decreases it when green light strikes them. A third set of cells fires in response to blue or yellow light striking the cones. All three sets are paired with cells that react in exactly the opposite way. So Hering was not completely wrong.

It now seems plausible that there are, as Helmholtz believed, three kinds of receptors for color. The messages they transmit, however, are translated by either the bipolar or ganglion cells into opponent-process form. These complex patterns of "on" and "off" firing of neurons are what communicate the message "color" to the brain. In the brain itself there are cells that respond only to color (Mollon, 1982). They too appear to work according to the opponent-process principle. In fact, it is possible to see certain kinds of afterimages by adapting these brain cells. For example, certain computer video displays feature green letters. When heavy users look away from the screen, they often notice that white objects seem to have pink edges (Personal Computing, December 1983). This phenomenon, which can last for several days, appears to be an afterimage caused by adaptation of color cells in the brain itself.

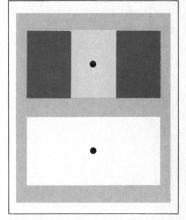

Figure 3-16

An afterimage is always in the complementary colors. After staring at the center dot of the top rectangle for about 30 seconds and then shifting your gaze to the center dot of the bottom rectangle, you will again see blue and yellow.

Hearing

There is an ancient question that asks, "If a tree falls in the forest and there is no one there, is there a sound?" A psychologist would answer, "There are sound waves, but there is no sound or noise." Sounds and noise are psychological experiences created by your brain in response to stimulation. What kinds of stimuli cause us to hear sounds?

Sound

The physical stimuli for the sense of hearing are sound waves—changes in pressure caused when molecules of air or fluid collide with one another and then move apart again, transmitting energy at every bump. The simplest sound wave—what we hear as a pure tone—can be pictured as a sine wave (see Figure 3-17). The tuning fork vibrates, causing the

Frequency The number of cycles per second in a wave; in sound, the primary determinant of pitch.

Hertz (Hz) Cycles per second; unit of measurement for the frequency of waves.

Pitch Auditory experience corresponding primarily to frequency of sound vibrations, resulting in a higher or lower tone.

molecules of air to first compress and then expand. The **frequency** of the waves is measured in cycles per second, expressed in a unit called **hertz (Hz)**. Frequency primarily determines the **pitch** of the sound—how high or how low it is. The human ear responds to frequencies from about 20 Hz to 20,000 Hz. A bass viola can reach down to about 50 Hz, a piano to as high as 5,000 Hz.

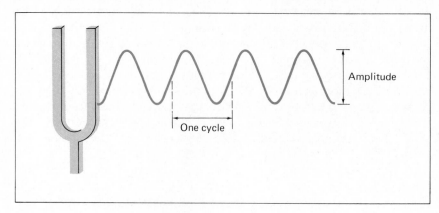

Figure 3-17

As it vibrates, the tuning fork alternately compresses and expands the molecules of air, creating a sound wave.

Figure 3-18

A decibel scale for several common sounds. Prolonged exposure to sounds above 85 decibels can cause permanent damage to the ears.
(After Dunkle, 1982.)

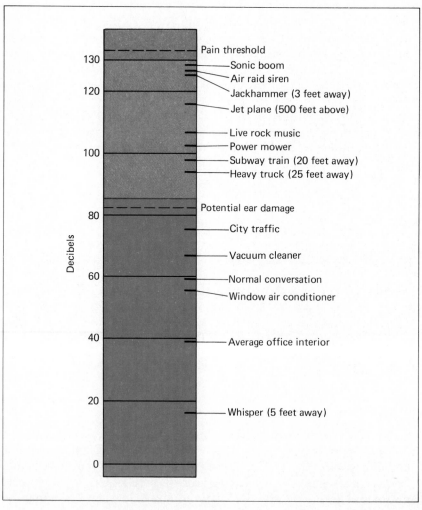

The height of the wave represents its **amplitude,** which, together with pitch, determines the *loudness* of a sound. Loudness is measured in **decibels** (see Figure 3-18). As we grow older, we lose some of our ability to hear low-intensity sounds (McBurney & Collings, 1977). We can hear high-intensity sounds, however, as well as ever. This is why elderly people may ask you to speak louder and then, when you oblige by speaking much louder, respond, "There's no need to shout!"

The sounds we hear seldom result from pure tones. Most fundamental tones also carry with them a load of **overtones**—accompanying sound waves that are different multiples of the frequency of the basic tone. A violin string, for example, does not only vibrate as a whole; it also vibrates in halves, thirds, quarters, and so on, all at the same time. Each set of vibrations produces a tone. The complex pattern of overtones determines the **timbre**—or "texture"—of the sound.

Amplitude The magnitude of a wave; in sound, the primary determinant of loudness.

Decibel Unit of measurement for the loudness of sounds.

Overtones Tones that result from sound waves that are multiples of the basic tone; primary determinant of timbre.

Timbre Tone quality or texture produced by overtones of a sound.

The Ear

Hearing begins when sound waves bump up against the eardrum (see Figure 3-19) and cause it to vibrate. The quivering of the eardrum causes

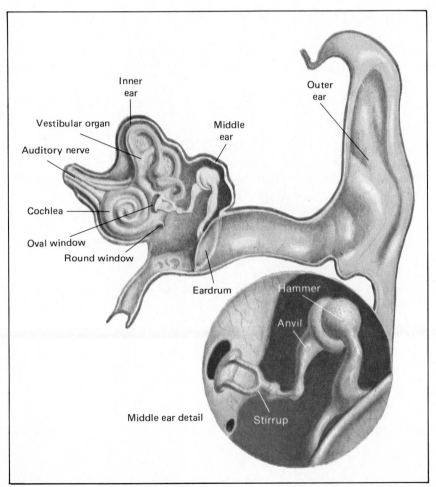

Figure 3-19

The structure of the human ear.

Inner
ear

Vestibular organ

Auditory nerve

Outer
ear

Middle
ear

Cochlea

Oval window

Round window

Eardrum

Hammer

Anvil

Middle ear detail

Stirrup

Hammer, anvil, stirrup The three small bones in the middle ear that relay vibrations of the eardrum to the inner ear.

Oval window Membrane across the opening between the middle ear and inner ear that conducts vibrations to the cochlea.

Round window Membrane between the middle ear and inner ear that equalizes pressure in the inner ear.

Cochlea Part of the inner ear containing fluid that vibrates, which in turn causes the basilar membrane to vibrate.

Basilar membrane Vibrating membrane in the cochlea of the inner ear that contains sense receptors for sound.

Organ of Corti Structure in the cochlea that contains the receptor cells for hearing.

Auditory nerve The bundle of neurons that carries signals from the ear to the brain.

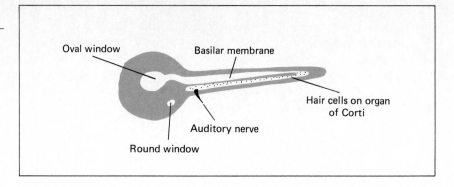

Figure 3-20

If the cochlea were uncoiled, it would look something like this.

three tiny bones in the middle ear—called the **hammer,** the **anvil,** and the **stirrup**—to hit each other in sequence and to carry the vibrations to the inner ear. The last of these three bones, the stirrup, is attached to a membrane called the **oval window.** Just below the oval window is another membrane, called the **round window,** which equalizes the pressure in the inner ear when the stirrup hits against the oval window.

The air waves are magnified during their trip through the middle ear. Thus, when the oval window starts to vibrate at the touch of the stirrup, it has a powerful effect on the inner ear. There, the vibrations are transmitted to the fluid inside a snail-shaped structure called the **cochlea.** The cochlea is divided lengthwise by the **basilar membrane** (see Figure 3-20). The basilar membrane is stiffer near the oval and round windows, and gets gradually more flexible as it coils inward toward its other end. When the fluid in the cochlea begins to move, the basilar membrane is pushed up and down, bringing the vibrations deeper into the inner ear.

Lying on top of the basilar membrane, and moving with it, is the **organ of Corti.** It is here that the messages from the sound waves finally reach the receptor cells for the sense of hearing. Embedded in the organ of Corti are thousands of tiny hair cells—the receptors. As you can see in Figure 3-21, each hair cell is topped by a bundle of fibers. These fibers are pushed and pulled by the vibrations of the fluid inside the cochlea. If the fibers bend so much as 100 trillionths of a meter, the receptor cell sends a signal to be transmitted through the **auditory nerve** to the brain. The brain pools the information from thousands of these cells to create sounds (Hudspeth, 1983). Recently it has been discovered that each hair cell not only sends messages to the brain but also receives messages from the brain. The brain apparently can send signals to the hair cells that reduce their sensitivity to sound in general or to sound waves of particular frequencies. It appears that the brain can in effect "shut down" the ears somewhat, but for what purpose remains one of the mysteries of research on hearing (Hudspeth, 1983).

NEURAL CONNECTIONS. The sense of hearing is truly bilateral. Each ear sends messages to both cerebral hemispheres. The switching station where the nerve fibers from the ears cross over is in the medulla, part of the hindbrain. From the medulla other nerve fibers carry the

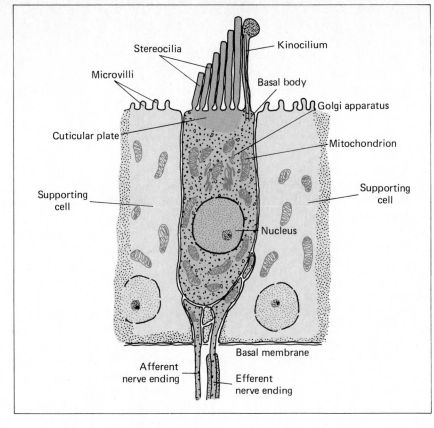

Stereocilia

Kinocilium

Microvilli

Basal body

Golgi apparatus

Cuticular plate

Mitochondrion

Supporting
cell

Supporting
cell

Nucleus

Basal membrane

Afferent
nerve ending

Efferent
nerve ending

Place theory of hearing Theory that the location of greatest vibration of the basilar membrane changes in response to sound waves of different frequencies.

Figure 3-21

A detailed drawing of a hair cell, the receptor for hearing. At the top of each hair cell are a bundle of fibers. If the fibers bend so much as 100 trillionths of a meter, this causes the receptor cells to transmit a sensory message to the brain.
(From Hudspeth, 1983)

messages from the ears to the higher parts of the brain. Some messages go to the brain centers that coordinate the movements of the eyes, head, and ears. Others travel through the reticular formation (which we looked at in Chapter 2), which probably tacks on a few special "wake-up" or "ho-hum" postscripts to the sound messages. The primary destinations, of course, are the auditory projection areas in the temporal lobes of the two cerebral hemispheres. Along the way, the auditory messages pass through at least four levels of neurons—a much less direct route than in the visual system. At each stage auditory information becomes more precisely coded.

Theories of Hearing

The thousands of tiny hair cells in the organ of Corti send messages about the infinite variations in the frequency, amplitude, and overtones of sound waves. But so far we have said nothing about how the different sound-wave patterns are coded into neural messages. One aspect of sound, loudness, seems to depend on how many neurons are activated—the more cells that fire, the louder the sound seems to be. The coding of messages about pitch is more complicated. There are two basic views of pitch discrimination: place theory and frequency theory. **Place theory** states that the brain determines pitch by noting the place on the basilar membrane where the message is strongest. Helmholtz, who helped de-

Frequency theory of hearing
Theory that pitch is determined by the frequency with which hair cells in the cochlea fire.

Volley principle Theory that receptors in the ear fire in sequence, with one group responding, then a second, then a third, and so on, so that the complete pattern of firing corresponds to the frequency of the sound wave.

Vestibular senses Senses of equilibrium and body movement and position.

Semicircular canals Structures in the inner ear particularly sensitive to body rotation.

Vestibular sacs Sacs in the inner ear that are responsible for sensing gravitation, and forward, backward, and vertical movement.

Utricle Organ in the inner ear that provides information about horizontal movement of the body.

velop the trichromatic theory of color vision, proposed that for any given sound wave, there is a point on the basilar membrane where vibrations are most intense. As the frequency of the wave changes, the point of maximum vibration also changes. According to Helmholtz, high-frequency sounds cause the greatest vibration at the stiff base of the basilar membrane. Low-frequency sounds do the same at the more flexible opposite end of the membrane (Zwislocki, 1981). The brain detects the location of most intense nerve cell activity and uses this to determine the pitch of a sound. Georg von Bekesy won the Nobel Prize in 1961 for a series of ingenious experiments that confirmed in general the place theory of pitch discrimination.

The **frequency theory** of pitch discrimination states that the frequency of vibrations of the basilar membrane as a whole, not just parts of it, is translated into an equivalent frequency of nerve impulses. Thus, if a hair bundle is pulled or pushed rapidly, its hair cell sends a high-frequency message to the brain. Neurons cannot fire as rapidly as the frequency of the highest-pitched sound that can be heard, however, and this problem has led theorists to suggest a **volley principle.** The nerve cells, they maintain, fire in sequence: One neuron fires, then a second one, then a third. By then, the first neuron has had time to recover and can fire again. If necessary, the three neurons together can send a rapid series of impulses to the brain.

Neither the place theory nor the frequency theory alone fully explains pitch discrimination, so some combination of the two is needed. The volley principle, for example, explains quite well the ear's responses to frequencies up to about 4,000 Hz. Above that, however, the place theory provides a better explanation of what is happening.

The Vestibular Senses

The **vestibular senses** monitor equilibrium and the awareness of body position and movement. Birds and fish rely on them to tell them which way is up and in which direction they are headed when they cannot see well. Like hearing, the vestibular senses arise in the inner ear, and the sense organs are hair cells that send their signals out over the auditory nerve. There are actually two kinds of vestibular sensation. The first is the sensation of body rotation, and it arises in the three **semicircular canals** of the inner ear (see Figure 3-22). Like the cochlea, each canal is filled with fluid that shifts when the head is moved in any direction. The movement of the fluid bends hair bundles, which in turn stimulate hair cells, sending a message to the brain about the speed and direction of body rotation.

The second vestibular sense is that of gravitation and movement forward and backward, up and down. This sense arises from the two **vestibular sacs** that lie between the semicircular canals and the cochlea. Both sacs are filled with a jellylike fluid that contains millions of tiny crystals. The **utricle** is positioned so that when the body moves horizontally, the crystals bend hair bundles and thus start a sensory message. The

saccule does the same thing for vertical movement. But even when your head is motionless, the crystals bend some hair bundles because they are pulled down by gravity. This gives you a sense of the position of your head at all times.

The nerve impulses from several vestibular organs travel to the brain on the auditory nerve, but their ultimate destinations in the brain are not fully known. Some messages from the vestibular system go to the cerebellum, which controls many of the reflexes involved in coordinated movement. Others go to the areas that send messages to the internal body organs, and some go to the cerebral cortex for analysis and response.

Saccule Organ in the inner ear that provides information about vertical movement of the body and gravitation.

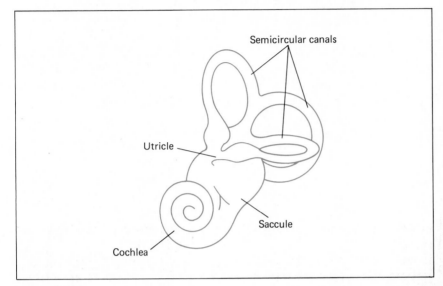

Figure 3-22
The vestibular organs.

While the vestibular senses usually monitor our sense of equilibrium and bodily position, when confused by things like rocking boats and twisting amusement-park rides, they can produce motion sickness.

Olfactory epithelium Nasal membranes containing receptor cells sensitive to odors.

Olfactory bulb Either of the two smell centers in the brain.

Sensations of Motion

Motion sickness arises in the vestibular organs. Certain kinds of motion (riding in ships, cars, airplanes, even on camels and elephants) trigger strong reactions in some people. The effect is made worse if the person's head moves relative to his or her body. One theory is that motion sickness results from discrepancies between visual information and vestibular sensations: Trying to read a book while your body is being bumped up and down in a bus is one example of conflict between visual and vestibular information.

Occasionally the vestibular sense can be completely overwhelmed by information from the visual sense. This is what happens when we watch an automobile chase scene that was filmed from inside a moving car. We feel a sensation of movement because our eyes are telling our brain that we are moving, even though the organs in our inner ear insist that we are sitting still. In fact, the sense of motion can be so strong that some people get motion sickness while sitting absolutely still watching a movie filmed from an airplane or a boat! This visual trick has an advantage. People who have had one or even both vestibular organs removed can function normally as long as they have visual cues on which to rely.

Smell

Unlike many lower animals, which must use their noses to detect mates, predators, and prey, humans do not depend on their sense of smell for survival. Nevertheless, the sense of smell in humans is incredibly sensitive. Only a few molecules of a substance reaching the smell receptors are necessary to cause humans to perceive an odor (DeVries & Stuiver, 1961). Certain substances that give off a large number of molecules that dissolve easily in the moist, fatty tissues of the nose can be detected in especially small amounts. Decayed cabbage, lemons, and rotten eggs are examples. According to one estimate, the sense of smell is about 10,000 times as sensitive as that of taste (Moncrieff, 1951), though sensitivity to odors appears to decrease with age (Engen, 1973).

Our sense of smell is activated by substances that are carried by airborne molecules that enter the nose. The receptors for this sense are located high in each nasal cavity, in a patch of tissue called the **olfactory epithelium** (see Figure 3-23). The olfactory epithelium is only about one-half the size of a postage stamp, but it is packed with millions of receptor cells. As we breathe, airborne molecules are carried into the nasal cavities, and they activate the receptors in the olfactory epithelium, which are specialized neurons. Apparently these nerve cells die and are replaced by new ones every few weeks (Graziadei, Levine, & Graziadei, 1979).

The axons from nerve cells in the nose carry the messages directly to the two **olfactory bulbs** in the brain. Since these fibers do not pass through the thalamus, as other sensory fibers do, the sense of smell's route to the cerebral cortex is the most direct. The olfactory bulbs can cam-

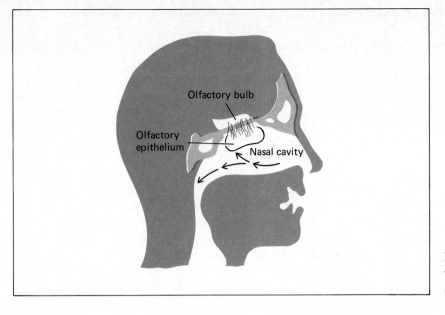

Figure 3-23

The location of the olfactory
epithelium.

municate "across the hall" to each other and "upstairs" to the olfactory
projection areas in the cerebral cortex.

Humans can discriminate thousands of different odors. For centuries
scientists have tried to classify these odors into basic smells and to link
these smells to distinct receptors in the nose. The most promising
classification system suggested so far is based on the structure of odor-
producing molecules. According to the *stereochemical theory of odors* put
forth by J. E. Amoore, J. W. Johnston, and M. Rubin (1964), there are
seven primary categories of odors. In five of these categories the molecules have a distinctive shape or size and fit into a corresponding "hole"
in the olfactory epithelium, much as a key fits into a lock. The other two
basic odors seem to depend on their electrical charge rather than on their
molecular shape or size. Unfortunately this theory does not explain why
changes in some molecules that do not affect their size and shape nevertheless radically affect smell (Schiffman, 1976).

Humans are less adept at identifying the source of odors than they are
at detecting their presence. When given common household substances
to smell, blindfolded people often cannot identify a substantial proportion of them, even though the odors seem familiar. But if they are told
what the odor is, they quickly learn to identify it on later trials (Cain,
1981). Nonetheless, certain kinds of odors seem to be consistently
identifiable without training. Body odor is an example. In a recent study
23 out of 24 mothers could identify by smell alone which T-shirts had
been worn by their own children (Porter & Moore, 1982). Interestingly,
although men and women have equal biological capacity to sense odors,
women are much better at identifying odors.

Earlier in the chapter we mentioned the capacity of the eyes to adjust
to shifts in the intensity of light. Sensory adaptation occurs in the sense
of smell as well, only here it is much more rapid. People who live in a
paper-mill town rarely notice the putrid smell that tends to repel visitors.
The rate of adaptation, however, appears to differ in degree for various
odors.

Taste

To understand taste, we must first distinguish it from *flavor*. The flavor of food is a complex combination of taste and smell. If you hold your nose when you eat, most of the food's flavor will be eliminated, although you will still be able to experience sensations of *bitterness*, *saltiness*, *sourness*, or *sweetness*. In other words, you will get the taste, but not the flavor.

The receptor cells for the sense of taste lie inside the **taste buds,** most of which are found on the tip, sides, and back of the tongue. An adult has about 10,000 taste buds. The number of taste buds decreases with age, which may partly explain why older people lose interest in food—they simply cannot taste it as well as they used to.

The taste buds are contained in the tongue's **papillae,** small bumps you can see if you look at your tongue in the mirror. Each taste bud contains a cluster of taste receptors, or hair cells (see Figure 3-24). About every 7 days these hair cells die and are replaced. The chemical substances in the foods we eat are dissolved in saliva and are carried down into the crevices between the papillae of the tongue, where they come into contact with the hairs of the taste receptors. The chemical interaction between food substances and the taste cells causes adjacent neurons to fire, sending a nerve impulse to the brain. This happens very fast: People can accurately identify a taste within 1/10 of a second after something salty or sweet has touched the tongue (Cain, 1981). The same nerves that carry messages about taste also conduct information about chewing, swallowing, and the temperature and texture of food.

We experience only four primary taste qualities: sweet, sour, salt, and bitter. All other tastes result from combinations of these four. The tip of the tongue is most sensitive to sweetness, the back to bitterness, and the sides to saltiness and sourness. The tip and sides together are most sensitive to saltiness (see Figure 3-25). But each area can distinguish all of the four qualities to some degree (Collings, 1974; McBurney & Collings, 1977). The middle of the tongue does not respond to taste at all.

Sourness is one of the four primary taste qualities.

Figure 3-24

A diagram of a single taste bud.

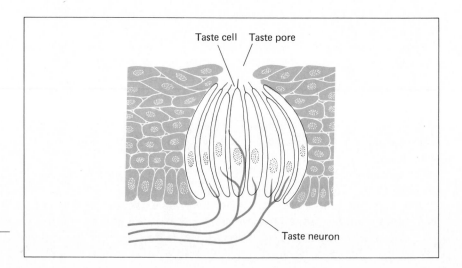

Taste cell   Taste pore

Taste neuron

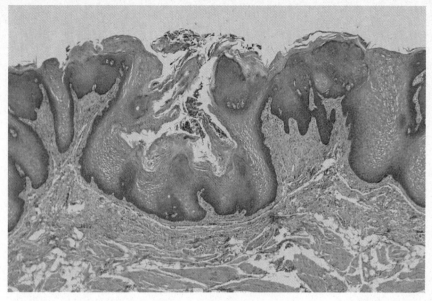

Photomicrograph of the human tongue.

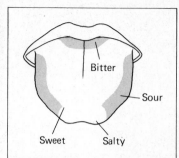

Figure 3-25
A schematic drawing of the tongue, showing the locations most sensitive to the four primary taste qualities.

The sense of taste, like smell, adapts quickly. Taste adaptation is quite complicated. For instance, adaptation to one kind of salt lowers the threshold of sensitivity to other salts, and adaptation to one kind of acid usually affects the sensitivity to other acids. This kind of cross adaptation in the sense of taste will not be fully understood until we have more information about the activities of the taste cells and about how their messages are coded and interpreted by the nervous system.

Once experimenters realized that there were four primary tastes, they tried to isolate four kinds of taste receptors to match each taste. They have not succeeded. Taste seems to be coded by the overall pattern of neural firing rather than by separate receptors for each taste. Further processing for taste may occur as the nerve impulse travels to the brain, but exactly where or how this occurs is unknown.

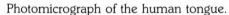

Pressure and Temperature

What we normally think of as the sense of touch is really several sensations: *pressure, warmth, cold,* and *pain.* All other tactile sensations result from some combination of these four. Usually messages from all these senses are combined, but it is possible to separate them and to map the areas of the skin that respond most strongly to each sense. In general, the most numerous areas are the skin areas that respond to pain, followed by those that record pressure. The least numerous are the areas that are sensitive to cold and to warmth.

Some parts of the body are more sensitive than others to all of these sensations. For example, the hands, the feet, and the face (especially the

Free nerve endings Finely branched nerve endings in the skin that serve as receptors for pain, pressure, and temperature.

Basket nerve endings Nerve endings wrapped around the base of hairs that are sensitive to pressure.

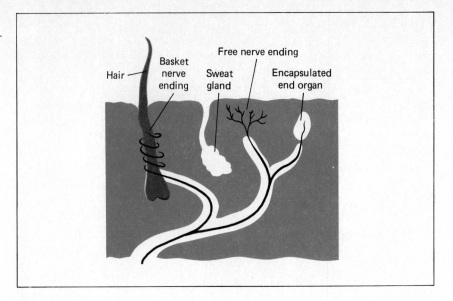

Figure 3-26

The three types of sensory receptors in the skin.

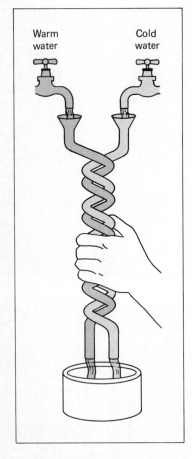

lips and tongue) are much more sensitive than the back, the upper arms, or the calves of the legs. The most sensitive areas are represented in the cerebral cortex by the most fiber endings; they also seem to contain more receptors.

Many kinds of receptors have been located in the skin. At one time, physiologists confidently pointed to one receptor or another as the specific receptor for each of the four skin sensations. Studies have not revealed, however, a consistent set of relations between the various types of receptors and the separate sensations. Skin sensations may not be caused by separate receptors for each kind of stimulus, but by the rate at which these receptors fire. In other words, it may be the way these messages are *coded* that determines the sensation we feel (McBurney & Collings, 1977).

The receptors in the skin fall into three general categories: free nerve endings, basket nerve endings, and encapsulated end organs (see Figure 3-26). **Free nerve endings,** which cover most of the skin area, are found just below the surface of the skin. Free nerve endings are usually thought to be involved with the sensation of pain, but they are also probably sensitive to warmth and cold, and may even send messages about pressure.

Basket nerve endings are nerve fibers that are wrapped around the base of hairs. They are distributed over about 90 percent of the body's surface. They respond to touch or light pressure; when the hair they are

Figure 3-27

Touching a warm pipe and a cold pipe at the same time causes two sets of skin receptors to signal at once to the brain. The brain reads their combined pattern of firings as "hot," a phenomenon known as paradoxical heat.

entwined around is moved, they fire off a message about the intensity and direction of the touch. But recall that some of the most sensitive areas of the body—such as the lips and the fingertips—have no hair at all, and thus no basket nerve endings.

The third general class of receptors in the skin, **encapsulated end organs,** vary in location, size, and structure. They all share one feature: a nerve fiber ending inside of some sort of capsule or shell. Most of these receptors are found quite near the surface of the skin and are responsive to pressure; some are also sensitive to temperature.

The nerve fibers from all of these receptors travel to the brain through the spinal cord. Before they reach the top of the spinal cord and enter the brain, all the nerve fibers have crossed over: Messages from the left side of the body reach the projection areas in the right cerebral hemisphere; messages from the right side of the body go to the left hemisphere.

The sense of temperature appears to depend on at least two kinds of receptors: those that respond to temperatures at least 1 to 2 degrees centigrade (3 to 6 degrees Fahrenheit) warmer than body temperature, and those that respond only to temperatures of at least 1 to 2 degrees centigrade colder than body temperature. When one set of receptors sends in messages, the brain reads them as "warm." When the other set signals, the brain reads "cold." If both sets are activated at once, the brain reads their combined pattern of firings as "hot." Thus you might sometimes think you are touching something hot when you are really touching something warm and something cool at the same time. This phenomenon is known as **paradoxical heat** (see Figure 3-27). It is easier to study cold receptors because they are easier to find. They fire constantly at about 5 to 15 impulses per second. This rate increases to over 100 impulses per second when there is a sudden drop in temperature.

Encapsulated end organ Pressure and temperature receptor in the skin, consisting of a nerve ending enclosed in a shell or capsule.

Paradoxical heat Simultaneous stimulation of "warm" and "cold" receptors that is experienced as "hot."

Pain

Pain differs from the other senses in the extent to which people react to it. Most of us react to the pain caused by a burn by pulling our hands away. But one person may calmly run some cold water over the burn, while another may scream with pain. In other words, people *perceive* and respond to pain differently. This is the psychological component of pain. People also have differing physiological reactions to pain. For example, there is the case of a Canadian girl who felt nothing when she inadvertently bit off part of her tongue and who got third-degree burns on her knee from kneeling on a hot radiator (Baxter & Olszewski, 1960; McMurray, 1950).

How do we explain the differences in how people respond to painful stimuli? There are three main approaches. The first stresses the actions of a specific set of nerve fibers that are responsible for conducting pain impulses. The primary pain receptors, as we mentioned above, are the networks of free nerve endings that overlap and penetrate many layers of skin. According to this approach, a painful stimulus activates several networks at once and sends several simultaneous messages to the brain.

Gate-control theory of pain Holds that the pain-signaling system contains a gatelike mechanism that controls the degree to which the receptors transmit pain messages to the brain.

Psychologists have not found pain receptors for each type of pain, but they have recently discovered two kinds of nerve fibers that appear to carry different pain messages. One kind of fiber carries "fast, sharp, well-localized" pain messages, while another kind carries "slow, aching or burning, long-duration, and poorly localized pain" (Leibeskind & Paul, 1977).

A second approach is the pattern theory of pain. According to this theory, pain does not have its own set of special receptors. Instead, pain perception is based on the intensity of the stimulus and how the nervous system codes it (Weisenberg, 1977).

A third theory, known as the **gate-control theory,** contains elements of the other two approaches to the study of pain. It also tries to explain

Acupuncture: Shutting the Gate on Pain

Acupuncture, as most of us know, is an analgesic (or painkilling) technique. Special needles are inserted at specific sites in the body. These needles may be rotated rapidly or used to conduct mild electric currents. Although the needles are inserted in areas that are far from the area of pain, they have been shown to be effective in relieving that pain. In one documented thyroid operation, pain was relieved by inserting one needle into a site on each forearm of the patient. In another case, during an operation to remove a patient's stomach, four needles were inserted into the patient's ear lobes (Dimond, 1971). Unlike patients who are anesthetized during surgery, these patients are conscious and alert throughout their operations. Postsurgical pain seems to be decreased, as the pain-relieving effects last for several hours after the needles have been removed. There is also some evidence that healing after surgery is accelerated. According to Chinese tradition, acupuncture brings the yin (spirits) and the yang (blood) forces back into harmony. But why does it work?

It now seems likely that the stimulation of the nervous system that is involved in acupuncture produces a greater amount of the body's natural painkillers (enkephalins and endorphins). How do we know this? Scientists reached this conclusion when they electrically stimulated areas of the brain and found that this increased the body's production of enkephalins and endorphins and blocked the sensation of pain. By contrast, drugs that inhibited the production of the body's internal painkillers also blocked the effects of acupuncture. Thus it appears that the mysterious painkilling effects of acupuncture may be understandable in terms of the release of the body's own painkilling substances (Olson et al., 1979).

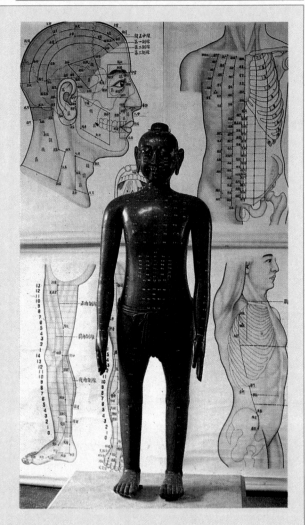

the psychological differences in how people experience pain. According to this theory, there is a neural "gate" mechanism in the spinal cord that controls the transmission of nerve impulses to the brain (Melzack & Wall, 1965). The theory states that large fibers exist in the sensory nerves that can be stimulated to "close the gate" on pain by preventing the impulses from reaching the brain. There are also small fibers that react with interneurons in the spinal cord to let the pain through, or to "open the gate." Certain areas of the brain stem can also send out signals to fibers connected to the spinal cord, which can effectively block pain. Gate-control theory offers the hope that manual or electronic stimulation of the large fibers can be used to help diminish pain.

The gate-control theory also explains how pain messages can be modified considerably on their trip to the brain. Messages from the other senses can inhibit or enhance the nerve impulses from the pain receptors. Interference in the higher brain centers can also reduce, or even block, sensations of pain. For example, people under hypnosis can be made to feel no pain (Hilgard, 1969). The same principles may be important in the dramatic success of acupuncture in China (see box on p. 98).

The specifics of gate-control theory have been challenged by other findings, but research has also supported the idea that pain messages can be blocked by intense stimulation and that the brain can send pain-blocking signals to fibers in the spinal cord. Some of the most intriguing support comes from recent experiments on powerful painkilling drugs such as morphine and other members of the opiate family. There is evidence that these drugs do not dull the brain, as you might expect; rather, they stimulate parts of the brain that in turn inhibit transmission of pain impulses in the spinal cord (Levinthal, 1979).

The body's natural painkillers, the endorphins, which were discussed in Chapter 2, also work by stimulating portions of the brain, which then "turn down" pain messages coming from sensory receptors. Thus the gate-control theory seems to have considerable support, even though it may be wrong in its details.

Application

Two Hearing Disorders: Too Little Sound and Too Much

Because the ear is so complicated, the number of possible problems that can affect our hearing is large. Deafness is one of the most common problems. Some instances of deafness result from defects in the outer or middle ear—for instance, the eardrum may be damaged or the small bones of the middle ear may not work properly. Other cases of deafness occur because the basilar membrane in the cochlea or the auditory nerve itself has been

damaged. Disease, infections, and even long-term exposure to loud noise can harm the ear and cause partial or complete deafness.

Hearing aids can relieve many hearing problems, but not all. If the hairlike receptor cells in the cochlea have been damaged severely, hearing aids cannot help. During the last decade, however, a new surgical technique, the cochlear implant, has offered some hope to people who suffer from deafness due to cochlear damage. The implant operation consists of inserting a platinum electrode into the cochlea of one ear. The electrode bypasses the damaged hair cells and conveys electrical signals directly to the auditory nerve. A microphone that can be attached to the ear converts sound waves into electrical pulses, which are sent to a small sound processor worn on clothing near the chest. The processor sorts out the frequencies of sounds most relevant to human needs—the sounds of speech, for instance—and sends the corresponding electrical signals through a series of devices to the implanted electrode. The electrical signals reaching the auditory nerve vary with the frequency and amplitude of the sound waves that reach the microphone.

Unfortunately the implant devices are not yet sophisticated enough to reproduce sounds clearly. Most of the 300 Americans who have received implants cannot understand speech. But the implant does provide sound cues that improve their lip reading and allow them to adjust their own voice to appropriate levels as they speak. Recipients can also learn to distinguish warning signals such as car horns and alarm bells. Despite their present limitations, cochlear implants may give young children a vital link to spoken language at the stage during which exposure to words is crucial to learning how to speak normally. Many profoundly deaf children never develop normal speech. Those who have received the implant, however, have learned words and proper pitch and loudness more easily than they would have without it. Improvements in the implant technology are on the horizon and should greatly enhance sound quality, making the benefits of the operation even greater (Grady, 1983).

Far from not hearing enough sound, some people hear too much of the wrong kind and suffer greatly because of it. Almost everybody at some time has heard a steady, high-pitched hum that seems to persist, even in the quietest room. The apparent sound seems to come from inside the head. In about 1 percent of the population, this tone, called a tinnitus (tin-NYE-tus), becomes unbearably loud—like the screeching of subway brakes—and it does not go away (Dunkle, 1982). In a few cases, tinnitus is caused by blood flowing through vessels near the inner ear. Generally, though, tinnitus originates somewhere in the brain.

Unfortunately, medical research has not yet found a cure for this problem. Many of those who suffer from severe tinnitus gain some relief from masking. A device mounted in the ear much like a hearing aid produces a sound that mutes the annoying hum. Oddly enough, in about a third of the cases, any weak sound has the desired effect (McFadden & Wightman, 1983). The tinnitus often remains masked for seconds or even minutes after the masking tone has been withdrawn. Researchers are at a loss to explain how masking devices work, but it is clear that they do not simply drown out the tinnitus. Another line of attack has been drugs, but those that have been tested have produced side effects worse than the problem they were designed to cure. Researchers are working on this problem, though, and safer drugs may someday bring relief to even the most unbearable cases of tinnitus.

Summary

1. The study of *sensation* is the study of how the various receptor cells in the sense organs translate forms of physical energy into neural messages; how those messages reach the central nervous system; and the different experiences that result. The related process of perception is the interpretation of sensory data by the brain.

2. In all sensory processes some form of energy stimulates a receptor cell in one of the sense organs. The receptor cell then changes the energy it receives into a neural signal. As the neural signal travels along the sensory nerves to the central nervous system, it is coded further. By the time it reaches the brain, its message is quite precise. The brain creates the "illusion" of sensory experience by interpreting the "clicks" on various nerve fibers,

such as the optic and auditory nerves.

3. The minimum intensity of physical energy that is required to produce any sensation at all in a person is called the *absolute threshold.* The absolute threshold for each of our senses is remarkably low. The smallest change in stimulation that a person can detect is called the *difference threshold* or the *just noticeable difference (jnd).* Generally, the stronger the overall stimulation, the bigger the change needed for you to be able to sense it.

4. Light enters the eye through the *cornea* and passes through the *pupil,* which expands or contracts to let more or less light through. The colored part of the eye around the pupil is the *iris.* Inside the pupil, the light passes through the *lens,* which focuses it onto the *retina.* Images are in sharpest focus on the *fovea,* a depressed spot on the retina directly behind the lens.

5. The physical stimulus for the sense of vision is only a small segment of the spectrum of electromagnetic energy. There are two kinds of receptors in the retina—*rods* and *cones.* Cones operate mainly in daylight and respond to colors. Rods are chiefly responsible for night vision when there is not enough light to stimulate the cones. The fovea contains thousands of cones but no rods.

6. Several rods generally connect with a single bipolar neuron, while most cones are connected to their own bipolar neuron. The one-to-one connection in the fovea between cones and bipolar neurons allows for maximum *visual acuity,* the ability to distinguish fine details. Thus vision is sharpest when the image falls directly on the fovea; outside the fovea acuity drops dramatically.

7. When the intensity of light shifts, the receptor cells change their own sensitivity. This is known as *adaptation.* In *dark adaptation* both the rods and cones become more sensitive to light in response to lowered levels of illumination; in *light adaptation* the rods and cones become less sensitive to light as illumination increases. In addition, small involuntary eye movements keep an image moving around slightly on the retina, so that the receptors never adapt completely.

8. Neural messages originate in the retina, but they must get to the brain for a visual sensation to occur. Within the retina rods and

cones connect to bipolar neurons, which in turn connect to the *ganglion cells.* The axons of the ganglion cells converge to form the *optic nerve,* which carries messages from the eye to the brain. The optic nerve fibers from the right side of each eye travel to the right hemisphere of the brain; those from the left side travel to the left hemisphere. The fibers cross one another at the *optic chiasm.* Some messages travel to parts of the brain that control retinal movements. Others are headed for the visual projection areas in the brain.

9. *Hue, saturation,* and *brightness* are three separate aspects of our experience of color. *Hue* refers to what most of us call *color* (e.g., red, green, blue). *Saturation* refers to the purity of the hue; and *brightness* refers to the intensity of the hue (from bright to dark).

10. There are two processes of mixing colors. In *additive color mixing,* lights of different colors are mixed to create a new hue. Two colors that are far apart on the spectrum and that create a neutral gray when mixed are called *complementary colors.* Color mixing can produce colors that are not on the spectrum (*nonspectral colors*). Three colors that when mixed in equal intensities produce gray and when mixed in various unequal intensities can match any visible color are *primary colors. Subtractive color mixing* involves the mixing of pigments that reflect only the hues that are reflected by all pigments in the mixture.

11. There are two main theories of color vision. According to the *trichromatic theory,* the eye contains three different kinds of color receptors that respond to red, green, and blue light, respectively. By mixing these three basic colors, the eye can detect any color in the spectrum. The *opponent-process theory* accepts the notion of three different kinds of receptors, but claims that each receptor responds to either member of three basic color pairs: red-green, yellow-blue, and black-white (dark and light).

12. Trichromatic theory provides a convincing explanation of *color blindness,* the partial or total inability to perceive hues. People with normal vision can match any hue by combining just three primary colors; they are

called *trichromats*. *Monochromats*, who have a rare color deficiency, see no color at all; while *dichromats* are blind either to red-green or to yellow-blue. Opponent-process theory can most easily account for *afterimages*, sense experiences that occur when a stimulus is removed.

13. Modern research has established support for the operation of both theories. We now know that there are three types of color receptors in the retina. In addition, bipolar neurons or ganglion cells process coded signals from the receptors according to an opponent-process principle. When these signals reach the brain, color receptors in the visual cortex process them further, in an opponent-process manner. Thus both Helmholtz and Hering were partly right.

14. The physical stimuli for the sense of hearing are sound waves. The frequency of the waves determines the *pitch* of a sound; their *amplitude* determines loudness; and their *overtones* determine *timbre*.

15. Sound waves produce vibration of the eardrum. Vibration of the eardrum causes three bones in the middle ear—the *hammer, anvil,* and *stirrup*—to vibrate in sequence. These vibrations are magnified in their passage through the middle ear deep into the inner ear. There the vibrations cause fluid inside the *cochlea* to vibrate, pushing the *basilar membrane* and *organ of Corti* up and down. Inside the organ of Corti are tiny hair cells that are the receptors for hearing. Stimulation of these receptors produces auditory signals that are transmitted through the *auditory nerve* to the brain.

16. The *place theory* of hearing states that the brain determines pitch by noting the place on the basilar membrane where the message is strongest. *Frequency theory* states that the frequency of vibrations of the basilar membrane as a whole is translated into an equivalent frequency of nerve impulses. Neurons, however, cannot fire as rapidly as the frequency of the highest pitched sound. This suggests a volley principle, whereby nerve cells fire in sequence to send a rapid series of impulses to the brain.

17. The *vestibular senses* tell us what position our body is in, whether it is moving, and which way is up. The receptors for this sense are located in the vestibular organs in the inner ear. Motion sickness originates in the vestibular organs and may result from discrepancies between vestibular sensations and visual information.

18. The sense of smell is activated by substances that are carried by airborne molecules into the nasal cavities. There they activate the receptors for smell, which are located in a patch of tissue called the *olfactory epithelium*. The messages are then carried directly to the two *olfactory bulbs* in the brain. The *stereochemical theory of odors* is a classification system of odors based on the structure of odor-producing molecules. Humans are more adept at detecting the presence of odors than identifying their source.

19. The receptor cells for the sense of taste lie in the *taste buds* on the tongue. Each taste bud contains a cluster of taste receptors, or hair cells, that cause their adjacent neurons to fire when they become activated by the chemical substances in food. We experience only four primary taste qualities—sweet, sour, salty, and bitter—and these combine to form all other tastes.

20. The receptors in the skin fall into three general categories. *Free nerve endings*, found just below the surface of the skin, are responsible for pain, as well as temperature and perhaps even pressure. The *basket nerve ending* wraps around the base of a hair and responds to tough or light pressure. In *encapsulated end organs* a nerve fiber ends inside some sort of capsule or shell. The nerve fibers from all these different receptors travel to the brain through the spinal cord, crossing at various points so that messages from the left side of the body reach the right cerebral hemisphere, and vice versa.

21. The sense of temperature depends on two sets of receptors: one set for warmth and one for cold. If both sets are activated at the same time, the brain reads their combined pattern of firing as hot. This is known as *paradoxical heat*.

22. Pain is subject to more individual interpretation than the other senses. There are three approaches to the theory of pain. One

states that the primary pain receptors are the free nerve endings, which act in networks to send messages to the brain. The second, the pattern theory, states that pain perception is based on the intensity of the stimulus and the way the nervous system codes it. The third approach to pain, which has elements of the other two theories, is *gate-control theory*. According to this theory, our pain-signaling system contains a gatelike mechanism that, depending on the level of activity in large fibers, may be open, partially open, or closed. If the gate is closed, no pain message will get through to the brain and there will be no sensation of pain. The exact mechanism proposed by gate-control theory appears to have been disproved, but its basic principles have been successfully applied in the area of pain research.

23. *Enkephalins* and *endorphins* reduce pain by inhibiting the firing of neural pain impulses to the brain. Acupuncture therapy seems to work by chemically stimulating the release of these substances, which then block pain impulses.

Review Questions

1. The first step in the sequence of events that produces a sensation is that a receptor cell converts some form of energy into an electrochemical impulse.   T/F
2. The absolute/difference threshold is the smallest change in stimulation that can be detected 50 percent of the time.
3. Match the following terms with their definitions:
   ___ cornea   A. colored part of the eye
   ___ pupil   B. center of the visual field
   ___ iris   C. receptor cell responsible for color
   ___ lens   vision
   ___ fovea   D. protective layer over front part of the
   ___ retina   eye
   ___ rod   E. contains the receptor cells that
   ___ cone   respond to light
                   F. focuses light onto the retina
                   G. receptor cell responsible for night
                       vision
                   H. opening in the iris through which
                       light enters
4. In the process known as dark/light adaptation, the rods and cones adjust to become more sensitive to lowered levels of illumination.
5. The place on the retina where the axons of all the ganglion cells come together to leave the eye is called the:
   a. fovea   c. optic chiasm
   b. blind spot   d. visual cortex
6. _____ , _____ , and _____ are three separate aspects of our experience of color.
7. Additive/subtractive color mixing is the process of mixing pigments.
8. According to the opponent-process/trichromatic theory, color perception derives from three different color receptors in the retina.

9. Dichromats/trichromats are people who have normal color vision.
10. As a sound wave moves from the outer ear to the inner ear, number the following in the order that it would reach them:
    ___ oval window
    ___ anvil
    ___ cochlea
    ___ auditory nerve
    ___ round window
11. Match the following theories with their definitions:
    ___ frequency theory   A. groups of cells fire in
    ___ volley principle   sequence, not each
    ___ place theory   individually
                            B. rate at which hair cells
                                in the cochlea fire deter-
                                mines pitch
                            C. different parts of basilar
                                membrane respond to
                                different frequencies
12. Equilibrium and the awareness of body movement and position are monitored by the _____ _____ .
13. Our sense of smell is activated when airborne molecules are received by receptor tissue in the nasal cavities called the:
    a. saccule   c. olfactory bulb
    b. olfactory epithelium   d. papillae
14. The receptor cells for taste lie in the _____ _____ on the tongue and respond to the four basic taste sensations _____ , _____ , _____ , and _____ .

Outline

Perception and Altered States

4

Without the ability to make sense of sensory information, even the most mundane activities would become impossible. Take driving a car: As you negotiate traffic on a city street, accurate visual information about your surroundings becomes especially important. From a complicated array of colors, shapes, and patterns, you must be able to distinguish a road sign that tells you how to get where you are going from one that tells you when to stop. You depend on visual cues to judge the distance of other cars, bicycles, and pedestrians. If you see a motorist trying to enter the flow of traffic from a driveway just ahead of you, you must be able to determine whether a collision is possible. And as you drive, if you hear a siren, you must be able to determine quickly where it is coming from and how close it is so that you can yield the right of way. In all these cases, you have to make sense out of raw sensory information and act accordingly.

In this chapter we will discuss the ways in which we create meaningful perceptual experiences out of sensory information. We will examine how patterns, distance, and movement are perceived, and how we are able to identify an object despite changing or sometimes even contradictory information. We will look at how characteristics of the observer influence perception. And finally we will explore the ways in which sensory deprivation, meditation, hypnosis, daydreams, sleep, dreams, and drugs can alter perception and other aspects of normal consciousness.

Perception Process of creating meaningful patterns from raw sensory information.

Perception

The eye records patterns of light and dark, but it does not "see" a pedestrian crossing the street. The eardrum vibrates in a particular fashion, but it does not "hear" a symphony. Seeing and hearing meaningful patterns in the jumble of sensory information is what we mean by **perception.**

Ultimately it is the brain that interprets the complex flow of the information from the senses. Using sensory information as raw material, the brain creates perceptual experiences that go beyond what is sensed.

105

Figure Object perceived to stand apart from the background.

Ground Background against which the figure appears.

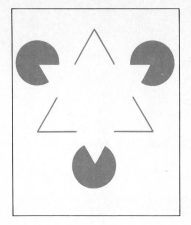

Figure 4-1

When sensory information is incomplete, we tend to create a complete perception by supplying the missing details. In this figure we fill in the lines that let us perceive a white triangle in the center of the pattern.

Figure 4-2

Knowing beforehand that the black blotches in this figure represent a person riding a horse changes our perception of it.

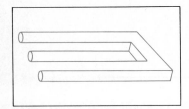

Figure 4-3

An optical illusion. In the case of the two-pronged trident, we go beyond what is sensed (black lines on flat white paper) to perceive a three-dimensional object that isn't really there.

For example, looking at Figure 4-1, we tend to perceive a white triangle in the center of the pattern, although the sensory input simply consists of three circles from which "pie slices" have been cut and three 60-degree angles. Or take Figure 4-2. At first glance, most people see only an assortment of black blotches. If you are told that the blotches represent a person riding a horse, suddenly your perceptual experience changes. What was meaningless sensory information now takes shape as a horse and rider.

Sometimes, as in some optical illusions, you perceive things that could not possibly exist. The "two-pronged trident" shown in Figure 4-3 is an example of such an "impossible" figure; on closer inspection you discover that the object you "recognize" is not really there. In all these cases, the brain actively creates and organizes your perceptual experiences out of raw sensory information.

Perceptual Organization

Early in this century a group of German psychologists called "Gestalt psychologists" set out to discover the principles through which we interpret sensory information. The word *gestalt* has no exact English equivalent, but essentially it means "whole" or "pattern." The Gestalt psychologists believed not only that the brain creates a coherent perceptual experience that is more than simply the sum of the available sensory information, but also that it does so in regular and predictable ways.

One important part of the perceptual process involves our being able to distinguish **figures** from the **ground** against which they appear. A colorfully upholstered chair stands out from the bare walls of a room. A marble statue is perceived as a whole figure standing out from the red brick wall behind it. The two-pronged trident in Figure 4-3 stands out from the white page. In all these cases, we perceive some objects as "figures" and other sensory information as just "background."

The figure-ground distinction pertains to all our senses, not just vision. We can distinguish a violin solo against the ground of a symphony orchestra, a single voice amid cocktail party chatter, and the smell of roses in a florist shop. In all these instances, we perceive a figure apart from the ground around it.

Reversible figure Stimulus in which figure and ground continually reverse.

Closure Inclination to perceive an object whole even when it is incomplete.

Continuity Tendency to group together items that continue a pattern or direction.

Proximity Tendency to group together objects that are close together, rather than perceive them as distinct units.

Figure 4-4
There are not enough cues in this pattern to allow us to easily distinguish the figure of the Dalmation dog from the ground behind it.
(Gregory, 1970)

The sphinx moth is well camouflaged against the tree bark.

Sometimes, however, there are not enough cues in a pattern to permit us to easily distinguish a figure from its ground. The horse and rider in Figure 4-2 illustrate this problem, as does Figure 4-4, which shows a spotted dog investigating shadowy surroundings. It is hard to distinguish the dog because it has few visible contours of its own, and as a result it seems to have no more form than the background. This is the principle behind camouflage—to make a figure blend into its background. Nature has succeeded quite well with the Dalmatian dog.

Sometimes a figure with clear contours can be perceived in two very different ways because it is unclear which part of the stimulus is figure and which part is ground. Examples of such **reversible figures** are shown in Figures 4-5 and 4-6. At first glance you may perceive figures against a background, but a second glance may result in just the opposite experience.

Another important principle of perceptual organization is **closure.** This refers to our inclination to overlook incompleteness in sensory information and to perceive a whole object even where none really exists. In Figure 4-7, for example, we tend to see a series of rectangles rather than a series of brackets. The same thing happens with auditory sensations. Often during overseas telephone calls we hear only bits and pieces of words and sentences, but we can usually fill in the gaps and perceive the sounds as whole words and sentences.

Gestaltists also identified the principle of **continuity.** Items that continue a pattern or direction tend to be grouped together as part of the pattern (see Figure 4-8). In Figure 4-9 we tend to perceive a continuous wavy line crossing three square humps, even though the figure could justifiably be perceived as two separate lines.

Closely allied to this is the principle of **proximity.** When objects are close to each other, we tend to perceive them together rather than

Figure 4-5 (left)

The reversible figure and ground in this Escher woodcut cause us to see first black devils and then white angels in each of the rings.

Figure 4-6 (below)

A reversible figure-ground drawing. The figure can be perceived as either a white cup against a dark background, or as two faces against a white background.

Figure 4-7

The principle of closure accounts for the fact that we overlook incompleteness and instead perceive whole objects—in this case a series of rectangles rather than a series of brackets.

Figure 4-8

Because of continuity, we are likely to see this figure as two curved lines, one from point A to point B, and the other from point C to point D.

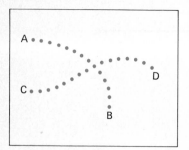

Figure 4-9

Even though we could justifiably perceive the top figure as two separate lines (below), we tend to perceive a wavy line crossing three square humps.

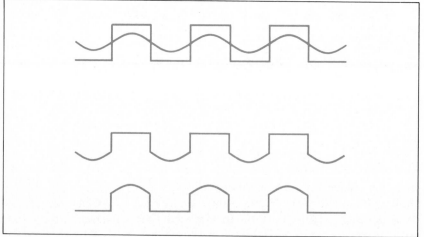

Figure 4-10 (right)

Because of the proximity of the pairs of lines, we tend to perceive three pairs and an extra line at the right, rather than seven separate lines.

Similarity Tendency to perceive objects of a similar color, size, or shape as belonging together.

Common fate Tendency to perceive objects in motion together as distinct from the objects around them.

Perceptual constancy Tendency to perceive objects as stable and unchanging despite changes in sensory stimulation.

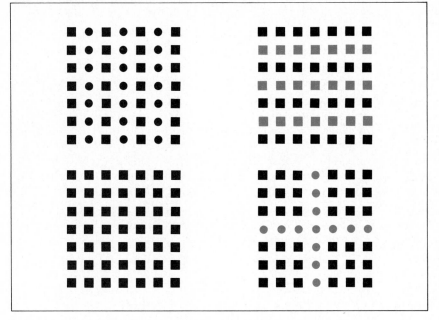

Figure 4-11

Similarity of shape or color can lead to the perception of patterns in these figures.

separately. Most people would perceive the seven lines shown in Figure 4-10 as three pairs and an extra line at the right because of the relative proximity of the pairs of lines. This principle also extends to auditory perception. "Did he tell you what the nitrate is?" means something quite different from "Did he tell you what the night rate is?" Both sentences contain the same sounds, but how the speaker groups the sounds—where he or she pauses—will usually determine how the sounds are perceived.

Similarity is another principle of grouping. Objects that are of a similar color, size, or shape are usually perceived as part of a pattern(see Figure 4-11). Gestalt theorists also recognized the principle of **common fate.** Objects that are in motion together—a precision flying team, runners in a marathon race—are perceived as distinct from the objects around them.

Gestalt psychology no longer exists as a separate school of thought, but contemporary psychology has built on many of the Gestalt principles in trying to understand how we create perceptual experiences out of sensory information.

Perceptual Constancies

Surprisingly, we often continue to have the same perceptual experience even as the sensory data change. **Perceptual constancy** refers to this tendency to perceive objects as relatively stable and unchanging despite changing sensory information. Without this ability, we would find the world completely confusing. Once we have formed a stable perception of

Size constancy Perception of an object as the same size regardless of the distance from which it is viewed.

an object, we can recognize it from almost any position, at almost any distance, under almost any illumination. A white house is perceived as a white house by day or by night and from any angle. We see it as the same house. The sensory information changes, but the object is perceived as constant.

Objects tend to be perceived as being their true size regardless of the size of the image they cast on the retinas of our eyes. As Figure 4-12 shows, the farther away an object is from the lens of the eye, the smaller the retinal image it casts. For example, a 6-foot-tall man standing 20 feet away casts a retinal image that is only 50 percent of the size of the retinal image he casts at a distance of 10 feet. Yet he is not perceived as having shrunk to 3 feet.

Size constancy depends partly on experience—information about the relative sizes of objects is stored in memory—and partly on distance cues. When there are no distance cues, size constancy has to rely solely on what we have learned from our previous experience with an object. Naturally, more errors occur when there are no distance cues, but fewer than one would expect in view of the radical changes in the size of the retinal image. We might guess that a woman some distance away is 5 feet 4 inches tall instead of 5 feet 8 inches, but hardly anyone would perceive her as being 3 feet tall, no matter how far away she is. We know from experience that adults are seldom that short.

Familiar objects also tend to be seen as having a constant shape, even though the retinal images they cast change as they are viewed from different angles. A dinner plate is perceived as a circle, even when it is tilted and the retinal image is oval. A rectangular door will only project a rectangular image on the retina when it is viewed directly from the

Figure 4-12

The relationship between distance and the size of the retinal image. Object A and object B are the same size, but A, being much closer to the eye, casts a much larger image on the retina.

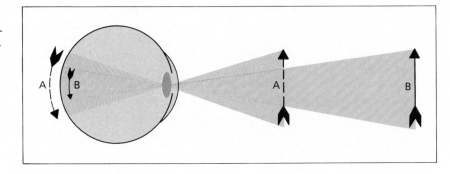

Figure 4-13

Examples of shape constancy. The opening door is actually many different shapes, but we still see it as basically a rectangular door.
(Boring, et al., 1976)

front. From any other angle, it casts a trapezoidal image on the retina, but it is not perceived as having suddenly become a trapezoidal door. These are examples of **shape constancy** (see Figure 4-13).

Two other important constancies are **brightness constancy** and **color constancy.** The former principle means that although the amount of light available to our eyes varies greatly, the perceived brightness of familiar objects hardly varies at all. We perceive a sheet of white paper as white whether we see it in candlelight or under a bright bulb. Likewise, we perceive a piece of coal as black whether we see it in a dark cellar or in noonday sunlight. This may seem obvious, but bear in mind that coal in sunlight reflects more light than white paper in candlelight, yet we always perceive white paper as being brighter. The explanation for brightness constancy is that a white object—or a black or gray one—will reflect the same percentage of the light falling on it whether that light is from a candle, a fluorescent lamp, or the sun. What is important is not the absolute amount of light the object reflects, but how the relative reflection compares to the surrounding objects.

Similarly, we tend to perceive familiar objects as keeping their color, regardless of the information that reaches the eye. If you own a red automobile, you will see it as red whether it is on a brightly lit street, or in a dark garage, where the small amount of light may send your eye a message that the color is closer to brown or black than red. But color constancy does not always operate. When objects are unfamiliar or there are no customary color cues, color constancy may be distorted—as when we buy a pair of pants in a brightly lit store, only to discover that in ordinary daylight they are not the shade we thought they were.

Throughout our discussion of these various principles, the common theme has been that our perceptual experiences often go far beyond the sensory information we are provided. In fact, our perceptual experiences rarely if ever correspond exactly to the information we receive through our senses.

Observer Characteristics

Clearly our perceptual experiences depend greatly on experience and learning. Several other factors can also affect perception, such as our particular motivations and values, expectations, cognitive style, and experiences growing up in a certain culture.

MOTIVATION. Our desires and needs may strongly influence our perceptions. People in need are more likely to perceive something that they think will satisfy that need. For example, several interesting experiments have tested the influence of hunger on perception. Sanford (1937) found that if people were deprived of food for some time and were then shown vague or ambiguous pictures, they were apt to perceive the pictures as being related to food. Similarly, McClelland and Atkinson (1948) showed blurred pictures to people who had not eaten for varying times. Some had eaten 1 hour before; others had gone as long as 16 hours without food. Those who had not eaten for 16 hours perceived the blurred images as pictures of food more often than those who had eaten just 1 hour before.

Shape constancy Tendency to see an object as the same shape no matter what angle it is viewed from.

Brightness constancy Perception of brightness as the same, even though the amount of light reaching the retina changes.

Color constancy Inclination to perceive familiar objects as retaining their color despite changes in sensory information.

Figure 4-14

Look first at the drawing on the top and ask someone else to look at the one on the bottom. When you both look at the one in the middle, you will see it very differently because your expectations are different.

(From R. W. Leeper, 1935)

Another experiment showed how strongly perceptions can be affected by a person's values. Nursery-school children were shown a poker chip. Each child was asked to compare the size of the chip to the size of an adjustable circle of light until the child perceived the chip and the circle of light as being the same size. The children were then shown a machine with a crank. When a child turned the crank, he or she received a poker chip, which could be exchanged for candy. Thus the children were taught to value the poker chips more highly than they had before. After the children had been rewarded with the candy for cranking out the poker chips, they were again asked to compare the size of the chips to a circle of light. This time the chips seemed larger to the children (Lambert, Solomon, & Watson, 1949).

EXPECTATIONS. Knowing in advance what we are supposed to perceive can also influence our perception. For example, in a well-known children's game, a piece of cardboard with a red stop sign is flashed in front of you. What did the sign say? Nearly everyone will say that the sign read "STOP." But, in fact, the sign is misprinted "STOPP" or STTOP." Because we are used to stop signs reading "STOP," we tend to perceive the familiar symbol rather than the misprint. Siipola (1935) demonstrated how prior expectations can affect people's responses to certain words. He told one group of people that they would be shown words related to animals. For a brief moment he then showed them combinations of letters that really did not spell anything—like "sael," "dack," and "wharl." Most of the group perceived the letters as the words "seal," "duck," and "whale." He then told a second group that he was going to show them words about boats, and showed them the same letter combinations. This group, expecting to see nautical terms, tended to perceive the same letter combinations as the words "sail," "deck,'" and "wharf." Try the experiment suggested in Figure 4-14 for another example of the effect of prior expectations.

COGNITIVE STYLE. As we mature, we develop a *cognitive style* —our own general method of dealing with the environment—and this also affects how we see the world. Some psychologists distinguish between two general approaches people use in perceiving the world (Witkin et al., 1962). The first is the "field-dependent" approach. A person taking this approach perceives the environment as a whole and does not clearly differentiate the shape, color, size, or other qualities of individual items. If field-dependent people are asked to draw a human figure, they usually do not draw it so that it stands out clearly against the background. People who are "field independent," on the other hand, tend to perceive the elements of the environment as separate and distinct from one another and to draw each element as standing out from the background.

Another way of defining cognitive styles is to distinguish between "levelers" and "sharpeners"—those who level out the distinctions between objects and those who magnify them. To investigate the differences between these two styles, Klein (1951) showed people sets of squares of varying sizes and asked them to estimate the size of each of the squares. One group, the "levelers," failed to perceive any difference in their size. The "sharpeners," however, were aware of the differences in the size of the squares and made their size estimates accordingly.

CULTURAL BACKGROUND. Cultural background can also influence people's perceptions. As we will see in Chapter 8, the language people speak can affect how they perceive their surroundings. Other cultural differences can influence how people use perceptual cues. The Mbuti pygmies of Zaire, for example, seldom leave the forest and rarely encounter objects that are more than a few feet away. On one occasion, Colin Turnbull (1961), an anthropologist, took a pygmy guide named Kenge on a trip out onto the plains. When Kenge looked across the plain and saw a herd of buffalo, he asked what kind of insects they were. He refused to believe that the tiny black spots he saw were buffalo. As he and Turnbull drove toward the herd, Kenge believed that magic was making the animals grow larger. Because he had no experience of distant objects, he could not perceive the buffalo as having constant size.

Let us now look at two basic perceptual phenomena—distance and depth, and movement—to see how we use both stimulus information and past experience to create perceptual experiences.

Monocular cues Visual cues that require one eye.

Binocular cues Visual cues requiring the use of both eyes.

Perception of Distance and Depth

We constantly have to judge the distance between us and other objects. When we walk through a classroom, our perception of distance helps us to avoid bumping into desks or tripping over a wastebasket. If we reach out to pick up a pencil, we automatically judge how far to extend our arms. We also constantly judge the depth of objects—how much total space they occupy. In doing so, we seem to ask ourselves, often without being aware of the question, "How big is this object? How thick or thin is it?"

We use many of the same cues to determine the distance and the size of objects. Some of these cues depend on visual messages that one eye alone can transmit; these are called **monocular cues.** Others require the use of both eyes; and these are called **binocular cues.**

MONOCULAR CUES. Having two eyes allows us to make more accurate judgments about distance and depth, particularly when objects are relatively near. But the monocular cues for distance and depth often let us judge distance and depth successfully by using only one eye.

SWIFTSURE EXPRESS LINE.

This artist's mural creates a visual illusion and relies on monocular cues of depth perception.

Superposition Monocular distance cue in which one object, by partly blocking a second object, is perceived as being closer.

Linear perspective Monocular cue to distance and depth based on the fact that two parallel lines seem to converge at the horizon.

Aerial perspective Monocular cue to distance and depth based on the fact that more distant objects are likely to appear hazy and blurred.

Elevation Monocular cue to distance and depth based on the fact that the higher on the horizontal plane an object is, the farther away it appears.

Superposition, when one object partly blocks a second object, is an important relative distance cue. The first object is perceived as being closer, the second as more distant (see Figure 4-15).

As all students of art know, there are several ways perspective can help in estimating distance and depth. Two parallel lines that extend into the distance seem to come together at some point on the horizon. This cue to distance and depth is known as **linear perspective.** In **aerial perspective** distant objects have a hazy appearance and a somewhat blurred outline. On a clear day, mountains often seem to be much closer than on a hazy day, when their outlines become blurred. The **elevation** of an object is another perspective cue to depth. An object that is on a higher horizontal plane seems to be farther away than one on a lower plane (see Figure 4-16).

Figure 4-15

Because the king of clubs has been superimposed on the blank card, we perceive it as being closer to us than the king of spades. When the cards are spaced out, however, we can see that the king of spades is actually no farther away than the king of clubs. The notching of the cards helps create the illusion.

Figure 4-16

Because of the higher elevation and the suggestion of depth provided by the road, the tree on the right is perceived as being more distant and therefore larger.

Still another helpful monocular cue to distance and depth is **texture gradient.** An object that is close seems to have a rough or detailed texture. As distance increases, the texture becomes finer, until finally the original texture cannot be distinguished clearly, if at all. A man standing on a pebbly beach, for example, can distinguish the gray stones and gravel beside his feet. As he looks off down the beach, however, the stones will seem to become smaller and finer until eventually he will be unable to note individual stones.

Shadowing can provide another important cue to distance and to the depth and solidity of an object. Normally, shadows appear on the parts of objects that are farther away. The shadowing on the outer edges of a spherical object, such as a ball or globe, gives it a three-dimensional quality (see Figure 4-17). Without this shadowing, the object might be perceived as a flat disk. The shadow an object casts behind itself can also give a cue to its depth. And the presence of shadows either before or behind objects can help to indicate how far away they are.

People traveling on buses or trains often notice that the trees or telephone poles that are close to the road or the railroad tracks seem to flash past the windows, while buildings and other objects that are farther away seem to move slowly. The objects close to you are perceived as moving very quickly; those that are farther away seem to move more slowly. These differences in the speeds of *movement* of images across the retina as you move give an important cue to distance and depth. You can observe the same effect if you stand still and move your head from side to side. Also, if as you move your head from side to side, you focus your gaze on something in the middle distance, objects close to you seem to move in the direction opposite to the direction in which your head is moving, while objects far away seem to move in the same direction as your head. This distance cue is known as **motion parallax.**

In the process known as **accommodation** the lens of the eye changes

Texture gradient Monocular cue to distance and depth based on the fact that objects seen at greater distances appear to be smoother and less textured.

Shadowing Monocular cue to distance and depth based on the fact that shadows often appear on the parts of objects that are more distant.

Motion parallax Monocular distance cue in which objects closer than the point of visual focus seem to move in the direction opposite to the viewer's moving head, and objects beyond the focus point seem to move in the same direction as the viewer's head.

Accommodation Monocular distance cue based on the adjustment of the lens in the eye to focus on objects at different distances.

(Right)   Texture is a monocular cue that helps us to determine the distance and depth of objects.

Figure 4-17

Shadowing on the outer edges of a spherical object, such as a ball or globe, gives it a three-dimensional quality. Without shadowing, it might be perceived as a flat disk.

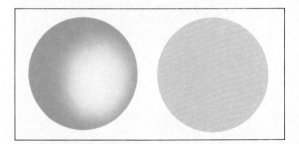

Stereoscopic vision Combination of two retinal images to give a three-dimensional perceptual experience.

Retinal disparity Binocular distance cue based on the difference between the images cast on the two retinas when both eyes are focused on the same object.

Convergence Binocular distance cue based on sensations from the muscles that turn the eyes toward or away from each other.

Because the lion's visual fields overlap, as do ours, he has more accurate perception of depth and distance. A horse, whose visual fields do not overlap, must rely entirely on monocular cues.

to focus different objects on the retina. If the object is close, the lens is made rounder; if the object is farther away, the lens is flattened. Sensations from the muscles that cause these changes provide another cue to how near or far an object is.

BINOCULAR CUES. All the cues discussed so far depend on the action of only one eye. Many animals, such as horses, deer, and fish, rely entirely on monocular cues. Although they have two eyes, because their eyes are set on the sides of their head, the two visual fields do not overlap. Humans, apes, and many predatory animals—such as lions, tigers, and wolves—have a distinct physical advantage over these animals. Because both eyes are set in the front of the head, the visual fields overlap. The **stereoscopic vision** obtained from combining the two retinal images makes the perception of depth and distance more accurate.

Because our eyes are set approximately 2½ inches apart, each one has a slightly different view of things. The difference between the two images the eyes receive is known as **retinal disparity.** The left eye receives more information about the left side of an object, and the right eye receives more information about the right side. You can easily prove that each of your eyes receives a different image: Close one eye and line up a finger with some vertical line, like the edge of a door. Then open that eye and close the other one. Your finger will appear to have moved a great distance. When you look at the finger with both eyes, however, the two different images become one.

Another binocular cue to distance comes from the muscles that control the **convergence** of the eyes. When we look at objects that are

fairly close to us, our eyes tend to converge—to turn slightly inward toward each other. The sensations from the muscles that control this movement of the eyes provide another cue to distance. If the object is very close, such as at the end of the nose, the eyes cannot converge and two separate images are perceived. If the object is more than 60 or 70 feet away, the sight lines of the eyes are more or less parallel and there is no convergence.

BINOCULAR DEPTH INVERSION. Under certain special conditions, the brain appears to ignore depth and distance cues and construct incorrect three-dimensional perceptions that more closely match our past experience. This tendency—called **binocular depth inversion**—is especially likely if the available sensory information comes from an improbable object that strongly resembles a familiar object. The best example of such an object is an inside-out human face, say the inside of a Halloween mask. If you stare at the inside of a mask that is lit from behind, you are likely to perceive a normal, right-side-out face, despite all the visual cues to the contrary. This is a particularly powerful demonstration of our tendency to create perceptual experiences that agree with past experience, despite sensory information to the contrary. A lifetime of perceiving normal faces prompts us to reinterpret the sensory data from the inverted mask in order to create a more plausible object (Yellott, 1981).

LOCATION OF SOUNDS. So far we have looked only at the perception of visual depth and distance. But sounds also occur in three-dimensional space, and to a large extent we are able to locate the source of sounds. When someone calls your name, you turn your head immediately in the direction from which the voice came. This ability to determine where a sound originates, **sound localization,** depends in part on **monaural** (single-ear) **cues** (see Figure 4-18). Loud sounds are perceived to be closer than faint sounds. If a sound is familiar—your best friend's voice, for instance—you can judge its distance fairly well, even with one ear covered. Changes in loudness are perceived as changes in distance, so if your friend's voice becomes louder each time he or she calls out your name, you conclude that your friend is approaching.

If you have the use of both ears, your perception of the location of sounds will be much more accurate. If your friend is off to one side of you, the sound waves of his or her voice will reach one ear slightly before the other. The difference in arrival time is slight—about 1/1000 of a second—yet the brain is able to detect and process this information. The source of a sound is always located in the direction of the ear that detected the sound waves first. A second important **binaural** (two-ear) **cue** comes from the fact that sound signals arriving from a source off to one side of you are slightly louder in the near ear than in the ear farther from the source. The slight difference occurs because your head in effect casts a "shadow" over the ear opposite the sound source, thus reducing the intensity of sound in that ear. This relative difference between signals is enough for the brain to locate the sound source and to judge its distance. Stereo recordings sometimes use these cues to provide the illusion of depth and distance. When sound engineers record your favorite band, they may place microphones at many different locations. On playback, the two speakers or headphones project sounds at slightly

Binocular depth inversion Tendency to create three-dimensional perceptual experiences that agree with past experience, despite sensory information to the contrary.

Sound localization Ability to determine where a sound originates.

Monaural cue Cue to sound location that requires just one ear alone.

Binaural cue Cue to sound location that involves both ears working together.

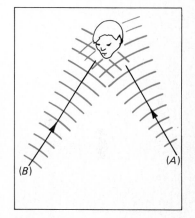

Figure 4-18

Cues used in sound localization. Sound waves coming from source B will reach both ears simultaneously. A sound wave from source A reaches the left ear first, where it is also louder. The head casts a "shadow" over the other ear, thus reducing the intensity of the delayed sound in that ear. (Boring, et al., 1976)

During a stereo recording session, microphones are generally placed at many different locations. On playback, the twin speakers or headphones project sounds picked up by the microphones at slightly different instants, mimicking what would occur if you were hearing a "live" performance.

It is possible to perceive movement in a stationary object, as in a portion of the painting *Current* by Bridget Riley.

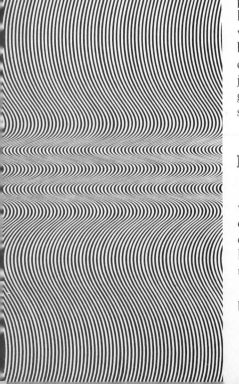

different instants to mimic what would occur if you were actually listening to the group perform in front of you (Schiffman, 1976).

What happens if a sound comes from directly in front of or above you rather than from one side? Then both ears receive the sound signals at exactly the same time, so differences in arrival time and loudness cannot be used to judge the location of the sound. In cases such as this, people tend to tilt their heads one way and another in order to create a difference in signals between the two ears, and thus to produce cues that will help them locate the sound.

Most of us rely so heavily on visual cues that we seldom pay much attention to the rich set of auditory information available in the world around us. Experiments with blind people, who often compensate for their lack of vision by improving their ability to perceive sounds, have shown just how much information about the environment our ears can provide. The blind can discover the presence of obstacles in their path by listening to the echoes from a cane, their own footsteps, and their own voice. In one notable case, a blind boy was so adept at avoiding obstacles by sound that he could ride a bicycle in public places. Many blind people can judge the size and distance of one object in relation to another using just sound cues. They can also discriminate contrasting surfaces such as glass and fabric by listening to the difference in the echo produced when sound strikes a surface (Schiffman, 1976).

Perception of Movement

The perception of movement is a complicated process involving both visual messages from the retina and messages from the muscles around the eye as it follows the object. At times, our perceptual processes play tricks on us and we think we perceive movement when the objects we are looking at are, in fact, stationary. We must distinguish, therefore, between real and apparent movement.

Real movement means the physical displacement of an object from one position to another. The perception of real movement depends only in part on the movement of images across the retina of the eye. If you stand still and move your head to look around you, the images of all the objects in the room will pass across your retina. Yet you will probably perceive all these objects as stationary. Even if you hold your head still and move only your eyes, the images will continue to pass across your retina. But the messages from the eye muscles seem to counteract those from the retina, so the objects in the room will be perceived as motionless.

The perception of real movement seems to be determined less by images moving across the retina than by how the position of objects changes in relation to a background that is perceived as stationary. When we perceive a car moving along a street, for example, we see the street, the buildings, and the sidewalk as a stationary background and the car as a moving object. Remarkably, the brain can distinguish between these retinal images of an object moving against an immobile background and all the other moving images on the retina.

It is possible, under certain conditions, to see movement in objects that are really standing still. One form of *apparent movement* is the **auto-kinetic illusion**—the perceived motion created by a single stationary object. If you stand in a room that is absolutely dark except for one tiny spot of light and stare at the light for a few seconds, you will begin to see the light drift. In the darkened room your eyes have no visible framework; there are no cues telling you that the light is really stationary. The slight movements of the eye muscles, which go unnoticed all the time, make the light appear to move.

Another form of illusory movement is **stroboscopic motion**—the apparent motion created by a rapid series of images of stationary objects (see Figure 4-19). A motion picture, for example, is not in motion at all. The film consists of a series of still pictures showing people or objects in slightly different positions. When the separate images are projected in sequence onto the screen, the people or objects seem to be moving because of the rapid change from one still picture to the next.

Stroboscopic motion also causes a perceptual illusion known as the **phi phenomenon.** When a light is flashed on at a certain point in a darkened room, then flashed off, and a second light is flashed on a split second later at a point a short distance away, most people will perceive a single spot of light moving from one point to another. Of course, the distance between the two points, the intensity of the two lights, and the time interval between them must be carefully controlled for the illusion to succeed. The same perceptual process causes us to see motion in neon signs or theater marquees, where words appear to move from one side to the other as different combinations of stationary lights are flashed on and off.

Autokinetic illusion Perception that a stationary object is actually moving.

Stroboscopic motion Apparent movement that results from flashing a series of still pictures in rapid succession, as in a motion picture.

Phi phenomenon Apparent movement caused by flashing lights in sequence, as on theater marquees.

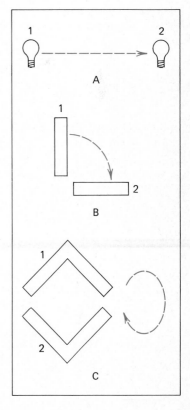

Figure 4-19
If after just the right delay (50 to 100 msec) form 1 is replaced by form 2 in A, B, or C, stroboscopic motion will be perceived as indicated by the dotted line. In A this will be a horizontal motion of the bulb from left to right. In B it will be a tipping of the bar from vertical to horizontal. In C the top angular bar will appear to flip over. In all these cases you perceive the most "reasonable" pattern of movement.

So far we have seen that we are able to create true perceptual experience from sensory information that is sometimes quite sketchy. As in the case of the inverted masks lit from behind, however, we can be fooled. This is especially likely when there are false distance or depth cues hidden in the stimulus.

Many visual illusions depend on cues that give misleading information

Extrasensory Perception

Some people claim to have an extra power of perception, beyond those known to the normal senses. This unusual power, known as extrasensory perception, or ESP, has been defined as "a response to an unknown event not presented to any known sense" (McConnell, 1969). Examples of ESP cover a variety of phenomena, including *clairvoyance*—awareness of an unknown object or event; *telepathy*—knowledge of someone else's thoughts or feelings; and *precognition*—foreknowledge of future events. The operation of ESP and other psychic phenomena is the focus of a field of study called *parapsychology*.

Modern experimentation with ESP is often done with special cards called Zener cards. A deck of Zener cards contains 25 cards showing five different symbols. To test a subject for clairvoyance, the target cards are first arranged randomly; the order is unknown to both the subject and the experimenter. The subject is then asked to "call" the cards in order. If the number of correct guesses, called "hits," is consistently higher than would be expected by chance, ESP is presumed to be operating. In tests for telepathy, the experimenter goes through the cards concentrating on each symbol in turn. Without being able to see the cards, the subject is asked to write down what he or she "reads" about the card in the experimenter's mind. Precognition tests call for the subject to recite the order of cards in advance. The experimenter then selects cards at random, using a computer or a pair of dice, and checks to see if the subject has called them in correct order.

C. E. M. Hansel (1966), a severe critic of ESP studies, has expressed the doubts most psychologists feel about the whole subject of ESP. The most serious objections concern the unscientific manner in which experiments are conducted and reported. Most ESP experiments, Hansel feels, are poorly designed—there are relatively few safeguards against dishonesty. Another drawback is that the reporting of results is often inadequate or biased in favor of supporting evidence. Hansel is particularly dismayed that researchers often do not seek to confirm results by conducting follow-up experiments, either with the same subjects or with different ones. To make matters worse, subjects themselves are not able to explain how they perform acts of ESP. As a result, most scientists feel that positive results with ESP are due to sloppy experiments, misinterpretation of data, and even out and out trickery (Cornell, 1984).

In view of so much professional skepticism, what accounts for the rather widespread willingness to believe in ESP? Some psychologists relate it to the difficulty people have in sorting out random from nonrandom events. According to psychologist Lee Ross, we do not have enough information about probability in the world at large to properly distinguish natural coincidence from causal events. Another speculation is that people tend to convert what they think is likely or possible into what is actual, hoping to have science eventually prove them right. Whatever the reason, studies indicate that people tend to persevere in beliefs about ESP and other paranormal phenomena even after experiments have been discredited (Cornell, 1984).

The study of ESP is admittedly far too complex and controversial to cover fully in the space we have. But it does remain an open question. If you are interested in doing further reading, you might start with these suggested sources:

Abell, G. O. & Singer, B. eds. (1981). *Science and the Paranormal.* New York: Scribner.
Hansel, C. E. (1980). *ESP and Parapsychology: A Critical Evaluation.* New York: Prometheus Books.

about distance or depth. In Figure 4-20, for example, the strange triangle contains a false and misleading depth cue that leads us to perceive a three-dimensional figure that clearly cannot exist. Other figures that fool us by presenting false depth cues are Figure 4-21E, where the top line is perceived as shorter; the visual illusion in Figure 4-21F; and the Ames room in Figure 4-22, in which there are misleading three-dimensional cues.

The effects of a misleading distance cue can be seen even in nature. The full moon seems larger when it first rises over the horizon than later in the evening, when it is higher in the sky. Yet photographs prove that its size does not change at all. Why the moon, the sun, and constellations all seem larger when they are nearer the horizon has puzzled people for thousands of years. Today most researchers explain it with the *apparent-distance theory* proposed by Kaufman and Rock (1962). To most people, the horizon seems farther away than the sky directly overhead. Thus we perceive the moon at the horizon as larger to make up for its apparently greater distance from us, just as in Figure 4-21F we perceive the bar at the top as farther away and therefore larger. When the terrain is blocked out, the moon at the horizon does not appear larger than the moon at the zenith.

In other illusions the visual information is so ambiguous that we cannot decide which of our perceptions is correct. In Figure 4-21A, is the cube facing to the left or to the right? Which way can you pass through the coils in Figure 4-21B—left or right? Do you see a flight of stairs or an overhanging cornice in Figure 4-21C? The answer to these questions usually is "both." Moreover, the more you stare at the figures, the more confusing they become—shifting first one way, then another.

Reversible figures like these clearly show that without adequate information from the visual stimulus, we continually search for the right interpretation. Since the visual information does not provide enough clues to tell us which perception is correct, we keep shifting from one to the other (Gregory, 1966, 1978). It is clear from all of this that we use all available information to create a perceptual experience that makes sense of the information available to us, even if the result is sometimes "impossible."

Sensory deprivation Total or near-total removal of normal sensory stimuli.

Figure 4-20

In these visual illusions there are misleading depth cues. For example, the strange triangle is constructed so that a fake depth cue signals a three-dimensional object that cannot exist.
(Adapted from Gregory, 1966)

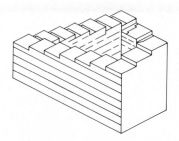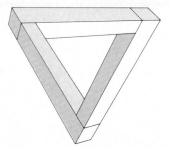

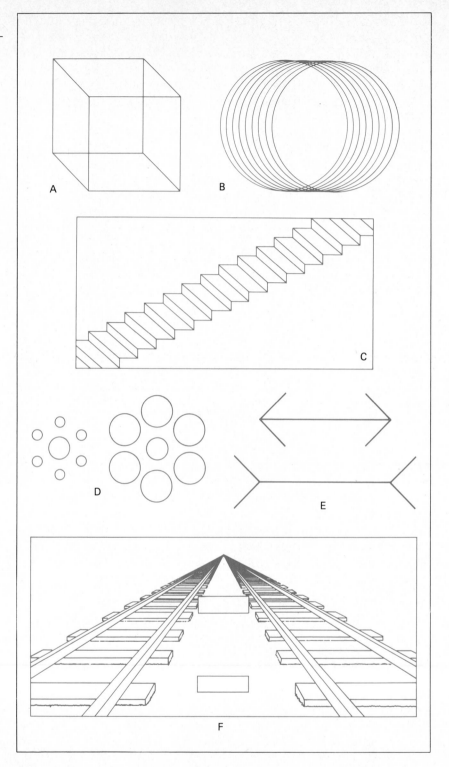

Figure 4-21

A, B, and C are examples of reversible figures. D, E, and F show that through the effects of misleading depth cues we misjudge the size of objects. The middle circles in D are exactly the same size. The lines in E are both the same length, and the rectangular bars in F have the same dimensions.

Figure 4-22

The Ames room. Most people watch with disbelief as the man seems to grow taller as he crosses the room. False depth cues—and the fact that the room has a tilting floor—are what mislead us.

Sensory Deprivation

We have been talking about our ability to make perceptual sense of a variety of sensory information. Ordinarily there is no lack of sensory material to work with—the brain is virtually bombarded with messages from the eyes, ears, nose, tongue, and skin. But what would happen if this flow of sensory information suddenly ceased almost completely? Would it just leave us feeling deeply restful? Or would it have more noticeable effects on our perceptual experiences?

In the 1950s and 1960s experimenters explored the effects of such **sensory deprivation**—the radical reduction of sensory stimuli. The results were somewhat surprising. The primary study was done at McGill University in Montreal in the late 1950s. Student volunteers were put in special sensory deprivation chambers (see Figure 4-23). They were then masked and bandaged, severely restricting their visual, auditory, and tactile stimulation. They were only released from these constraints for three meals a day and for trips to the bathroom. The results were dramatic. The subjects were increasingly unable to do the mental tasks they had set for themselves. Some had planned to mentally review their studies. Others had intended to think about a paper they had to write. The subjects grew increasingly irritable and eventually began to hallucinate. When released from their cubicles, they performed poorly on a number of tests in comparison with a control group given the same tests (Heron, 1957).

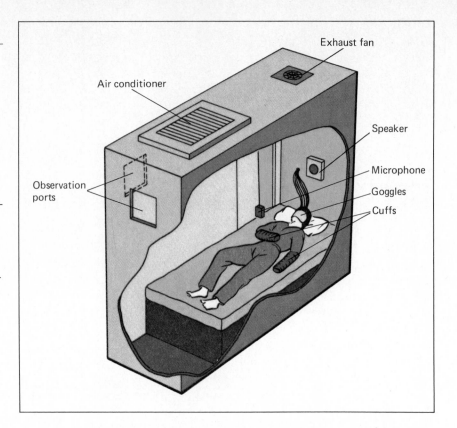

Figure 4-23

A schematic drawing of a sensory deprivation chamber. The subject lies on a cot. Cardboard cuffs are placed over the subject's hands and forearms and translucent goggles over the eyes. The only sound is the monotonous noise of the exhaust fan. A microphone allows experimenters to monitor any speech, and the wires attached to the subject's head record brain waves.
(After W. Heron, 1961)

Other research has modified both the techniques for studying deprivation and the initial findings of the McGill study. Investigators learned to vary the mode of sensory deprivation in three ways. First, the patterns that normally characterize stimulation could be eliminated with translucent goggles or white noise. Second, the variability of sensory input could be reduced by immobilizing part or all of the subject's body in a frame. Third, the absolute level of sensation could be reduced by placing volunteers in dark, quiet chambers or by immersing them in water (Suedfeld & Borrie, 1978).

No matter how deprivation was induced, its effects were fairly similar. Subjects hallucinated, although not as often as first reported; experienced altered perceptions, both like and unlike those discovered among the McGill subjects; and dreamed, daydreamed, and fantasized. The term *hallucination* generally applies to the perception of apparently real visual and auditory stimuli in the absence of any real object. By this definition, most of the phenomena produced by sensory deprivation were not hallucinations. Instead, subjects reported flashes of light, geometrical forms, noises, and various complex images of objects or living beings that did not seem to be external. While confined to their deprivation chambers, some volunteers also described nonexistent odors such as tobacco smoke and the feeling that the room or they themselves were moving.

A second effect of sensory deprivation is misinterpretation of real stimuli. Subjects emerging from solitary confinement to face a battery of perceptual tests had impaired color perception and reaction time. Visual acuity and perception of brightness remained relatively unimpaired, and some faculties were actually heightened by systematic deprivation. Auditory vigilance, tactile acuity, pain sensitivity, and taste sensations all improved in this kind of experiment. Furthermore, the negative effects of deprivation were sometimes canceled out by countermeasures such as drugs, prior experience in isolation, and pre-isolation training (Zubek, 1973). Some of these effects, which are most powerful after about 2 days of deprivation, last for up to a day after the end of the experiment (Suedfeld & Borrie, 1978).

A third major response to sensory deprivation consists of dreaming, daydreaming, and fantasy. After being alone in the deprivation chamber for a few hours, many subjects began to pass through alternating states of drowsiness, sleep, and wakefulness. Suedfeld (1975) explains the resulting imagery as the subject's attempt to maintain a normal level of stimulation under deprived conditions. Because the distinctions among wakefulness, drowsiness, and sleep become blurred in the chamber, many of the "hallucinations" reported in the McGill research may in fact have been dreams or daydreams (Suedfeld, 1975). Bad dreams sometimes occur, but the type of dreams and other imagery a person experiences may depend on how that person reacts to deprivation.

In recent years sensory deprivation has become a sought-after means of altering one's consciousness, and businesses have sprung up to satisfy the demand. After a hard day's work, customers are paying $14 or more an hour to relax in enclosed tanks filled to a depth of 10 inches with a solution of warm water and Epsom salts. Some devotees of sensory deprivation claim that the experience makes them more creative, while others merely say that it helps them collect their thoughts.

The desire to alter one's state of consciousness in order to change perceptual experiences as well as other aspects of awareness is not limited to the trendy or to those who can afford "tank time." Sensory deprivation is only one of many ways to alter one's perceptual state. Little children all over the world play at making themselves dizzy by turning rapidly in circles and eventually falling down to watch the world spin. Some people seek meditation, hypnosis, or drug-induced experiences. And, of course, daydreams, sleep, and dreams are universal. The means to altering one's state of consciousness may vary, but the interest in doing so is commonplace.

Non-experimental sensory deprivation. Customers spend "tank time" relaxing in enclosed tanks filled to a depth of 10 inches with a warm water and Epsom salt solution.

Altered States of Consciousness

Friday night on a college campus is special. Late in the afternoon powerful sound systems begin to pound out competing rhythms. By dinnertime, most of the mental activity valued so highly by professors during the rest of the week—rational thought, problem solving, memorization—have become bad form. By midevening, many students have gone from a change of pace to a change of consciousness. This is especially true at bars, parties, and the more notorious fraternity and sorority houses. Early the next morning, however, the drinkers, the pot smokers, and almost everyone else share the same **altered state of consciousness (ASC)**—sleep.

An ASC has been broadly defined as any mental state caused by physiological, psychological, or pharmacological intervention that can be recognized either by the person experiencing it or by an objective observer as producing behavior substantially different from the person's normal behavior when alert and awake. According to Ludwig (1969), most ASCs demonstrate one or more of the following characteristics: an impaired ability to think clearly and to perceive reality; a distorted sense of time; a loss of self-control; a change in how emotions are displayed; a change in body image; perceptual distortions such as hallucinations and increased visual imagery; a change in the significance given to experience; a sense of having experienced something that cannot be verbalized or communicated; feelings of rebirth; and a very high degree of suggestibility. ASCs may vary not only in character but also in degree (Suedfeld & Borrie, 1978). At one extreme are mental states distinguishable from normal ones only by an increase in the number of perceptions, intellectual activities, and emotional responses; at the other extreme are drastic qualitative changes.

Ludwig also lists three general functions of ASCs that have been traditionally socially acceptable: healing; gaining new knowledge; and providing a ritualized outlet for a group's conflicts and goals. Weil (1972) adds a controversial fourth function—counteracting the limiting effects of "straight," logical, uninsightful thinking. With this brief general introduction, let us now examine the major kinds of ASCs other than sensory deprivation.

Meditation

Like sensory deprivation, **meditation** brings about an altered state of consciousness, but unlike sensory deprivation, it is extremely common in human cultures, and is a part of almost all religions (Benson, 1975). Each form of meditation—Zen, yoga, Sufi, Christian, transcendental meditation (TM), and so on—focuses the meditator's attention in a slightly different way. Zen and yoga concentrate on respiration. The Sufi discipline, on the other hand, involves both frenzied dancing and a technique that is similar to the use of a mantra in TM (Schwartz, 1974). A mantra is an Indian sound specially picked for a student by the teacher. According to proponents of TM, concentrating on the mantra keeps all other images and problems at bay and lets the meditator relax more deeply (Deikman, 1973; Schwartz, 1974).

Meditation often creates a sense of unity between a person and his or her surroundings. The meditator may experience increased sensory awareness, euphoria, strong emotions, and a sense of timelessness and expanded awareness (Deikman, 1973). Peace of mind, a sense of well-being, and total relaxation have also been reported (Dean, 1970).

Meditation has been used to treat certain medical problems and drug abuse. Some studies found that a high percentage of meditators who had used drugs stopped using them. One survey of people who practiced TM found a dramatic decrease in drug use among them (Benson & Wallace, 1972). The proportion using marijuana fell from 78 percent before practicing TM to 12 percent after 21 months of meditation. Of all LSD users, 97 percent had ceased taking the drug after an average of 22 months of meditation. The subjects of this study were already committed to TM when they were surveyed. Among another population—high-school drug users—meditation apparently was a less attractive alternative to drugs. Of 460 students offered the chance to learn TM, only 6 accepted. These 6, however, subsequently did tend to use fewer drugs (Benson et al., 1979). Meditation may also moderate high blood pressure. TM and techniques related to yoga have lowered blood pressure among subjects matched by age, sex, and race (Stone & DeLeo, 1976). Relaxation techniques have also helped to make the heart beat more regularly (Benson, Alexander, & Feldman, 1975).

Despite its diverse forms, meditation seems to produce consistent physiological changes. These changes appear to be related to decreased

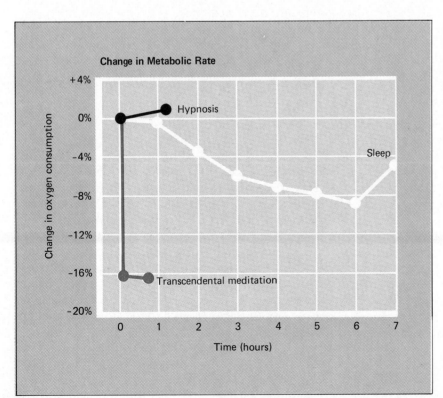

Figure 4-24

A graph depicting the lowered rate of metabolism during meditation, as measured by reduced absorption of oxygen in the bloodstream.
(Wallace et al., 1972)

Hypnosis Trancelike state in which the hypnotized person responds readily to suggestions.

activity of the sympathetic nervous system. In Chapter 2 we stated that this system of nerve fibers helps prepare the body for strenuous activity during an emergency. Meditation produces a lower rate of metabolism, which is shown by reduced absorption of oxygen in the bloodstream and elimination of carbon dioxide (see Figure 4-24). Heart and respiratory rates also decrease. Alpha brain waves noticeably increase during meditation, and there is a decrease in blood lactate, a chemical that may be linked to stress. Wallace and Benson (1972) have reported a sharp rise in skin resistance and interpret this as a sign of increased ability to cope with or shut out stressful occurrences, but other research (Schwartz, 1974) does not support this finding. In any event, there is no experimental evidence that these bodily responses are different from what one would obtain simply by resting (Holmes, 1984).

Hypnosis

Hypnosis first came to general attention in mid-18th-century Europe, when Anton Mesmer, a Viennese physician, fascinated audiences by putting patients into trances and by curing a variety of illnesses. Although some scientists studied and applied Mesmer's techniques to medical problems, for over a century hypnosis remained largely a sideshow amusement. When Freud successfully used hypnosis to cure symptoms of hysteria, however, scientific interest in the subject revived.

People in a hypnotic trance may appear to be blind, deaf, or immune to pain. They may display heightened conscious powers. For example, when told to relive their childhoods, people under hypnosis appear to be able to recite forgotten childhood memories. When awakened, they may be unable to recall anything they described while they were hypnotized. Some hypnotized subjects can even write a letter without being aware that the writing is taking place. Hypnosis can also create hallucinations that are so realistic that subjects cannot easily determine whether they are real or the products of their own minds.

Some people are more susceptible to hypnosis than others. One leading researcher (Hilgard, 1975) finds that the best subjects are those with vivid imaginations, often people who had imaginary childhood playmates or who use their imagination to escape from unpleasant realities. Hilgard hypothesizes that an active imagination enables the subject to create another world that shuts out stimuli from the external environment.

Individual differences in hypnotic susceptibility were demonstrated in an experiment by Hilgard (1974). First, the subjects immersed a hand and forearm in ice water while awake and rated the intensity of the pain they felt. After receiving the hypnotic suggestion that their hands and arms were insensitive, they immersed them again in ice water and rated the pain a second time. Hilgard found that 67 percent of the "highly hypnotizable" subjects showed a 33 percent reduction in pain, while only 13 percent of the least hypnotizable subjects obtained such dramatic results.

The classification of hypnosis as an ASC is controversial. Perhaps the most widely accepted criterion by which hypnosis is recognized as an ASC is the increase in suggestibility it produces. But many people are highly suggestible even in a normal state of consciousness; some, in fact, are just as susceptible to suggestion as the best hypnotized subjects. Therefore hypnosis cannot be distinguished from a normal state solely by the degree of suggestibility it produces.

Weitzenhoffer (1978) argues that hypnosis is indeed an ASC because under its influence subjects lose their sense of identity, which they retain in a normal state, no matter how susceptible to suggestions they are then. According to him, hypnotized subjects reach a state of effortless, concentrated attention, free from distraction by sensations or random thoughts—a condition somewhat like dreamless sleep. They lose their sense of self and respond more or less automatically to the directions of the hypnotist.

The dispute over the nature of hypnosis is unresolved partly because of two major research problems. First, there is no physiological condition that can clearly be characterized as unique to a hypnotic state (Hilgard, 1974). This makes it hard to know when the hypnotic trance state has occurred, which makes it difficult to study. Second, researchers must rely to some degree on the reports of people who have been hypnotized, and their reactions are necessarily subjective and varying (Dalal & Barber, 1970). Nevertheless, some objective measures of the perception and performance of people under hypnosis have been devised. While this research has not resolved the theoretical debate over hypnosis, it has shown that, for whatever reason, some people's perceptions can be dramatically altered by systematic forms of suggestion.

Daydreaming

It takes a special effort to enter an altered state of consciousness through meditation or hypnosis, but special effort is not necessary to enter some kinds of ASCs. All of us experience altered states every day without even trying to do so. Sometimes just sitting in class on a warm spring day can cause your mind to wander. You may be busy with thoughts of bicycling down a country road when a question from the professor suddenly makes you realize that you have been daydreaming. Interestingly, people who daydream a lot report that the content varies widely from one daydream to the next (Singer, 1974).

Daydreams usually occur when you would rather be somewhere else or doing something else—escaping from the demands of the real world for the moment—or when you are doing something that requires little conscious thought—like driving a car on a deserted highway. Sometimes you replay a scene from the past in your daydream; at other times you project into the future. Daydreams provide the opportunity to write, act in, direct, and stage manage a private drama for which you are the only audience.

Although the content of daydreams varies, at least three daydream patterns have been identified by Singer (1975). These patterns are closely linked to personality type. The first is marked by fleeting, loosely connected daydreams, usually related to worries. People who have this kind of daydream tend to score high on personality tests designed to measure anxiety. They appear to take little pleasure in their daydreams.

The second pattern of daydreams centers on guilt, hostility, achievement, and fear of failure. These fantasies often reflect self-doubt and questioning in the daydreamer. People who report this pattern frequently are strongly oriented to achievement, yet suffer from fear of failure and resentment of others.

The third pattern is characteristic of "happy daydreamers." It consists of fantasies about the future and pleasant daydreams uncomplicated by anxiety or guilt. Happy daydreamers enjoy their daydreams and use them to solve problems, think ahead, or distract themselves. In some groups of people that have been studied, a fourth daydreaming pattern appears, which is related to the third. These daydreams are tied more closely to the objective world and are often marked by controlled lines of thought. Many of these daydreamers display unusual curiosity about the natural world and place great emphasis on orderliness and objective thinking.

Some psychologists believe that daydreams are a kind of wishful thinking that occurs when inner needs cannot be expressed in actual behavior. We daydream, they claim, when the world outside does not meet our needs, or when we want to do something but cannot. Freudian theorists have traditionally held that daydreams reflect repressed desires, generally about sex or hostility, that makes us feel guilty (Giambra, 1974).

By contrast, other psychologists have stressed the positive value of daydreaming and of fantasy. Pulaski (1974) suggests that daydreaming can build cognitive and creative skills and can help people survive difficult situations. She notes that daydreaming helped prisoners of war endure torture and deprivation. Her view suggests that daydreaming and fantasy can provide relief from everyday—and often unpleasant—reality, and can reduce internal tension and external aggression.

Singer (1969) proposed that daydreams are not just a substitute for reality or an important form of relief, but part of the information-processing system (which we will discuss in Chapter 7). Singer suggests that when we process the vast, potentially overwhelming array of information we receive through our senses, we single out some of the material for later review. Whether asleep or awake, we work on this information and on the contents of long-term memory, coding or restructuring it.

We are usually unaware of this activity. But in dull moments, when we are only occupied with a few or with repetitive external stimuli, we can focus on the results of this mental activity, and "unfinished business" is the material most likely to emerge for reconsideration. By responding to these inner stimuli when daydreaming, we may briefly lose some contact with the outside world. But in the long run, shifting to an inner channel lets us organize and integrate pressing unfinished business and cope with the environment more effectively.

Sleep and Dreaming

We spend about one-third of our lives in an ASC—namely, sleep. Throughout history, people have paid varying degrees of respect to sleep and to its product, dreams. Some societies believe that great universal truths are revealed in dreams, while others view sleep as an essential, but basically nonproductive, activity. Only recently have sleep researchers begun to analyze the fascinating complexity of sleep, its function, and its influence on human perceptual activity.

SLEEP. Nobody who has tried to stay awake for any length of time can doubt that sleep is a necessity. Yet its functions are unknown. Many scientists believe that sleep somehow restores or repairs the body, but little evidence has been found to support this idea: If sleep destroys substances produced during waking hours or creates substances needed when we are awake, no such substances have been found so far. Protein synthesis in the brain speeds up during sleep, but whether this is a cause or effect of sleep is not clear. Sleep may also help in memory formation, but it seems unlikely that this is the reason we sleep. Other investigators believe that sleep has evolved as an adaptive device to keep organisms inactive during times of the day when their food supplies are low or their predators are especially numerous. Despite considerable research and some clues, however, scientists have so far failed to piece together an explanation for why we sleep.

Nonetheless, scientists have recently learned a great deal about sleep itself, and about the dreams that accompany it. Researchers do not usually enter people's homes to study the ways in which they sleep. Instead, they find volunteers to spend some nights in what is called a "sleep lab." With electrodes that are painlessly attached to their skulls, the volunteers sleep comfortably while their brain waves, eye move-

Biological Clocks

In a world organized by mechanical clocks, time schedules, and calendars, it is easy to forget that our body has its own natural rhythms. Many of these rhythms follow a roughly daily circadian cycle—from the Latin *circa diem:* "about a day." If we try to ignore them, circadian rhythms have a way of reminding us of their existence.

Workers whose shifts change frequently are apt to experience problems with sleeping. At one factory, employees were required to change to an earlier shift every week. For one week they would work from midnight to 8 A.M.; the next week they would work from 4 P.M. to midnight; and the third week, 8 A.M. to 4 P.M. Faced with low productivity and complaints of insomnia during sleeping hours and drowsiness on the job, management called in a team of sleep researchers. The team recognized immediately that the workers' natural sleep-wake cycle was continually being disrupted by the factory schedule. The team recommended that workers be given 3 weeks to adjust to each new shift and that they be rotated to later rather than earlier shifts. These changes did, in fact, eliminate many of the problems.

Even people with regular working hours may experience sleep-related disorders, especially on Mondays. Scientists relate Monday morning grogginess to the fact that people tend to go to bed later on Friday and Saturday nights. Returning to the weekday schedule on Sunday night produces the "blue Mondays" many people feel when they go back to work.

The sleep-wake cycle is only one of a number of circadian rhythms. Body temperature and many endocrine secretions follow daily cycles as well. And scientists now believe that the daily cycle of light and dark serves to synchronize the various circadian cycles in the body so that they work together.

One piece of evidence in support of this idea is that when experimental subjects were isolated in a room with constant lighting, their biological clocks soon began to keep different times. Among some subjects, for example, the sleep cycle speeded up while the temperature clock slowed down. And after 2 months of living under constant illumination, volunteers in another study only slept every 36 to 50 hours, but they still spent a third of their total time sleeping.

Scientists are certain that other cycles also affect our behavior, although these have not yet been fully identified and classified. The menstrual cycle clearly can affect mood, but there may be "mood cycles" of varying lengths in all people. Depression and elation, accident proneness and efficiency, have all been shown to vary in cycles.

Delta sleep Fourth and deepest stage of sleep, characterized by slow, even brain waves.

REM sleep Rapid-eye-movement sleep; characterized by jagged brain wave activity, muscle relaxation, and a rapid movement of the eyes; most dreams occur during REM sleep.

NREM sleep Non-rapid-eye-movement sleep; Stages 1–4, which alternate with REM sleep during the sleep cycle.

ments, and other physiological data are monitored.

Although there are significant individual differences, researchers using information gathered from these "sleep labs" have identified several stages that everyone goes through while sleeping (Kleitman, 1963). "Going to sleep" means losing awareness and failing to respond to a stimulus that would produce a response in the waking state. Often this involves a floating or falling sensation, followed by a quick jolt back to consciousness, especially if the sleeper has entered Stage 1 of sleep. Stage 1 is marked by irregular and low-voltage brain waves, slower pulse rate, muscle relaxation, and side-to-side rolling movements of the eyes. This eye movement is the most reliable indication of the initial sleep process (Dement, 1974). Stage 1 lasts only a few minutes. The sleeper is easily awakened at this point, and if awakened may be unaware of having been asleep. Stages 2 and 3 form a continuum of deeper and deeper sleep. In Stage 2 brain waves show bursts of activity called "spindles." In Stage 3 these disappear and brain waves become long and slow, about 1 per second. At this stage the sleeper is hard to awaken and does not respond to stimuli. Heart rate, blood pressure, and temperature continue to drop. Stage 4 is **delta sleep,** the deepest stage, which is marked by slow, even brain waves. In young adults delta sleep occurs in 15 to 20-minute segments—interspersed with lighter sleep—mostly during the first half of the night. Delta sleep lessens with age, but continues to be the first sleep to be made up after sleep has been lost.

About 30 or 40 minutes after going to sleep, the sleeper begins to ascend from Stage 4, a process that takes about 40 minutes. At the end of this time, the brain waves exhibit a saw-toothed quality much like that of the brain during waking hours, although the muscles of the body are more relaxed than they had been at any previous point in the sleep cycle. The eyes move rapidly under the closed eyelids. This is called **REM** (rapid eye movement) **sleep,** as opposed to the four non-REM **(NREM) sleep** stages that precede it (see Figure 4-25).

During REM, sleep activity in the brain strongly resembles that of full wakefulness, or arousal, yet this arousal cannot be translated into movement of the body because the muscles are virtually paralyzed at this time. This paralysis lasts throughout the period of REM sleep. When researchers made lesions on the brain stem of cats to reverse this paralysis, the effects were spectacular. Although sound asleep, the cats raised their heads, tried to stand up, and sometimes succeeded. Other cats even seemed to search for prey and attack it (Morrison, 1983). Obviously the ability to inhibit this kind of activity makes REM sleep safer for all of us.

The first REM period lasts about 10 minutes and is followed by Stages 2, 3, and 4 of NREM sleep. This sequence of sleep stages repeats itself all night long, averaging 90 minutes from beginning to end. Normally a night's sleep consists of four to five complete sleep cycles. But the pattern of sleep changes as the night progresses. Stages 3 and 4 dominate at first, but as time passes, the REM periods gradually become longer, up to 40 minutes, with NREM Stage 2 the only interruption. Over the course of a night, Stage 2 makes up 45 to 50 percent of sleep, while REM sleep takes up about 25 percent of the total.

This nightly pattern of sleep varies considerably from person to person. Some adults need hardly any sleep. Researchers have documented the cases of a Stanford University professor who slept for only 3 to 4 hours

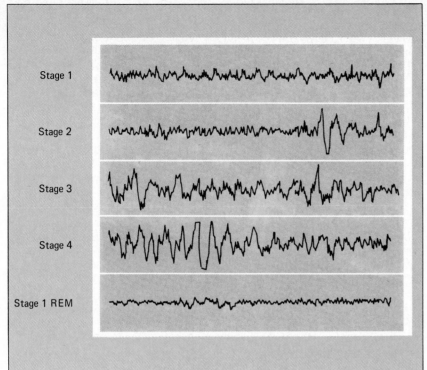

Stage 1

Stage 2

Stage 3

Stage 4

Stage 1 REM

Insomnia Inability to sleep.

Apnea Sleeping disorder associated with difficulty in breathing during the night and bouts of sleeping during the day.

Narcolepsy Sleeping disorder marked by sudden nodding off during the day and sudden loss of muscle tone upon emotional excitement.

Figure 4-25
The brain wave patterns typical of the five stages of sleep—the four NREM stages and the first REM stage. The brain waves in REM sleep closely resemble stage 1 of NREM sleep, but the person in REM is very deeply asleep.
(From Luce and Segal, 1966)

a night over the course of 50 years and a woman who lived a healthy life on only 1 hour of sleep per night (Rosenzweig & Leiman, 1982). Sleep patterns also change with age. Infants tend to sleep much longer than adults—13 to 16 hours during the first year—and much more of their sleep is REM sleep. Infants also enter REM sleep immediately after falling asleep, unlike adults, and change stages often. The elderly, on the other hand, tend to sleep less than younger adults, wake up more often during the night, and spend about half as much time in the deep sleep of Stages 3 and 4.

Sleeping disorders are another source of variation in patterns of sleep. Not all of us can take it for granted that 7 or 8 hours after we put our head on the pillow we will wake up refreshed. In the United States about 30 million people suffer from **insomnia.** The problem usually grows out of stressful events and is temporary. But for some victims insomnia persists, disrupting their lives. The problem is made worse by the fact that over time sleeping pills lose their effectiveness. In some cases, psychotherapy seems to help eliminate insomnia.

Up to 15 percent of the adult population suffers from the reverse problem—too much sleepiness. A major cause of this problem is **apnea,** a condition associated with breathing difficulties during the night. In severe cases, the victim seems to make no effort to breathe after falling asleep. When the level of carbon dioxide in the blood rises to a certain point, apnea sufferers are spurred to a state of arousal just short of consciousness. Because this can happen hundreds of times in a night, apnea patients typically feel exhausted the next day and fall asleep repeatedly. Another source of too much sleepiness is **narcolepsy,** a heritable condition that causes victims to nod off during the day without warning.

The Long and Short of Sleep

If you are like most people, you need between 7 and 8 hours of sleep a night. If you get any less, you drag through the day hoping to get a good night's sleep the next night. If you get more sleep, you feel groggy from too much. Not everyone needs 7 or 8 hours of sleep; some people need a lot less and some need much more.

Ernest L. Hartman (1973) investigated the characteristics of long sleepers—those who need 9 or more hours of sleep a night—and short sleepers—those who need fewer than 6 hours—to learn whether their personalities as well as the quality of their sleep differed.

Short sleepers, according to Hartman, tend to be more sociable and less nervous than long sleepers. They are also relatively efficient, energetic, adroit, and optimistic about life. Long sleepers, by contrast, are more likely to be mildly depressed, experience greater personal stress, and worry more than other people. In particular, people who worry about political and social issues are disproportionately represented among long sleepers (Hartman, 1973).

When Hartman tested the sleeping patterns of long and short sleepers, he found that both got about the same amount of NREM sleep. But long sleepers spent more time than short sleepers in REM sleep. What is the value of these extra REM periods to the long sleeper? According to Hartman, "Longer sleep and more REM time may have some function in dealing with or restoring the brain and psyche after days of worry, depression, or disequilibrium or after difficult new learning—perhaps after any intrapsychic conflict" (Hartman, 1973). The research suggests that short sleepers do not have the same need to resolve conflicts as they sleep. Their easygoing nature carries on through the night.

Narcoleptics also often experience a sudden loss of muscle tone upon expression of any sort of emotion. A joke, anger, sexual stimulation—all bring on a feeling of weakness. Another symptom of the disease is immediate entry into REM sleep, a condition that produces frightening hallucinations that are in fact dreams that the narcoleptic experiences while still partly awake. Narcolepsy is thought to arise from a defect in the central nervous system. The disorder can be successfully treated with drugs such as antidepressants and stimulants.

DREAMS. Dreams occur primarily during REM periods, although they can also take place during NREM states. Subjects awakened from REM sleep report dreams 80–85 percent of the time (Berger, 1969). Compared to NREM dreams, REM dreams are less like normal thought; they are also more vivid, emotional, and distorted than NREM dreams (Dement, 1974; Foulkes, 1966). Thus dreams become progressively more visual and less related to reality throughout the night as REM sleep becomes increasingly dominant (Broughton, 1975). There is also some evidence of dream activity during the day. In one experiment subjects who were monitored during the day and periodically questioned reported a considerable amount of dreamlike activity (Foulkes & Fleisher, 1975). We may dream off and on, night and day, but only when competing external stimuli are minimal do our dreams become coherent enough to recall (Koulack & Goodenough, 1976). People dream an average of 2 hours a night, even if they do not remember their dreams.

The dreams we have at night are in many ways like the daydreams we experience while awake. They may be influenced by something in everyday waking life, but they reshape and re-create that material into new and "illogical" forms. A little boy who wishes his baby sister were dead knows it is unacceptable to have fantasies of killing her, much less to perform the act. When he dreams that she is dead, the dream is "not his fault" because he had no say in whether to have it. A dream may reflect a person's unconscious wishes, needs, and conflicts. It may draw on any part of one's history, from earliest childhood to events that happened the other day.

Dreams, like daydreams, can also be a rich source of creative ideas. Franz Kafka got most of the material for his short stories from his dreams. René Descartes "dreamed up" the axioms of analytic geometry while sleeping one night. The high regard in which dreams have been held throughout history can be seen in the biblical story of the pharaoh's dreams of "fat and lean cattle," which Joseph interpreted as omens of 7 years of feast and 7 years of famine. Aristotle believed that dreams arose from the psychic activity of the sleeper. From ancient times most people have felt that the content of their dreams was significant—even if they could not interpret it.

Psychologists have spent considerable effort investigating the content and meaning of dreams. According to Freud, all dreams are symbolic expressions of repressed—and "forbidden"—desires that are hidden from awareness. Today investigators of dreams rely on what dreamers remember about their dreams just after waking. Such recall shows that individual differences and daytime experiences help form the content of dreams, along with what happens during sleep itself. When you are closest to waking, your dreams are apt to be about recent events. In the middle of the night, when body temperature is lowest, more of your dreams involve childhood or past events. The last dream you have before waking is the one you are likely to remember.

Dreams vary according to age and sex. Children's dreams, like those of adults, seem to represent their waking life. Disturbed children have disturbed dreams, but most children dream about scary animals, while few adults, except in primitive cultures, dream about animals. Men dream more about men than about women. Women dream equally about both men and women. Men's dreams are more adventurous and aggressive and less emotional than women's dreams. Both sexes dream equally about being pursued or victimized. Before menstruation, women often dream about waiting. Before childbirth, they are likely to dream more about babies or their mothers than about their husbands. The dreams of women have more characters, warmer interactions, more indoor settings, and more family subjects than men's dreams.

Events near bedtime also affect a night's dream. We may have dreams about snow when we are cold or about deserts when we are hot. Eating salty food before bedtime made Freud dream of cold water. In one experiment thirsty people who dreamed about drinking water drank less upon waking than those who did not dream about drinking. People who have been isolated tend to dream more about social interaction. It is difficult, however, to study how presleep experiences relate to dreams because people may respond to the same situation in terms of a different set of conflicts and defenses. These different conflicts and defenses affect the nature of dreams and must be understood before an experimenter can know if a subject's dreams are consistent with his or her waking emotional states (Webb & Cartwright, 1978).

Most dreams last about as long as the events would in real life; they

The Hypnagogic State

One afternoon in 1865, the chemist Friedrich von Kekule turned his chair toward the fireplace and dozed off. For some time he had been trying to determine the shape of the benzene molecule. As he began to fall asleep, what looked like rows of atoms danced before his eyes, twisting like snakes. When one of the snakes seized hold of its own tail and whirled before him, von Kekule awoke immediately with the solution to his problem—the benzene ring. This discovery became a cornerstone of modern chemistry (Koestler, 1964).

Psychologists call the mental state from which von Kekule drew his inspiration the *hypnagogic state*. It occurs during the drowsy period between waking and sleeping and is marked by visual and auditory images that arise unwilled. They appear to the observer to be part of the external world. Also characteristic of the hypnagogic state are highly unusual patterns of thought and verbal constructions that sound at first as if they have a meaning, but dissolve into nonsense. The phenomenon seems to be quite common, with recent estimates of the proportion of people experiencing the hypnagogic state ranging from 72 to 77 percent (Schachter, 1976).

Like other ASCs, the hypnagogic state varies from person to person. According to Schachter (1976), visual imagery is most common. Typically, flashes of color, light, and geometric patterns appear first, then faces and other objects, and later landscapes or complex scenes. The faces often appear in vivid detail and, surprisingly, are usually those of complete strangers. Sometimes these faces are so grotesque that they scare children. Landscapes are typically described as unusually beautiful and striking.

Less commonly, people seem to hear sounds. Sometimes they hear their names called or see and hear someone speak to them. Music has also been reported. One subject heard Rachmaninoff's *Second Piano Concerto* so clearly that he felt his experience rivaled an actual performance (McKellar, 1957). Sometimes people experience bodily sensations such as the feeling of falling. Bizarre sequences of thought and speech are also associated with the hypnagogic state. Archer, for instance, reported hearing the phrases, "A savory pudding—raw in the market," and "A little management of Killie-krankie," as he fell asleep (1935).

Is the hypnagogic state similar to or related to other ASCs? Hypnagogic experiences are clearly distinct from dreams in two ways: Dreamers usually dream about themselves, while people seldom participate in their own hypnagogic imagery; and dreams are usually longer and better organized than the "snapshot" imagery of the hypnagogic state.

Thus, although the contents of both experiences are often strange, hypnagogic imagery is probably not closely related to dreaming (Schachter, 1976). And although there seem to be some similarities in the form and quality of hypnagogic and drug-induced imagery, the little research that has been done generally supports the unique nature of the hypnagogic state.

do not flash on your mental screen just before waking, as was once believed. Generally, they consist of a sequential story or a series of stories. Stimuli, both external and internal, may modify an ongoing dream, but they do not initiate dreams. One interesting experiment used three different external stimuli on subjects who were dreaming: a 5-second tone just below the waking threshold, a flashing lamp, and a light spray of cold water. The water was incorporated into 42 percent of the dreams, the light into 23 percent, and the tone into 9 percent (Dement & Wolpert, 1958). Another experiment by Dement and Wolpert (1958) showed that when a tape recording of the subject's voice was played back to the subject while dreaming, the principal actor in the dream became more active and self-assertive. Thus, while these external stimuli are perceived

Throughout history,
significance has been
attached to dreams,
even if their meaning
was unclear. The
woman in *The
Nightmare* by Henry
Fuseli, seems to be
dreaming of monsters
of her own creation.

during dreaming, their origin is often not perceived as being external. Their presence in the dream is usually personal and subjective rather than literal. Interestingly, significant external stimuli such as the sleeper's name being spoken are most likely to spur awakening.

Are all the dreams dreamt in a single night related? Unfortunately experimenters run into a methodological problem when they try to answer this question. Each time the subject is awakened to be asked about a dream, the natural course of the dream is interrupted and usually lost forever. If one particular problem or event weighs heavily on the dreamer's mind, however, it will often show up in dreams throughout the night (Dement, 1974).

What if you set up a tape recorder to play back information while you sleep? Will you painlessly absorb this material? Unfortunately no learning of complex material during sleep has ever been demonstrated. Even experiments designed to teach sleepers simple pairs of words have failed. Very rudimentary forms of learning may be possible, however. The first time that a stimulus such as a loud noise is presented to a sleeper, it produces signs of arousal. Repetition of the stimulus causes less and less arousal, suggesting that the sleeper has learned that the stimulus is not a cause for alarm.

Attempts to influence dream content through presleep suggestions have also had mixed results. Success seems to depend on subtleties such as the phrasing of the suggestion, the tone in which it is given, the relationship between the suggester and the subject, and the setting

(Walker & Johnson, 1974). If these variables could be refined and controlled, the presleep suggestion technique could be important for both sleep researchers and psychotherapists.

NEED FOR SLEEP AND DREAMS. People have often lamented about how much time we "waste" while sleeping. Think what we must be missing! What we actually miss by sleeping are things like hallucinations, increased irritability, difficulty in concentrating, disorientation, lapses of attention, and stress. These are the effects of extreme sleep deprivation, seen in people who have stayed up, on a bet or for a television marathon, for over 200 hours. Among people who go without sleep for 60 hours or less, the primary effect is, not surprisingly, sleepiness. A loss of sleep also affects the nervous system. Sleep-deprived people perform certain tasks less efficiently; they also experience hand tremors and lower pain thresholds. Reflexes and the autonomic nervous system seem to be affected very little by moderate deprivation. In the long run, however, the human body needs sleep to function, just as it needs food and water.

The need to dream appears to be less crucial than the need to sleep. Dement (1965) studied the effects of dream deprivation on people by awakening subjects just as they entered REM sleep. He found that subjects who went without REM sleep became anxious, testy, hungry, had difficulty concentrating, and even hallucinated in their waking hours. But we now know that some dreams occur in NREM sleep, so eliminating REM sleep isn't the same as eliminating all dreams. Moreover, in later experiments on the loss of REM sleep, Dement found no evidence of harmful changes in people who were kept from REM sleep for 16 days, nor in cats deprived for 70 days (Dement, 1974). "A decade of research," he wrote, "has failed to prove that substantial ill effects result even from prolonged selective REM deprivation" (Dement, 1974, p. 91).

This does not mean that stopping people from entering REM sleep does not affect them in any way. When people have been deprived of REM sleep, and are then allowed to sleep undisturbed, the amount of REM sleep nearly doubles. This phenomenon is called "REM rebound." Interestingly, schizophrenics show little or no REM rebound. Persons who show signs of dreaming during the day also show less REM rebound (Cohen, 1976). This suggests that we can make up for the loss of dream-like fantasy characteristic of REM sleep either in NREM sleep or in waking life (Dement et al., 1970). Many people who take drugs or drink alcohol, or who lose dream time because of illness or worry, say that when these inhibiting factors are removed, they compensate by dreaming more intensely, often having nightmares (Dement, 1965). Studies of alcoholics indicate that REM deprivation caused by a disturbance in sleeping patterns may even break through to waking life. The result is delirium tremens, or d.t.'s which are vivid hallucinations experienced during alcohol withdrawal (Greenberg & Pearlman, 1967).

REM sleep may also be essential to the normal operations of certain emotional and cognitive processes. There is some evidence, drawn mainly from studies of animals, that a loss of REM sleep may hinder the later storage and recall of important or meaningful information. The learning of simple or irrelevant information, however, is not greatly affected by the amount of REM sleep (McGrath & Cohen, 1978).

So far we have confined our discussion to altered states of consciousness that are produced without drugs. Meditation, hypnosis, daydreams, sleep, and dreaming all occur without fundamentally changing normal physiological processes. In the final section of this chapter we will look at ASCs that are produced with the help of drugs.

Since ancient times drugs have been used to alter consciousness for social, religious, medical, and personal reasons. Wine is mentioned often in the Old Testament. Marijuana first appeared in the herbal recipe book of a Chinese emperor in 2737 B.C. Today, with widespread education about psychology and much interest in—and misinformation about—drugs, many people take drugs in a conscious and deliberate effort to change their cognitive and perceptual styles, to get away from "straight" modes of thinking (Weil, 1972). The effects of some of these drugs may depend on the set—the expectations that people bring to the drug experience and their emotional state at the time—and the setting—the physical, social, and emotional atmosphere in which the drug is taken. Other drugs affect everyone in similar ways.

ALCOHOL. Are you surprised that alcohol is discussed in this section? Our society recognizes many appropriate occasions for the use of alcohol: to celebrate important events, to reduce tension, to break down social isolation, and to promote group harmony. According to a government survey, 39 percent of American adults and 34 percent of American youths do not regard alcohol as a drug; and only 7 percent of the public think alcoholism is a serious social problem, compared to 53 percent who hold this attitude toward all other drugs. However, alcoholism is the most serious drug problem in the United States today. Users of alcohol outnumber users of all other drugs, largely because alcohol is readily available and aggressively marketed. It is also highly "reinforcing," that is, it tends to encourage repeated use and can result in both physical and psychological dependence. One out of every ten Americans uses it compulsively, and 50 percent of them are seriously dependent on it (National Commission on Marijuana and Drug Abuse, 1973a). Furthermore, there are signs of a sharp upsurge in alcoholism among adolescents.

Alcohol is a depressant and can lessen a person's normal inhibitions. Because you may feel more free to act in certain ways when drinking, you may think that the drug is a stimulant. It is not, but the excitement of feeling "free" certainly can be. During the euphoric period a person's diminished self-control can result in social embarrassment, injury, or automobile accidents. Prolonged and excessive use of alcohol can damage the brain, liver, and other internal organs and can change the personality of the drinker.

Alcohol has mixed effects on visual perception. It heightens perception of dim lights, but it impairs perception of the differences between brighter lights, colors, and depth. The same is true of auditory perception. Some aspects of hearing, like perception of loudness, are not affected. The ability to discriminate between different rhythms and pitches, however, is impaired by a single dose of the drug. Smell and taste

Amnesia Loss of memory.

perception are uniformly diminished. Perception of time is also distorted. Most people report that time seems to pass more quickly when they are "under the influence" (NCMDA, 1973b).

While alcohol can certainly produce an ASC, some of the effects of alcohol are due not to the alcohol itself but to expectations about what it is supposed to do to people. For example, experimental evidence indicates that men become more aggressive when they believe they are drinking alcohol, even if in fact they are drinking only tonic. They also become more sexually aroused and less anxious in social situations when they mistakenly believe they are drinking alcohol (Marlatt & Rohsenow, 1981).

MARIJUANA. Although marijuana use in the United States has risen markedly since the 1960s, there is no indication of significant compulsive use (NCMDA, 1973a). Moderate use seems to produce no mental or physical deterioration (Grinspoon, 1969). The most recent research, however, suggests some negative effects of long-term use, including damage to lung and brain cells and lowered sperm count among males (Zimmerman, 1979). On the positive side, marijuana seems to relieve some of the symptoms of glaucoma and asthma, as well as the nausea resulting from chemotherapy. Repeated use of marijuana produces a reverse-tolerance effect. Newcomers to the drug can absorb large quantities with little or no change in consciousness, while users with more experience are able to get high on much smaller amounts.

Marijuana is far less potent than the hallucinogens—LSD, peyote, mescaline, and psilocybin—and affects consciousness far less profoundly. A user who becomes "high" for the first time is likely to be anxious. This is usually followed by euphoria, a heightened sense of humor, a feeling of being bodiless, a rapid flow of ideas but confusion in relating them—due to impairment of short-term memory—heightened sensitivity, increased visual imagery, and a distorted sense of time. Cognitive tests administered to subjects after use of marijuana show mixed results: Some functions are unaffected, some are mildly impaired, and others may be slightly heightened (Grinspoon, 1969).

AMPHETAMINES AND BARBITURATES. Amphetamines (or "uppers") produce feelings of optimism and boundless energy. They are thus a highly reinforcing kind of drug. Compulsive use can eventually lead to severe problems, however.

Amphetamines have a stimulating effect, while barbiturates ("downers") are depressants. Barbiturates are pharmacologically similar to alcohol and have the same potential for creating physical and psychological dependence (NCMDA, 1973a). They relax all muscles—including the heart—and are therefore used to relieve anxiety. An overdose can relax muscle function so completely that death results.

Both amphetamines and barbiturates affect perception, primarily the perception of time. People's self-perceptions can also be affected—users of amphetamines may rate their abilities higher than they really are. But drugs also affect memory. Barbiturates can cause **amnesia,** but they can also enhance long-term memory; "truth serums" are actually barbiturates (NCMDA, 1973a). Amphetamines can make it hard to concentrate, thus disrupting both attention and perception. When taken to excess, they may also cause a condition called "amphetamine psychosis" (Groves & Rebec, 1976). The symptoms of this condition, including fear, suspicion, paranoid delusions, and hallucinations, strongly resemble those associated with paranoid schizophrenia.

THE OPIATES. Heroin is the best known member of the **opiate** family. Heroin use has tremendous social implications because the most likely users are urban young men whose drug habit prevents them from gaining an economic and social niche in society. Also, because it is illegal and expensive, heroin, more than any other drug, generally results in criminal behavior. Most people who use heroin inject it intravenously, which leads relatively quickly to physical dependence and **addiction.** An overdose can kill.

Heroin use produces a feeling of well-being and relaxation. Because of the rapid development of tolerance, however, the addict must take increasingly larger doses to achieve these effects; smaller doses simply prevent the terrible pains of withdrawal. Since heroin is expensive, addicts must spend so much time and energy getting it that when they do, the primary feeling is generally one of relief rather than well-being. At this stage, heroin is less a means to alter consciousness than a medicine or a painkiller.

COCAINE. Cocaine is a stimulant and a member of a group of substances that includes nicotine, caffeine, and morphine. The drug is extracted from the leaves of the coca shrub, which grows throughout the eastern highlands of the Andes, in Ecuador, Peru, Bolivia, and Colombia. The Indians of South America have been using cocaine for at least 5,000 years. Among the Inca, coca leaves had religious significance and they were chewed by the ruling classes. Today the drug has developed a mystique and has been widely adopted in the United States. According to one estimate, about 10 million Americans in 1979 had taken cocaine in the previous 12 months.

The effects of cocaine vary with the quantity consumed, the way in which it is taken, and the setting in which it is used. It is most common to inhale cocaine powder through the nose, but the drug can also be injected or smoked. Cocaine stimulates the sympathetic nervous system, increasing the heart rate, raising the blood pressure, and constricting the blood vessels. Large doses raise the body temperature and dilate the pupils of the eyes. The drug tends to create a feeling of euphoria as well as a sense of improved powers of thought. These sensations peak within 15 to 30 minutes. In part, the euphoria appears to be produced by the user's expectations and the social setting. After relatively large doses wear off, some users experience anxiety, depression, fatigue, and a strong desire for more cocaine. Those who inject or smoke the drug often experience a "crash" or extreme discomfort as the effect of the cocaine fades.

Although cocaine is not physically addictive, it is strongly habit forming, especially among users who smoke or inject it. Persistent use of the drug over a period of time leads people to reorganize their lives around the need to finance and procure the drug. Regular use can also cause loss of sleep and appetite, and may bring about an anxious paranoid state, marked by hallucinations if large doses are involved (Van Dyke & Byck, 1982).

Opiates Addictive drugs, such as heroin and opium, that dull the senses and induce a feeling of lethargic well-being.

Addiction Strong physical need for a substance, such as some drug.

A cocaine user about to inhale the white powdery substance.

Hallucinogen Any of a number of drugs that distort perception, such as mescaline and LSD.

HALLUCINOGENS. The **hallucinogens** include LSD ("acid"), mescaline, peyote, psilocybin, and other drugs. These drugs have a rather low dependency rate (NCMDA, 1973*a*). Contrary to some popular thinking, they seldom induce psychosis, and only rarely in people with no previous history of instability (Barron, Jarvik, & Bunnell, 1964). The effects of hallucinogens last considerably longer than those of most drugs—12 hours or longer is common. This length of time can cause unstable people to panic unless they are reassured that the effects are temporary.*

The problem with studying hallucinogens is that, even more than most drugs, their effects are determined not only by the properties of the

How LSD Works

Some of the first experiments with LSD were described as "mind trips." As it happens, the term is a remarkably accurate one. Scientists studying hallucinogenic drugs have now determined the steps by which LSD "trips" the mind by altering chemical transmission in the brain.

The first lead in LSD research was discovery of a structural similarity between a molecule of LSD and serotonin, one of the important brain transmitters we saw in Chapter 2. Because of this similarity, early researchers proposed that LSD might lock into the receptor sites for serotonin and thus prohibit the transmitter from doing its job. The blocking of serotonin was thought to cause the characteristic LSD hallucinations. This theory soon came into question, however, when testing with related drugs produced conflicting results. Most notably, brom-LSD, a close chemical cousin of LSD, was indeed found to block serotonin, but without producing hallucinations (Jacobs & Trulson, 1979). While scientists continued to believe that LSD interfered in some important way with serotonin, it was not yet known where and how in the brain this happened.

Other researchers then began to look for areas of the brain where serotonin was especially important.

With the aid of a new technique, it was possible to look at sections of rat brain under ultraviolet light and see exactly where nerve cells producing serotonin were located. A small group of such neurons was found clustered in an area of the forebrain known as the "raphe nucleus." What's more, the axons of these neurons spread out over a very large distance, eventually reaching brain areas involved in vision and emotion. And it turned out that this concentration of serotonin in the raphe nucleus is much the same for a number of mammal species. This suggested that LSD might also

have its effects on humans through the raphe nucleus.

In 1968 George Aghajanian inserted microelectrodes into the brain stems of anesthetized rats and injected a low dose of LSD. He watched as serotonin cells in the area abruptly ceased activity. In later experiments Aghajanian was able to prove that LSD acts directly on the cell body of these neurons, and not at the synapses, as was originally thought (Jacobs & Trulson, 1979).

From this and other evidence, scientists now have a model for the way LSD works. First, the drug acts directly to inhibit the action of serotonin neurons in the raphe nucleus of the forebrain. This, in turn, causes a burst of activity in those portions of the brain responsible for vision and emotion. This two-step process is what causes the hallucinations and other effects associated with LSD. Moreover, several laboratories have reported recently that LSD also seems to mimic the action of dopamine, another brain transmitter. Thus it may be that the most potent hallucinogenic drugs are those that both inhibit serotonin and mimic dopamine. The clinical evidence for this is very striking. When patients who are having "bad trips" on LSD are given blockers against dopamine, they report that the overall intensity of the experience diminishes but not the hallucinations themselves.

Scientists are now using the model to help answer unresolved questions about LSD and other hallucinogens. One interesting question is whether the LSD effect occurs naturally under any normal conditions, such as during sleep. Another line of investigation is whether some cases of severe mental illness that involve hallucinations and emotional disorder might be due to natural hallucinogens in the nervous systems of these people. We will examine this possibility more closely in Chapter 14.

drug itself but also by a person's expectations and the setting in which the drug is taken. Moreover, subjects under the influence of these drugs often find a researcher's questions hilarious or irrelevant and either refuse or are unable to answer them (NCMDA, 1973a).

We do know that hallucinogens have profound effects on visual and auditory perception. At a minimal level, colors seem more vivid and surface details stand out more. With a higher dose of the drug or greater sensitivity to it, a person may see kaleidoscopic patterns and images, or fully integrated and often bizarre scenes (Barron, Jarvik, & Bunnell, 1964). Spatial distortions and changed body images are also common. Sometimes these visual effects are described as breathtakingly beautiful, at other times as extremely unpleasant and upsetting.

Auditory perception also changes in a fascinating variety of ways. Some people report hearing imaginary conversations, or fully orchestrated and original symphonies, or foreign languages previously unknown to them. Auditory acuity may be increased, making the person keenly aware of low sounds like breathing, heartbeats, or the light rustle of leaves in the wind (Barron, Jarvik, & Bunnell, 1964).

Some students of hallucinogens view all of these effects as shallow aspects of the drug experience compared with the mystical and transcendental qualities that are often noted. For example, Pahnke and Richards (1969) suggest that the various perceptual and sensory effects are paltry compared with the consciousness attained when one goes through the drug pattern toward a mystical sense of harmony, unity, and serenity. In a similar way, Deikman (1973) cites the LSD experience as another means of achieving "deautomatization"—the abolition of psychological structures that normally limit, select, and interpret sensory stimuli.

It should be noted that scientists are still debating whether any or all of the hallucinogens have harmful physiological effects.

Application

Perception and the Blind

A woman who had been blind from birth finally had an operation that would enable her to see. One of her first sights after the operation was her own reflection in a mirror. Her response: "I thought I was better looking."

This story illustrates what many people have always suspected: Blind people have visual images, though they may never have actually seen anything. The question of *how* blind people visualize the world and where they get their information from is of great interest to psychologists and researchers in the field of perception and sensation.

In the 1930s Marius von Senden, a German scientist, studied the perceptions of people who had been born blind and were later cured. One patient thought that people and trees looked alike, because they both have a central trunk that you can put your arms around, no sharp edges, and limbs that emerge from the trunk. She was quite surprised to discover, upon being cured, that people and trees look so different.

John Kennedy, a psychologist at the University of Toronto, has studied how blind people perceive by asking them to draw various objects. Since the blind perceive objects only through touch, Kennedy wished to see if they could convey their sense of objects through line drawings. He was surprised to note that the blind people in his study quickly realized that some aspects of reality must be sacrificed in a drawing—that you cannot draw all

Drawn by people blind from birth, these illustrations portray, from top to bottom, crossed fingers, a figure running (one leg is foreshortened), and a wheel with curved spokes.
(From Hechinger, 1981 and Kennedy, 1980a.)

sides of an object, for example. The blind artists devised ways to represent objects, such as a cup or a table, that were readily understood by people who could see. Kennedy was especially fascinated to find that his blind subjects understood the idea of occlusion—that objects in front will partly or totally obscure objects behind them.

Other studies designed by Kennedy have revealed that blind people have an intuitive grasp of several other principles of graphic imagery. The blind seem to understand linear perspective, which—as we saw earlier—is the tendency of parallel lines to converge at a point in the distance. Some blind subjects were also able to represent the near edge of a surface with a thick line and the far edge with a thin line. When blind subjects touched tactile drawings, they understood that lines can represent changes in depth. Thus they could distinguish between foreground and background, just as sighted people can. Finally, in a fascinating series of experiments, Kennedy asked people who had been blind from birth to portray the idea of movement. They accomplished the task in a number of ways. Some showed figures in postures of movement, such as a man with knees bent. Others represented movement abstractly instead of literally. One subject, for example, indicated that a figure of a man was running by drawing a line trailing behind one foot. Another drew a wheel with curved spokes (Kennedy, 1983).

Apparently, when blind people are cured, their initial sense impressions are very much like a newborn baby's—they see patches of brightness and darkness, but can barely perceive the details of objects. One blind man, who was cured at age 53, could not discern what a lathe was—although he had worked with one every day for years while blind—until he could touch and handle it. In the blind, touch appears to fill much of the void left by the lack of sight. It also seems that active blind people when they are cured learn to see more quickly than passive blind people.

Summary

1. *Perception* is creating meaningful sensory experiences out of raw sensory information. Perceptual experiences go beyond what is sensed and may even lead us to perceive objects that couldn't possibly exist.

2. Gestalt psychologists were the first to describe

some of the ways in which perceptions are created. A *figure* is distinguished from the *ground* against which it appears. In a *reversible figure* parts of the stimulus shift from being figure to being ground. The principle of *closure* refers to the tendency to overlook incompleteness in sensations and to perceive a whole object where none really exists. The concept of *continuity* states that objects that continue a pattern or a direction tend to be perceived as a group. Likewise, the principle of *proximity* supposes that objects seen or heard close together tend to be perceived as a group. The principle of *similarity* states that objects that look alike are perceived as part of a pattern. According to the principle of *common fate*, objects that are in motion together are perceived as distinct from the objects around them.

3. *Perceptual constancy* refers to the tendency to perceive objects as relatively stable and unchanging, despite changing sensory information. Experience seems to compensate for the changing sensory information, leading to *size constancy*, *shape constancy*, and *brightness* and *color constancy*.

4. Our desires and needs may strongly influence our perceptions. We tend to perceive things as we wish them to be. How an object is interpreted also depends on a person's values, expectations, cognitive style, and cultural background.

5. We can perceive *distance* or *depth* through *monocular cues*—from one eye—or *binocular cues*—which depend on the interaction of both eyes.

6. Monocular cues include *superposition, perspective, texture gradient, shadowing, movement, motion parallax,* and *accommodation*.

7. Binocular cues increase the accuracy of depth and distance perception. Each eye has a slightly different view of things. The difference between the images that the two eyes receive is called *retinal disparity*. Other binocular cues include *stereoscopic vision* and *convergence*.

8. Under special conditions the brain may ignore depth and distance cues and create an erroneous three-dimensional object that more closely matches our experience. This is called *binocular depth inversion*.

9. *Sound localization* is the ability to determine where a sound originates. *Monaural cues* such as loudness convey information about distance, while *binaural cues* such as discrepancies in arrival time of sound waves and their volume help to locate the source of a sound. Blind people are particularly adept at using sound cues to determine information about their environment.

10. Perception of *movement* is a complicated process involving both the visual messages from the retina and messages from the muscles around the eye as they shift to follow a moving object.

11. The perception of *real movement*—the physical displacement of an object from one position to another—seems to be determined chiefly by changes in the position of objects in relation to a background that is perceived as stationary.

12. *Apparent movement* involves the perception of movement in objects that are actually standing still. The *autokinetic illusion* refers to the apparent motion of a stationary object such as a point of light in a dark room. *Stroboscopic motion* is the apparent motion created by a rapid series of images of stationary objects such as in motion pictures. It is responsible for the perceptual illusion known as the *phi phenomenon*.

13. At times our senses mislead us into perceiving objects that cannot exist. *Visual* or *optical illusions* usually arise because misleading depth cues are hidden in the figure. Other illusions arise because the sensory information is ambiguous.

14. *Sensory deprivation* results from the radical reduction of sensory stimuli. It produces an altered state of consciousness, which can lead to hallucinations, altered perceptions, dreams, daydreams, and fantasies. Research indicates that hearing, touch, sensitivity to pain, and taste become more acute after sensory deprivation, while other sensory capacities are either unaffected or reduced.

15. *Altered states of consciousness* include sensory deprivation, meditation, hypnosis, daydreaming, sleep, dreaming, and drug-induced experiences.

16. *Meditation* can take many different forms. Suc-

cessful meditation produces deep relaxation and may be useful in reducing drug use and other problems.

17. Psychologists disagree about whether the trance induced by *hypnosis* is a true altered state of consciousness. Nonetheless, hypnosis has been shown to alter some people's perceptions and behavior.

18. Daydreaming allows you to escape from the demands of the real world and be somewhere else for the moment. Daydreams vary with personality and may be a way of processing "unfinished business" that is made possible by a reduction of external stimuli. There are three main patterns of daydreams. The first type reflects anxiety in the dreamer; the second reflects self-doubt and fear of failure; the third type reflects happier fantasies uncomplicated by guilt or anxiety.

19. Although its function remains unclear, *sleep* is a necessity. There are four stages of sleep. Stage 1 lasts only a few minutes and is a borderline between true sleep and waking. Sleep becomes progressively deeper in Stages 2 and 3. Stage 4, *delta sleep,* is the deepest stage. After Stage 4, *REM* (rapid eye movement) *sleep* begins. The other stages of sleep are referred to as *NREM* (nonrapid eye movement) *sleep.*

20. The sequence of sleep repeats itself four or five times per night, with Stage 2 taking up about half of total sleep time and REM about a quarter. Sleep patterns vary with age and are subject to disorders such as *insomnia, apnea,* and *narcolepsy.*

21. Dreams occur in both REM and NREM sleep, but are more frequent and detailed in REM sleep. Dreams reshape and re-create material into new and often illogical forms and can be a source of creative ideas. A dream may reflect the dreamer's unconscious wishes, needs, and conflicts. Most dreams last about as long as the actual events would in real life; internal and external stimuli can apparently modify dreams but not initiate them.

22. Thus far evidence shows that no real learning of complex material is possible during sleep. The need to dream appears to be less crucial than the need to sleep. People deprived of the effects of REM sleep appear to make up for it in NREM sleep or in waking life. REM sleep may also be a necessary part of emotional and cognitive processes.

23. The use of drugs to alter consciousness has a long history. The effect any drug has on consciousness depends on *set*—the person's state of mind at the time the drug is taken—and *setting*—the physical, social, and emotional atmosphere in which the drug is taken.

24. The most commonly used drug is alcohol. Alcohol is a depressant that can lessen a person's normal inhibitions, but has a temporary stimulating effect. Alcohol impairs some kinds of perception. The behavior of people who have been drinking is influenced by ideas about how drinkers should act as well as by the alcohol itself.

25. Marijuana, if used moderately, does not appear to cause mental and physical deterioration. Long-term use, however, may cause physical harm. Its effects include euphoria, a heightened sense of humor, impairment of short-term memory, heightened sensory sensitivity, increased visual imagery, and distortion of the sense of time.

26. Amphetamines produce feelings of optimism and boundless energy. Amphetamine use can become compulsive and may eventually lead to severe problems. Barbiturates are depressants and have the same potential as alcohol for creating physical and psychological dependence. Both amphetamines and barbiturates affect perception of time, self-perception, and memory.

27. Heroin use results in physical and psychological dependence. Its users become tolerant of the drug and need larger doses to achieve the same effects after using it for a period of time.

28. As a stimulant of the sympathetic nervous system, *cocaine* increases the heartbeat, raises blood pressure, and constricts the blood vessels. It also produces euphoria. Cocaine is not physically addictive, but compulsive use can cause loss of sleep, paranoia, and hallucinations.

29. The *hallucinogens* include LSD, mescaline, peyote, and psilocybin. They have a low dependence rate and rarely cause psychosis. Hallucinogens have profound effects on visual and auditory perception.

1. The process by which we create meaningful experiences out of the jumble of sensory information is called _____ .

2. It has been suggested by what school of psychology that the brain creates a whole perceptual experience that is much more than the sum of sensory "bits"?
   a. parapsychology   c. gestalt
   b. psychoanalytic   d. hypnagogic

3. In the case of reversible figures, we have difficulty distinguishing the _____ from the _____ behind it.

4. Match the following principles of perception with their definitions:

   ___ similarity
   ___ continuity
   ___ common fate
   ___ proximity
   ___ closure

   A. tendency to perceive a whole object even where none exists
   B. objects in motion together appear to stand out from their surroundings
   C. elements that continue a pattern are likely to be seen as part of the pattern
   D. objects that are like one another tend to be grouped together
   E. elements found close together tend to be perceived as a unit

5. The inclination to perceive objects as relatively stable and unchanging, despite changing sensory information, is known as _____ _____ .

6. A wide variety of monocular and binocular cues help us to perceive the _____ and _____ of objects.

7. Next to each depth cue, put B if it is a binocular cue and M if it is a monocular cue:

   ___ retinal disparity
   ___ texture gradient
   ___ shadowing
   ___ convergence
   ___ motion parallax
   ___ accommodation
   ___ stereoscopic vision
   ___ linear perspective
   ___ superposition

8. The perception of loud sounds being closer than faint sounds is a common monaural/binaural cue to sound localization.

9. Autokinetic illusion, stroboscopic motion, and phi phenomenon are three examples of _____ _____ .

10. Figures like the "two-pronged trident" are examples of _____ _____ , perceptual experiences that result from misleading depth or distance cues.

11. If the flow of sensory data is stopped, the following may be said to exist:
    a. hypnagogic state   c. meditation
    b. sensory deprivation   d. hypnosis trance

12. Meditation, sleep and dreaming, daydreaming, hypnosis, and drug intake are different ways of experiencing a(n) _____ _____ .

13. While _____ is the inability to fall asleep, both _____ and _____ are conditions that result in too much sleepiness.

14. The deepest stage of sleep, marked by slow, even brain waves, is REM/delta sleep.

15. We need to dream at night as much as we need to sleep. T/F

16. Match the following types of drugs with their descriptions:

    ___ alcohol
    ___ amphetamines
    ___ barbiturates
    ___ opiates
    ___ cocaine
    ___ hallucinogens

    A. produces feelings of optimism and boundless energy
    B. addictive drugs that dull the senses
    C. effects vary with quantity consumed, and manner and setting in which it is taken
    D. responsible for the most serious drug problem in the U.S. today
    E. causes profound effects on visual and auditory perception
    F. depressants that affect memory and perception of time

Outline

Motivation and Emotion

5

To see the manipulation of motivation and emotion at a sophisticated level, we might turn to a detective story. At the beginning, all we know is that a murder has been committed: After eating dinner with her family, sweet little old Miss Jones collapses and dies of strychnine poisoning. "Now, why would anyone do a thing like that?" everybody asks. The police ask the same question, in different terms: "Who had a *motive* for killing Miss Jones?" In a good mystery the answer is, "Practically everybody."

The younger sister—now 75 years old—still bristles when she thinks of the tragic day 50 years ago when Miss Jones stole her sweetheart. The next-door neighbor, a frequent dinner guest, has been heard to say that if Miss Jones's poodle tramples his peonies one more time, he will . . . The nephew, a major heir, is deeply in debt. The parlor maid has a guilty secret that Miss Jones knows. All four people were in the house on the night that Miss Jones was poisoned. And all four had easy access to strychnine, which was used to kill rats in Miss Jones's basement. All of these people also had emotional reactions to Miss Jones; envy, anger, shame, and guilt.

These are the first things that come to mind when we think of a murder mystery. But look at some of the day-to-day happenings in the same story. Motivated by hunger, the family gets together for meals. The next-door neighbor is lonely and visits because he wants company. The parlor maid's guilty secret involves her sex drive. The poodle's presence in the peonies may spring from its need to eliminate wastes or from sheer curiosity. When Miss Jones dies, the tragedy draws the family together; their need for affiliation makes them seek one another out. Yet they quickly become fearful; the drive for self-preservation makes each one wonder if the other is actually the killer. In all these less spectacular acts motivation and emotion are also present.

As we can see from the story of Miss Jones, motivation and emotion are closely related and distinctions between them are difficult to draw. A **motive** usually refers to a specific need, desire, or want that energizes and directs behavior toward some goal. **Emotion** usually refers to the experience of feelings such as fear, joy, surprise, and anger. Like motives, emotions also energize and affect behavior, although the goal is often less obvious than with motives. If someone is hungry, we can be reasonably

Motive A specific need, desire, or want, such as hunger, thirst, or achievement, that energizes and directs goal-oriented behavior.

Emotion A feeling, such as fear, joy, or surprise, that energizes and directs overt behavior.

149

Primary drive A physiologically based unlearned motive (e.g., hunger).

sure that person will seek out something to eat. But if someone is feeling joy or surprise, it is not always clear what the effect will be on that person's behavior.

The important thing about both motives and emotions is that they move us to some kind of action—whether it be as drastic as murder, or as mundane as drumming our fingers on a table because we are nervous. Motivation takes place whether we are aware of it or not. We do not have to know we are feeling hungry to go to the refrigerator, or to be aware of a need for achievement to study for an exam. We do not have to know we are feeling fearful to step back from a precipice, or know we are angry to raise our voice at someone. And the same motivation or emotion may produce different behaviors in people. Ambition might motivate one person to go to law school and another to join a crime ring. Feeling sad might lead one person to cry and another to seek out a friend. On the other hand, the same behavior may spring from different motives or emotions: You may buy liver because you like it, because it is cheap, or because your body "knows" that you need iron. You may go to a movie because you are happy, or depressed, or bored. The workings of motives and emotions can be very complex, as we shall see during the rest of this chapter. We begin by looking at different kinds of motives, and then turn our attention to emotions and how they are expressed.

Primary Drives

All motives are triggered by some kind of stimulus—a bodily need such as hunger or thirst, or a cue in the environment such as a picture of a juicy hamburger and a cool milkshake. When a motive is triggered, the result is goal-directed behavior, perhaps a trip to the nearest fast-food restaurant. Thus one or more stimuli create a motive, which in turn activates and directs behavior (see Figure 5-1). But motives differ in the kinds of stimuli that trigger them, as well as in the effects they have on behavior.

Some motives are unlearned and are common to every animal, including humans. These motives are called **primary drives.** Primary drives, such as hunger, thirst, and sex, are strongly influenced by stimuli from within the body. These stimuli are part of the biological arousal associated with the survival of the organism or, in the case of sex, the survival of the species. The behavior that results from primary drives is usually directed, at least in part, toward reducing the state of arousal. This behavior may be the result of learning, but the drives themselves are

Figure 5-1

A motive is triggered by some kind of stimulus—a bodily need or a cue in the environment. A motive, in turn, activates and directs behavior.

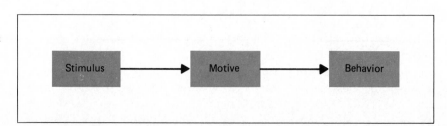

unlearned. Babies do not have to be taught to be hungry or thirsty, but they can learn to eat certain foods and drink certain liquids at certain times.

Glucose A simple sugar that is the main source of body energy.

Hunger

When you are hungry, you eat. If you cannot do so, your need for food will increase the longer you are deprived of it. But your appetite, your feeling of hunger, will not necessarily increase. Suppose you decide to skip lunch in order to play tennis. Your need for food will remain, nonetheless, and will increase throughout the day. But your hunger will come and go. You will probably be hungry around lunchtime; then your hunger will probably decrease during the tennis game. But it is likely that by dinnertime no concern will seem as pressing as getting something into your stomach. The psychological state of hunger, then, is not the same thing as the biological need for food, although it is often set in motion by biological processes.

We now know that two centers in the brain control hunger. One, the *hunger center,* stimulates eating, while the other, the *satiety center* ("satiety" means being full to satisfaction), reduces the feeling of hunger. Both centers are located in a part of the brain called the hypothalamus.

Since the 1950s scientists have learned more about how these two centers function. If the neurons in either center are stimulated, the neurons in the other center will fire less often. Thus, if your hunger center "tells" you that you are hungry, you will get few signals from the satiety center to contradict this message (see Figure 5-2). It has also been discovered that these two centers alone do not regulate hunger. Neurons that pass through the hunger and satiety centers to other parts of the brain also have some influence. So does another part of the brain near the hypothalamus, called the amygdala, but its exact role has not been precisely defined (Rosenzweig & Leiman, 1982).

How do these areas of the brain "know" when to signal hunger? It appears that the brain monitors the level of a simple sugar called **glucose** in the blood. When the level of glucose falls, nerves in the hunger center are stimulated, while those in the satiety center are inhibited. An increase in the level of fats in the blood as the body draws down reserve

An external cue like the sight of a pizza truck can trigger the hunger drive at almost any time of day.

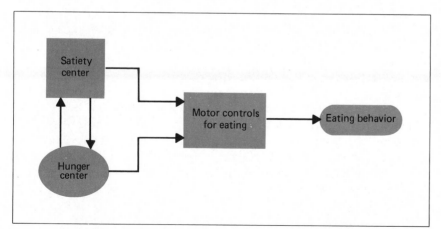

Figure 5-2

A diagram of the dual mechanisms in the brain that control hunger and eating. The hunger center signals when you are hungry and stimulates eating. The satiety center reduces the feeling of hunger and the desire to eat.

There's More to Being Fat Than Consuming Calories

Fitness is America's obsession; people now worry about cellulite the way they used to worry about crabgrass. Thin is in, and the generous proportions so admired in the past by artists like Rubens and Renoir are decidedly not chic today.

But unfashionable or not, many people *are* overweight, and some are heavy enough to be considered obese. Why do people become fat? It is not simply that they eat too many calories. Two similarly active people can consume exactly the same number of calories, yet one will gain weight and the other will not (Rodin, 1981). The causes of obesity are many and complex, and they underscore the idea that eating is more than a simple response to a chemical imbalance in the blood.

In part, biological factors can contribute to being overweight. Some people are born with an oversupply of fat cells—a condition that increases the body's ability to store excess calories. Heredity can also cause abnormalities in regulation of digestion and energy storage.

Eating experiences early in life also influence body weight. People who were overfed as babies may retain fat cells that stay with them in later life through thick and thin. Bad eating habits learned as a child may also persist into adulthood. Yesterday's child with a hand constantly in the cookie jar may become today's obese adult—still with a hand constantly in the cookie jar.

Sociocultural forces also play a role in body weight. A higher proportion of poor people than well-to-do people are fat. This may be due in part to stronger social pressure on wealthier people to conform to norms of thinness, and in part to eating patterns among subcultures of the poor that contribute to obesity.

Finally, psychologists have proposed several theories of obesity that focus on sensitivity to internal and external hunger cues. One of the most influential of these is the so-called internal-external hypothesis put forth by Schachter (1971a, 1971b). According to Schachter, overweight people are less sensitive than people of normal weight to internal signals of hunger such as hunger pangs and low blood sugar. Because they have a hard time distinguishing when they are hungry from when they are not, fat people have less control over how much they eat. In addition, Schachter argues that fat people are unusually sensitive to environmental cues related to food, and that their eating is mainly controlled by these cues. Stimuli such as the sight and smell of food can trigger hunger in all of us, but Schachter believes that fat people are particularly vulnerable to such cues.

More recent research casts some doubt on parts of Schachter's theory. Most people, not just fat people, have difficulty interpreting internal body signals to determine how much food their bodies really need (Speigel, 1973; Wooley, 1971). Moreover, the experiments showing that obese people are more sensitive to external food cues have proved hard to reproduce. And when the results have been reproduced, the relationship between weight and sensitivity to external food cues has proved weak. Still, sensitivity to external cues does seem to contribute to obesity, even though many people who are sensitive to these cues do not become fat. The reason is that all of the other causes mentioned earlier can increase or reduce the amount of eating and weight gain as well (Rodin, 1981).

---

energy supplies appears to have the same effect (Rosenzweig & Leiman, 1982).

The brain also monitors the amount and kind of food you have eaten. Receptors in the stomach apparently can sense not only how much food it holds but also how many calories the food contains. A stomach full of salad is far less satisfying than a stomach full of filet mignon with all the trimmings. Signals from these receptors are sent to the brain, where they stimulate the satiety center, with the result that you feel less hungry. In addition, there is some evidence that when food enters the small intestine, a hormone is released into the bloodstream, which carries it to the brain, where it also stimulates the satiety center (Smith & Gibbs, 1976).

These hunger mechanisms regulate our day-to-day intake of food. But there appears to be yet another hunger regulator, one that operates on a long-term basis to regulate the body's weight. With the exception of humans and some domesticated animals, very few animals ever become grossly overweight. The body seems to have a way of monitoring its own fat stores and regulating the intake of food to provide just enough energy to maintain normal activities without storing up excessive fat deposits (Kennedy, 1953).

As we mentioned earlier, hunger need not stem from nutritional requirements alone. External cues like the smell of a cake baking in the oven or the sight of golden brown french-fried potatoes can trigger the hunger drive at almost any hour of the day. In fact, sometimes just looking at the clock and realizing it is dinnertime can make us hungry. Psychologists have discovered recently that cells in the hypothalamus of hungry monkeys respond to the sight of foods (Rosenzweig & Leiman, 1982). The discovery of similar cells in the human brain might explain in part why the mere sight of food can make us hungry.

The response to hunger also varies greatly with the experience of the eater. For example, most people learn to eat three meals a day at more or less regular intervals, and to a large extent what they choose to eat is governed by learning. Most Americans, for example, love milk, but the Chinese have a strong aversion to it (Balagura, 1973). A cola drink may provide both the sweetness of orange juice and the stimulation of coffee, but you would probably not choose to have it with bacon and eggs for breakfast. Emotions can also affect hunger. You may be starving when you sit down at the table, but then hear about a traffic accident that "turns off" your desire to eat. Social factors can make a meal a ceremony, and elaborate rituals have grown up around the offering and accepting of food.

All types of social occasions have grown up around the offering and acceptance of food—from the informal American picnic to the ritualized Japanese tea ceremony.

"Ammonia! Ammonia!"

Drawing by R. Grossman; © 1962 The New Yorker Magazine, Inc.

Thirst

The physiology of thirst is very similar to that of hunger. When you are hungry, your stomach growls. Similarly, when you are thirsty, your mouth is dry and your throat feels scratchy. However, as we have seen with hunger, the thirst drive goes much deeper than that. It is controlled by two delicate balances within the body: the level of fluids outside the body's cells and the level of fluids inside the body's cells.

One thirst regulator monitors the level of fluid inside the cells of the body. Salt causes water to leave the body's cells, and a high level of salt in the blood would therefore cause the cells to become dehydrated. When the level of sodium in the blood reaches a certain point, indicating that the tissues need more water, a thirst center in the hypothalamus is stimulated, which activates the thirst drive. We drink until we have consumed enough fluid to restore water to our tissues, but scientists do not fully understand how we know when to stop drinking (Rosenzweig & Leiman, 1982). Normally we stop drinking long before the new supply of water makes its way to the tissues. One theory is that receptor cells in the small intestine send a message to the brain when we have consumed enough liquid (Rolls, Wood, & Rolls, 1980).

Scientists believe that a second thirst regulator monitors the amount of fluid outside the body's cells. When the level of extracellular fluid drops, less blood flows to the kidneys. The kidneys react by releasing a substance into the bloodstream, which carries it to the brain, where it triggers the thirst drive (Epstein, Fitzsimmons, & Simons, 1969). Under normal conditions, the two regulators appear to interact and to strengthen each other, although either can function alone if the other is damaged.

Learned, individual, and cultural factors can also affect how we respond to the thirst drive. On a hot summer day, seeing a glass of lemonade can make us feel thirsty. And what we drink is greatly affected by learning and experience. Water is water, but in chic restaurants people pay $2 a glass for water imported from France. Some people avoid coffee, having been raised to believe that stimulants are harmful. And as magazine advertisements indicate, our self-image may be linked to what we choose to drink: One beer is said to appeal to a "man's thirst," another to someone who wants to "stay on the light side."

Sex

Like hunger and thirst, sex is a primary drive. It gives rise to reproductive behavior. Like other drives, it can be turned on and off both by biological conditions in the body and by environmental cues. Erotic fantasies, the sight of our lover, the smell of perfume or after-shave lotion—all of these can arouse sexual excitement. As with other drives, experience shapes our response to the sexual drive. Ideas about what is moral, appropriate, and pleasurable help determine our sexual behavior. As much as sex resembles other drives in these respects, it differs from them in one important way: Hunger and thirst are vital to the survival of the individual, but sex is vital only to the survival of the species.

BIOLOGICAL FACTORS IN AROUSAL. The sex drive is powerfully affected by hormones, the chemical messengers secreted into the bloodstream by the various endocrine glands.* The circulatory system carries hormones to the sites in the body where they act. For both men and women, **testosterone** is the major biological influence on the sex drive (Masters, Johnson, & Kolodny, 1982). A decline in the level of testosterone in either men or women can lead to a drop in sexual desire. Men may have difficulty in getting and sustaining an erection (Kolodny, Masters, & Johnson, 1979). Too much testosterone, on the other hand, spurs intense interest in sex. It is important to keep in mind, however, that testosterone level does not completely determine sexual desire. Despite low testosterone levels, some people maintain an active interest in sex. As we'll see, in humans psychological influences are at least as important as biological factors.

The possibility also exists that the sex drive in human beings, as in other animals, may be affected by subtle smells. Many animals have been found to secrete substances called **pheromones** that, when smelled by the opposite sex, affect sexual readiness. Some evidence indirectly suggests that humans may secrete such pheromones through the sweat glands of their armpits as well as from the genitals (Le Magnen, 1952; Michael et al., 1974). Researchers are far from agreed, however, that pheromones actually exist in humans and affect their sexual response.

The nervous system also exerts controls over the sex drive. Once sexual arousal begins, stimulation of the genitals and other parts of the body becomes important. In the male, signals are sent to an "erection center" located at the bottom of the spinal cord. This center in turn sends neural messages to muscles that control an erection. A similar reflex center higher in the spine stimulates ejaculation, except that this process is subject to some voluntary control. Little is known so far about how similar mechanisms may affect the sexual drive in women (Hyde, 1982).

Not surprisingly, the brain exerts a powerful influence on the sex drive. Just how the brain affects sex remains unclear, although some evidence suggests that the limbic system, located deep in the brain, influences sexual excitement.† When experimenters implanted electrodes in the limbic system of male monkeys, they located three areas that when stimulated caused erections (Hyde, 1982). Two human subjects who had electrodes placed in their limbic systems for therapeutic reasons reported intense sexual pleasure when the electrodes were electrically stimulated (Heath, 1972).

PSYCHOLOGICAL INFLUENCES ON SEXUAL MOTIVATION. In both human beings and other animals the sex drive is affected by hormones and by the nervous system. But human sexual motivation, especially in the early stages of excitement and arousal, is much more dependent on experience and learning. In fact, the number of stimuli that can activate and shape the sex drive in humans is almost infinite.

What kind of stimulus can have this effect? It need not be anything

Testosterone Hormone that is the primary determinant of the sex drive in both men and women.

Pheromones Substances secreted by some animals that, when scented, enhance the sexual readiness of the opposite sex.

---

*The endocrine system is discussed in detail in Chapter 2.
†See Chapter 2 for a more detailed discussion of the limbic system.

Sexual dysfunction The loss or impairment of the ordinary physical responses of sexual function.

as immediate as a sexual partner. People respond sexually to fantasies, pictures, words, and to things they see, touch, or hear. Magazines stress the aphrodisiac effects of soft lights and music. One person may be unmoved by an explicit pornographic movie, but aroused by a romantic love story, while another may respond in just the opposite way. Popular music captures some of the many things that can be sexually attractive. The Beatles sang about "something in the way she moves." Fred Astaire told Audrey Hepburn, "I love your funny face." And Cole Porter admired "the way you sing off-key." Human sexual response is also affected by social experience, sexual experience, nutrition, emotions—particularly feelings about one's sex partner—and age. In fact, just thinking about or having fantasies about sex can trigger the sex drive in humans.

Some systematic research has been done on sexual stimuli, including erotic material. Given equal opportunity to view or hear erotic materials, men and women respond to them similarly. Both men and women are aroused by explicit material. One study demonstrated this by exposing sexually experienced college students to tape recordings with four kinds of content: (1) explicit descriptions of heterosexual sex; (2) romantic expressions of affection, but no sex; (3) romantic expressions of affection and explicit descriptions of sex; and (4) a control tape containing only neutral conversation. Both men and women found the tapes with explicit contents (tapes 1 and 3) the most arousing. Those in which women initiated the activity were most arousing to both sexes. And both sexes responded physiologically to the tapes (Heiman, 1977). Although men and women are equally arousable by explicit material, and although neither sex is partial to a particular medium—whether it be words, photographs, movies, or tapes (Byrne, 1977)—men and women tend to prefer different kinds of content. Men seem to favor closeups of sexual behavior, while women respond to details of style, setting, and mood (Masters, Johnson, & Kolodny, 1982).

SEXUAL DYSFUNCTION. Loss of sexual drive can come from both biological and psychological sources. About 10 to 20 percent of such cases of **sexual dysfunction** are caused by physical problems. Diseases affecting the circulatory system, diabetes, or damage to the spinal erection center may undermine a man's ability to have an erection. Fatigue can have the same effect. Similarly, severe illness, fatigue, and depression sometimes contribute to sexual dysfunction in women. Most sexual dysfunction, however, comes from psychological sources. Because their sex drive is so strongly influenced by psychological factors, humans are uniquely vulnerable to sexual problems. In some cases the sex drive is reduced by things a person has learned about sex in the past, while in other cases the cause is to be found in events that occurred during a particular sexual encounter (Kaplan, 1974). Sometimes as the result of a traumatic event such as rape, attempted seduction by kin, or punishment by parents for sexual activity, a person may learn to associate fear or anxiety with sex, and these emotions can interfere with sexual motivation. A fear of failure, blocking out of erotic sensations, lack of communication between partners about what is pleasurable, hostility toward one's mate, or fear of the intimacy that sexual contact brings can all lead to reduction in sexual drive (Hyde, 1982). Sexual dysfunctions will be discussed further in Chapter 14.

Stimulus motives seem to be largely unlearned, but in all species these motives depend even more on external stimuli—things in the world around us—than primary drives do. Moreover, unlike the primary drives, their main function extends beyond the bare survival of the organism or species to a much less specific end—dealing with information about the environment in general. Motives such as *activity, curiosity, exploration, manipulation,* and *contact* push us to investigate, and often to change, the environment. Most often, external stimuli set these motives in action. We, in turn, respond with stimulus-seeking behavior.

Activity

People need to be active. Most people get bored when they are confined to a small space with nothing to do: They wander around, drum their fingers on the table, or study the cracks in the wall. Of course, age, sex, health, genetic makeup, and temperament affect the need for *activity* to various degrees. One person may be comfortable sitting in the same position for hours, while another may begin to fidget in 5 minutes.

Although all animals need activity, scientists are not sure if it is a motive in itself or a combination of other motives. Most of the experiments to determine if there is a separate "activity motive" have been done with rats. A rat put into a cage so small that it cannot move around will be more active than normal when it is released (Hill, 1956). But before we conclude that activity is an unlearned motive, we should consider other experiments. Food deprivation increases activity, but running is affected more than other types of restless behavior (pawing, climbing, moving around aimlessly). Experiments with female rats (Wang, 1923) show that peak activity coincides with peak sexual receptivity. So it is still unclear whether the need for activity is a separate motive by itself or simply the result of other motives.

Exploration and Curiosity

Where does that road go? What is that dark little shop? How does a television set work? What is that tool used for? Answering these questions has no obvious benefit for you. You do not expect the road to take you anywhere you need to go, or the shop to contain anything you really want. You are not about to start a TV-repair service or use an unknown tool. You just want to *know.* Exploration and curiosity appear to be motives activated by the new and unknown and directed toward no more specific goal than "finding out." Even animals will learn a behavior just to be allowed to explore the environment. The family dog will run around a new house, sniffing and checking things out, before it settles down to eat its dinner.

Animals also seem to prefer complexity, presumably because more complex forms take longer to know and are therefore more interesting

Stimulus motive An unlearned motive, such as curiosity or activity, that depends more on external stimuli than on internal physiological states.

This monkey showed stimulus-seeking behavior in learning to unlock a window with a novel view of an electric train on the other side.

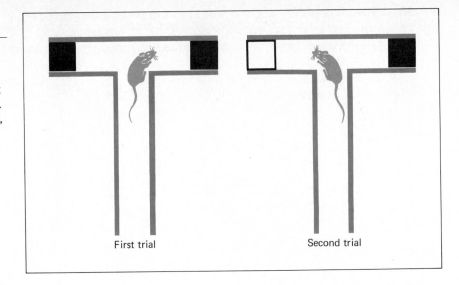

Figure 5-3
On the first trial, a rat explores either one of the black arms of the maze at random. On the second trial, however, given a choice between a black arm and an arm of another color, a rat will consistently choose the unfamiliar one.
(After W. N. Dember, 1965)

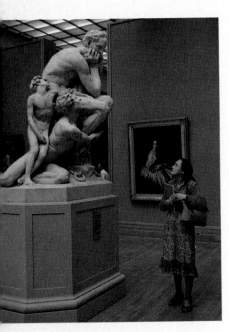

Stimulus motives depend on external stimuli to push us to investigate the new and unknown.

(Dember, Earl, & Paradise, 1957). Placed in a maze that is painted black, a rat will explore it and learn its way around. The next time, given a choice between a black maze and a white one, it will choose the white one (Dember, 1965). Apparently the unfamiliarity of the unknown maze has more appeal. The rat seems to be curious to see what the new one is like (see Figure 5-3).

There are, of course, reservations. At times we have all found the unknown more distressing than stimulating, or found something—an argument, a symphony, or a chess game—too complex for us. A young child accustomed only to her parents may withdraw from a new face and scream with terror if that face has a beard. Unusual clothing or a radical piece of art or music may be rejected, scorned, or even attacked. But here again, learning is important. Familiarity may change the face, the clothing, or the symphony from the unacceptable to the novel and interesting. A child who at age 2 is only up to "Three Blind Mice" welcomes the complexity of a popular song at age 12, and perhaps of a Mozart string quartet at age 22. As we learn—and as we continually explore our environment—we raise our threshold for the new and complex, and our explorations and our curiosity become much more ambitious.

Manipulation

Why do you suppose that museums have "Do Not Touch" signs everywhere? It is because the staff *knows* from experience that the urge to touch is irresistible. Unlike curiosity and exploration, manipulation is directed toward a specific object that must be touched, handled, played with, and felt before we are satisfied. Manipulation is a motive that seems to be limited to primates, which have agile fingers and toes.

The desire to manipulate seems to be related to two things: a need to know about something at a tactile level, and sometimes a need to be soothed. The Greek "worry beads"—a set of beads on a short string that are moved back and forth during a conversation—are examples of this

Is Work a Stimulus Motive?

Studies suggest that rats, pigeons, and children sometimes work to gain rewards even if they can get the same rewards without working (D'Amato, 1974):

> Rats will run down an alley tripping over hundreds of food pellets to obtain a single, identical pellet in the goal box, . . . and pigeons will peck a key, even on intermittent schedules of reinforcement, to get exactly the same food that is freely available in a nearby cup. Given the option of receiving marbles merely by waiting an equivalent amount of time for their delivery, children tend to prefer to press a lever . . . to get the same marbles. (p. 95)

Why would animals or humans work for food or other rewards when they can get the same payoff without working? Isn't there an inherent tendency to "freeload"? Apparently just the opposite is true: There seems to be an inherent need to work. Both animals and people prefer to earn their rewards. In fact, external rewards may even undermine the *intrinsic* motivation to perform a task. In one experiment monkeys manipulated puzzles without any reward until the puzzles were baited with a raisin. Once they realized they could get a raisin by manipulating a puzzle, the monkeys lost interest in the unbaited puzzle (de Charms, 1968).

Why would people and animals prefer to work for their rewards? Working for rewards may help us to control our environment. Such control is necessary for survival and is basic in both animals and human beings. In a number of experiments animals that could not control their rewards and punishments became passive, apathetic, and simply "gave up." This "learned helplessness" has recently received considerable attention as an explanation for some cases of severe depression (see Chapter 13).

second type of manipulation. Under stress, people "fiddle" with a cigarette, a paper napkin, a fountain pen. Children are always manipulating the objects around them. Eyeglasses, earrings, flowers, dogs' tails—everything must be touched and played with. The brighter the object, the more mixed its colors, the more irregular its shape, the more appealing it is as a potential object for manipulation.

Contact

People also want to touch other people. The need for contact is broader and more universal than the need for manipulation. Furthermore, it is not limited to touching with the fingers—it can involve the whole body. Manipulation is active, but contact can be passive.

In a famous series of experiments (Harlow, 1958; Harlow & Zimmerman, 1959) newborn baby monkeys were separated from their mothers and given two "surrogate mothers." Both were the same shape, but one was made of wire and offered no soft surfaces. The other was cuddly—layered with foam rubber and covered with terry cloth. A nursing bottle was put in the wire "mother," and both "mothers" were warmed by means of an electric light placed inside them. Thus the wire "mother" fulfilled two physiological drives for the infant monkeys: the need for food and the need for warmth. But it was to the terry-cloth "mother," which did not provide food, that the babies went. When they were frightened, they would run and cling to it as they would to a real mother. Since both mothers were warm, it seems that the need for affection, cuddling, and closeness goes deeper than a need for mere warmth.

An infant monkey with Harlow's "surrogate mothers"—one made of wire, the other covered with terrycloth. The monkey clings to the terrycloth "mother," even though the wire "mother" provides both food and warmth.

Learned Motives

Social motive Learned motive associated with relationships among people, such as needs for affiliation, achievement, and power.

Aggression Behavior aimed at doing harm to others; also the motive to behave aggressively.

We are not born with all our motives intact. We have already seen that even motives that appear to be unlearned—such as hunger, thirst, and sex—are actually learned in part. As we develop, our behavior becomes governed by new motives that are almost entirely learned. Although these new motives are learned rather than innate, they can exert just as much control over our behavior as unlearned drives and motives do.

One very important learned motive is aggression. Another major class of learned motives, **social motives,** centers around our relationships with other people. We will first look at aggression and then consider some of the most important of these social motives.

Aggression

Aggression in human beings includes all behavior that is intended to inflict physical or psychological harm on others. Intent is an important element of aggression (Beck, 1978). If you accidentally hit a pedestrian with your car, you have inflicted harm, but without intent to do so. If, however, you spot the man who mugged you last week and try to hit him with your car as he crosses the street, you are doing something intentionally harmful. This is an act of aggression.

Judging from the statistics, aggression is disturbingly common in America. In 1981, 22,500 people were murdered in the United States. Nonfatal violence in the family is also common. In a study of some 2,000 married couples in this country, investigators found that more than 25 percent of those questioned had engaged in some form of physical violence in their married lives (Straus, 1977). Frequently aggression is directed at children: Hundreds of thousands of children are known to be abused each year, and these are only the cases that are reported (Kempe & Kempe, 1978). Murder, violence in the family, and child abuse are easily recognized as acts of aggression. One that is not so obvious is rape, which is primarily motivated by aggression rather than sexuality. Rape is an expression of hate and the desire to inflict harm, not lust (Brownmiller, 1975). Like child abuse, rape is very common. The FBI estimates that about 500,000 rapes occur outside of marriage each year (Gager & Schurr, 1976).

Human aggression is so widespread that it appears to be an inevitable part of our existence. In fact, some ethologists believe exactly that: Aggression in humans is part of an unlearned instinct to kill and to destroy, a vestige of our primitive past (Lorenz, 1968).

Freud also believed that aggression is an innate drive, although he did not try to explain it in quite the same way as the ethologists. For Freud and his followers, the aggressive urge, like the sexual urge, arises from bodily processes and must be released periodically. If it is not released, aggression can cause tension, pain, and irrational behavior. Freud believed that one important function of society is to direct the expression of the aggressive drive into constructive and socially acceptable channels such as sports, debating, and various forms of competition.

People who behave aggressively are intending to inflict physical or psychological harm on others. In the U.S., aggression is disturbingly common within the family as well as among strangers.

Freud's ideas on aggression are still acknowledged. But most psychologists today believe that aggression is a learned response. Lazarus (1974) observed, for example, that there is no substantial research showing that people have a built-in, uncontrollable urge to fight and kill. Moreover, the evidence suggests that expressing aggression does not always reduce aggressiveness, as Freud would predict. There is some evidence that when angry people are encouraged to express aggression, they do in fact become less angry and aggressive. But nonangry people who are encouraged to express aggression are either unaffected by doing so or actually become more aggressive (Doob & Wood, 1972).

Other factors besides anger may play a part in releasing aggression. It appears that aggression may be triggered in part by frustration, especially when the frustration is unexpected or arbitrary. In one experiment members of a group became quite aggressive when someone seemed to be deliberately thwarting a task that had been assigned to the group. But they were much less aggressive when their work was impaired unintentionally (Worchel, 1974).

While studies such as this one indicate a link between frustration and aggression, this is not always the case. In response to frustration, some people seek help and support, others withdraw from the source of frustration, and some even escape into drugs or alcohol. In other words, it appears that frustration generates aggression only in those people who have learned to be aggressive as a means of coping with unpleasant situations (Bandura, 1973). Moreover, aggression may be learned as a response to a number of different stimuli. According to Berkowitz (1983), research indicates that almost any unpleasant event can lead to aggression. Foul odors, high room temperature, frightening information, irritating cigarette smoke, and disgusting scenes have all been found to increase hostility in human subjects. Thus frustration is only one of many types of unpleasant experiences that can provoke aggression.

According to both Bandura and Berkowitz, although the aggressive behavior of lower animals can be explained in terms of instinctual "drives," aggression in humans is learned. One important way of learning aggression is by observing aggressive models. For example, studies of parent-child relationships have consistently shown that children who are severely punished grow up to be aggressive adults prone to using violence themselves (Aronson, 1980). As we will discuss in Chapter 6, when punishing their children, parents may be serving as models of aggressive behavior and demonstrating how effective aggression can be.

But what if the aggressive model is itself not particularly effective or is even punished? The concept behind the ancient custom of public executions and punishments like flogging and stocks is that punishing a person for aggressive acts will deter others from committing those acts. In one study, one group of children was shown a film in which an aggressive character was punished. Another group was shown a film in which the character was rewarded for the same behavior. A third group watched a film with no violence in it at all. Then all the children were given the chance to act aggressively under circumstances like those depicted in the violent films. Those children who had seen the aggressive model being punished were less aggressive than those who had seen the aggressive model rewarded, but both groups of children were *more* aggressive than those who had seen *no* aggressive model at all. Simply seeing an ag-

Achievement motive The need to excel, to overcome obstacles; a social motive.

nAch Need for achievement (see Achievement motive).

gressive model seems to increase aggression among children, whether the model is punished or rewarded (Aronson, 1980).

Aggression can also be "unlearned." For example, aggression can be ignored and nonaggressive behavior rewarded. Davitz (1952) used this approach with two play groups of children. One was rewarded for constructive behavior, while the other was rewarded for aggressive behavior. Next, the children in both groups were deliberately frustrated, a situation that would ordinarily trigger aggression. The children who had been rewarded for constructive behavior were far less aggressive than the children in the other group.

These data support the idea that aggression is a learned motive. A number of important social motives also seem to be learned, and we turn to them now.

Achievement

Climbing Mount Everest "because it is there," sending rockets into space, making the dean's list, rising to the top of a giant corporation—all these actions probably have mixed underlying motives. But in all of them there is a desire to excel, "to overcome obstacles, to exercise power, to strive to do something difficult as well and as quickly as possible" (Murray, 1938, pp. 80–81). It is this interest in achievement for its own sake that leads psychologists to suggest a separate **achievement motive.**

As with all learned motives, need for achievement, or **nAch,** varies widely from person to person. McClelland (1958) has developed ways to measure *nAch* experimentally. One method uses responses from the Thematic Apperception Test (see Chapter 12). For example, one picture in the test shows an adolescent boy sitting at a classroom desk. A book lies open in front of him, but the boy's gaze is directed outward toward the viewer. Subjects are asked to make up stories about the picture. One person responded: "The boy in the picture is trying to reconcile the philosophies of Descartes and Thomas Aquinas—at the tender age of 18. He has read several books on philosophy and feels the weight of the world on his shoulders." Another response was in sharp contrast: "Ed is thinking of leaving home for a while in the hope that this might shock his parents into getting along." The first response comes from someone who scored high in the need for achievement, the second from someone who scored low (Atkinson & Birch, 1970; Atkinson & Raynor, 1975).

Why do some people have a high need for achievement? McClelland et al. (1953) suggest two reasons. First, as children, these people saw that their actions or efforts could change the world around them for the better. Second, the success of their actions was measured and reinforced by adult standards of excellence. Children who are exposed to such standards will soon learn how to tell a good performance from a bad one. They know that they will be praised for achievement and this leads to a desire to excel.

From tests and personal histories, psychologists have discovered some general traits of high *nAch* people. These people do best in competitive situations and are fast learners. They are driven less by the desire for fame or fortune than by the need to live up to a high, self-imposed standard of performance. They are self-confident, take on responsibility willingly,

and are relatively resistant to outside social pressures. They are energetic and let little obstruct their goals. But they are also apt to be tense and to have psychosomatic illnesses.

How does high *nAch* relate to occupational choice? In a study of 55 college graduates who were tested for achievement levels while in college, McClelland (1965) found that 83 percent of those who had high *nAch* scores went into "entrepreneurial occupations." (p. 389). These occupations, which include sales, owning and operating a business, management consulting, and the like, are marked by a high degree of risk and challenge, decision-making responsibility, and objective feedback on job performance. McClelland also found that 70 percent of those who chose professions that were not entrepreneurial had low *nAch* scores.

A desire to overcome hurdles is one mark of the achievement motive.

Avoidance of Success

Is there a motive to *avoid* success? According to Matina Horner (1969), both men and women develop the need to achieve, but women also develop a fear of success. Horner asked undergraduate men at the University of Michigan to finish a story that began: "After first-term finals, John finds himself at the top of his medical school class." Undergraduate women got the same story, but with "Anne" substituted for "John." Only about 10 percent of the men revealed doubt or fear about success. But the women worried about social rejection, picturing Anne as "acne-faced," lonely and dateless, and "unsexed."

Horner attributed this fear of success to how women are raised in our society. A girl grows up hearing women who achieve outside the home called "sexless," "unfeminine," or "hard," so that achievement—or the prospect of it—makes her feel guilty and anxious. Horner believes that unless these feelings can be resolved, women will not make full use of their opportunities.

Power motive The need to win recognition or to influence or control other people or groups; a social motive.

nPower Need for power (see Power motive).

Cultural stereotypes about appropriate sex roles for women may account for a learned motive to avoid success. But this may be changing as women observe more role models who demonstrate the value of achievement. Pictured here at the White House is Sandra Day O'Connor, the first woman Supreme Court justice.

Horner's work has received widespread publicity, but some of her methods and conclusions have been questioned. Tresemer (1974) noted the small size of Horner's sample and various inconsistencies and problems in the coding of fear of success (FOS). Tresemer was also skeptical of Horner's connection between FOS imagery and women's actual behavior. He claimed that Horner's work did not show that fear of success is a clear motive for the lack of achievement in many women. For example, nonachievement imagery in women subjects may represent "fear of sex-role inappropriateness" rather than "fear of success."

A more serious problem is that the situations that arouse the motive to avoid success have never been identified. Do the situations occur only when women compete with men, or only when sex roles are involved? Or is this motive aroused by any situation in which it is possible to succeed? Studies so far have been inconclusive (Zuckerman & Wheeler, 1975).

Interestingly, other studies using the "Anne" story showed that men rated high on FOS too. This indicates that men and women with high FOS may simply be responding to cultural stereotypes about appropriate sex roles (de Charms & Muir, 1978). Women may fear becoming doctors because "men are supposed to be doctors"; but men may fear becoming nurses or librarians because these activities are traditionally "women's work." These people may be less afraid of success than of reversing sex roles.

Whatever its cause, this fear of success may be changing. Using undergraduates from the University of Michigan once again, Hoffman (1974) repeated Horner's study several years later with some surprising results. She found that about 65 percent of the women showed fear of success—about the same percentage Horner found. However, 77 percent of the men also expressed this fear, a dramatic increase from Horner's study. Hoffman suggests that this turnaround may relate to men's questioning of the value of achievement—something they would have been less likely to do six years earlier. Moreover, the wide publicity that Horner's original study received may have influenced the subjects of the later studies (de Charms & Muir, 1978).

Power

Another important learned motive is the **power motive,** or need for power **(nPower).** The power motive may be defined as the need to win recognition or to influence or control other people or groups. Like the achievement motive, the power motive can be scored from stories written in response to pictures in the Thematic Apperception Test. Images that concern vigorous actions, behavior that greatly affects others, and interest in reputation or position lead to high scores on the power motive (Winter, 1973).

College students who are high on *nPower* tend to occupy "power positions" such as offices in student organizations, residence counseling positions, and membership on important committees. They tend to participate in sports involving direct contact between competitors. They also tend to be interested in such careers as teaching, psychology, and business (Beck, 1978).

Winter (1973) studied the power motives of 12 American presidents, from Theodore Roosevelt to Richard Nixon. He scored the concerns, aspirations, fears, and plans for action of each president as revealed in his inaugural speech. The highest scorers in terms of power drives were Theodore Roosevelt, Franklin Roosevelt, Harry Truman, Woodrow Wilson, John Kennedy, and Lyndon Johnson. Except for Theodore Roosevelt, all were Democrats, and all six men were action-oriented presidents. All also scored high in the need for achievement. By contrast, Republican presidents—such as Taft, Hoover, and Eisenhower—were more restrained and scored much lower in power motivation and in the need for achievement. Richard Nixon scored quite high in the need for achievement but relatively low in power motivation. According to Winter, the effect of this kind of mixed achievement/power score is a tendency to vacillate in the exercise of power. Winter (1976) studied Jimmy Carter when he was still a presidential candidate and found his power motive to be about average and his need to achieve somewhat above average—about the same as Theodore Roosevelt's. Winter suggests a number of interesting relationships between the power motive and specific presidential policy decisions and actions:

1. Those presidents in power when the country entered wars tended to score high on power motive.
2. Power motive scores of presidents seem to be related to the gain or loss of territory through wars, expansion, treaties, and independence struggles.
3. Presidents with high power motive scores tended to have the highest turnover in cabinet members during their administration.

Affiliation motive The need to be with others.

John F. Kennedy is among the six recent American presidents scoring highest on the power motive. Kennedy also scored high on the need for achievement.

Affiliation

Sometimes you want to get away from it all—to spend an evening or a weekend alone, reading, thinking, or just being by yourself. But generally, people have a need for affiliation, a need to be with other people. If people are isolated from social contact for a long time, they may become anxious. Why do people seek one another out? How are groups formed, and why does a handful of isolated people become a group?

For one thing, the **affiliation motive** is aroused when people feel threatened. Esprit de corps—the feeling of being part of a sympathetic group—is important among troops going into a battle. A football coach's pregame pep talk is also important to the team. Both are designed to make people feel they are working for a common cause or against a common foe.

Often affiliation behavior results from another motive entirely. For example, you may give a party to celebrate getting a job because you want to be praised for your achievement. It has also been suggested that fear and anxiety are closely linked to the affiliation motive. When rats, monkeys, or humans are put in anxiety-producing situations, the presence of a member of the same species who is not anxious will reduce the fear of the anxious one. If you are on a plane during a bumpy flight and are nervous, you may strike up a conversation with the calm-looking woman sitting next to you because the erratic flight of the plane does not seem to be worrying her.

Unconscious Motives

A new car is advertised, and a man decides he would like to own one. Why? He may tell you that his old car was running down and this one looks "pretty good" to him. But there may be other reasons why he wants this new car of which he is unaware.

Theories of *unconscious motivation* vary. Freud's is probably the most extreme. Freud believed that every act—however trivial—derives from a host of unconscious motives. A Freudian might see the man's choice of car as the desire to conquer a sexual object—a desire encouraged by advertisements touting it as "sleek," "purring," and "packed with power." Freudian theory also proposes aggression as a possible reason—the man may feel a need to zoom down Main Street with as much horsepower as possible under his control.

Some psychologists maintain not only that behavior is influenced by unconscious motives, but also that some kinds of behavior occur *only* when we are unaware of our motives (Brody, 1980). This is in line with the Freudian theory of the unconscious.

But we do not need to explain all acts in Freudian terms to realize that they can spring from unconscious motives. The man who buys a certain car may be expressing a desire for social approval—"Be the first one on your block to own one!"—or he may be rewarding himself for hard work. He could be trying to bolster a sagging self-image, or he could be consoling himself for the loss of a promotion or a girlfriend.

It should be emphasized that unconscious motives are not a particular *class* of motives, as physiological, learned, and stimulus motives are. As we pointed out in the discussion of physiological drives, we do not have to be aware of hunger and thirst to act to satisfy them. An unconscious motive is one that we are acting to satisfy without quite knowing why.

It is difficult to learn about unconscious motives because we have to rely on what people *say* about their motives. For example, when people report their motives they are recalling something that has already occurred, and their memories may be inaccurate. People may also experience things on different levels of consciousness, and these experiences may be too subtle to put into words.

In one experiment, for example, people were hypnotized and told that they would experience no pain. Subsequently they said they had felt no pain, but other behaviors indicated that they were indeed suffering (Hilgard, 1973, 1977).

How does the motive for affiliation develop in people? Many conclusions are still tentative, but the desire to be with others clearly goes back to the family, the first group we were ever in. It has been found (Sarnoff & Zimbardo, 1961) that firstborn or only children have stronger affiliation motives than those born later, perhaps because they were used to receiving more parental attention during their early years. People who were brought up to be dependent, or who were raised with close family ties, show stronger affiliation motives than those whose families encouraged early independence.

A Hierarchy of Motives

You have probably noted that our discussion has gradually moved from primitive motives, shared by all creatures, to motives that are more sophisticated, complex, and human. Maslow (1954) arranged all motives in such a hierarchy, from lower to higher. The lower motives are relatively simple: They spring from bodily states that *must* be satisfied. As the

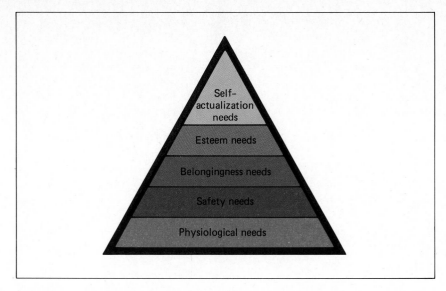

Figure 5-4
A pyramid representing Maslow's hierarchy of emotions. From bottom to top, the stages correspond to how fundamental the motive is for survival and how early it appeared in both the evolution of the species and the development of the individual. According to Maslow, the more basic motives must be satisfied before higher motives can appear.
(After A. H. Maslow, 1954)

motives become higher, they arise from other things: the desire to live as comfortably as possible in our environment, to deal as well as we can with other human beings, and to make the best impression on others that we can. Maslow's hierarchy of motives is shown in Figure 5-4.

According to Maslow's theory, higher motives appear only after the more basic ones have been satisfied. This is true on both an evolutionary and an individual scale. If you are starving, you will probably not care what people think of your table manners.

Maslow believed that the most highly "evolved" motive in the hierarchy is self-actualization. This may be described as a desire to make the best one can out of oneself. It does not concern the respect of other human beings and their judgments of us, but rather what we ourselves want to be. People differ in how important self-actualization is in their behavior, but to some extent all of us are motivated to live according to what is necessary for our personal growth. The people who are the most self-actualizing, Maslow said, think of themselves as whole beings, not as parcels of hunger, fear, ambition, and dependency.

Although Maslow's hierarchy theory is useful as a way of thinking about motives, it is extremely difficult to test (Wahba & Bridwell, 1976). Research has questioned in particular the evidence supporting the classification of human needs into five separate categories, and the placement of these categories in a hierarchical structure.

Emotions

In the first part of this chapter we saw that motives can both arouse and direct our behavior. Emotions do the same. "She shouted for joy," we say, or, "I was so angry I could have strangled him." The fact that emotions arouse and shape behavior provides a rich source of profits for advertising

Figure 5-5

Graph illustrating the Yerkes-Dodson Law. A certain amount of arousal is needed to perform, but a very high level of arousal interferes with performance. The level of arousal that can be tolerated is higher for a simple task than for a complex one. (After Hebb, 1955)

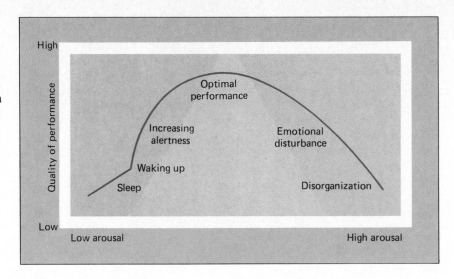

agencies. By manipulating our emotions, advertisers can get us to buy everything from cars to mouthwash.

To some extent, we can classify emotions in terms of whether they cause us to turn to or away from objects (Arnold, 1960). On this basis, there appear to be three fundamental categories of emotion. Imagine that you overhear this conversation among three people whose television set has just gone out during a midsummer thunderstorm:

A. Just when the movie was getting good! I've wanted to see it for years, and now *this* happens. (*Fiddles with set, to no avail, and switches it off disgustedly.*) Things like this always happen at the worst time. It makes me furious.

B. I *hate* thunderstorms, I always have. Don't you think we ought to turn off all the lights so we won't attract the lightning? My grandmother used to hide in a closet till it stopped, and I don't blame her. She used to say it was God's vengeance for our sins.

C. (*Going to window.*) Look at it, it's fantastic—the way the blue flashes light up everything. It makes the whole world different. I've always loved thunderstorms—they're so wild and happy. They make me feel liberated and crazy.

"A" is frustrated and angry. This category of emotions moves us to approach something, but in an aggressive or hostile way. "B" is fearful and anxious. These emotions make us want to avoid something. "C" is happy and experiencing a sense of release and joy. These emotions make us want to approach something in a positive way.

But emotions, like motives, can begin a chain of fairly complex behavior that goes far beyond simple approach or avoidance. If we are anxious about something, for instance, we may collect information about it, ask questions, and then decide whether to approach it, to flee from it, or to stay and fight it. Leeper (1948) gives the example of a family that heard an arsonist was in their neighborhood. First the family saw how the situation related to them, finding that one of their rooms was a firetrap. Next they learned about possible protective devices and had them installed. Their anxiety about fire focused their performance.

Sometimes our emotions seem like uninvited guests. Most of us have been in situations where we desperately wanted to think rationally but could not because our emotions had disrupted our concentration. Under what circumstances does emotion hinder what we do, and when does it help? There seems to be no single, simple answer. It is largely a question of degree—of both the strength of the emotion and the difficulty of the task. The **Yerkes-Dodson law** puts it this way: The more complex the task, the lower the level of emotion that can be tolerated without interfering with performance. You may feel very angry while boiling an egg, and it may not make much difference, but the same degree of emotion may interfere with your ability to drive safely. Moreover, although a certain minimum level of emotional arousal is necessary for good performance, a very high level may affect your performance for the worse (see Figure 5-5).

Yerkes-Dodson law States that the more complex the task, the lower the level of emotion that can be tolerated before performance deteriorates.

Basic Emotional Experiences

As we saw earlier, emotions can be broadly grouped according to how they affect our behavior—whether they motivate us to approach or to avoid something. But within these broad groups, how many different emotions are there?

One of the most influential attempts to identify and classify emotions was made by Robert Plutchik (1980). He proposed that animals and

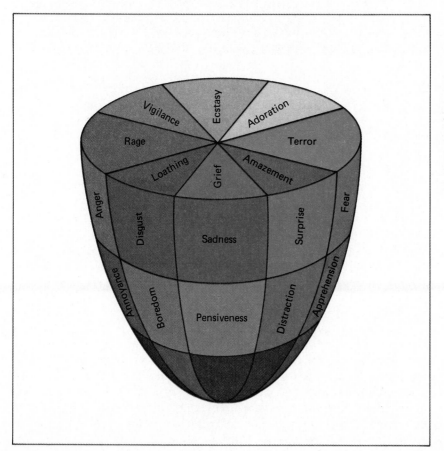

Figure 5-6

Robert Plutchik identifies eight basic categories of emotions. Emotions that lie next to one another on his emotion "circle" are more similar than those that lie opposite one another or are further apart. When adjacent emotions are combined, they yield new but related emotions. For example, sadness mixed with surprise leads to disappointment. (R. Plutchik, 1962)

Figure 5-7

Plutchik's three-dimensional model of the eight basic emotions. Within any of the categories emotions vary in intensity. Intensity is represented on the vertical dimension of the model, ranging from maximum intensity at the top to a state of deep sleep at the bottom. The model tapers inward at the bottom to indicate that emotions are less clearly distinguishable from one another at low intensities.
(R. Plutchik, 1980)

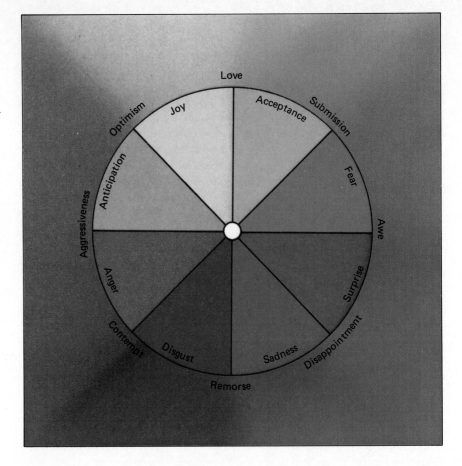

human beings experience eight basic categories of emotions that help to motivate various kinds of adaptive behavior. Fear, surprise, sadness, disgust, anger, anticipation, joy, and acceptance each help us to adjust to the demands of our environment, though in different ways. Terror, for example, is related to flight, which helps protect animals from their enemies, while rage is related to attack or destruction.

Emotions that lie next to each other on the "circle" are more similar than those that lie opposite each other, or that are farther away from each other (see Figure 5-6). Amazement is more similar to terror than to rage. Ecstasy and adoration are more similar to each other than either is to loathing. Moreover, according to Plutchik's model, different emotions can combine to produce an even wider range of experience. Anticipation and joy, for example, combine to become optimism. Joy and acceptance make us feel love. Disappointment is a blend of surprise and sadness.

Within any of Plutchik's eight categories, emotions vary in *intensity* (represented by the vertical dimension of the model in Figure 5-7). At the top—the most intense—end of the model lie rage, vigilance, ecstasy, adoration, terror, amazement, grief, and loathing. As we move toward the bottom, each emotion becomes less intense and the distinctions among the emotions become less sharp. Anger, for example, is less intense than rage, and annoyance is even less intense than anger. But all three emotions—annoyance, anger, and rage—are closely related. In general, the more intense the emotion, the more it motivates behavior.

If you want to mail an important letter and you get to the post office one minute after it closes, your basic emotion might be "anger," and you might respond with a muttered curse. If you only wanted to buy some stamps, you would probably feel "annoyed," and you might just walk away. But if you wanted to mail an income tax form that had to be postmarked by midnight that night, you might feel "rage," and end up banging on the post office door or perhaps even kicking it.

Thus, although Plutchik claims there are only eight categories or families of emotions, within each category the emotions vary in intensity, and this greatly expands the range of emotions we experience. From a very simple model such as this it is possible to account for a large number of different emotions.

James-Lange theory of emotion
States that physical reactions precede experienced emotions.

Theories of Emotion

Why do we feel on top of the world one minute and down in the dumps the next? What causes emotional experiences?

In the 1880s William James formulated the first modern theory of emotion, and at almost the same time a Danish psychologist, Carl Lange, reached the same conclusions. According to the **James-Lange theory,** stimuli cause physiological changes in our bodies, and emotions are the result of those physical changes. If you come face-to-face with a grizzly bear, the perception of the stimulus (the bear) causes your muscles, skin, and viscera (internal organs) to undergo changes: faster heart rate, enlarged pupils, deeper or shallower breathing, flushed face, increased perspiration, butterflies in the stomach, and a gooseflesh sensation as the body's hairs stand on end. The emotion of fear is simply your awareness of these changes (Strongman, 1978). All of this, of course, happens almost instantaneously and in a reflexive, automatic way.

We now know that this view of emotion is at least partly right. It is clear that peripheral body changes are important in experiencing emotion. When 25 men with lesions in their spinal cords were asked to describe their feelings of anger, sex, and fear, they reported that these *feelings* were decreased, although they could *act* emotionally (Hohmann, 1966). One subject had been caught in a sinking fishing boat and described his experience as follows: "I knew I was sinking, and I was afraid all right, but somehow I didn't have that feeling of trapped panic that I know I would have had before." Another subject explained that he no longer felt anger in the way he had before his spinal cord had been cut: "Now, I don't get a feeling of physical animation, it's sort of cold anger. Sometimes I act angry when I see some injustice. I yell and cuss and raise hell, because if you don't do it sometimes, I've learned people will take advantage of you, but it doesn't have the heat to it that it used to. It's a mental kind of anger" (Carlson, 1980, p.506).

But if peripheral body changes alone *cause* specific emotions, then we should be able to pinpoint different body changes for each emotion. Perhaps butterflies in the stomach make us afraid and blushing causes shame or guilt. There is some evidence that the physiological changes associated with fear and anxiety are somewhat different from those associated with anger and aggressiveness (Funkenstein, King, & Drolette,

Cannon-Bard theory of emotion
States that the experience of emotion occurs simultaneously with biological changes.

Cognitive theory of emotion
States that emotional experience depends on one's perception or judgment of the situation one is in.

1953; McGeer & McGeer, 1980). But beyond this, psychologists simply have not found distinct bodily states that could cause all of our various emotions. All strong emotions, for example, are accompanied by a rapid pulse rate. But a rapid pulse rate does not tell you which strong emotion you are feeling. Most of the physiological "signs" of emotion say only that some kind of emotion is present and tell how intense it is. They cannot tell us whether we are experiencing terror or joy.

How, then, can we explain the differences among emotions? Nearly 70 years ago an alternative theory of emotions, the **Cannon-Bard theory,** proposed that emotions and bodily responses occur simultaneously, not one after the other. Thus when you see the bear, you run-and-are-afraid—with neither reaction preceding the other. This model makes an important point: What you see (or hear or otherwise perceive) plays an important role in determining the emotional experience you have. Recently cognitive psychologists have developed and extended this idea by suggesting that our perception or judgment of situations (cognition) is absolutely essential to our emotional experience (Lazarus, 1982). All emotional states consist of a diffuse and general arousal of the nervous system. According to the **cognitive theory** of emotion, the situation we are in when we are aroused—the environment—gives us clues as to what we should call this general state of arousal. Thus our cognitions tell us how to label our diffuse feelings in a way suitable to our current thoughts and ideas about our surroundings (see Figure 5-8).

Schachter and Singer (1962) tested the interaction of cognition and physiological arousal to study how emotional states are labeled. The experimenters told a group of subjects that they would be injected with a dose of "Suproxin"—a fictitious vitamin compound that affected vision—and that they would be tested for its effects. They divided the subjects into two groups. They gave one group a placebo that produced no physiological effect whatsoever. Then they injected the rest of the subjects with epinephrine, which produces general physiological arousal similar to that of strong emotional states. They divided these latter subjects into three subgroups. They told the first subgroup about epinephrine's real effects. They told the second subgroup nothing. And they misinformed the third subgroup by telling them to expect side effects other than those epinephrine would produce. The placebo group was not told to expect any side effects.

The experimenters then exposed each subject separately to a stooge, supposedly another subject, who pretended to be either euphoric and friendly or angry and resentful. The experimenters observed the subjects through a two-way mirror to determine how much they appeared to adopt the stooge's emotional state. Afterward they gave the subjects a self-report questionnaire to find out how angry and irritated or happy and contented they felt.

Schachter and his co-workers discovered that those who were ignorant or misinformed about the effects of epinephrine-Suproxin were much more emotionally aroused—that is, more euphoric or angry—than those who knew what the drug would do and knew what to expect. These data support Schachter's idea that if there is little physiological difference between emotional states, then our cognitions—perceptions and expectations—must tell us what emotion we are experiencing.

Additional support for Schachter's theory comes from the fact that

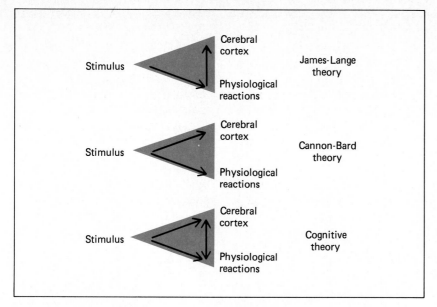

Figure 5-8

A summary of the three major theories of emotion. According to the James-Lange theory, the body first responds physiologically to a stimulus, and then the cerebral cortex determines which emotion is being experienced. In the Cannon-Bard theory, impulses are sent simultaneously to the cerebral cortex and peripheral nervous system. Thus the response to the stimulus and the emotion are experienced at the same time, but independently. Cognitive theorists propose that the cerebral cortex and peripheral nervous system work jointly to determine which emotions we feel.

people have to learn from others which emotions to experience when smoking marijuana. In a way marijuana is similar to epinephrine. It produces vague, diffuse physiological arousal that first-time users find hard to describe. Beginning smokers learn to label their physiological symptoms as a "high"—that is, other people teach them to name and interpret the physiological changes.

A fascinating test of the cognitive theory of emotion was undertaken by Spiesman (1965). People were shown a gory film that aroused strong emotional responses, both as measured by autonomic responses like heart rate and skin conductivity, and as reported in interviews.

Spiesman decided to explore how different kinds of sound tracks would affect the level of emotional response to this stress-inducing film, as measured by skin conductivity. He compared the arousal effects of the original silent film with three different sound tracks. The first he called the *trauma* track. This track simply narrated what was happening in the film. The second track was *intellectual.* Its description was detached and clinical. It allowed the viewer to maintain emotional distance from the events on the screen. The third sound track was the *denial* track. It tended to gloss over, deny, or speak in glowing terms about what was depicted.

The subjects were selected from two groups: university students and business executives. Each person saw the film alone, seated in a comfortable chair, with the device to measure skin conductivity attached throughout the showing. The results clearly show that the different verbal settings provided by each sound track affected the people's emotional response. Those who heard the trauma track were much more emotional than those who had seen the film with no accompanying narration. Those who heard the intellectual and denial tracks were much less emotional. These results show quite clearly that our emotional responses are directly and sharply affected by how we interpret a situation.

C. E. Izard (1971) developed a theory that challenges head on some of the assumptions of the cognitive theory of emotions. Cognitive the-

The Growth of Emotions

How do we become emotional beings? A newborn baby seems to experience only one emotion—a state of general excitement. A baby will react with this diffuse excitement to a red rattle, a large dog, a loud noise, or a mother's breast. A newborn girl smiles and her delighted aunt says, "Oh, look, she's happy!" Someone else says grumpily, "It's only gas." Apparently, it is neither. Instead, smiles in newborns indicate fluctuations in central nervous system activity (Ekman & Oster, 1979).

More specific emotional responses soon follow. In the first few weeks of life babies can communicate interest, distress, and disgust through their facial expressions. Well before they can talk, they have added other emotions to their repertoires, including joy, anger, surprise, shyness, and fear (Trotter, 1983). All of these emotions have been found to correspond to unique facial expressions that are recognized by people in all cultures (Izard, 1971). This universality suggests that the facial expression of these emotions is part of the innate capacity of the human nervous system.

The sequence in which the emotions emerge as an infant matures may itself be preprogrammed by the genes. According to Carroll Izard, a leading authority on emotions in infants whose work is discussed in this chapter, the development of the emotion is governed by a sort of biological clock. An infant simply cannot express some emotions until its nervous system has adequately matured. Izard noticed, for example, that 2-month-olds tended to react to an inoculation with a display of pain or physical distress. By the time they were 9 months old, however, the infants had developed the capacity for anger, which they typically expressed along with pain. Izard believes that anger adapts the child to cope with the source of pain more aggressively and more effectively than distress alone would (Trotter, 1983).

Emotions in both infants and adults are the result of many simultaneous processes—all of which influence the emotions that are displayed (Haith & Campos, 1977). As the number of stimuli that can trigger the emotions increases, so does the range of emotions that the child can express. Much of this occurs simply because the child's capacity to connect experiences increases. To the extent that thought precedes a given emotional response, a child's capacity to display the emotion is tied to the development of cognitive abilities. However some emotions, such as guilt, may depend on complex mental representations of the child's relationships with his or her social environment. So until children acquire the power to manipulate symbols adequately, they may be unable to feel guilt and certain other emotions (Lazarus, 1982).

A major landmark in a child's emotional development is the ability to hide emotions in certain situations. The child learns that it is sometimes wrong to show anger, disgust, or other emotions, although he or she feels them. In order to conceal an emotion, we must gain control over muscles in our face. Some people learn to do this better than others, and are therefore more skilled at hiding their feelings. According to one theory, children learn emotional restraint by interacting with a parent. For example, mothers may at first mimic the baby's emotional responses, but eventually they tend to limit their mimicry to a more adult range of emotions. By imitating the mother, the child learns what emotional responses are considered appropriate (Goleman, 1981).

orists tend to believe that infants do not experience distinct emotions because they have not yet learned to interpret the physiological arousal that accompanies all emotion. Izard, however, thinks that babies are born with ten basic, distinct emotions that are quite similar to Plutchik's eight fundamental emotions. The ability to experience these basic emotions is innate and has evolved over thousands of generations because emotion helps both infants and adults to survive. Disgust, for instance, promotes removal of possibly dangerous things from the mouth.

Also contrary to cognitive theory, Izard claims that emotions can be experienced without the intervention of cognition. In his view, a situation such as separation or pain provokes a unique pattern of facial movements and body postures. These responsive patterns are unlearned and are the result of activity in the nervous system that may be completely independent of conscious thought (Trotter, 1983). When information about our facial expressions and posture reaches the brain, we automatically experience the corresponding emotion. We experience surprise, for instance, once a complex pattern of muscular—and especially facial—activities has "told" the brain that we are feeling surprise, rather than anger or shame. According to Izard, then, the James-Lange theory was essentially right in suggesting that emotional experience arises from bodily reactions. But Izard stresses the face and body posture as crucial to the experience of emotion, while James-Lange emphasized visceral reactions. If Izard is right, one important element in determining our emotional experience is our expressive behavior, which is the next—and final—topic in this chapter.

The Expression of Emotion

Sometimes you are vaguely aware that a person makes you feel uncomfortable. When pressed to be more precise, you might say, "You never know what he is thinking." But you do not mean that you never know his opinion of a film or what he thought about the last election. It would probably be more accurate to say that you do not know what he is *feeling*. Almost all of us conceal our emotions to some extent to protect our self-image or to conform to social conventions. But usually there are some clues to help us determine another person's emotions.

Verbal Communication

It would be simplest, of course, if we could just ask people what they are feeling. Sometimes we do, with varying results. If your roommate finishes washing the dishes and says acidly, "I hope you are enjoying your novel," her words are quite clear, but you know very well that she is not saying what she means. If she were to say, "I am furious that you did not offer to help," she would be giving you an accurate report of her emotions at that moment.

For many reasons, we may not be able or willing to report our emotions accurately. In some situations people simply do not know what their emotions are. A father who abuses his child may sincerely profess affection for the child, yet act in ways that reflect another set of emotions that are hidden from his own awareness. Even when we are aware of our emotions, we sometimes diminish the degree of emotion we are feeling, as when we say we are "a little worried" about an upcoming exam, when in fact we are terrified. Or we may deny the emotion entirely, especially if it is negative. This may be done out of politeness or out of self-protection, as when we claim to like someone either because we do not want to hurt that person or because we feel he or she has some kind of power over us.

"Actions speak louder than words," and people are often more eloquent with their bodies than they realize or intend. We transmit a lot of information to others through our facial expressions, body postures, vocal intonations, and physical distance; in fact, our bodies often send emotional messages that contradict our words.

At a county fair, a political rally, or a football game, a pickpocket goes to work. Standing behind someone, the nimble-fingered thief prepares to relieve him of his wallet. Slowly the hand moves toward the back pocket, is almost touching the wallet, when suddenly it pulls back empty. The pickpocket moves casually through the crowd, whistling unconcernedly. What went wrong? What gave the thief a clue that his intended victim might have been about to reach for his wallet? It could have been any one of many signs to a pickpocket skillful enough to stay out of jail. The hairs on the back of the intended victim's neck might have bristled slightly; there might have been a slight stiffening of the back, a twitch in a neck muscle, a subtle change in skin color, a trickle of sweat. The man might not yet have been aware that his pocket was about to be picked, but these physiological signals showed an awareness that something was afoot.

As we noted earlier, these physiological changes are not normally

Angry Faces Around the World

Some Americans speak loudly and wave their arms when they are angry. Others speak softly and carry the proverbial big stick. Yet most of us have no difficulty recognizing when someone is angry, which suggests that certain features of angriness are common to all displays of anger. Several investigators have studied variations in emotional expression, but their conclusions are sometimes at odds, in part because their methods differ.

The psychologist Otto Klineberg (1938) became interested in cultural differences in emotional expression and devised a unique method to study them. His "novel" approach was to take several classic and modern Chinese works of fiction and examine how the emotions of the characters were represented in physical descriptions. He discovered both similarities to and differences from Western styles of expressing emotion.

Fear, for instance, is described in a similar fashion in both Chinese and Western literature. Chinese examples include, "Everyone trembled with a face the color of clay," and "All of his hairs stood on end, and the pimples came out on the skin all over his body."

Other emotions, however, were manifested quite differently. "They stretched out their tongues," conveys surprise to the Chinese, not the insolence or teasing it suggests to us. In Chinese fiction anger is exhibited by the eyes growing round and also opening wide.

Since Klineberg's work, the study of emotion has become much more systematic and precise, largely under the influence of Paul Ekman (1980), professor of psychology at the University of California medical school. For over 20 years Ekman has studied facial expressions in cultures around the world. One of his techniques was to show members of various societies photographs of American faces expressing basic emotions. People in these societies easily recognized the emotions projected in the faces. This result is especially interesting in the case of the Fore, a Stone Age society isolated in the jungles of New Guinea: even they had little difficulty interpreting the facial expressions of Americans. Ekman found that from one society to the next, anger, for example, is usually depicted on the face by means of lowered eyebrows, a hard stare, and lips tightly pressed together or slightly open in a square shape. However, the rules that define when and how these expressions should be displayed vary from culture to culture. Thus Ekman's work, guided by a different methodology, partly refines and partly contradicts that of Klineberg.

under our control. They tend to function independently of our will, and often, indeed, against it. *Facial expressions* are the most obvious emotional indicators. We can tell a lot about a person's emotional state by observing whether he or she is laughing, crying, smiling, or frowning. Many facial expressions are innate, not learned. Children who are born deaf and blind use the same facial gestures to express the same emotions as normal children do. Charles Darwin observed that most animals share a common pattern of muscular facial movements. For example, dogs, tigers, and men all bare their teeth in rage. Some human facial expressions of emotion are universal; others are unique to particular cultures (Izard, 1971).

While most people can recognize widely differing emotions in facial expressions, they tend to confuse some emotions with others, such as fear with surprise (Tomkins & McCarter, 1964). Thompson and Meltzer (1964) designed an experiment to see if certain emotions were easier to express facially than others. They found that most people have no trouble expressing love, fear, determination, and happiness, but suffering, disgust, and contempt are significantly more difficult to express—and to recognize.

The rest of the body also sends messages, particularly through position and posture. This has been called *body language.* When we are relaxed, we tend to sprawl back in a chair; when tense, to sit more stiffly with our feet together. Slumping, crossing of the arms and legs, straightness of the back, all these supply clues about which emotion someone is feeling. Birdwhistell (1952) has made the study of body language into a science called *kinesics.* He believes that every movement of the body has a meaning, that no movement is accidental, and that all of our significant gestures and movements are learned. Moreover, these body gestures may contradict our verbal messages about what we are feeling (Birdwhistell, 1974). In a family, for example, one might first notice that the mother verbally defers to her husband and children by asking for and taking their advice. But a closer inspection reveals her to be the true leader when she crosses her legs and all the other family members unconsciously imitate her (Fast, 1970). And in some cases, we may fail to communicate emotions effectively simply because we are not very good at deliberately controlling emotional expression. Beier (1974) videotaped subjects acting out six emotions: anger, fear, seductiveness, indifference, happiness, and sadness. He found that most of his subjects could successfully portray two out of the six emotions, but that the rest of their portrayals did not reflect their intentions. One girl appeared angry no matter what emotion she tried to project; another was invariably seductive.

Just as people send out complex and contradictory emotional messages by nonverbal cues, they also show considerable variety in their ability to read such messages. Rosenthal and his colleagues (1974) developed a test of sensitivity to nonverbal cues—the Profile of Nonverbal Sensitivity (PONS)—that assesses people's ability to judge the meaning of vocal intonations and face and body movements. In the test the subjects watch a film that shows an actress or actor portraying various emotional states. Sometimes the portrayal is accompanied by spoken phrases, but certain tones and rhythms that identify them as distinct words have been removed. The viewer then picks one of two possible interpretations of the scene.

Facial expressions are the most obvious indicators of emotions, but body language also communicates strongly about a person's inner state.

The study showed that women were consistently better than men at understanding nonverbal cues, although men in the "nurturant" professions—psychiatrists, psychologists, mental hospital aides, and teachers—along with artists, actors, and designers, scored as high as women. The study also showed that sensitivity to nonverbal cues increases with age, probably because as we grow older, we accumulate more experience in judging vocal tones and observing body movements.

Closely related to the ability to read other people's emotions is *empathy,* the arousal of emotion in an observer that is a vicarious response to the other person's situation (Parke & Asher, 1983). Empathy depends not only on the ability to identify other people's emotions but also on the capacity to put yourself in their place and to have an appropriate emotional response (Parke & Asher, 1983). Just as sensitivity to nonverbal cues increases with age, so does empathy: The cognitive and perceptual abilities required for empathy develop only as a child matures.

In addition to body language, another kind of body communication is *distance.* The normal distance between people definitely differs from culture to culture. Two Swedes standing around and talking would ordinarily stand much farther apart than two Arabs or Greeks. Within every culture there seems to be a distance that is generally thought appropriate for normal conversation. If someone is standing closer than usual to you, it may indicate aggressiveness or sexuality; if farther away than usual, it may indicate withdrawal or repugnance.

Explicit *acts,* of course, can also be nonverbal clues. When we receive a 2:00 A.M. telephone call, we expect that what the caller has to say is

Anger: Should You Hold It In or Let It Out?

At least since the 1960s popular wisdom has advised people who feel angry to vent their hostility, because repressing it can only threaten one's health. Indeed, various studies indicate that bottled-up rage can contribute to ulcers, high blood pressure, heart disease, and possibly states of severe anxiety.

Unfortunately it now appears that venting your anger may cause problems too. Leonard Berkowitz (1973) points out that therapists who reward patients for acting out their anger in the therapist's office may indeed reduce anxiety by lowering inhibitions. But by rewarding hostile behavior, these therapists may unintentionally be teaching people to be overly aggressive. Moreover, expressing anger often does not get rid of the source of the anger, and in some cases it does not reduce blood pressure either. Finally, Carol Tavris (1982) suggests that even talking about your hostility reinforces it and may make you more angry than you were before!

What, then, should we do about the anger we all inevitably feel sometimes? Tavris and others agree that we should first determine why we are angry and then decide if anger is the appropriate response. We will probably decide that a great many grievances are not worth getting excited about. Another strategy is to reinterpret the situations that make us angry. Tavris (1982) calls this the reappraisal method. Laughing off an infuriating encounter is one form of reappraisal. So is re-

Expressions of emotion vary in intensity. In complaining to the front desk, this hotel guest may well have progressed from annoyance, to anger, and finally to outright rage.

sponding with empathy to another's behavior: "He must be under a lot of pressure lately" or "She must not be feeling well to be acting like that." Attitudes like these help reduce tension by taking away the feeling of being under attack.

Most of the time the best way to deal with anger is to avoid the source. But when the expression of anger is definitely called for, polite assertiveness rather than outright aggression is probably the most constructive and healthful approach you can take.

urgent. A slammed door tells us that the person who left the room is angry. If friends drop in for a visit and you invite them into the living room, you are probably less at ease with them than you are with people you would ask to sit down at the kitchen table. *Gestures* such as a slap on the back or an embrace can also indicate feelings. Whether a person shakes your hand briefly or for a long time, firmly or limply, can tell you something about what he or she feels toward you.

A word of caution is needed here. Although overt behavior can be a clue to emotion, it is not always infallible. Laughing and crying sound alike, for example, and we bare our teeth in smiles as well as in snarls. Crying can "mean" sorrow, joy, anger, nostalgia, or that you are slicing an onion. Moreover, as with verbal reports, it is always possible that someone is putting out false clues. And we all have done something thoughtlessly—turned our backs, frowned because we were thinking about something else, laughed at the wrong time—that has given offense because these acts were taken to express an emotion that we were not, in fact, feeling at that time.

Truth Is More Than Skin Deep— The Lie Detector

As credibility and trust have declined in American society, the popularity of lie detectors has increased. Once limited to law enforcement applications, lie detectors (also called polygraphs) are now routinely used by corporations, banks, and even fast-food chains to question job applicants about their honesty in past jobs. And in 1983 President Reagan ordered polygraph tests of certain federal employees in an effort to plug leaks to the press of classified or embarrassing information.

The growing use of the polygraph has brought to the fore a controversial question: What does a lie detector measure? Is it only the act of telling a lie that produces the telltale patterns of inked needles on graph paper? Or can other factors such as emotional reactions to the content of the questions or the testing situation itself cause truthful people to appear to be liars?

Lie detectors rely on the fact that emotions and inner conflict typically are accompanied by physiological changes. When a person lies, there are changes in blood pressure, in breathing, and in the resistance of the skin to electrical current, known as *galvanic skin response,* a function of sweating. There is no single pattern of responses unique to lying, however; the pattern varies from person to person.

Lie detectors make use of the fact that inner emotions are typically accompanied by measurable physiological changes.

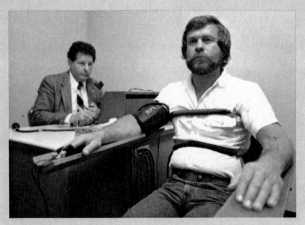

In a typical lie-detector examination, failing the test can have serious consequences. Hence subjects are generally quite nervous as a blood-pressure cuff is strapped to one arm, sensors designed to measure breathing are attached to the chest and stomach, and electrodes are placed on the fingertips to measure galvanic skin response. Because the blood-pressure cuff soon becomes uncomfortable, the examination must be short—3 to 4 minutes long.

The form and mix of questions is a key to the examination. A typical set of questions includes just a few that are critical: "Did you take money from the cash register on the evening of July 21?" The rest are control questions, designed to be answered dishonestly even if the subject is telling the truth about the relevant questions. For example, to a control question such as, "Have you ever taken anything in your life?" even most truthful people will choose to lie, given the circumstances, since just about everyone has stolen something sometime. Polygraph examiners assume that an otherwise truthful person will react more strongly to the control questions, while an untruthful subject will react more strongly to the relevant ones (Meyer, 1982).

Lie detectors are far from error free, and when they err, it is usually on the side of injustice. Figures vary widely, but according to one estimate, examinations in the field correctly identify about 75 percent of those lying. Unfortunately about 49 percent of those telling the truth are also identified as lying (Horvath, 1977). One major source of possible error is the fact that galvanic skin response changes in reaction to all kinds of emotions, not just those connected with deception (Lykken, 1975). When someone is asked if she committed a murder, the lie detector is likely to jump. Of course this may reflect guilt, but it may also reflect anxiety, fear, or loathing—all possible reactions to being questioned about a murder. If a suspect were questioned about marital problems, relationships with parents, or even attitudes toward work, the polygraph might make a similar jump in emotional response regardless of whether the person is telling the truth when answering (Stern et al., 1981).

It is also easy to fool the polygraph machine, given the proper knowledge. Some tactics do not work, however. Conscious efforts not to sweat or not to alter one's respiratory patterns will not succeed. Nor will efforts to increase one's response to control items, say by clenching one's teeth (Waid & Orne, 1982). But taking tranquilizers does seem to reduce the physiological response to lying. So does not paying attention to the questions. In one experiment subjects counted backward by sevens during their examinations to distract themselves from the questions, and they were able to escape detection more often as a result (Waid et al., 1981).

Personal and social factors can also affect the physiological signs monitored by the machine. The galvanic skin response of some people changes spontaneously at a high rate, thus increasing the chances that their truthful answers will appear to be lies. Finally, the degree to which examiner and subject are matched in terms of sex, age, race, or ethnicity may also have an effect. In one study the lie detector was least successful when examiner and subjects shared the same ethnicity, possibly because in this situation the subjects felt most at ease (Waid & Orne, 1981).

It is possible to increase the accuracy of polygraphs by testing only for "guilty knowledge"— that is, knowledge about details of the crime that only the guilty person could know. For example, if a list of banks is read, a guilty suspect should react more strongly to the name of the bank that he or she actually robbed. However, in many of the 500,000 to 1 million testings that take place each year in the United States, the most sophisticated methods are not used in formulating the questions or interpreting the results, partly because the vast majority of the 4,000 to 8,000 examiners have had negligible training in physiology or psychology (Lykken, 1975).

Summary

1. Motives and emotions both energize and direct our behavior. The two are closely related and can activate us even without our awareness. *Motive* usually refers to specific needs, desires, or wants that move us to attain some goal. The goals are often less obvious with *emotions*, which usually refer to complex feelings such as anger, fear, or love.

2. *Primary drives* are unlearned motives that are common to every animal. They include hunger, thirst, and sex. The primary drives are triggered by physiological stimuli and by both internal and external cues. All of them are subject to learning and experience.

3. Hunger is regulated by two centers in the brain. The *hunger center* stimulates the desire to eat while the *satiety center* signals when to stop. The hunger center is stimulated in response to a drop in the level of *glucose* in the blood or an increase in the level of fats in the blood. Receptors in the stomach send signals to the brain, where they stimulate the satiety center. Another hunger regulator operates on a long-term basis to regulate the body's weight.

4. The thirst drive is related to balances of fluids within the body. One thirst regulator monitors the level of fluid inside the body's cells, and a second thirst regulator signals when there is a drop in the level of fluid outside the cells. We drink until we have consumed enough fluid to restore water to our tissues, but it is not fully understood how we know when to stop drinking.

5. Sexual desire is affected by hormones, mainly *testosterone;* it is also affected by sensory stimulation, and by stimulation of a portion of the brain called the limbic system. In humans, as in other animals, it may also be affected by the smell of *pheromones*. Erotic materials, fantasy, and a great variety of other learned cues can also trigger the sex drive in humans. *Sexual dysfunction,* the loss or impairment of ordinary sexual function in men and women, is sometimes caused by organic factors, but more often is due to psychological factors.

6. A second set of motives that is largely innate depends more on external stimuli than on internal physiological states. These *stimulus motives,* such as curiosity, activity, exploration, manipulation, and contact, push us to investigate, and often to alter, our environment.

7. All animals seem to need *activity*, but we do not know if activity is a motive in itself or a combination of other motives. *Exploration* and *curiosity* appear to be triggered by the new and unknown and to be directed toward finding something out. *Manipulation* is directed toward a specific object that must be touched, handled, played with, and felt. The need for *contact* with others is broader and more universal than the need for manipulation. It can involve the whole body and can be passive.

8. Some motives are learned as we develop. Aggression is one of these *learned motives*. *Aggression* includes all behavior that is intended to inflict physical or psychological harm on others. It implies intent to do harm. Some theorists, such as Lorenz and Freud, believed that aggression is an innate drive, but most psychologists today, such as Bandura and Berkowitz, hold that people learn aggression as a response to frustration or other aversive stimuli. It follows that aggression can also be unlearned.

9. Various *social motives* are also learned, including achievement, power, and affiliation. The need for achievement, or *nAch*, is a desire to excel, to overcome obstacles, to achieve for its own sake. A high percentage of women experience a *motive to avoid success*, which may be a fear of success or simply a desire to avoid behavior that is thought to be inappropriate to their sex. The *power motive* is the need to control or influence other people or groups. Finally, the *affiliation motive*, the need to be with others, is usually aroused when people feel threatened. Fear and anxiety are closely linked to the affiliation motive.

10. Abraham Maslow proposed that all motives can be arranged in a hierarchy, from lower to higher. Higher motives will appear only after the more basic ones have been satisfied. The most evolved motive in Maslow's hierarchy is self-actualization.

11. Emotions, like motives, arouse and direct our behavior. We can classify emotions in terms of whether they cause us to avoid something (fear), approach something aggressively (anger), or approach something with acceptance (joy, love). Emotions can both help or hinder performance. The *Yerkes-Dodson law* states that the more complex the task, the lower the level of emotion that can be tolerated before performance declines.

12. Robert Plutchik proposed a more detailed classification of eight basic emotions, each of which helps the individual adapt to the environment in some way. Each emotion also varies in intensity. Different basic emotions can combine like primary colors to produce more complex emotions.

13. There are three basic theories about emotion. The *James-Lange theory* maintains that emotion is the result of visceral, or peripheral reactions. The perception of a stimulus causes the body to undergo certain physiological changes that are the cause of emotion.

14. The *Cannon-Bard theory*, unlike the James-Lange theory, holds that emotions and bodily responses occur simultaneously, not one after the other. Thus one's perception of the situation strongly influences one's emotional experience. This theory is a forerunner of cognitive theories of emotion.

15. *Cognitive theories* state that emotion results from interaction of cognitive and physiological processes. Most emotional states are diffuse, and many emotions are accompanied by essentially the same physiological reaction, which we interpret to create our emotion.

16. Izard has challenged the cognitive theory of emotions by proposing that humans are born with the ability to experience a number of distinct emotions. In his view, situations evoke a unique pattern of facial expressions and body postures, which the brain translates into an appropriate emotional experience.

17. Verbal reports do not always give a complete picture of what a person is feeling, because people may be unable or unwilling to report their emotions accurately.

18. Nonverbal communication—facial expressions, position, posture, distance between people, explicit acts, and gestures—can be a useful clue to emotion. Often nonverbal communication contradicts a person's verbal message. Many *facial expressions* do not appear to be learned, but are universal in humans. The rest of the body also sends messages through its position and posture, an idiom called *body language*. Women, on average, tend to understand nonverbal cues better than men.

1. Both _____ and _____ direct our behavior and can activate us even without our awareness.

2. Motivation begins with which of the following:
   a. emotion   c. stimulus
   b. drive   d. arousal

3. Primary motives are not at all affected by learning or experience. T/F

4. In the brain, signals from the _____ _____ stimulate eating, while those from the _____ _____ reduce the desire to eat.

5. Thirst regulators monitor the level of _____ inside and outside the body's cells.
   a. water   c. sodium
   b. nutrients   d. fluids

6. The hormone _____ stimulates sexual arousal in both men and women.

7. A class of wants or needs that are set in action by external stimuli and push us to investigate our environment are called _____ _____.

8. Next to each of the motives listed below, mark U if it is an unlearned motive and L if it is a learned motive.

   ____ sex   ____ aggression
   ____ curiosity   ____ manipulation
   ____ affiliation   ____ achievement
   ____ activity   ____ contact
   ____ power   ____ avoidance of success

9. You might accidentally hit a dog that is crossing the street, but deliberately running over your neighbor's dog would be considered an act of _____.

10. A person who is willing to contend with the high risks of a career in sales is probably motivated by a high _____ motive.

11. The _____ motive is sometimes aroused when a person needs to be consoled or supported by a group of peers.

12. According to Maslow's hierarchy the higher motives can only appear after the basic ones have been satisfied. T/F

13. According to the _____ _____ law, there is a relationship between the complexity of a task and the level of emotion that can be tolerated while performing the task.

14. According to Robert Plutchik, emotions vary in _____, a fact that accounts for the great range of emotions we experience.

15. Match the following theories of emotion with their definitions:

    ____ Cannon-Bard   A. says that physical reactions come before experienced emotions.
    ____ cognitive theory
    ____ James-Lange   B. says that emotions and bodily responses occur simultaneously.

                            C. says that emotional experience depends upon perception of a given situation.

16. Izard's theory of emotion stresses the importance of cognition/expressive behavior.

17. Two important nonverbal clues to emotion are _____ _____ and _____ _____.

Outline

Learning

6

As unlikely as it seems, the following situations have something in common.

Upon completion of a training course at the National Zoo, the star students demonstrate their special behaviors: Junior, a young orangutan, cleans up his cage for the chance to blow on a whistle; a pair of 18-inch-long lizards jump 2 feet in the air to snatch insects from the tip of a forceps; a chinchilla weighs itself by hopping into a basket on top of a scale; and Peela the tiger retrieves a floating keg from the moat in his exhibition area.

In the chronic schizophrenia ward of a mental hospital, patients who once had to be fed, cleaned, and clothed by caretakers now do their own laundry, eat meals together in a dining room, and wash and comb their own hair. The ward operates as a token economy. For performing tasks, patients earn tokens that will buy things like candy, soap, magazines, and trinkets.

Joey, a city kid, goes away to summer camp for the first time. Being from the city, he hasn't done much in the way of boating, hiking, camping, and so on. But by the end of 8 weeks at Camp Winnepesaka, Joey can row a canoe and sail a sunfish, pitch camp, and blaze a trail; he can even distinguish poison ivy from poison sumac and pick out constellations in the nighttime sky.

Although all these situations take place outside a classroom or school setting, **learning** is nonetheless going on. Most people think of learning as "studying." But psychologists define it more broadly as the process by which experience or practice results in a relatively permanent change in behavior. This certainly covers classroom learning and studying, but it covers many other types of learning too: learning to turn off lights when we leave a room; learning which way to put the key into a car ignition; learning how to avoid falling down on skis; learning how to dance.

Some kinds of learning are quite simple. Young children and even animals have little difficulty in learning to avoid a hot flame. Learning other things, such as how to play the violin or how to calculate the volume of an irregular solid object, is difficult for many people and impossible for others.

Some of the simplest, most basic learning is called conditioning. **Conditioning** is a general term—used for animals as well as for human

Learning The process by which experience or practice results in a relatively permanent change of behavior.

Conditioning The acquiring of fairly specific patterns of behavior in the presence of well-defined stimuli.

Learning is the process by which experience or practice results in a relatively permanent change in behavior.

beings—that refers to the acquiring of fairly specific patterns of behaviors in the presence of well-defined stimuli. There are two main types of conditioning: classical conditioning and operant conditioning.

Our discussion begins with the first of these processes—classical conditioning. This simple kind of learning provides a convenient starting point for examining the learning process—what it is and how we can observe it.

Classical Conditioning

Pavlov's Conditioning Experiments

Classical conditioning was discovered almost by accident by Ivan Pavlov (1849–1936), a Russian physiologist who was studying the digestive processes. Since animals salivate when food is placed in their mouths, Pavlov inserted tubes into the salivary glands of dogs to measure how much saliva they produced when they were given food. He noticed, however, that the dogs salivated before the food was in their mouths: The mere sight of food made them drool. In fact, they even drooled at the sound of the experimenter's footsteps. This aroused Pavlov's curiosity. What was making the dogs salivate even before they had the food in their mouths? How had they learned to salivate to the sound of the experimenter's approach?

To try and answer these questions Pavlov set out to teach the dogs to salivate when food was not present. He devised an experiment in which he sounded a bell just before the food was brought into the room. A

Figure 6-1

Pavlov's apparatus for classically conditioning a dog to salivate. The experimenter sits behind a two-way mirror and controls the presentation of the conditioned stimulus (bell) and the unconditioned stimulus (food). A tube runs from the dog's salivary glands to a vial, where the drops of saliva are collected as a way of measuring the strength of the dog's response.

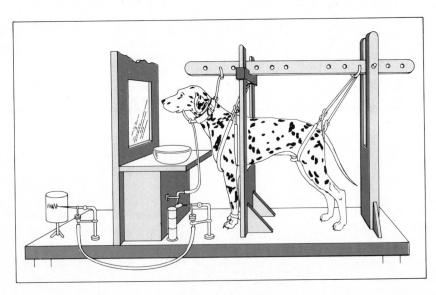

ringing bell does not usually make a dog's mouth water, but after hearing the bell many times just before getting fed, Pavlov's dogs began to salivate as soon as the bell rang. They had learned that the bell signaled the appearance of food, and their mouths watered on cue, even if no food followed. The dogs had been conditioned to salivate in response to a new stimulus, the bell, which would not normally have caused that response (Pavlov, 1927)(see Figure 6-1).

Generally speaking, **classical conditioning** involves learning to transfer a natural response from one stimulus to another, previously neutral stimulus. Pavlov's experiment illustrates the four basic elements of classical conditioning. The first is an **unconditioned stimulus (US),** like food, which invariably causes a certain reaction—salivation, in this case. That reaction—the **unconditioned response (UR)**—is the second element and always results from the unconditioned stimulus: Whenever the dog is given food (US), its mouth waters (UR). The third element is the neutral stimulus—in this case, the ringing of the bell—which is called the **conditioned stimulus (CS).** At first, the conditioned stimulus does not bring about the desired response. Dogs do not normally salivate at the sound of a bell—unless they have been conditioned to react in this way. Such a reaction is the fourth element in the classical conditioning process: the **conditioned response (CR).** The conditioned response is the behavior the animal has learned to produce in response to the conditioned stimulus. Usually the unconditioned response and the conditioned response—salivation, in our example—are basically the same (see Figure 6-2).

Classical Conditioning in Human Beings

So far we have been focusing on classical conditioning in animals, but humans respond to these same principles. For example, the sight of a menu, the sound of silverware being placed on the dinner table, the ring of the oven timer signaling that a favorite casserole is ready to be served—all of these can cause a hungry person to salivate.

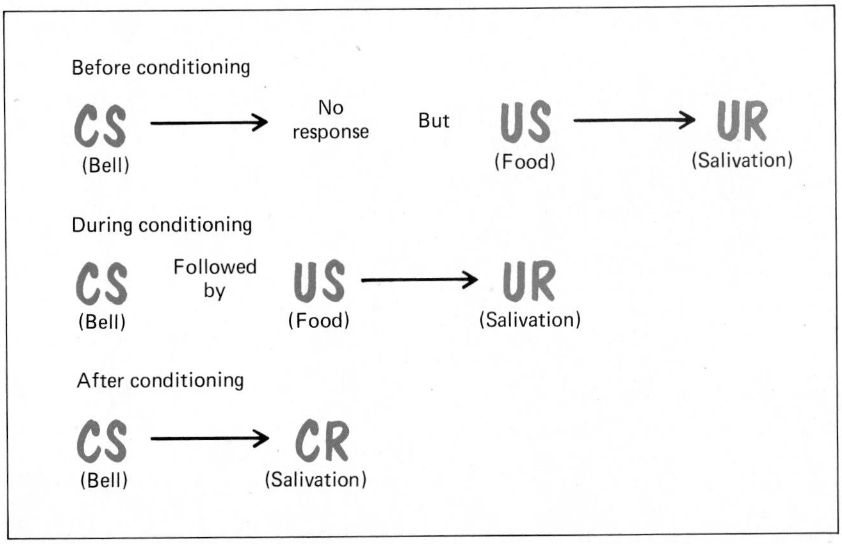

Classical conditioning Type of learning in which an organism learns to transfer a natural response from one stimulus to another, previously neutral stimulus.

Unconditioned stimulus (US) Stimulus that invariably causes an organism to respond in a specific way.

Unconditioned response (UR) Response that takes place in an organism whenever an unconditioned stimulus occurs.

Conditioned stimulus (CS) Originally neutral stimulus that is paired with an unconditioned stimulus and eventually produces the desired response in an organism when presented alone.

Conditioned response (CR) Response an organism learns to produce when a conditioned stimulus is presented.

Figure 6-2

A paradigm of the classical conditioning process.

Desensitization therapy Conditioning technique designed to gradually reduce anxiety about a particular object or situation.

One of the best known examples of classical conditioning in humans is the case of John Watson's experiment with Little Albert, an 11-month-old boy (Watson & Rayner, 1920). The experimenters started by showing Albert a white rat. At first the child displayed no fear. He crawled toward the rat and wanted to play with it. But every time he approached the rat, the experimenters made a loud noise by striking a steel bar. Since nearly all children are afraid of loud noises, Albert's natural reaction was fear. After just a few times Albert began to cry and crawl away whenever he saw the rat. This is a simple case of classical conditioning. An unconditioned stimulus—the loud noise—caused the unconditioned response of fear. Next, Albert learned to associate the loud noise with the rat, so that the rat (conditioned stimulus) then caused him to be afraid (conditioned response).

Several years later the psychologist Mary Cover Jones demonstrated a method by which children's fears can be unlearned using classical conditioning (Jones, 1924). Her subject was Peter, a 3-year-old boy who, like Little Albert, had a fear of white rats. Jones paired the sight of a rat with a pleasant experience—eating ice cream, Peter's favorite dessert. While Peter sat alone in a room, a caged white rat was brought in and placed far enough away so that he would not be frightened. At this point Peter was given plenty of ice cream to eat. On each successive day of the experiment the cage was moved closer and was followed by ice cream, until eventually Peter was not afraid around the rat. In this case, eating ice cream (US) elicited a pleasant response (UR). By pairing the ice cream with the sight of the rat (CS), it was possible to teach Peter to respond with pleasure (CR) when the rat was present.

Many years later the psychiatrist Joseph Wolpe adapted Jones's method to the treatment of certain kinds of anxiety (Wolpe, 1973). In step 1 of this treatment, called **desensitization therapy,** the person is taught how to achieve a state of deep relaxation. In step 2, the person helps to create a list of situations that evoke the anxiety and ranks them on a scale from least fearful to most fearful. For instance, a person who is afraid of cats might put being attacked by a vicious cat at the top of the list of fears, while the experience of hearing the word "cat" might go at the bottom. The final step of the therapy consists of having the person enter a state of deep relaxation during which he or she imagines the least distressing situation on the list. When the person succeeds in remaining relaxed while imagining that situation, he or she progresses to the next one, and so on until the person experiences no anxiety even when imagining the most frightening situation on the list. We will discuss desensitization therapy in greater detail in Chapter 15.

Classical conditioning can even be used to teach newborn infants. Babies who are only 5 to 10 days old can learn to blink their eyes when they hear a tone (Lipsitt, 1971). Babies blink naturally when a puff of air is blown in their eyes. The puff of air is an unconditioned stimulus. Blinking—the babies' natural reaction—is an unconditioned response. If a tone—a conditioned stimulus—is sounded just before the puff of air is blown into their eyes, the babies soon begin to blink their eyes whenever they hear the tone. By blinking as soon as they hear the tone, the babies are producing a conditioned response.

Classical conditioning can also result in some strange kinds of learning. For example, one group of experimenters conditioned a group of asthma sufferers to react to substances that had not previously affected them. They first exposed the asthmatics to something they were allergic to, like dust or pollen—an unconditioned stimulus. Of course, the dust or pollen caused an attack of asthma (an unconditioned response). Then the experimenters presented a neutral substance (a conditioned stimulus). Initially the asthmatics had no reaction to this neutral substance. But when the neutral substance was repeatedly followed by dust or pollen, the asthma sufferers began to wheeze and sniffle as soon as the neutral substance was presented. These attacks were conditioned responses: The subjects had to learn to react in this way. In one study, even a picture of the conditioned stimulus could trigger an attack of asthma (Dekker, Pelser, & Groen, 1957). This study and others like it help to explain why asthma attacks are sometimes brought on by such seemingly neutral events as hearing the national anthem, seeing a waterfall, or listening to a political speech!

Interstimulus interval Time lapse between the presentation of the conditioned stimulus and the unconditioned stimulus.

Necessary Factors in Classical Conditioning

We have seen that classical conditioning can occur quite easily, but it is not automatic. Learning does not occur unless certain requirements are met. The more carefully all these factors are controlled, the more likely it is that learning will take place. For example, the conditioned stimulus must be strong and distinctive enough for the subject to perceive it easily. Another factor that significantly affects the success of the learning process is the order in which the conditioned stimulus and the unconditioned stimulus are presented. The most effective method is the one used in all of the experiments we have described: presenting the conditioned stimulus just before the unconditioned stimulus. Remember that Pavlov rang his bell just before he gave the dogs their food. Presenting the conditioned stimulus and the unconditioned stimulus together is usually less effective. If the bell had rung at the same time that the dogs had gotten their food, they probably would not have salivated later at the bell alone. Backward conditioning—presenting the unconditioned stimulus before the conditioned stimulus—seldom results in effective learning. It would have been very difficult for Pavlov's dogs to learn to salivate when they heard a bell if they had already received their food before the bell rang.

The amount of time between the occurrence of the conditioned stimulus and the unconditioned stimulus is also critical to the success of learning. If this time lapse—called the **interstimulus interval**—is either too short or too long, it will impair learning. The most effective interstimulus interval is usually somewhere between a fraction of a second and a few seconds, depending on which animal is being conditioned and what it is supposed to learn. Pavlov found that if he waited too long after sounding the bell before he gave the dogs their food, the dogs would not learn. Moreover, one trial is usually not enough for any significant learning to occur. Most classical conditioning requires repeated trials to build up the learned association between the conditioned stimulus, like Pavlov's bell, and the unconditioned stimulus, like food. Pavlov had to pair the bell with the food several times before the bell alone would cause a dog's mouth to water.

Conditioning is usually cumulative. Each trial builds on the learner's previous experience. But this does not mean that learning will increase

Intermittent pairing Pairing the conditioned stimulus and the unconditioned stimulus on only a portion of the learning trials.

indefinitely or by an equal amount on each successive trial. At first the strength of the conditioned response—one way of measuring the effectiveness of classical conditioning—increases greatly each time the conditioned stimulus and the unconditioned stimulus are paired. Learning eventually reaches a point of diminishing returns: The amount of each increase gradually becomes smaller and smaller. Finally, the rate of learning levels off and continues at the same strength on subsequent trials.

The spacing of learning trials is as important as the number of trials conducted. Learning is more effective if the pairing of the conditioned stimulus and unconditioned stimulus is experienced at evenly spaced intervals, neither too far apart nor too close together. If trials follow each other very quickly or are too far apart, more trials are needed before learning will occur.

What if, on some of the trials, either the conditioned stimulus or the unconditioned stimulus is missing? This is called **intermittent pairing.** It reduces both the rate of learning and the final level of learning, though learning does still occur.

As we just mentioned, classical conditioning generally requires a short interval between presentation of the conditioned stimulus and the unconditioned stimulus and more than one occasion on which the two are paired. An interesting exception to these principles is food aversion. If an animal just once tastes a new food and later becomes ill, the animal may learn to avoid that food in the future. Not only does the learning take place with only one trial, but the interval between eating the food (the CS) and falling ill (the US) can be quite long—up to 12 hours among rats. In one experiment, after rats experienced a single pairing of salty water (CR) with illness (US) induced by drugs, they avoided salty water

Learning Curves

Learning can be measured in many ways. In classical conditioning, we can look for an increase in the strength of the conditioned response, or more often we look for an increase in the likelihood of getting the conditioned response when the conditioned stimulus is presented. When we plot any of these measures on a graph, over trials or blocks of trials, we have a *learning curve.*

The shape of the learning curve will vary, depending on what we are measuring. If we are measuring the strength of the conditioned response or the numbers of trials on which we get the conditioned response, the curve will be low on the left and move upward to the right.

In most cases, whether we are drawing a graph of strength of response or of percentage of trials showing the conditioned response, the steepest part of the curve will be at the left. This is because most improvement comes early in the learning

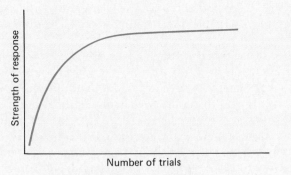

A typical learning curve based on strength of response.

process. Then, as the increase in learning on each trial becomes smaller, the curve will gradually level off.

for more than a month (Garcia, Hankins, & Rusiniak, 1974). Another unusual feature of food aversion is that an animal that has been poisoned learns to avoid only the food it ate but not any of the other stimuli that were present while it was eating, such as the room in which it ate the food or the container in which the food was kept (Dickinson & Mackintosh, 1978). In fact, if the animal eats both familiar and novel foods before it becomes ill, it subsequently avoids only the novel foods!

The research on food aversion suggests that some behaviors can be learned by classical conditioning much faster than others. Taste-illness combinations may be one of several pairs of stimuli that produce rapid learning because they increase an organism's chances of survival. John Garcia, who has done much of the key research in this area, believes that evolution plays a part in the rat's ability to quickly learn what foods to avoid. Over thousands of generations, rats have evolved a nervous system that helps them remember taste-illness combinations (Garcia & Koelling, 1966). Clearly this is an advantage to a scavenger like the rat, which comes into contact with potential toxic foods quite often.

Food aversion is an exceptionally well developed response in rats, but other animals, including humans, display signs of it. If we become ill several hours after trying a new dressing on our regular salad, we are apt to develop a strong aversion to that dressing, no matter how much we enjoyed it. Some of the more recent research on food aversion has focused on cancer patients, who often show severe appetite loss. Bernstein (1978) tested the possibility that this is due to a learned association between food and the nausea caused by many drugs used in chemotherapy. Patients in the test group were given an unusual flavor of ice cream to eat shortly before receiving chemotherapy that would cause illness. A control group was given the same ice cream before treatment that did not cause illness. In a follow-up 4 months later, most of the patients for whom the ice cream had been paired with illness refused it when given a choice, or else ate substantially smaller amounts of it than did the patients in the control group. The results suggest that humans do have some built-in facility for learning tastes related to illness.

Extinction Decrease in the strength or frequency of a learned response due to withholding of reinforcement (operant conditioning) or to failure to continue pairing the US and CS (classical conditioning).

Extinction and Spontaneous Recovery

Going back to Pavlov's dogs, what happens when the dog has learned to salivate upon hearing a bell, but after hearing the bell repeatedly fails to get food? The dog's response to the bell—the amount of salivation—will gradually decrease until eventually the dog will no longer salivate when it hears the bell. This process is known as **extinction.** If the conditioned stimulus (the bell) appears alone so often that the learner no longer associates it with the unconditioned stimulus (the food), and stops making the conditioned response (salivation), extinction has taken place.

Once a response has been extinguished, is the learning gone forever? Pavlov trained his dogs to salivate when they heard a bell, then caused the learning to extinguish. A few days later the same dogs were again taken to the laboratory. As soon as they heard the bell, their mouths began to water. The response that had been learned and then extinguished reappeared on its own, with no retraining. This phenomenon is

Spontaneous recovery The reappearance of an extinguished response after the passage of time, without further training.

Inhibition Learning to suppress a learned response.

External inhibition Reduction in a response because of a change in the learner's environment.

Figure 6-3

From point *A* to point *B* the conditioned stimulus and the unconditioned stimulus were paired and learning continued to increase. From *B* to *C*, however, the conditioned stimulus was presented alone. By point *C* the response had been extinguished. After a rest period from *C* to *D*, spontaneous recovery occurred—the learned response reappeared at about half the strength it had at point *B*. When the conditioned stimulus was again presented alone, the response extinguished rapidly (point *E*).

known as **spontaneous recovery**. The dogs' response was only about half as strong as it had been before extinction, but spontaneous recovery does indicate that learning is not permanently lost (see Figure 6-3).

To understand spontaneous recovery we have to take a closer look at what happens during extinction. Let us begin with a dog that has learned a particular response, like salivating when it hears a bell. If the bell is rung over and over again but is not followed by the appearance of food, the conditioned response becomes extinguished—the animal's mouth no longer waters when it hears the bell. This learning to suppress a learned response is called **inhibition**. We are not, however, simply teaching this learned behavior and then erasing it. Inhibition is the result of new learning that works in the opposite direction from the original learning. When inhibition becomes as strong as the original learning, the animal will no longer produce the conditioned response. Extinction has occurred.

We have been talking about inhibition as something that temporarily blocks a learned response. A sudden change in the learner's surroundings or routine can also block a conditioned response. When Pavlov's assistants would ask him to come and look over their projects to see how well the dogs were doing, the animals sometimes failed to perform. Pavlov realized that his presence had disrupted the dogs' usual routine and interfered with their performance. He called this effect **external inhibition**. Something in the dogs' surroundings—the presence of a strange person in the room—made it seem that extinction had occurred.

Generalization and Discrimination

Certain situations or objects may resemble one another enough so that the learner will react to one as he or she has learned to react to the

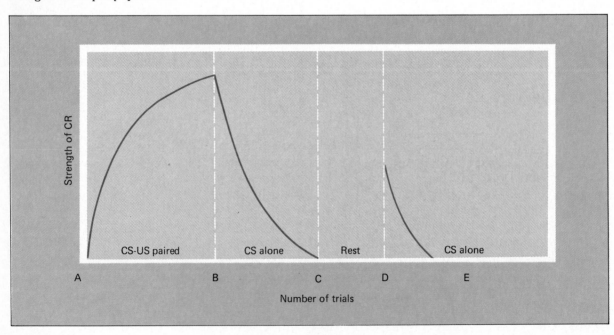

other. Pavlov noticed that after his dogs had been conditioned to salivate when they heard a bell, their mouths would often water when they heard a buzzer or the ticking of a metronome. Their conditioned response had been generalized to other noises that sounded like the bell. Reacting to a stimulus that is similar to the one you have learned to react to is called **stimulus generalization.**

Stimulus generalization Transfer of a learned response to different but similar stimuli.

Recall the case of Little Albert and his conditioned fear of white rats. When the experimenters later showed Albert a white rabbit, he cried and tried to crawl away. He had generalized his fear from the white rat to the similar stimulus of the white rabbit. In fact, his fear generalized to a number of white furry objects—cotton balls, a fur coat, and even a white Santa Claus mask.

Wolpe's desensitization therapy, mentioned earlier, provides another example of stimulus generalization. In the example we used, while the

Who's Afraid of the Big Bad Wolf?

One interesting aspect of human learning is the formation of phobias. *Phobias* are irrational fears of things like high places, cats, spiders, snakes, and the dark. Sigmund Freud explained phobias in terms of unresolved inner conflicts. A different explanation has been suggested by Wolpe and Rachman (1960), who see phobias simply as a case of

classical conditioning: An object comes to be feared after being linked with a frightening stimulus. Although phobias can be classically conditioned in this way, in other respects they do not follow most rules of classical conditioning.

In the first place, phobias are not affected by standard extinction procedures. For example, a woman has developed a fear of dogs because of one frightening experience in the past. According to traditional learning theory, each time she sees a dog and nothing frightening happens, her fear of dogs should decrease. But this does not happen. Her fear may become stronger each time she sees a dog or even thinks about dogs.

Furthermore, phobias, like food aversions, can sometimes be learned in one trial, which is not the case with typical laboratory fear conditioning. Moreover, the range of stimulus objects that result in phobic fear is limited. Classical conditioning theory would lead us to expect that any object could become a source of a phobia if it were paired with a stimulus that arouses fear and anxiety. But this is not true for most phobias. "Only rarely, if ever, do we have pajama phobias, grass phobias, electric-outlet phobias, hammer phobias, even though these things are likely to be associated with trauma in our world" (Seligman, 1972, p. 455).

Seligman suggests that all these nonconformities can be explained by the concept of preparedness. All the common objects of phobia—heights, snakes, cats, the dark, and so on—represent "events related to the survival of the human species through the long course of evolution" (p. 455). Thus humans may be prepared to develop phobias about these things.

Discrimination Learning to respond to only one stimulus and inhibit the response to all other stimuli.

Higher-order conditioning Conditioning based on previous learning; the conditioned stimulus is used as an unconditioned stimulus in further training.

person most fears being attacked by a vicious cat, cat-related stimuli also evoke fear; in fact, even hearing the word *cat* elicits a slight amount of fear. In other words, the fear response has generalized to a wide range of more or less similar stimuli.

It is also possible to train animals and people not to generalize, but to give a learned response only to a single specific object or event. This process is called **discrimination,** and in effect it is the reverse of generalization. The subject learns to respond to only one stimulus and to inhibit the response in the presence of all other stimuli.

Pavlov's method for training an animal to discriminate was to present two similar sounds but to follow only one of them with an unconditioned stimulus. The dog learned to salivate only when it heard the sound that was followed by the unconditioned stimulus (food), but not when it heard the other sound. It had learned to discriminate.

Learning to discriminate is very important in everyday life. As we noted earlier, most children fear all loud noises. Since thunder cannot harm a child, however, it would be helpful if children learned not to be afraid every time they heard it. Not all mushrooms are good to eat, and not all strangers are unfriendly. Thus discrimination is one of the most important parts of learning.

Higher-order Conditioning

After Pavlov's dogs had learned to salivate when they heard a bell, he decided to teach them to salivate when they saw a black square. But this time, instead of showing them the square and following it with food, he showed them the square and followed it with the bell. The dogs eventually learned to salivate when they saw the square. The bell was used as an unconditioned stimulus and the black square was used as a conditioned stimulus. This procedure is known as **higher-order conditioning,** not

Experimental Neurosis

When an animal is taught to discriminate between two similar stimuli—two sounds or two shapes projected on a screen—it learns to respond to one but not to the other. In one experiment a dog learned to salivate when it saw a circle, but not when it saw an ellipse (Pavlov, 1927). The shape of the ellipse was gradually changed, making it more and more circular. When the distinction between the circle and the ellipse was too fine for the dog to detect, discrimination broke down. Not only was the animal unable to discriminate between the two shapes that were now very similar, but it also lost the ability to discriminate between the original circle and the ellipse.

At this point an interesting side effect showed up: The dog became agitated and upset. It began

to bark, tried to attack the conditioning apparatus, and acted fearful. Pavlov termed the dog's condition *experimental neurosis*. He believed that this abnormal behavior was produced by the prolonged stress of being unable to decide which shape to respond to.

The reliability of these findings has been questioned in recent years by psychologists who have not always been able to create the same effects that Pavlov observed. His attribution of the dog's agitation to "stress" has also been challenged. Nevertheless, it is possible that at least some behavior disorders in humans are related to conflicts and uncertainty arising from ambiguous stimuli somewhat like those confronting Pavlov's dog (Schwartz, 1980).

because it is more complex or because it involves any new principles, but simply because it is learning based on previous learning.

Higher-order conditioning is more difficult to learn because it races against extinction. The dogs that learn to respond to a square are no longer getting any food. In fact, the square is a signal that the bell will follow and that the bell will *not* be followed by food. Without the food, the dogs will soon stop salivating when they hear the bell. If this happens, they cannot learn to salivate when they see the square. To avoid this problem, food must be given to the dogs once in a while at the sound of the bell, so that their mouths will continue to water when they hear the bell.

Operant behavior Behavior designed to operate on the environment in a way that will gain something desired or avoid something unpleasant.

Instrumental or **operant conditioning** Type of learning in which desired voluntary behavior is rewarded and incorrect responses are ignored or punished.

Operant Conditioning

As it has traditionally been viewed, classical conditioning is concerned with behavior that invariably follows a particular event: the salivation that automatically occurs when food is placed in the mouth; the blink of the eye that always results when a puff of air strikes the eye. In classical conditioning, we usually learn to transfer this reaction to another stimulus that would not normally produce it: salivating at the sound of a bell, blinking to a tone. In a sense classical conditioning is passive. The behavior is initially *elicited* by the unconditioned stimulus.

Most behavior, however, initially seems to be *emitted* rather than elicited; that is, most behavior is usually voluntary rather than inevitably triggered by outside events. You wave your hand to hail a taxi. A dog begs at the dinner table for food. A child stops crying to avoid further scolding. These and similar actions are sometimes called **operant behavior.** They are designed to operate on the environment in a way that will gain something desired or avoid something unpleasant.

To explain how operant behavior is learned, we turn to a second major kind of learning: **instrumental** or **operant conditioning.** This kind of learning also occurs both in animals and in people. Anyone who has ever trained a dog to do tricks such as sitting up, fetching, or rolling over knows that the best method of training is to reward the dog with a bit of food each time it gives the desired response. This is operant conditioning. You use the food to *reinforce* the correct behavior. Incorrect behavior may be either ignored (no reward) or punished (by a swat with a rolled-up newspaper, for example). This is the essence of operant conditioning. Correct responses are reinforced; incorrect responses are either ignored or punished.

The first problem in operant conditioning is to make the desired response occur so that it can be reinforced and learned. The animal trainer uses shaping, reinforcing smaller bits of behavior to teach animals complicated tricks.

Response Acquisition

We have said that classical conditioning deals with behavior that is initially a natural, automatic response. This implies that it is relatively easy to produce the desired responses. All Pavlov had to do when he wanted his dogs to salivate was to put food in their mouths. But operant

Skinner box Box equipped with a bar, in which an animal is placed during operant conditioning; pressing the bar releases food, which reinforces the bar-pressing behavior.

"Boy, do we have this guy conditioned. Every time I press the bar down, he drops a pellet in."

behavior does not automatically follow from a stimulus. Thus the first problem in operant conditioning is to make the desired response occur so that it can then be reinforced and learned.

One of the most common ways of getting the desired behavior is simply to wait for the subject to hit upon the correct response. The first time babies say "Mama" is by accident. But if their mothers smile and hug them, they will learn to repeat the sound. However, this can be a slow and tedious process: If you were an animal tamer for a circus, imagine how long you would have to wait for a tiger to decide to jump through a flaming hoop so you could reward that behavior!

In the laboratory there are several ways to speed up the process and make it more likely that the desired response will occur. One possibility is to increase motivation: A hungry laboratory rat is more active and thus more likely to give the response you are looking for than a well-fed rat. But imagine that you want the rat to learn to press a bar or lever in order to get food. A rat has a set of natural responses to hunger, but pressing a bar is not one of them. So until it learns to press the bar, you will have to see that the rat goes hungry.

One way to further speed up the process of learning is to narrow down a large number of potential responses, thereby improving the chances that the correct response will occur. This can be done by restricting the environment and then allowing the subject to respond freely within these bounds. One of the many kinds of equipment used in laboratory experiments on operant conditioning is the **Skinner box,** named after B. F. Skinner, the American psychologist who developed many of the techniques of operant conditioning. A Skinner box for rats is small and bare except for a bar with a cup underneath it. The rat must learn to press the

Learning and the Birds and the Bees

Birds, bees, and other animals can learn about their environment in remarkable detail, but their genes seem to rigidly define when and how this learning takes place (Gould & Gould, 1981). In order to survive, honey bees must be able to record and recall the location of nectar-bearing blossoms and the location of the home hive. Thus a bee must learn the sensory details of the two locations and landmarks in between. Many people have difficulty with such tasks, yet bees perform them easily and consistently. But bees, unlike many other organisms (including people), are greatly constrained in terms of when this learning can occur. For example, they can learn the location of their hive only when they first leave it in the morning. If the hive is moved at all after the first flight out, the returning bees become confused. Similarly, bees can learn the odor of a flower only when they are perched directly on it. Their remarkable learning abilities are inflexibly programmed by their genetic makeup to act only under certain very specific conditions.

Because genetic programming varies from species to species, animal species differ in terms of what and when they can learn. This is especially apparent in imprinting—extremely rapid learning that occurs only when a certain kind of stimulus is presented at a certain time (see Chapter 10). Newborn animals quickly learn to recognize their mother when they hear her make a call that triggers in them the response of following her. As they follow her around, they memorize certain traits of the mother that distinguish her from all other possible mothers. Interestingly, animals differ in how they identify their mothers. Some species record the odor of their mother, some depend on minute physical details, and still others rely on the sound of the mother's call. Despite such variation, this kind of imprinting serves the same function for all species: Being able to recognize their mother greatly improves the chances for survival of the young.

bar, which releases food pellets into the cup. In the simple environment of a Skinner box a rat quickly discovers bar pressing, since there are relatively few other possible responses.

But outside of the laboratory, it is rarely possible to arrange the environment so conveniently. And in some cases, as with the tiger and the flaming hoop, you would probably wait forever for the desired behavior to occur. In these situations a very effective procedure for acquiring a new response is to start by reinforcing partial responses—the small bits of behavior that make up the whole. Little by little, the complete response is shaped by successive approximations. This approach, called **shaping,** was used to get a severely disturbed boy named Dickey, who had just had cataracts removed from his eyes, to wear glasses. A doctor had predicted that if Dickey did not start to wear glasses within 6 months, he would go blind. But the boy stubbornly refused to wear his glasses and even threw terrible temper tantrums at the mere mention of them. Eventually researchers at the University of Washington tried a shaping procedure consisting of several steps. Dickey was first deprived of his breakfast so that bits of food could be used as reinforcers. Next, he was rewarded with food for simply picking up an empty frame for glasses that had been placed in his room. Later he was given food for putting on the glasses, and later still he had to keep them on in order to get food. Dickey was rewarded for correct behavior every step of the way until after 18 days he had learned to wear the glasses 12 hours a day (Wolf, Mees, & Risley, 1964).

Shaping has also proved useful in managing uncooperative animals at some of the nation's zoos. By offering an animal something that it wants (food and caresses are popular) when the animal comes close to a desired behavior, zookeepers have made their own work much easier. For example, at the National Zoological Park in Washington, D.C., shaping was used to teach a polar bear with a broken tooth to stick its nose out through a slot in the cage door and permit a keeper to lift its lip. A vet later inspected the tooth without having to shoot the bear with a tranquilizer gun, a risky undertaking for both vet and bear (Pryor, 1981).

Reinforcement

Once the desired response has been produced, how do we ensure that it will be repeated? We do just what the animal trainer does—we reward the correct response. Psychologists call this reward a **reinforcement,** since it strengthens the desired response and increases the likelihood that it will be repeated.

Whenever something we do is followed closely by a reinforcement, we will tend to repeat the action—even if the reinforcement is not produced directly by what we have done. In one of Skinner's experiments (1948) a pigeon was placed in a cage that contained only a food hopper. There was nothing the bird could do directly to get food, but at random intervals Skinner dropped a few grains of food into the hopper. He found that the pigeon began to repeat whatever it had been doing just before it was given food: standing on one foot, hopping around, or strutting around with its neck stretched out. None of these actions had had anything to do with getting the food. It was pure coincidence that the food appeared when the

Shaping Reinforcing successive approximations to a desired behavior.

Reinforcement Anything that follows a response and makes it more likely to recur in the future.

A rat in a Skinner box.

Shaping can also be used for some types of human learning. Through successive approximations, the girl will learn to use the cello bow correctly.

Primary reinforcer Reinforcer that is rewarding in itself, such as food, water, and sex.

Secondary reinforcer Reinforcer whose value is learned through association with primary reinforcers.

Skinner found that the bird would repeat whatever action it had been doing just before food was dropped into the box—a form of superstitious behavior.

bird was standing on one foot, for example. But that action would usually be repeated. Skinner called the bird's behavior "superstitious." It is possible that some human superstitions are learned in the same way. If we happen to be wearing a particular piece of jewelry or carrying a rabbit's foot when we are reinforced, we may come to believe that our behavior caused the reinforcement. This was illustrated in a laboratory study conducted by Catania and Cutts (1963) in which college students were asked to push one of two buttons when they saw a light. Reinforcement was given only when they pushed the right-hand button, but not every time they pushed this button. Virtually no subjects learned to push only the right-hand button. Instead most of the students developed elaborate sequences of left/right button pushing that they later said were the "key" to getting reinforced!

Psychologists distinguish several kinds of reinforcers. A **primary reinforcer** is one that is rewarding in and of itself, without any association with other reinforcers. Food, water, and sex are primary reinforcers. A **secondary reinforcer** is one whose value has to be learned through association with other reinforcers. It is referred to as secondary not because it is less important, but because it is learned. A rat learns to get food by pressing a bar; then a buzzer is sounded every time the rat presses the bar and gets food. Even if the rat stops getting the food, it will continue to press the bar just to hear the buzzer. Although the buzzer by itself has no value to the rat, it has become a secondary reinforcer.

Money is a secondary reinforcer. Although money is just paper or metal, through its association with food, clothing, and other primary reinforcers, it becomes a powerful reward. Children come to value money only after they learn that it will buy such things as candy (primary reinforcer). Then the money becomes a secondary reinforcer. Chimpanzees have learned to work for poker chips, which they insert into a vending machine to get the primary reinforcer, raisins. The poker chips have become secondary reinforcers for the chimps.

Usually there is a delay between the time the desired behavior occurs and the time that reinforcement is given. The length of this delay is important to the success of learning: The longer the interval, the less effective the reinforcement. In one study (Azzi, Fix, Keller, & Rocha e Silva, 1964) the experimenters varied the time interval between when rats pressed a lever and the delivery of reinforcement. As Figure 6-1 shows, a delay of only a few seconds sharply reduced the rate at which the rats pressed the bar.

The reduced effectiveness of delayed reinforcement appears to be due to distracting events that interfere with the learning process (Wickelgren, 1977). By minimizing the distractions that the learner is subjected to between the behavior and the reinforcement, it is possible to delay reinforcement without decreasing learning too much. The same effect may be achieved with humans by repeatedly reminding the learner that the reinforcement is coming or by explaining why the person is being reinforced when it finally does arrive. This forms a link between the learner's response and the delayed reinforcement that follows.

There are some cases in which behaviors are intrinsically reinforcing so there is no delay at all in reinforcement. For example, the stalking and sexual behaviors of animals are considered to be intrinsically reinforcing, that is, reinforcing all by themselves. As the behavior occurs, the animal is immediately rewarded by the behavior itself. As you might expect, such behaviors are very hard to eliminate.

Schedules of Reinforcement

Seldom, either in life or in laboratory, are we rewarded every time we do something. And this is just as well, for *partial reinforcement,* in which rewards are given for some correct responses but not for every one, results in a behavior that will persist longer than one learned by continuous reinforcement. The program for choosing which responses to reinforce is called the **schedule of reinforcement.** Schedules can be either fixed or varied and can be based either on the number of responses or on the elapsed time between responses. The most common reinforcement schedules are the fixed-interval and the variable-interval schedules, which are based on time, and the fixed-ratio and the variable-ratio schedules, which are based on the number of correct responses.

On a **fixed-interval schedule** subjects are reinforced for the first correct response after a certain time has passed: They learn to wait for a set period before responding. Subjects begin making responses shortly before the set amount of time has gone by, in anticipation of the reinforcement that is to come. For example, although a cake recipe may say, "Bake for 45 minutes," you will probably start checking to see if the cake is done shortly before the time is up. With fixed-interval schedules, performance tends to fall off immediately after the reinforcement, and tends to pick up again as the time for the next reinforcement draws near. A rat learns to press a bar to get food only for the first response in any 5-minute period. The rat will stop pressing the bar right after it gets its food, but will begin pressing it more frequently as the next time for getting the food approaches.

A **variable-interval schedule** reinforces correct responses after varying lengths of time. One reinforcement might be given after 6 minutes, the next after 4 minutes, the next after 5 minutes, the next after 3 minutes. Subjects learn to give a slow, steady pattern of responses, being careful not to be so slow as to miss all the rewards. If they are too slow and fail to respond at the appointed time for reinforcement, they will not get their reward. When exams are given at fixed intervals—like midterms and finals—students tend to increase their studying just before an exam; studying then decreases sharply right after the exam until shortly before the next one. On the other hand, if several exams are given during a semester at unpredictable intervals, students have to keep studying at a steady rate all the time, because on any given day there might be an exam (see Figure 6-4).

On a **fixed-ratio schedule** a certain number of responses must occur before reinforcement is presented. This results in a high response rate because it is advantageous to make many responses in a short time in order to get more rewards. Being paid on a piecework basis is

Schedule of reinforcement In partial reinforcement, the program for choosing which responses to reinforce.

Fixed-interval schedule Reinforcement schedule that calls for reinforcement of a correct response after a fixed length of time.

Variable-interval schedule Reinforcement schedule in which the first correct response is reinforced after various lengths of time.

Fixed-ratio schedule Reinforcement of the correct response after a fixed number of correct responses.

A fixed-ratio schedule—such as being paid on a piecework basis—usually results in a high response rate. There is incentive to make many responses in a short time in order to get more rewards.

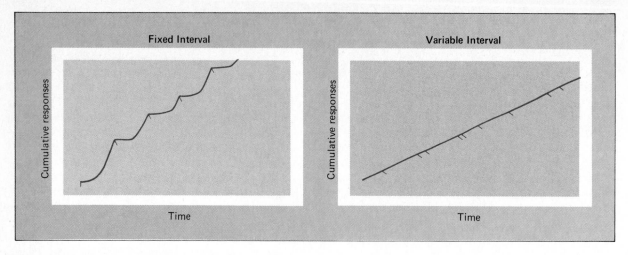

Figure 6-4

(Above) The typical pattern of responses on a fixed-interval schedule of reinforcement. The small markings along the colored line indicate points at which reinforcement is given. As the time for reinforcement approaches, the number of responses increases and the slope becomes steeper. The rate of responding is low immediately after reinforcement, so the curve is nearly flat at that point. **(Right)** On a variable-interval schedule of reinforcement, the rate of responding is relatively constant.

After Skinner, 1961

Figure 6-5

(Below) A high rate of responding and a moderate pause after each reinforcement are characteristic of the fixed-ratio schedule of reinforcement. **(Right)** The variable-ratio schedule of reinforcement leads to a high rate of responding, with a slight pause after each reinforcement. Sometimes an animal will even forego eating the food that it has earned, preferring to get on with the business of earning the next reinforcement.

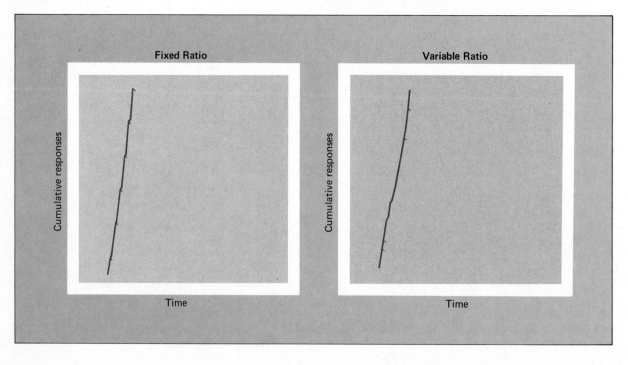

an example of a fixed-ratio schedule. A migrant worker might get $3 for every 10 baskets of cherries he picks. The more he picks, the more money he makes. A fixed-radio schedule results in a pause after reinforcement is received, then a rapid and steady response rate until the next reinforcement.

On a **variable-ratio schedule,** the number of responses necessary to gain reinforcement is not constant. The slot machine is a good example of a variable-ratio schedule. It may pay off, but you have no idea when. Since there is always a chance of hitting the jackpot, the temptation to keep playing is great. Subjects on a variable-ratio schedule tend not to pause after reinforcement and have a high rate of response over a long period of time. Since they never know when reinforcement may come, they keep on trying (see Figure 6-5).

Aversive Control

Up to this point we have concentrated on the effect of positive reinforcers on behavior. A **positive reinforcer** can be anything that increases the likelihood that a response will be repeated when it is presented after the response. Praise, food, money, a smile—all are positive reinforcers for most of us. If they follow some behavior, we are more likely to behave that way again in the future.

But behavior can also be controlled by **punishment.** For most of us, receiving a fine for speeding or littering reduces the likelihood that we will speed or litter in the future. Being rudely turned down when we ask someone for a favor makes it less likely that we will ask that person for a favor again. In all these cases, the unpleasant aftereffect makes it less likely that we will repeat our behavior.

It seems obvious, therefore, that punishment works. But we can think of situations where it does not work. Children often continue to misbehave even after they have been punished repeatedly. Some drivers continue to drive recklessly despite repeated fines. The family dog continues to sleep on the couch at night despite being punished for this every morning. So it is important to ask, "Under what conditions does punishment work?" (Schwartz, 1980).

The effectiveness of punishment depends entirely on how and when it is used. Punishment should be *swift*. Children who misbehave should be punished right away so that they know what they have done is wrong. If punishment comes too late, it may not be clear to children why they are being punished. Punishment should also be *sufficient*, without being cruel. If a parent merely warns a child not to bully other children, the effect may be less than if the warning is accompanied by a slap on the hand or by being "grounded" for a day. Moreover, the common practice of making the punishment for each successive misdeed more severe than the last is not so effective as maintaining a constant level of punishment. Effective punishment is also consistent, or *certain*. The parent should try to punish the child each and every time he or she misbehaves. Otherwise the misbehavior may persist.

One of the problems with using punishment is that it can often disrupt the learning process. When children are learning to read and the teacher scolds them every time they mispronounce a word, they may only become

Variable-ratio schedule Reinforcement schedule in which a varying number of correct responses must occur before reinforcement is presented.

Positive reinforcer Any event whose presence increases the likelihood that ongoing behavior will recur.

Punishment Any event whose presence decreases the likelihood that ongoing behavior will recur.

Because the reinforcement is unpredictable, a variable-ratio schedule tends to yield a very high rate of response. This is the attraction of slot machines and lotteries. Since there is always a chance of hitting the jackpot, the temptation to keep playing is great.

Negative reinforcer Any event whose reduction or termination increases the likelihood that ongoing behavior will recur.

Avoidance training Learning a desirable behavior in order to prevent an unpleasant condition such as punishment from occurring.

frightened. As they become more frightened and confused, they mispronounce more words and get scolded more. In time they may become so scared that they will not want to read at all. Moreover, punishment can provoke aggressive behavior. Laboratory studies show that monkeys that are punished tend to attack other monkeys, pigeons other pigeons, and so on (Schwartz, 1980). Similarly, punishment often makes people angry, and angry people are likely to be more aggressive and hostile.

Despite obvious negative side effects, punishment when used properly works quickly, and in some cases speed is especially important. A child who likes to play in the street or who likes to poke things into electric outlets must be stopped quickly, and in these cases punishment has a role to play. Similarly, some autistic children repeatedly injure themselves by banging their heads against the wall or by hitting themselves in the face with their fists. Punishment can be effective in stopping this self-destructive behavior so that other forms of therapy can proceed.

By itself, punishment simply inhibits or suppresses behavior. It doesn't teach an alternative behavior to replace what is being punished. Scolding a child for misbehaving does not in itself teach the child how he or she should have behaved. But when punishment *is stopped,* any behavior going on at the time is reinforced and is more likely to occur in that situation in the future. If a child is scolded for eating spaghetti with his fingers (punishment) and the scolding stops when he picks up a fork and uses it, he is more likely to use a fork in the future. This is an example of a **negative reinforcer.** Reducing or terminating unpleasant events (such as punishment) increases the likelihood that behavior going on at the time will recur. And if at the same time you add positive reinforcement ("Good boy! That's the way grown-ups eat their spaghetti."), the new behavior is even more likely to happen again in the future. Thus, if punishment must be used to suppress undesirable behavior, it should be terminated when more desirable behavior occurs (in order to negatively reinforce that behavior); and positive reinforcement (praise, rewards) should also be used to strengthen the desired behavior. This approach is more productive than punishment alone, since it teaches an alternative behavior to replace what is being punished. The positive reinforcement also makes the learning situation less threatening in general.

Note that both positive and negative reinforcement result in learning new behaviors. A child might practice the piano in order to receive praise (positive reinforcement) or to escape for doing tedious homework for a while (negative reinforcement). A dog that learns to open the back door with its paws may be doing so either for the positive reinforcement of getting outside to play or for the negative reinforcement of getting away from the bothersome family cat.

As a method of controlling behavior, punishment is an unpleasant alternative. It is often carried out ineffectively, and it can have negative side effects. Most of us would prefer to avoid using punishment at all, perhaps relying only on the *threat* of punishment if behavior is getting out of control. In this case, a change to more desirable behavior can prevent the punishment from ever occurring. Psychologists call this **avoidance training.**

Avoidance training with animals usually includes some sort of warning device, like a light or a buzzer. For example, an animal might be placed in a box with a wire floor that can deliver a mild shock. The experimenter first sounds a buzzer, then a few seconds later turns on the shock. If the animal presses a bar after hearing the buzzer, no shock will be delivered. Pressing the bar after the shock has already started will have no effect. The animal must learn to press the bar after hearing the buzzer, but before the shock starts, in order to prevent the shock from occurring. At first this usually happens accidentally. But once the animal learns that pressing the bar prevents the shock, it will run to the bar whenever it hears the buzzer and will avoid the shock altogether.

Avoidance training is usually helpful to us, as when we learn to carry an umbrella when it looks like rain or not to drink from bottles labeled "Poison." But sometimes avoidance learning persists after it is no longer effective. A child who learns not to go into deep water may build up a fear that remains even after he or she has learned how to swim. In other cases, avoidance behavior may persist even after the fear has been removed. It seems that the fear that was essential for learning the avoidance response is not necessary in the long run for sustaining the learned response.

Generalization and Discrimination

As we saw in classical conditioning, a response can generalize from one stimulus to a similar one. Conversely, the same stimulus will sometimes bring about different, but similar, responses. Generalization also occurs in operant conditioning.

An example of stimulus generalization in operant conditioning is a baby who is hugged and kissed for saying "Mama" when he or she sees the mother, and begins to call everyone "Mama"—including the mailman. Although the person the baby sees—the stimulus—changes, the baby responds with the same word. In the same way, the skills you learn when playing tennis may be generalized to badminton, Ping-Pong, and squash.

Response generalization occurs when the same stimulus leads to different, but similar, responses. The baby who calls everyone "Mama" may also call the mother "Dada" or "gaga"—other sounds that have been learned—until he or she learns that only "Mama" is correct. In response generalization the response changes, but the stimulus remains constant.

The ability to tell the difference or discriminate between similar stimuli—or even to determine whether the right stimulus is present—is as essential in operant conditioning as it is in classical conditioning. Knowing what to do has little value if the learner does not know when to do it.

Discrimination in operant conditioning is taught by reinforcing a response only in the presence of certain stimuli. In this way, pigeons have been trained to peck at a red disk, but not at a green one. First the pigeon is taught to peck at a disk. Then it is presented with two disks, one red and one green. The bird gets food when it pecks at the red one, but not when it pecks at the green one. Eventually it learns to discriminate between the two and will only peck at the red disk. Babies who call everyone "Mama" learn to discriminate between their own mothers and other people and to use "Mama" only for their own mothers. Of course, this could be done by punishing the children for calling other people

Response generalization Giving a response that is somewhat different from the response originally learned to that stimulus.

Quality Control Through Operant Conditioning

The scene is a drug factory. A conveyor belt carries the tiny gelatin capsules that will soon be filled with one of our modern wonder drugs. A quality control inspector stands by the moving belt and scrutinizes each capsule as it passes by. If a capsule is bumpy or dented, if its color is not quite right, the inspector pushes a button and the defective capsule is removed from the belt. There is nothing unusual about this—except that the inspector is a pigeon.

So far, no human quality control inspector need worry about being replaced by a bird. But psychopharmacologist Thom Verhave has successfully conditioned pigeons to perform the exact discrimination task outlined above—to look at drug capsules as they move by on a belt and, whenever an imperfect capsule appears, to signal by pecking at a disk (Verhave, 1966).

Verhave's conditioning procedure was very simple: He placed the bird in a cage that contained a small window, a lighted disk, and an automatic food hopper. When the bird correctly identified a defective capsule by pecking twice on the disk, it was rewarded with food. Eventually the bird learned to perform the whole inspection process. It would peck at the disk once to turn on a light behind the window so it could see the capsule. If the capsule was acceptable, the pigeon then pecked one more time at the disk, which turned off the light and moved the next capsule up. One out of every ten capsules was misshapen or off-color, and when the bird saw one of these, it pecked twice at the disk and was rewarded with food. Within a week, Verhave's pigeons were signaling defective capsules with 99 percent accuracy, no small achievement for any inspector—human or pigeon.

If the expected reinforcement for an action does not occur—the woman shown here expects to receive food for the money she put in the machine—the behavior of the subject often becomes more intense (here the woman kicks the machine) before it disappears altogether (extinction).

"Mama." But more commonly we teach children to discriminate by reinforcing them for using "Mama" correctly and not reinforcing them when they use the term for other people.

Extinction and Spontaneous Recovery

Extinction was discussed earlier in connection with classical conditioning. In operant conditioning, extinction is the result of withholding reinforcement. Withholding reinforcement does not usually produce an

1 "THIS IS A STICKUP!"

2 "THIS IS A STICKUP!"

Merely paying attention to someone's behavior can be reinforcing, particularly if the person is "starved for attention." Withdrawal of the reinforcing attention results in the elimination of the behavior.

"THIS IS A STICKUP!"

Drawing by Opie; © 1961.
The New Yorker Magazine, Inc.

immediate decrease in the frequency of the response. When reinforcement is first discontinued, there is often a brief increase in responding before it declines. The behavior itself also changes at the start of extinction. It becomes more variable and often more forceful. For instance, if you try to open a door by turning the knob and pushing the door, but find that it will not open, you may continue to try. You may turn the knob more violently and you may even kick or pound on the door. But if the door still will not budge, your attempts will decrease, and you will finally stop trying to get the door open altogether.

Several factors affect how easy or how hard it is to extinguish learned actions. The stronger the original learning, the harder it is to stop the action from being performed. The greater the variety of settings in which learning takes place, the harder it is to extinguish it. Rats trained to run in a single straight alley for food will stop running sooner than rats trained in several different alleys that vary in width, brightness, floor texture, and other features. Complex behavior is also much more difficult to extinguish than simple behavior. Since complex behavior consists of many actions, each single action that makes up the total behavior must be extinguished.

The schedule of reinforcement used during conditioning has a major effect on the extinction process. Partial reinforcement creates stronger learning than continuous reinforcement. This is because the subject does not expect reinforcement for each response and has learned to continue responding in anticipation of eventual reinforcement. During extinction it will take the subject longer to learn that no reinforcement will be presented and to stop responding.

Avoidance training is especially hard to extinguish, because it is based on fear of an unpleasant or painful situation. But if the unpleasant situation no longer exists, then continued response to the warning is pointless and may even be harmful. The usual method of extinction—withholding reinforcement—will not work. Responding to the warning is reinforced because the unpleasant event does not happen. This reinforcement obviously cannot be withheld by the event's ceasing to exist, because the subject has no way of finding that out as long as he or she continues to respond to the warning. For this reason, standard conditioning procedures are generally ineffective and special means must be used to extinguish avoidance responses.

Extinction will be easier if the nonreinforced experiences occur in rapid succession. This is just the opposite of learning, which occurs in fewer trials if the trials are distributed over time. Extinction can also be

Autonomic conditioning Learning
to voluntarily control responses
of the autonomic nervous
system.

speeded up if the learner is put in a situation that is different from the one in which the response was learned. The response is weaker in a new situation, and will disappear much more rapidly.

Removing the reinforcement will eventually cause a response to be extinguished, but punishment can be used to eliminate the response even faster. Punishing a response adds another deterrent. If the punishment is used correctly and consistently, the response will be eliminated quickly.

Spontaneous recovery, which was defined in the classical conditioning section as the reappearance of the original learning after it has been extinguished, also occurs in operant conditioning. Rats that have their bar-pressing behavior extinguished will sometimes start pressing the bar spontaneously when they are placed in the Skinner box again after a lapse of time.

Contemporary Views of Learning

Early research on conditioning produced several concepts that seemed to make complex behavior more understandable. But the life span of concepts, especially scientific ones, is becoming shorter as the pace of research speeds up. The work of Pavlov, Skinner, and others has generated a huge amount of interest and investigation. Today neither the basic distinction between classical and operant conditioning nor the body of assumptions central to conditioning itself remains unquestioned.

Classical Conditioning Versus Operant Conditioning

Traditionally, classical and operant conditioning have been regarded as very different learning processes. Work done in the last fifteen or twenty years, however, has suggested that aside from the different procedures used, the two kinds of learning may not really be that different. In fact, they may be the same kind of learning simply brought about in two different ways (Schwartz, 1980). At least four differences originally thought to distinguish classical from operant conditioning have been questioned in recent years (Hearst, 1975).

1. Psychologists tend to assume that classical conditioning is associated with involuntary behavior such as salivation and fear, while operant conditioning is associated with voluntary actions. Research suggests, however, that classical conditioning can also be used to shape voluntary movements (Brown & Jenkins, 1968). Moreover, operant conditioning of involuntary processes has occurred in **autonomic conditioning** studies in which both humans and animals have been taught to control certain biological functions such as blood pressure, heart rate, and skin temperature. (In the "Application" at the end of this chapter, we'll discuss how autonomic conditioning, incorporated into a technique called biofeedback, has become an important tool for treating a variety of health problems.)

2. It has been assumed that in classical conditioning the unconditioned response and the conditioned response are similar, if not identical, and that in operant conditioning the learned response need bear little or no resemblance to what the "normal" response in that situation would be. Both of these assumptions have recently been called into question. For example, Pavlov's dogs salivated in response to both the food and the bell. But recent research suggests that in classical conditioning the conditioned response and the unconditioned response can be quite different from each other. This is especially likely to occur when some other conditioned response is more adaptive and the organism is free to make that alternative response. For example, a recent series of experiments suggests that in Pavlov's studies, salivation was both the CR and the UR because the dogs were strapped into a harness that prevented them from responding to the bell (CS) with anything other than salivation. When dogs are free to react to the bell as they wish, they salivate but they also move toward the bell and make contact with it. In a natural setting, too, a conditioned stimulus such as the sound of dinner plates being put on the table provokes not only salivation but also other highly adaptive responses such as movement toward the food (Schwartz, 1980).

In operant conditioning, the subject typically learns a response that is very unlike the normal response the subject would make to the same stimulus. For example, a rat may be taught to open a door when a light goes on. Whatever the rat's normal response would be to such a light, it certainly would not involve opening a door! In fact, in operant conditioning experiments the experimenters go out of their way to teach animals purely arbitrary behaviors that they would never perform under normal conditions. This way the experimenters can be reasonably sure that if the animal gives the unusual response—rats pressing levers or pigeons pecking at lights, for example—it is the result of learning during the course of the experiment.

Research indicates, however, that there are limits on how far a learned response can diverge from the normal response to the stimulus (Rescorla & Holland, 1982). Keller and Marian Breland, besides being psychologists, trained animals to perform in shows. Their experiences provide delightful examples of how hard it is to ignore an animal's innate responses in operant conditioning (Breland & Breland, 1972). For example, a bantam chicken that they tried to condition to stand on a platform for 12 to 15 seconds scratched so much that they finally gave up and billed it instead as a "dancing chicken." A raccoon that had been trained to insert a coin into a container for food suddenly became a miser. It reverted to its natural "washing" response, rubbing the coins together and refusing to drop them into the slot.

3. In our initial discussion, we said that in classical conditioning the unconditioned stimulus draws out the desired response from the subject. In operant conditioning, the subjects spontaneously come up with the response, which is then reinforced. The behavior to be learned is elicited in one case and emitted in the other. But in operant conditioning, once the operant response becomes linked to a stimulus, the operant response looks and acts very much like an unconditioned response. If a rat is trained to open a door when a light goes

Cognitive learning theorists Theorists who conceive of learning in terms of cognitive processes that cannot be observed directly.

Contingency theory Proposes that for learning to take place, the stimulus must provide the learner with information about the likelihood of other events occurring.

on, the light elicits the door-opening behavior just like an unconditioned stimulus in classical conditioning.

4. Finally, if the two forms of learning are truly different, they should also differ in such things as extinction, generalization, or discrimination. In fact, as we have seen, there are very few differences between the two kinds of learning in any of these processes.

All of this evidence suggests that classical and operant conditioning may simply be two different procedures for achieving the same end. If so, psychologists have been overstressing the differences and paying too little attention to the similarities between the two. Learning occurs in both cases, and the nature of learning itself remains open to new theories. In the next section we shall discuss several theories that also challenge traditional views of conditioning.

Cognitive Learning

Traditional theories of learning give only "objective" definitions of the learning process and have little use for "inner causes," such as individual cognition: "If you cannot measure it, forget it." Many psychologists, however, are no longer content with this description of what goes on in learning. They have begun to reassess classical and operant conditioning to take into account *cognitive*, or internal, factors that may be involved in learning. Lower species may learn only simple stimulus-response associations, but higher forms of cognitive mediation, such as the learning of expectations, seem to occur among birds and mammals, including, of course, human beings. **Cognitive learning theorists** have by no means abandoned the classic notions of stimulus-response conditioning, but they do maintain that cognitive processes are important in all human and in some animal learning. They want to explain what actually goes on inside of us when we learn. Let us now take a closer look at the kinds of learning that cognitive theorists tend to study.

Cognitive learning theorists maintain that cognitive, or internal, factors are involved in all human learning.

CONTINGENCY THEORY. Conditioning has been seen as a process of pairing things together in time. In classical conditioning, an unconditioned and a conditioned stimulus are paired, while in operant conditioning, a response is paired with reinforcement. In the late 1960s psychologists took a major step toward refining these concepts when they began to ask if something more than simple pairing was behind conditioning. Did Pavlov's dogs salivate when they heard a bell only because the bell and food had appeared within a short time of one another? Or did the bell tell them something about the coming of food?

Psychologist Robert Rescorla (1967) argues that the close appearance in time of two objects does not explain classical conditioning. In his view, the conditioned stimulus must be able to tell you something about whether the unconditioned stimulus is going to occur. The buzzer must signify contingency—that if one thing occurs, something else is likely to occur. This and related proposals have since been grouped under the heading of **contingency theory.** Rescorla tested his ideas by pairing a tone (the CS) with electric shocks (the US), which were administered in different ways to several groups of dogs. One group received the tone followed consistently by a shock, just as in classical conditioning studies. These dogs showed fear at the sound of the tone, much as Pavlov would have predicted. Another group received an equal number of tones and shocks, but the tone was never followed by a shock. The two were always unpaired. According to classical conditioning, no learning should occur, but Rescorla found that this was not so. Instead, the dogs learned that when the tone was not present, shocks were more apt to occur, and that when the tone was present, they were safe. In other words, although the CS and US were never paired, the dogs learned. For still another group, the tone and shock occurred randomly, entirely independently of one another. Occasionally tone and shock were paired by chance. According to Pavlov's theory, this should have led to classical conditioning. But the dogs did not learn to fear the tone, apparently because it told them nothing about the likelihood of a shock. Thus Rescorla concluded that a stimulus must "tell" the organism something about the other stimulus for classical conditioning to occur.

This same line of reasoning has been extended to operant conditioning (Rescorla & Holland, 1982). One especially interesting line of

Drawing by Chas. Addams; © 1981
The New Yorker Magazine, Inc.

Learned helplessness Apathy and passivity learned in a situation where one's behavior has no effect on reward and punishment.

Social learning theory View of learning that emphasizes the ability to learn by observing a model or receiving instructions, without first-hand experience by the learner.

research concerns **learned helplessness** (Seligman, 1975). In one experiment dogs restrained in a harness received shocks at random. Skinner might argue that the harnessed dogs would learn only "superstitious" behavior, since none of the dogs' behaviors was consistently paired with a reward of relief from pain. In fact, the dogs seemed to learn that nothing they could do would deliver them from their discomfort, that they had no control over the shocks. When they were placed in another context and given the chance to escape, these dogs whined and finally lay down, passively accepting shock after shock long after other dogs had learned to escape. Contingency theorists believe that this passivity, or learned helplessness, was learned in the harness and then mistakenly generalized to the new context in which escape was possible.

Young infants also seem to be able to distinguish situations in which they can control delivery of a reward from those in which they cannot. This was the conclusion of experimenters who worked with infants lying in a crib, their heads resting on a pillow. For one group, beneath the pillow was a switch; whenever the infant shifted its head, a mobile on the opposite side of the crib would move for a few seconds. For the other group, the mobile was moved by the experimenters, independent of what the infant did. The first group quickly learned to move the mobile and repeatedly shifted their heads, taking obvious pleasure in the result. The second group also smiled and cooed when the mobile moved, but only for a time. Apparently because they realized they could not control the mobile, the rate at which they turned their heads stayed even and they soon lost interest in the mobile. The reinforcing power of the mobile seems to have depended on the infants' awareness that they controlled its movement (Watson, 1971).

Contingency theory is a more cognitive approach to simple learning than traditional theories of conditioning. Contingency theorists believe that animals and humans continually collect, code, and distill information about their environment. Classical and operant conditioning procedures are simply two ways of providing that information to the subjects, and in this sense the distinction between classical and operant conditioning has been further reduced. Moreover, contingency theory suggests that there may be other, more effective procedures to provide this information and thus to cause learning to occur, at least for some organisms.

SOCIAL LEARNING THEORY. In the past two decades another group of psychologists has challenged the idea that most or all human learning involves classical or operant conditioning. The foremost representative of this group is Albert Bandura, and the point of view he represents is called **social learning theory** (Bandura, 1977). Social learning theorists are impressed by the extent to which we can learn not just from first-hand experience—the kind of learning explained by classical and operant conditioning—but also from watching what happens to other people or by being told about something. In fact, we can learn new behaviors without ever actually carrying them out or being reinforced for them. The first time you drive a car, you are likely to drive carefully because you have been told to do so, you have been warned about driving carelessly, you have watched people drive carefully, and you've seen what happens if people drive carelessly. In other words, you have learned a great deal about driving without ever actually sitting behind the wheel of a car.

This kind of **vicarious** or **observational learning** seems to be quite common. By watching models, we can learn such things as how to start a lawn mower and how to saw wood. We can also learn how to show love or respect or concern, as well as hostility and aggression. When the Federal Communications Commission (FCC) banned cigarette commercials on TV, they showed their belief that modeling a response—lighting up a cigarette—would encourage people to imitate it. They removed the model to discourage the habit. More recently, the close scrutiny given to violence on television (especially in children's cartoon shows) also reflects an awareness that models can shape people's behavior. (TV violence is discussed in more detail at the end of Chapter 10.)

But obviously we do not imitate everything that other people do. Social learning theory accounts for this in several ways (Bandura, 1977). First, you must not only see but also pay attention to what the model does; this is more likely if the model (such as a famous or attractive person or an expert) commands attention. Second, you must remember what the model did. Third, you have to convert what you learned into action: It is quite possible to learn a great deal from watching the model, but have no particular reason to convert what you learned into behavior. This distinction between *learning* on the one hand, and *performance* on the other, is very important to social learning theorists: They stress that learning can occur without any change in outward behavior.

In a classic experiment Bandura (1965) demonstrated that people can learn a behavior without being reinforced for doing so, and that learning a behavior and performing it are not the same thing. Bandura randomly divided a group of 66 nursery-school children (33 boys and 33 girls) into three groups of 22 subjects. Next, each child was led individually into a darkened room, where he or she watched a film. In the film an adult model walked up to an adult-size plastic Bobo doll and ordered it to clear the way. When the doll failed to obey, the model exhibited a series of aggressive acts. He set the doll on its side, punched it in the nose and exclaimed, "Pow, right in the nose, boom, boom." He also hit it with a rubber mallet, kicked the doll around the room, and threw rubber balls at it.

The film ended differently for children in each of the three groups. Children in the *model-rewarded condition* watched the model being rewarded by a second adult, who brought a large supply of candies and soft drinks and praised him. Children in the *model-punished condition* observed the second adult shaking his finger, scolding, and spanking the model for his bullying behavior. Children in the *no-consequences condition* saw the same film, but without an ending showing either of these consequences to the model. Immediately after seeing the film the children were escorted individually into a room in which a Bobo doll, rubber balls, a mallet, and many other toys were available for play. While the child played alone for 10 minutes, observers coded his or her behavior from behind a one-way mirror. Every time a child spontaneously repeated any of the aggressive acts seen in the film, he or she was coded as *performing* the behavior. After 10 minutes, an experimenter entered the room and offered the child treats in return for imitating or repeating things the model had done or said to the Bobo doll. Bandura used the number of successfully imitated behaviors as a measure of how much the child had *learned* by watching the model.

Vicarious or **observational learning** Learning by observing other people's behavior.

In observational or vicarious learning, we learn by watching a model perform a particular action, and then trying to imitate it correctly.

Modifying Your Own Behavior

Can people modify their own behavior? The answer is yes. The first thing to do is to decide what behavior you want to acquire—the "target" behavior. What if you want to get rid of some behavior? Behavior modification specialists emphasize a positive approach called "ignoring." Much better results are achieved when the emphasis is on the new behavior to be acquired rather than on the behavior to be eliminated. For example, instead of setting a target of being less shy, you might define the target behavior as becoming more outgoing or more sociable. Other possible target behaviors are behaving more assertively, studying more, and getting along better with your roommate. In each case, you have focused on the behavior that you want to acquire rather than on the behavior you want to reduce or eliminate.

The next step is to define the target behavior precisely: What exactly do you mean by "assertive" or by "sociable"? One way to do this is to imagine situations in which the target behavior could be performed. Then describe these situations in writing and the way in which you now respond to them. For example, in the case of shyness, you might write: "When I am sitting in the lecture hall, waiting for class to begin, I don't talk to the people around me." Next, write down how you would rather act in that situation: "Ask the people sitting next to me how they like the class or the professor; or ask if they have seen any particularly good films recently."

The next step is to monitor your present behavior, keeping a daily log of activities related to the target behavior in order to establish your present rate of behavior. At the same time, try to figure out if your present, undesirable behavior is being reinforced in some way. For example, if you find yourself unable to study, record what you do instead and try to determine how that undesirable behavior is being reinforced.

The next step—the basic principle of self-modification—is to provide yourself with a positive reinforcer that is contingent on specific improvements in the target behavior. You may be able to use the same reinforcer that now maintains your undesirable behavior, or you may want to pick a new reinforcer. Watson and Tharp (1981) use the example of a student who wanted to improve his relationship with his parents. He first counted the times he said something pleasant to them and then rewarded himself for improvement by making his favorite pastime, playing pool, contingent on predetermined increases in the number of pleasant remarks he made. You can also use tokens: Give yourself one token for every 30 minutes of studying and cash in those tokens for reinforcement. For an hour of TV, you might charge yourself three tokens, while the privilege of going to a movie might cost six.

Remember that behavior need not be learned all in one piece. You can use shaping or successive approximations to change your behavior bit by bit over a period of time.

If you would like to attempt a program of self-modification, a book by David Watson and Roland Tharp entitled *Self-Directed Behavior* (1981) is extremely useful, as it provides step-by-step instructions and exercises.

Analysis of the data revealed that (1) children who had observed the model being rewarded were especially likely to *perform* the model's behavior spontaneously; but (2) children in the three groups had *learned* equal amounts about assaulting the doll. That is, when they were offered rewards for showing what they had learned, the children in all three groups could imitate the model's behavior equally well, and quite accurately at that.

Notice that the children in this study learned aggressive behavior without being reinforced for it. In fact, the children learned even when the model was neither reinforced nor punished for behaving aggressively. While reinforcement of the model is not necessary for vicarious learning to occur, seeing a model reinforced or punished nonetheless provides us with useful information. It tells us what the correct or incorrect behavior is, and what is likely to happen to us if we imitate the model. In short, we learn what behaviors are valued and are therefore able to anticipate the consequences of acting in various ways. Human beings have not only sight but also insight, hindsight, and foresight. We use all of these to interpret our own experience and that of others (Bandura, 1962).

Finally, Bandura stresses that human beings are capable of setting performance standards for themselves and then rewarding (or punishing) themselves for achieving or failing to achieve those standards. In other words, people can be their own source of reinforcement or punishment and can thus regulate their own behavior. Because of its emphasis on expectations, insight, information, self-satisfaction, and self-criticism, social learning theory has great potential for widening our understanding not only of how people learn skills and abilities, but also of how attitudes, values, and ideas pass from person to person. Social learning theory can also teach us how *not* to pass something on. For example, suppose you want to teach a child not to hit other children. A traditional learning theorist would advise you to slap the child as punishment to change the behavior, while reinforcing more desirable behavior. But a social learning theorist would tell you that slapping the child only demonstrates a better way of hitting. It also supports the child's suspicion that hitting can be effective. You and the child would both be better off if you demonstrated a less aggressive model of dealing with other people (Bandura, 1973, 1977). Such advice, combined with traditional discrimination training and reinforcement, can indeed help people to change their behavior. Because social learning theory takes the best from operant conditioning and combines it with the "human element" ignored by traditional learning theories, it has attracted a great deal of interest and has become a major trend in research into learning.

Application

Shaping Better Health Through Biofeedback

"Operant conditioning is a good way of teaching pigeons and rats to do unusual things," you might find yourself thinking at this point, "but does it have any practical value for humans?" The answer is definitely yes. Principles of operant conditioning can be applied to some extent to the delivery of rewards in schools, the workplace, and other settings. One of the most exciting applications in recent years is in the area of health care. Consider the following case.

From the time she was 9 years old, a 29-year-old woman had suffered from tension headaches. The dull aching would begin in the morning and last all day. Members of the clinic where she sought help knew that one major cause of tension headaches is constant excessive contraction of the frontalis muscle, the main muscle in the forehead. So they set about teaching her to relax this muscle by means of a technique called *biofeedback*. Biofeedback is essentially a form of operant conditioning in which instruments are used to inform the learner about some biological response over which he or she wishes to gain control. In the case of the headache sufferer, electrodes attached to her forehead measured the degree of contraction in the frontalis muscle below. The amount of contraction was converted into an audible tone that lowered in pitch as the muscle relaxed: If she relaxed the muscle even slightly, the tone dropped. This drop in the tone served as a secondary reinforcer, which increased the future likelihood of muscle relaxation. At first, she was capable of only slight relaxation. But over the course of several dozen 30-minute training sessions spread over 9 weeks, she exhibited increasing ability to control the level of contraction. At a follow-up 3 months after therapy had begun, the woman reported virtually no further tension headaches (Budzynski, Stoyra, & Adler, 1970). This technique has succeeded in reducing tension headaches in about 70 percent of the people who have used it over the years.

We use this case as an example to illustrate the major elements of biofeedback. First, special equipment is used to collect information about a biological response—in this instance, muscle contraction—about which people normally have little or no information. Second, feedback about the response is provided to the subject by means of lights, tones, or some other signal that varies with the response being measured. In the tension headache case, the tone signaled changes in muscle tension. Third, the subject uses this information to improve control over the response. In this case, the subject could tell from the tone whether she was succeeding in reducing tension.

The effectiveness of biofeedback depends on some of the same factors that determine success in operant conditioning. Feedback should be rapid, consistent, and precise. When feedback is *rapid*, reinforcement is most effective. Each time the tone dropped, it immediately reinforced the muscle relaxation response. *Consistent* feedback is also crucial. Suppose that early in the training, the tone dropped several times, but the muscle had actually contracted rather than relaxed. Learning how to relax the muscle would have been much harder, if not entirely impossible. Finally, especially at the start of training, feedback must be *precise*, indicating even the slightest changes in response. This permits the shaping of the desired behavior by successive approximations.

In recent years biofeedback has become a well-established treatment for a number of medical problems, including not only tension headaches but also migraine headaches, asthma, and peptic ulcers. Migraine headaches, which plague about 10 percent of the population to varying degrees, can be eased or stopped by a biofeedback approach that differs in some details from that used to treat tension headaches. Migraines typically affect a localized area of the head, cause intense pain, and are sometimes associated with nausea, vomiting, and sensitivity to light. Just before the headache starts, blood vessels carrying blood to the brain constrict,

reducing the blood supply to nerve cells in the brain. Shortly afterward, these vessels expand rapidly, causing nerve cells surrounding the vessels to fire off messages of intense pain. Research has discovered that with migraine sufferers, changes in the blood supply to the hands, and hence changes in the skin temperature of the hands, are associated with changes in the supply of blood to the brain. The mechanism behind this effect is not fully understood, but biofeedback therapists can teach victims to change the skin temperature of their hands and thereby counteract the changes in brain blood supply that cause migraines. Generally, a temperature sensor placed on a finger causes changes in a tone, which can be used effectively as feedback to increase or decrease skin temperature and blood supply to the brain. The training period is longer and more difficult than for tension headaches. Nevertheless, significant reductions in the frequency of migraines have been reported consistently (Olton & Noonberg, 1980).

Biofeedback has effectively relieved medical problems other than headaches, including asthma. During an asthma attack the victim suffers from shortness of breath and difficulty in breathing. These symptoms are due in part to the contraction of muscles around the air passages in the lungs, partly blocking the movement of air through the lungs. In order to keep the passages partly open, the lungs must remain partly inflated, limiting the efficiency with which air is exchanged. Biofeedback has been employed successfully to train people to change the volume of air they exhale. In one approach a device measures resistance to breathing in the lungs and converts this into an audible tone, which in turn can be used to learn to reduce resistance in the air passages.

Finally, peptic ulcers—small areas of the lining of the stomach or small intestine that have been destroyed by digestive acids—have also been treated by means of biofeedback. The behavior to be shaped in this case is a reduction in the amount of acid that is secreted by the stomach. Acid levels in the stomach are measured either by extracting liquid through a tube inserted into the nose and swallowed, or by swallowing a meter that transmits readings to a receiver outside the body. When acid measurements are converted into a biofeedback signal, subjects have successfully trained themselves to reduce the amount of acid secreted. So far, however, although the amount of reduction has been great enough to be valuable, it has not been so great that biofeedback can be clearly recommended over other modes of treatment.

Biofeedback has some drawbacks. Patients must invest considerable time and effort in shaping their behavior. They must also have the discipline to practice their new technique, a quality that many patients do not display. Nevertheless, biofeedback does place the control of treatment in the patient's own hands, a major advantage over other kinds of treatment, and has achieved impressive success in treating certain kinds of problems (Olton & Noonberg, 1980).

Summary

1. *Learning* is the process by which relatively permanent changes in behavior are brought about through experience or practice. Some of the simplest kinds of learning are called *conditioning* responses—the acquisition of a particular pattern of behavior in the presence of certain stimuli.

2. *Classical conditioning* involves learning to transfer a response from a stimulus that invariably elicits the response to some stimulus that does not normally produce such a response. Ivan Pavlov first demonstrated this process when he conditioned dogs to salivate upon hearing a bell.

3. In classical conditioning, the stimulus that invariably causes the desired response is called the *unconditioned stimulus* (US). The reaction to the unconditioned stimulus is called the *unconditioned response* (UR). The neutral stimulus that the subject learns to respond to is known as the *conditioned stimulus* (CS); and the response to the conditioned stimulus is called the *conditioned response* (CR).

4. Humans also respond to principles of classical conditioning. Humans have been conditioned to develop certain responses, such as a fear of rats, and also to unlearn them. In *desensitization therapy*, conditioning is used to gradually reduce a person's anxiety about a particular object or situation.

5. Effective classical conditioning generally depends on a strong, distinctive stimulus, presentation of the conditioned stimulus just before the unconditioned stimulus, and repeated pairing of the US and CS.

6. An exception to some of the principles of classical conditioning is food aversion. Animals that experience a food-related illness learn to avoid that stimulus in the future even if a long time passes between eating and illness. Such learning occurs after only one trial.

7. A learned response will generally stop occurring if the conditioned stimulus fails to be followed by the unconditioned stimulus. This process is known as *extinction*. After a while the response may suddenly reappear on its own. This is known as *spontaneous recovery*.

8. Once a response has been conditioned to a particular stimulus, it may also be elicited by similar stimuli. This is *stimulus generalization*. The opposite of generalization is *discrimination*. This is the process by which a subject learns to respond to one specific stimulus and to inhibit the response to all other stimuli.

9. After a response to a conditioned stimulus has been learned, the conditioned stimulus itself can be used as the unconditioned stimulus in further training—a procedure known as *higher-order conditioning*.

10. In *operant conditioning*, subjects learn to operate on their environment in some way that will get them something they desire or allow them to avoid something unpleasant. The conditioning is done by reinforcing correct responses and ignoring or punishing incorrect ones.

11. For operant conditioning to occur, the desired response must be made. There are several ways to make the correct response occur. The most common method is to wait for the subject to hit upon the correct response. Other effective methods are to increase motivation and restrict the environment as within a *Skinner box*.

12. Once the desired response has been made,

reinforcement ensures that it will be repeated and learned. A *primary reinforcer* is one that is rewarding by itself. A *secondary reinforcer* is one whose value has to be learned through association with other reinforcers.

13. Minimizing the interval between a response and reinforcement is important for learning to be successful. Delayed reinforcement is more effective when distractions from intervening events are minimized.

14. Not every correct response need be reinforced for learning to occur. *Schedules of reinforcement* can be based either on the number of responses or on the time lapse between responses. On a *fixed-interval schedule* reinforcement is given for the first correct response after a specific time has passed. The amount of time always stays the same. On a *variable-interval schedule* the amount of time between reinforcements varies. On a *fixed-ratio schedule* reinforcement is given after a certain number of responses. The number of responses always stays the same. On a *variable-ratio schedule* the number of responses between reinforcements varies.

15. A *positive reinforcer* is anything that increases the likelihood that ongoing behavior will be repeated. *Punishment* tends to inhibit or suppress behavior although it does not teach alternative behaviors. Punishment is most effective when it is swift, sufficient, and certain. Punishment has a number of negative side effects, including a tendency to provoke aggressive behavior; nonetheless, there are times when it is needed to stop certain behavior. In such cases, the ending of punishment acts as a *negative reinforcer,* and any ongoing behavior at the moment is likely to be repeated in the future. Following negative reinforcement with positive reinforcement makes it even more likely that the desirable behavior will recur in the future.

16. An alternative to the use of punishment is *avoidance training,* whereby a behavior is learned in order to avoid an unpleasant situation.

17. Generalization and discrimination occur in operant conditioning as well as in classical conditioning. In *response generalization* the stimulus remains the same but the response changes. Discrimination is taught by reinforcing a response only in the presence of certain stimuli. Operant responses are extinguished by withholding reinforcement, but they may recover spontaneously. Several factors affect how easy or difficult it is to distinguish operant responses, including the strength of the original learning and the number of settings in which learning took place. It is especially difficult to extinguish avoidance training.

18. Recent research has blurred the distinction between classical and operant conditioning to the point that many psychologists believe the two may simply be different methods of bringing about the same process of learning. Research now suggests that classical conditioning can be used with voluntary behaviors and operant conditioning with involuntary ones; that in classical conditioning the conditioned response and unconditioned response are not necessarily the same; that there apparently are limits on how far a learned response can differ from natural behavior; and that the relatively few differences in such things as generalization, discrimination, and extinction reinforce similarities between the two types of learning.

19. *Cognitive learning theorists* do not agree that learning involves only observable stimuli and responses. In their view, learning also involves unobservable cognitive processes that link stimulus and response. One kind of cognitive theory, *contingency theory,* proposes that a simple pairing of the unconditioned stimulus (US) and the conditioned stimulus (CS), or of the desired response and reinforcement, is not enough to explain learning. Only when one stimulus provides information that something else will (or won't) happen does learning occur.

20. *Social learning theory* emphasizes *observational learning*—the ability to learn by watching other people's behavior. Whether observation leads to imitation, however, depends upon (1) paying attention to the model; (2) remembering what the model did; and (3) converting observed learning into action. Social learning theorists hold that human beings can reinforce—or punish—themselves, and thus can regulate their own behavior. Their views differ in a number of important respects from those of traditional learning theorists.

1. The simplest type of learning is called _____ . It refers to the establishment of fairly predictable behavior, in the presence of well-defined stimuli.

2. The most effective method in classical conditioning is to present the conditioned stimulus (CS) before/after the unconditioned stimulus (US).

3. In classical conditioning, extinction requires breaking the association between which of the following pairs:
   a. CS and the CR
   b. US and the UR
   c. CS and the US
   d. US and the CR

4. Once extinction has occurred, a CS may still bring about a CR at a later time; this phenomenon is known as _____ _____ .

5. The process by which a learned response to a specific stimulus comes to be associated with different but similar stimuli is known as _____ .

6. A type of learning that essentially involves rewarding correct responses and ignoring or punishing incorrect responses is known as _____ _____ .

7. By means of a technique called _____ , a new response is acquired by successively reinforcing partial responses.

8. Food, water, and sex are examples of primary/secondary reinforcers.

9. Match the following terms with their correct definitions:
   ___ fixed-ratio schedule
   ___ variable-ratio schedule
   ___ fixed-interval schedule
   ___ variable-interval schedule

   A. subject is rewarded for the first response after a certain amount of time has passed
   B. subject is rewarded after a fixed number of correct responses
   C. subject is rewarded after a varying number of responses
   D. subject is rewarded after varying lengths of time have passed

10. The goal of both positive and negative reinforcement is to increase/decrease the likelihood that a certain behavior will be repeated.

11. Punishment is an effective way of both controlling behavior and of teaching new ways of behaving. T/F

12. A monkey is taught to eat only green bananas and to avoid eating bananas of any other color; this is an example of discrimination/avoidance learning.

13. Which of the following occurs in both classical and operant conditioning:
   a. generalization and discrimination
   b. extinction and spontaneous recovery
   c. neither a nor b
   d. both a and b

14. The emphasis in social learning theory is on _____ learning, the process of learning by watching other people's behavior.

15. Cognitive theorists argue that in order for learning to take place, the CS must be able to provide the learner with information about whether the US is likely to occur. This proposal is known as _____ theory.

Outline

Memory

7

The famous conductor Toscanini was known to have memorized every single note of every instrument of about 250 symphonies and all the music and lyrics of about 100 operas. Once, when he could not locate a score of Joachim Raff's Quartet No. 5, he sat down and reproduced it purely from memory. He had not seen or played the score for decades. Nonetheless, when a copy of the Quartet was finally found, it was discovered that with the exception of one single note Toscanini had reproduced it perfectly! (Neisser, 1982)

A waiter named John Conrad never writes down a single item of a customer's order. He routinely handles parties of 6 and 8 in a busy Colorado restaurant, remembering everything from soup to salad dressing. Once he handled a party of 19, serving 19 complete dinners to the correct person without a single error (Singular, 1983).

Before being stricken with a viral illness, a young woman of 29 (known as "MZ") could remember "the exact day of the week of future or past events of almost anything that touched my life . . . all personal telephone numbers . . . colors of interiors and what people wore . . . pieces of music . . . recalling a picture, as a painting in a museum, was like standing in the museum looking at it again" (Klatzky, 1980).

These accounts of people with extraordinary memories raise lots of questions about the nature of memory. Why are some people so much better at remembering things than others? Are they simply born with good memories or do they learn to remember unusually well? Could I learn to remember as much as these people do? And why is it that remembering can be so simple sometimes (as when a baseball fan remembers every batting average on his favorite team), and yet so difficult at others (such as groping for answers on an exam)? Why do we find it so difficult to remember something that happened only a few months ago, yet find ourselves able to recall every vivid detail of some other event that happened ten or twenty or even thirty years ago? Just how does memory work and what makes it fail? We will be exploring all these and other questions about memory in this chapter.

Since we can only remember those things that we perceive in the first place, we will start by looking at what happens to the vast amounts of information that continually bombard our senses. We begin by selecting some of this information to think about and potentially remember.

The Sensory Registers

If you look slowly around the room you are in, you will see that each glance—which may last for only a fraction of a second—takes in an enormous amount of visual information, including colors, shapes, textures, relative brightness, shadows, and so on. At the same time you are taking in sounds, smells, and other kinds of sensory data. All this raw information flows from your senses into what are known as the **sensory registers.** These are like waiting rooms. Information enters, stays for a very short time, and then is either processed further or lost. Though there are registers for each of our several senses, the visual and auditory registers have been studied most extensively, and it is to them that we now turn.

Visual and Auditory Registers

To understand how much visual information we take in, and how quickly it is lost, take an instant camera into a darkened room and take a photograph using a flashbulb. During the split second that the room is lit up by the flash, your visual register will take in a surprising amount of information about the room and its contents. Try to hold on to that visual image, or *icon,* as long as you can. You will find that it fades rapidly and, in a few seconds, is gone. Then compare your remembered image of the room with what you actually saw at the time, as captured in the

Just a glance around a room takes in an enormous amount of visual and often other kinds of sensory information. All this raw data from the senses flows into the sensory registers.

photograph. You will notice that there was far more information taken in by the visual register than you were able to retain for even a few seconds.

In this experiment, the image faded out by itself over several seconds. But under normal circumstances, new visual information keeps coming into the register and this new information replaces or "erases" the old information. This is just as well, because otherwise the visual information would simply pile up in the sensory register and get hopelessly scrambled. Phillips (1974) has determined that under normal viewing conditions, visual information is erased from the sensory register in about ¼ second and is replaced by new information, long before it has a chance to simply fade out by itself.

Auditory information fades more slowly than visual information. The auditory equivalent of the icon is the *echo*. The echo tends to last for several seconds, which, given the nature of speech, is fortunate. Otherwise, "*You* did it!" would be indistinguishable from "You *did* it!" because we would be unable to remember the emphasis on the first words by the time the last words were registered.

Initial Processing

If information disappears from the sensory registers so rapidly, how do we remember anything for more than a second or two? The answer is that we select out some of the incoming information and hold it for further processing and, perhaps, for remembering permanently (see Figure 7-1). No matter how hard we try, we simply cannot be aware of all the details that bombard our senses. We constantly select which information is chosen for further processing. This is what we call **attention:** the process

Attention Selection of some incoming information for further processing.

Figure 7-1

The sequence of information processing in memory. Raw information flows from the senses into the sensory registers, where it is either further processed or lost. Information chosen for further processing enters short-term memory, from which it is either forgotten or transferred into long-term memory.

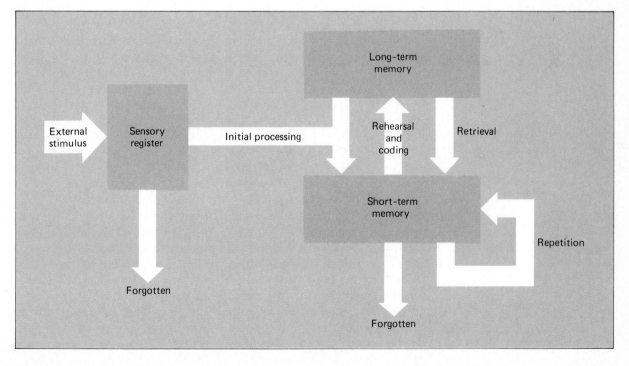

of selective looking, listening, smelling, tasting, and feeling. In the process of attending, we also give *meaning* to the information that is coming in. Information in the sensory registers is just meaningless raw data. Look at the page in front of you. You will see a series of black lines on a white page. Until you recognize these lines as letters and words, they are just meaningless marks. To make sense of this jumble of data, the information in the sensory registers must be processed for meaning.

Suppose you are sitting at a desk reading this book. Your roommate is listening to a talk show on the radio. There are traffic sounds outside. The water you are heating to make tea starts to boil. Even if you turn off the kettle and ask your roommate to take the radio into the other room, there will still be at least a vague hum from the radio, the traffic noises will continue, and you will taste the tea as you read. In situations like this one, how do we select which information to pay attention to?

Broadbent (1958) suggested that there is a filtering process at the entrance to the nervous system. All incoming stimuli are accepted into the sensory registers where they are sorted out by physical properties such as color, size, loudness, location, shape, and so on. Only those stimuli that meet certain requirements are allowed through the filter. According to Broadbent, only those stimuli that get through the filter are compared with what we already know, so that we can recognize them and figure out what they mean. If you are sitting at a restaurant table listening to a friend talk, you filter out all other conversations taking place around you. Although you may be able to describe certain physical characteristics of those other conversations, such as whether they were spoken by men or women, or spoken loudly or softly, according to Broadbent you would normally be unable to describe what was being said. Because the conversations were filtered out, processing did not reach the point where you could understand the meaning of what you heard.

According to Broadbent's theory, information will draw our attention if it is made to stand out because of its physical properties—intensity, color, sudden starts or stops. Yet most of us have had the experience of reading a book only to have our attention swing to a particularly meaningful word farther down the page—perhaps our own last name, or the name of our hometown. Or, to return to the restaurant example, if someone around us were to speak our name, in all likelihood our attention would shift to their conversation. This is called the "cocktail-party phenomenon" (Cherry, 1966). There is no physical reason why that one word should have stood out. In fact, according to Broadbent's theory, since we were not attending to it and it was presumably filtered out, we should not even have heard the word, much less understood what it meant!

Treisman (1965), among others, modified the filter theory to account for these exceptions. She suggested that the filter is not a simple on or off switch, but a variable control like the volume control on a radio that can "turn down" unwanted signals without rejecting them entirely. According to this view, many signals are passed on from the sensory registers at the same time. All this information gets at least some processing, during which time it begins to become meaningful—we begin to understand what we are seeing and hearing, tasting and touching. Although we may be paying attention to only some of this incoming information, we monitor the other signals at a low level. In this way, although we are not

The "cocktail-party" phenomenon states that we can shift our attention if we sense something particularly meaningful. Thus if someone around us in a restaurant were to speak our name, we would very likely shift our attention to their conversation.

normally aware of extraneous stimuli, we can shift our attention if we sense something particularly meaningful. This process works even when we are asleep: A classic example is the mother who wakes immediately to the sound of her baby crying yet sleeps through other, louder noises. Similarly, most of us would wake up immediately to the words "The house is on fire," while we would probably sleep through less important phrases like "The car is for sale."

Let's look more closely at the evidence for this alternative view of attention. How do we know that apparently "unattended" messages are not completely filtered out (and thus forgotten) at the level of the sensory registers? Norman (1969) gave subjects separate messages in each ear at the same time and asked them to *shadow*, or verbally repeat, one of these messages and to ignore the other. Nonetheless, he found that people could remember parts of the irrelevant message if they were interrupted during the experiment or asked to recall the message immediately afterward. Moray (1959) also found that part of an unattended message could be remembered immediately after the message ended if it had been preceded by the subject's own name. But without this "signal," Moray's subjects could remember little or nothing of the unattended message. In another experiment, MacKay (1973) asked subjects to shadow ambiguous sentences delivered to one ear while ignoring information in the other ear that clarified the meaning of those sentences. For example, the word "bank" can refer to a financial institution or to the sides of a river. All subjects shadowed an ambiguous sentence delivered to one ear which contained the word "bank." For some subjects, an unattended message in their other ear suggested that the word "bank" referred to a financial bank, while for other subjects the unattended message suggested that "bank" referred to a riverbank. Even though subjects were subsequently unable to recall the unattended message, it affected their interpretation of the word "bank." In other words, the meaning of the unattended message was understood.

To summarize, we know that we attend to very little of the informa-

Short-term memory (STM) Working memory; briefly stores and processes selected information from the sensory registers.

tion in our sensory registers. In part, we select information based on certain physical characteristics—such as color, a certain voice quality—and process those signals further in an effort to recognize and understand them. But other, "ignored" signals get at least some initial processing, so that we can shift our attention to focus on something particularly meaningful. But what happens to the information that we do attend to? It enters our short-term memory.

Short-Term Memory

Chess players demand complete silence as they ponder their next move. This is due to the fact that there is a definite limit on how much information STM can handle at any given moment.

Short-term memory (STM) is what we are thinking about at any given moment. It is sometimes referred to as "consciousness." When you listen to a conversation or a piece of music, when you watch a ballet or a tennis tournament, when you become aware of a leg cramp or a headache—in all these cases you are using STM to both hold onto and think about new information coming in from the sensory registers. STM therefore has two main tasks: to briefly store new information and to work on that (and other) information. Thus STM is sometimes called *working memory*.

Capacity of STM

The arcade fanatic absorbed in a game is oblivious to the outside world. Chess masters at tournaments demand complete silence while they ponder their next move. And you shut yourself in a quiet room to study for final exams. All these examples illustrate the fact that there is a definite limit on how much information STM can handle at any given moment. In fact, psychologists have determined that STM can hold only five to ten bits of information at the same time. You can demonstrate this for yourself. Read the first row of letters in the list below just once. Then close your eyes and try to remember the letters in the correct sequence before going on to the next row:

1. C X W
2. M N K T Y
3. R P J H B Z S
4. G B M P V Q F J D
5. E G Q W J P B R H K A

Like most people, you probably found rows 1 and 2 fairly easy, row 3 a bit harder, row 4 very hard, and row 5 impossible to remember after just one reading. This gives you an idea of the relatively limited capacity of STM.

Now try reading through the following set of twelve letters just once and see if you can repeat them: TJYFAVMCFKIB. How many letters were you able to recall? In all likelihood, not all twelve. But what if you had been asked to remember the following twelve letters instead: TV FBI JFK YMCA. Could you do it? Almost certainly the answer is yes (Klatzky, 1980). These are the same twelve letters as before, but here grouped into four separate "words." This way of grouping and organizing information to fit into meaningful units is called **chunking.** The twelve letters have been chunked into four meaningful items that can be readily handled by STM.

By chunking words into sentences or sentence fragments, we can process an even greater amount of information in STM (Aaronson & Scarborough, 1976, 1977; Tulving & Patkau, 1962). For example, suppose you want to remember the following list of words: *tree, song, hat, sparrow, box, lilac, cat.* One strategy would be to cluster as many of them as possible into sentences: "The sparrow in the tree sings a song;" "a lilac hat in the box;" "the cat in the hat." But isn't there a limit to all this? Would five sentences actually be as easy to remember for a short time as five single words? Simon (1974) found that as the size of any individual chunk increases, the number of chunks that can be held in STM declines. Thus STM can easily handle five unrelated letters or words simultaneously, but five unrelated sentences are much harder to remember.

Keep in mind that STM usually has more than one task to perform at once. During the brief time you spent memorizing those rows of letters, you probably gave them your full attention. But normally you have to attend to new incoming information while you work on whatever is already present in short-term memory. Competition between these two tasks for the limited workspace in STM means that neither task will be done as well as it could be. In one experiment, subjects were given six random numbers to remember and repeat while performing a simple reasoning task. As a result, they performed their reasoning task more slowly than subjects who had simply been asked to repeat the numbers 1 through 6 throughout the task (Baddeley & Hitch, 1974). Similarly, if you had been asked to count backward from 100 while trying to learn the rows of letters in our earlier example, you would have been much less successful in remembering them. Try it and see.

Coding in STM

There has been a good deal of controversy over how we *code* information for storage in STM. Much of the early research on STM looked at how we remember strings of letters or numbers, like our earlier lists. And the evidence seemed to indicate that these kinds of information were stored acoustically in STM—in sounds rather than in shapes. In other words, we code verbal information according to its sound, even if we see the word, letter, or number on a page rather than hear it spoken. How do we know that information is stored acoustically? Because numerous experiments have shown that when people try to retrieve material from STM, they are likely to mix up items that sound alike even if they are visually dissimilar. Thus, the letters B and V are often confused, while V and Y seldom are. The sequence PTGZDBVC is generally harder to remember than FJYQKRMH for the same reason (Reed, 1982).

Acoustic coding also seems to play a part in reading. This is particularly true for poor or beginning readers; but even experienced readers tend to *subvocalize*, that is, to pronounce words to themselves silently or audibly. This slows our reading down, of course, to the rate of speaking. In fact, the technique of speed reading is based in part on learning to

Chunking Grouping of information into meaningful units for easier handling by short-term memory.

Information like strings of letters or numbers is coded acoustically in STM—in sounds rather than in shapes.

process printed words visually only (Reed, 1982). Yet Levy (1978) and others have found that subvocalizing printed words helps us to understand more complex material better. You can test this for yourself very simply. Try to suppress subvocalizing by counting from 1 to 10 quickly and steadily while reading something simple like a shopping ad; then try it again while reading something more complex, like an editorial. You will probably have much greater difficulty understanding and remembering the editorial than the shopping ad when you are prevented from subvocalizing.

But not all material in short-term memory is stored acoustically. At least some material is stored in visual form, while other information is retained in terms of its meaning. For example, we don't have to convert things like maps, diagrams, and paintings into sound before we can code them into STM and think about them. And, of course, deaf people rely primarily on shapes rather than on sounds to retain information in STM (Conrad, 1972; Frumkin & Anisfeld, 1977).

In fact it appears that the capacity of STM is actually greater with visual coding than it is with acoustic coding (Reed, 1982). A good illustration of the superiority of visual coding in STM is the experiment done by Nielsen and Smith (1973). They asked subjects to pay close attention either to a verbal description of a face or to an actual picture of a face for four seconds. The subjects were then asked to match features of a test face with the features they had just seen or heard described. It took much longer to recognize the face from the verbal description ("large ears," "small eyes," etc.), which suggests that visual images tend to be more efficiently coded and decoded than verbal ones.

Retention and Retrieval in STM

Without looking back, try to recall the five rows of letters you learned on page 224. In all likelihood, if you haven't gone back to study those lists again, you have forgotten them. In fact, material in short-term memory will disappear in 15 to 20 seconds unless it is rehearsed or practiced (Klatzky, 1980; Reed, 1982).

Why do we forget material stored in short-term memory? According to the **decay theory,** the passing of time in itself will cause the strength of memory to decrease, thereby making it harder to remember. Most of the evidence for the decay theory comes from experiments known as *distractor studies.* For example, Peterson and Peterson (1959) gave subjects a sequence of letters to learn, like *PSQ.* Then subjects heard a 3-digit number, like 167. They were then asked to count backward from 167 by 3s: 167, 164, 161, and so on, for up to 18 seconds. At the end of that period, they were asked to recall the 3 letters. The results of this test astonished the experimenters. The subjects showed a rapid decline in their ability to remember the letters (see Figure 7-2). Since counting backward was assumed to be a task that would not interfere with remembering, the fact that subjects forgot the letters seemed to prove that the letters had simply faded from short-term memory in a very short time. Later experiments by Reitman (1974) and Shiffrin and Cook (1978) led to the same conclusion. Decay, then, seems to be at least partly responsible for forgetting in short-term memory.

But Shiffrin and Cook also found that interference can lead to forgetting from STM. **Interference theory,** unlike decay theory, holds that information gets mixed up with, or pushed aside by, other information and thus becomes harder to remember. Interference can come from two

Decay theory Holds that the passage of time itself causes forgetting from short-term memory.

Interference theory Holds that interference from other information causes forgetting from short-term memory.

Drugs and Memory

Memory can be both enhanced and impaired by the use of drugs. To date, most of the research in this area has focused on the short- and long-term effects of alcohol. Overall, the results show that alcohol interferes with the ability to encode new information, but it has relatively little effect on the retrieval of data already stored in long-term memory (Birnbaum, Parker, Hartley, & Noble, 1978). Heavy use of alcohol, however, may result in significant memory loss. In some cases, *everything* that was said or done while intoxicated is completely blocked out of memory. The person may fail to remember even highly significant events—such has having injured somebody! In extreme cases chronic alcoholism may result in "Korsakoff's psychosis," a disorder characterized by gross memory defects and disorientation. Sufferers of Korsakoff's psychosis may lose track of their own names, where they came from, or where they are.

The effects of marijuana on memory are far less clear. In one study subjects who had smoked marijuana experienced unusual difficulty in transferring information from short- to long-term memory. They could recall items for a brief period, but as time progressed they forgot more and more of the information (Klatzky, 1980). Like alcohol, marijuana appears to interfere with the ability to encode and store data in long-term memory.

There are drugs that actually enhance memory. Perhaps the most promising of these is DDAVP, a synthetic drug related to the hormone vasopressin which is secreted by the pituitary gland. Vasopressin appears to increase a person's motivation and enjoyment of learning, and these are important factors in improving one's memory. Taken in the form of a nasal spray, DDAVP has significantly increased subjects' ability to recall information on cue.

Another hormone, epinephrine, may also aid memory. Gold and Delaney (1981) discovered that the memory-enhancing effects of epinephrine were greatest when it was administered right after a learning session. Delays in administering the epinephrine markedly reduced its effectiveness. These results suggest that naturally occurring memory problems may be due in part to inadequate levels of vasopressin or epinephrine (McGaugh, 1983).

Retroactive inhibition Process by which new information in STM interferes with old information already in STM.

places. New material can interfere with old material already in short-term memory. This is called **retroactive inhibition** (see Figure 7-3). If you are trying to remember a phone number by repeating it to yourself and you

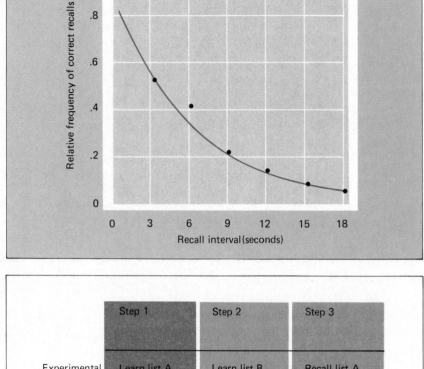

Figure 7-2

Graph showing the results of Peterson and Peterson's (1959) distractor study. The experiment measured the length of time that short-term memory lasts without rehearsal. Subjects showed a rapid decline in their ability to remember a sequence of letters.

Figure 7-3

A diagram of the experiment measuring retroactive inhibition. The experimental group usually does not perform as well on tests of recall as the control group, which does not suffer from retroactive inhibition from the second list of words or syllables.

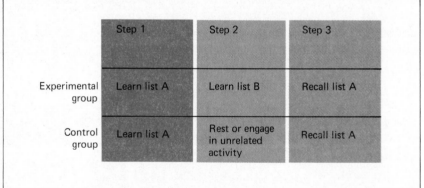

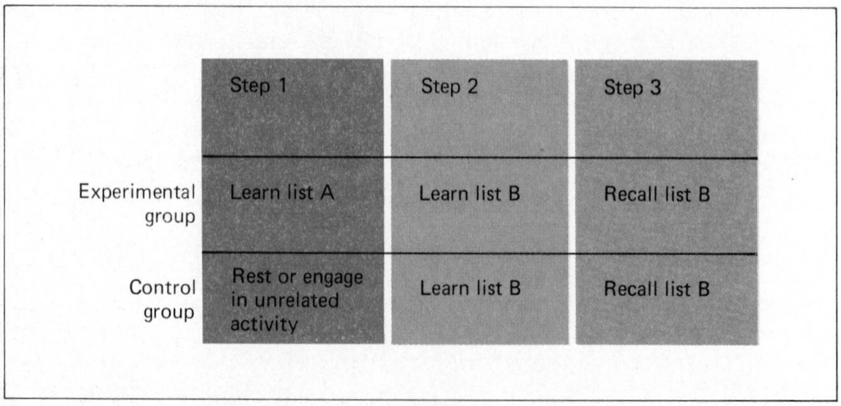

Figure 7-4

A diagram of the experiment used to measure proactive inhibition. The experimental group suffers the effects of proactive inhibition from List *A* and, when asked to recall List *B*, performs less well than the control group.

become aware of someone else in the room repeating another number, you may become confused and lose track of the number you were trying to keep in mind. Alternatively, old material in short-term memory can interfere with incoming information, which is called **proactive inhibition** (see Figure 7-4). In both cases, the more similarity there is between the old and the new learning, the more interference there is likely to be.

Decay theory clearly points to a storage failure. If an item has faded away to nothing, it is simply not there. But interference could work in either of two ways: Information could push other information out of STM—storage loss—or simply make it harder to get at the information that is still in STM—retrieval loss.

It appears that proactive inhibition is due primarily to retrieval problems. Old information in STM makes it harder to retrieve new, similar information that is also still in STM. To a lesser extent, the old information may actually push some new information out of STM completely. Retroactive inhibition appears to work largely by storage loss. To the extent that the new information interferes with the old, it is likely to push the old out of STM. In any case, forgetting in short-term memory appears to be due both to decay and to interference. Decay is a storage problem, while interference may be due to both storage and retrieval loss.

Once information is lost from STM, it is gone forever. If you can't recall now those lists of letters from earlier in the chapter, you probably never will! Usually it is just as well that this sort of forgetting takes place. Not only does this give space in STM for new information, but it keeps us from being overwhelmed with a jumble of irrelevant, trivial, or unrelated data. In this sense, forgetting from STM is usually not a "problem." But there are two exceptions to this: Sometimes we need to hold on to some information for a bit longer than 15 or 20 seconds, while other times we need to remember a new piece of information permanently. How can we avoid forgetting these kinds of information?

Rote Rehearsal

If you want to hold onto information for just a minute or two, the most effective device to use is **rote rehearsal.** You talk to yourself, repeating information over and over, silently or out loud. Through constant rote rehearsal, information can be held indefinitely in short-term memory (Klatzky, 1980). Although this is hardly the most efficient way to remember something permanently, it can be quite effective for a short while. In fact, if you repeat something to yourself long enough, even if you cannot recall it later, you may recognize the information when you hear or use it again. If you look up a telephone number and then twenty minutes later you are asked "What was the telephone number?" you are not likely to recall it. But if someone asks instead, "Were you dialing 555-1356?" you might recognize the number if you had repeated it often enough (Glenberg, Smith, & Green, 1977).

Rote rehearsal, simply repeating material over and over, is a very common memory strategy. Millions of students have learned their ABCs and multiplication tables by doggedly repeating letters and numbers. But mere repetition without any intent to learn does not seem to enhance memory (Glenberg, Smith, & Green, 1977). A child may see the same

Proactive inhibition Process by which old material already in STM interferes with new information in STM.

Rote rehearsal Retaining information in STM simply by repeating it over and over.

Rote rehearsal is a very common memory strategy. Doggedly repeating numbers is one way to learn the multiplication tables.

mailboxes day after day for years on the way to school and still be unable to recall the names on the mailboxes along the way. The mail carrier, however, probably could. Or think of the number of times in your life you have handled (and presumably recognized) pennies. Stop here and try to draw from memory the front side of a U.S. penny. When you have finished your drawing, turn to Figure 7-5 on p. 233 and pick the illustration you believe matches a real penny. For most people this task is surprisingly difficult: Despite seeing and handling tens of thousands of pennies, most people cannot accurately draw one or even recognize one when it is shown in a drawing (the correct penny, incidentally, is C in Figure 7-5) (Nickerson et. al., 1979). A well-known example of this same phenomenon is the case of Edmund Clarke Sanford, a noted psychologist of the early 20th century. Professor Sanford described his inability to recall a group of prayers that he had read aloud "at least 5,000 times in the last 25 years, usually at 24-hour intervals." He was so used to reading these prayers that he could do so with very little attention. Still, when he actually tested his memory of them, he found that he could only repeat an average of three to six words before having to refer to the text for help.

Laboratory experiments have also shown that repeating an item more often does not always improve later recall. Craik and Watkins (1973) asked subjects to keep track of the last word beginning with a given letter in a 21-word list. For example, if the given letter was G, a typical list might include: *daughter, oil, rifle, garden, grain, table, football, anchor, giraffe,* etc. Subjects would hold *garden* in short-term memory by repeating it silently until *grain* was heard; *grain* until *giraffe* was heard, and so on. As you can see from the list, *garden* was held in STM for just an instant since *grain* followed it immediately. But *grain* was held in STM for quite a while until *giraffe* finally replaced it. Nonetheless, subjects were equally likely to recall that *garden* and *grain* were on the list, despite the difference in rehearsal times for the two words.

Elaborative rehearsal The linking of new information in short-term memory to familiar material stored in long-term memory.

Elaborative Rehearsal

What do we have to do to assure that information in STM will be remembered for a long time if simple rote repetition isn't sufficient? Most researchers believe that **elaborative rehearsal** is necessary (Postman, 1975). Elaborative rehearsal involves relating new information to something that we already know. Suppose that you had to remember that the French word *poire* means *pear*. You are already familiar with *pear*, both as a word and as a fruit. *Poire*, however, means nothing to you. To remember what it means, you have to link it up with *pear*. To do this you might make up a sentence: *Pear* and *poire* both begin with "*p*." Or you might associate *poire* with the familiar taste and image of a pear.

You can see that elaborative rehearsal involves a deeper and more meaningful processing of new data than does simple rote repetition. Unless material gets rehearsed in this way it will quickly be forgotten. For example, consider for a moment what happens when elaborative rehearsal is either interrupted or prevented. Frequently, a person who has suffered a concussion cannot recall what directly preceded the injury, even though he or she can remember what happened some time before the injury. A severe electric shock can have the same effect. This condition is known as **retrograde amnesia.** The events right before the accident were at the short-term memory level and had not been rehearsed enough to be remembered for more than a short time. Thus, they were completely forgotten.

A person who suffers a concussion may not be able to recall what directly preceded the injury. This happens because the injury interferes with elaborative rehearsal.

Dreams also occur in STM, and unless they are rehearsed or repeated, they will quickly be forgotten. Cohen (1974a) asked one group of subjects to call the weather report on the telephone immediately after they woke up and to write down the day's expected temperature. This effectively prevented them from rehearsing their dreams. A second group of students was instructed to lie still for 90 seconds upon waking—the approximate time the first group took to call the weather report—and then to write down their dreams. This group could think about and rehearse their dreams while waiting. Only 33 percent of the first group could recall their dreams, while 63 percent of the second group remembered theirs.

Barring disruptions such as these, elaborative rehearsal seems to be necessary if you want to remember something more or less permanently. But before we go much further in understanding the nature of this process, we need to understand more about long-term memory.

Pathology of Memory

Forgetting is a normal, even healthy part of remembering. As we have seen, both decay and interference commonly lead to forgetting in short-term memory. And information that has been poorly encoded may be very difficult to retrieve from long-term memory. These are fairly normal occurrences of forgetting. But sometimes forgetting can become uncontrollable and persistent. When it actually interferes with our normal memory processes, we consider it to be a pathology of memory. Most often, pathological memory conditions result from traumatic events like accidents or disease.

Head injuries like concussions are a common cause of retrograde amnesia, ordinarily a temporary condition in which events just prior to an accident cannot be recalled. Also, damage to the hippocampus region of the brain may cause "hippocampal amnesia." This too entails a breakdown in the transference of data from short- to long-term memory and usually results in more extended memory loss. More devastating still is the memory damage caused by a brain disorder known as "Milner's syndrome." In 1959, Brenda Milner studied one young man who had lost part of his temporal lobes and hippocampus in a brain operation. His IQ did not decline after the operation. He could remember events that preceded the operation as well as anyone else, but nothing that had happened *since* the operation stuck in his mind. His family moved to a new house shortly after his stay in the hospital, and although he remembered his old address perfectly well, the new one eluded him. He might use the lawn mower on a Tuesday, but on Wednesday his mother would have to tell him all over again where to find it. He read the same magazines over and over—and each time the material was new to him (Milner, 1966).

A person with this syndrome can remember events from the distant past before brain damage occurred. He or she can also retain new information for a short time if it is repeated. The person cannot transfer new material from short-term memory to long-term memory, however, even though long-term memory is still "working" well enough to retrieve "old" memories from the distant past (Klatzky, 1980).

Forgetfulness also plays a prominent role in various degenerative diseases. Alzheimer's disease, for example, is an untreatable neurological disorder that involves severe memory loss.

The causes of memory pathology are invariably traced to brain damage. But what causes brain damage? Nutritional imbalances may be an important factor in some cases. Accidents, including those caused inadvertently during surgical operations, are another. Other research shows that supposedly beneficial drugs like antibiotics can cause varying degrees of forgetfulness, apparently by inhibiting essential protein synthesis (Rosenweig & Leiman, 1982).

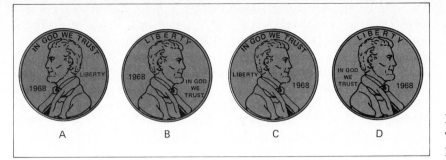

Figure 7-5
Which of these accurately illustrates a real U.S. penny?

Long-Term Memory

Everything that we "know" is stored in **long-term memory (LTM):** the words to a song, the results of the last election, the meaning of "justice," and so on. Some of this information is general knowledge: we know that 2 and 2 make 4, and that George Washington was the first president of the United States. We also understand the meaning of the various words in this sentence as well as abbreviations like TV, FBI, JFK, and YMCA. Psychologists call this portion of LTM **semantic memory.** Semantic memory is much like a dictionary or encyclopedia, filled with general facts and information. Other information in LTM is more personal and specific: what you ate for dinner last night, the date you were born, and what you are supposed to be doing tomorrow at 4 p.m. This personal kind of knowledge is called **episodic memory** (Tulving, 1972). Episodic memory is made up of specific events that have personal meaning for us. If semantic memory is like an encyclopedia or dictionary, episodic memory is more like a diary.

Long-term memory (LTM) Portion of memory that is more or less permanent and that corresponds to everything we "know."

Semantic memory Portion of long-term memory that stores general facts and information.

Episodic memory Portion of long-term memory that stores more specific information that has personal meaning.

Information in LTM is highly organized and cross-referenced like a cataloging system in a library.

Surface structure The particular arrangement of verbal information, such as words in a sentence.

Deep structure The underlying meaning conveyed by verbal information.

You might guess from this brief description that LTM is quite different from STM, and you would be right. We saw that the capacity of STM is very limited, but LTM apparently has a virtually unlimited capacity for information (Bourne et al., 1979; Loftus, 1980). Lack of storage is simply not a problem in LTM: there is enough room not only for the sum total of everything we know, but also for everything we will ever know—with room left over! Moreover, as we will see, there is some evidence that once information gets into LTM it stays there permanently (Loftus, 1980; Klatzky, 1980). Thus LTM contains virtually all the events of one's lifetime.

It should be clear by now that unlike STM, LTM contains a staggering amount of information, yet we nonetheless reach down and retrieve almost instantly such things as the number of days in a year, the name of the current president, and the temperature at which water freezes. How can we retrieve isolated facts like these so quickly from the vast storehouse of LTM? The answer is *organization*. The information in LTM is highly organized and cross-referenced like a cataloging system in a library or the index at the back of this book. The more carefully we organize and cross-reference information when it goes into LTM, the more likely it is that we will be able to retrieve it later. Let's look more closely at the ways in which information is placed in LTM and then see how this affects the storage and retrieval of long-term memories.

Coding in LTM

Can you picture the shape of Florida? Do you know what a trumpet sounds like? Can you recall the smell of a rose or the taste of coffee? When you answer the telephone, can you sometimes identify the caller immediately, just from the sound of their voice? The fact that you can do most or all of these things suggests that at least some long-term memories are coded in terms of nonverbal images: smells, tastes, and so on (Bourne et al., 1979; Klatzky, 1980; Reed, 1982).

But most of the information in LTM seems to be coded in terms of meaning. If material is especially familiar (the national anthem, perhaps, or the opening of Lincoln's Gettysburg Address) you may have stored it verbatim in LTM and with a little luck you can retrieve it word-for-word when you need it (Neisser, 1982). More often, however, we do not use verbatim storage in LTM. If someone tells you a long, rambling story, complete with flashbacks, you may listen to every word but you certainly will not try to remember the story verbatim. Instead, you will extract the main points of the story and try to remember those. Even simple sentences are usually coded in terms of their meaning. For example, the sentences "Tom called John" and "John was called by Tom" differ in what psychologists call their **surface structure**—the particular arrangement of words in each sentence. But they both mean the same thing— their **deep structure** is identical—and under normal conditions they are both stored in LTM in the same way. Thus when people are asked to remember that "Tom called John," they often find it impossible to remember later whether they were told "Tom called John" or "John was called by Tom." They usually remember the meaning of the message (the deep structure) but not the exact words (the surface structure) (Bourne et al., 1979).

Do you know what a motorbike sounds like? Can you recall the feeling of rocks underfoot? The fact that you can suggests that at least some long-term memories are coded in terms of sounds, feelings, tastes, and so on.

You will remember that information in STM gets transferred to LTM if it is rehearsed. "Elaborative rehearsal" involves extracting the meaning of the information and then linking the new information to as much of the material in LTM as possible. The more links or associations you can make, the more likely you are to remember the new information later, just as it is easier to find a certain book in a library if it is catalogued under many headings, rather than just one or two. This is one reason why we tend to remember semantic material better than episodic. Episodic material is quickly "dated"; we code fewer cross-references for it. For instance, you may remember that you ate a hamburger last night, but normally there is no good reason to relate that piece of information to anything else in LTM and so it is not something you are likely to remember for very long. But if you have been a vegetarian for years and find the very thought of eating beef disgusting, then eating that hamburger was a very meaningful event, and it is probably linked to all kinds of other facts in your LTM. As a result you are unlikely to forget it for quite some time. Later in the chapter we will see how this same principle can be used to help you improve your memory and also to study more effectively.

Retrieval cue A piece of information that assists in retrieving information stored in long-term memory.

Storage and Retrieval in LTM

We saw earlier that information in short-term memory disappears in less than 20 seconds unless it is repeated. But information placed in long-term memory apparently does not disappear over time. In fact, under the proper circumstances we can often dredge up an astonishing amount of information from LTM. In one study, for example, elderly adults who had graduated from high school more than 40 years earlier were still able to recognize the names of 75 percent of their classmates (Bahrick, Bahrick, & Wittlinger, 1974).

But not everything stored in LTM can be remembered when we need it. The information may still be *available* somewhere in LTM, but it is *inaccessible* because we are unable to retrieve it (Mandler, 1967). Usually the problem can be traced to inadequate **retrieval cues.** Cues are extremely important in helping to "jog" our memory. When an actor forgets a line, a word or two whispered from backstage will usually suffice to solve the problem. In daily life, almost anything can serve as a retrieval cue: "the creaking of a hinge, the whistling of a tune, the smell of seaweed, the sight of an old photograph, the taste of nutmeg, the touch of a piece of canvas" can all trigger memories that we thought we'd forgotten (Loftus, 1980).

The more cues we have, and the more extensively the information was linked to other material when it was first entered in LTM, the more likely it is that our search will end in success. For example, if someone asks you to recite a poem you once learned, you may be able to do it without help: You have perfect *recall* of the poem. But suppose you get stuck halfway through and cannot remember the next line or phrase. When someone tells you what it is, you probably *recognize* it as soon as you hear it. If you are asked "Who was the 22nd President of the United States" you might have difficulty recalling his name, since the only useful retrieval cue is "22nd." If you were told, "His name is the same as that of a large city on Lake Erie" the additional cues might help you recall his name. But if you were asked "Was it John Sherman, Thomas Bayard, or

Information placed in long-term memory apparently does not disappear over time. With the aid of retrieval cues, elderly adults attending a class reunion are often able to recognize the names of a high percentage of their classmates.

Grover Cleveland?" you would probably recognize the correct answer as Grover Cleveland immediately. His name is a powerful retrieval cue.

We have talked about retrieval mostly in terms of a conscious search for a piece of information. But retrieval cues can also trigger memories without your deliberately trying to remember anything. If a professor mentions Napoleon you may remember something about the Battle of Waterloo. But Napoleon may also conjure up a French pastry, a trip to Naples, or a man you know who is shorter than you are. The smell of an apple pie in the oven, the taste of apple pie, or the words *apple pie* printed in a book can all lead you to remember a particular experience of apple pie. Marcel Proust has attested to the gripping power of retrieval cues in this moving and poetic passage from *Swann's Way:*

Flashbulb Memories

"I was standing by the stove getting dinner; my husband came in and told me." "I was fixing the fence, can go within a rod of the place where I stood. Mr. W. came along and told me. It was 9 or 10 o'clock in the morning." "It was in the forenoon; we were at work on the road by K's mills: A man driving past told us." These are three responses to the question, "Do you recall where you were when you heard that Abraham Lincoln was shot?" Other accounts were even more detailed. In fact, of 179 people interviewed, 127 recalled precisely the time and place at which they first heard of the assassination. That is a very high percentage, considering that the question was asked by a researcher 33 years after the event! (Colegrove, 1899)

Being able to vividly remember a certain event and the incidents surrounding it for a long time has come to be known as "flashbulb memory." Events that are shocking or otherwise highly significant are often remembered in this way. The death of a close relative, a time when we were seriously hurt, a graduation or wedding day may all elicit flashbulb memories.

There are several ideas about how people form such memories. According to the "now print" theory, a mechanism starts up in the brain when something especially significant, shocking, or noteworthy is at hand. The entire event is captured and then "printed," much like a photograph. The "print" is then stored, like a photograph in an album, for long periods, perhaps a lifetime. It is periodically reinforced, since such an important event is bound to be remembered and discussed many times throughout the years.

But this theory raises other questions. Why are very insignificant features remembered along with the main event—"standing by the kitchen stove," "mending the fence?" The answer given by the "now print" theory is that the entire event is registered, not just the main subject. Again, this is like a photograph. We may decide to photograph our mother sitting on the couch on her silver wedding anniversary. Our mother is the main subject, yet that same picture may show how the living room furniture was arranged, the family dog, the crack in the window. We were not taking a picture of those things, but because they were in the background, they too are registered (Brown & Kulik, 1977).

The "now print" theory implies, among other things, that flashbulb memories are accurate, that they are created at the time of an event, and that they are remembered better because of their highly emotional content. All these implications have been questioned. First of all, flashbulb memories are certainly not always accurate. Although this is difficult to test, let us consider just one case in point. The psychologist Ulric Neisser recalled the day he heard about the Japanese attack on Pearl Harbor. He was listening to a baseball game on the radio, and it was interrupted with the shocking announcement. The problem with this vivid flashbulb memory is that baseball is not played in December when the attack took place! The vivid memory was simply incorrect (Neisser, 1982).

Moreover, even if an event is registered accurately, it may undergo periodic revision. We are bound to discuss and rethink a major event many times over. As a result the flashbulb memory may become more (or less) accurate over the years until it bears little or no resemblance to what we initially remembered (Loftus, 1980).

. . . the smell and taste of things remain poised a long time, like souls, ready to remind us, waiting and hoping for their moment, amid the ruins of all the rest; and bear unfaltering, in the tiny and almost impalpable drop of their essence, the vast structure of recollection. (p. 36)

Our discussion thus far has focused on the ordinary workings of memory. In the next section we take a brief look at some examples of extraordinary memory and then turn our attention to ways in which memory can be improved. As you will see, exceptional memory essentially relies on developing the skills used in ordinary memory.

Eidetic imagery Ability to reproduce unusually sharp and detailed images of something that has been seen.

Mnemonist Someone with highly developed memory skills.

Special Topics in Memory

Extraordinary Memory

Some people seem to have truly extraordinary memories. For example, from time to time the newspaper will carry a report of a person with a "photographic memory." Such people can apparently create unusually sharp and detailed visual images of something that has been seen—a picture, a scene, a page of text. **Eidetic imagery,** as this phenomenon is called by psychologists, enables a person to see the features of an image in minute detail, sometimes even to read a page of a book that is no longer present. Eidetic imagery is much more common in children, but some adults also seem to have it.

Haber (1969) screened 500 elementary school children before finding 20 with eidetic imagery. The children were told to scan a picture for 30 seconds, moving their eyes to see all its various parts. The picture was then removed, and the children were told to look at a blank easel and report what they saw. They needed at least 3 to 5 seconds of scanning to produce an image, even when the picture was familiar. Once the image had been described, it faded away. Imagery usually could not be prolonged or recalled, but the children could "erase" the images by blinking or looking away from the easel.

The quality of eidetic imagery seems to vary from person to person. One girl in Haber's study could move and reverse images and recall them several weeks later. Three children could produce eidetic images of three-dimensional objects, and some could superimpose an eidetic image of one picture onto another and form a new picture. However, the children with eidetic imagery performed no better than their noneidetic classmates on other tests of memory.

No less dramatic are the more frequent cases of people who dazzle their friends and acquaintances with what seem to be impossible feats of memory. Such people are called **mnemonists.** One of the most famous mnemonists is the Russian newspaper reporter named Shereshevskii ("S"), who was studied for over 20 years by a distinguished psychologist, Alexander Luria. In *The Mind of a Mnemonist* (1968), Luria described how "S" could recall masses of senseless trivia as well as detailed mathematical formulas and complex arrays of numbers. He could easily repeat

Motivated Forgetting

Our discussion in this chapter generally assumes that we want to remember things accurately. But this may not always be a reasonable assumption. Without realizing it, we may blank out memories that are unpleasant or that conflict with our ideas of the people we want to be or the world we want to live in. *Repression* protects us from remembering things that are so painful that we would rather not think about them. There is a general desire on the part of human beings to see themselves—and to some extent, the world around them—as friendly, civilized, and reasonable. The memories that are in harmony with this view are acceptable to us, but those that conflict with it are often blotted out.

Freud often attributed the forgetting of names and places to repression. One of his patients, whom he called Mr. Y, fell in love with a woman who did not love him. She married another man, Mr. X. Although Mr. Y was well acquainted with Mr. X and had business dealings with him, after the marriage he found himself unable to remember Mr. X's name and had to ask what it was every time he wrote to him about business. Since Mr. X was his rival and had married the woman he loved, Mr. Y, Freud believed, subconsciously did not want to remember anything about him (Freud, 1928).

At its most extreme, repression can cause hysterical amnesia. Screenwriters have gotten a lot of footage over the years with amnesia victims, and we are all familiar with some form of the story: A man wakes up in a strange city, unable to remember his name or where he came from, or how he got there, but perfectly capable of reciting the alphabet or frying an egg. The memory of any personal information is gone. It makes a good melodramatic story—and it does happen. In hysterical amnesia there is no apparent organic reason for the failure of memory. Usually something in the person's life has been so frightening or so unacceptable that he or she has totally repressed all personal memories rather than remember that one incident.

The conditions of hysterical amnesia have been approximated experimentally. In one study, college students were taught a list of word pairs. After learning the list of pairs, they were read a second list of words, some of which were consistently accompanied by a mild but unpleasant electrical shock. This second list was composed of words that appeared to be related to the word pairs in the first list. If the students had learned the pair *thief* and *steal*, for example, the corresponding word on the second list was *take*. When they were tested for their retention of the first list, the apparent association of the "shocked" word with the word pair led to a significant drop in their ability to remember the original pair even though the paired words had had no shock directly attached to them (Glucksberg & King, 1967).

lists of up to seventy words or numbers after having heard or seen them only once.

These and other people with exceptional memory were not born with a special "gift" for remembering things. Rather, they have carefully developed memory techniques using the principles we have been discussing in this chapter. For example, Luria (1968) discovered that as "S" studied long lists of words, he would form a graphic image for every item. As these images became more numerous and complex, he would find a way of "distributing" them in a "mental row or sequence" so that one followed from another. "S" became so adept at this that he could repeat lengthy lists backward or forward, and even years later could recall them perfectly. His technique essentially involved coding verbal material visually in a way that allowed him to see various complexities and relationships. By organizing his data in a way that was meaningful to him, he could more easily link it to existing material in his long-term memory. In turn this provided him with many more retrieval cues than he would have had for isolated, meaningless facts.

Developing an exceptional memory takes time and effort. Virtually all the mnemonists discussed thus far had strong reasons for developing their memories as they did. "S" used it to advantage as a newspaper reporter. The waiter we spoke about in our introduction used it to establish a clientele who gave him significantly larger tips for his memory feats (Singular, 1982). As we will see in the next chapter, chess masters also sometimes display astonishing recall of meaningful chess board configurations (Chase & Simon, 1973; de Groat, 1966). For example, some master chess players are able to recall the position of every single piece on the board after only a 5-second exposure to a particular pattern. Yet when these same masters are shown a totally random and meaningless array of chess pieces, their recall is no better than yours or mine (Ericsson & Chase, 1982).

One memory researcher concluded:

> One of the most interesting things we've found is that just trying to remember things does not insure that your memory will improve. It's the active decision to get better and the number of hours you push yourself to improve that makes the difference. Motivation is much more important than innate ability. (Singular, 1982, p. 59)

But even if you are motivated, what should you do to improve your memory? That is the subject of the next section.

Improving Your Memory

The key to improving memory lies in organizing and coding material more effectively when it is first entered into LTM. There are certain techniques called **mnemonics** that can be used to assist in this task. Such devices are based on the coding and retrieval principles that we have discussed in this chapter. When we use mnemonic devices, we deliberately impose some sort of order on the material we want to learn.

Some of the simplest mnemonic devices are the rhymes and jingles we often use to remember dates and other facts. "Thirty days hath September, April, June, and November," helps us recall how many days there are in a month. "*I* before *E*, except after *C*, or when sounded like *A*, as in *neighbor* and *weigh*," helps us spell certain words. Other simple mnemonic devices involve making words or sentences out of the material to be recalled. The colors of the visible spectrum—red, orange, yellow, green, blue, indigo, violet—can be remembered by using their first letters to form the name *ROY G. BIV.* In remembering musical notes, the spaces in the treble clef form the word *FACE*, while the lines in the clef may be remembered by "Every Good Boy Does Fine."

Greek and Roman orators used a topical system of mnemonics to memorize long speeches. They would visit a large house or temple and walk through the rooms in a definite order, noting where specific objects were placed within each room. When the plan of the building and its contents were memorized, the orator would go through the rooms in his mind, placing images of material to be remembered at different places in the rooms. To retrieve the material during the speech, he would imagine himself going through the building and, by association, would recall each point of his speech as he came to each object and each room.

Imagery is also a great aid to understanding and recalling verbal

Mnemonics Techniques that make material easier to remember.

material. In experiments, subjects who are taught to memorize word lists by forming mental pictures related to the meaning of each word show better recall than subjects who use other learning strategies. If you were asked to recall the word pair "man—horse," your best bet would be to imagine a horse and man somehow interacting. You could visualize the horse trying to throw the man, for instance (Bugelski, 1979). This strategy can also be applied to large pieces of writing. As you read, try to picture the people, events, and ideas described by the author. Sometimes a single image can bring meaning to an entire paragraph. The more you visualize, and the more dynamic your images, the better you will recall what you have read.

Most memory improvement books are filled with mnemonic devices such as these, and they do in fact work if you are willing to spend the time to learn how to use them. For example, a study by Bower (1973) showed that mnemonic techniques were far more effective than simple rehearsal for remembering long lists of items. College students were asked to study 5 successive "shopping lists" of 20 unrelated words each. They were given 5 seconds to study each word, and time to study each list as a whole. At the end of the session, they were asked to recall all 100 items. Subjects using mnemonic devices remembered an average of 72 items, but the control group—generally relying on simple rehearsal—remembered only 28. The subjects trained in mnemonic techniques were also much more successful at recalling the position of each item and the list on which it appeared.

How can you use the principles in this chapter to help you remember the material you have been reading? You could simply reread the chapter until you have drummed it into your head. A more efficient approach, however, is active rehearsal, or recitation. After reading the chapter, close the book and try to remember what you have read. The more time that you spend recalling or attempting to recall the material, the better you will learn it within a given time. But there is an even more efficient strategy that begins *before* you have read the chapter.

THE SQ3R METHOD. Probably the most effective system for studying written material is known only by the letters of its five stages: SQRRR (or *SQ3R*, for short). SQRRR involves 5 steps.

Survey (1). Before you even start to read, quickly look at the chapter outline, the headings of the various sections in the chapter, and the chapter summary. This will give you an overview of what you will read and make it easier to organize and interrelate the material in the chapter.

Question (2). Also before you start to read, translate each heading in the chapter into a question about the text to follow. This helps you compare the new material with what you already know. It gets you actively involved in thinking about the topic. It also helps to bring the main points into sharp relief. Before you had read this chapter, for example, you might have translated the heading "Short-Term Memory" on page 224 into questions such as "Why is it called 'short-term'?" "Is there another type of memory that lasts longer?" "What good is a short-term memory?" "Why do memories fade?" It is usually helpful to write these questions out.

Read (3). Now read the first section in the chapter. Look for the answers to the questions you have posed. If you find major points not

Strategies for improving memory include the use of mnemonic devices, visual imagery, and active rehearsal.

directly related to your questions, try either to revise or refine your old questions to include the new material, or make up new questions especially for this material.

Recite (4). When you have finished reading the section, close the book and recite from memory the answers to your questions and any other major points you can remember. It may help to jot down your answers in outline form or even to recite them aloud to somebody. Then open the book and check to be sure that you have covered all the major points in the section. Repeat steps 2, 3, and 4 for each section of the chapter.

Review (5). After you have completed the chapter, review your notes and then recite your questions and answers from memory. Relate the material to other ideas, to your life, or to things with which you are familiar. Try to think of particularly good examples or illustrations. Get involved. The *SQ3R* method forces you to react, to have a kind of dialogue with the text. This interaction makes the material more interesting and meaningful and improves your chances of recalling it. It also organizes the material and relates it to what you already know. As we have seen, this is important for transferring the material to long-term memory. Although this seems time-consuming, you will probably spend less time overall because studying for exams later should go much more quickly.

Biological Bases of Memory

What physiological processes take place inside of us when we are remembering something? Where is memory stored and retrieved? These are the questions that we address now.

The Location of Memory

For the past 100 years, psychologists have attempted to determine if memory is localized in a certain part of the brain. In Chapter 2 we learned that some functions, such as vision and speech, are localized in this way. Early in the 19th century, it was believed that this was also true of memory.

We now know that no single part of the brain is solely responsible for memory. Lashley (1950) performed a pivotal experiment in which he removed various parts of rats' brains. Although their memories were found to be weakened by losing any part of the brain, the memories were still present. The amount of memory remaining seemed to depend primarily on the amount of brain tissue that Lashley removed, not the particular portion of the brain that was removed. From this Lashley concluded that a single memory can be stored in numerous parts of the brain, so that removal of any one part can diminish but not erase the whole memory.

More recent experiments have supported this theory, although with some qualifications. For example, recent experiments with rats indicate that one form of memory, that of the location of objects, is localized in the region of the brain known as the hippocampus (Olton, 1977). Thus evidence seems to indicate that some memories may be stored in specific regions of the brain, while other memories are stored throughout many regions of the brain (Carlson, 1977).

One possible explanation for the widespread storage of most memories is that several different senses seem to be involved in any one memory. A single experience might be stored in the brain's visual areas, auditory areas, and areas for smell and touch—all at the same time. Another explanation is that the processing centers that retrieve stored material are widely distributed. Damaging the brain may interfere with only some retrieval mechanisms. Evidence to support these two theories comes from studies in which one area of an animal's brain is damaged and retrieval cues are limited to the particular sense controlled by that area. For example, if the visual area is removed and retrieval cues are limited to only black-and-white visual images, with no sounds or smells to accompany them, retrieval does seem to be seriously impaired by specific brain damage.

Finally, recent evidence suggests that specific parts of the brain are necessary for the formation of memory. At the base of the cortex is a section of the brain called the limbic system (see Chapter 2). It appears that in humans the hippocampus—which is part of the limbic system—is instrumental in transferring verbal information from short-term to long-term memory. People with hippocampal damage can remember events that have just occurred (STM), but often have to write everything down to remember it for any length of time (LTM).

Application

Eyewitness Testimony

Jurors in court cases are generally willing to believe eyewitnesses. Faced with conflicting or ambiguous testimony, it is tempting to put faith in someone who actually "saw" an event with his or her own eyes. However, this faith in eyewitnesses may be unjustified (McCloskey & Egeth, 1983). While there is no denying that eyewitness accounts are a unique and essential form of courtroom testimony, studies show clearly that people who say "I know what I saw," often mean "I know what I *think* I saw." And they can be wrong (Loftus, 1983).

Consider this scenario. Two women enter a bus station and leave their belongings unattended on a bench while they check the bus schedule. A man enters, reaches into their baggage, stuffs something under his coat, and leaves. One of the women returns to her baggage and, after checking its contents, exclaims, "My tape recorder has been stolen!" Eyewitnesses sitting nearby confirm her story when contacted by insurance investigators; many eyewitnesses are able to provide a detailed description of the missing tape recorder, including its color, size, and shape. But in fact there never was a tape recorder! The man and women were assisting psychologist Elizabeth Loftus in a study of the fallibility of eyewitness testimony (Loftus, 1983).

The courts have begun to recognize the eyewitness problem. Judges increasingly instruct juries to be skeptical of eyewitness testimony and to evaluate it critically. In recent years, some courts have even begun admitting "expert testimony" from psychologists about eyewitness testimony in an effort to inform jurors of the potential pitfalls.

What do psychologists tell jurors about eyewitness testimony? First of all, they make them more aware of factors that may interfere with a witness's memory. For example, information is subject to change or distortion even after it has been encoded in long-term memory. There is a marked tendency, especially with highly meaningful information, to shift it around until it is more to our liking or matches up more favorably with other recollections. Juries are also warned that cross-racial identification by eyewitnesses is extremely questionable. People have more trouble recognizing faces belonging to people of other races than they do remembering someone of their own race. And whites tend to be less accurate than other racial groups in identifying minority members.

Other errors in testimony may result from the way in which eyewitnesses are questioned by police, lawyers, and investigators. In one classic experiment, a group of students were shown a film of a car accident. They were then questioned about the film. Some were asked, "How fast was the car going when it passed the barn while traveling along the country road?" A week later, all the students were asked whether there had been a barn in the film. Nearly 20 percent of the students "remembered" the barn. In fact there was no barn in the film (Bazelon, 1980; Loftus, 1980; Loftus, Miller, & Burns, 1978). Obviously, then, the posing of questions can make a difference in subsequent eyewitness accounts.

Expert psychological testimony has itself recently become the target of considerable controversy. Lower courts have often denied the need for expert testimony, maintaining that it is within the scope of juries to decide on the merit of eyewitness testimony. Higher courts, however, have sometimes ruled differently, citing the usefulness of expert testimony. Psychologists, too, have expressed their own reservations. Some question whether expert testimony is either useful or necessary. Others maintain that research in this area is not sufficiently developed. Still others are wary of intruding into judicial proceedings where they may potentially do some harm (Loftus, 1984).

Summary

1. The *sensory registers* receive sensory information from the external world. They may be thought of as the "waiting rooms" of memory. They have a huge capacity, but retention time is extremely brief; if old information is not replaced by new information it fades from the sensory registers in only a few seconds.

2. We are continually bombarded by sensory information; some of this information is selected for further processing. According to Broadbent (1958), we pay *attention* to information that in some way stands out because of its physical properties. Other material is filtered out immediately and receives no further processing.

3. An alternative view of attention holds that unattended signals get at least some initial processing for meaning. This allows us to shift attention to something particularly meaningful even if it doesn't otherwise stand out from the background.

4. The information that we select for further processing enters our *short-term memory* (STM). The main tasks of short-term memory are to briefly store new information and actively process it and other information. STM is sometimes referred to as "consciousness" or "working memory."

5. It is generally thought that the capacity of STM is limited to about 7 items at a time. We can process greater amounts of information by *chunking* material into meaningful units. However, as individual chunks increase in size, the number of them that can be held in short-term memory declines.

6. There has been considerable debate over how we code information for temporary storage in short-term memory. It is now known that some verbal information is coded acoustically,

while other information is coded in visual form. The capacity of short-term memory is greater with visual coding than with acoustic coding.

7. Material in short-term memory will disappear rapidly unless it is rehearsed or practiced. There are two basic explanations for why this happens. The *decay theory* states that time causes the strength of the memory to fade. The *interference theory* claims that other information simply gets in the way of remembering.

8. It now appears that decay and interference both cause short-term memory loss. Decay is a storage problem, while interference seems to affect both storage and retrieval.

9. *Proactive inhibition* occurs when old material in STM gets in the way of new material and causes retrieval problems. *Retroactive inhibition* is the result of new material in STM either pushing the old material out of STM or making it difficult to retrieve any old material still in STM.

10. Forgetting from short-term memory leaves room for new information and keeps us from being overwhelmed by meaningless and unrelated data.

11. Some information can be held indefinitely in STM by *rote rehearsal*—repeating the item over and over again, either out loud or silently. The amount of repetition an item gets does not always improve later recall, particularly if there is little or no intent to remember the material permanently.

12. To retain material more or less permanently, *elaborative rehearsal* is necessary. When elaborative rehearsal is either interrupted or prevented, information in STM is lost. For example, a blow to the head can cause *retrograde amnesia,* the inability to recall what was stored in short-term memory immediately preceding the injury. Dreams, which also occur in STM, will be quickly forgotten upon waking unless they are rehearsed.

13. *Long-term memory* (LTM) is the storehouse for all we know. It has a seemingly unlimited capacity. It is also a highly organized and relatively permanent storage. The portion of long-term memory known as *semantic memory* stores general facts and information. Another portion, *episodic memory,* stores more personally meaningful kinds of knowledge.

14. Although some information in LTM is coded visually, most of the information in LTM seems to be coded according to its meaning. People usually remember the meaning of a verbal message (its *deep structure*) but not the exact arrangement of words (the *surface structure*).

15. The more links that can be made between new and old information in LTM, the easier it is to retrieve new information later on. Organizing and cross-referencing information when it enters LTM makes it more likely that we will be able to retrieve it later. As a general rule, it is easier to remember semantic material than episodic material because more "cross-references" exist for it.

16. Information may be available in long-term memory but it remains inaccessible unless it can be retrieved. We use *retrieval cues* to help search out information from LTM. Sometimes cues can trigger memories we are not even trying to retrieve.

17. Information may be available in long-term memory but it remains inaccessible unless it can be retrieved. We use *retrieval cues* to help search out information from LTM. Sometimes cues can trigger memories we are not even trying to retrieve.

18. One form of exceptional memory is *eidetic imagery,* the ability to reproduce images photographically. This ability is inborn, but other exceptional memory skills are ones that are carefully developed and practiced. Most memory experts, or *mnemonists,* are individuals who are strongly motivated to improve their memories.

19. The key to improving memory lies in organizing and coding material more effectively when it is first entered into long-term memory. *Mnemonics* are techniques that help us remember material by imposing a meaningful order upon it. Forming images or mental pictures is another aid in recalling verbal material.

20. SQ3R is a study method designed to improve retention of material. The method generally calls for organizing one's material step by step and relating it to known information in long-term memory.

21. Some memories are stored in specific regions of the brain, and others are stored throughout the brain. One explanation for the widespread storage of memories is the involvement of different senses in any one memory. Another is that the processing centers are widely distributed. Finally, there is some evidence that a part of the brain called the limbic system is specifically involved in the formation of memories.

Review Questions

1. Raw information from the senses flows into the _____ _____ before being either lost or processed further.
2. The selection process that allows us to retain information after it has arrived from the senses is termed _____ .
3. We sometimes find ourselves shifting our attention to something that we had supposedly tuned out. This is called the _____ _____ phenomenon.
4. _____ _____ _____ is what we are thinking about at any given moment. Its function is to briefly store new information and to work on that and other information.
5. According to _____ theory, the passing of time in itself will cause the strength of memory to decrease. By contrast, _____ theory holds that information gets mixed up with, or pushed aside by, other information and thus becomes harder to remember.
6. When the operator gives you the telephone number you requested, you have trouble remembering it because it resembles your friend's number. This is an example of retroactive/proactive inhibition.
7. To assure that information in short-term memory will be remembered for a long time, the best strategy to use is _____ _____ , which involves relating new information to something that we already know.
8. _____ _____ , or simply repeating information over and over, is an effective way of retaining information for just a minute or two.
9. Two parts of long-term memory are _____ memory, which is filled with general facts and information, and _____ memory, made up of events that have personal meaning for us.
10. Usually the inability to recall items from long-term memory can be traced to inadequate _____ _____ .
11. The psychological term for the detailed visual images that serve as the basis for photographic memory is _____ imagery.
12. Mnemonists are able to accomplish their feats of memory by
    a. repeating facts until recall is automatic
    b. making use of unrefined natural ability
    c. using carefully developed memory techniques
    d. using the SQ3R method
13. Arrange the following steps of the SQ3R method in the proper sequence: question, read, review, survey, recite.
14. Some memories are stored in specific regions of the brain, while others are stored throughout many regions. T/F

Outline

Cognition

8

If someone were to ask you, "What is **cognition** or thinking?" your first response might be that thinking means pondering some deep problem, the way Rodin's sculpture *The Thinker* seems to be doing. Or you might say something as broad and vague as "Thinking is what goes on inside your head." The last answer, because it covers more, is probably more correct. Thinking is so complex a process and includes such a wide range of activities that we can only hope to touch upon them in this chapter.

A clue to the vast range of things that are involved in thinking can be seen in different ways we use the word. "I think I will go to the store," indicates intention. "You were just not thinking!" is the same as saying that you were behaving absentmindedly. "I've given it some thought," implies reflection or meditation. "What does he think of all this?" is a way of asking for an evaluation. "I think this solution is the better choice," indicates a decision.

These are all examples of thinking. Thinking includes the processing and retrieval of information from memory. But in addition, it requires manipulation of the information in various ways. In this chapter we will first look at the building blocks of thought—the kinds of things we think *about*—and then study the ways in which we use these building blocks in problem solving and decision making.

Cognition The processes of thinking.

Image A mental recollection of a sensory experience.

Concept A mental category for classifying objects, people, or experiences.

Building Blocks of Thought

Images and **concepts** are the two most important building blocks of thought. When you say you are "thinking about" your brother, you may have an image of him—probably his face, but perhaps also how he sounds when he is talking, or the scent of his favorite after-shave lotion. But you can also think about your brother by using various concepts or categories that help you recall him—like "boy," "brother," "high-school sophomore," "butterfly collector," "gentle," "strong." In the first part of this chapter we will explore concepts and their relationship to language.

247

Then we will look at how concepts and language together are related to thought. Finally we will consider the role that images play in thinking.

Concepts

Concepts are mental categories for classifying specific people, things, or events. "Dogs," "books," and "cars" are all concepts that let us categorize objects in the world around us. "Fast," "strong," and "interesting" are also concepts that we can use in categorizing objects. When you think about an object—say a Ferrari—you usually think of the concepts that apply to it: for example, "fast, sleek, expensive car." Thus concepts let us think about things.

"If only he could think in abstract terms . . . ."

Concepts also give meaning to new experiences. We do not stop and form a new concept for every new experience. We draw on the concepts we have already formed and place the new object or event into the appropriate categories. In the process we may actually change or modify some of our concepts to better match the world around us. Say, for example, you go to the opera to see *Pagliacci*. You probably have some concept of "opera" even if you have never attended one before. But when you actually go to the opera for the first time, your concept may change. Perhaps it will become more accurate—you might realize now that members of the cast actually speak some of their lines instead of singing them. Probably your concept of opera will also become fuller, as you add new information about what you experience. Later, when you go to hear *La Traviata*, you will know what to expect—the orchestra will play the overture, the curtain will rise, the characters will be costumed and will sing. You will also know how you are expected to behave—you will follow the usher to your seat, listen quietly, show your appreciation of a good performance by applauding at certain times. Because of the concept you have already formed of opera, you will not have to respond to this performance as a totally new experience; you have a concept to assign it to. Conceptualizing "opera"—or anything else—is a way of grouping experiences so that every perception need not be surprising. We know, to some extent, what to think about it.

Concepts allow us to generalize, to differentiate, or to think abstractly. If you see a lizard, for example, you can assign it to your general concept "reptile." Like most reptiles, it has scales and a flat head. On the other hand, the concept "lizard" will help you to differentiate this reptile from others. You know—from personal experience, reading, or some other source—that most lizards are harmless, so you will not react to a lizard with the alarm you might show if you met a rattlesnake. Finally, you may use the concept "lizard" in an abstract way, without referring to any specific animals.

It is tempting to think of concepts as simple and clear-cut. But psychologists have discovered that most of the concepts people use in thinking are neither clear nor unambiguous (Rosch, 1973). Rather they are "fuzzy": They overlap with one another and they are often poorly defined. For example, most people can tell a mouse from a rat. But most of us would be hard pressed to come up with an accurate list of the critical differences between mice and rats.

If we cannot explain the difference between "mouse" and "rat," how can we use those concepts in our thinking? The answer seems to be that we construct a model (or *prototype*) of a representative mouse and another prototype of a representative rat, and then use those prototypes in our thinking. Our concept of "bird," for example, does not consist of a list of key attributes like "feathered," "winged," "two feet," and "lives in trees." Instead, most of us have a model bird or prototype in mind—such as a robin or a sparrow—that captures for us the essence of "bird." When we encounter new objects, we compare them to this prototype to determine if they are in fact birds. And when we think about birds, we usually think about our prototype bird.

But prototypes are seldom perfect models. Robins and sparrows do not contain every single feature that can be possessed by "birds." Because natural categories are fuzzy, prototypes are only the best and most suitable models of a concept, not perfect and exclusive representations of it. As Lindsay and Norman (1977) point out, "The typical dog barks, has four legs, and eats meat. We expect all actual dogs to be the same. Despite this, we would not be too surprised to come across a dog that did not bark, had only three legs, or refused to eat meat" (p. 386). We would still be able to recognize such an animal as a dog.

How, then, do we know which objects belong to a concept? For instance, how do we know that a lion is not a bird, but that a penguin is a bird. The answer is that we decide what is most probable or most sensible given the facts at hand. This is what Rosch calls relying on the

We decide that a penguin is a "bird" by relying on degree of category membership.

Phonemes The basic sounds that make up any language.

Morphemes The smallest meaningful unit of speech such as simple words, prefixes, and suffixes.

degree of category membership. For example, a lion and a bird both have two eyes. But the lion does not have wings, it does not have feathers, and it has four feet, all of which indicate that it is quite unlike our prototype bird. Thus we are able to eliminate lions from the general category of birds. On the other hand, penguins share many features that belong to our prototype for a bird. As a result, we tend to recognize these Arctic creatures as members of the bird family, even though they lack feathers.

You may have noticed in our discussion so far that each concept corresponds to a word in the English language. "Boy," "gentle," "opera," "reptile," "lizard"—these are all concepts we have discussed and each of them matches a word. By putting words together into sentences, we are able to link concepts to other concepts and form complex thoughts and ideas. Since our language determines not only the words we use but also the ways in which we combine those words into sentences, it seems obvious that language and thought are closely linked. In the next section we will examine language and its relationship to thinking.

Thinking and Language

Language is based on universal sound units called **phonemes**. The sounds of *t*, *th*, and *s*, for instance, are phonemes. There are 46 phonemes in English, and as many as 85 in some languages (Bourne, et al., 1979). By themselves, phonemes are meaningless. The sound *b*, for example, has no meaning by itself. But phonemes can be grouped together to form words, prefixes (un-, pre-), and suffixes (-ed, -ing). These are called **morphemes**, which are the smallest meaningful units in a language. Morphemes are combined to make up complex words (pre-exist-ing, un-excell-ed). In turn, words are combined to form *phrases*, which are used in the construction of *sentences*. When thinking about something— say the ocean or a sunset—we develop "ideas" or "thoughts" about it. These thoughts rarely reflect single concepts as expressed in morphemes

The Brain of the Bilingual

Many people today speak two languages. They are known as bilinguals. Scientists have long been interested in how such people keep two—or even more—language systems separate. And how do they, in speaking or writing, call up the right word from two different sets of words with the same meaning (Benderly, 1981)?

It now appears that the two languages in part occupy different portions of the brain, and that the person's native language takes up less room than the second language. We saw in Chapter 2 that in most people's brains the left hemisphere handles language and logical thinking, while the right deals primarily with nonverbal imagery. Recent research has shown, though, that people learning a new

language appear to draw heavily on the right hemisphere. Moreover, bilinguals seem generally to place an unusually heavy reliance on the right side of the brain, even after the second language is completely mastered. As a result, they are especially sensitive to nonverbal stimuli. According to some researchers, the right-hemisphere dependence of bilinguals probably helps them do more than tell two sets of symbols and meanings apart. It seems likely that it results in specifically bilingual strategies for processing language. And more speculatively, it may even prompt bilinguals to think about people, objects, and ideas in a way that is very different from how single-language speakers view the world (Benderly, 1981).

like "red" or "calm." Instead, our ideas usually are made up of phrases and sentences, such as "The ocean is unusually calm tonight."

In Chapter 7, you may recall, we saw that sentences have both a "surface structure" (particular words and phrases) and a "deep structure" (underlying meaning). The same deep structure can be conveyed by various different surface structures, as in the following example:

The ocean is unusually calm tonight.
Tonight the ocean is particularly calm.
Compared to most nights, tonight the ocean is calm.

When you wish to communicate an idea, you start with deep structure or meaning, then choose words and phrases that will express the idea, and finally produce the speech sounds that make up those words and phrases. This movement from deep structure to surface structure is called **top-down processing**. You can see in Figure 8-1 that the movement is indeed from the top down. When you want to understand a sentence, your task is reversed. You must start with surface structure (sounds) and work your way up to the meaning of those sounds. This movement from surface structure to deep structure is called **bottom-up processing**, as also shown in Figure 8-1.

This brief review of language illustrates just how tightly thinking is linked to language. Is it possible, then, that the language we use determines how we think and what we think about? Some theorists think this is true. Recall that in Chapter 7 we discussed the fact that language affects long-term memory. For example, Brown and Lenneberg (1954) asked subjects to look at color patches and assign each one a name. Colors that were quickly and easily named (like *blue*) were more readily coded and later retrieved than those that took longer to name and were given less common labels (like *sky blue* or *pale blue*). This indicates that the ease with which we are able to retrieve an experience such as that of colors is closely related to the ease and speed with which we are able to name and encode that experience. As Lindsay and Norman (1977) point out, "Memory for single perceptual experiences is directly related to the ease with which language can communicate that experience" (p. 483).

If language affects our ability to store and retrieve information, it seems reasonable to suggest that it should also affect our ability to think about things. Benjamin Whorf (1956) is the strongest spokesman for this position. According to Whorf's **linguistic relativity hypothesis**, the language that one speaks determines the pattern of one's thinking and one's view of the world. For Whorf, if a language lacks a particular expression, the thought that the expression corresponds to will probably not occur to the people who speak that language. Whorf notes that the Hopi Indians have only two nouns for everything that flies. One noun refers to birds. The other is used for everything else: airplanes, kites, or dragonflies. Thus the Hopi would interpret all flying things in terms of either of these two nouns—something in the air would be either a bird or a nonbird.

Think for a moment about how linguistic relativity might apply to what you are learning in this course. Phrases like *top-down processing* and *bottom-up processing* capture very complex ideas. To the extent that you understand those phrases, you probably do find it easier to think about the relationship between language and thought, between words and sentences and their underlying meaning. The technical vocabulary of any

Top-down processing Progressing from deep structure (meaning) to surface structure (sounds and words that express the meaning).

Bottom-up processing Progressing from the essential components of a sentence (phonemes and morphemes) to the deep structure (meaning) of the sentence.

Linguistic relativity hypothesis Whorf's idea that patterns of thinking are determined by the specific language one speaks.

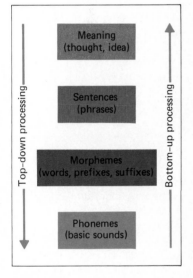

Figure 8-1

The direction of movement in top-down and bottom-up processing. Producing a sentence involves top-down processing; understanding a sentence requires bottom-up processing.

field of study is intended to permit people to think and communicate more easily, more precisely, and in more complex ways about the content of that field. But this example also illustrates some of the criticisms of Whorf's hypothesis. The idea of bottom-up processing occurred before someone thought up that particular phrase. Similarly, you were able to identify and think about basic speech sounds before you learned that they are called phonemes. And you certainly recognize the difference between what someone says and what that person means without having to know that these are called surface structure and deep structure, respectively.

In the same vein, some critics of the linguistic relativity hypothesis point out that it is more likely that the need to think about things differently changes a language than vice versa. For example, if the Hopi Indians had been subjected to air raids, they probably would have quickly created a word to distinguish a butterfly from a bomber! Closer to home, most English-speaking people know only one word for snow. But expert skiers, realizing that different textures of snow can affect their downhill run, have coined such specific words for snow as *powder, corn,* and *ice* (Clark & Clark, 1977). But Whorf may still be correct in pointing out that once such phrases as *powder snow* and *corn snow* make their appearance, they shape the way skiers subsequently think about snow. In short, experience may shape language, which in turn may shape subsequent experience.

A related criticism of the linguistic relativity hypothesis is that a language may capture only some of the experiences of the people who speak it. Nonskiers may call all types of snow *snow*, but they can think about the differences between icy snow, slush, wet snow, and snow flurries. The Dani of New Guinea have no words for colors—everything

According to the linguistic relativity hypothesis, once expressions such as "powder snow" make their appearance in the language, they shape the way skiers subsequently think about snow.

Chimpanzees and the Use of Language

Language has long been regarded as a uniquely human capability that sets us apart from all other animals. But what if language can be linked to certain thought processes found in other species? Certain animals are capable of representational thought; they can relate a symbolic representation of an object to the object itself. Animals' ability to use such thought in simple experiments has opened the question of whether they are also capable of using it in the same way as humans—to represent their world through language. Several experiments with chimpanzees have investigated this question.

Robert Gardner and Beatrice Gardner (1969) taught Washoe, a young chimpanzee, to communicate in American Sign Language (Ameslan), the system of gestures and hand movements used by many deaf people. By the time Washoe was 7 years old, she knew more than 175 signs and could generalize some of them. The sign for "open," for example, was first learned with one particular door, but Washoe soon began to use it when referring to all closed doors, briefcases, cupboards, boxes, and even faucets. She was soon able to construct six-word sentences, note things that interested her, and make requests ("gimme sweet eat please"). She even tried to communicate through sign language to other chimpanzees.

Psycholinguists have been skeptical of language learning in chimpanzees, and specifically of Washoe's achievements (Baur, 1975). A number of critics, including Eric Lenneberg, Ursula Bellugi-Klima, Roger Brown, and John Limber, have stated that the multi-*sign* combinations formed by Washoe are not equivalent to the multi-*word* formulations of a child. For them, the way words are ordered is crucial in determining linguistic sophistication. Human children learn quickly that "Come Daddy home" is not proper word order. Because the Gardners never recorded data on word order during their years of work with Washoe, some psycholinguists are still unconvinced about whether Washoe used sophisticated language.

A different approach to teaching language to a chimpanzee was devised by David Premack (1970), who made his language written rather than gestured. The basic unit of the language is a magnetized "word" that adheres to a slate. Sarah was first taught to place a particular "word" on the slate to get fruit. Then she learned to associate "words" with different fruits. Sarah formed sentences by writing the name of the person giving her the food. If the experimenter was Randy, Sarah would have to put "Randy apple" on the slate before she would get a bit of apple to eat. She would have to use correct word order—sentences like "apple Randy" were not acceptable. Sarah learned to form simple and compound sentences; to label things "same" or "different"; to answer questions; and to classify things by color, shape, size, and object class. She also learned how to construct sentences that involve conditional relationships ("If Sarah take apple, then Mary give Sarah chocolate. If Sarah take banana, then Mary no give Sarah chocolate").

No matter how promising chimpanzees' ability to think with and use language seems to be, there is no evidence that their language skill will progress toward the achievement level of human adults. Whether chimps, like children, can learn to think with and use language that has correct and complex syntax is still an open question (Premack, 1976).

---

is either "dark" or "light"—but nonetheless they remember basic colors such as red, green, and yellow better than other colors. Furthermore, when taught the names of these basic colors they learn them faster than they learn the names of other colors. And they judge the similarity of colors much as English-speaking people do (Heider & Olivier, 1972; Heider, 1972; Rosch, 1973). In other words, the Dani seem to be able to think about colors much as we do even though their language has no words for specific colors. Thus people from different cultures with very different languages nonetheless seem to think about some things—such as color—in remarkably similar ways. Even though language and thought are intertwined, people can think about things they have no words for in their language.

Images

Stop reading and think for a moment about Abraham Lincoln. Then think about being outside in a summer thunderstorm. Your thoughts of Lincoln probably included such words as President, slavery, Civil War, and assassinated. But you probably also had some mental images concerning Lincoln—his bearded face, perhaps, or his lanky body, or a log cabin. When you thought about the thunderstorm, you probably had mental images of wind, rain, and lightning. An image is a mental recollection of a sensory experience, and images can be used to think about things. We can visualize the Statue of Liberty or astronauts hopping around the surface of the moon; we can smell Thanksgiving dinner; we can hear Martin Luther King, Jr. saying "I have a dream. . . ." In short, we can think using sensory images.

Moreover, researchers have found that we not only visualize things to help us think about them, but we even manipulate our mental images. Shepard and Metzler (1971), for example, presented subjects with pairs of geometrical patterns (see Figure 8-2). In some cases, the two pictures were of the same pattern simply rotated to provide different views (e.g., Figures 8-2A and 8-2B). In other cases, the two pictures were of different patterns (Figure 8-2C). Subjects were asked to determine whether each pair of patterns was the same or different. The researchers discovered that

Figure 8-2

Examples of the pairs of geometrical patterns used in Shepard and Metzler's (1971) experiment. The researchers found that subjects first rotated an image of one pattern in their minds until they could see both patterns from the same perspective. They then matched the mental images of the pairs of patterns to decide if they were the same (A and B) or different (C).

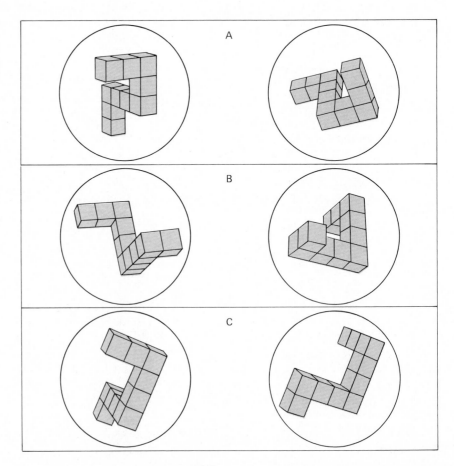

the subjects invariably rotated an image of one pattern in their minds until they could see both patterns from the same perspective. The next step was simply to see if the mental image of one pattern matched the other pattern. Moreover, Shepard and Metzler found out that the more a pattern had to be rotated, the more time it took to match the two patterns. In other words, if a pattern had to be mentally rotated 180 degrees, it would take longer for subjects to make the comparison than if it had to be mentally rotated only 90 degrees. Subsequent tests have supported these findings. It seems that we can and do freely manipulate mental images to help us think about things.

Images may help us think about things because they are more concrete than words. Even Albert Einstein relied heavily on visualizing ordinary, concrete things that later found their way into his complex mathematical formulas. Einstein believed that his extraordinary genius resulted in part from his skill in "visualizing effects, consequences, and possibilities" (Shepard, 1983, p. 67). Although few of us manage to match Einstein's brilliance, we nonetheless use imagery as an effective aid in thinking about and solving problems (Adams, 1976). All of us have watched a teacher clarify a cloudy concept by drawing a quick, simple sketch on a blackboard. Many times when words make a tangled knot of an issue, a graphic image drawn on paper straightens out the confusion. Images also invite us to ponder and manipulate a concrete form. For example, you have no doubt seen "budget pies," in which each item receives a "piece of the pie" according to the percentage of the budget that the item represents. You can mentally compare the sizes of each wedge, and perhaps imagine how the pie would look if a particular item received a larger or smaller wedge.

We have seen so far that images and concepts are the building blocks of thought. Let's turn our attention now to the ways in which we use thought to solve problems and make decisions.

Problem Solving

Consider the following problems:

1. Six disks are placed on a stake, with the smallest disk on the bottom of the pile and the largest on top. Transfer these disks to another stake so that the largest disk is on the bottom and the smallest is on top.

2. You have three jugs; one is filled with 12 cups of water, the other two are empty but have a capacity of 3 cups of water each. Divide the water among the jugs so that the largest jug has just 6 cups of water left in it.

Most people find these two problems very easy to solve. But now consider more elaborate versions of the same two problems:

3. There are three identical spikes and six disks, each with a different diameter but each having a hole in the center large enough for a spike to go through. At the beginning of the problem, the six disks are placed on one spike, one on top of another, with the largest disk on the bottom, then the next largest, and so on, in order of decreasing size until the smallest disk, which is on top

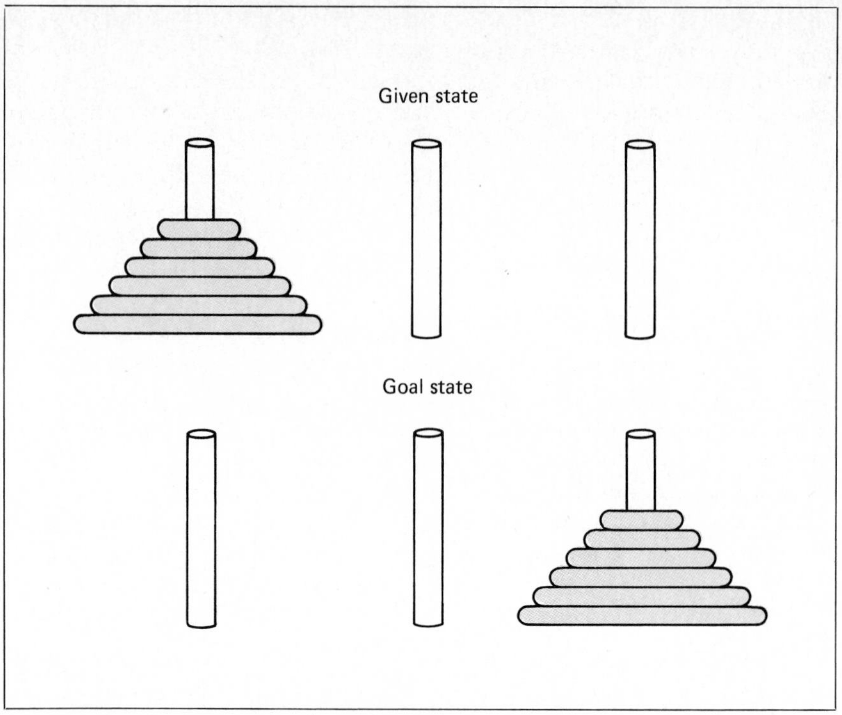

Given state

Goal state

Figure 8-3

The given state (top) and goal state (bottom) for the disk transfer problem. The goal is to transfer all six disks to one of the other two spikes without ever permitting a larger disk to rest on top of a smaller disk.

(see Figure 8-3). You are permitted to move only one disk at a time from one spike to another spike, with the restriction that a larger disk must never be moved on top of a smaller disk. The goal is to transfer all six disks to one of the other two spikes (without ever permitting a larger disk to rest on top of a smaller disk) (Wickelgren, 1974, p. 102).

4. You have three jugs, which we will call A, B, and C. Jug A can hold exactly 8 cups of water. B can hold exactly 5 cups, and C can hold exactly 3 cups (see Figure 8-4). A is filled to capacity with 8 cups of water. B and C are empty. We want to find a way of dividing the contents of A equally between A and B so that both have 4 cups. You are allowed to pour water from jug to jug (Mayer, 1983, p. 173).

Most people find the last two problems much more difficult to solve than the first two. Why should this be the case? In part, it is because the solutions to problems 3 and 4 simply take longer to work out than the solutions to the first two problems. But there is more to it than that. The first two problems are considered trivial because what you are asked to do is obvious; the strategy for solving them is simple and easily identified, and it is easy to verify that each step is moving you closer to a solution. The last two problems, however, require some interpretation, the strategy for solving them is not at all obvious, and it is much harder to know whether any given step has actually helped move you closer to a solution.

Let's examine each of these aspects of the problem-solving process. After we have looked at the principles of solving a problem and the steps and strategies involved in the process, we will turn to common obstacles people face when they tackle a problem. To conclude, this section will present several techniques for sharpening your skills at problem solving.

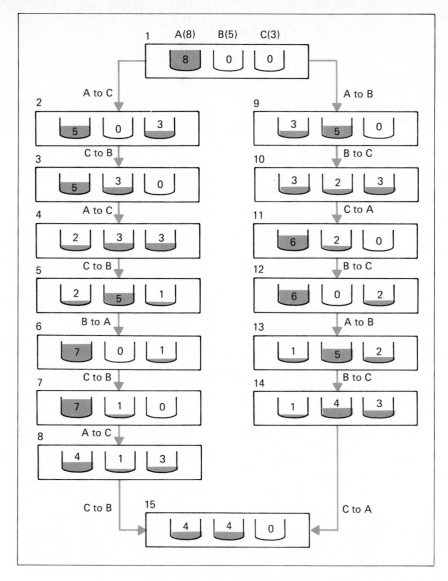

Problem representation Defining or interpreting a problem.

Figure 8-4

A version of a water jug problem. The given state is 8 cups of water in jug A and none in jugs B and C. The goal is to have 4 cups of water in jug A and 4 in jug B.

Interpretation of Problems

The first step in solving a problem is called **problem representation,** which means interpreting or defining the problem. It is tempting to leap ahead and try to solve a problem just as it is presented, but this impulse often leads to poor problem solutions. For example, if your business is losing money, you might sit down to "figure out how to cut costs." But by defining the problem narrowly as "cost cutting," you have ruled out the possibility that the best way to stop losing money might be to increase income rather than to cut costs. A better representation of this problem would be "to discover ways to cut costs or increase income or both."

Let us turn to a thornier example. Carroll, Thomas, and Malhotra (1980) asked two groups of subjects to work on two different problems. One group was given a problem that dealt with time: organizing seven stages of a manufacturing process, taking into account specific guidelines or "constraints." The other group received a problem that dealt with space: organizing the location of seven business offices on a corridor, again taking into account specific constraints. Although the two problems appeared to be quite different, they were actually the same: They had the same number of variables and constraints, and they had the same solution. Nonetheless, the subjects who worked on the spatial problem were far more successful than those who worked on the time problem. Why should this be so? The answer seems to be that both groups simply accepted the initial representation of the problem. The subjects who received the space problem automatically represented or interpreted the problem in visual terms. They all drew diagrams that showed how the offices could be arranged. This approach made this particular problem relatively easy to solve. Most of the subjects working on the time problem, however, did not interpret it visually. They used no maps or other visual images. After many attempts, they became tangled in a complex maze of language and logic. When the researchers repeated the experiment, but instructed all subjects to use a graphic approach to solving the problem, the two problems turned out to be equally easy to solve.

Another aspect of problem interpretation is deciding what class or category of problem the problem belongs to. Properly categorizing a problem can provide clues about how to solve it. In fact, in the case of simple problems, once a problem has been properly categorized, its solution may be as simple as painting by numbers. For example, many people find the following problem difficult to solve:

> A farmer is counting the hens and rabbits in his barnyard. He counts a total of 50 heads and 140 feet. How many hens and how many rabbits does the farmer have? (Reed, 1982, p. 320)

This problem becomes much easier to solve when you realize that it belongs in the same category as the following, more familiar problem:

An experienced football coach can draw upon game plans stored in long-term memory.

Bill has a collection of 20 coins that consists entirely of dimes and quarters. If the collection is worth $4.10, how many of each kind of coin are in the collection? (Reed, 1982, p. 320)

Quite often, people who seem to have a knack for solving problems are actually just very skilled at interpreting and representing them in effective ways. Star chess players, for example, can readily categorize a new game situation by comparing it to various standard kinds of situations stored in their long-term memory. This strategy helps them to interpret the current pattern of chess pieces with greater speed and precision than the novice chess player. A seasoned football coach may quickly recognize that a certain situation on the gridiron calls for a particular kind of defense. He has interpreted the game in terms of familiar categories. To a great extent, gaining expertise in any field, from football to physics, consists of increasing your ability to represent and categorize problems in such a way that they may be solved more quickly and effectively (Mayer, 1983).

Algorithm A step-by-step method of problem solving that guarantees a correct solution.

Producing and Evaluating Solutions

Once you have properly interpreted a problem, the next step is to select a solution strategy that best suits the problem. When casting about for the right strategy, we must choose from a rich assortment of possibilities. One possibility is simple trial-and-error, but this strategy usually leads to many wasted hours since it may take a very long time until the solution appears by accident. Moreover, many problems can never be solved strictly through this scattershot approach. How many guesses would it take, for example, to come up with the name of the seventh caliph of the Islamic Abbasid dynasty? Or, how soon could you guess the square root of the product of two sides of a given triangle? You could well go on guessing for the rest of your life.

To solve most problems, it is necessary to choose some strategy other than trial-and-error. The particular strategy you use should be based on an accurate categorization and representation of the problem. But it should also take into account the limits of short-term memory. We have to be able to retrieve information and work on it without overcrowding the limited work space of short-term memory. With this in mind, let's look at some of the problem-solving strategies that are available.

In some cases, the solution to a problem may be as simple as retrieving information from long-term memory. For example, as a pilot you are expected to memorize the slowest speed at which you can fly a particular airplane before it stalls and heads for the ground. When you need this information, there is simply no time to sit back and calculate the correct answer. Time is of the essence, so you simply refer to long-term memory for an immediate answer.

More complex problems require more complex methods. In some cases, you may be able to use an **algorithm.** Algorithms are problem-solving methods that guarantee a solution if they are appropriate for the problem and are properly carried out. For example, an algorithm for solving an anagram (a group of letters that can be rearranged to form a word) entails trying every possible combination of letters until we come

Algorithms are problem-solving methods that guarantee a solution—if they are appropriate to the problem and are correctly carried out.

Heuristics "Rules of thumb" that help in simplifying and solving problems, though they do not guarantee a correct solution.

Hill-climbing A heuristic problem-solving strategy in which each step moves you progressively closer to the final goal.

Subgoals Intermediate, more manageable goals used in one heuristic strategy to make it easier to reach the final goal.

up with the hidden word. Suppose we are given the letters *acb*. We try *abc, bac, bca, cba*, and finally come up with *cab* and the problem is solved. To calculate the product of 323 and 546, we multiply them according to the rules of multiplication (the algorithm). If we do it accurately, we are guaranteed of getting the right answer. To convert temperatures from Fahrenheit to Celsius, we use the formula $C = \frac{5}{9}(F-32)$. This formula, like all formulas, is an algorithm.

Many of the problems we encounter in everyday life, however, cannot be solved by using algorithms. In these cases, we often turn to heuristics. **Heuristics** are "rules of thumb" that help us to simplify problems. They do not guarantee a solution, but they may bring it within reach. Some heuristic methods work better in some situations than in others. Some heuristics have special purposes only, such as those applied to chess or word puzzles. But other general heuristics can be applied to a wide range of human problems. Part of problem solving is to decide which heuristic is most appropriate for a given problem (Bourne et al., 1979).

A very simple heuristic method is **hill-climbing.** In this process we try to move continually closer to our final goal without ever digressing or going backward. At each step we evaluate how far "up the hill" we have come, how far we still have to go, and precisely what the next step should be. On a multiple-choice test, for example, one useful strategy in answering each question is to eliminate the alternatives that are obviously incorrect. Even if this does not leave you with the one correct answer, you are closer to a solution. In trying to balance a budget, each reduction in expenses brings you closer to the goal and leaves you with a smaller deficit with which to deal.

There are other problems, however, for which the hill-climbing heuristic is not optimal. Problems 3 and 4 on page 256 are of this sort. In each case, there comes a point where you *must* digress, or actually move backward, in order to make ultimate progress toward your goal. In Problem 4, for example, there are at least two solutions (see Figure 8-4). The hill-climbing heuristic might cause you to start by filling up the second jar as shown in Step 9. Since the goal is to get 4 cups of water in both A and B, this step has brought you closer to that goal. But by moving from Step 9 to 10, and from 11 to 12, you must move away from the ultimate goal. By Step 12, you have actually returned almost to your starting point, yet you are more than halfway toward solving the problem!

Let us consider some other examples for which the hill-climbing strategy is inappropriate. You have probably played checkers at one time or another. At a decisive moment you may have had to "give up" a piece in order to maneuver toward a more strategic position on the board. Although losing that one piece seemed to push you further from victory, the move in fact nudged you closer to your goal. In baseball a pitcher can prevent a good hitter from batting in runs at a critical time by giving him an "intentional walk." This tactic puts an extra player on base and seems to work against the goal of keeping runners off the bases. But the shrewd pitcher knows that by conceding a walk to a strong batter, he will get to pitch to the next batter, a weaker hitter who is less likely to score runs.

Another problem-solving heuristic is to create **subgoals.** By setting subgoals, we can often break a problem into smaller, more manageable pieces, each of which is easier to solve than the problem as a whole. A student whose goal is to write a history paper might set subgoals in the following order: Decide on a topic; collect and read the research; prepare an outline; write a first draft; reread the draft; and write a second and final draft. Subgoals make problem solving more manageable because they free us from the burden of having to reach the "top of the hill" at the first crack. This tactic allows us to set our sights on closer, easier goals. Of course, the overall purpose of setting subgoals is still to reach the ultimate goal—the solution to the problem.

One of the most frequently used heuristics combines hill-climbing and subgoals. **Means-end analysis** involves analyzing the difference between the current situation and the desired end, then doing something to reduce that distance. We progress through a series of points involving choices about how to proceed further, and we assess each choice in terms of whether it will bring us closer to our goal. At each point we make the most likely choice, and continue to the next point. Wickelgren (1979) notes, for example, that a woman driving toward a clear landmark—a mountain range—with no specific directions to guide her will probably choose roads that appear, from her present position, to be headed in that direction. If the road then curves and leads in a different direction than was expected, she might decide, "I'll go another mile and if I'm not any closer by then, I'll turn around and go back."

Means-end analysis moves very carefully through subgoals from one step to another. Like hill-climbing, it is always forward-looking. Such attention to what lies ahead is often helpful because if we stray too far from the end goal, it may vanish from sight altogether. And, like hill-climbing, this strategy may prompt us to overlook digressions or temporary steps backward that are absolutely necessary for the solution of a problem.

An alternative heuristic method that is not so short-sighted is called **working backward** (Bourne et al., 1979). With this strategy, the search for a solution begins at the goal and works backward toward the "givens." This method is often used when the goal has more information than the givens, and when the operations can work both forward and backward. If, for example, we wanted to spend exactly $100 on clothing, it would be difficult to reach that goal by simply buying some items and hoping they totaled exactly $100.

Nim games are another fine example of working backward: 15 pennies are placed on a table in front of two players. Each player is allowed to remove at least 1 penny but not more than 5 pennies a turn. The players alternate turns, each removing from 1 to 5 pennies, until one player takes the last penny on the table, and wins all 15 pennies (Wickelgren, 1974). Is there a method of play that will guarantee victory? If so, what is it?

In this case, in order to win you must reach your final turn with 1 to 5 pennies left on the table. This means that your opponent must be faced with just 6 pennies on the table when it is his or her last turn: If your opponent removes 1 penny, you will be left with 5 for your last move; if your opponent removes 5 pennies, you will be left with 1 for your last move. By working backward in this manner, you will come to this conclusion: If at any point your opponent is faced with either 6 or 12 pennies, no matter what he or she does, you will be in position to win the game (Wickelgren, 1974).

To this point we have seen how various strategies can be used to solve problems. Yet in real life, problem solving often bogs down and we are

Means-end analysis A heuristic strategy that aims to reduce the discrepancy between the current situation and the desired goal at a number of intermediate points.

Working backward A heuristic strategy in which one works backward from the desired goal to the given conditions.

Set Tendency to perceive and to approach problems in certain ways.

either unable to arrive at a solution or our solution is not an effective one. In the next section we will examine various obstacles to problem solving.

Obstacles to Solving Problems

Problem solving is affected by many factors other than those we have already discussed. In Chapter 5 we saw that the "peak" or optimum state of performance in problem solving is achieved at intermediate levels of excitement or arousal (Reed, 1982). Moreover, the more complex the problem-solving task, the lower the level of emotion that can be tolerated without interfering with performance. Generally, we must whip up a certain surge of excitement in order to adequately motivate ourselves to solve a problem, but too much arousal can hamper our ability to find a solution.

Another obstacle to problem solving is the fear of taking risks. Albert Ellis notes that people become convinced that failure makes them look "bad" in other people's eyes, while success makes them appear "good" (Ellis, 1973). Such feelings have been fostered over a lifetime of being called (directly or implicitly) good for putting our toys away, getting a good grade on a test, and bringing home fat paychecks. At the same time, we have been called bad for spilling our milk, getting a traffic ticket, and losing our job. Such criticisms may create a highly emotional fear of failure, even though this fear is rooted in the irrational assumption that failure means we are worthless and unloved. Many people would rather not risk losing the approval of others, and so fail to put a sincere effort into solving problems. As a result, their attempts are half-hearted, feeble, and doomed from the start.

A factor that can either help or hinder problem solving is **set,** which refers to our tendency to perceive and to approach problems in certain ways. This can be helpful if we have learned certain operations and perceptions in the past that we can apply to the present. For example, people tend to do better when they solve problems for the second or third time because they have learned more effective strategies for choosing moves, and because they understand the problem better (Reed, Ernst, & Banerji, 1974). Much of our education involves learning sets and ways to solve problems (i.e., heuristics and algorithms), although it may seem that we are learning only specific information. We are taught to integrate new information into forms we already know, or to use methods that have proved effective in the past. In fact, the strategies we use in problem solving are themselves a set. We have learned that approaching a problem in a certain logical order is the best way to solve it.

But sets do not always help solve problems. If a problem requires you to apply your previous experience in a new and different way, a strong set could become a serious obstacle. People who are most successful in solving problems often are those who have many different sets at their disposal, and can judge when to change sets or when to give up a set entirely. Great ideas and inventions come out of such a balance. Copernicus was familiar with the sets of his time, but he had the flexibility to see that they might not be relevant to his work. Only by putting aside these sets could he discover that the earth revolves around the sun. The point is to use a set when it is appropriate, but not to let the set use you—not to be so controlled by learned ways of approaching a problem that you are closed to new approaches to solving it.

One set that can seriously affect creative problem solving is **functional fixedness**. The more you use an object in one way, the harder it is to see new uses for it. When you get used to seeing something one way and only one way, you have assigned it a fixed function. To some extent, of course, part of the learning process is assigning correct functions to objects. We teach a child that the "right" function of a spoon is stirring, not pounding. Much of how we form concepts involves learning the "right" functions of objects. But it is important to remain open enough to see that a coin can be used as an emergency screwdriver, or that a book can be used

Functional fixedness The tendency to perceive only a limited number of uses for an object, which interferes with the process of problem-solving.

Creative Insight

People sometimes report solving problems by using insight, a seemingly arbitrary flash "out of the blue" that solves a problem. Most of us explain creative problem solving in terms of such inspiration. When we have an original idea and somebody says, "How did you arrive at that?" we realize that we did not get there step by step. We may answer with something like, "The idea just came to me while I was walking home." Henri Poincaré, the French mathematician, has described this process at work:

> One evening, contrary to my custom, I drank black coffee and could not sleep. Ideas rose in crowds; I felt them collide until pairs interlocked, so to speak, making a stable combination. By the next morning, I had established the existence of a class of Fuchian functions. . . . I had only to write out the results, which took but a few hours (Poincaré, 1924).

Many people have provided strikingly similar accounts of their own processes of creative thinking. In these cases, the solution does not, in any direct way, appear to follow logically from the preparation. Poincaré knew what the problem was and what facts it involved. In his hours at his desk he may have sought to solve the problem by normal means, but such a solution eluded him. The way in which his thinking at his worktable "led to" the sudden flash of insight that presented the solution is much less direct than the step-by-step method of problem solving. Note that Poincaré does not say that he brought the ideas together, but that he "felt them collide." Something other than logic appears to have been involved, and that something is what we call "inspiration" or "insight."

Many psychologists are still unsure, however, if insightful or creative problem solving is much different from step-by-step problem solving. Some believe that the same processes are involved but are unrecognized by the thinker. We still do not know why people have sudden insights after "taking a vacation" from a task, as Poincaré did, but there are several possible explanations, none of which involves magic!

First, and obviously, concentrating on a task for a long time can cause mental fatigue. We may do better after a break. Or, a rest may allow us to take a new approach when we return to the problem, to look at it from a new angle (Murray & Denny, 1969). Moreover, although we may think we are taking a break, we may actually be thinking— consciously or not (Neisser, 1967)—about the same old problem. Moreover, solving a problem creatively sometimes involves taking risks. You are more likely to pursue an absurd idea when you are relaxed and off-guard than when you feel pressed to solve a problem in a more traditional way (Adams, 1976).

Another possible explanation for flashes of insight has to do with hemispheric specialization of the brain. Scientists generally believe that the left hemisphere attacks problems in a linear fashion. It handles them one at a time, like links in a chain. The right hemisphere, however, may allow us to approach a problem by looking at the whole picture. This holistic perspective may show at once how all the elements of a problem fit together. After a prolonged and tiring bout with pieces of information, we may become so entangled with the parts of a problem that we lose the overall picture. But when we take a break from our work, perhaps to eat dinner or wash the car, the right hemisphere may have an opportunity to view the problem as a whole and provide new insights.

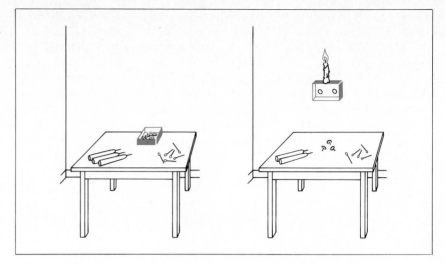

Figure 8-5
To test the effects of functional fixedness, subjects might be given the items shown on the table at left and asked to mount a candle on the wall. One solution is shown in the figure on the right. A common obstacle is that people tend to think of the tack box as a container only and overlook how it can be used as a candleholder.

as a prop for a wobbly table leg (for example, see the problem in Figure 8-5).

We have been talking about functional fixedness in terms of objects, but the idea can also be applied to problems with people. For example, the problem of the elderly has been given much attention recently. Putting older people into institutions can make them feel useless and depressed. Unwanted children also live in institutions that cannot always give them the time and care they need. Instead of seeing the elderly as people to be looked after, someone grasped the idea that they might serve as "foster grandparents" to the children in institutions. This was a case of suspending the fixed function of both groups. The "grandparents" gave the children love and attention, and the children gave older people the feeling of being useful. Two human problems were solved with one wise, new, and compassionate solution.

Despite the many pitfalls that we may encounter when trying to solve problems, there are many techniques for sharpening our performance on such tasks. Let us take a look at some of the ways to become better and more efficient problem solvers.

Becoming Better at Solving Problems

As you will recall, the first step in reaching a solution to a problem is to try out various ways of interpreting or representing the problem. You can then experiment with a number of solution strategies, shifting your perspective of the problem from one angle to another. Let's look more closely at how some of these strategies work.

If in a given problem you are more sure of what you do not want than of what you do want, the tactic of elimination can be very helpful. The best approach is to first create a working list of all the possible solutions you can think of. Then you evaluate and discard choices by applying the appropriate criteria. When working with this strategy, however, you will want to keep in mind that you have assumed that a good solution to the problem does exist in your list of possible choices. But this assumption may prove false, and as a result you could very well eliminate all the possible solutions! Other useful tactics are visualizing, diagraming, and charting various courses of action (Adams, 1976).

Various "thinking aids" can also be effective in the process of solving tough problems. One such aid is listing all the uses or attributes of an object; the list then may suggest ways to solve a problem involving that object. For instance, suppose we are asked to find new uses for the common red brick. We might start out by listing some of the attributes of a typical brick: color, weight, rectangular shape, sturdiness, and ability to store and conduct heat. The list then suggests some novel uses for bricks. For example, the weight of a brick brings to mind such uses as a doorstop, a paperweight, and a projectile during a riot. The key to this approach is to list whatever uses or attributes you can think of, regardless of how absurd they may sound at first (Adams, 1976).

Compensatory model A rational decision-making model in which choices are systematically evaluated on various criteria.

Decision Making

Many of the problems that you must solve each day require that you make decisions. What to wear, what to say to your boss, what to eat—these are just a few examples. Usually you must pick one of several choices. For instance, do you wear the red striped shirt, the yellow one, or the blue plaid one? Do you ask your boss about your next assignment, your vacation plans, or your next raise? When you are pushing your cart along the aisles of the supermarket, which bread do you buy? Do you choose the dark or light rye, the brand for which you have saved a coupon, or the loaf that is the most nutritious?

In making such decisions, we use a predetermined set of criteria in evaluating the possible choices. Sometimes we have to juggle a fairly large and complex set of criteria. As this set grows, so do the difficulties in reaching a good solution. For example, suppose we are looking for an apartment. The amount of rent is important, but so are the neighbors, location, level of noise, and cleanliness. If we find a noisy apartment with undesirable neighbors but a bargain-basement rent, should we take it? Is it a better choice than the apartment in a more desirable location, with less noise, but with a somewhat higher rent? How can we weight the various characteristics to ensure that we make the best possible decision from among the various choices?

If you were to proceed logically, you would use some kind of **compensatory model** to arrive at a decision (Reed, 1982). In this case, you would rate different choices on each of several criteria in order to see how the attractive features of each choice might compensate for the unattractive ones. For example, if you are buying a house, one criterion might be that you prefer a brick house. You might, however, buy a wooden house if it is located in a good school district, has a pleasing floor plan, and is reasonably priced. In this case, the attractive features compensate for the fact that the house is not brick.

One of the most useful compensatory models is shown in Table 8-1.

Even everyday decisions, such as what brand to buy at the supermarket, call for rating and choosing among alternatives.

When it comes to major decisions, such as which house to buy, compensatory models are the best choice in decision making.

The various criteria are listed, with each assigned a weight according to its importance. Here the decision involves the purchase of a new car, and only three criteria are considered: price (which is not weighted heavily), and gas mileage and repair record (which are given fairly heavy weights). Each car is then rated from 1 (poor) to 5 (excellent) on each of the criteria. You can see that Car 1 has an excellent price but relatively poor gas mileage and service record; Car 2 has a less desirable price but a fairly good mileage and repair record. Each rating is then multiplied by the weight for that criterion (e.g., for Car 1, the price rating of 5 is multiplied by the weight of 4) and the result is put in parentheses next to the rating. Then the numbers in parentheses are added to give a total for each car. Clearly Car 2 is the better choice: It has a less desirable price, but that is offset by the fact that its mileage and service record are better and these are more important than price to this particular buyer.

Using a table such as Table 8-1 allows you to evaluate a large number of choices on a large number of criteria. It can be extremely helpful in making choices such as which college to attend, which job offer to accept, which career to pursue, and where to take a vacation. If you have

Table 8-1 Compensatory Decision Table for Purchase of New Car

	Price (weight = 4)	Gas mileage (weight = 8)	Service record (weight = 10)	Weighted total
Car 1	5 (20)	2 (16)	1 (10)	(46)
Car 2	1 (4)	4 (32)	4 (40)	(76)

Ratings: 5 = Excellent
1 = Poor

properly weighted the various criteria and correctly rated each alternative in terms of each criterion, then you can be sure that the alternative with the highest total score is in fact the most rational choice.

Most people, however, do not follow such a precise system of making decisions. Rather, they use various **noncompensatory models**. Especially popular is the *elimination-by-aspects* tactic (Reed, 1982). In this case, we toss out specific choices if they do not meet one or two of our requirements, regardless of how good they are on other criteria. For example, we might eliminate Car 2, regardless of all its advantages, because "it costs more." As you might guess, noncompensatory models tend to be short-sighted. They do not help us weigh the values of particular features, nor do they invite us to compare all the alternatives. As a result, such a model is likely to lead to a decision that is merely adequate, but not the best.

Sometimes we mix both compensatory and noncompensatory strategies to settle on a decision (Payne, 1972). When there are many alternatives and many criteria, we use a noncompensatory approach to eliminate any choices that are especially weak on one or more criteria, even though they may be strong on other criteria. When the field has been narrowed to a few alternatives, all of which are at least average on the various criteria, then we adopt some form of compensatory decision model.

We also decide among different decision models according to how much is at stake. We are more likely to use a compensatory model when the stakes are high: buying a home or car or choosing a college. When the stakes are low, the noncompensatory model usually helps us to decide such casual matters as which shoes to wear or who we think might win an Academy Award.

But even in important matters it is not always easy to make rational decisions. Sometimes, for example, information about an alternative is uncertain. In the case of the two cars, we may not know the repair record of either car, perhaps because both are new models. In this case, we have to make some estimates based on information about past repair records, which then help us to predict the repair records of these new models. In the absence of any reliable information at all, we may have to guess about some of the facts that we need to make a decision, and research indicates that in many cases our guesses may not be correct. For example, in making informed guesses people tend to rely on the most readily available information, even though it is often inaccurate. Tversky and Kahneman asked subjects whether the letter r appears more frequently as the first or third letter in words. Most people said "first," although "third" is actually the correct answer. Their estimates were incorrect because they simply relied on the most readily available information. Since it is easier to recall words that begin with r most people assume that these words are more prevalent than words that have r as their third letter (Mayer, 1983).

Decision making is one of the most important functions of human thought. Government leaders shape policy (e.g., how to regulate the nuclear power industry) and individuals shape their private lives (e.g., how to lose 20 pounds) by choosing among alternatives. Since most of us can tolerate poor decisions in areas that are of minor importance, it does not much matter that such decisions are often biased and somewhat irrational. However, there are cases where decision making is critical and errors can be quite serious. Medical decision making falls into this category and is the subject of the following Application.

Noncompensatory models
Decision-making models that do not try to systematically weigh comparisons among alternatives.

Medical Decision Making

You have a sore throat and a high fever accompanied by severe back pains. You are examined by a doctor who asks a few questions, listens to your heart and lungs, looks down your throat, and then takes your blood pressure. Finally, you are given a drug prescription and told that you should be feeling better by the day after tomorrow. How did your doctor arrive at that decision so quickly?

Medical decisions are not nearly as clear-cut and objective as they might seem. Elstein, Shulman, and Sprafka (1978) found that most physicians tend to form a few initial general hypotheses

Medical decision making involves forming a few initial general hypotheses almost immediately.

almost immediately. These guide the search for additional information, and the choice of diagnostic tests and perhaps some initial medication. These hypotheses are then modified or changed as new data are found. If evidence refutes this initial diagnosis, new hypotheses will be generated partly on the basis of the results of the tests and partly on the basis of the doctor's knowledge and past experience. These, too, will be tested until it appears that the problem has been correctly diagnosed, though a well-trained physician will remain alert for evidence that a diagnosis is still not quite correct.

If all possible diagnoses are considered, each one tested thoroughly, and the results evaluated according to a compensatory model, then medical decision making can be very effective. But because

subjective judgment plays such a large role in the medical decision process, it can also go awry relatively easily, especially when an inexperienced physician is making the decision. With this in mind, Elstein and his colleagues (1978) recommend following three stages in medical decision making: (1) produce a list of alternative hypotheses, (2) collect data selectively, and (3) assemble all the data and plot a course of action. In Stage 1, physicians should start with the most common diagnoses that fit the case. However, they should also keep in mind other, less common diagnoses that, if overlooked, could seriously endanger the patient. In the second stage, physicians should order laboratory tests that will either confirm or rule out the most common diagnoses as well as those for which the patient would be at serious risk if he or she were not treated. At this stage the physician must balance the harm these tests might cause the patient—as well as the costs of the tests—with the likely benefits. When interpreting the data in Stage 3, it is important to remember that a patient with several complaints may well suffer from more than one ailment. Moreover, in sifting through all the data in an effort to confirm or rule out hypotheses, it is critical to remember that the patient may have an uncommon illness, and as a result *none* of the preliminary diagnoses may be correct. Finally, when charting a course of treatment, the physician must weigh the probability that the diagnosis is accurate against the benefits and risks that can follow from the chosen regimen of treatment.

Summary

1. *Cognition*, or thinking, involves various ways of manipulating the information that we have processed and stored in memory.
2. *Images* and *concepts* are the two most important building blocks of thought.
3. Concepts are categories that we use in classifying objects, people, or experiences. We draw upon previously formed concepts to give meaning to new experiences. Concepts allow us to generalize, to differentiate, and to think abstractly. Our concepts can change or become modified as a result of contact with new objects, people, or experiences.
4. In practice, concepts tend to be "fuzzy" and ambiguous rather than clear-cut and precise. In everyday thinking we rely on models or prototypes of concepts. We decide which objects belong to a particular concept according to what seems most probable and sensible given the facts at hand.
5. Concepts match up with words. We use language to link concepts with other concepts and in that way form more complex thoughts and ideas.
6. *Phonemes* are the basic, universal sounds of all languages. Phonemes are meaningless in themselves but are combined to form *morphemes*, the smallest meaningful units in language. We express our ideas in phrases and sentences (combinations of morphemes) rather than in single concepts.
7. We use *top-down processing* (movement from deep structure to surface structure of language) to communicate ideas. We use the reverse process, *bottom-up processing* (movement from surface structure to deep structure of language) in order to comprehend ideas.
8. Language itself significantly affects our ability to think about things. The *linguistic relativity hypothesis* maintains that thinking is patterned by language and that the language one speaks determines one's view of the world. Although this theory has been strongly criticized, evidence suggests that the way we think affects the words we use, and that once words make their appearance in a language, they shape the way we think about things. People from different language backgrounds appear to think about some things—like color—in very similar ways. Thus people are able to think about things for which no equivalent words exist in their language.
9. Images are mental recollections of sensory experience. We freely manipulate images in our minds in order to think about things. Because

images are more concrete than words, they are useful aids in problem solving.

10. *Problem representation*, or interpretation, is the first step in figuring out a solution to a problem. People show a strong tendency to accept the initial representation of a problem, even though it may not be the most appropriate. Those who are skilled at problem solving are adept at representing problems in various ways.

11. Step 2 in problem solving is choosing a solution strategy. Trial-and-error is a common but ineffective strategy. The most effective strategies are based upon accurate problem representation.

12. Different types of problems require different solutions. In some cases, solving a problem is simply a matter of retrieving information from long-term memory and applying it to the situation at hand.

13. *Algorithms* are problem-solving methods that guarantee the correct solution if they are appropriate for the problem and are properly carried out.

14. *Heuristics* are rules of thumb that help in simplifying problems and bringing solutions within reach. Part of problem solving is deciding which heuristic best fits the problem at hand. *Hill-climbing, subgoals, means-end analysis,* and *working backward* are four heuristic methods.

15. Hill-climbing and means-end analysis are strategies that call for steady progress toward a goal. Working backward allows for digressions or temporary steps backward in order to realize a final goal.

16. In setting subgoals we break a problem into smaller and more manageable goals. Means-end analysis is a combination of hill-climbing and subgoals.

17. A number of conditions can affect problem solving. The peak state of performance in problem solving is achieved at intermediate levels of arousal. A state of high emotional arousal can interfere with problem solving.

18. Both the fear of taking risks and the fear of failure may weaken our efforts at problem solving.

19. *Set* refers to our tendency to perceive and approach problems in certain ways. Set can be helpful since it enables us to benefit from past experiences in learning certain operations and ways of perceiving. But if we rely too heavily on set so that we don't look for new methods to solve problems, we may overlook more creative strategies. *Functional fixedness* occurs when we get used to perceiving something in a certain way and cannot perceive it in any other way.

20. Becoming better at problem solving requires trying out various ways of representing problems and experimenting with different solution strategies.

21. We can use the tactic of elimination to narrow down a list of possible solutions. The disadvantage of elimination is that it assumes a good solution to the problem exists among the various possible choices being considered, which is not always true.

22. Listing items is a helpful thinking aid in problem solving.

23. In decision making, we evaluate possible choices using a predetermined set of criteria. The more complex our set of criteria, the greater the difficulty we encounter in reaching a solution.

24. *Compensatory models* allow us to rate and compare different choices on each of several criteria. Such rational models of decision making allow us to evaluate a large number of criteria. They are the models of choice in making important decisions.

25. In everyday decision making we tend to use less logical and formal methods. *Noncompensatory models*, such as the elimination-by-aspects method, do not involve weighing the various criteria and making comparisons among alternatives. Because they are short-sighted, noncompensatory models result in adequate but not always the best decisions.

26. People very often use a mix of compensatory and noncompensatory models in decision making. The choice of decision model is greatly affected by how much is at stake in making the decision.

27. We do not always have the information that we need to weigh criteria and make decisions. In these cases, we are likely to make informed guesses using the most readily available information. Readily available information, however, is not always correct and may result in erroneous guesses.

1. The term that psychologists use to refer to the processes of thinking is _____ .
2. _____ and _____ are the two most important building blocks of thought.
3. Categories for classifying specific people, things, or events are
   a. concepts   c. phonemes
   b. images   d. morphemes
4. People decide which objects belong to a concept by comparing the facts to a model or prototype.   T/F
5. We use _____ to link concepts with other concepts and thus form more complex thoughts.
6. In language, universal sounds called _____ are combined to form the smallest meaningful units, which are called _____ . These meaningful units can then be combined to create words, which in turn can be used to build phrases and whole _____ .
7. According to the _____ _____ _____ hypothesis, the language that one speaks determines the pattern of one's thinking and one's view of the world.
8. Movement from deep structure to surface structure is termed _____ _____ processing, while movement from surface structure to deep structure is _____ _____ processing.
9. Images help us think about things because images are more concrete than words.   T/F
10. Match each problem-solving strategy with its definition:

    ___ algorithm
    ___ heuristics
    ___ hill-climbing
    ___ means-end analysis
    ___ working backward

    A. rules of thumb that help in simplifying and solving problems, although they do not guarantee a correct solution.
    B. Strategy in which each step moves you progressively closer to a solution.
    C. Step-by-step method that guarantees a solution.
    D. A strategy in which one moves from the goal to the starting point
    E. Strategy that aims to reduce the discrepancy between the current situation and the desired goal at a number of intermediate points.

11. All of the following are potential obstacles to problem solving except
    a. sets   c. functional fixedness
    b. excitement   d. hill-climbing
12. Bill is trying to decide between taking a ski vacation in Vermont and a beach vacation in the Caribbean. To make the choice, he sets up some criteria for a good vacation and then rates the two alternatives on each in order to see how they stack up against each other. Bill is using a _____ model of decision-making.
13. Our tendency to perceive and to approach problems in certain ways is termed a _____ .
14. The tendency to perceive only a limited number of uses for an object, a tendency which interferes with the process of problem solving, is known as _____ _____ .
15. In making decisions, most people use a compensatory model.   T/F
16. Decision-making models that do not try to systematically weigh comparisons among alternatives are _____ models.
17. People are most likely to use a compensatory model when
    a. the stakes are low
    b. the stakes are high
    c. others are observing them
    d. the problem is simple

Outline

Intelligence

9

1. Describe the difference between laziness and idleness.

2. Which direction would you have to face so your right hand would be toward the north?

3. What does *obliterate* mean?

4. In what way are an *hour* and a *week* alike?

5. Select the item that completes the series of four figures below:

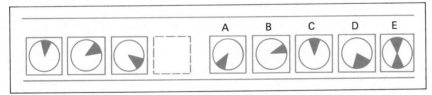

6. Choose the lettered block that best completes the pattern in Figure 1.

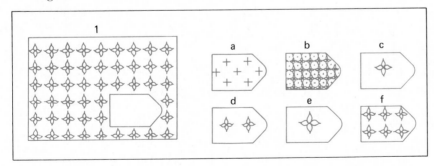

7. The opposite of hate is:
   (a) enemy (b) fear (c) love (d) friend (e) joy

8. If 3 pencils cost 25 cents, how many pencils can be bought for 75 cents?

9. A bird does not always have:
   (a) wings (b) eyes (c) feet (d) a nest (e) a bill

10. Choose the word that is most nearly *opposite* in meaning to the word in capital letters:

SCHISM: (a) majority (b) union (c) uniformity (d) conference (e) construction

11. Choose the set of words that, when inserted in the sentence, *best* fits in with the meaning of the sentence as a whole:

From the first, the islanders, despite an outward _____, did what they could to _____ the ruthless occupying power.
(a) harmony . . . assist (b) enmity . . . embarrass (c) rebellion . . .foil (d) resistance . . . destroy (e) acquiescence . . . thwart

12. Select the lettered pair that best expresses a relationship similar to that expressed in the original pair:

CRUTCH: LOCOMOTION: (a) paddle: canoe
(b) hero: worship (c) horse: carriage (d) spectacles: vision
(e) statement: contention

13. The first three figures are alike in some way. Find the figure at the right that goes with the first three.

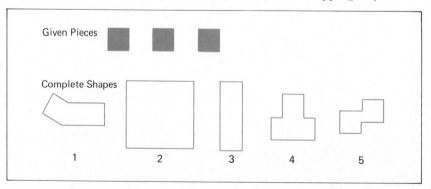

14. Decide how the first two figures are related to each other. Then find the one figure at the right that goes with the third figure in the same way that the second figure goes with the first.

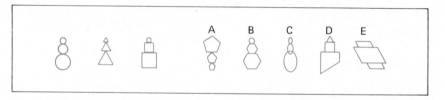

15. For each figure, decide whether or not it can be completely covered by using all the given black pieces without overlapping any.

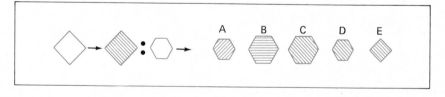

These questions have been taken from various **intelligence tests,** which were designed to measure general mental abilites. Obviously we cannot see the complex mental processes that are involved in **intelligence.** We have to approach the subject indirectly—by watching what people do when situations require the use of intelligence. But what do these tests actually tell us? Do they sample all the kinds of ability we consider "intelligence"? What is intelligence anyway? And is it related to creativity? If you do well on tests such as these, will you be more successful in school, in a job, or in your personal life than someone who does less well? We will address these and related questions in this chapter. We'll begin by looking at what is meant by intelligence.

Intelligence tests Tests designed to measure a person's general mental abilities.

Intelligence A general term covering a mixture of intellectual abilities, and defined in various ways by different psychologists.

Intelligence

What does "intelligence" mean to you? Take a few minutes to write down on a sheet of paper some behaviors that you think are characteristic of intelligent people. In particular, what behaviors distinguish them from unintelligent people?

Sternberg and his associates (Sternberg et al., 1981; Sternberg, 1982) conducted a study to find out how various people define intelligence. They studied both laypersons with no expertise in psychology and psychologists who specialize in studying intelligence. In each group the researchers asked a large number of people to list characteristics of intelligence and then to rate various kinds of people on those characteristics. The results showed that most laypersons think of intelligence as practical problem-solving ability, verbal ability, and social competence. Practical problem-solving ability includes using logic, connecting ideas, and viewing a problem in its entirety. Verbal ability includes using and understanding both written and spoken language in well-developed ways. Social competence concerns interacting well with others—being open-minded about different kinds of people and showing interest in a variety of topics. Experts described intelligence as being made up of verbal intelligence, problem-solving ability, and practical intelligence. This corresponds fairly closely to the layperson's view (see Table 9-1). The main difference in thinking between the two groups is one of emphasis. Whereas laypersons stress social competence, experts do not consider this an essential component of intelligence. Experts, on the other hand, consider motivation an important factor, while this characteristic does not appear on the layperson's list. Before we go on, you might find it interesting to compare your own description of intelligence with those of Sternberg's laypersons and experts. Which one seems to match your own definition most closely? Now that you can compare all three definitions, which one do you think is the best? Why do you think so?

Psychologists have thought about these same questions for many years and in the process they have developed several formal theories of intelligence. We will turn our attention first to those formal theories and then to the ways in which psychologists go about measuring intelligence.

Table 9-1   Some Characteristics of Intelligence as Seen by Laypersons and Experts

Laymen	Experts
I. Practical problem-solving ability	**I. Practical intelligence**

I. Practical problem-solving ability

Reasons logically.
Makes connections among ideas.
Can see all sides of a problem.
Keeps an open mind.
Responds thoughtfully to the ideas of others.
Good at sizing up situations.
Interprets information accurately.
Makes good decisions.
Goes to original source for basic information.
Good source of ideas.
Perceives implied assumptions.
Deals with problems in a resourceful way.

I. Practical intelligence

Sizes up situations well.
Determines how best to achieve goals.
Shows awareness of world around him or her.
Shows interest in the world at large.

II. Verbal ability

Speaks articulately.
Converses well.
Is knowledgeable about a particular field.
Studies hard.
Reads widely.
Writes without difficulty.
Has a good vocabulary.
Tries new things.

II. Verbal intelligence

Has a good vocabulary.
Reads with high comprehension.
Is intellectually curious.
Sees all sides of a problem.
Learns rapidly.
Shows alertness.
Thinks deeply.
Shows creativity.
Converses easily on a wide range of subjects.
Reads widely.
Sees connections among ideas.

III. Social competence

Accepts others as they are.
Admits mistakes.
Shows interest in the world at large.
Arrives on time for appointments.
Has social conscience.
Thinks before speaking and acting.
Shows curiosity.
Avoids snap judgments.
Makes fair judgments.
Assesses the relevance of information to the problem at hand.
Is sensitive to others.
Is frank and honest with self and others.
Shows interest in the immediate environment.

III. Problem-solving ability

Makes good decisions.
Displays common sense.
Shows objectivity.
Is good at solving problems.
Plans ahead.
Has good intuition.
Gets to the heart of problems.
Appreciates truth.
Considers the results of actions.
Approaches problems thoughtfully.

Source: Sternberg, 1982.

Formal Theories of Intelligence

Charles Spearman, a British psychologist, began working on a theory of intelligence around 1900. It struck him that people who are bright in one area often seem to be bright in other areas. So Spearman argued that intelligence is more than an accumulation of specific skills. Instead, he maintained, intelligence is quite general, a kind of well, or spring, of mental energy that flows into every action. The intelligent person understands things quickly, makes good decisions, carries on interesting conversations, and so on. He or she behaves intelligently in various situations. All of us are quicker in some areas than in others. We may find math easy, for example, but will spend hours writing an essay. But Spearman saw these differences as simply ways in which the same underlying general intelligence is revealed in different activities. To return to the image of a well or spring, general intelligence is the fountain from which specific abilities flow like streams of water in different directions.

L. L. Thurstone, an American psychologist, partly agreed with Spearman, but he thought the differences between various abilities needed more attention. From the results of various intelligence tests, Thurstone made a list of seven primary mental abilities (Thurstone, 1938):

S–Spatial ability*	M–Memory
P–Perceptual speed	W–Word fluency
N–Numerical ability	R–Reasoning
V–Verbal meaning	

Operations According to Guilford, the act of thinking.

Contents According to Guilford, the terms we use in thinking, such as words or symbols.

Products According to Guilford, the ideas that result from thinking.

Unlike Spearman, Thurstone believed that these abilities are relatively independent of one another. A person with high spatial ability might be low on word fluency, for example. But together, Thurstone felt, these primary mental abilities are what we mean when we speak of general intelligence. According to Thurstone, one or more of these abilities can be found in any intellectual activity. To read a book, you need verbal meaning, word fluency, and reasoning. To study that same book for an exam, you also need memory. Thurstone thus presented a somewhat more complex model of intelligence than Spearman's.

J. P. Guilford found both Spearman's and Thurstone's models of intelligence incomplete. Guilford distinguished three basic kinds of mental ability: **operations,** the act of thinking; **contents,** the terms in which we think—such as words or symbols; and **products,** the ideas we come up with (Guilford, 1961). Each of these categories can be broken down further. The result is the three-dimensional model shown in Figure 9-1.

According to Guilford, all mental activity involves an operation on some kind of content and results in some product. For example, you are reading a newspaper column about the candidates in a mayoral election. Reading involves three operations: cognition, memory (you recall the candidates' speeches and ads), and evaluation (Does the columnist make sense? Do the candidates make sense?). In performing these operations you use two kinds of contents: semantic (the words) and behavioral (the activities or behavior described). The products of your reading are infer-

According to Thurstone, one or more primary mental abilities is involved in any intellectual activity. To read a book, for example, you need verbal meaning, word fluency, and reasoning.

*Spatial ability is the ability to perceive distance, recognize shapes, and so on.

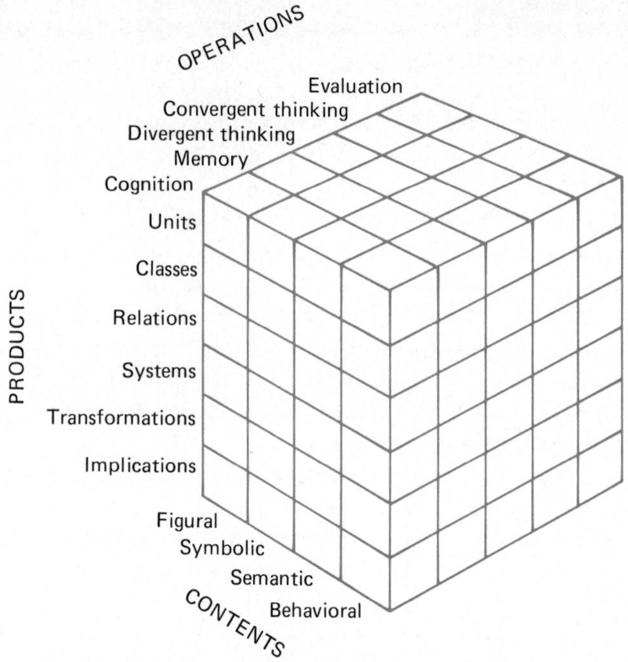

Figure 9-1

Guilford's three-dimensional model of intelligence. The model consists of 120 small cubes, or factors. Each factor can be classified according to operation, product, and content.

ences (this person would make a good mayor, that person would not) and classes (two candidates are liberal, the third is conservative). You may also discover some relationships: perhaps the candidate born in the central city understands its problems better than the two who were raised in the suburbs.

The formal theories about intelligence have become increasingly complex. For example, most people find the 120 cubes in Guilford's model overwhelming! However, one line of research has been directed at developing a simpler theory of intelligence. Psychologist R. B. Cattell believes that there are just a few clusters of mental abilities, with only minor differences between the specific abilities within each cluster (Cattell, 1971). In fact, Cattell has found repeatedly that the various aspects of intelligence fall into just two clusters. The first is what he calls *crystallized intelligence,* or abilities such as reasoning and verbal and numerical skills. These are the kinds of abilities stressed in school, and as a result, Cattell believes, the scores on tests of crystallized intelligence are greatly affected by experience and formal education. The second cluster of abilities makes up what Cattell calls *fluid intelligence,* or skills such as spatial and visual imagery, the ability to notice visual details, and rote memory. Scores on tests of fluid intelligence are much less affected by experience and education.

There are some striking similarities and differences between the way intelligence is defined in these formal theories and the way it was defined in the informal theories of both laypersons and experts in Sternberg's studies. Both laypersons and experts included verbal ability and problem-solving ability in their informal definitions of intelligence; these abilities also appear in the formal definitions. But neither social competence nor practical intelligence appears in formal definitions of intelligence.

Despite the differences between them, both informal and formal concepts of intelligence are useful (Sternberg, 1981). We all use informal, everyday notions of intelligence in making judgments about others. The fact that we include social competence in our judgment of people's intelligence suggests that it is an important ability in normal encounters with people. But this concept of intelligence would be less useful than a formal theory in selecting engineers to design a new spacecraft.

Formal theories of intelligence are also important because they provide a standard view of intelligence that can be used as the basis for the measurement of intelligence. Formal theories supply the means to develop intelligence tests to measure the abilities of large numbers of people and to compare them to one another. From formal definitions of the components of intelligence, psychologists can create corresponding questions and problems to tap those elements. But because intelligence tests are not based on everyday views of intelligence, they will not precisely match people's ideas about what they should include.

Binet-Simon Scale The first test of intelligence, developed for testing children.

Intelligence quotient (IQ) A numerical value given to intelligence that is determined from the scores on an intelligence test; based on a score of 100 for average intelligence.

Stanford-Binet Scale Terman's adaptation of the Binet-Simon Scale.

Intelligence Tests

The Stanford-Binet Intelligence Scale

The first "intelligence test" was designed for the French public school system by Alfred Binet, director of the psychological laboratory at the Sorbonne, and his colleague, Theodore Simon. Binet and Simon developed a number of questions and tested them on schoolchildren in Paris to find out which children were retarded, or had trouble learning.

The first **Binet-Simon Scale** was issued in 1905. It consisted of 30 tests arranged in order of increasing difficulty. With each child, the examiner started at the top of the list and worked down until the child could no longer answer questions. By 1908 enough children had been tested to predict what the normal average child could do at each age level. From these average scores Binet developed the concept of *mental age*. A child who scores as well as an average 4-year-old has a mental age of 4; a child who scores as well as an average 12-year-old has a mental age of 12.

In the next 10 years a number of Binet adaptations were issued, the best known of which was prepared at Stanford University by L. M. Terman and issued in 1916. Terman introduced the now famous term **IQ (intelligence quotient)** to mean a numerical value of intelligence, and set the score of 100 for a person of average intelligence.

The **Stanford-Binet Scale** has been revised twice since 1916, for two reasons. First, any test must be updated as word meanings and styles change. Second, Terman and his colleagues found that some questions were easier for people from one part of the country than for those from another, that some were easier for boys than for girls (and vice versa), and that some failed to discriminate among age levels since nearly everyone tested could answer them. Such questions were replaced. Questions 1 and

The Stanford-Binet is given individually and used to determine the subject's intelligence.

2 at the start of the chapter were drawn from the revised Stanford-Binet.

The Stanford-Binet test is not simply passed out to a roomful of students. Instead, each test is given individually, by trained examiners. The test resembles an interview. It takes about 30 minutes for young children and up to 1½ hours for older ones. For instance, 3-year-olds are asked to identify a toy cup as something "we drink out of," and to name objects such as *chair* and *key*; 6-year-olds are asked to define words such as *orange* and *envelope* and to complete a sentence such as "An inch is short; a mile is _____." A 12-year-old might be asked to define *skill* and *juggler* and to complete the sentence: "The streams are dry _____ there has been little rain" (Cronbach, 1970).

The standard procedure is to begin by testing just below the expected mental age of the subject. If a person fails that test, he or she is then given the test at the next lowest level, and so on, until the subject can pass the test. This level is then established as the person's *basal age*. Once the basal age is known, the examiner continues testing at higher and higher levels until the person fails *all* the tests. Then the tests stop. After scoring the tests, the examiner determines the subject's mental age by adding to the basal age credits for each test passed above that age level.

The Wechsler Adult Intelligence Scale

The individual test most often given to adults is the **Wechsler Adult Intelligence Scale—Revised (WAIS-R).** The original WAIS was developed by David Wechsler, a psychologist at Bellevue Hospital in New York. Wechsler objected to using the Stanford-Binet for adults on three grounds. First, the problems had been designed for children and seemed juvenile to adults. Second, the mental age norms of the Stanford-Binet did not apply to adults. Finally, the Stanford-Binet emphasizes verbal skills and Wechsler felt that adult intelligence consists more in the ability to handle the environment rather than in the skill to solve verbal and abstract problems.

The WAIS-R is divided into two parts. One part stresses verbal skills, the other performance skills. The verbal scale includes tests of information ("How many nickels make a dime?") ("Who wrote *Paradise Lost*?"); tests of simple arithmetic ("Sam had three pieces of candy, and Joe gave him four more. How many pieces of candy did Sam have then?"); and tests of comprehension("What should you do if you see someone forget a book on a bus?") The performance scale also measures routine tasks. People are asked to "find the missing part"—buttonholes in a coat, for example; to copy patterns; and to arrange three to five pictures so that they tell a story (Anastasi, 1982). Questions 3 and 4 at the start of this chapter are taken from the WAIS.

Although the questions and instructions might be more sophisticated on the WAIS-R than on the Stanford-Binet, the problems are not especially adult ones. Wechsler's chief innovation was in scoring. First, the person is given separate verbal and performance scores, as well as an overall IQ score. Second, on some items the person can earn one or two extra points, depending on the complexity of the answer given. This innovation credits the reflective qualities we expect to find in adults. Third, on some questions both speed and accuracy affect the score.

Group Tests

The Stanford-Binet and the WAIS-R are individual tests. The examiner takes the person to an isolated room, spreads the materials on a table, and spends from 30 to 90 minutes giving the test. The examiner may then spend another hour or so scoring the test according to detailed instructions in the manual. Obviously this is a time-consuming, costly operation. Moreover, the examiner's behavior may greatly influence the score.

For these reasons, test makers have devised **group tests,** written intelligence tests that a single examiner can give to large groups. Instead of a person sitting across the table asking you questions, you receive a test booklet that contains questions for you to answer within a certain amount of time. Questions 6–12 in the introduction to this chapter are all from group tests.

When people talk about intelligence tests, they most often mean group tests, because this is how they were tested in school. Schools are among the biggest users of group tests. From fourth grade through high school, tests such as the *School and College Ability Tests* (SCAT) and the *California Test of Mental Maturity* (CTMM) are used to measure students' specific abilities. The *Scholastic Aptitude Tests* (SAT)—questions 10–12 in the introduction—and the *American College Testing Program* (ACTP) are designed to measure a student's ability to do college-level work. The *Graduate Record Examination* (GRE) plays the same role on the graduate level. Group tests are also widely used in different industries, the civil service, and the military.

Group tests have some distinct advantages. They eliminate bias in the examiner. Answer sheets can be scored quickly and objectively. And since more people can be tested in this way, better norms can be established. There are also some distinct disadvantages of group tests, however. There is less chance that the examiner will notice if a person is tired, ill, or confused by the directions. People who are not used to being tested tend to do less well on group tests than on individual tests. Emotionally disturbed children also seem to do better on individual tests (Anastasi, 1982).

Group tests Written intelligence tests administered by one examiner to many people at one time.

Performance tests Intelligence tests that do not involve language.

Schools are among the biggest users of group tests of intelligence.

Performance and Culture-Fair Tests

Deaf children take longer to learn words than children who can hear. Immigrants, who may have been lawyers or teachers in their own countries, may need time to learn English. Infants and preschool children are too young to understand directions or answer questions. How can we test these people? One way is to use problems that minimize or eliminate the use of words; that is, **performance tests** or nonverbal tests of various sorts.

One of the earliest performance tests, the *Seguin Form Board,* was devised in 1866 to test the mentally retarded. The form board is essentially a puzzle. The examiner removes the cutouts, stacks them in a predetermined order, and asks the person to replace them as quickly as possible. Another performance test, the *Porteus Maze,* consists of a series of increasingly difficult printed mazes. The examiner asks the person to trace his or her way through the maze without lifting the pencil from the

Culture-fair tests Intelligence tests designed to eliminate cultural bias by minimizing skills and values that vary from one culture to another.

Reliability Ability of a test to produce consistent and stable scores.

paper. This test gives the examiner the equivalent of a mental age based on the most difficult maze a person negotiates.

One of the most effective tests used for very young children is the *Bayley Scales of Infant Development*. The Bayley Scales are used to evaluate the developmental abilities of children from ages 2 to 2½. One scale tests perception, memory, and the beginning of verbal communication. Another scale measures sitting, standing, walking, and manual dexterity. The Bayley Scales can detect early signs of sensory and neurological defects, emotional problems, and troubles in a child's home (Anastasi, 1982).

Culture-fair tests try to measure the intelligence of people who are outside of the culture in which the test was devised. Like performance tests, culture-fair tests minimize or eliminate the use of language. Culture-fair tests also try to minimize skills and values—such as the need for speed—that vary from culture to culture. A good example of this is the *Goodenough-Harris Drawing Test*. The subject is asked to draw the best picture of a person that he or she can. The drawing is scored for proportions, correct and complete representation of the parts of the body, detail in clothing, and so on. It is not scored for artistic talent.

Cattell's *Culture-Fair Intelligence Test* combines some questions that demand verbal comprehension and specific cultural knowledge with other questions that are "culture-fair." By comparing scores on the two kinds of questions, cultural factors can be isolated from "general intelligence." An example of culture-fair items from the Cattell test is question 5 in our introduction.

Another culture-fair test, developed in England by Raven, is the *Progressive Matrices* (question 6 in our introduction). This test consists of 60 designs, each with a missing part. The person is given six to eight possible choices to replace the part. The test involves various logical relationships and requires discrimination. It can be given to one person or to a group.

What Makes a Good Test?

All the tests we have looked at so far claim to measure a broad range of mental abilities or "intelligence." How can we tell if they really do measure intelligence? And how can we decide whether one test is better than another? Psychologists answer these questions by referring to a test's reliability and validity.

Reliability

By **reliability** psychologists mean whether a person's score is dependable and consistent. If your alarm clock is set for 8:15 A.M. and goes off at that time every morning, it is reliable. But if it is set for 8:15 and rings at 8:00 one morning and 8:40 the next, you cannot depend on it; it is unreliable. Similarly, a test is reliable when it yields consistent results. But if you score 90 on a verbal aptitude test one week and 60 on the same or an equivalent test a week or two later, something is wrong.

How do we know if a test is reliable? The simplest way to find out is to give the test to a group and then, after a short time, give the same people the same test again. If they score the same each time, the test is reliable. For example, look at Table 9-2 which shows the IQ scores of eight people tested one year apart on the same test. This is a very reliable test. Although the scores did change slightly, none changed by more than 6 points.

But there is a serious problem with this way of determining reliability. Because the exact same test was used on both occasions, people might simply have remembered the answers from the first testing and repeated them the second time around. To avoid this, *alternate forms* of the test are often used. In this method two equivalent tests are designed to measure the same ability. If a person gets the same score on both forms, the tests are reliable. One way to create alternate forms is to split a single test into two parts—for example, to assign odd-numbered items to one part and even-numbered items to the other. If scores on the two halves agree, the test is said to have **split-half reliability.** Most intelligence tests do have alternate equivalent forms—for example, there are many versions of each college admission test.

These methods of testing reliability can be very effective. But is there some way of being more precise than simply calling a test "very reliable" or "fairly reliable"? Psychologists express reliability in terms of **correlation coefficients,** which measure the relationship between two sets of scores.* If test scores on one occasion are absolutely consistent with those on another occasion, the correlation coefficient would be 1.0. If there is no relationship between the scores, the correlation coefficient would be zero. In Table 9-2 where there is a very close, but not perfect, relationship between the two sets of scores, the coefficient is .96.

How reliable are intelligence tests? In general, the reliability coefficients are around .90—that is, people's IQ scores on most intelligence tests are about as stable as the scores in Table 9-2. For the Stanford-Binet, the chances are about 20 to 1 that a child's true IQ score is within 10 points of the score obtained on any one occasion. On the WAIS-R, the chances are about 20 to 1 that a person's true IQ score is within 5 points of the score obtained on any one occasion. Performance and culture-fair tests are somewhat less reliable.

Scores on even the best tests vary a bit from one day to another, however. Many testing services, therefore, now report a person's score along with a range of scores that allow for variations due to chance. The person might be told that his or her score was 105, with a range of 95–115. This implies that the true score almost certainly lies somewhere between 95 and 115, but is most likely within a few points of 105. But even with the *best* intelligence tests, differences of a few points in IQ scores have little meaning, and should not be the basis for major decisions, such as putting a child in an accelerated or remedial program.

We have seen that many intelligence tests are reliable. But do these tests really measure "intelligence"? We know that the scores on intel-

Split-half reliability A method of determining test reliability by dividing the test into two parts and checking the agreement of scores on both parts.

Correlation coefficients Statistical measures of the degree of association between two variables.

Table 9-2 IQ Scores on the Same Test Given One Year Apart

Person	First Testing	Second Testing
A	130	127
B	123	127
C	121	119
D	116	122
E	109	108
F	107	112
G	95	93
H	89	94

*For more information on correlation coefficients, consult the appendix on measurement and statistical methods at the end of this book.

ligence tests are fairly consistent from day to day, but how do we know that the consistency is due to "intelligence" and not to something else? This is what psychologists mean by test validity.

Validity

Validity Ability of a test to measure what it has been designed to measure.

Content validity Refers to a test's having an adequate sample of the skills or knowledge it is supposed to measure.

Validity is a test's ability to measure what it has been designed to measure. How can you determine if a given test actually measures what it claims to measure?

CONTENT VALIDITY. One measure of validity is known as **content validity,** or whether the test contains an adequate sample of the skills or knowledge that it is supposed to measure. We have already seen that social competence and practical intelligence are not reflected in formal theories of intelligence. Not surprisingly, measures of these skills do not appear on intelligence tests, either. This omission has led to a lot of criticism of the content validity of IQ tests, as we will see shortly.

But what about the other components of intelligence? Do IQ tests adequately cover the kinds of mental abilities that they set out to include? The answer is somewhat mixed. Alfred Binet specifically designed his test to measure qualities like judgment, comprehension, and reasoning. The test was more heavily verbal than perceptual or sensory. Binet himself felt that his intelligence test did not measure a single entity called "intelligence." Instead, he believed that his test sampled various different mental operations, all of which are part of intelligence. As we saw earlier, Binet's original test has been revised and updated several times. At the earliest age levels, the test now requires eye-hand coordination, discrimination, and the ability to follow directions. Children build with blocks, string beads, match lengths, and so on. Older children are tested on skills they learn in school, like reading and math. The tests still rely heavily on verbal content: vocabulary, sentence completion, and interpreting proverbs, for instance. And the tests that are not strictly verbal require understanding of fairly complex verbal instructions.

Most people would agree that the content of the Stanford-Binet is at least part of what we commonly consider "intelligence," so we can conclude that the Stanford-Binet does have at least some content validity. But the heavy emphasis on verbal skills suggests that the test may not adequately sample all aspects of intelligence equally well.

As we saw earlier, it was partly the Stanford-Binet's emphasis on verbal skills that prompted Wechsler to devise the WAIS. Wechsler believes that his 11 subtests together do adequately measure what we call "intelligence," which he defines as "the aggregate or global capacity of the individual to act purposefully, to think rationally, and to deal effectively with his environment." In fact, the WAIS-R does appear to cover many of the primary abilities that Thurstone included under "intelligence" and that Cattell grouped under the headings of "fluid" and "crystallized" intelligence. So the WAIS-R also appears to have some content validity as an intelligence test.

Most group intelligence tests, such as those from which questions 6 through 12 at the beginning of this chapter were taken, also seem to measure at least some of the mental abilities that make up intelligence.

They rely on written questions and answers, and do not require nonverbal behavior, like moving blocks around. They do include tests that ask people to make quantitative decisions—for example, to decide if 5×0 is greater, less than, or equal to 5—to work with geometric figures, and to solve mathematical tasks. Of course, to solve a math problem, the person must also be able to read and understand verbal instructions.

In general, then, the content of most intelligence tests does cover many of the abilities considered to be components of intelligence. These include concentration, planning, memory, understanding language, and writing (Carroll & Horn, 1981). As we saw earlier, most people would agree that these abilities are part of intelligence. Yet intelligence tests do not cover every type of mental ability. Some tests cover skills that other tests leave out, and each intelligence test emphasizes the abilities it measures in a slightly different way.

CRITERION-RELATED VALIDITY. Is test content the only way to determine if an intelligence test is valid? Fortunately, it is not. If both the WAIS-R and the SAT measure intelligence, high scores on one should go with high scores on the other. And if school grades reflect intelligence, then students with good grades should be high scorers on the Stanford-Binet and other intelligence tests. In each case, we can compare scores on the test with some other "direct and independent measure of that which the test is designed to predict" (Anastasi, 1982, p. 137) to determine **criterion-related validity.**

In fact, various intelligence tests do relate well with each other, despite the differences in their content. People who score high on one test tend to score high on the others. Again, we can use the correlation coefficient to describe the strength of the relationship. The Stanford-Binet and Wechsler Scales correlate around .80. The SAT and Wechsler Scales correlate about .60 to .80. Raven's Progressive Matrices and the Porteus Maze Test correlate .40 to .80 with other intelligence tests. The Goodenough-Harris Drawing Test correlates about .50 or better with other tests. Thus, despite their differences in surface content, most intelligence tests do seem to be measuring similar things.

Do IQ tests predict academic achievement? Even the strongest critics agree that this is one thing IQ tests do well. The Stanford-Binet was designed specifically to predict school performance, and it typically does this quite well. Correlations between grades and IQ of .50 to .75 are quite common. Like the Stanford-Binet, the Wechsler Scales also correlate highly with school grades, especially the verbal IQ score. The SAT and ACT college admission tests correlate around .40 with college grades, and the GRE is a good predictor of performance in graduate school. Evidence on the various performance and culture-fair tests is scanty but suggests that these tests do not predict school grades as well as other intelligence tests do (Blum, 1979).

We have seen that intelligence tests are quite reliable: Scores on these tests are consistent from day to day. These tests also seem to include many of the qualities that psychologists define as components of intelligence. And intelligence test scores seem to agree as they should with one another and with other indicators of intelligence, such as school grades. Nonetheless, in the past decade or so, intelligence tests have been the subject of severe criticism.

Criterion-related validity Validity of a test as measured by a comparison of the test score and independent measures of that which the test is designed to measure.

Criticisms of IQ Tests

TEST CONTENT AND SCORES. One major criticism of IQ tests is directed at their content. Many critics believe that intelligence tests are actually concerned with only a very narrow set of skills: passive, verbal understanding; the ability to follow instructions; common sense; and, at best, scholastic aptitude (Ginsberg, 1972; Sattler, 1975). For example, one critic observes, "Intelligence tests measure how quickly people can solve relatively unimportant problems making as few errors as possible, rather than measuring how people grapple with relatively important problems, making as many productive errors as necessary with no time factor" (Blum, 1979, p. 83).

These critics suggest that if there is one thing that all intelligence tests measure, it is the ability to take tests. This would explain why people who do well on one IQ test also tend to do well on others. And it would also explain why intelligence tests correlate so closely with school performance, since academic grades also depend heavily on test scores. But whether this ability applies to other, real-life situations that require thinking is questionable (Blum, 1979). Thus it should not be surprising that there is a growing trend to "abandon the term IQ and replace it with a more accurate descriptor, such as school ability or academic aptitude" (Reschly, 1981, p. 1097).

Still other critics suggest that the content and administration of IQ tests discriminate against minorities. In part, this may be because minority children tend to see such tests as "just a game" and so make less of an effort to do well (Palmer, 1970). But it is also suggested that the unique language skills of black and minority children are not measured by most IQ tests (Blum, 1979). Moreover, examiners often complain that they "cannot understand" how poor black children talk, and this obviously does not encourage good test performance (Sattler, 1975).

Certain questions may have very different meanings for a white middle-class child and for a black ghetto child. The Stanford-Binet, for instance, asks, "What's the thing for you to do if another boy hits you without meaning to do it?" The "correct" answer is, "Walk away." But for a ghetto child, whose survival may depend on being tough, the logical answer might be, "Hit him back." This answer, however, receives zero credit on the Stanford-Binet (Williams, 1970).

Even the culture-fair tests may accentuate the very cultural differences they were designed to minimize (Linn, 1982). Nonverbal tests, for example, can be more culturally loaded than verbal ones. For example, when given a picture of a head with the mouth missing, one group of Oriental children responded by saying that the body was missing, thus receiving no credit. To them, the absence of a body under the head was more remarkable than the absence of the mouth (Ortar, 1963). And nonverbal tests often require abstract thinking styles that are typical of Western middle-class cultures (Cohen, 1969). Cattell's Culture-Fair Test, for example, may be easier for those cultural groups accustomed to working with pencils and paper or those that are motivated to do well on tests.

There are many other reasons why minority children might do less well on IQ tests than middle-class whites (Sattler, 1975). Studies suggest that minority children are more wary of adults, more eager for adult approval, less motivated to get "the right answer" just for the sake of

The content of IQ tests, including culture-fair tests, has been criticized for discriminating against minorities. The best evidence to date, however, indicates that the major and widely used IQ tests are not biased against minorities.

being right, and less driven to achieve. These emotional and motivational deficits could be reflected in test performance.

Although these concerns are real, the best evidence available indicates that "the major, widely used and widely studied tests" are not biased against minorities (Cole, 1981, p. 1075; Reschly, 1981; Bersoff, 1981). While some test items do appear to be biased, these items are so few that they have little or no effect on the IQ scores of various groups. Nonetheless, as Cole (1981) points out, this does not mean "that the use made of the tests is necessarily socially good nor that improvements in the tests cannot be made" (p. 1075).

USE OF IQ SCORES. If IQ tests were just used for some obscure research purposes, perhaps the criticisms would carry less weight. But because IQ tests have been used for so many significant purposes, their evaluation is very important.

Alfred Binet developed the first IQ test to help the French public school system identify students who needed to be put in special classes. In fact, Binet believed that courses of "mental orthopedics" could be used to help those with low IQ scores. But using IQ tests to put a person into a "track" or "slot," as in school classes, can backfire. To the extent that a child gets a low score on an IQ test because of test bias, language handicap, or disinterest, labeling the child "slow" or "retarded" and putting him or her into special classes apart from "normal" students can have a disastrous effect, one that may get worse, not better, with time. Although the American Medical Association's Council on Mental Deficiency defines mental retardation as "subaverage general intellectual functioning . . . associated with impairment in adaptive behavior," Jane Mercer found that 42 percent of children labeled retarded by public schools had IQs above 70 and suffered from no physical disabilities (Mercer, 1972). Mercer and her colleagues also found that most of the adults who were considered retarded were competent in their social roles for people their age. Almost all of them could take care of themselves; 65 percent of them were employed. Mercer concluded that adaptive behavior is as important as IQ scores in judging if a person is retarded. We will look more closely at these issues later in the chapter when we examine mental retardation in detail.

In this section, we have reviewed several criticisms that have been leveled at IQ tests and their use. But criticism does not always mean that the critics want IQ tests to be altogether eliminated. Instead, many of these critics want simply to make IQ tests more useful. For example, Mercer has developed a "System of Multicultural Pluralistic Assessment" (SOMPA), which can be used to test children between the ages of 5 and 11. SOMPA takes into account both the dominant school culture and the family background, and IQ scores (based on the Wechsler Scales) are then adjusted accordingly (Rice, 1979).

In any event, it is important to remember that an IQ score is *not* the same as intelligence. Tests measure a person's ability level at a certain point in time, in relation to the norms for his or her age group. IQ scores do not tell us why someone performs poorly or well. Moreover, "intelligence" is not a single entity. Rather it is "a combination of abilities required for survival and advancement within a particular culture" (Anastasi, 1982). Obviously, these abilities will vary from culture to culture and from one age to another. Those abilities considered most important in one culture will tend to increase in that culture; abilities that are deemphasized will tend to decrease (Levinson, 1959). And finally, IQ score is really a very simplistic way of summing up an extremely complex set of abilities. Maloney (1978) points out that we do not describe a person's personality with a two- or three-digit number. Why, then, he asks, should we try to sum up something as complex as intelligence by labeling someone "90" or "110"?

Although IQ tests are useful for predicting academic performance and for reflecting past learning, there is much that they do not measure—motivation, emotion, and attitudes, for example. Yet in many situations these other characteristics may have more to do with one's success and effectiveness than intelligence does. Let's look briefly at the relationship between IQ scores and success.

IQ AND SUCCESS. Despite their limitations, IQ tests do predict school performance. What does this fact mean and how important is it?

IQ scores should correlate well with academic performance because both involve some intellectual activity and stress verbal ability. Moreover, both academic achievement and high IQ scores require similar kinds of motivation, attention, and continuity of effort (Ginsberg, 1972). And since academic success depends largely on test-taking ability, the correlation is not surprising. But critics suggest that there may be another, less attractive, reason for the relationship between school performance and IQ test scores. If teachers expect a student to do well in school—on the basis of his or her IQ scores—they may encourage that student. By the same token, a student with a low IQ score may not be expected to perform as well, and may be neglected as a result.

Whatever the reason, IQ scores do predict success in school with some accuracy. Moreover, people with high IQ scores get into high-status occupations: Doctors and lawyers tend to have high IQs; truck drivers and janitors tend not to have high IQs. But critics point out that this can be explained in various ways. For one thing, because people with higher IQs tend to do better in school, they stay in school longer; they get advanced degrees, which in turn open the door to high-status jobs. Moreover, children from wealthy families are more likely to have the motivation and the money needed for graduate school and occupational training. They also tend to have helpful family connections. Perhaps most important, they grow up in an environment that encourages academic success and rewards good performance on tests (Blum, 1979).

In fact, studies have shown that IQ scores and grades in college have very little to do with later occupational success (McClelland, 1973). In fact, we now know that when education and social class are held constant, in a wide range of jobs people with high IQs do not perform better than people with lower IQs. As early as 1921 Thorndike observed that the Stanford-Binet test was useful in predicting a child's academic achievement, but less helpful in determining "how well he will respond to thinking about a machine that he tends, crops that he grows, merchandise that he buys and sells and other concrete realities that he encounters in the laboratory, field, shop, and office. It may prophesy still less accurately how well he will succeed in thinking about people and their passions and in responding to these" (Sattler, 1975, p. 21).

IQ scores do predict academic success with some accuracy. By themselves, they are less able to predict career success.

Heredity

About 30 years ago R. C. Tryon began wondering if the ability to run mazes could be bred into rats. Horse breeders and cattle farmers have long known that selective breeding—for example, crossing a fast horse with a strong one—can change the physical characteristics of animals. Could the same technique alter mental abilities? Tryon isolated eligible pairs of "maze-bright" rats in one pen and "maze-dull" rats in another. The animals were left free to breed. Within a few generations the difference between the two groups was astounding: The maze-dull rats made many more mistakes learning a maze than their bright counterparts (Tryon, 1940; see Figure 9-2).

It is difficult to explain how maze ability was transmitted. Perhaps the brighter rats inherited better eyesight, larger brains, quicker reflexes, greater motivation, or a combination of these things. Still, Tryon did show that a specific ability can be passed down from one generation of rats to another.

Obviously laboratory experiments in selective breeding of humans are impractical. Nature, however, gives us nearly perfect experimental subjects for measuring heredity in humans: identical twins. Unlike siblings and fraternal twins, whose genes come from the same parents but have combined differently, identical twins have exactly the same genetic inheritance. If, as Tryon's experiment suggests, intelligence is inherited, they should have identical IQs. Any difference between them can be attributed to environment.

Studies of twins begin by comparing the IQ scores of identical twins who have been raised together. The correlation, shown in Figure 9-3, is very high. But these twins grew up in the same environment: They shared parents, home, schoolteachers, vacations, and probably friends and clothes, too. These common experiences may explain their similarity. To check this possibility, researchers look for identical twins who were separated early in life—generally before they were 6 months old—and raised

Figure 9-2

Errors made by Tryon's maze-bright and maze-dull rats in learning a maze. The colored line shows what percentage of the parent group made equal numbers of errors. The black lines show the errors of the eighth generation of rats. Notice that almost all the maze-dull rats made more errors than the maze-bright rats.

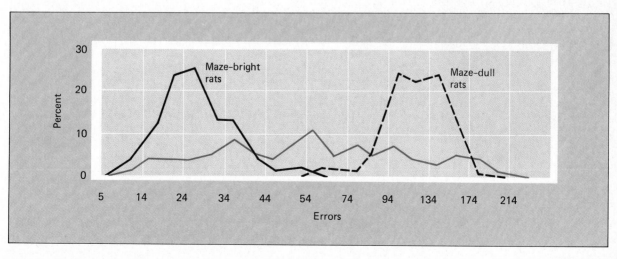

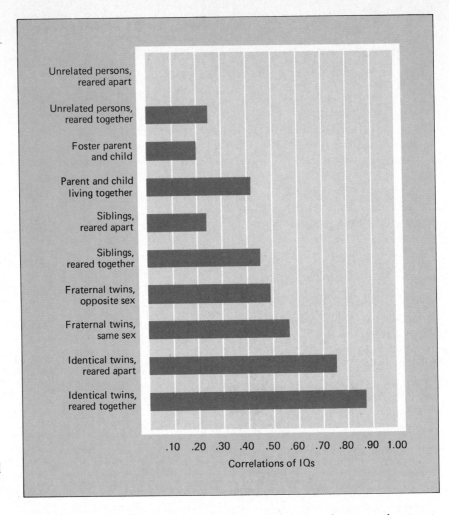

Figure 9-3

Correlations of IQ scores and familial relationships.

According to Tryon, identical twins should have the same IQ. Any differences between them is the result of environment.

in different families. The correlation between IQs of separated twins is nearly as high as that between twins raised together, but there is some evidence of environmental influence.

At this point the case for heredity seems to be won: Identical twins have about equal IQ scores, even when they have not been raised together. For several reasons, however, twin studies are not "final proof." First, it is so difficult to find identical twins who were separated at birth that very few such pairs have been studied. Second, adoption agencies tend to match natural and foster parents. If the twins were born to middle-class, educated parents, it is highly likely that the adopted twin was placed with middle-class, educated foster parents. Finally, even if the twins grew up in radically different environments, for 9 months they lived in the same mother: Their prenatal experiences were identical. Therefore at least some of their similarity may actually be due to similar environment. It is here that the environmental case begins.

Environment

Environmentalists do not deny that some part of intelligence is inherited, but they feel this is only the start. Each of us inherits a certain body build from our parents, but our actual weight depends on what we eat and how much we exercise. Similarly, environmentalists argue, we inherit certain mental capacities, but how our intellectual abilities develop depends on what we see around us as infants, how our parents respond to our first attempts to talk, the schools we attend, the books we read, the TV programs we watch—and even what we eat.

The environmental case begins even before birth. A number of studies show that prenatal nutrition affects IQ scores. For example, one group of psychologists studied a group of pregnant women who were poor and therefore rarely got "three square meals a day." Half the women were

IQ Scores, Family Size, and Birth Order

Zajonc and Markus (1975) present some striking findings about the relationship between IQ scores, family size, and birth order. After reviewing research conducted by Belmost and Marolla (1973), who collected IQ and birth-order statistics on 386,114 young men in the Netherlands, Zajonc and Markus concluded:

> Intelligence declines with family size; the fewer children in your family, the smarter you are likely to be. Intelligence also declines with birth order; the fewer older brothers or sisters you have, the brighter you are likely to be.

Zajonc and Markus constructed a model of the intellectual environment of a family in order to account for these findings. Their model suggests that when a newborn baby enters a family, the average intellectual environment of the family is lowered. Each parent is arbitrarily given an "intellect score" of 100. But the zero score assigned to the newborn baby lowers the average intellectual environment in the family to a level of 67. If a second child is born 2 years later, the family's average score will drop to nearly 50. One simple way to explain this is to imagine the intellectual capacity of the parents being spread among a number of young children. The more children there are, the smaller the amount that will be passed to each child.

To maximize the intellectual environment of your children, the authors suggest that you have no more than two children and that you have them at least 3 years apart. One of the benefits firstborn children have is the opportunity to teach things to their younger siblings. Contrary to popular belief, only children are not better off intellectually. This is probably because they lack this teaching opportunity.

There is some doubt about Zajonc and Markus's conclusions. Other studies have sug-

One of the benefits firstborn children have is the chance to teach their younger siblings.

gested that when we look at individual families rather than aggregate statistics, the results are very different. In fact, family size appears to be much less important in determining mental abilities than social class and ethnic background. Although there is not enough research on the question, the origins of these influences may be related to such factors as education and environment. Children with well-educated parents who provide a rich intellectual climate are likely to have a better chance to develop their intellectual skills than children whose parents cannot provide them with these benefits (Page & Grandon, 1979).

given a dietary supplement, and half were given placebos—to guard against the possibility that merely taking pills would make the women feel better and that this, not nutrition, would affect their babies. When given intelligence tests between the ages of 3 and 4, the children of the mothers who had taken the supplement scored significantly higher than the other children (Harrell, Woodyard, & Gates, 1955).

Extreme malnutrition during infancy can lower IQ scores and may lead to retardation that cannot be cured by improved diet in later years. For example, severely undernourished children in South Africa averaged 20 points lower in IQ than similar children with adequate diets (Stock & Smythe, 1963). If children do not get an adequate diet early in their development, both their mental and their physiological growth will be stunted.

None of this is surprising: Common sense tells us that we need food to grow. But is that all we need? Apparently not. Many psychologists think that surroundings are as important to mental development as diet. The first hint of this came from studies of the effect of light deprivation on sight. Chimpanzees, kittens, rabbits, and other animals raised in total darkness for 16 to 18 months and then moved to a normal environment could never see as well as animals exposed to daylight since birth. There was nothing wrong with these animals' eyes at birth. It seems the cells and nerves we use to see with do not develop without stimulation (Wiesel & Hubel, 1963).

Even more revealing was a further study of Tryon's maze-bright and maze-dull rats conducted in the 1950s. Psychologists raised one group of mixed bright and dull rats in absolutely plain surroundings, and another group in a stimulating environment that contained toys, an activity wheel, and a ladder. When the rats were grown, they were tested on the mazes. There was no difference between genetically bright and dull rats that had been raised in a restricted environment: The inherited abilities of the bright rats had failed to develop and they acted just like dull rats. Among the rats raised in the unusually stimulating environment there was also little difference in performance. Apparently the genetically maze-dull rats were able to make up through experience what they lacked in heredity. The researchers performed autopsies on both groups and found that the rats brought up in a stimulating environment had heavier brains than the others, whether or not they had inherited maze-brightness (Cooper & Zubek, 1958).

Quite by chance, one researcher found evidence that IQ scores among children also depend on stimulation. In the 1930s psychologist H. M. Skeels was investigating orphanages for the state of Iowa. Then, as now, the wards were terribly overcrowded: Often 3 or 4 attendants were responsible for washing, dressing, feeding, and cleaning up after as many as 35 children. There was rarely time to play with the children, to talk to them or to read them stories. Many of the children were classified as subnormal. It was fairly common for the state to transfer them to institutions for the mentally retarded when the orphanages ran out of space. Skeels became interested in two such children who, after 1½ years in an orphanage, were sent to a ward for severely retarded adult women. When Skeels first tested these girls, they did seem retarded, but after a year on the adult ward their IQs were normal (Skeels, 1938). This was quite remarkable. After all, the women they had lived with were themselves

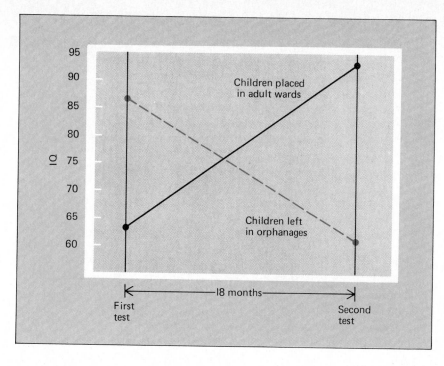

Figure 9-4

Changes in IQ of the institutionalized children studied by Skeels.

severely retarded. Skeels decided to repeat the experiment and placed 13 slow children as houseguests in adult wards (Skeels, 1942) (See Figure 9-4). Within 18 months the mean IQ of these children had risen from 64 to 92 (within the normal range), all because they had had someone to play with them, to read to them, to cheer when they took their first steps, to encourage them to talk. During the same period the mean IQ of a group of children who had been left in orphanages dropped from 86 to 61. Such dramatic changes could not occur if intelligence were stable and hereditary. Skeels found 30 years later that all 13 of the children raised on adult wards were self-supporting, their occupations ranging from waitress to real estate salesperson. Half of the contrasting group were unemployed; four were still in institutions, and all those who had jobs were dishwashers (Skeels, 1966).

Taking their cue from Skeels, some researchers suggest that child-rearing patterns explain class differences in IQ. They point out that lower-class mothers, especially mothers with large families, often do not play with their children as much as middle-class mothers do. Nor do they reward them consistently for achievements—such as learning to crawl or to tell time. Middle-class parents encourage their children to talk. They ask them to describe what they are building with blocks, to identify shapes, colors, and sizes. Those who claim that intelligence depends on stimulation explain the lower IQs of some poor children in terms of thwarted curiosity, an underdeveloped attention span, and a general mistrust of adults.

This is the essence of the environmentalist case: True, some general abilities are inherited, but without stimulation a child's intelligence will not develop. The effects of early deprivation—whether the extreme loneliness of the institutionalized child or the relative isolation of some lower-class children—may not be reversible in later life.

Environmentalists claim that intellectual development depends upon environmental stimulation and encouragement.

The Jensen Controversy

The recent furor over IQ testing was triggered in large part by a 1969 article by psychologist Arthur Jensen that criticized compensatory education programs such as Head Start. The purpose of Operation Head Start was to act as a kind of foster-middle-class environment for disadvantaged children. Its purpose was not only to teach children basic concepts, but also to encourage them to put their perceptions into words. The program sought to teach children to trust adults, to feel comfortable in a schoolroom, and to exercise their curiosity—in other words, to get children ready for school. We will examine Head Start and other compensatory programs more closely in the Application at the end of this chapter. But for the moment we will focus on Jensen's argument that race differences in IQ scores are largely inherited.

In the first part of his article Jensen examines the evidence that intelligence is inherited and concludes that heredity accounts for at least 80 percent of the variation in IQ scores. He then turns to the question of the effect of race differences on intelligence: Black Americans average 15 points lower than whites on most IQ tests. Jensen claims that socioeconomic class does not explain these differences. For one thing, blacks in the upper and middle classes, as well as those in the lower class, have lower IQ scores than their white counterparts. For another, American Indians, who are worse off than blacks in every way, score higher on IQ tests than blacks. Jensen concludes that discrimination and prejudice cannot explain the gap. According to Jensen, one must conclude that the gene pool of blacks differs from that of the general population. Although Jensen concluded that heredity is strongly implicated in IQ differences between groups, he did caution against drawing conclusions about any one person's IQ on the basis of such group generalizations.

Jensen's views on racial differences in IQ are highly controversial. As both sides point out, however, comparisons of average scores of any group tell us very little about what we can expect of any one member of the group.

Jensen's work caused a furious controversy among educators and social scientists over the validity of IQ testing, the heritability of intelligence, and the relationship between race and intelligence. Between 1969 and 1973 alone, 117 articles were published in response to his original piece in the *Harvard Educational Review* (1969). Critics have pointed out that for generations blacks were told that they belonged to an inferior race. The effects of such discrimination show in the fact that IQ scores for blacks from the northern part of the United States are significantly higher than those for southern blacks, suggesting that a higher level of discrimination in the South depresses IQ scores.

Second, teachers tend to expect less from black students and will communicate this, however subtly. The effects of low expectations and low self-esteem mount over the years.

Jensen assumes that blacks and whites from the same class live in the same environments. Few researchers would agree. For example, the average white construction worker owns his own home. His black coworker, with the same salary and references, finds it much more difficult to find a home and to get a mortgage.

It is difficult to sort out the conflicting data and claims involved in the argument over Jensen's work. This is especially true since most of the participants, including Jensen and many of his critics, agree that *both* hereditary and environmental factors affect IQ. Dobzhansky (1973) insists that we simply do not have conclusive evidence to prove that there is, or is not, a genetic basis for racial differences in IQ scores. Moreover, as Jensen himself points out, we should remember that comparisons of average scores of any group tell us very little about what we can expect of any *one* member of the group.

Gender Differences in Cognitive Abilities

Another area of recent concern is the relationship between gender and cognitive abilities. Do males show greater abilities than females in some areas? Do females have more abilities in some areas than males? These questions have become increasingly important since women have entered the work force in larger numbers. Employment statistics show that many occupations are dominated by one sex or the other. Engineering, for example, is almost exclusively a male field (U.S. Bureau of the Census, 1981). Is it possible that these occupational differences reflect real gender differences in cognitive abilities?

In 1974 psychologists Eleanor Maccoby and Carol Jacklin published a review of psychological research on sex differences in a number of areas. In most of the studies they examined, these researchers found no differences at all between the two sexes. But a few differences did appear in the area of cognitive abilities. Maccoby and Jacklin found that girls tend to have greater verbal ability than boys and that boys tend to have greater visual-spatial and mathematical abilities.

Do these findings mean that girls should be encouraged to enter careers that emphasize their greater verbal skills and boys to go into fields that will make use of their visual-spatial skills and mathematical abilities? Even more important, should we discourage girls from trying to enter fields like engineering and computer science and boys from trying to become writers and psychotherapists? Exactly how great are these sex differences in cognitive abilities, and how important are they?

Psychologist Janet Shibley Hyde (1981) believes that as a result of the Maccoby and Jacklin study many people have exaggerated the importance of these male-female differences. She points out that although the differences Maccoby and Jacklin found were consistent, they were also very small. In fact, the differences appear only in studies with very large numbers of subjects. In small groups these differences are often too slight to detect. Hyde also investigated sex differences at the extremely high end of the ability scales. If nearly everyone who scored very high on tests of visual-spatial skills also happened to be male, for example, this might explain the relative absence of females in engineering. Hyde found that the ratio of males to females at the high end of the visual-spatial ability scale was 2 to 1. Males were clearly the majority of high scorers on tests of visual-spatial skills, but the difference was not even close to the ratio of men to women in engineering.

It seems clear that these gender differences in cognitive abilities should not be used for vocational counseling of individuals. Considering how small the differences are, it would be a mistake to conclude that females as a group should not enter careers that rely on visual-spatial skills or math abilities or to expect that individual women cannot show outstanding skills in these areas. By the same token, it would be a mistake to assume that these small differences in cognitive abilities should keep men out of professions that rely on strong verbal skills. It is also important

The very slight gender differences in cognitive abilities make it clear that they should not be used in vocational counseling.

Mental retardation Condition of significantly subaverage intelligence combined with deficiencies in adaptive behavior.

to remember that, on many tests, the sex differences do not appear at all, so it is difficult to determine how important they are when they do appear. Finally, as we discussed earlier, since overall IQ scores are not good predictors of career success, very small sex differences on specific abilities are even less likely to be reliable predictors of future job performance.

Extremes of Intelligence

The average IQ score on intelligence tests is 100. Nearly 70 percent of all people have IQs between 85 and 115, and all but 5% of the population falls between 70 and 130. In this section we will focus on those people who score at the two extremes of intelligence, the mentally retarded and the gifted.

Mental Retardation

In some cases the effects of mental retardation can be greatly reduced by education and social contact.

Mental retardation is a broad heading that covers a large number of very different kinds of mental deficits with a wide variety of causes, treatments, and outcomes. The American Association on Mental Deficiency (AAMD) defines mental retardation as "significantly subaverage intellectual functioning existing concurrently with deficits in adaptive behavior and manifested during the developmental period" (Grossman, 1973, p. 11). There are several important points to this definition. First, mentally retarded people are well below normal in intelligence. *Mild retardation* corresponds to Stanford-Binet IQ scores ranging from a high of 68 down to a low of 52. *Moderate retardation* includes people with IQ scores ranging from 51 to 36. Those with IQ scores between 35 and 20 are considered *severely retarded,* and the *profoundly retarded* are those whose scores are below 19.

But a low IQ score is not in itself sufficient for identifying someone as mentally retarded. The person must also exhibit maladaptive or inappropriate behavior. Therefore evaluations of the mentally retarded usually include tests of motor development and social adaptation as well as of intelligence. One widely used group of motor development tests is the *Oseretsky Tests of Motor Proficiency.* These tests measure control of facial muscles, hand and finger coordination, and posture. Two measures of social adaptation are the *Adaptive Behavior Scale* (ABS) and the *Vineland Social Maturity Scale.* Both are based on observations of the individual's behavior in everyday situations. In the ABS the person is scored in such areas of adaptation as language development, understanding and use of number and time concepts, domestic activity, responsibility, and social action. Another section focuses on the individual's maladaptive behaviors, such as withdrawal, hyperactivity, and violent behavior.

What causes mental retardation and what can be done to overcome it? Most causes of mental retardation are genetic or physiological. One cause is a genetically based disease known as phenylketonuria, or PKU. In a person with PKU the liver fails to produce a certain enzyme necessary for early brain development. PKU occurs in about 1 person out of 25,000 (Minton & Schneider, 1980).

Another cause of mental retardation is chromosomal abnormality, as in Down's syndrome. Mental retardation can also be caused by brain damage in infancy or early childhood and by severe environmental deprivation.

As you might guess, there is little that can be done to reverse the biological conditions that underlie mental retardation once they have developed. But steps can be taken to reduce the effects of retardation through education and training. For those with severe brain damage combined with other physical limitations, learning abilities may be only slight. For others with no physical impairment but a history of social and educational deprivation, education and social contact may have a dramatic impact.

In order to fully assess individuals and to place them in appropriate treatment and educational programs, mental health professionals need information on emotional adjustment, physical health, and social adjustment. The passage of the Education for All Handicapped Children Act in 1977 instituted four required procedures. First, handicapped children must be tested to identify their disabilities. Second, a team of specialists must determine each child's educational needs. Third, an educational program that meets those needs must be provided. Finally, children are to be periodically retested to determine if the program is adequate.

In the assessment phase special attention must be paid to possible biases in measuring instruments. In a recent landmark case in California a judge ruled that the state's education department may not place black children in self-contained classes for the "educable mentally retarded" (EMR) on the basis of standardized intelligence tests. The judge's ruling was based on the assertion that standardized intelligence tests can be used to limit some minority students' educational achievement by labeling and classifying them as EMR and then restricting their school experience to special classes outside of the mainstream (Reschly, 1981; Bersoff, 1981).

Giftedness

At the other extreme of the intelligence scale are "the gifted," those with exceptional mental abilities as measured by scores on standard intelligence tests. Unlike mental retardation, the causes of **giftedness** are largely unknown.

Recently, there has been a national movement to recognize gifted children and to establish special educational programs for them. Even so, questions remain as to what mental abilities are involved in giftedness and how these abilities can best be measured. And there is the related question of whether giftedness is a matter of potential alone, or a combination of both potential and demonstrated achievement (Fliegler & Bish, 1959).

The first and now classic study of giftedness was begun by Lewis Terman and his colleagues in the early 1920s. Terman's (1925) was the first major research study in which giftedness was defined in terms of academic talent and measured by an IQ score in the top 2 percent. More recently, there has been an effort to broaden the definition of giftedness beyond that of simply high IQ. Renzulli (1978), for instance, proposes

Giftedness Refers to superior IQ combined with demonstrated or potential ability in such areas as academic aptitude, or creativity, or leadership.

thinking of giftedness as the interaction of above-average general ability, exceptional creativity, and high levels of commitment. Sternberg (1981) defines giftedness as exceptional skill in problem-solving.

In 1971, a very broadened definition of giftedness was drafted by Congress. Gifted children were to include those with demonstrated achievement and/or potential ability in any of the following areas, singly or in combination: (1) general intellectual ability; (2) specific academic aptitude; (3) creative or productive thinking; and (4) leadership ability.

Various criteria have been used to identify gifted students, including scores on intelligence tests, teacher recommendations, and scores on achievement tests. Most school systems also use diagnostic testing, interviews, and evaluation of student academic and creative work. These selection methods seem to work well for identifying students with a broad range of talent, but they do not do the best job of distinguishing specific abilities, such as a talent for mathematics or music. This has led to the development of specialized programs, such as the Study of Mathematically Precocious Youth (SMPY), to identify children who are gifted in one or more specific areas without necessarily exhibiting general intellectual superiority overall (Fox, 1981).

The gifted movement is not without its critics who have pointed out that some fundamental assumptions about gifted children may simply not be true. One such notion is that gifted people are a distinct group, demonstrably superior to other people in all areas of intelligence and creativity. People gifted in one area, however, may not be gifted in others. For example, Gardner (1983) found that gifted children performed no better than other bright children on tests of moral and social reasoning.

A second assumption is that gifted children will contribute greatly to society when they become adults. As we have seen, there is no evidence that high IQ scores by themselves predict such things as professional success or leadership. Even in Terman's group, where there was a remarkably high level of professional achievement overall, not everyone was successful in their chosen field. While some minimal level of intelligence may be required for success, more recent studies show that other factors— determination, self-reflection, daringness, and encouragement, among others—are needed as well (Gardner, 1983). These data indicate that it makes little sense to identify giftedness in terms of IQ alone. However, to the extent that educational programs select gifted students using a broad range of criteria, including such things as outstanding achievement, leadership, creativity, and initiative, it is possible that the students selected for these programs are indeed tomorrow's leaders.

Critics of the gifted movement have also expressed concern that present measures may fail to identify gifted students in minority populations. Some of the alternatives devised thus far are an abbreviated Stanford-Binet for the disadvantaged (Bruch, 1971) and the Mercer and Lewis (1978) System of Multicultural Pluralistic Assessment. In both cases, intelligence test scores are adjusted to take into account a child's socio-cultural group. In addition, the multiple screening methods used by many schools tend to increase the participation of minority students in special programs. But it is still too soon to predict the effectiveness of these alternatives (Fox, 1981).

Yet another reservation about gifted programs is how students themselves feel about being labeled exceptional students. Some children, it would seem, would rather not be thought of as "brains." And gifted children may chafe under the pressure to perform. Finally, there is the growing controversy over creativity and its relationship to giftedness. Guilford (1967), among others, has pointed out that some types of thinking involved in creative problem solving are not adequately assessed by achievement and aptitude tests. And Getzels and Jackson (1962) have found that some children who score only moderately high on intelligence, but high on creative measures, are capable of high levels of achievement. We will look more closely at the relationship between creativity and intelligence in the next section.

Creativity

In ancient Greece the mathematician Archimedes noticed that the water overflowed when he got into his bath. From this observation he formulated his theory of displacement: A body or an object immersed in water will displace an amount of water equal to its own volume. Centuries later the Impressionist painters noticed that as the sun moves across the sky, the light on a haystack changes. They realized that they could paint this light just as easily as they could paint the haystack. Few previous artists had never regarded light itself as a subject for painting. Creativity is not, of course, limited to inventors and artists. Shoppers who compare prices, looking for bargains, are acting intelligently—they are examining the available information and making rational decisions. But the shopper who first thought of organizing a co-op, with one family going to the wholesale market every week to buy food for the group, was exercising **creativity,** the ability to produce novel and unique ideas or objects ranging from philosophy to paintings, from music to mousetraps.

Creativity The ability to produce novel and unique ideas or objects.

Some researchers believe that creative ability is simply one aspect of intelligence. For example, in the Sternberg (1981) study discussed earlier in the chapter it was found that experts on intelligence included creativity as part of verbal intelligence (though laypersons did not include creativity in their view of intelligence). Guilford also included creativity as part of what he called intelligence. His complex model of intelligence (Figure 9-1) includes five kinds of operations, one of which is "divergent thinking." Divergent thinkers expand on the facts, letting their minds go wherever each piece of evidence leads. Instead of looking for the "right" answer, divergent thinkers develop all possibilities, producing different solutions that can then be evaluated or combined.

Although some psychologists believe that creativity is one aspect of intelligence, most IQ tests do not include measures of creativity and many researchers in the area would argue that "intelligence" and "creativity" are not the same thing. What is the relationship between intelligence and creativity? Are people who score high on IQ tests likely to be more creative than those who score low?

In one study Getzels and Jackson (1962) gave creativity and IQ tests to a group of bright 5th- through 12th-graders in a private school. Scores

Scores on IQ and creativity tests may not adequately reflect real-life creativity.

Though many psychologists consider creativity a function of intelligence, there is less certainty about the best way to go about testing creativity. How can we measure creative responses with questions that can only be answered true or false, *a* or *b*? One solution has been the development of more open-ended tests. Instead of asking for one set answer to a problem, the examiner asks the test taker to think of as many answers as possible. Scores on the tests are based on the number and originality of the subject's answers.

In one such test, the *Torrance Test of Creative Thinking,* the examiner shows the subject a picture and then asks the subject to explain what is happening in the picture, how it came about, and what its consequences are likely to be. The *Christensen-Guilford Test* asks the subject to list as many words containing a given letter as possible; to name things belonging to a class—such as liquids that will burn; and to write four-word sentences beginning with the letters *RDLS*—Rainy days look sad, Red dogs like soup, Renaissance dramas lack symmetry, and so on.

One of the most widely used creativity tests, Mednick's (1962) *Remote Associates Test* (RAT), asks the subject to produce a single verbal response that relates to a set of three apparently unrelated words. For example, the three stimulus words might be *poke, go,* and *molasses.* A desirable response—though not the only possible one—relates them through the word *slow:*

slow-poke, go *slow, slow* as molasses. Arriving at such responses is not easy, especially since the stimulus words have no apparent connection to one another.

The newer *Wallach and Kogan Creative Battery* centers on having the subject form associative elements into new combinations that meet specific requirements. Children are asked to "name all the round things you can think of" and to find similarities between objects—for example, a potato and a carrot. It is possible for people who do not have high IQs to receive high scores on the Wallach and Kogan test. The Torrance test, on the other hand, seems to require a reasonably high IQ for adequate performance. But the validity of neither of these tests is conclusive (Crockenberg, 1980; Anastasi, 1976).

How creative are people who do well on creativity tests? The correlation between test scores and the products we associate with creativity—paintings, poems, operas, inventions, cures for cancer—is relatively ·low. Some psychologists explain these disappointing results by pointing out that creativity appears to depend on more than intellectual abilities alone. For example, Tyk (1968) sees *motivation* as a critical factor in creative output. Great artists, scientists, and writers have more than simple "talent" or "genius." They have intense dedication, ambition, and perseverance.

on the creativity tests correlated .27 on average with the tests of intelligence. That is, there was a slight tendency for those children who scored high on the creativity tests also to score high on the IQ tests, but the relationship between the two scores was not very strong. Wallach and Wing (1969) studied the divergent-thinking ability of a sample of college freshmen and compared this to the students' scores on Scholastic Aptitude Tests as a measure of intelligence. Again, there seemed to be little direct relationship between scholastic aptitude and divergent-thinking ability.

One criticism of both these studies is that they used only bright students. For example, the average IQ of the students tested by Getzels and Jackson was 132! Perhaps there is little relationship between creativity and IQ once IQ reaches a certain level. In fact, there is considerable evidence that this may be the case.

The "threshold theory" of the relation between intelligence and creativity states that in order for a person to be considered creative, he or she must first be at least slightly more intelligent than average. But above that point, there seems to be little relation between the two variables. Yamomoto (1965) found that intelligence and creativity correlated .88

for people with IQs below 90, .69 for those with IQs ranging from 90 to 110, − .30 for those with IQs between 110 and 130, and − .09 for those with IQs above 130. That is, below an IQ of 110, higher IQ scores were accompanied by higher creativity, but above this point there was little or no relationship between IQ and creativity. Other studies have borne out these findings (Barron, 1963; Yamomoto, 1964; Yamomoto & Chimbidis, 1966). This evidence supports the view that creativity is based on a certain amount of intelligence, but once intelligence passes a threshold level, creativity and intelligence are only mildly related, if at all.

Since all these studies rely heavily on tests of creativity, any conclusions drawn from them must be qualified by what many experimenters regard as the dubious relationship between creativity test scores and real-life creativity. But other studies at least partially avoid this problem by studying adults who have demonstrated outstanding creativity in their lives. These studies (e.g., Barron, 1969; Cattell, 1971; Helson, 1971; Bachtold & Werner, 1973) show that creative people tend to be highly intelligent—that is, highly creative artists, writers, scientists, and mathematicians tend, as a group, to score high on intelligence tests. But for individuals in this special group there is little relationship between IQ scores and levels of creative achievement. These data further support the threshold theory of creativity and intelligence.

Interestingly, creative people are often *perceived* as more intelligent than less creative people who have equivalent IQ scores. In one study of architects, for example, psychology staff members perceived creative architects as more intelligent than less creative architects, even though their IQ scores were, in fact, equivalent (MacKinnon, 1962). This finding brings us back to everyday ideas of intelligence that we discussed early in the chapter. Perhaps some characteristic that creative people share—possibly "effectiveness" or some quality of social competence— conveys the impression of intelligence even though it is not tapped by IQ tests (Barron & Harrington, 1981).

Application

Intervention Programs— Do They Improve IQ?

We have seen that to some extent IQ scores are affected by experience. Nutrition, environmental stimulation, and child-rearing patterns all can influence scores on IQ tests. A number of researchers have become interested in whether it is possible to increase IQ scores deliberately.

One way to go about this is to provide *coaching*. Coaching includes specific instruction and practice in taking intelligence tests in order to raise scores. Sometimes this means just practicing the kinds of questions and problems that may appear on the test. Coaching may also include some tutoring in an educational area in which the student is deficient. While intensive short-term coaching with practice questions may increase an IQ score, the increase is seldom great. Also, while this kind of coaching may achieve the desired results in the form of higher test scores, it does not seem to produce any improvement in underlying mental abilities, since school and college grades do not also improve (Linn, 1982).

Apart from coaching, efforts have been made to intervene in more substantial ways to actually increase mental abilities. These intervention programs attempt to increase not only IQ scores but also "intelligence" itself, and thereby to improve academic performance as well as test scores. In 1961 Heber launched the Milwaukee Project. Its purpose was to see if intervening in a child's family life could alter the effects of cultural and socioeconomic deprivation on IQ. Heber and his associates worked with 40 poor, mostly black families in the Milwaukee area in which the average IQ of the mothers was under 75 on the Wechsler Scales. The pregnant women were split into two groups. One group was given job training and sent to school. As they found jobs, they were also instructed in child care, home economics, and personal relationships. The control group received no special education or job training. When all 40 women had had their babies, the research team began to concentrate on the children. The children of the mothers who were being given special training were taken to an infant education center at the age of 3 months. For the next 6 years these children spent the better part of each day at the center. They were given nourishing meals and an educational program that included a wide range of educational toys. They were cared for by paraprofessionals who behaved like nonworking mothers in affluent families.

All of the children were periodically given IQ tests. Those in the experimental group ended with an average IQ score of 126—51 points higher than their mothers' scores. The average score of the children in the control group, whose lives had not been changed as much, was 94—still much higher than their mothers' average scores, perhaps because they had become accustomed to taking tests, an experience their mothers had never had.

Sandra Scarr-Salapatek and Richard Weinberg went a step further than Heber and his associates. They studied black children who had been adopted by well-educated white families with moderate incomes. They found that children who had been adopted early in life and who had warm, intellectually enriched family environments got higher IQ scores than the national average score for blacks, and also did better in school (Scarr-Salapatek & Weinberg, 1976).

The largest program designed to improve educationally disadvantaged children's chances of school achievement is Head Start, a program that began almost 20 years ago. Head Start focuses on preschoolers between the ages of 3 and 5 who are from low-income families. The purpose of the program is to provide the children with some educational and social skills before they get to school,

as well as to provide information about nutrition and health to the children and their families. The Head Start program has stressed parental involvement in all its aspects, from daily activities to administration of the program itself. The acceptance of cultural differences between children, as opposed to an emphasis on the poverty of their families and what they lack in comparison with middle-class children, has distinguished Head Start from other intervention programs (Zigler & Berman, 1983).

Several studies have evaluated the long-term effects of Head Start. Brown and Grotberg (1981), after reviewing many of these studies, concluded that the program has indeed brought about lasting improvements in children's cognitive abilities. There is also some evidence that the involvement of parents in the Head Start program has been crucial to its success (Ryan, 1974).

Another study evaluated the effects of the Perry Preschool Program in Ypsilanti, Michigan. The children in this study were 123 black preschoolers from poor families, 58 of whom attended the program, while 65 did not. The children who participated in the program scored higher on tests of academic skills, were more likely to finish high school and plan to go to college, and had a higher employment rate and lower arrest rate than those who did not participate in the program (Schweinhart & Weikart, 1980).

These studies provide clear evidence that cognitive abilities can be enhanced through extensive training in educational skills. Most of these programs focus on preschoolers. Some researchers believe that the effectiveness of programs introduced later in life is limited, though older children, adolescents, and adults may benefit from such training (Anastasi, 1981).

Hobbs and Robinson (1982) propose that intervention programs have overemphasized the early-childhood period. These researchers believe that academic skills can be taught at any age through adolescence and that the development of intelligence occurs over a lifetime, rather than stopping at some point during childhood. Problem-solving skills and abstract thinking abilities, according to these authors, also appear to be modifiable in adolescence and early adulthood. Hobbs and Robinson recommend further research on junior and senior high school students and an increase in programs designed to develop cognitive abilities in adolescents who show learning deficits.

1. Laypersons define *intelligence* as a combination of practical problem-solving ability, verbal ability, and social competence. Experts view intelligence similarly, as a combination of verbal ability, problem-solving ability, and practical intelligence. *Intelligence tests* are intended to measure a person's mental abilities.

2. Spearman viewed intelligence as a single kind of mental energy that flows into every action. Thurstone identified seven somewhat independent mental abilities that combine to form general intelligence. Guilford constructed a three-dimensional model of intelligence composed of *operations* performed on *contents* with a resulting *product*. Cattell views intelligence as two clusters of abilities: "crystallized intelligence" (reasoning and verbal and numerical skills) and "fluid intelligence" (visual-spatial skills and rote memory).

3. The first test of intelligence was the *Binet-Simon Scale*, designed by French psychologists for use in the French public school system. This was later adapted by Terman into the *Stanford-Binet Scale*. Terman also introduced the term *IQ (intelligence quotient)* to mean a numerical value of intelligence and based it on a score of 100 for average intelligence. The Stanford-Binet Scale emphasizes verbal skills and is administered individually by a trained examiner. The test score is used to calculate the mental age at which the subject performs. The *Weschler Adult Intelligence Scale–Revised* was designed especially for adults. It includes a verbal scale and a performance scale, and yields separate scores on the two scales, as well as an overall IQ. Like the Stanford-Binet, it is administered individually.

4. *Group tests* are written tests of intelligence designed to be administered by a single examiner to many people at one time. Two advantages of group tests are efficiency in testing and the elimination of bias on the part of the examiner. One of the disadvantages is that there is less chance of the examiner detecting problems a subject might be experiencing at the time of the test that could interfere with the score. Examples of group tests are the School and College Ability Tests (SCAT), the Scholastic Aptitude Tests (SAT), and the Graduate Record Examination (GRE).

5. *Performance tests* are nonverbal intelligence tests for people who are unable to take standard intelligence tests, such as non-English-speaking people, the handicapped, and preschool children. These tests generally substitute puzzles or mazes for written questions. The Bayley Scales of Infant Development, for example, are used to measure the developmental abilities of very young children. *Culture-fair tests* are an attempt to measure the intelligence of people who are outside the culture in which the test was devised. These intelligence tests try to minimize the use of skills and values that vary from one culture to another.

6. In a test, *reliability* means that scores are consistent and stable. Reliability can be measured by retesting people at different times and comparing the results, by using alternate forms of the same test, or by dividing the test into two parts and checking for *split-half reliability*. Reliability is expressed in terms of *correlation coefficients*. If test scores correlate perfectly, the correlation coefficient is 1.0; if there is no correlation between the scores, the coefficient is zero. The most widely used individual tests—the Stanford-Binet and the WAIS-R—are very reliable.

7. *Validity* is a test's ability to measure what it has been designed to measure. *Content validity* is a measure of whether the test contains an adequate sample of the skills or knowledge it is supposed to measure. Most intelligence tests are thought to have content validity in that they cover many of the abilities considered to be components of intelligence. *Criterion-related validity* is measured by a comparison of the test score and independent measures of that which the test is designed to measure. The independent measure against which the test is evaluated is called the criterion. With the exception of various performance and

culture-fair tests, most IQ tests are good predictors of academic performance. In addition, most IQ tests relate well with one another, despite differences in content.

8. Many critics have found fault with the content of intelligence tests, claiming that they are actually concerned with only a narrow set of skills, particularly academic abilities and the ability to take tests. Others believe that for many reasons IQ tests discriminate against minorities, though recent evidence suggests that most major, widely used intelligence tests are not biased. In any case, standardized intelligence tests should not be used to place children in an educational "slot" that may do them more harm than good by restricting their possibilities for educational achievement.

9. IQ scores predict success in school fairly reliably, but they are of little value in predicting career success. However, even though there is no evidence that people with high IQ scores do better in their careers than those with lower scores, they are more likely to hold high-status jobs. A probable reason for the low correlation between IQ scores and career success is that success in a chosen field also depends on a variety of factors—such as motivation, emotional stability, and adaptability—that IQ tests do not measure.

10. Heredity and environment are both determinants of intelligence. In support of heredity, psychologists point to significantly higher correlations between IQ scores of identical twins than between those of fraternal twins or other members of the same family. Environmentalists agree that some part of intelligence is inherited, but state that how intelligence develops depends on environmental factors as we grow up. Several studies have demonstrated that stimulating a child's family life to alter the effects of deprivation can dramatically improve IQ scores. Without such early stimulation, it appears that the effects of childhood deprivation may not be reversible in later life.

11. The Jensen controversy refers to the claim made by psychologist Arthur Jensen that race differences, as revealed in IQ scores, are largely inherited. Jensen's work stirred furious argument over the validity of IQ testing, the heritability of intelligence, and the relationship between intelligence and race. Research on the question continues, but most critics strongly insist that we have no conclusive evidence to prove that there is, or is not, a genetic basis for racial differences in IQ scores.

12. Some recent studies on cognitive abilities have found that girls tend to have greater verbal ability than boys and that boys tend to have greater visual-spatial and mathematical abilities. Critics argue, however, that these findings should not be used for vocational counseling of individuals. Given that IQ scores are not good predictors of career success, very small sex differences on specific abilities are even less likely to be reliable predictors of job performance.

13. *Mental retardation* refers to significantly subaverage intellectual functioning combined with deficiencies in adaptive behavior. Mild retardation corresponds to IQ scores between 68 and 52, moderate retardation to scores between 51 and 36, and severe retardation to scores between 35 and 20. The profoundly retarded are those whose scores are below 19. The causes of mental retardation include genetic disease, chromosomal abnormality, brain damage, and severe environmental deprivation. Educational and social contact may have a dramatic effect on some forms of mental retardation, and federal law requires that handicapped children be properly evaluated and placed in educational programs appropriate to their needs.

14. *Giftedness* refers to a combination of superior IQ and demonstrated or potential achievement in such areas as academic performance, creativity, or leadership. The gifted movement seeks to identify gifted students and to place them in special educational programs. This movement has been criticized on a number of counts, including its ability to predict future leadership and professional success. While critics have objected to identifying giftedness in terms of IQ alone, the selection methods now used by most school systems include a broad range of criteria.

15. *Creativity* is the ability to produce novel and unique ideas or objects. Most IQ tests do not include measures of creativity, despite the fact

that many psychologists consider it an important component of intelligence. The "threshold theory" of the relation between intelligence and creativity states that a certain level of intelligence is a necessary precondition for creativity. Beyond this threshold level, however, creativity and intelligence appear to be only mildly related, if at all. Creative people are nonetheless very often perceived as being more intelligent than less creative people who have equivalent IQ scores.

Review Questions

1. Match each of the following with his concept of intelligence:
___ Cattell
___ Spearman
___ Thurstone
___ Guilford
   A. Identified 7 somewhat independent mental abilities.
   B. Argued that intelligence is general.
   C. Proposed two clusters of mental abilities.
   D. Proposed that operations performed on contents result in a product.

2. According to Guilford, mental abilities include the act of thinking, which he termed _____ , the terms in which we think, such as words or symbols, which he called _____ ; and _____ , the ideas we come up with.

3. In 1916, the Stanford psychologist L. M. Terman introduced the term _____ and set the score of _____ for a person of average intelligence. His test was based on the first intelligence test, the _____ _____ _____ , designed by Alfred Binet.

4. The IQ test that L. M. Terman constructed is called the Stanford-Binet Scale.   T/F

5. The individual IQ test most often given to adults is the _____ _____ _____ _____ .

6. Written tests of intelligence designed to be administered by a single examiner to many people at one time are termed _____ _____ . Which of the following is NOT such a test?
   a. GRE   c. Wechsler Adult Intelligence Scale
   b. SAT   d. SCAT

7. _____ tests eliminate or minimize the use of words. They are designed for people who cannot speak English and for preschoolers and handicapped people. Like these tests. _____ _____ tests also minimize the use of language, but they also include questions that minimize the use of skills and values that vary across cultures.

8. Which of the following makes a good test?
   a. high reliability   c. correlation coefficients
   b. high validity   d. a and b

9. If you take a test several times and score about the same each time you take it, your results suggest that the test is _____ .

10. Which of the following is a measure of reliability?
   a. correlation coefficient   c. criterion validity
   b. median   d. average

11. _____ is a test's ability to measure what it has been designed to measure.

12. IQ scores predict success in school and career success fairly reliably.   T/F

13. Arthur Jensen argued that
   a. the races do not differ in terms of average IQ.
   b. racial differences in IQ are largely due to environmental factors.
   c. racial differences in IQ are largely due to genetic factors.
   d. racial differences in IQ are due equally to environmental and genetic factors.

14. Sex differences in mental ability have not been established.   T/F

15. The ability to produce novel and unique ideas or objects, ranging from philosophy to paintings, from music to mousetraps, is termed
   a. creativity   c. fluid intelligence
   b. IQ   d. wit

Outline

Infancy and Childhood   10

Developmental psychology Study of the psychological and physical changes that take place throughout life.

An old king, realizing that his end was near, summoned his three sons to his bedside. "My sons," said the dying monarch, "I must decide which among you is to inherit my kingdom. I will ask each of you one question, and this is it: If you could spend your childhood over again, how would you spend it?"

The first son sprang forward. "I would spend it with reckless abandon!" he said. "Childhood is the only time we are not held accountable for the consequences of our actions."

The second son regarded his brother reproachfully. "I would not spend it at all," he said. "I would save it carefully until I grew old enough to appreciate it fully."

"And you, my son?" said the aged ruler to his third son. "If you could spend your childhood over again, how would you spend it?"

"I would neither spend it foolishly nor hoard it selfishly," said the third son. "I would invest in the pursuit of love, knowledge, and experience so that my later years might reap the dividends."

"Truly, such a wise answer should not go unrewarded," said the king. "The kingdom shall be yours."

If each of us were asked to answer the old king's question, our responses would be varied and would reflect our individual experiences from our earliest moments of life to the present day. We may remember our childhood with fondness or with regret—or we may hardly remember it at all. Yet none of us can deny the importance and the seeming miracle of childhood: When it ends, a helpless infant should have acquired most of the capabilities of an adult.

Methods and Issues in Developmental Psychology

Developmental psychology is the study of the psychological and physical changes that take place throughout a person's life. Some developmental psychologists are mainly interested in charting the course of significant psychological changes as people grow older. For example, when do chil-

307

Longitudinal method Research method in developmental psychology that studies a fixed group of people at selected intervals over an extended period of time.

Cross-sectional method Research method in developmental psychology that makes comparisons between people of different ages at just one point in time.

dren first learn to speak, and how does their speech change as they develop and mature? Do creativity and intelligence increase, decline, or remain unchanged as we get older? How early can we identify gifted children, and what becomes of such children later in life?

To study such changes over the life span, developmental psychologists use two methods. In the first method, the **longitudinal method,** the researcher studies a fixed group of people over a period of time. The same subjects are observed, interviewed, or tested at several ages. In our example, this might mean studying the creativity of the same people at ages 4, 12, 30, and 60. In the second method, the **cross-sectional method,** a sample of people of different ages is selected and studied at one point in time. Then comparisons are made between the different age groups. Again, in our hypothetical study, this might mean simultaneously comparing the creativity of 4-year-olds with that of 12-year-olds, and so on.

Other developmental psychologists are more concerned with the reasons *why* developmental changes occur. What causes changes in the way we speak as we grow older? What causes increases or declines in creativity or intelligence as we age? What causes some children to be "gifted," and why do some gifted children make outstanding contributions as adults, while others never distinguish themselves? To answer these kinds of questions, developmental psychologists use the same basic research methods we discussed in Chapter 1: the naturalistic-observational method, the correlational method, and the experimental method.

Suppose, for example, that a psychologist wants to know how children's environments influence their IQ scores. Using the first method, the psychologist might go to children's homes and observe how high- and low-IQ children and their parents interact. To do a correlational study, the psychologist might simply have the parents answer a questionnaire about their home environment, how they behave with their children, and so on. The psychologist could then correlate these responses with the children's IQ scores. In the experimental method the psychologist might split a group of children into two groups. Let us say that for a year one group would be placed during the day in a special enriched environment designed to promote high IQ scores. The other group would receive no special treatment at all. At the end of the year the psychologist would then test both groups' IQ scores and compare the results.

Each of these methods is useful for studying developmental issues: hence psychologists often use data gathered from all of them. These *converging data* are then combined to provide a much fuller picture than any one method could give (Craig, 1983). In this chapter and the next one we will see examples of all these research methods as they are used to help us understand psychological development.

Besides using various methods to study human development, psychologists often approach their studies from varying points of view. Some psychologists, as we saw in Chapter 2, emphasize the importance of heredity, while others stress experience or environmental influences. Some see change as abrupt and discontinuous while others view development as a gradual, continuous process. In this chapter and in the next we shall see how these differing viewpoints come into play as we discuss the various aspects of human development from infancy through adulthood.

Scientists once thought that the development of the child before birth was simply a process of physical growth. Only at birth, they believed, did experience and learning begin to influence development. Today we know that the unborn baby is profoundly affected by its environment. Some experts, such as psychologist Leni Schwartz, have even gone so far as to say that "the most important time in our lives may well be the time *before* we were born" (Spezzano, 1981). Schwartz and some other psychologists have argued that what happens to us while we are still *in utero* has a definite effect on the kind of person we turn out to be. Although most experts don't go as far as Schwartz, they do agree that there is much more going on during the prenatal period than mere physical growth.

Prenatal development Physical and psychological changes in an organism before birth.

Placenta Organ that connects the developing fetus to the mother's body, providing nourishment to it and filtering out some harmful substances.

Fetus An unborn infant at least 8 weeks old.

The Prenatal Environment

During the earliest period of **prenatal** (before birth) **development,** survival is the most important issue. Immediately after conception, the fertilized egg divides many times, beginning the process that will change it from a one-celled organism into a highly complex human being. The cell ball implants itself in the uterus. Around it grows a **placenta,** which carries food to it and waste products from it as the organism grows. In time, the major organ systems and physical features develop. If all goes well, by the end of this stage of development the organism is recognizably human and is now called a **fetus.** The fetal period begins in the eighth week after conception and lasts until birth. (It is usually early in this period that a woman discovers that she is pregnant.) The important role of this period is the preparation of the fetus for independent life.

From the second week after conception until birth, the baby is linked to its mother, and thus to the outside world, through the placenta. Many changes in the mother's body chemistry, whether as a result of nutrition, drugs, disease, or prolonged stress or excitement, affect the fetus directly through the placenta. The placenta is not merely a passive tube connecting mother and fetus; it is an active organ with some ability to select and provide substances that the developing fetus needs. Unfortunately, although it can filter out some harmful substances, it cannot protect the fetus from the toxic effects of alcohol, narcotics, medications, and a variety of other chemicals.

Good nutrition is at least as important for the fetus as it is for us. Yet many mothers, especially in developing countries, subsist on diets that are not substantial enough to nourish them or their babies properly. Even in the United States expectant mothers' diets are often inadequate. Malnutrition in the prenatal period can result in seriously deprived babies and often permanent damage. These babies may have smaller brains and bodies and be weak, listless, and disease-prone (Stechler & Halton, 1982). In childhood they often show impaired intellectual functioning that is usually difficult or impossible to improve.

Besides malnutrition, drugs constitute a particular threat to the unborn child. If the mother is a heavy drinker, her baby may be born

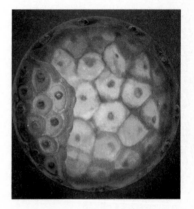

A fertilized human egg, shortly after conception when it has divided many times.

This 2-month-old human fetus can be affected by changes in its mother's body.

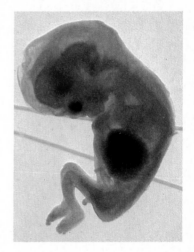

Neonate A newborn baby.

mentally retarded, be unusually small and slow to develop, and suffer from other serious abnormalities (Clarren & Smith, 1978). If the mother is a heavy user of narcotics, her baby may actually be born addicted to them and may experience withdrawal symptoms immediately after birth. If she smokes, the baby may be premature, underdeveloped, or deformed (Evans, Newcombe, & Campbell, 1979).

Certain diseases can also injure the fetus, particularly early in pregnancy. German measles (rubella) is especially dangerous. It can lead to eye damage, heart malformations, deafness, and mental retardation. Other diseases, such as syphilis and diabetes, can also produce serious defects in the fetus.

Moreover, prolonged stress or excitement on the part of the mother can directly affect the health of the fetus. There is some evidence that when pregnant women experience emotional stress, their fetuses move more frequently and forcefully than usual (Sontag, 1964). In one study, it was found that women who were under severe stress (most often from extremely unhappy marriages) gave birth more often to children who were sickly and slow to develop, and whose behavior was abnormal. Critics of these and similar studies have pointed out, however, that the connection between maternal stress and developmental problems in children is by no means clear. For example, since many of the mothers under stress in these studies were also poor, it may have been that growing up in a deprived household was more responsible for the children's problems than was prenatal stress (Sameroff, 1975).

It should be kept in mind that despite the hazards to the fetus that we have mentioned, most babies develop normally. If a pregnant woman is careful to eat well, maintain her health, and avoid exposure to harmful substances and communicable diseases, she should not worry about whether stress at home or on the job will harm her child. Young children are resilient and with proper care can often recover completely from minor problems related to prenatal development. As human beings, we have a long period of childhood, and most of our development, as we shall see, occurs after we are born.

The Newborn Baby

Recent research has challenged the traditional idea that newborn babies—or **neonates,** as they are sometimes called—are passive creatures that merely eat and sleep, oblivious of the world around them. We now know that newborn babies see, hear, and understand far more than they've been given credit for. Most of their senses operate fairly well at birth or shortly thereafter. They absorb and process information from the outside world almost as soon as they enter it. And they quickly learn who takes care of them and begin to form close attachments to those persons.

It's easy to see why neonates were once thought to be passive and relatively unresponsive to the outside world. For one thing, they sleep most of the time—up to 16 or 20 hours a day. For another, they are helpless. Left lying in their cribs, they can neither lift their heads nor turn over by themselves. They are totally dependent on the care of the adults around them. They are, however, equipped with a number of reflexes. When someone picks up a newborn, the baby begins searching for a nipple with its head and mouth, grasping the adult with surprising strength. The **rooting reflex,** as this is called, directs babies toward the food they need. Another reflex that is crucial for the neonate's survival is the **sucking reflex.** Shortly after birth, newborns will suck on anything that touches their faces: a bottle, a pacifier, a finger. Within a few days, if all goes well, they suck rhythmically and efficiently while being fed. Another reflex is **grasping,** which will lead the newborn to cling vigorously to any adult's hands or fingers or to any object that is put in their hands. All these reflexes help ensure that babies can cling to their mothers and receive the nourishment vital to life.

But newborns are capable of much more than reflex behavior. They seem prepared by nature to make contact with adults and to communicate with them. Neonates will turn their heads toward a voice (interestingly,

Rooting reflex A reflex in newborn babies that causes them to turn their heads and search for a nipple when they are picked up.

Sucking reflex A reflex in newborns that causes them to suck on anything that touches their faces.

Grasping reflex A reflex in newborns that causes them to clasp their fingers around anything that is put in their hands.

Temperament

It is tempting to talk about children as if they were all the same, but from birth infants show individual differences. One baby curls quietly in an adult's arms; another squirms and kicks. One sleeps through a rock concert in the next room; another wails when a dog barks two houses away. One baby feels almost limp when picked up; another is always tense and rigid. What do these differences mean? Some researchers have suggested that these individual characteristics express the child's inborn temperament. One study concluded that there are three general kinds of babies: "easy," "difficult," and "slow-to-warm-up" (Thomas, Chess, & Birch, 1970). "Easy" babies are those who are relaxed and adaptable from birth. In later life such children find school quite agreeable and learn rather easily how to make friends and how to play by the rules. "Difficult" babies, on the other hand, are moody and intense. They react violently to new people and new situations, sometimes withdrawing from them, at other times protesting until the well-meaning adult gives up. "Slow-to-warm-up" babies are relatively inactive, withdrawn, and slow to react. Unlike tantrum-prone "difficult" babies, these children seem reluctant to express themselves. In later life they often have difficulty in competitive and social situations. More recently Brazelton (1983) has proposed a similar set of distinctions: quiet babies, active babies, and average babies. In both sets of distinctions it is suggested that children retain the same general temperament from birth to adolescence.

Other psychologists are cautious about categorizing babies as "quiet" or "active," "easy" or "difficult." These psychologists point out that the same baby may go through all these states in a single day. While one style or another will usually dominate, it should not be thought of as unchanging. Moreover, about one-third of the children in the Thomas et al. study did not fit any of the three categories.

Still other psychologists flatly reject the idea that temperament is inborn or predetermined. True, some children who were grumpy at birth are nasty at the age of 8 and impossible at 12, but this is not necessarily because they were "born that way." Rather, these psychologists suggest that infants behave the way they do because they are part of a social system in which various people— the infant, the mother, the father, siblings, and so on—influence one another's behavior and temperament (Bronfenbrenner, 1977). Suppose, for example, that an infant has digestive troubles and cries constantly. An inexperienced mother or father might consider such a child difficult and hard to please. Yet another set of parents might react quite calmly to the same situation. Since the two sets of parents would treat a child who cries a lot differently, their children would probably grow up having different temperaments. It's important to keep in mind the extremely important role that parents and others play in the development of the child.

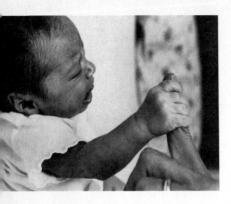

Within a few days of birth, newborns display the grasping reflex, which causes the baby's fingers to close around anything that is put in their hands.

they prefer the higher-pitched voices of women). They will wave their arms and legs in time with the rhythms of human speech. They will follow a human face (or a picture of one) with their eyes—but will not follow a scrambled drawing of a face. Within a few weeks newborns can recognize their parents and can tell their voices from those of other adults.

Most parents will testify that their babies seem to have distinctive personalities—recognizable almost from birth. Psychologists have found that there is some basis for this notion. Differences in temperament can sometimes be observed in the earliest days of life. Some babies cry much more than others, and some are much more active than others. Some are cuddly, and some seem to dislike being picked up and held. Neonates have even been found capable of expressing several basic emotions: for example, their faces show different expressions for surprise, distress, and disgust (Trotter, 1983). And they have their likes and dislikes: In one experiment babies only a few hours old showed pleasure at the taste of sweetened water and the smell of vanilla, but grimaced at the taste of lemon juice and the smell of rotten eggs (Steiner, 1979).

It is obvious from this new evidence that neonates are aware of the world around them—and research continues to document how sophisticated their perception is. In one recent experiment, for example, 2-week-old babies were shown either a cube or the image of a cube that seemed to be moving toward them. As the cube moved closer and appeared to be about to hit them, the neonates squirmed away in an effort to avoid being hit. When the cube merely came close to them, but not on a collision course, the babies merely watched it as it moved along. This experiment showed that even very young babies could somehow predict the course of a moving object and understood that they could avoid its path by moving away (Friedrich, 1983). Yet only a few decades ago neonates were thought to have such poor vision and coordination that this would have been impossible.

Newborn babies, then, are advanced in some ways, but they have a long way to go. The simple act of picking up a toy, for example, requires that the baby judge how far away the toy is, crawl or walk up to it, and coordinate an arm and hand to pick it up. It takes most babies almost a year to be able to cross a room and grab something they want. Much of the rest of this chapter concerns how babies develop these and other abilities.

Physical and Motor Development

Certainly one of the most visible changes during infancy and childhood is physical growth. The child increases in size, of course, but there are also marked changes in body proportion (see Figure 10-1). The body becomes longer and the head proportionally smaller, so that the child's overall shape becomes more like that of an adult. Height and weight increase steadily from early childhood, with an additional spurt taking place during adolescence.

The physical development of a child follows a regular course known as **maturation,** a more or less automatic unfolding of development that begins with conception. It is as if the body had certain goals—say, a height of 6 feet. Physical maturation follows a somewhat different sequence in boys and girls. Girls develop more quickly in the prenatal period then boys do, but boys grow faster in their first few months of life. Girls then surpass boys in growth until they are about 4. After the age of 4, both sexes grow at approximately the same rate until puberty. There are, however, sex differences in children's body composition. Proportionately, girls have more fat than boys and less muscle tissue. Girls' skeletal systems are more mature than those of boys of the same age throughout childhood. The greatest sex differences, of course, become evident at puberty, which girls experience as much as 2 years earlier than boys do. With puberty, both sexes go through a period of rapid growth, followed by the development of the secondary sexual characteristics.

Physical maturation follows such a predictable timetable that psychologists have been able to establish **developmental norms** or standards that indicate the age by which an average child should reach various developmental milestones. By about 10 months, for example, infants can stand up; by about 13 months, they can begin to walk by themselves. Some infants, however, develop much faster than these norms, and others do so more slowly. There is a *range* of normal development: Some babies may be several months ahead of or behind schedule and yet be perfectly normal. Norms, then, are general guidelines—they can't predict the day or the week at which a child should develop a particular skill. They do, however, alert parents and doctors to extremes. For example, brain damage may not be discovered until a parent notices that an infant has not tried to lift his or her head by the age of 4 months. At the opposite extreme, the infant who walks at 11 months, starts talking at 14 months, and is throwing a ball at 3 years may be ready to start school a year early.

Maturation Automatic unfolding of development in an organism over time.

Developmental norms Ages when the average individual reaches various milestones of development.

Figure 10-1

Body proportions at various ages. As the child grows, the head becomes relatively smaller and the legs longer in proportion to the rest of the body.
(From Bayley, 1956)

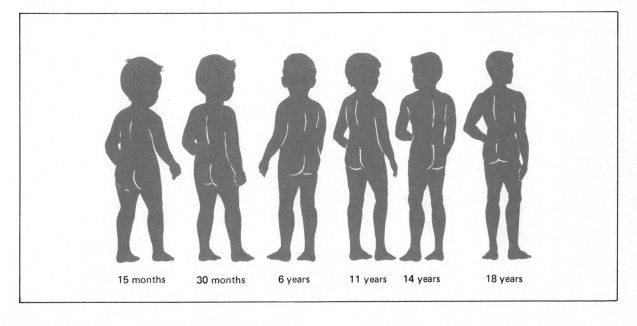

15 months 30 months 6 years 11 years 14 years 18 years

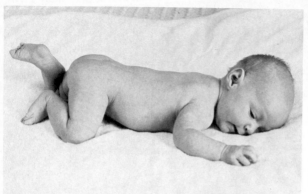

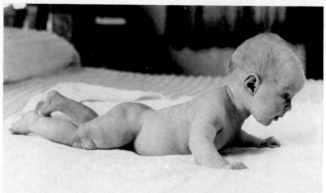

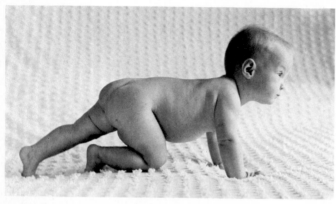

The normal sequence of motor development. Newborns are only capable of simple reflex movements. At about 1 month they begin to lift their shoulders. They start to crawl at about 4 to 6 months. By 9 months they can sit up by themselves. They can stand upright at about 10 months and they begin to walk at about 13 months.

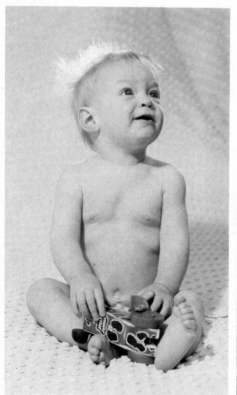

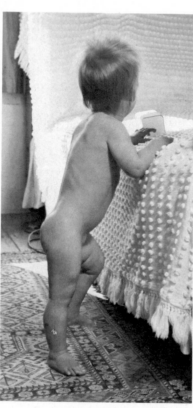

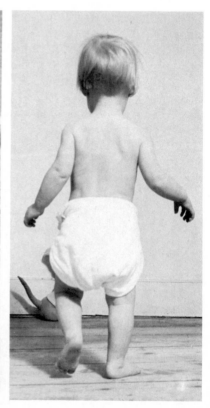

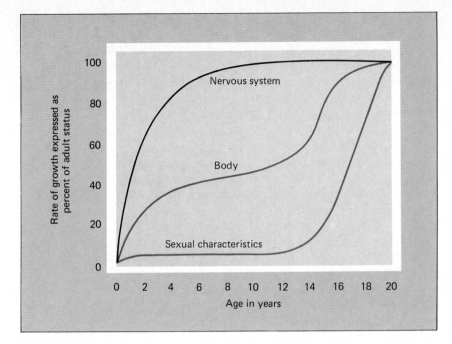

Figure 10-2

Patterns of growth of various parts of the body. The nervous system develops relatively early; sexual characteristics do not appear until puberty (see Chapter 11).

(Adapted from Jackson, 1928)

The child who develops more slowly than the norm will not always lag behind. Albert Einstein, the story goes, did not begin to talk until he was 3 years old—1½ years late, according to most norms. Given these individual differences, parents should not be alarmed if their babies seem a little "behind schedule" in developing a particular skill. Virtually all babies eventually catch up. What should be cause for concern is a lengthy developmental lag.

Less visible than growth during the infant's first years is the development of the central nervous system (see Figure 10-2). An infant's brain grows rapidly, reaching three-quarters of its adult size by the time the child is 2. Besides simply becoming larger, the infant's brain becomes more complex. Interconnections among nerve cells and among regions of the brain are formed. It is this brain development that makes it possible for babies to get their bodies under control, first raising their heads, then sitting up, crawling, and walking.

The physical maturation of infants also makes new behavior possible. Within a year after birth, most babies are sitting up, crawling around, and beginning to walk with a little help. As soon as they can walk unaided, they try to jump and climb. At each stage their view of the world changes markedly. By the age of 7 months, they are curious about everything they see; by 10 months, they can act on their curiosity, crawl through open doors, and push books off tables. Along the way, they work out a number of techniques, like crawling, that they will later abandon.

In describing infants' motor development, psychologists focus on walking and grasping. Although both appear as reflexes in newborns, neither is of much use to them at that point. Held up, with their bodies dangling, infants pump their legs up and down like runners. This reflex seems to disappear after 7 to 9 weeks. When they begin to practice walking again at 6 to 11 months, the picture is quite different, for by then infants can pull themselves up. Gradually their attempts become more deliberate, and with only a little support they begin to walk forward. They soon learn heel-to-toe coordination, and after practice (and many falls) they straighten up and walk.

What happens if parents do not encourage their babies to walk even when they are ready? Hopi Indian babies who have been strapped to stiff, confining cradleboards from birth learn to walk just as easily as Hopi babies who have been allowed to scramble around as they liked (Dennis & Dennis, 1940). There seem to be critical periods when a child is most able to start certain activities. Children who are bedridden from the age of 13 to 18 months (the average "walking readiness" period) find learning to walk after this period much more difficult.

Does encouragement or training help a child to walk sooner? One experiment indicated that early encouragement does, indeed, produce results. A group of 1-week-old babies was trained by their mothers in walking and "foot-placing" exercises each day for a 7-week period, while a second group of babies was not. The babies who had been helped through the motions of walking were significantly more active and walked sooner than the others. Thus the first 8-week period of life, before the newborn's walking reflex disappears, seems critical for developing walking ability (Zelazo, Zelazo, & Kolb, 1972).

Walking, of course, is not the only motor skill young children master: They quickly learn to run, skip, climb, and balance themselves as their muscles and bones mature and their coordination develops. At 3 and 4 they begin to attempt to use their hands for increasingly complex tasks— first learning how to put on mittens and shoes, then grappling with buttons, zippers, and shoelaces. Grasping a crayon firmly in the fist gives way to holding it in a more controllable way with the fingers. All these skills develop rapidly, some after considerable adult coaching and others almost spontaneously as children imitate the motions of their older siblings and parents.

We have described physical and motor development as gradual, steady processes. That is, as children get older and bigger, most seem to become more proficient at any kind of task. But T. G. R. Bower (1976) points out that this isn't always the case. Sometimes infants acquire a particular ability, lose it for a while, and then regain the skill later in their development. For example, newborn infants show a striking aptitude for imitation—a talent that requires a high degree of coordination between the baby's senses and muscles. Newborns can mimic adults who stick out their tongues, open their mouths, or widen their eyes. Yet as the infant develops, this remarkable ability seems to disappear quickly and does not return until the end of the child's 1st year. Also, as we saw earlier, infants show the reflex of "walking" in their first 2 months. The reflex then disappears until real walking begins near the end of the 1st year. So although much human development is gradual and steady, it is important to remember that development sometimes occurs in "fits and starts" that are much less orderly.

Newborn babies, as we saw earlier, are now given credit for being far more aware of their environment than was once thought. Babies, in fact, were once considered to be virtually blind at birth, but we now know that this is not the case. Normal babies can both see and hear at birth, although not as well as adults can, and their vision and hearing continue to improve during infancy. One question that has intrigued developmental psychologists is: To what extent does perception develop naturally with the growth of a child? Is it a process of maturation and therefore relatively independent of experience? Many psychologists do not think so.

Animals have been studied to determine how experience relates to the development of perception. In one of the earliest studies Riesen (1947) sought to discover whether chimpanzees that had been raised in darkness for 16 months could perform visually oriented tasks when exposed to light. He found that the chimpanzees' visual responsiveness had been severely inhibited. Objects with which they were familiar through touch—their feeding bottle, for example—were not visually recognized for a long time. "Visual learning," Riesen explained, "so characteristic of the normal adult primate, is thus not an innate capacity independent of visual experience, but requires a long apprenticeship in the use of the eyes" (p. 108).

Studies with young kittens have shown that the *kind* of visual stimulation that infants receive may also affect their visual functioning. Blakemore and Cooper (1970) placed one group of 2-week-old kittens in cages covered with black-and-white vertical stripes. They placed another group in similar cages covered with horizontal stripes. After 5 months, both groups of kittens showed permanent visual defects, including clumsy movements and the inability to perceive objects properly. Moreover, kittens raised in a horizontally striped cage ignored vertically oriented objects, and those raised in a vertically striped cage ignored horizontally oriented objects. The researchers concluded that the brain's visual cortex may adjust permanently to the kind of visual stimulation it receives during maturation.

Another experiment with kittens seems to support this idea. In this case, kittens that had had one eye covered between their 4th and 12th weeks of life never developed normal binocular vision—that is, sight involving the coordination of a different image from each eye. If the eye was covered only before the 4th week or only after the 12th week, this effect did not occur. This suggests that there is a critical period for the development of binocular vision in cats, and perhaps in human infants as well (Pines, 1982).

Other factors besides the quantity and quality of visual stimulation may also affect visual functioning. Studies have shown that feedback from movements that are self-produced may also influence the development of perception. Held and Hein (1963) placed two young kittens in a special apparatus that allowed one kitten to move relatively freely as it pulled the other kitten, whose movements were restrained. Although both kittens received the same visual stimulation, the passive, restrained kitten failed in a number of visual tests. It had not received the sensory-

Visual acuity Ability to distinguish fine details.

motor feedback needed to develop normal visual functioning.

Do the effects of visual deprivation from an early age also apply to humans? Research on this question has, of course, been limited. Evidence suggests that people who are born blind and whose sight is restored through surgery often have permanent visual defects that may stem from a lack of early visual stimulation (Riesen, 1950). Less severe eye disorders may also interfere with visual development, resulting in permanent deficits. Thus there is good evidence to suggest that stimulation, experience, and learning all contribute to perceptual development. The ability to perceive is inborn, but without experience it will not develop properly.

Acuity and Pattern Perception

How well can infants see? How "sharp" are their eyes? As we've suggested, neonates cannot see as well as adults. For one thing, they lack **visual acuity,** or the ability to distinguish fine details (Acredolo & Hake, 1982). If you hold this book about 18 inches from your eyes, you should have little or no difficulty identifying separate letters on the page, and even seeing parts of each letter. But an infant would not see separate letters. Rather, words would appear simply as gray blurs with white spaces between them and between lines.

We know, then, that infants can perceive lines and dots as long as they are not too small or too thin. But can they perceive patterns? Can they tell the difference between, say, a human face and a balloon? Some of the first experiments that sought to answer this question were conducted by Robert Fantz. His method was simple: He showed infants a variety of pictures and patterned cards to see which they liked best. Preference

Figure 10-3

Fantz's experiment on pattern perception. Infants were shown the three shapes at the side of the graph. At almost every age, the babies spent more time looking at the patterned faces and less time looking at the plain oval.

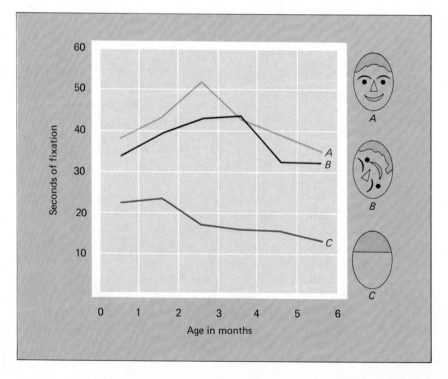

was measured by how long the infant looked at a card. In one experiment Fantz showed 1- to 15-week-old babies two cards with black-and-white facial patterns and one card that was a plain oval. All the infants spent more time looking at the patterned cards (Fantz, 1961) (see Figure 10-3). Similar techniques show that infants prefer faces to other stimuli and bright colors to pastels. Other studies have demonstrated that infants can abstract various kinds of information from a series of pictures. They can recognize a woman's face as being different from a series of men's faces, for example. Not only can infants perceive such differences in the stimuli presented to them; they also have been found to prefer more and more complex stimuli as they grow older (Acredolo & Hake, 1982).

We know from these studies that infants perceive patterns and can recognize the human face at an early age. But what about depth and distance perception? Before babies learn to crawl and learn from experience that it takes effort to go from the crib to the door, do they realize that the door is far away? Before they have dropped a rattle from their crib a hundred times, do they perceive depth?

Distance and Depth Perception

Psychologists created an ingenious device—the visual cliff—for some classic experiments on depth perception. The device consists of a table divided into three parts. The center is a solid board. On one side, the table surface is dropped 1 inch or so; on the other side (the visual cliff) the drop is about 40 inches. The side with the visual cliff is covered with

When placed on the visual cliff, babies 6 months of age and older will not cross the deep side, even to get to their mothers. This is evidence that 6-month-olds perceive depth. Younger infants sense the problem but are unsure how to react.

glass an inch below the center board so that infants who cross over will not fall. The three parts are covered with a checkerboard pattern to make it easier to tell where one part ends and the next begins. An infant is placed on the center board, and his or her mother stands on one side or the other, encouraging the infant to crawl toward her.

All of the 6- to 14-month-old infants tested by Walk and Gibson (1961) refused to crawl over the deep side to their mothers. Some peered down over the cliff, others cried, and still others patted the glass with their hands. When their mothers stood on the shallow side, however, the babies crawled to them. Obviously, then, 6-month-olds perceive depth. What about younger babies? Because infants younger than 6 months cannot crawl, they were placed on one side or the other of the center board and their pulse rates measured (Campos, Langer, & Krowitz, 1970). When they were placed on the deep side of the board, the infants' hearts slowed down—a reaction typical of infants and adults who stop to orient themselves in new situations. Thus babies younger than 6 months seemed to know that something was different on the deep side, but did not know how to react.

More recently scientists have developed another technique to measure babies' depth perception. This method, known as the loom-zoom procedure, presents the infant with a shape that seems to approach on an apparent collision course (loom) and then zoom back to its original position. Although some experiments with this technique have suggested that infants can perceive an object's motion toward them (Bower, 1977), it is not clear that this constitutes depth perception.

Since babies younger than 6 months have imperfect vision and immature nervous systems, it is likely that if they have any depth perception, it is limited. It also seems likely that the experience of seeing and touching objects at various distances—for example, reaching out to a piece of furniture for support and finding it too far away to grasp—helps develop depth perception.

Object Perception

Adults take it for granted that people and objects are solid. At the movies we know that if we reach out to touch the actors, all we will feel is the screen. But does an infant understand this?

It seems that even as young as 1 or 2 months of age, infants can tell the difference between a flat photograph or drawing of an object and the three-dimensional object itself. Given the choice, babies prefer to look at a three-dimensional object (Fantz, 1961). Other studies, with 3-month-olds, have found that infants are more likely to reach out to a three-dimensional object than to a picture, which suggests that they somehow sense the graspable nature of the object (Bower, 1972; DiFranco et al., 1978). Going a step further, other investigators have found that 5-month-old infants can identify a person in a photograph. After looking at a person for a while, the babies were shown two photos, one of the person they'd been looking at and one of a strange face. The babies preferred to look at the photograph of the strange face—as if they'd become bored with the face they'd already seen in the flesh (Dirks & Gibson, 1977).

Another aspect of three-dimensional objects that adults take for granted is **object permanence.** We assume that a box locked in the closet will be there when we come back. But does an infant realize that a ball that rolls under a chair does not change into something else or even disappear forever?

Experiments done by Bower (1971) suggest that infants develop a sense of object permanence when they are about 18 weeks old. In his experiments Bower used a toy train that went behind a screen. When 16-week-old and 22-week-old infants watched the toy train disappear behind the left side of a screen, they looked to the right, expecting it to reappear. If the researcher took the train off the table and lifted the screen, all the babies seemed surprised not to see the train. This seems to indicate that both the 16-week-old and the 22-week-old infants had a sense of object permanence. But the second part of the experiment showed that this was not really the case. After the train went behind the screen, the researchers substituted a ball for it. When the screen was lifted, the 22-week-old babies seemed puzzled and looked back to the left side for the original object, but the 16-week-old infants did not seem to notice the switch. Thus, the 16-week-old babies seemed to have a sense of "something permanence," while the 22-week-old babies had a sense of object permanence based on a specific object.

Bower also tested the concept of *person permanence*. Using mirrors, he showed infants multiple images of their mothers. Bower found that infants less than 20 weeks old were generally pleased with the multiple images. However, older infants were disturbed; they seemed aware that there should be only one mother (Bower, 1971).

Other Senses

Babies don't experience the world only through their eyes. Normal newborns, as we have seen, can hear fairly well. This fact is familiar to all new mothers and fathers who have seen their baby wake up when a door slams or produce a wail when a fire truck screeches down the street. Beyond simply taking in sounds, infants can also tell sounds apart. They react differently to speech sounds, for example, than to nonspeech sounds. And infants only a few months old can distinguish between different consonant sounds; they can recognize the difference between *pa* and *ba,* for example (Eimas & Tartter, 1979). Infants thus seem especially well prepared to hear speech, even at a remarkably early age.

Infants also make contact with the world by touching, tasting, and smelling it. They squirm or cry if clothing binds them or a pin pokes them. But they also eagerly reach out to touch things, exploring the folds of their clothes and blankets and grasping whatever toys or objects are held out to them. As for taste and smell, even newborns have been found to have their preferences. They like sweet flavors, and this choice persists through infancy and childhood. They also seem to prefer many of the smells that adults find pleasant, although some things that smell good to most adults (shrimp, for example) provoke expressions of disgust in babies.

It should be kept in mind that the senses do not work in isolation. When you shake a jingling toy in front of an infant, he or she will

Object permanence Realization that objects hidden from view nonetheless still exist.

probably grab the toy and chew on it. This simple action involves all five senses: hearing the toy jingle, seeing it held within reach, touching it, and finally tasting and smelling it. Babies are born with some "communication" between their senses: Shortly after birth, they will turn their eyes toward a soft tone played at one side of their head. Somewhat older infants will search for the source of a sound by moving their eyes and turning their heads. Even as early as 3 or 4 months, babies appear to know that certain sights and sounds go together (mother's face and her voice, for example). Vision and touch likewise seem to be coordinated in infants only a few months old. In one experiment (Bruner & Koslowski, 1972) babies from 8 to 22 weeks were shown two balls—one small enough to grasp and one too large to grasp. The babies reacted differently to the balls, reaching out more often to the one they could grasp.

Even though infants can sense many things, their perceptions of the world grow sharper and increasingly meaningful as they grow older. Two factors are important in this development. The first is nervous system maturation, which progresses rapidly in infancy. The second is experience in the world—taking in sights, sounds, textures, smells, and tastes through the senses. As children become able to experience the world more actively, their perceptions sharpen, and the people and things immediately at hand come more clearly into focus.

Memory Development

We've just seen that infants are capable of perceiving a great deal. But do they remember what they see or hear? To attempt to answer this question, one investigator showed infants a pattern displayed on a screen over and over until they became familiar with it. Then a new pattern was displayed alongside the old one. The babies preferred the novel pattern, apparently recognizing the other as one they knew well already (Fantz, 1965).

What does this tell us? For one thing, it tells us that babies, too, can become bored. But more important, the experiment implies that the babies could *remember* the old pattern. Otherwise they would not prefer the new one. In one study, 18-, 24-, and 30-week-old babies were shown photographs of a familiar female face looking in various directions, and of another female face that they had never seen before. The younger babies reacted only to the changes in direction. They did not show that they understood either that it was the same face seen from different angles or that there were two different faces in the photographs. But the 30-week-old babies appeared to recognize both the changes in direction and the change to an unfamiliar face (Cohen, 1979). In another experiment, 5-month-old infants who were given only 2 minutes to become familiar with a face still remembered things about that face 2 weeks later (Fagan, 1973). And another, more recent study has shown that infants as young as 2 to 4 weeks can remember for several days a word that has been repeated to them over and over (Ungerer, Brody, & Zelazo, 1978).

So very young infants apparently can remember. But their memories are primitive compared with those of older children. Memory improves dramatically as children develop, and psychologists have long sought to identify what causes this expansion of memory. Age alone cannot account for it, nor can some kind of age-related increase in brain capacity. But the acquisition of language profoundly affects our ability to "record" and store what we experience. Related to children's acquisition of language is their ever-increasing store of knowledge about the world. (A child is more likely to remember, for example, that the striped animal encountered at the zoo is a zebra if she already knows that it's something like that familiar creature called a horse, which is an animal, not a plant or an inanimate object.) As their knowledge grows, children are better able to sort out new bits of information they encounter and relate that information to what they already know. During middle childhood, when children begin formal schooling, they also develop specific strategies for remembering. Some of these are taught directly by the school ("*i* before *e* except after *c*"), and others are learned less formally as part of the whole school experience. (Chapter 7 discusses in detail the effects of language, previous experience, and learning strategies on our ability to remember.) In addition, as children grow older, they learn for the first time that remembering things is important, and this further contributes to memory development.

Language Development

Infants, as we have seen, are well prepared to perceive speech. They also seem eager to use sounds to communicate, quickly producing a variety of noises to attract the attention of those around them. Parents eagerly await their children's first words, knowing that this dramatic event is a turning point in their development.

A Brief Chronology

At about 2 months of age the infant begins to coo—a rather nondescript word for rather nondescript sounds. In another 1 or 2 months the infant enters the "babbling" stage and starts to repeat sounds. Gradually the infant's babbling starts to resemble the rhythms of adult speech. Between 8 and 10 months infants seem to take special pleasure in "talking" aloud to themselves as they work at grabbing hold of things and at crawling. At this age vocalizing is still primarily nonsocial. Soon, however, infants start to imitate sounds and use their voices to get attention. By 10 or 11 months, they show signs of understanding things said to them.

By about 12 months of age, infants utter their first word, usually "Dada." During the next 6 to 8 months they build a vocabulary of one-word sentences: [Pick me] "Up!"; [I want to go] "Out!"; [Tickle me] "Again!" They may also use compound words, such as "Awgone" [all gone]. To these they add words that they use to address people—"Bye-

Without a social environment, children are slow to learn language. "Feedback"—in the form of listening to oneself and to others—greatly influences language development.

bye" being a favorite—and a few exclamations such as "Ouch!" Most small children are also interested in possessives: [The shoes are] "Daddy's." But perhaps the overwhelming passion of 2-year-olds is naming. For example, at play the child will say the word *block* over and over, looking at a parent for approval each time.

Soon the child begins to form two- and three-word sentences. A typical beginner's sentences are "Baby crying," "My ball," "Dog barking." A number of psychologists have recorded mother-child conversations at this age to see just what children pick up and what they omit. Children at this age most noticeably omit auxiliary verbs—[Can] "I have that?" "I [am] eating it"—and prepositions and articles—"It [is] time [for] Sarah [to] take [a] nap." Apparently children seize on the most important words, probably those their parents stress.

During the next few months (at 3 to 4 years of age) children begin to fill in their sentences: "Billy school" becomes "Billy goes to school." They start to use the past tense as well as the present. They ask more questions and learn to use "Why?" effectively—and sometimes monotonously. By age 5 or 6 years, a child usually has a vocabulary of over 2,500 words and can make sentences of 6 or 8 words.

Theories of Language Development

This chronology shows that most children seem to enjoy making sounds and learning words, and that they pick up the complex rules for putting words together to make sentences quite easily. But what prompts children to learn to talk in the first place? And how do they learn to speak so well so quickly?

There are two very different theories about how language develops. B. F. Skinner (1957) believes that parents and other people around the infant listen to the cooing and babbling and *reinforce* or reward the child for making the sounds that most resemble adult speech. If a child says something that sounds like "Mama," his mother gives him a hug. As the child gets older, he or she is only reinforced for sounding more and more like an adult and for using words correctly. If the child calls an aunt "Mama," there is less likely to be a rewarding hug. In other words, by this time children are only reinforced when they call the right person "Mama." Similarly, children slowly learn by trial and error what words belong where in a sentence, how to use prefixes and suffixes, and so on. All these little bits of language learning are put together into what Whitehurst (1982) has called "a patchwork of thousands of separately acquired frames, patterns, responses, rules, and small tricks. The elegance of the final product belies the chaos of its construction" (p. 368).

But most psychologists and linguists now believe that simple reinforcement alone cannot explain the impressive speed, accuracy, and originality with which children learn to use language. Noam Chomsky (1965), the most influential advocate of this alternative point of view, rejects the notion that children must be *taught* language. Instead he argues that children are born with an *internal* device for processing the adult speech they hear around them. This mechanism enables them to understand the basic rules of grammar, to make sense of what they hear, and to form their own sentences. This internal "language acquisition

The Strange Silence of Genie

In 1970 a 50-year-old Los Angeles woman separated from her husband after a violent domestic dispute. When she subsequently applied for public assistance, she brought her 13-year-old daughter with her to the welfare office. The social workers there, after observing the daughter and questioning the mother, called the police.

A horrible and tragic story then unfolded. The girl, Genie, had spent almost her entire life shut into a small dark bedroom. Isolated from her family by her psychotic father, fed only milk and baby food, she had never been toilet trained or taught to speak. She had spent her days harnessed to a child's potty chair (the harness, made by her father, left her unable to move anything but her hands and feet). At night Genie had been put into a tight sleeping bag and confined in a crib with a wire mesh cover—in effect, a cage. If Genie made any noise, she was beaten. Virtually her only contact with people took place when her father brought her food or moved her from the harness-chair to the crib. Instead of speaking to her, he regularly barked and growled at her as if he were a dog.

When she was found, Genie weighed only 59 pounds. She could not stand up straight and did not know how to chew. And she was strangely silent, both because she had learned to suppress her own sounds to avoid being beaten by her father and because she had had almost no opportunity to learn human speech. She had hardly ever been spoken to (Pines, 1981).

After Genie was found, she was taken to Los Angeles Children's Hospital, where she was cared for and examined by doctors, psychologists, and therapists. She was given an intelligence test for young children, on which she achieved the score of a 1-year-old. She seemed able to recognize only two words: the word *sorry* and her name. Eventually she began to repeat two phrases over and over: "Stop it" and "No more." Psychologists and linguists were called in to determine whether Genie was capable of learning language. One of them, Susan Curtiss, began to work regularly with Genie, taking her for outings and encouraging her to speak. Eventually Genie began to use words to describe the things she saw around her, much as toddlers do: "big teeth," "little marble."

Despite much help and encouragement from Curtiss, Genie's speech development progressed very slowly. She never learned to ask questions, nor did she seem to understand much grammar. Even after several years of careful teaching, her speech consisted primarily of short combinations of simple nouns, verbs, and adjectives ("Father hit arm. Genie cry.")

Genie's difficulty in learning language is consistent with the idea that there may exist a critical period for learning human language—that is, a span of time during which children either must learn to speak their native language or remain language-deficient for life (Pines, 1981). Eric Lenneberg, who has advanced this theory (1967), argues that the critical period for language acquisition is from age 2 until puberty. Genie, who was at the age of puberty when she was found, did acquire some language, as we have seen, although it seems unlikely that she will ever speak normally.

Despite her language handicap, Genie showed ability in other forms of expression. This is an example of Genie's art.

device" can be thought of as something like a street map (Whitehurst, 1982). Children don't approach language as a stranger without a map might encounter a new city—blundering this way and that, taking wrong turns, getting lost, and finally learning what leads where. Instead they are already provided with a kind of internal "map" of language, an overview of the terrain and how it's divided up (into "doers" and "what they do," for example—what we know as nouns and verbs).

Most psychologists today agree that children are born with a biological capacity for language, but this potential must be stimulated by their environment—the speech they hear from the day they are born. For example, a child points to a pair of shoes, and the mother says, "Those shoes are Daddy's." We know that without a social environment—people to talk with—children are slow to pick up words and rules that enable them to communicate and learn. Institutionalized children, who cannot expect an adult's smile to reward their efforts, and deaf children, who lack the self-satisfaction of hearing themselves make noises, babble like other children. The institutionalized child, however, takes much longer to start talking than the child who is raised in a family, and the deaf child requires special training. Clearly "feedback," in the form of listening to oneself and to others, influences language development.

The way children speak, what they say, and the errors they make tell us a great deal about not only their memory of language but also their thinking process. For example, when a child first uses actual words, the process is very concrete—that is, the child identifies words with situations and functions. Stone and Church (1968) described a child who called all red cars "engines"—for fire engines—long before he used the word *red* or had grasped the more abstract concept of colors. On word-association tests in which people are asked to listen to a word and then say the first word that comes into their minds, adults associate the cue word *table* with *chair*. Given the same cue, children associate *table* with *eat*. At this stage, then, children are more aware of what things do or are used for than of similarities or compatibilities between them (Brown & Berko, 1960).

Later children begin forming sentences, at first by joining two words together. One key element in this learning process seems to be *practice*. One mother put a tape recorder in her little boy's bedroom and recorded his talk after he had been alone for the night. When she played the tape back, she heard "what color . . . what color blanket . . . what color mop . . . what color glass . . . what color TV . . . red ant . . . fire . . . like lipstick . . . blanket . . . now the blue blanket." The child was playing with words and phrases, trying them on for size (Moskowitz, 1978).

Children between the ages of 2 and 3 commonly make certain mistakes that indicate they are beginning to learn more sophisticated grammatical rules. Often the children will proudly announce, "I saw some sheeps" or "I digged a hole." Obviously the words *sheeps* and *digged* were not learned by imitating adults. Rather, the child applied the logical rules for making plurals and past tenses, unaware that some words are irregular. In other words, children seem to know what they *want* to say before they can say it correctly by adult standards. In another case, a child was talking about a "fis" (Moskowitz, 1978). The adult repeated "fis" and the child became indignant. "Fis!" the child said impatiently. Eventually the adult tried "fish" and the child, satisfied at last, said, "Yes, fis."

Cognitive Development

In this section we look at changes in the way children think about the world. Perhaps the most influential view of children's cognitive development is that of the Swiss psychologist Jean Piaget. We will look at his theory in some detail and then consider some recent criticisms of that theory.

Schemes Piaget's term for the frameworks one uses to organize experience, which change as one develops.

Piaget's Approach

Jean Piaget (1896–1980) entered the field of cognitive development through a back door: He was trained as a zoologist, a perspective that shows in his work. For example, Piaget saw all behavior in terms of a person's adaptation to the environment. Unlike animals, people have few reflexes, so they must learn how to deal with their environment.

Piaget first became interested in human adaptation while watching his own children at play. Observing them with the trained eyes of a scientist, he began to see their games as confrontations with their surroundings. In other words, through play they were learning to adapt.

As Piaget's children grew, he noticed that their approach to environmental problems changed dramatically at different ages. Was it simply that their coordination improved, or did the older children think differently from their younger brothers and sisters? Piaget became an avid child watcher: He played with children, asked about their activities, and devised games that would show how they were thinking.* Gradually he discerned a pattern, a series of stages through which, in his view, all children pass.

SENSORY-MOTOR STAGE *(birth–2 years)*. As Piaget saw it, the baby's first step is to apply the skills that he or she has at birth—sucking and grasping—to a broad range of activities. Small babies delight in putting things into their mouths: their own hands, their toys, and so on. Gradually they divide the world into what they can suck and what they cannot. Similarly, young babies will grasp a rattle instinctively. Then, at some point, they realize that the noise being produced comes from the rattle. They begin to shake everything they get hold of, trying to reproduce the sound, and eventually start to distinguish between things that make noise and things that do not. In this way infants start to organize their experiences, fitting them into categories. **Schemes,** as these simple frameworks are called, are the first step toward intentional behavior and adaptive problem solving. Unusual things that do not fit into existing schemes, such as a strange adult or a moving mechanical dog, are apt to disturb children at this stage (Kagan, 1976).

By the end of the sensory-motor stage, as we saw earlier, children have developed a sense of object permanence. When a ball rolls under a chair,

*Piaget's approach is unusual. In developing theories, most researchers test as many children as they can to arrive at solid generalizations. Piaget chose instead to study a small number of children intensively as they went about their daily lives. This is a form of naturalistic observation, which is discussed in Chapter 1.

the child realizes that the ball still exists. Also, by the end of this stage, children have a sense of self-recognition—the ability to name themselves correctly in a mirror (Berntenthal & Fischer, 1976). Object permanence is crucial to cognitive development, for it enables the child to begin to see how things happen.

PREOPERATIONAL THOUGHT (*2–7 years*). Children are action oriented when they enter the preoperational stage. Their thought is tightly bound to physical and perceptual experiences. But as their ability to remember and anticipate grows, children begin to use symbols to represent the external world. The most obvious example of representation is language, and it is in this stage that children begin to use words to stand for objects.

But preoperational thinking differs in many ways from the thinking of older children and adults. Small children, for example, are extremely egocentric: They cannot distinguish between themselves and the outside world. They assume that objects have feelings, just as they do; they consider their own psychological processes—for example, dreams—to be real, concrete events. According to Piaget, children in the preoperational stage cannot put themselves in someone else's place.

Although they may be self-centered most of the time, under certain conditions even 4-year-olds seem to take into account the perspectives of other people (M. L. Hoffman, 1977). In one study 4-year-olds chose birthday presents that were appropriate for their mothers. If the children had been entirely self-centered, they probably would have picked toys they liked as gifts for their mothers (Marvin, 1975). In other studies 4-year-olds were found to use simple forms of speech when talking to 2-year-olds (Gelman, 1979), and they gave very detailed directions to people who they thought could not see (Maratsos, 1973)—both of which suggest that preoperational children do not always think in egocentric ways.

Piaget also suggested that children in the preoperational stage tend to focus on the one aspect of a display or event that attracts their attention and to ignore all the others. In a famous experiment he asked preoperational children to fill two identical short, wide containers with

Figure 10-4

In this experiment, Piaget pours the beads from one of the short, wide containers into the tall, narrow one. Children in the preoperational stage will usually say that the tall container has more beads in it.

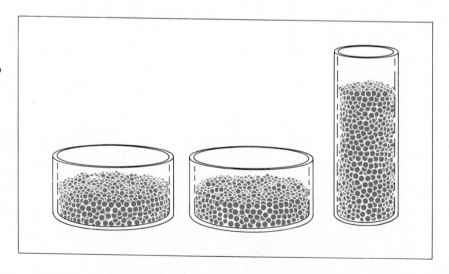

beads (Figure 10-4). When they had finished, he poured the beads from one container into a tall, narrow container and asked the children whether it had more beads in it than the other. The children always said yes, the tall one had more, even though Piaget had not added or taken away any beads. In a more recent experiment Gelman (1979) found that very young children (age 2½ to 4 years) could identify changes that occurred in the number of objects solely from adding or subtracting—even if they did not see the changes occur. If the color or shape of the objects also changed, however, the children became confused and could not perceive any change in the number of the objects. These results indicate that very young children can only concentrate on one aspect of a thing at a time: height, width, number, or color. The dominant feature of what a child sees becomes the center of his or her attention.

The children were also confused in these experiments because young children cannot mentally retrace their steps to reach a conclusion: "If we poured the beads back into the original container, it would look the same as before. The number of beads must therefore be the same." Both self-centeredness and irreversibility are shown in an example cited by Phillips (1969). A 4-year-old boy was asked if he had a brother, and he replied, "Yes." The child was then asked the brother's name: "Jim." "Does Jim have a brother?" "No." The child could not think of himself as somebody else's brother, nor could he work backward to reason that if Jim was his brother, he must be Jim's brother.

CONCRETE OPERATIONS (7–11 years). During this stage children become more flexible in their thinking. They learn to retrace their thoughts, correct themselves, and start over if necessary. They learn to consider more than one dimension of a problem at a time, and to look at a single object or problem in different ways.

Another bead game illustrates all these abilities and shows how children between the ages of 7 and 11 have grown intellectually. Piaget gave children of different ages a box of 20 wooden beads: 2 were white, the rest brown. He asked them whether the wooden beads or the brown beads would make the longest necklace. Children under 7 decided that there were more brown beads, ignoring the fact that *all* the beads were wooden. Children 7 and older laughed at the question: They knew that all the beads were wooden (Piaget & Szeminska, 1952).

By about age 10, children also become more able to infer what another person knows or may be thinking (Shantz, 1975). At about the same time, they become aware that the other person may be equally capable of inferring their thoughts.

Although quite logical in their approach to problems, children in the concrete operations stage can think only in terms of concrete things that they can handle or imagine handling. In contrast, adults can think in abstract terms, can formulate hypotheses and accept or reject them without first testing them. This ability develops in the next stage.

FORMAL OPERATIONS (11–15 years). To test the development of abstract thinking, children in the concrete and the formal operations stages were given a variety of objects and asked to separate them into two piles: things that would float and things that would not (Inhelder & Piaget, 1958). The objects included cubes of different weights, matches, sheets of paper, a lid, pebbles, and so on. Piaget then let the children test

Concepts Categories of objects that share some characteristic.

their selections in a pail of water, asking them to explain why some things floated while others sank.

The younger children were not very good at classifying the objects. When questioned, they gave *individual* reasons for each object's performance: The nail sank because it was too heavy, the lid floated because it had edges, and so on. The older children seemed to know what would float. When asked to explain their choices, they began to make comparisons and cross-comparisons, gradually concluding that neither weight nor size alone determined if an object would float: It was the relation between these two dimensions that was important. Thus they approximated Archimedes' law: Objects float if their density is less than that of water.

Younger children solve complex problems by testing their ideas in the real world; their explanations are concrete and specific. Adolescents can think in abstract terms and can test their ideas internally, with logic. As a result, they can go beyond the here and now to understand things in terms of cause and effect, to consider the possibilities as well as the realities, and to develop **concepts,** or categories of objects that share some characteristic. We will explore in greater detail the kinds of cognitive changes that occur during adolescence and adulthood in Chapter 11.

Criticisms of Stage Theory

Piaget's work has led to a good deal of research. Developmental psychologists have focused on two of his assumptions: that there are distinct stages in cognitive development, and that a person must go through each stage to reach the next.

T. G. R. Bower (1976) has argued that development does not always progress in this smooth way. For example, he found that during their first 11 or 12 years, children appear to master and then to lose the concept of conservation of weight; for example, they do not realize that a pound of feathers weighs the same as a pound of lead, even though the feathers make a bigger pile. Children finally reach a stable understanding of this concept when they are about 13 years old. There also appear to be "fits and starts" in children's memory development that do not follow Piaget's outline (Liben, 1974; Samuels, 1974).

Horn (1976) feels that much of the evidence that seems to support the idea of developmental stages has been misinterpreted. For example, simple observation tells us that an average child can do things at the age of 4 that he or she could not do at the age of 2. But that does not necessarily mean that something happens to a child of 2 that prepares him or her to have the skills of a 4-year-old. Horn suggests that a child can reach a later developmental stage (and perform the tasks associated with it) without having gone through the earlier stages, just as some children can walk without ever having crawled.

Perhaps it would be better to see Piaget's model as an ideal rather than a real picture of cognitive development. The interests and abilities of a particular child and the demands of the environment may influence development of cognitive abilities in ways not accounted for by Piaget (Kagan, 1976). Thus cognitive development might be better viewed as an ongoing process rather than separate stages with "breaks" between them.

One of the important aspects of human development is how a child learns to relate to other people. Early in life, a child's primary relationship is to its parents or other caregivers. By early childhood, various other relationships begin to form—with siblings, playmates, and others outside the family circle. The social world expands still further as children begin school and encounter an increasing number and variety of social relationships—with teachers, classmates, friends, teammates, neighbors, and so forth. As we will see, social development is the result of both constant and changing influences over time. How does social development occur?

Imprinting Rapid formation by a young animal of a strong bond to the first moving object with which it comes into contact, generally its mother.

Social Development During Infancy

In nature, young animals of many species follow their mothers around. Why? Because they have **imprinted** on their mothers. That is, in a short period of time the young animals have formed a strong bond to the first moving object with which they have come into contact. In nature, this object is the mother. In laboratory experiments, certain species of animals, such as ducks and geese, have been hatched away from their mothers, and have imprinted on decoys, toy balls, and even human beings (Hoffman & DePaulo, 1977; Lorenz, 1935).

Surviving Childhood Trauma

In 1959 psychologist Harry Harlow published the results of an experiment with rhesus monkeys—a bit of research that has since become very famous (Harlow, 1959). Harlow separated baby monkeys from their mothers and raised them in cages by themselves. Even though they were adequately fed, some of the monkeys died. Those that survived were decidedly abnormal—they were irritable, antisocial, and withdrawn. This experiment provided dramatic evidence that mothering is important to normal development. It also supported an idea widely held at least since the time of Sigmund Freud: that trauma in childhood, such as separation from the mother, produces abnormalities in the adult personality.

Although there is a large body of additional research in abnormal psychology that supports this notion, some experimental and child psychologists have begun to suggest that the relationship between youthful trauma and adult maladjustment is not so clear-cut. Children may be far more resilient than was once thought. For example, Jerome Kagan, a developmental psychologist at Harvard University, has said, "You can predict very little from experiences at ages 0 to 3, even when they include a number of traumatic events" (Newsweek, January 18, 1982).

Kagan's view is supported by a later study by Harlow and one of his associates, Stephen Suomi. Suomi and Harlow (1977) found that much of the trauma of maternal separation in rhesus monkeys could apparently be erased if 1-year-old monkeys raised in isolation were put into a cage with normal 2- and 3-month-old monkeys. The normal monkeys, outgoing and sociable, apparently rehabilitated the maladjusted monkeys. It seems that under some circumstances early traumas can be overcome if social support and affection are forthcoming. This discovery has implications for the treatment of children who have the misfortune to suffer child abuse, the death of a parent or sibling, or some other painful event. If family members, teachers, friends, or some other people are available to comfort the child, he or she may recover from the trauma with no ill effects.

Attachment Social bond that develops between an infant and its primary caregiver.

Imprinting of this particular type clearly does not occur with human babies. A newborn child separated from its mother will not attach itself to a manikin or a toy. But infants will form a close **attachment**, or social bond, to the person who cares for them, and in most cases in our society this person is the mother. For a long time, it was thought that feeding of the infant is the primary source of attachment. After all, feeding is the infant's first and most important experience of the world. To the extent that the mother satisfies her baby's need for food, the infant should begin to see her in a positive way, and this might cause the baby's first social attachment to form. Certainly the experience of feeding contributes to the development of attachment, but researchers no longer think that food and oral gratification are so overwhelmingly important. Parents and caregivers also provide warmth and "contact comfort": They talk to, hold, and smile at the baby. All these actions help to develop attachment, although psychologists disagree about which is most important.

The infant's attachment to his or her mother grows slowly over the first months of life. By six months, infants normally show a clear preference for their mothers, reacting with smiles and coos at her appearance and whimpers or cries when she goes away. At around seven months, infants begin to appear even more deeply attached. They will reach out their arms to be picked up and will crawl into their mother's lap and cling to her. They begin to be wary of strangers, sometimes reacting with tears and wails at even the friendliest approach by someone they don't know. Infants of this age also may react negatively if they are separated from their mothers, even for a few minutes. Parents are sometimes puzzled by these new reactions in their previously friendly, well-adjusted infants, but they are perfectly normal developments. Psychologists think that anxiety over strangers and separation from mother show that the infant is becoming more aware of the world: he or she knows that mother is a

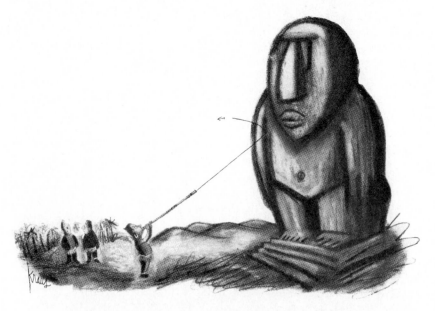

"Pointless rebellion against authority, if you ask me."
Drawing by Kraus; © 1960 The New Yorker Magazine, Inc.

comforting force and that there are people and things "out there" that may pose a threat.

Eventually infants do learn that the world beyond mother's lap is not necessarily frightening. They crawl away cautiously, then more boldly, to investigate things and people around them. This exploration is necessary for children to develop **autonomy,** or a sense of independence and trust in their own abilities and powers. At first glance, autonomy and attachment may seem to be polar opposites, but in fact they are simply different sides of the same coin. Recent research indicates that the stronger the attachment between mother—or principal caregiver—and child, the more autonomous the child is likely to be. This may seem paradoxical, but it makes more sense if we reflect that a strong mother-child attachment provides a sense of *security*.

Studies of children with varying degrees of attachment to their mothers have shown that, in new situations, children who feel they have a secure "home base"—a secure relationship with their mothers—are more likely to venture out from that base to explore these new situations. These children apparently know that when they finish exploring, they can return to the haven of maternal protection (Ainsworth et al., 1979). Studies of children from the age of one through six years have shown that babies who are securely attached to their mothers at the age of one are later more at ease with other children, more interested in exploring new play situations, and more enthusiastic and persistent when presented with new tasks (Main, 1973; Matas, Arend, & Sroufe, 1978; Waters, Wittman, & Sroufe, 1979). Therefore, mother–child attachments, far from being a sign of excessive dependency, actually seem to strengthen the child's growing desire for autonomy.

At about 2 years of age, children begin to test their strength by refusing everything: "No, I won't get dressed." "I won't go to sleep." The child's first efforts to be independent, however, may not be entirely welcome to the parents. The parents' attachment to the child, the mischief children get into as they begin to explore, and the extra demands on the parents' time and energy may explain this, although research on these questions is far from conclusive (Haith & Campos, 1977). The usual outcome of these first moves toward independence is that the parents begin to discipline the child. Children are expected to eat at a particular time, not to pull the cat's tail or to kick their sisters, and to respect other people's rights. The constant push-and-pull between such restraints and the need for independence often causes difficulties for both parents and children. But it is an essential step in developing a balance between dependence and autonomy.

Social Development During Childhood

As children grow up they are **socialized,** that is, they learn the behaviors and attitudes appropriate to their family and culture. Their social world expands—they play with their siblings; they make friends; they go off to nursery school, kindergarten, and finally school itself. But it is important to remember that throughout this period of encounters with new people and influences, children's parents continue to have a major

Autonomy A sense of independence and trust in one's own abilities and powers.

Socialization Process by which children learn the behavior and attitudes appropriate to their family and culture.

As soon as they can crawl, all infants begin to leave their mothers to investigate things and people around them. This exploration is necessary for children to develop autonomy.

Day Care: Rearing Children Away From Home

More mothers than ever before are working at full-time jobs—in many cases because their income is needed to help support their families, but in some cases because they are pursuing rewarding careers. When mothers of young children work outside the home—and about half now do—some provision for the children is obviously needed. Some mothers hire full-time baby sitters, if they can afford to, or leave their children in the care of relatives during the day. But a small percentage of young children are cared for in commercial day care centers. Is it a good idea to leave young children with substitute caregivers in day care centers?

The answer to this question depends most of all on the particular facility and the services it offers. If the center is well run (clean, attractive, with well-scheduled activities) and adequately staffed (no more than three or four children per adult attendant), the likelihood is that children will do as well in day care as they would at home with mother (Craig, 1983). The important thing to consider is that whoever cares for the child is consistently there (frequent staff turnover is undesirable) and is a loving, supportive person—a "second mother," in short (Browning, 1982). Some experts recommend enrolling children either before or after the stranger/anxiety period (approximately 7 to 15 months) so that they don't have to adjust to life at a center at just the time when they are most distressed at separation from mother and interaction with strangers (Hall, 1982).

It now appears that in some respects good day care may be even better for the child than staying at home. Children reared in day-care centers are sometimes more sociable with other children and at ease with strangers than are children brought up in the more isolated environment of home (Moore, 1975). Hall has found in a long-term study that older children from disadvantaged backgrounds

may actually benefit intellectually from day care if it offers a structured educational program (Scarr, 1984). And Hoffman (1983), who has reviewed all the studies done in the last fifty years on maternal employment, has found no consistent effects on children of mothers working outside the home and leaving children in the care of others.

It should be noted that we know rather little about the long-term effects, if any, of day care. Studies have yet to be done comparing the adolescent and adult adjustment of day-care vs. home-care children. Evidence now available, however, suggests that it is not so much the setting (whether home or center) that is important, but the quality of care the child receives there. Most psychologists seem to agree that *good* day care has no ill effects on children (Rutter, 1982).

influence on their social development (Craig, 1983).

When children are still tiny, most parents are mainly concerned with seeing to their physical and emotional needs. Yet even at this early stage in parents' interaction with their children, some rudimentary teaching is going on. For example, a mother will vary the way she talks or plays with an infant in order to keep the child's interest and match what appear to be the child's competencies at that point (Hodapp & Mueller, 1982). When children reach the toddler stage, the parents' role shifts very strongly to one of teaching (although the physical and emotional needs of the child still demand attention, of course). From using the toilet, to tying shoelaces, to holding a crayon, children need the help of patient teaching—and their first teachers are usually their parents.

Parents instruct their children in how to do things, but they teach them in other and more indirect ways as well. They serve as models of behavior and they make their expectations known through punishing and rewarding children's behavior. There is a large body of evidence showing that styles of parenting—the ways in which parents act toward their children and the demands they make of them—may have a lasting effect on children's behavior. Baumrind (1972), who has done extensive research on parenting, has found that authoritarian parents, who control their children's behavior rigidly and require total obedience, are likely to produce children who are withdrawn and distrustful. On the other hand, the children of parents who exert little control are likely to be dependent and to have little self-control. Other researchers have also found that restrictiveness often leads to dependence and submissiveness in children, and that extremes of either restrictiveness or permissiveness can lead to social problems later on (Craig, 1983). The best parenting approach, according to Baumrind, seems to be firmness combined with a great deal of warmth and encouragement. Parents who use this approach seem most likely to have children who are self-reliant and socially responsible, but this does not mean that this approach is correct for every parent or every child at every stage of growing up. There are simply no guarantees that any single method or combination of methods will produce a socially competent child. The best evidence thus far is that certain approaches are more likely to succeed than others, and that the appropriate parenting style for a given child is likely to change somewhat as the child grows, especially as new influences from the world outside the family begin to intrude (Hall, 1972).

Along with parents, brothers and sisters also play an important socializing role in a child's life. Siblings are more than occasional playmates—they are a younger child's first peer group. Like parents, they act as powerful models. Indirectly or directly, older siblings teach motor skills and language to their younger brothers and sisters. They show them how to play with toys or put on clothes or answer the telephone. And if siblings are close in age (and especially if they are of the same sex), they also provide the child's first experience with competition as they struggle to establish their own identities and outdo the other.

Besides siblings' direct influence on one another, a child's early social development is influenced by birth order. The evidence available thus far indicates that certain personality traits are connected with birth order. Firstborn children are generally more achievement-oriented than later siblings and seem to have a greater need for adult approval. Second and third children are usually more socially adept than firstborns and better able to get along well outside the family. A probable reason for this is that later siblings do not get exclusive attention from parents and depend to a greater extent on social contact with older brothers and sisters. Although the connection between birth order and personality tendencies is fairly well established, psychologists agree that the effects are modified by other factors in need of more study, such as the number and sex of siblings in a family and how close siblings are in age (Craig, 1983).

Not all children have siblings, of course, but virtually all do have some contact with playmates and friends before going to school. Like siblings, these playmates help to teach and socialize the young child. Preschoolers quickly learn some of the rules of social life, such as sharing and cooperation, although adult prodding is often called for. They also learn new social behaviors, such as how to act at birthday parties. Children of this age learn in part by imitating and instructing one another, which can result in acquiring new skills, whether valuable (such as riding a tricycle) or not so valuable (such as flushing the family's washcloths down the toilet). But they also learn through reward and punishment. Children tend to do the things that are rewarded or reinforced by other children and to avoid the things that are punished (Hall, 1982).

Eventually, of course, all children leave the protection of home and family for the new world of school. Here they are separated from parents or caregivers, perhaps for the first time, and enter a world filled with unfamiliar adults and peers. The impact of school is felt immediately. No matter what kind of school a child attends, there are new codes of behavior that are different from those of home. In even the most favorable school environments, individual attention is limited and children must learn quickly to ask questions, to explore things independently, and to do certain things (e.g., tie a shoelace, put on a coat) for themselves. While the school environment encourages independence and self-sufficiency, at the same time it demands cooperation with others and participation in structured group activities. Children are expected to be self-controlled and to follow orderly procedures, such as raising their hands before speaking, lining up for recess, and asking permission to leave the room. And in all their various school activities, children must learn to control aggression, to consider others, and to follow basic rules of social behavior.

Not surprisingly, this restructuring of their social world can be quite an adjustment for many children. But the adjustment to school is likely to be easier if a child has had a supportive family and has already begun to develop social skills within family relationships (Craig, 1983). Teachers themselves may make a difference in the social development that takes place in the classroom. Like parents, teachers are models, and their role definitions of themselves have an influence on children's behavior (Strommen, McKinney, & Fitzgerald, 1983). Another important consideration is the role of teachers in helping children adjust to school. As they oversee classroom activities, teachers are often instrumental in reinforcing peer activities and encouraging more isolated children to take part in the group.

The school environment also calls upon children to develop the social skills needed to cope with a variety of peers. As we have seen, peers begin to have an influence on a child's social development as early as late infancy, but their influence is strongest now. We have also looked at some of the ways in which peers influence one another by serving as models and punishing or rewarding each other's behavior. But as peers begin to take on more definite roles in the school setting (the smartest, the most athletic, the most popular, the toughest) and thus to exert greater control over one another, there is far more pressure than before to cooperate with one's peers and feel accepted by them. Studies of schoolchildren show that the way in which children relate to their peers is an important determinant of popularity. Steven Asher (1978), for example, has pointed out that popular children have the ability to ini-

The influence of peers is strongest during the school years and successful peer relations are a factor in popularity.

tiate friendships and to communicate effectively and positively with other children.

The importance of being accepted by one's school peers shows up strongly when psychologists study unpopularity and its effects. Children without the acceptance of peers tend to be socially withdrawn and unhappy and may lack self-confidence. And isolated children are more likely to have significant social problems later on, ranging from emotional difficulties to dropping out of school (Ullman, 1957; Cowen et al., 1973). Thus children's relationships to their peers are important in reinforcing a sense of belonging and providing the opportunity to develop competence in social roles.

Along with the social environment that school provides, school is a major influence on a child's sense of competence and achievement. Once at school, children may find it necessary to revise their own expectations of themselves, depending on how well they do at school, and how their efforts compare with their classmates' (Entwisle & Hayduk, 1978). Studies show that children who are successful at school and who view themselves that way are likely to develop a positive outlook. Children who face more disappointments and frustration may begin to lower their expectations and even give up (Seligman, 1975). In many respects, then, school is the first encounter between a child and the social system outside the family; and success at school—or the lack thereof—in the early years can exert a lifelong influence.

Sex Typing and Sex Roles

Parents treat their sons and daughters differently, starting with the blue or pink blanket in which they wrap the new baby. Until recently this differential treatment was thought perfectly natural and appropriate since it was believed to reflect inherent differences between boys and girls. But in the last decade psychologists have begun to examine closely the extent to which differences between boys and girls are the *result* of different treatment, and the extent to which there may be few inherent differences between the sexes.

Clearly there are sex differences in behavior. From very early childhood, boys tend to be more aggressive than girls (Wolman, 1978) and girls tend to excel in verbal ability. From the preschool years to early adolescence, the verbal abilities of both sexes tend to become equal. But girls then spurt ahead again and continue to excel verbally, at least through the high-school years. Boys, however, begin in high school to excel in their ability to perceive figures in space and to understand the relations between these figures. This visual-spatial superiority continues into adulthood (Maccoby & Jacklin, 1974).

Are these differences the result of biology or culture? Boys might be more aggressive because they have higher levels than girls do of the hormone testosterone, which is thought to be related to aggressive behavior. But aggression is also an area where parents seem to have very different expectations for boys and for girls (Sears et al., 1957). As a result, any inborn sex differences in aggressiveness might be increased by learning and parents' teaching. As for the discrepancy between the sexes in verbal, mathematical, and visual-spatial abilities, there is evidence

Children are socialized into stereotyped sex roles by their parents, and parents' attitudes greatly influence how a child feels about being a boy or a girl.

that these differences, too, can be modified greatly by training (Craig, 1983).

In fact, most of the differences assumed to distinguish women from men now appear to be primarily, if not entirely, the result of culture rather than biology. Newborn baby girls behave like baby boys, and 2-year-old girls and boys are about equal in cognitive development and social skills. A 2-year-old boy is just as likely to be fearful, dependent, and interested in caring for others as girls have been thought to be (Williams, 1977). As children get older, however, their behavior conforms more and more to our culture's version of how men and women should act.

How are children socialized into these stereotyped sex roles? They first learn about sex-appropriate behavior from their parents, and parents' attitudes have a great influence on their children's feelings about being a boy or a girl. In one study parents were asked to describe their newborn children (Rubin, Provenzano, & Luria, 1974). The parents were much more likely to describe their newborn daughters as delicate, beautiful, and weak. Newborn sons, on the other hand, were seen as strong, well coordinated, and robust. As all the babies were the same height and weight, these descriptions appeared to reflect the parents' expectations rather than actual physical characteristics.

As children grow up, parents seem to increase their emphasis on sex-appropriate behavior (Block, 1975). Girls are more likely to be coddled, while boys are encouraged to be adventuresome and independent. Boys are more likely than girls to be discouraged from showing their emotions. A boy who bursts into tears may be told that "only sissies cry." Girls are trained to be mothers, boys to be breadwinners. Thus boys play doctor and cops-and-robbers, while girls play nurse and mother with their dolls. Parents dress children in sex-typed clothing and encourage them to act like adult men or women.

It is also possible that infants *themselves* notice differences between their father's and mother's roles. From the start, mothers are more apt to assume caregiving tasks, while fathers interact with their children through vigorous play. This continues for some months. The fact that mothers and fathers represent very different experiences for babies may affect children's ideas about what it means to be male or female (Lamb, 1979).

As more women work outside the home, fathers will become more active in child rearing (Hoffman, 1977). This trend pleases many observers. They believe that if both mother and father share in child care and work outside the home, children will have a family model that avoids rigid sex roles. The working mother provides a self-sufficient model for her children, especially if the father takes on some of the household chores. Children who see their parents sharing domestic duties learn that there is not "men's work" and "women's work"—there is just work.

But the effect may not work out as expected. In several studies fathers have been found to treat sons and daughters more differently than mothers do. Fathers are much more likely to prefer male children to female children (Coombs, 1975), and to describe infants in sex-typed language (Fagot, 1974; Rubin, 1974). Fathers are more concerned with their sons' than with their daughters' cognitive development; their daughters are more encouraged to develop social skills (Block et al., 1974). Fathers also tend to encourage their daughters to "daydream" or to wonder about life. They are more willing to comfort them, and they generally have warmer relations with their daughters than with their sons (Block, 1975).

These studies suggest that as fathers become more directly involved in child care, there could be *more* sex role differentiation and a resulting decrease in the options made available to young girls. Perhaps, however, as men become more aware of the rewards of nurturance and more flexible in their own parental roles, they will encourage their children to be equally "liberated" from traditional sexual stereotypes.

Of course, socialization only begins in the home. Schools and the mass media express cultural values and are apt to be slow to reflect changes in people's attitudes. Textbooks often portray women and girls in subordinate roles. Girls are steered toward classes in cooking and sewing, while boys are expected to learn such skills as woodworking and auto repair. Girls' interest in such traditional female careers as nursing or teaching is encouraged, while boys have a freer choice.

The mass media—particularly television—also portray sexual stereotypes. The harried housewife in commercials, the macho cops and private eyes, and the bikini-clad females who sell cars all teach children certain values about being men and women. Even *Sesame Street* has come under fire for rigid sexual stereotyping and negative female role models (Bergman, 1974).

Thus most children are subtly bombarded with pressures to conform to sexual stereotypes. Many girls still assume that they can only be happy as wives and mothers, that they should be beautiful, and that they must find a man to attach themselves to. Boys learn that they are expected to be domineering and that it is normal to be aggressive. Parents who do not accept such stereotypes can provide their children with more alternatives, but they also have to be aware that much socialization takes place outside the home.

Social Cognition

As children's social horizons begin to extend beyond their own families, they become more aware of a complex social world. They become capable of understanding other people, social relationships, and finally, social institutions. This mental understanding of the social world and their place in it is called **social cognition** (Strommen, McKinney, & Fitzgerald, 1983). Cognitive psychologists believe that there are predictable changes in children's social cognition. They believe, too, that the ability to understand the social world depends, in part, on where children are in other areas of their development (Strommen, McKinney, & Fitzgerald, 1983).

As we have seen in our discussion of cognitive development, there are limits to the way younger children can think about the world. An infant's view of the world is egocentric: Although the child soon forms an important attachment to his or her mother (or other caregiver), the relationship does not include the ability to understand the mother or her needs. A baby cannot understand how his or her mother feels. An infant can't think, "She's had a long day already, so I'd better not cry tonight

Social cognition A mental understanding of the social world and one's place in it.

and disturb her sleep." Further along in the socialization process, infants and young children are more aware of the existence of a surrounding social order, but they are still incapable of understanding that other people have thoughts and feelings of their own. And they remain egocentric in the belief that others see the world and respond to it exactly as they do (Hall, 1982). Only as children lose their egocentrism do they start to see themselves and others as distinct individuals and realize that there are many different perspectives in the world besides their own.

Overcoming egocentrism is a lengthy process, and it is only in middle childhood (around the time children begin school) that children begin to gain some real understanding of others. In coming to recognize that other people have their own thoughts and feelings, children develop a first and essential component of social knowledge: They can begin to infer what other people's thoughts and feelings are—"Mother is angry with me"; "Dad looks happy today." It will take years before a child is fully capable of understanding someone else's perspective, but children can begin to act on this new knowledge in their own social relationships and friendships.

Children in middle childhood also begin to see themselves in a way that indicates greater awareness of their own personal characteristics: "I'm shy"; "I don't like hard work"; "I want to be a doctor when I grow up." Moreover, Diane Ruble (1980) has observed that children in middle childhood begin to compare these attributes with other children's and in this way begin to evaluate their own relative strengths and weaknesses.

It is also in middle childhood that children develop the ability to think about social relationships. Selman (1981) has discovered, for example, that children under the age of 7 consider "friends" to be people who live nearby, who have nice toys, and who play with them. "Friend" means "playmate." Around age 7 children begin to define friends as "people who do things for me"; therefore friends are important because they meet the child's needs. Later, at about age 9, children begin to understand that "friendship" is a two-way street, and that while friends do things for us we are also expected to do things for them. But throughout these years, friendships come and go at a dizzying speed. Friendship lasts only as long as needs are being satisfied. It is not until late childhood or early adolescence that friendship is viewed as a stable and continuing social relationship that requires trust, confidence, and mutual support regardless of day-to-day problems or dissatisfactions.

Application

Television and Children

It may seem unlikely that watching cartoon characters flatten each other or TV cops and robbers shoot it out could cause children to behave aggressively themselves. But a large body of research on the relationship between television viewing and aggression shows that this is indeed what happens.

Over the last two decades, psychologists, educators, and parents have expressed a great deal of concern about the influence of television on children's behavior. Singer (1983) finds that preschoolers spend about 4 hours a day watching television and notes that viewing time increases as children get older. Singer also states that, overall, children spend more time watching television than they do attending school.

In 1982 the National Institute of Mental Health published a comprehensive review of research on the psychological effects of television on young viewers. The many conclusions of the study have ignited a new public fury over this issue, focused primarily on the findings that watching violent television programs can promote or increase aggressiveness in children.

Eron (1982) has conducted a number of long-term studies to determine when television violence begins to affect children and what it is about TV violence that impresses youngsters. He found that around age 8 children become more susceptible to what they see happening on the screen. Moreover, he determined that the degree to which children are affected by watching violence depends on how closely they identify with the programs' characters and how realistic they believe the programs to be. Eron also asked children to rate one another on aggressiveness and then tied these results to television viewing. Children who identified strongly with TV characters on programs that contained a lot of violence were rated highly aggressive by their peers; children who believed these programs to be very realistic were also rated highly aggressive.

The television networks often argue that although their programs may include a good deal of violence, they also conclude with good winning out over evil. Thus, claim the networks, these programs teach children a positive lesson. Much to the contrary, the NIMH report argues that young children have not yet reached a stage of cognitive development where they can connect the violent actions seen during the course of a show with their final consequences (punishment) at the end of the show (Rubinstein, 1983).

The NIMH report also shows that children who watch a lot of TV tend to develop a distorted view of the world. Heavy viewers see the world as a place in which many more unpleasant and scary events take place than actually occur.

While research confirms the negative impact of television on children, it also supports the idea that television can have positive influences. Singer and Singer (1976) report that programs designed for children of a certain age can teach them cognitive skills. While most children's programs tend to be fast paced, lively, and shift scenes often, programs that are deliberately slow and repetitive can also hold children's attention. A program such as *Mr. Rogers' Neighborhood* can stretch children's imaginations, acquaint them with letters and numbers, and teach them valuable social lessons. Singer and Singer (1983) have also found that for some children, a combination of certain parental attitudes with television-watching can aid academic performance in the early school years. In families of low socioeconomic status, in which the mother describes herself as curious and imaginative, these researchers found that heavier viewing can lead to better reading comprehension. For these children, television perhaps provides the opportunity to learn and practice certain skills they might otherwise find difficult to acquire.

Psychologists do not fully understand television's effects on children. However, many are committed to further investigation into this issue, particularly because television has become one of the major sources of knowledge for children.

Summary

1. *Developmental psychology* is the study of psychological and physical changes over time, from the fetal stage through adulthood. Developmental psychologists employ various methods to gather data and study changes in human development. Using the *longitudinal method,* a researcher studies a fixed group of people over a period of time. The *cross-sectional method* enables a researcher to compare a sample of people of different ages at one point in time.

2. To uncover the reasons why developmental changes occur, developmental psychologists can use the naturalistic-observational meth-

od, the correlational method, or the experimental method. Actually they often use converging data from all three of these methods, since this gives them a more complete idea of the reasons behind developmental changes.

3. Psychologists now know that the *prenatal* (before birth) environment profoundly affects the unborn fetus. The *placenta* links the *fetus* to its mother and filters food in and waste products out. The placenta cannot filter out all harmful substances, however, so the pregnant woman should maintain a healthy diet and avoid drugs (including alcohol), communicable diseases, and stressful environments.

4. Newborns, or *neonates*, begin to absorb and process information from the outside world almost as soon as they are born; most of their senses operate at birth or shortly thereafter. Neonates are equipped with reflexes that prepare them to make contact and communicate with the adults around them. Three important reflexes that are present at birth are *rooting*, *sucking*, and *grasping*. In addition, neonates will respond to human voices and faces by turning their heads or their eyes toward them. Newborns seem to be born with "personalities" and react differently to certain tastes and smells. In experiments 2-week-old infants seem to be able to predict the course of a moving object and to understand that they can avoid being hit by it by moving away.

5. *Maturation* is an automatic unfolding of development that begins with conception. Boys and girls mature at different rates and have different body compositions. The greatest sex differences become evident at puberty, when both boys and girls go through a period of rapid growth followed by the development of the secondary sexual characteristics. *Developmental norms* are standards of growth that indicate the ages by which an average child should reach various developmental milestones. Normal development can occur within a range of ages, so these norms are only general guidelines.

6. The development of the central nervous system makes it possible for babies to get their bodies under control. The brain grows rapidly and becomes more complex, making new behavior possible. Motor abilities such as walking and grasping are present at birth, but develop in sequence. Walking progresses from lifting up the head, sitting up, crawling around, and walking with help to walking unsupported. There seem to be critical periods when a child is most able to start certain activities. Much of human development is gradual and steady, but sometimes development occurs in spurts that are less orderly.

7. Normal babies can both see and hear at birth, although not as well as adults can, and vision and hearing continue to improve during infancy. Visual perception seems not to be an innate capacity independent of visual experience. There is good evidence to suggest that stimulation, experience, and learning all contribute to a child's perceptual development. The ability to perceive is inborn, but without experience it will not develop properly.

8. Neonates lack *visual acuity*—the ability to distinguish fine details. Infants can perceive lines and dots as long as they are not too small or too thin. They can also recognize patterns and have been found to prefer increasingly complex stimuli as they grow older.

9. Developmental psychologists use a device called a visual cliff to test infants' distance and depth perception. When allowed to crawl freely around the cliff, babies will not cross what appears to them to be a deep hole; they will, however, cross over a hole that appears to be shallow and therefore not dangerous. Because babies under 6 months have imperfect vision and immature nervous systems, it is likely that their depth perception is limited. The experience of seeing and touching objects at various distances probably helps develop depth perception.

10. Infants as young as 1 or 2 months old can tell the difference between a picture of an object and the actual object. They are also more likely to reach out toward an actual object than toward a picture of it, indicating that they sense the graspable nature of objects. *Object permanence* is the knowledge that an object continues to exist even if it is not in sight. Infants develop a sense of object permanence at about 18 to 20 weeks of age.

11. Infants experience and make contact with the

world through all their senses. Even very young infants can hear fairly well and can distinguish between speech and other types of sounds. Infants will often reach out to touch, smell, and taste objects around them; and they even demonstrate preferences in tastes and smells. Infants' perceptions of the world grow sharper and more meaningful as they grow older. This is both because the nervous sysem is maturing and because they are gaining in first-hand experience of the world.

12. Infants demonstrate some limited ability to remember patterns and words, but memory improves dramatically as children acquire language. Other factors that contribute to memory development are the steady acquisition of knowledge about the world, the learning of strategies for remembering, and the realization that remembering things is important and necessary.

13. Infants are well prepared to perceive speech and eager to use sounds to communicate. Infants begin vocalizing with rather nondescript sounds but soon begin to imitate the sounds of speech. Children usually utter their first word around 12 months of age. They then normally go through a stage of naming objects repeatedly before beginning to learn more complex rules for putting words together into sentences.

14. There are two very different theories about how language develops. B. F. Skinner believes that children develop language skills through trial and error and reinforcement. The more current belief is that children have an innate capacity for learning language which is stimulated by hearing speech and by having people around with whom to communicate.

15. When children start speaking, they use words that reflect their awareness of what things do or what they are used for. Both practice and making mistakes are essential to learning the rules of language. Children seem to know what they want to say before they are able to say it correctly.

16. Cognitive development refers to changes in the way children think about the world as they grow older. Jean Piaget saw all behavior in terms of a person's adaptation to the environment. He noticed that as children grow older their strategies for adapting and coping with their surroundings become more sophisticated. From his observations Piaget developed his theory of cognitive development, consisting of a series of stages through which all children must pass.

17. The first stage in Piaget's theory of cognitive development is the sensory-motor stage (birth–2 years). Babies in this stage apply the reflexes of sucking and grasping to a broad range of activities. Infants will begin to organize their experiences into categories and devise *schemes* with which to deal with their world. At the end of the sensory-motor stage children develop object permanence and a sense of self-recognition.

18. Preoperational thought (2–7 years) is the next stage in Piaget's theory. During this time the child learns to use symbols to represent the external world. The child is egocentric most of the time and can center on only one aspect of an event at a time. In this stage a child cannot mentally reverse a situation.

19. During the concrete operations stage (7–11 years), the child learns to retrace his or her thoughts, to consider more than one dimension of a problem at a time, and to look at a single object or problem in several ways. By about age 10, children usually become more able to infer what another person knows or may be thinking and also become aware that another person may be able to infer what they are thinking.

20. The formal operation stage (11–15 years) marks the development of abstract thinking and the ability to formulate *concepts.*

21. Piaget assumed that there are distinct stages of cognitive development and that an individual must go through each stage in order to reach the next. Other developmental psychologists question these assumptions and suggest that cognitive development may proceed by "fits and starts," that there may be no sharp "breaks" between stages, and that it may not be necessary to go through earlier stages to reach a later stage.

22. In nature, young animals of many species *imprint* on the first moving object they come in contact with after birth, usually the mother,

and will follow her around. Imprinting creates a strong bond between the young animal and its mother.

23. Human babies form a close *attachment* to their mothers during the first few months of life. This attachment is the beginning of the child's social development. The mother satisfies the infant's need for food and gives warmth, contact, and auditory and visual stimulation. At around 7 months, children begin to show anxiety around strangers and react negatively to being separated from their mothers.

24. As soon as most babies can crawl, they begin to explore and to separate themselves from their mothers. They begin to develop a sense of *autonomy*. A strong mother-child relationship actually fosters autonomy because it provides the child with a secure base from which to explore new situations.

25. Throughout childhood, children continue to develop socially both within and outside the family. Parents significantly influence their children's social development through direct teaching as well as by serving as models of behavior. Research shows that styles of parenting can have a lasting effect on children's behavior. Certain parenting approaches seem more likely to succeed than others in producing a socially competent child, and in any event it is necessary that parenting styles change somewhat as children grow older.

26. Siblings also play an important socializing role in a child's life. Older siblings help teach younger ones language and behaviors. Sibling relationships expose children to competition, as siblings seek to establish their own identities. Among siblings, firstborns tend to be more achievement-oriented and to seek adult approval; later siblings are often more competent socially. Besides siblings, other peers help to teach and socialize the preschool child.

27. School is a child's first encounter with the social system outside the family and it calls for learning new social behaviors and skills. School encourages independence but at the same time it demands cooperation, interaction with peers, and conformity to the rules of social behavior. The socializing influence of peers is strongest during the school years. Successful relationships with peers become an important determinant of popularity and are a means of developing competence in social roles. Successes and failures at school may have a lasting effect on a child's sense of competence and achievement.

28. Psychologists have begun to examine the extent to which differences between the sexes are the result rather than the cause of differences in treatment. Most research on the subject does not support the notion of profound sexual differences. Males, however, do tend to be more aggressive than females. This difference may be hormonal at first, but socialization probably accounts for the discrepancy later. Females tend to excel in verbal abilities, while males excel in visual-spatial abilities. But these differences apparently can be significantly modified through training.

29. Many societies presume the existence of significant sex differences, and assign distinctive (and often opposite roles) to each sex. In the United States, females have been expected to be unaggressive, nurturing, and caring; males have been expected to be assertive, competent, and emotionally tough. Children are socialized into stereotyped sex roles through pressure at home (such as the use of sex-typed toys and clothing), and through sex stereotyping in the schools and the influence of the mass media.

30. Children gradually develop *social cognition*, a mental understanding of the social world and their place in it. Infants and very young children are egocentric. As they lose their egocentrism, children in middle childhood develop a greater understanding of others and can make assumptions about others' thoughts and feelings. They are also more self-aware and begin to assess their own strengths and weaknesses relative to others. Around this time children start to think about social relationships. Before age 7 they consider friends simply as playmates. After age 7 friends are important because they meet certain needs. Around age 9 there begins an understanding of the reciprocal nature of friendship. The fuller understanding of friendship as a stable social relationship does not come until late childhood or adolescence.

1. The longitudinal/cross-sectional method of research involves comparisons between people of different ages at one point in time.
2. The very earliest, or _____ period of development, is now thought to involve psychological as well as physical changes in an organism.
3. Neonates are only capable of simple reflexes and thus remain relatively unresponsive to the outside world.   T/F
4. Match the following terms with their correct definitions:

____ rooting reflex
____ grasping reflex
____ sucking reflex

   A. causes newborns to clasp anything that is put in their hands
   B. causes newborns to suck on anything that touches their faces
   C. causes newborns to search for a nipple when they are picked up

5. Physical development follows a regular, more or less automatic, course, which psychologists refer to as _____ .
6. Psychologists have agreed on some general guidelines and timetables in predicting the course of development. These guidelines are called _____ _____ .
7. Match the following terms with the appropriate definition:

____ perceptual ability
____ depth perception
____ visual acuity
____ object permanence

   A. ability to distinguish fine details
   B. is innate, but requires experience for proper development
   C. awareness that objects hidden from view still exist
   D. awareness of how close or far away an object is relative to oneself

8. Through a special device called the _____ _____ , psychologists are able to measure the extent of depth perception in infants.
9. The fact that an infant prefers a new pattern to an old one shows that it has the ability to _____ . The acquisition of language will further enhance this ability.
10. Most psychologists today believe that children are born with a biological capacity for learning language.   T/F
11. Match Piaget's stages of cognitive development with their appropriate descriptions:

____ sensory-motor stage
____ preoperational thought
____ concrete operations
____ formal operations

   A. marked by egocentrism and a narrow focus of attention
   B. increased logical aptitude and intellectual flexibility, but no ability to think abstractly
   C. marked by the development of abstract thinking
   D. a sense of self-recognition and object permanence develops by the end of this stage.

12. According to Piaget, the schemes/concepts one first uses to organize experience change as one grows older.
13. The bonding between an infant and its primary caregiver is the result of imprinting/attachment.
14. Children's development of _____ _____ gives them a fuller picture of the social world and their place within it.

Outline

Adolescence, Adulthood, and the Aging Process

11

William James, the 19th-century American psychologist and philosopher, believed that our character was "set like plaster" by the age of 30. Since James's day, psychologists have suggested ever earlier ages as the point at which our personalities are more or less "finished products." Sigmund Freud, for example, thought that the crucial events in personality development all took place before the age of 6. And until recently most psychologists also tended to see early childhood as the critical period of human development. Although it was acknowledged that people did change throughout life, these changes were considered routine and predictable—such as the physical changes of middle and old age.

Recent research suggests that development does not stop when childhood ends. In fact, some aspects of development are not even normally completed until adolescence or adulthood—sexual, cognitive, and moral development, for example. And experiences after childhood can change even those parts of ourselves that are already well developed. Adolescence and adulthood, then, are important developmental periods for human beings—not just long spans of years during which people simply play out their lives according to the patterns established in early childhood. In this chapter we will explore the ways in which adolescents and adults grow and change—physically, intellectually, morally, and socially.

Puberty The age at which sexual reproduction becomes possible.

Adolescence

Adolescence begins when a child's body shows signs of becoming an adult's body. Starting around the age of 11 or 12 and lasting until around 17, this stage is one of dramatic change. It begins with a rapid growth spurt and the changes of **puberty**—when sexual reproduction becomes

347

Menarche The onset of menstruation.

possible—and it ends with physical maturity.

Of course, adolescence is not just a time of physical change. During these years the adolescent becomes more able to comprehend the world, more able to make thoughtful moral decisions, and more socially autonomous. The years of adolescence are thus an important stage of transition between the dependence of childhood and the independence of adulthood.

Physical and Motor Development

One of the most striking changes of adolescence is sexual maturation. Boys and girls reach puberty at different ages, with girls maturing about 2 years before boys, on average (Harris & Liebert, 1984). For most girls, the first visible evidence of puberty (usually development of the breasts) appears between the ages of 8 and 13. Rapid growth in height begins just over a year later, and by the midteens most girls have reached their adult height. The appearance of pubic hair usually accompanies the growth spurt. **Menarche,** or the onset of menstruation, usually occurs somewhere between the ages of 10 and 17. For boys, puberty begins between the ages of 10 and 15 with the growth of the testes and the scrotum and the appearance of pubic hair. About a year later the penis begins to grow larger and the male growth spurt takes place. By the age of 17 or 18 the average boy has attained 98 percent of his adult height—and acquires that hallmark of adult masculinity, a beard (Conger & Petersen, 1984).

Adolescence is also a period in which boys and girls grow larger and heavier and begin to take on noticeably different physical shapes. Although girls experience the adolescent growth spurt first, sometimes standing a head taller than boys at the age of 12 or 13, boys eventually catch up and then surpass girls in height, on average. Boys also begin to develop heavier bones and a much more substantial musculature than girls, particularly in the upper body. (This change, like that in height, is one that persists throughout adulthood.) Girls' bodies, on the other hand, begin to accumulate proportionally larger amounts of fat than boys'. The increase in body fat on girls' arms, chests, hips, and legs begins to impart to them the shape of an adult woman's body.

The greater muscle growth in adolescent boys not surprisingly gives them an advantage in strength and motor development. Although girls' earlier growth spurt may allow them to surpass boys in agility and speed in early adolescence, this advantage decreases as boys' skeletal and muscular development catches up. By the age of 16 or 17, most boys have the edge in motor development (Chumlea, 1982).

The psychological consequences of these various physical changes are of special interest. Adolescents are acutely aware of the rapid changes in their bodies and as a result they are particularly concerned about whether they are the "right" shape or size, whether they measure up to the "ideal" adolescent portrayed on television and in magazines (Craig, 1983). Predictably, few real-life adolescents match the media image of an attractive, energetic, athletic person with a nearly perfect body, no pimples, absolutely straight teeth, and hair that is always "just right." Thus it is not surprising that when young adolescents are asked what they dislike about themselves, physical appearance is mentioned more often than anything else (Conger & Petersen, 1984). Moreover, satisfaction with one's ap-

Adolescents are acutely aware of the physical changes that are taking place. Many become anxious about measuring up to an ideal physical attractiveness.

pearance is tied to satisfaction with one's self, especially among adolescent girls (Lerner & Karabenick, 1974; Conger & Petersen, 1984). It is as though the adolescent says, "If I look unattractive, then I am not a worthwhile person." It is perhaps understandable why many adolescents react with anxiety if their appearance does not match their ideal.

The fact that puberty does not happen to everyone at the same age also has psychological consequences. Among boys, reaching puberty relatively early seems to have distinct advantages (Dreyer, 1982; Siegel, 1982). Boys who mature earlier do better in sports and social activities, which earns them the respect of other boys (Conger & Petersen, 1984). Boys who mature later are more likely to feel inadequate, anxious, and self-conscious (Jones, 1958; Jones & Bayley, 1950; Mussen & Jones, 1957, 1958). Longitudinal studies show that these personality characteristics tend to persist into early adulthood, though they become less marked as time goes by (Jones, 1965; Conger & Petersen, 1984). And a few studies (Peskin, 1967, 1973) indicate that as an adult, the late-maturing boy is more likely to be uninhibited, flexible, curious, expressive, and less rigid and cautious than the early maturer. Peskin suggests that this is because the late maturer has more time to prepare for and deal with the physical and emotional changes of adolescence.

For girls, early maturation appears to be a mixed blessing. A girl who develops earlier may be admired by other girls, but she is likely to be taunted or treated as a sex object by boys (Clausen, 1975). Her larger size and more adult physique may make her feel conspicuous and awkward, especially compared with the smaller, less developed boys of her age. For these reasons the late-maturing girl may find adolescence an easier period than her early-maturing peer (Siegel, 1982). But as with boys, the differences between girls tend to decrease with age. Early-maturing girls who find adolescence a stressful time are often quite well adjusted and at ease with themselves in adulthood (Peskin, 1973).

Cognitive Development

Just as the body changes during adolescence, so too does the mind. During the adolescent years a person thinks more and more like an adult and less like a child. This does not mean that adolescents simply know more than younger children do. They *do* know more, of course, but they can also use that knowledge in new ways.

The change in cognitive abilities that takes place in adolescence has been described by Piaget as the change from concrete operations to **formal operations.** In a nutshell, this means a change from a concrete to an abstract way of thinking about the world. Recall that in Chapter 10 we discussed an experiment in which children were asked to sort objects into things that would float and things that would not float. The children were also asked to explain *why* particular objects floated or sank (Inhelder & Piaget, 1958). Children from 7 to 11 years of age showed little skill in classifying the objects. They also gave *individual* reasons for each decision. But adolescents—who are at Piaget's stage of formal operations—not only knew what would float, but also could make a general rule for predicting whether an object would float.

It is particularly significant that adolescents search for general rules.

Formal operations The fourth and final stage in Piaget's theory of cognitive development, characterized by the appearance of abstract thinking.

Preconventional level Kohlberg's first level of moral development, during which children interpret behavior according to its physical consequences.

Conventional level Kohlberg's second level of moral development, during which children define right behavior according to what is approved of by others or what is required by the social order.

Younger children can think logically, but only in terms of concrete things. Adolescents can manipulate and understand abstract concepts (Piaget, 1969). With this ability adolescents can formulate general rules about the world and then test them against the facts. In other words, adolescents can deal with ideas systematically and scientifically, rather than in the haphazard way that younger children do. The formal operations stage, then, is a higher, more abstract way of thinking about the world. Thought is detached from any direct connection with experience. The adolescent who reaches this cognitive stage can speculate about alternative possibilities, can reason in hypothetical terms, and can understand analogies and metaphors.

The ability to think more abstractly accounts in part for some profound changes in the way adolescents relate to other people and to the world around them. For, unlike children, adolescents are able to think not only about the way things are, but also about how they might be different (and perhaps better). Conger and Petersen (1984) relate this new cognitive skill to the "relentless criticism by many adolescents of existing social, political, and religious systems and their preoccupation with the construction of other elaborate or highly theoretical alternative systems" (p. 168). Adolescents also tend to become immersed in introspection and self-analysis (Elkind, 1968). As they come to reflect in a more complex way on their feelings, attitudes, and actions, they may decide that they are "onstage," that their peers are always judging their appearance and behavior. This makes them continually play to an imaginary audience by dressing in a particular way, cultivating a distinctive image, and so on. Newly introspective adolescents may also believe that their feelings are unique in content and intensity. This sense of self-importance is what Elkind (1969) has called a "personal fable." The adolescent feels that no one else can reach the same heights of ecstasy or descend to the same depths of misery. This self-preoccupation has led many an adolescent to pour out anguished feelings in poetry or love letters. It is only toward the end of adolescence that a more mature perspective is gained. As older teenagers reach out to others and form more mature relationships, they begin to judge themselves more realistically (Elkind, 1969).

Moral Development and the Growth of Conscience

Another change of adolescence is moral development. Prior to the onset of adolescence children adopt what Kohlberg (1979, 1981) calls a "preconventional" perspective on morality. At the **preconventional level,** very young children interpret behavior in light of its concrete consequences—whether they are rewarded or punished for it. Somewhat older children at this level define "right" behavior as that which satisfies needs, particularly their own.

With the arrival of adolescence and the gradual shift to formal-operational thought, the stage is set for the progression to Kohlberg's second, or **conventional,** level of moral development. At this level the adolescent at first defines right behavior as that which pleases or helps others and is approved by them. Around mid-adolescence there is a further shift toward considering various abstract social virtues such as "doing one's duty," being a "good citizen," respecting authority, and maintaining the social order. Both forms of conventional morality require an ability to think about abstract values such as "duty" and "social order," to consider the intentions that lie behind behavior, and to put oneself "in the other person's shoes." In turn, these require formal-operational thinking. But, as we will see shortly, being able to think in formal-operational ways does not in itself guarantee that moral thought will progress to the conventional level.

The third, or **postconventional, level** of morality also requires advanced formal-operational thought. This level is marked by an emphasis on abstract principles quite apart from the concern with existing social rules and the power of those who enforce them. Justice, liberty, and equality become the guideposts for deciding what is moral and correct, whether or not this corresponds to the rules and laws of a particular society at a particular time. For the first time the person may become aware of discrepancies between what appears to be "moral" and what is "legal," and this awareness may lead to conflicts over following one's conscience as opposed to obeying the law.

Several points are worth making about Kohlberg's view of moral development in adolescence. First, research indicates that most people—both adolescents and adults—never progress beyond conventional morality (Conger & Petersen, 1984; Lerner & Shea, 1982). In fact, in one study a number of college students and young adults were found to be reasoning predominately at the preconventional level (Haan, Smith, & Block, 1968). Second, although one type of moral reasoning may predominate in an individual, that person's moral judgments may at times fit into a lower level and at other times fit into a higher level. Many of our day-to-day moral decisions (whether to put money in the parking meter, whether to play hooky from work) are based on preconventional or conventional reasoning, whatever our ability to engage in postconventional moral thinking. Third, although the development of formal-operational thought is necessary before a person can reach higher levels of moral development, it is no guarantee of advanced moral development (Kohlberg, 1976; Walker & Richards, 1979; Carroll & Rest, 1982). In other words, attaining the formal-operational level of thinking may make you capable of conventional and postconventional moral reasoning, but this does not mean that you will necessarily reason about morality in those ways. Nor does your ability to engage in higher levels of moral reasoning necessarily mean that you will behave more morally, although this is some evidence that this tends to be the case (Blasi, 1980; Lerner & Shea, 1982).

Kohlberg's moral-stage theory has had its critics. Some have pointed out that Kohlberg's levels of development may not be present in societies with different ideas of morality than our own (Baumrind, 1978). Since conventional and postconventional moral reasoning rely on formal-operational thought, which, in turn, is related to schooling, cultures in which schooling is less widespread than our own seem unfairly condemned by Kohlberg's theory to a low level of moral reasoning. Kohlberg has also been criticized for not acknowledging the difference between moral reasoning and moral behavior (Power & Reimer, 1978). As we have seen, ability to reason at a high level about moral issues is not the same as behaving according to such reasoning in a given situation.

Postconventional level Kohlberg's third level of moral development, during which a person uses abstract moral principles to reason about morality.

In the not-so-distant past the young person about to enter the adult world had a familiar path to follow. The boy whose father worked in a factory would probably do so as well; the girl whose mother reared children and ran the household was likely to follow the same pattern. In our era, however, the adolescent faces a number of decisions: what kind of people to associate with, what course of schooling to pursue, what kind of career goal to follow—in short, what kind of person to be.

According to Erik Erikson (1968), this quest for identity is the main task of adolescence. The young child's roles—son or daughter, brother or sister, friend, student—have largely been determined by his or her family. Few 6-year-olds choose the school they will attend or debate with their parents about whether a sibling should be added to the family. Yet many 16-year-olds do participate in choosing a college, and some even choose to become parents themselves. The family can no longer oversee every aspect of the adolescent's life, and most young people are eager to start making decisions for themselves, whether about clothes, friends, or school. In theory, this new independence from the family should be exhilarating. In practice, however, it may be stressful, particularly for the adolescent who finds a great deal of conflict between her choice (hanging out with a motorcycle gang) and her parents' choice (having a conventionally feminine daughter). Sometimes the conflict may be between the young person's *own* desires: He or she may want to remain a member of a strict religious group and yet also to experiment with sex or drugs. When such conflicts are extensive and serious, the person may feel pulled in many directions at once and be unable to make any decisions about the future. This problem is popularly known as an "identity crisis."

Not all adolescents have difficulty in establishing their identity. Many seem to weather this period fairly easily, perhaps with a few periods of uncertainty. The influence of parents seems to be the most important factor affecting the adolescent's ability to establish a clear and independent sense of self (Siegel, 1982). Adolescents who have rewarding relationships with *both* parents have a better chance to develop a strong identity (Conger, 1977). One study found that children of parents who stressed "democratic" child-rearing practices—such as open discussion of issues concerning behavior and discipline—were the most likely to develop confidence and independence (Elder, 1963).

The peer group is also important in the adolescent's quest for identity. At a time when the adolescent must choose among a confusing number of occupations, life-styles, ideologies, and sex role models—and is caught in a twilight zone between childhood and adulthood—the understanding and support of peers can be essential (Conger, 1977). Peers are all the more important at this time because the adolescent, in trying to become more independent of parents and older siblings, may cling to friends instead.

Unfortunately an adolescent's peers are not always a source of support and encouragement. Peer pressures often encourage the adolescent to conform to group norms rather than to be genuinely independent. What appears at first as rebellion against parental values may actually be a desperate need to follow the rules of the peer group and maintain peer popularity and approval.

Adolescents who have rewarding relationships with both parents have a better chance to develop a strong identity.

Caution: Youth Working

A 15-year-old girl leaves school at 4:00 P.M. and walks a few short blocks to a neighborhood restaurant, where she dons an apron and goes to work as a kitchen helper for 4 hours. In exchange for her work she receives the minimum wage, a free dinner—and the benefits of working: discipline, a sense of responsibility, and job skills. Her work experience is likely to make her more mature, more self-reliant, and a better student.

According to Ellen Greenberger, a professor of psychology at the University of California at Irvine, this story reflects a popular misconception: that after-school work experience is necessarily a good thing for teenagers (Greenberger, 1983). Americans, with their high regard for work, tend to assume that it is valuable for everyone—even 14- and 15-year-olds. When the U.S. Department of Labor in 1982 proposed to increase the number of hours that young teenagers might legally work (from 18 to 24 hours per week during the school year), Greenberger testified against the proposal before a House of Representatives subcommittee.

According to Greenberger, who has done research on youth employment for several years, working while in school *does* have some of the benefits its proponents claim. Teenagers who work are likely to gain a better understanding of money and increased feelings of responsibility and self-reliance. But they are also likely to spend less time on their schoolwork and less time with their families, which she considers major disadvantages of working. Greenberger and her associates found a telling relationship between the number of hours that teenagers worked and their grade-point averages: generally, the more work, the lower the GPA. Moreover, working during the teenage years is associated with increased use of cigarettes, alcohol, and marijuana.

In other industrialized countries it is the exception rather than the rule for teenagers (even 16- and 17-year-olds) to work while attending school. For example, in 1979 over 60 percent of American 16- and 17-year-olds were working, while less than 2 percent of Japanese youth worked. And as Greenberger (1983) points out, employment of 14- and 15-year-old students is now higher than it has been since 1940 (the first year the U.S. Census compiled a separate record of working students). This movement of youth into the workplace, she suggests, may be one reason for our nation's declining educational performance. At a time when we are concerned with encouraging high school students to spend more time on their studies, it would seem poor public policy to urge them to spend additional hours on the job.

Teens who work are likely to spend less time on their schoolwork and less time with their families.

One important aspect of a peer relationship is the expression of sexuality, a major developmental task of adolescence. In the early years of adolescence there may be a preoccupation with self—watching the body change shape, for example, and wondering whether it will measure up to some ideal. There is likely to be considerable curiosity about sex, which may take the form of asking peers for information, consulting explicit magazines or books, and masturbating (Siegel, 1982). Depending on peer group influences, sexuality may develop slowly, through a lengthy progression of hand holding, timid good-night kisses, and necking. Alternatively, some adolescents experience mature sexuality when they are only a few years past puberty. Familial and cultural expectations and peer group norms are the most important influences on how adolescent sexuality develops (Siegel, 1982). For some young people, engaging in sexual activity is a way of asserting their independence from their parents (Masters et al., 1982). Sexual behavior is a subject on which adolescents and their parents often disagree: Many parents expect their nearly grown children to conform to a traditional no-sex-before-marriage standard. This becomes increasingly unlikely as teenagers (and even children) are exposed to more and more sexual messages from the society at large. Recent studies indicate that more than half of adolescents of high-school age approve of premarital sexual intercourse, at least under some conditions, such as being in love or engaged to be married (Dreyer, 1982). By the time they are in college, as many as 56 percent of young men and 44 percent of young women will have had sexual relations at least once (Dreyer, 1982).

The Transition to Adulthood

The transition from childhood to adolescence is fairly well defined by the physical changes of puberty. Yet there is no clear-cut line to cross at the end of adolescence: No rites of passage exist in our society to mark the official beginning of adulthood.

The period that we usually call "young adulthood"—in which a person is something more than an adolescent, yet not quite a full-fledged adult—has resulted in part from our culture's emphasis on higher education. Since most young people are encouraged to pursue at least some education beyond high school, many are unable to achieve financial independence from their parents. As we have no other obvious point at which we can declare that adolescents have assumed an adult identity (Siegel, 1982), the end of formal education and/or the assumption of a job adequate for self-support is often considered the beginning of the adult years.

Adulthood

In their efforts to understand the physical, cognitive, and personality changes that occur during adulthood, psychologists use the same two methods of research that we discussed in Chapter 10: cross-sectional and longitudinal studies. Of the two, cross-sectional studies are by far the more popular with researchers on adulthood, because a longitudinal study of the same people would take 50 years or more to complete! Cross-sectional studies, however, cannot establish the relative importance of age differences and of generational differences. For example, a woman who is 60 years old in 1985 lived the first 20 years of her life during the Great Depression and World War II. She may have been profoundly affected by the difficulties of those years. By contrast, her son, who is only 35 years old in 1985, grew up in the relatively prosperous 1950s and 1960s. His attitudes toward life will to some extent reflect the conditions he encountered during those years. Thus it is hard to know whether differences between mother and son reflect the aging process, the fact that they belong to different generations, or both.

It is also worth noting that adulthood is not homogeneous. People confront different developmental challenges at different times during the adult years. Young adults need to form close personal relationships and to decide on a life's work. Many people choose to marry at this time, and marriage brings a new sense of permanence and responsibility. When the first child arrives, still more adjustments are demanded. For women in particular, parenthood can become a real crisis. In their 30s people tend to settle down. They usually come to accept themselves, both their good and bad qualities. For some, the early 30s may produce a questioning of earlier commitments to career or marriage that may require change.

At the start of middle adulthood many people realize that time is getting short. The pressure to achieve life goals becomes acute. By this time, most children have "left the nest," which rejuvenates many women. Both men and women become aware of the physical aspects of aging during this period. Menopause is an obvious turning point for women, but men also become more concerned about their health. Later in middle adulthood the awareness that one's time is limited may cause some people to turn inward and become reflective. Personal needs often become important. A mark of adjustment during this period is the discovery of new interests to fill the gaps left by decreased career and family demands.

In late adulthood retirement may leave a person with little sense of identity or purpose, with more "free" time, but with not much to do. The physical realities of aging are unavoidable as people face illnesses and death. Perhaps one of the greatest challenges of late adulthood is coping with our society's negative attitudes toward old age.

The rest of this chapter is devoted to a discussion of these and other aspects of adulthood. We start with the physical process of aging.

Many people choose to marry during young adulthood. Marriage itself, and the arrival of the first child, call for many adjustments.

Physical and Motor Development

In the first few years of adulthood, most people reach the peak of their physical condition. In the 20s physical strength reaches its maximum, the cardiovascular system is strongest, vision is as sharp as it is ever likely to be, and psychomotor skills (running, gymnastics, skiing) are at their peak (Stevens-Long, 1984).

But beginning in the late 20s and continuing throughout adulthood, we all undergo a gradual and inevitable decline in life processes (Hendricks & Hendricks, 1977). Typically, most of us are unaware at first of the decline, in part because the changes are small and in part because we develop strategies for minimizing their impact—we rest a bit more before

The Change of Life

One of the physical changes of middle age with which men and—especially—women have to cope is the climacteric, or the decline in function of the reproductive organs. In women this change is known as menopause; its most characteristic feature is the gradual cessation of menstruation. Men's bodies do not go through so drastic a change as menopause, but their reproductive capacity, too, declines after the 40s.

Menopause, which usually takes place in a woman's mid- or late 40s, produces a number of physical changes. The amount of estrogen, the principal female hormone produced by the body, drops sharply. Breasts, genital tissues, and the uterus begin to shrink slowly, and the menstrual periods become scantier and finally stop altogether. The hormonal changes produce in most women a characteristic pattern of physical symptoms: hot flashes, shortness of breath, and sometimes pain in the breasts or lower abdomen (Newman, 1982).

Whether these physical symptoms—which may be mild or moderate, depending on the individual—are usually accompanied by psychological symptons is a debated issue. Current evidence suggests that women who strongly identify with the role of mother and who are anxious about growing old and losing their physical attractiveness may suffer the most psychological distress at menopause. These women may become depressed, irritable, or anxious (Newman, 1982). But popular opinion may be too quick to ascribe any personality changes in middle-aged women to menopause, when the real causes may be illness, conflict with children or husband, adjustment to widowhood, or other problems. Most women find that menopause isn't the difficult period they had been led to expect, either physically or psychologically (Newman, 1982).

In men, middle age sees the beginning of a series of changes in the sex organs. A gradual decline in the male hormone testosterone results in reduced production of sperm and seminal fluid. Erection occurs more slowly, ejaculation occurs with less force, and orgasm is shorter. Although these biological changes are less drastic and final than those that occur in women (men can father children at virtually any age), they, too, signal the waning of the active reproductive years. Since the changes in men are less clearly observable, and perhaps since society puts less stress on men's attractiveness and reproductive role, the male climacteric seems to produce few major psychological problems.

and after participating in vigorous exercise, we hold our reading material a little closer to the light, and we work harder to keep ourselves in shape. But eventually evidence of the decline is undeniable. Weight and blood pressure start to increase; speed, strength, and agility decrease; vision and hearing become less sharp; we react more slowly to stimuli around us. Wrinkles appear, gray hairs emerge, aches and pains are more common, and sleep comes less readily (Newman, 1982; Larue & Jarvik, 1982; Stevens-Long, 1984).

There are several theories about why we age. The most obvious is that our bodies simply wear out (Timiras, 1972). Yet since many bodily systems are able to replace or repair their worn components (wounds heal, for example, and skin cells are constantly being generated), this cannot be the whole story. A related theory is that as they undergo repeated divisions, more and more cells in our bodies contain genetic errors and do not function properly (Curtis, 1965). Yet another theory holds that our body chemistry loses its delicate balance over the years (Timiras, 1978). For example, our excretory system, after years of filtering pollutants from our bloodstream, becomes less efficient, and the resulting change in our blood chemistry can produce a variety of other malfunctions. Finally, according to another theory, our bodies, with age, tend to reject some of their own tissues (Beaubier, 1980).

Whatever the reason, the processes of aging go forward in everyone, though they do so at different rates in different people. Much depends, for example, on whether a person eats a nutritious diet and gets regular exercise. Lack of exercise is a primary reason for the physical decline that is often seen in the 40s and 50s (Newman, 1982). Heredity is also a factor: Some people are apparently genetically programmed to get wrinkles and gray or thinning hair earlier than others.

Cognitive Development

Piaget proposed that in adulthood a person simply continues to use the formal-operational thinking process that first emerged during adolescence. But other psychologists have proposed that adult thinking undergoes qualitative changes (Arlin, 1975; Commons, Richards, & Armon, 1982; Riegel, 1973). So far there is little agreement on the characteristics of these changes, and not much convincing evidence that they actually occur, but the issue is certain to attract continued attention (Denney, 1982; Stevens-Long, 1984).

As for other cognitive abilities such as intelligence, problem solving, and reasoning, most researchers agree that some abilities decline more than others, that the declines begin somewhat later in life than was previously assumed, and that there are large individual differences in the way age affects cognitive abilities (Horn & Donaldson, 1976; Denney, 1982; Horn, 1982; Stevens-Long, 1984). Moreover, there appears to be some agreement on what Turner (1982) calls "the classic aging pattern of intellectual change" (p. 918). "Performance intelligence" tends to peak in very early adulthood and decline steadily thereafter (see Figure 11-1). As we discussed in Chapter 9, tests of performance ability require arranging blocks in different patterns, completing pictures, identifying the next number or letter in a series, and so on. "Verbal intelligence" tends to peak in middle adulthood and declines slowly until old age, when it declines more rapidly. Verbal intelligence includes factual knowledge, vocabulary, analogies, and comprehension.

Denney (1982) has recently suggested that the differences between verbal and performance abilities are due to the fact that performance abilities simply are not exercised very much during adulthood, while verbal abilities are used far more often. She supports this argument by noting that performance on traditional laboratory problem-solving tasks also tends to decline steadily during adulthood; these tasks tend to involve abstract, artificial problems that have little bearing on real-world issues. But ability to solve practical, real-life problems actually increases into the 50s, when it starts to decline (See Figure 11-1). Again, Denney interprets the data as showing that those cognitive skills that are exercised or used regularly during adulthood decline little or not at all until quite late, while less used skills and abilities start to decline quite early in adulthood. The dictum "use it or lose it" seems to capture the essence of this process.

Does creativity decline with age? A classic study by Harvey Lehman (1953) found that most of a person's high-quality creative work is done in early adulthood and declines thereafter. Botwinick (1967) also pinpoints the age of peak production of high-quality work in the arts, sci-

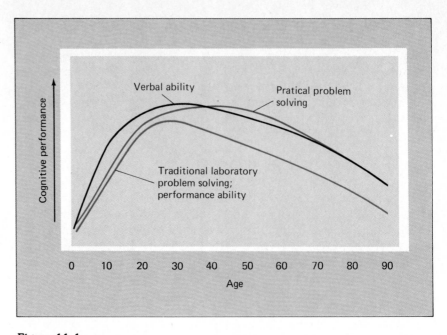

Figure 11-1

Graph showing patterns of cognitive development. Performance ability tends to peak in very early adulthood and decline steadily thereafter. Verbal ability tends to peak in middle adulthood and decline slowly there-after. Practical problem-solving ability actually increases into the 50s, when it starts to decline.

ences, and humanities as between the ages of 30 and 40. Wayne Dennis (1966) found evidence, however, that creativity continues well past middle age, especially in fields where much of the routine work can be done by younger people. Moreover, Stevens-Long (1984) notes that extraordinary creative achievements late in life can be found in almost any field. Leonardo da Vinci, Titian, Rembrandt, Rodin, and Le Corbusier stand out as creative geniuses whose best work appeared late in their lives. Other notable examples of this kind are shown in Table 11-1.

Personality Development

Until recently psychology paid relatively little attention to the development of personality in adulthood. As we saw at the beginning of this chapter, some of the most important thinkers in psychology, among them William James and Freud, believed that personality was essentially formed early in life. And some research data lend general support to the idea that at the age of 40 or 60, many people's personalities have changed little from what they were at age 20. To a degree, many of our personality traits *do* remain remarkably stable over the years (Rubin, 1981). A person who is quiet and introverted at 20 is unlikely to be a chatterbox or the "life of the party" at 40.

But this does not mean that we do not grow and change in adulthood (Rubin, 1981). Many adults can testify to the feeling that the problems of their 20s (stress at work, strained relations with parents) seemed to resolve themselves in their 30s (a new job, more independence from parents). Having children and launching them into the world more or less successfully can have a great effect on our sense of competence and self-esteem. Suffering through a divorce or the death of a spouse, though a traumatic experience at the time, may enhance our feelings of autonomy and integrity if we rise to the challenge of shaping a new life. Even without such dramatic events, the passage of the years seems to decrease the sex role differences between men and woman: Men become somewhat more nurturant and women more assertive with age (Turner, 1982). Thus it seems that the question of how much our personalities change and how much they stay the same has no simple answer. We both stay the same *and* change. We may grow with the years, resolving old problems and developing added competence as we come to grips with new ones, yet we seem to preserve a characteristic core of personality traits (Newman, 1982).

Changes in Social Relationships

In adolescence, as we saw earlier, relations with friends—one's peer group—are extremely important. In adulthood, social relationships expand greatly as people assume new social roles such as spouse, parent, neighbor, and co-worker. It is fair to say that changes in these social roles and relationships are among the most important factors in adult psychological development, and so we will study each of them in some detail.

FRIENDSHIP. The importance of friends fluctuates over a person's life span. For most people, the frequency, if not the intensity, of contact with friends declines over the life span. Newlyweds and young students enjoy daily contact with many friends. During young adulthood, when people are most inclined to form deep personal attachments, most people come to appreciate the support and affection of a smaller number of old and close friends. This has an important effect on the development of identity, on feelings of continuity, and on the perception of time. But Haan and Day (1974) report that by the end of young adulthood most people have as many close friends as they want, usually three or four. Friendships formed by adults are often quite strong, and they last as one grows older (Hess, 1971).

Emotional support, companionship, understanding, and caring are among the important values of close friendships. Such friendships also provide a sense of continuity to one's adult life. Despite employment changes, the growing up and departure of children, new interests and pastimes, and the physical and psychological changes we have already examined, close friends remain relatively constant and provide a stable point of reference.

Young adulthood is the time when people are most inclined to form deep personal attachments. By the end of young adulthood, most people have a small circle of close friends.

MARRIAGE AND SEXUALITY. Many cultures, including our own, regard marriage as an important social institution. Beyond that, marriage is viewed as the relationship in which adults are expected to continue their development and achieve goals such as intimacy and commitment, personal growth, and sexual satisfaction (Stevens-Long, 1984; Dogherty,

1982). Despite an increase in unmarried cohabitation and a trend toward the postponement of marriage into the late 20s and 30s, marriage remains an almost universal adult role: More than 90 percent of Americans will marry at some point in their lifetime (Dogherty, 1982). As well as having a significant social role in adult life, there is evidence that marriage is an important determinant of overall life satisfaction (Campbell, 1976). Married people report the highest levels of happiness, followed by the widowed, the separated-divorced, and the never-married or single (Dogherty, 1982).

In our society the usual prelude to marriage is the selection of a mate. Most Americans view love as the overriding factor in this selection; yet research indicates that most people are likely to marry someone of similar race, religion, education, and background. There are probably many reasons for this, including the fact that people from the same social background tend to come into contact more frequently and discover shared interests and compatibilities. In addition, many people find that social pressure from parents, relatives, and friends promotes association and ultimately marriage within one's social group (Stevens-Long, 1984).

The marital relationship itself may take various forms over the life cycle. Evelyn Duvall (1971), for instance, has described four stages of marriage and family structure—the newlywed marriage, the parental marriage, the middle-age marriage, and the retirement marriage—characterized by specific goals and tasks, and marked by role changes for both partners. Marital satisfaction, however, varies during the marriage and affects men and women in different ways: Husbands report most dissatisfaction during the years before retirement; wives report most dissatisfaction during the parental years (Rollins & Feldman, 1970).

Children complicate all marriages. Young children demand considerable time, attention, and energy, and this may leave the husband and wife with little time to be alone with each other. Working couples with children, who must depend on child-care arrangements, face added difficulties. Unexpected problems such as a child getting sick or a baby-sitter not showing up on time can be very difficult—and stressful—to resolve. Couples with adolescent children find themselves under special strains as they try to juggle many roles: parents, workers, homemakers, citizens, friends, members of civic and other groups, as well as being husbands and wives. Once children leave the home, many parents find renewed marital satisfaction. In fact, married couples with "empty nests" are often among the happiest (Campbell, 1975; Miller, 1976; Rollins & Feldman, 1970). For the first time in years they can be alone together and enjoy one another's company. In a study of older couples Stinnett et al. (1972) found that 90 percent saw their relationship as either "happy" or "very happy." More than 50 percent said that their marriage had improved with time; and most of those polled felt that the later years of their marriage were the best.

Another important part of successful marriage is a satisfactory sexual adjustment. Until fairly recently most American couples had little or no sexual experience on their wedding night; now fewer than 20 percent of newlyweds have had no sexual experience (Broderick, 1982). Increasingly, in fact, couples have already established a sexual relationship before marrying, and may have lived together for some time.

The greater sexual experience most people now bring to marriage, as

Expressions of affection between married couples do tend to decline over the years. Common reasons for sexual inactivity among older people are societal norms and the ill health or death of a spouse.

well as the greater availability of sexual information, may be contributing to a reported rise in sexual satisfaction in marriage (Stevens-Long, 1984). For one thing, Westoff (1974) has found evidence that married couples have been having sexual intercourse more frequently in recent years, perhaps because of a proliferation of popular books on sexual technique and an increasingly frank treatment of sexual themes in movies, TV, and magazines. Hunt (1974) has also found substantial gains in married couples' participation in sexual activity as well as in their enjoyment of it. There seems to be a correlation between couples' satisfaction with the frequency of intercourse and their marital satisfaction in general (Broderick, 1982).

Expressions of affection between married couples, from kissing to sexual intercourse, do tend to decline over the years (Masters & Johnson, 1971). Nevertheless, even with increasing age most couples remain interested in sex and continue to have sexual intercourse at least five times a month, on average (Broderick, 1982). Although aging may produce bodily changes that require some adjustment in technique or timing, a healthy person is able to continue sexual activity into advanced age. Contrary to popular belief, the physiological changes of menopause have no effect on a woman's level of sexual interest (Comfort, 1976). And although older men may respond more slowly to sexual stimulation, they, too, retain sexual interest. Common reasons for sexual inactivity among older people are acceptance of the stereotype that sexuality after a certain age is no longer expected or "nice," and the lack of a partner because of the ill health or death of a spouse.

PARENTHOOD. Establishing a family seems to be the major turning point in most adults' lives (Lowenthal & Chiriboga, 1972). With the birth of the first child, many adjustments have to be made in a marriage. "Husband" and "wife" become "father" and "mother." "Couple" becomes "family." This can be a real crisis, for the woman especially. If she has been involved in a career, she may suddenly have conflicting values. She may feel frustrated if she abandons her career, and anxious or guilty if she continues to work. Inexperienced parents may be terrified of responsibility, plagued by inadequacy, and stricken by guilt over mixed emotions about the baby. The husband may feel "left out." The wife may resent her husband's freedom from child care. One thing that seems to help couples cope with the transition to parenthood is preparation during pregnancy, such as attending childbirth classes (Parke & Asher, 1983).

Establishing a family is a major turning point in most adults' lives.

For women in middle adulthood, dealing with adolescent children can also be very difficult (Field & Widmayer, 1982). Most women cite this as the most unsatisfactory phase of their marriage. But men in middle adulthood often express increased interest in marriage and in family life. When the firstborn grows up and leaves home, the worst stage of family life for the woman seems to be over. Most women look forward to their children's leaving home and find renewed enjoyment in their marriages; they often feel rejuvenated by the freedom from responsibility. Often the sadder figure may be the father who decides to get to know his children just when they have left home or are struggling to define themselves as young adults outside the family.

At the same time that middle-aged parents are launching their children into the world, they are also faced with increasing responsibilities for their own aging parents. The role reversal that occurs at this stage can sometimes be difficult and filled with anxiety and resentment. Studies have shown, however, that most relationships between middle-aged adults and their parents are quite good (Hill et al., 1970). This is at least partly due to time and maturity. The middle-aged adult may at last be able to see a parent as a person, and the aging parents can step back from their parental role and let them run their own lives without interference.

DIVORCE AND THE DEATH OF A SPOUSE. One-third of all first marriages now end in divorce. Yet within 3 years of a divorce, 75 percent of both males and females remarry (Stevens-Long, 1984). As more women work and become more emotionally independent, they have fewer reasons to stay in unsatisfactory marriages—particularly since the religious, economic, social, and legal obstacles to divorce have weakened in the past 20 years.

Divorce and separation affect people in different ways, but going through either is an extremely stressful experience. Common responses are anger, depression, and psychological disequilibrium. These feelings may alternate with (or coexist with) feelings of continued attachment to one's spouse, relief that the marriage is ending, and a hope that the divorce will mean a chance to begin life on a new footing (Kelly, 1982). The end of a marriage seems to be more difficult for older people (Chiriboga, 1978), perhaps because the dissolution of a relationship of many years' standing involves so many changes in one's life.

Recovery from the death of a spouse is related to one's options, or resources—i.e., money, education, contacts outside the home, and so on (Lopata, 1973). When a woman's husband dies, she not only loses a friend, a companion, an escort, and a sexual partner, she often also loses a primary source of financial support. Twenty-six percent of all widows have never worked; 40 percent did not work while they were married. As a result, many widows cannot support themselves, and their social and financial standing plummets, causing them to become withdrawn and isolated. Widows are also much less likely to have the chance to remarry than are widowers (Turner, 1982).

Men have somewhat different problems. In studies involving widows and widowers of the same age, Atchley (1975) found that widows had more anxiety but that widowers seemed to feel more aimless. For many men, their wives are their only friends, and men are often not prepared to live alone. Although men of all ages find it easier to form new sexual relationships than women do—marriage between an older man and a younger woman is still socially more acceptable than marriage between an older woman and a younger man—women have social skills that they use to make friends with other women and that help assuage their grief. This is even more true for older women, who often have a more extensive social network than have older men. On the whole, however, most widows and widowers eventually adjust well to the changes in their lives (Turner, 1982).

WORK AND RETIREMENT. Young adulthood is consumed by the need for economic security and success. Deciding on a life's work is a central concern of most people in their 20s. Although some men wander from job to job, most men select, through education or experience, a career path by their mid-20s. Much of their identity and most of their time and energy are tied to that career. More women are making similar career choices in their 20s. At this point in their lives, if they want to start a family, some women may choose work that will not tie them down in one place, that will not stop them from getting home on time at night, or that will not interfere with child care. For similar reasons, some women do not start a professional career until after their 20s, if they have one at all. Women who combine marriage and family with a career may

The Myths of Aging

People over 65 constitute the fastest-growing segment of the U.S. population. If you are like most people, you probably assume that the majority of the elderly are lonely, poor, and troubled by ill health. But this view is not only inaccurate, it also causes many problems for older people. As Eisdorfer (1983) notes: "Our beliefs, based in fiction and nonfiction alike, have relegated the aged to a nonproductive, impaired, incapable, and useless status with the loss of virtually everything that contributes to the personal capacity, performance, roles, and status of individuals in the world" (p. 198). For example, doctors and other health professionals sometimes assume that it is "natural" for elderly patients to be ill. Symptoms that would indicate treatable disease in younger people are sometimes taken simply as signs that "Martha just isn't what she used to be." All manner of psychological problems, such as depression, can be wrongly blamed on a process of mental decline that is expected to begin in old age.

The most harmful idea of all is that *senility* is an inevitable part of growing old. Senility, a state marked by serious lapses of memory, haziness of thought, and other signs of mental decay, is by no means a natural or inevitable result of aging. Very few people actually become senile, and when they do, their condition is caused by a disease process. Two-thirds of all cases of senility, for example, are caused by Alzheimer's disease, an organic brain disorder (Olendorf, 1982). Senility is thus no more "natural" than a brain tumor or any other disease affecting the nervous system. When old people seem forgetful or want to reminisce about the past, we may incorrectly conclude that their minds have begun to wander. Thinking over the past is a natural stage in the later years of life, a kind of putting one's mental affairs in order (Craig, 1983). Many behaviors we may be quick to label signs of senility are actually the results of old people's exclusion from an active role in society. If they seem unable to comprehend current events, for example, it may be because they have given up reading the newspaper—since they have no one to discuss the news with or since they feel that their opinions don't matter to anyone anymore. The idea that senility is common—indeed, almost inevitable—among the aged is a most unfortunate misconception.

Other false notions about old people are that they are helpless and dependent on their families for care and financial support. This is true of a minority of the aged—mostly the very old. The majority of people over 65 live independently and maintain an acceptable style of life—they are not living in heatless tenements worrying about how to make it to the store to buy their next loaf of bread.

In 1975 the National Council on the Aging reported the results of a survey of the elderly. More than half of the people questioned reported that they were just as happy as they were when younger. Three-quarters thought that they were involved in activities that were as interesting as ever (Birren, 1983).

All this is not to deny that for a significant minority of old people, advancing age *does* present problems. For the poor, and especially for minorities, old age may be bleak. A lifetime of poor health care may culminate in serious illness, and lack of money may have made putting aside any assets for old age impossible. (And most jobs held by poor working people do not provide pensions or other retirement benefits.) These people face the same conditions in old age that they did earlier in life: poor housing, lack of opportunity, lack of resources. With advancing age, these problems are even more burdensome.

face conflicting demands in handling both roles (Hoffman, 1983; Stevens-Long, 1982).

In their early 30s many men go through a crisis in which they become dissatisfied with the shape of their lives and feel that it is their last chance to set things right (Levinson, 1978). Just how difficult this time of life is for men is debatable. Some researchers see midlife as a time of tremendous turmoil, and there is some evidence to support this view. At midlife, marriage is often least satisfying (Pineo, 1961), and neurotic disorders most frequent (Weintraub & Aronson, 1968). The rates for first-admission alcoholism are highest for people in middle adulthood. The number of suicides, especially among men, also increases at this time. Infidelity and desertion become major problems. And peptic ulcers, hypertension, and heart disease flare up (Rosenberg & Farrell, 1976).

Other researchers, however, find less evidence that a severe midlife crisis occurs. Some studies show that most people in middle adulthood believe themselves to be happy, satisfied, confident, and in control. They rarely, if ever, describe life as a crisis. Whether or not midlife is traumatic, many men and women turn to second careers at this point to find new rewards and challenges.

Ultimately, of course, everyone must face the prospect of retirement. Although retirement has become an accepted phase of life, the role of the retiree is, at best, ambiguous. Retired people are supposed to live their own lives, to pay their own way, to have reasonable self-respect, and to be socially responsible (Atchley, 1977; Donahue, Orbach, & Pollack, 1960). But exactly what does all that entail on a day-to-day basis? Unlike other roles in life, such as student, worker, child, or spouse, the expectations for retirees are unclear. Are retirees supposed to sit on the porch and watch life go by, or should they join civic groups, play golf, and be foster grandparents? Those who have trouble filling their work-free days find it hard to adjust to retirement.

Money clearly influences people's attitudes toward retirement. Shanas (1972) found that what Americans miss most about their work is not the responsibility, usefulness, power, fulfillment, or the sense of a job well done, but the money. If retirement means a major loss of financial freedom, a person will be less eager to retire.

But more than money is involved. In a general sense, people's attitudes toward retirement are tied to their attitudes toward work. People who are fulfilled by their jobs are often less interested in retiring than those whose jobs are unrewarding (Atchley, 1976). Blue-collar workers, for example, often look forward to retirement; professionals more often do not. Other factors, such as education and age, are also important. Highly educated men are less interested in retiring than uneducated ones, although well-educated women tend to leave the work force earlier than their less-educated counterparts.

Some researchers (e.g., Streib & Schneider, 1971) see retirement as a form of disengagement: People disengage themselves from the role of worker and move into another and more satisfying role in life. According to one view, this move out of the work world is only the first step in a general disengagement from society as a whole in old age (Cumming and Henry, 1961).

But research evidence shows that disengagement from society does not seem to be associated with either good physical or mental health, at

Older people stand to benefit from continued activity and satisfying use of time.

from good social relationships, physical and mental exercise, and satisfying use of time (Kahana, 1982). Of course, not all retirees need or want a life of whirlwind activity. Like young adults and those in middle age, older people get satisfaction from various life-styles. Problems with adjustment to old age occur when people cannot live lives that fulfill their own needs and desires. People who like to be active and highly involved can be happy and satisfied throughout their lives if they are given opportunities for continued involvement. People who choose to be less involved when they are young enjoy old age if they are allowed to avoid the responsibilities and activities they never wanted to begin with. Neugarten and Hagestad (1977) believe that one's earlier personality predicts how well one will adjust to the aging process. People with well-integrated personalities tend to adjust well to old age. Those who are less satisfied with their lives continue to have difficulty in old age.

Death and Dying

Death is seldom central to a person's final years. In fact, it may loom larger in young adulthood or in middle age, when the first awareness of mortality coincides with a greater interest in living (Kimmel, 1974). A study undertaken to compare attitudes toward death and dying among young adults and people over age 65 found that 19 percent of the young were afraid of death, compared with only 1.7 percent of the elderly (Rogers, 1980). When asked to describe the worst aspect of death, 36 percent of the young adults mentioned "an end to experience," while only 9 percent of the elderly felt that way.

According to Simone de Beauvoir (1972), the elderly person, while aware of the imminence of death, may be more concerned with taking stock of past accomplishments. If people have been successful in the main tasks of life, they will have a sense of integrity. If they cannot accept the events of their lives, however, the result will be despair, for it is now too late to change things (Erikson, 1968).

Robert Butler (1963) asserts that this kind of life review is universal among those near to death. This does not mean, however, that old people brood about the past. For example, Paul Cameron (1972) found that most people, including the elderly, concentrate on the present.

Recent research shows that nearness to death—apart from age or illness—may itself cause psychological changes. Lieberman (1965) tells of a nurse who could predict the death of her patients because they "just seemed to act differently." Several researchers have been startled to find an accurate sign of impending death, which they call the "terminal drop." The terminal drop is a noticeable decline in assertiveness, cognitive organization, and IQ as measured by psychological tests. As a person nears death, there is a sharp decline in these functions (Kleemeier, 1962; Lieberman & Coplan, 1969; Riegel, Riegel, & Meyer, 1967).

Psychiatrist Elisabeth Kübler-Ross (1969) interviewed more than 200 dying people of all ages to try to understand the different aspects of the dying process. From these interviews she isolated five sequential stages through which people pass as they react to their own impending death.

The first stage is *denial*. The person refuses to accept the prognosis, insists it is a mistake, and consults other doctors. In the second stage the person recognizes the verdict and feels intense *anger* and resentment. These emotions are directed at nurses, doctors, family—anyone with whom the dying person comes into contact. The patience and understanding of others is very important at this time. The third stage is marked by *bargaining*—with the doctor, with the illness, or with God—in a desperate attempt to buy time. The bargaining seems to be a healthy attempt to cope with the awareness of death. In the fourth stage the person accepts that death is coming, and the result is *depression*. Finally the dying person moves from depression to full *acceptance*. This stage is characterized by "quiet expectation." The person is typically tired, weak, and unemotional.

According to Kübler-Ross (1969), the central problem that Americans have in coping with death is that we fear and deny it. Because we do not believe we could possibly die of natural causes, we associate death with "a bad act, a frightening happening" (p. 2). She observes that while some other cultures are *death affirming*, American culture is *death denying*. "We are reluctant to reveal our age; we spend fortunes to hide our wrinkles; we prefer to send our old people to nursing homes" (Kübler-Ross, 1975, p. 28). We also shelter children from death and dying. By trying to "protect" children from unpleasant realities, we may actually make them very fearful of death (Kübler-Ross, 1975).

Kübler-Ross believes that we depersonalize dying people at a time when they badly need comfort and compassion. In part, this may be because relating to dying people can be very painful for family and friends—and for nurses, doctors, and mental health professionals as well (Pattison, 1977). Often dying people are separated from everyone and everything that is familiar and meaningful to them and are "segregated" with other sick and dying people in a hospital or nursing home. It is even more difficult to cope with fears about dying when a person feels alone and perhaps discarded (Kübler-Ross, 1975).

Kübler-Ross's work has increased our understanding of the emotional needs of the dying person (Kastenbaum & Costa, 1977). In the last decade medical and other professional schools have begun to teach that death is a natural event and that families should be helped to accept it.

There is, however, some doubt about the accuracy of Kübler-Ross's five-stage model of dying. Shibles (1974) suggests that the stages are too narrow and fixed. Kastenbaum (1977) has argued that there is no evidence that every person moves through all five stages. Pattison (1977) believes that a dying person, like someone who is not dying, has a continual ebb and flow of emotions.

Even more seriously, some health-care professionals apply the Kübler-Ross model in a rigid and destructive manner. Clinical personnel may patronize the dying person before he or she "is in the anger stage" (Kastenbaum & Costa, 1977, p. 242). Or *they* may become angry if a person does not move neatly into the "next" stage. In extreme cases, professionals actually demand that individuals "die in the right way"

(Pattison, 1977, p. 304). Pattison points out that Kübler-Ross cited many examples of people who did not precisely follow the five-stage model. He adds, "From my own personal contacts with Dr. Kübler-Ross, I believe she would be dismayed at the manner in which her stages of dying have been misused to force artificial patterns of dying upon the dying person" (p. 304).

Hospice A center for the dying that seeks to minister to their medical, psychological, and social needs.

Application

Hospice Care for the Dying

In the Middle Ages a "hospice" was a way station and a refuge where pilgrims and travelers could find food, rest, and comfort on their journey. Today's *hospice* is a center for the dying that seeks to minister to their medical, psychological, and social needs.

"I am less afraid of death than I am of dying," is a remark often heard by doctors and counselors from dying patients. And, in truth, the pain and loneliness of the dying are often fearsome—and to a certain extent inescapable. Yet the American way of dying may have made things worse. In the past most people who had a terminal disease suffered and died at home and were consoled somewhat by familiar faces and surroundings. Today the terminally ill are more apt to spend their last days, or even months, in a hospital or a nursing home. Seventy percent of all Americans now live part of their last year in one of these facilities (Wellborn, 1978).

There is now a new health-care facility for the terminally ill: the hospice. With in-patient facilities and home-care services, the hospice helps a dying patient and his or her family live with as little pain and as much comfort as possible until the patient's death. The first hospice in the United States was established in 1974; by 1981 there were more than 800 hospice programs nationwide (Vandenbos, DeLeon, and Pallak, 1982). Clearly the hospice movement has served a human need.

The key features that distinguish a hospice from a hospital or nursing home are the treatment of people who cannot be cured and the attention given to their families. Hospitals seek to help the patient recover from disease. Nursing and convalescent homes exist to provide long-term care for the elderly or the handicapped. Neither is

equipped to deal with those patients suffering from an incurable disease—especially cancer—who may expect to live for less than a year. Moreover, hospitals and nursing homes have only minimal resources for helping these patients' families deal with the emotional trauma of watching a loved one die. By contrast, hospices exist solely to deal with the dying and their survivors, not with the ill or the elderly.

The first goal of hospice care is to control pain, not to try to cure its causes. For example, Hospice, Inc., in New Haven, Connecticut, uses a mixture of morphine and water to relieve pain while still allowing the patient to be active and alert. But the hospice also recognizes that pain control succeeds best when it is related to the patient's mental and emotional well-being. Hospice treatment, there-

The hospice is a center for the dying that seeks to minister to their medical, psychological, and social needs.

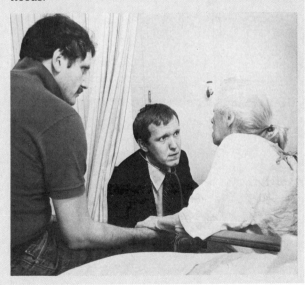

fore, includes a constant program of comfort, counseling, and care designed to help patients cope with the situation. Allaying patient fears is a major part of this program. At Hospice, Inc., Dr. Sylvia Lack, the head physician, tries to prepare dying patients for the inevitable. She explains that 50 percent of terminal patients do not experience pain; that pain, if it comes, does not have to be endured; and that pain control should start when pain is still mild—patients should not feel guilty for asking for relief even in the earliest stages (DuBois, 1981).

Hospice patients spend their last days either in the facility itself or, in most cases, at home with their families. An important goal of the hospice is to allow the patient to be comfortable and to live (as much as possible) in a familiar way. Patients wear their own clothes, not hospital gowns, and they are encouraged to bring in favorite possessions for their rooms. Family visits are welcome at any time, and when family members come, they find the person they know and love—not a supine body attached to tubes, dials, and machines. As one hospice visitor noted, "This was a 'home for the dying,' yet what we saw was people living" (Smyser, 1982).

Hospices also recognize the need to comfort the family and friends of the dying patient throughout the whole period of grief, which means after death as well as before it. Dr. Elisabeth Kübler-Ross found that it was often harder for the family to accept death than it was for the dying patient. Officials at Hospice, Inc., write, "The bereaved are more vulnerable to physical and psychological disease; care for the survivors . . . is needed until [they] can cope for themselves, or until other resources such as mental health services, family physician, extended family, or minister are found to provide the help needed" (DuBois, 1981). Outside professionals can advise the bereaved on insurance policies, bills, lawyers, and funeral preparations. A grieving person can turn to the hospice staff for help at any time.

Besides the psychological and spiritual uplift provided by hospices, there are also noteworthy dollar savings. Professional planners of the hospice movement report that "61 percent of one hospice's patients die at home (compared with the 2 percent of all American deaths which occur at home)" (DuBois, 1981). According to the American Hospital Association, in 1978 the average cost of a day's hospital care was $151.79. Hospice, Inc., placed the cost of its Home Care Service at approximately $750 per patient over a 3-month period (Wellborn, 1978).

All of the benefits of hospices, however, depend on how well they can overcome the negative American attitudes toward death and dying and toward institutions associated with them. People who lived near Hospice, Inc., for example, feared that a "death house" was coming to their neighborhood. To dispel this image, the hospice was designed to appear as pleasant as possible.

It is in accepting death as part of the life process that the hospice movement renders perhaps its greatest service to the dying and their families. Hospices can encourage people to share their needs and fears and thus help them overcome their dread of what they may not want to accept—but cannot avoid.

Summary

1. It was once thought that an individual's development ended with childhood. More recent evidence shows that development continues through childhood, adolescence, and adulthood. Human beings appear to undergo physical, cognitive, moral, personal, and social changes throughout life.

2. Adolescence begins when a child's body shows signs of becoming an adult's body. In both sexes it begins with the physical changes of *puberty*, accompanied by a rapid growth spurt. On the average, girls grow faster in the beginning and show signs of sexual maturity at an earlier age than boys. *Menarche* usually occurs somewhere between the ages of 10 and 17. Boys usually catch up and surpass girls in height; by about the age of 16 or 17 boys

usually have an advantage in strength and motor development due to greater muscle growth in adolescence.

Adolescence, Adulthood, and the Aging Process **369**

3. The physical changes that occur during puberty have a psychological impact on adolescents. Adolescents are acutely aware of these changes and are concerned about whether their physical appearance matches their image of the "ideal" adolescent. Some boys and girls mature faster physically during puberty than others. Maturing early or late contributes to psychological difficulties during adolescence. Eventually, however, everyone goes through puberty, and differences between early and late maturers become less marked as time goes on.

4. Cognitive development occurs as the adolescent begins to think more like an adult and less like a child. According to Piaget, adolescence marks the change from the *concrete operations stage* to the *formal operations stage.* Adolescents begin to think about the world in abstract ways. At this stage, adolescents often become preoccupied with problems in society and may speculate on how things could be different. They tend to become immersed in introspection and may feel as though they are always being watched and judged. To the adolescent his/her feelings are unique in content and intensity. Toward the end of adolescence, teenagers begin to form more mature relationships and judge themselves more realistically.

5. Prior to adolescence, children have a *preconventional* view of morality; they equate good and bad behavior with reward or punishment. Moral development in adolescents is related to the shift from concrete operational thought to formal-operational thought. According to Kohlberg, the adolescent begins moving toward the *conventional level* of morality when s/he defines right behavior as that which pleases or helps others. Eventually the adolescent begins to define right behavior according to society's definition of morality. Kohlberg's third or *postconventional level* of morality requires advanced formal-operational thought. At this point the person thinks of right and wrong in abstract terms of justice, liberty, and equality. It must be remembered, however, that most people never progress beyond the level of conventional morality, and that people's moral judgments may sometimes fit into a lower level and at other times into a higher level. Although a person may be capable of formal operational-thought, this does not guarantee advanced moral development.

6. According to Erikson, adolescence is the time when most young people search for an identity. They begin to make decisions for themselves—a process that is exciting but may also be stressful. The adolescent may be torn between choosing one style of life or another and may experience an "identity crsis." Parental influence appears to be the single most important factor in an adolescent's ability to establish a clear and independent sense of self. The peer group also plays an important role; but while the peer group provides support, it may also exert pressures to conform. Expression of sexuality in adolescence is influenced by both parental and peer group norms.

7. In our society there is no set time when one "officially" ends adolescence and enters adulthood. But commonly, it is the time when formal schooling ends and a person begins employment with the intention of self-support. For practical reasons, cross-sectional, rather than longitudinal, studies are more commonly used in doing research on adults. Adulthood is not homogeneous and people continue to confront developmental challenges during the adult years.

8. Most people reach the peak of their physical condition during their 20s. Beginning in the late 20s and continuing thereafter, everyone undergoes a gradual and inevitable decline in life processes. Several theories attempt to explain why we age. One is that our bodies simply wear out. A second theory states that with repeated divisions more and more cells in our bodies contain genetic errors and do not function properly. A third theory is that our body chemistry loses its delicate balance over the years. A fourth contends that our bodies tend to reject some of their own tissues as we age. People age at different rates and the effects of aging depend on how well a person takes care of his/her body. Heredity is also a factor, since some people are predisposed genetically to show earlier signs of age.

9. There is disagreement on what sort of cognitive changes occur through adulthood. According to Piaget, adults simply continue to use the *formal-operational* thinking process. Others have proposed that adults undergo further qualitative changes as they grow older. It has been shown that some mental abilities decline more than others; that decline begins later in life than was previously assumed; and that there are large individual differences in the way age affects cognitive abilities. In addition, there is evidence suggesting that cognitive skills that are used regularly during adulthood decline little or not at all until quite late, while less used skills start to decline quite early in adulthood. Whether or not creative ability declines or increases as a result of age is in question.

10. It appears that many aspects of personality do remain relatively stable through adulthood. However, many adults find that through different life experiences they grow and change. For example, through the years there is a decrease in many gender differences. It seems as if people both stay the same and change throughout life.

11. For most people the frequency of contact with friends declines while the intensity of friendship increases as they get older. The close friendship of a few friends has an important effect on the development of identity, on feelings of continuity, and on the perception of time. As other elements of life change, close friends remain relatively constant and provide a stable point of reference in adulthood.

12. Most people in our society marry at some point in their lives. People tend to choose partners from the same race, and of similar religious, educational, and social background. People who get married report the highest levels of happiness. Couples pass through different stages in their marriage that include role changes for both individuals. Marital satisfaction, however, varies during the marriage, and may be felt differently by men and women. A dual career marriage, raising children, and seeing children leave home create new situations that married couples must work out strategies to deal with. Most people feel that their marriage improves with time and that the later years of marriage are the best.

13. Satisfactory sexual adjustment is an important part of a successful marriage. The reported rise in sexual satisfaction in marriage may be a result of premarital sexual experience and increased access to sexual information. Expressions of affection and sexual relations between married couples tend to decline over the years. However, there is no age at which people become physiologically incapable of sexual expression. The decrease in sexual behavior in old age may be due to stereotypes imposed by society.

14. The experience of raising a family presents many new challenges, responsibilities, and role changes for men and women. For many women raising children through adolescence proves to be the most unsatisfactory phase of their marriage. As middle age approaches and children leave home, couples may find renewed satisfaction in their marriage. At the same time they are also faced with increasing responsibilities to their own aging parents. This role reversal can cause tension and anxiety but most people work through this and develop a more mature relationship with their parents.

15. Divorce and separation are stressful experiences that may bring feelings of anger, depression, and psychological disequilibrium. These feelings may alternate with (or coexist with) feelings of continued attachment to one's spouse, relief that the marriage is ending, and hope that the divorce will mean a chance to begin life on a new footing. Older men seem to feel aimless when their wives die, while women express feelings of anxiety about financial and social resources. Older women, however, often have a more extensive social network than do older men, which aids in readjustment.

16. Deciding on a life's work is a central concern of most people in their 20s. Men often choose a career path earlier in life than do women. More and more women are making similar career choices, although some choose to postpone it until after establishing a family. Midlife crisis is a time when many men feel dissatisfied with their lives and seek a change. However, some studies show that most people feel satisfied and happy with their lives. The

role of the retiree is ambiguous. People are expected to be self-sufficient, but retirement often brings economic insecurity. People's attitudes toward retirement are related to their attitudes toward work and the fulfillment they found in their jobs. Older people, like everyone else, benefit from good social relationships, physical and mental exercise, and satisfying use of time. One theory proposes that one's earlier personality predicts how well a person will adjust to the aging process.

17. Elisabeth Kübler-Ross has described five sequential stages through which people pass as they react to impending death: denial, anger, bargaining, depression, and acceptance. Her work has done much to promote greater understanding of the emotional needs of the dying. Some evidence exists, however, that not all dying people go through the experience in the way Kübler-Ross describes.

Review Questions

1. Adolescence begins with _____ , the point at which sexual reproduction becomes possible.
2. An important physical change for adolescent girls is _____ , the onset of menstruation.
3. A striking feature of the adolescent stage for *everyone* is:
   a. introspection
   b. formal operational thought
   c. sexual maturation
   d. delinquency
4. According to Piaget, adolescence is marked by a change in cognitive abilities from _____ to _____ .
5. Match each of Kohlberg's moral stages with its appropriate definition:
   ___ preconventional level
   ___ conventional level
   ___ postconventional level

   A. person differentiates right from wrong behavior and tries to live up to socially accepted standards
   B. behavior is interpreted in terms of physical punishment and rewards.
   C. person seeks to reconcile socially accepted norms with his/her own conscience

6. According to Erik Erikson, the quest for _____ , or what kind of person to be, is the main task of adolescence.
7. _____ intelligence, which involves laboratory problem-solving tasks, tends to decline more rapidly in adulthood than does _____ intelligence, which involves factual knowledge, vocabulary, and comprehension.
8. Americans are just as likely to marry outside their social group as within it.   T/F
9. One effect of physiological changes in later life is loss of interest in sexual activity.   T/F
10. Research indicates that the one thing most retired Americans miss about work is loss of money/ fulfillment.
11. Kubler-Ross has shown that people who know they are dying go through the following five stages: acceptance, bargaining, denial, anger, depression. Arrange them in the correct order.
12. According to Kubler-Ross, American culture as a whole is _____ _____ , as evidenced by our anxiety over growing old and tendency to depersonalize the dying.

Outline

Personality

12

Jaylene Smith is 30 years old, single, and shows plenty of promise as a physician. Yet she is troubled by some aspects of her social life and has entered therapy. Here is part of a profile of Jay:

Acquaintances describe Jay in glowing terms, for example, as being highly motivated, intelligent, effective, creative, attractive, and charming. "If they only knew," thinks Jay frequently. For Jay, unbeknown to others, is terribly insecure and anxious. When asked once by a psychologist to pick out some self-descriptive adjectives, Jay selected introverted, shy, overweight, inadequate, dull, unhappy, and afraid of people—not an enviable self-image!

Jay was the firstborn in a family of two boys and one girl. Their father, a successful medical researcher, loved all the children but favored Jay— there was something special, he thought, about his eldest child. And what dreams he had for Jay! Dr. Smith wanted to instill in her a strong desire for achievement so that someday she would strive to become successful, wealthy, and most of all, independent. He wanted very much to be proud of his little "bundle of joy," as he affectionately referred to Jay. Their relationship remains as close today as it was during Jay's childhood.

Jay's mother has always been career-oriented but she has frequently experienced considerable conflict and frustration over her roles as full-time mother, housekeeper, and financial provider. Much of this conflict, unfortunately, was communicated subtly to the children, especially when they were quite young. For some reason, these anxieties particularly affected Jay—as reflected perhaps in intense and frequent childhood fears of animals, darkness, and separation. Mrs. Smith was amicable toward all her children but tended to argue and fight more with Jay than with the others, at least until Jay was about 6 or 7 years of age (when the bickering subsided). Today their relationship is cordial but it lacks the dynamics, vitality, and closeness apparent between Jay and Dr. Smith.

Throughout elementary and high school Jay was popular and did well academically. Athletics, student government, newspaper reporting, performing in school plays, and dating were all regular parts of her social calendar. When asked once by a favorite teacher about future goals, Jay replied definitively, "I plan on going into medicine because I enjoy

373

Personality A person's unique pattern of thoughts, feelings, and behaviors that persists over time and situations.

helping people, particularly when they are sick and must be taken care of." The teacher, familiar with Jay's talents, abilities, and physical handicap (a slight congenital hearing impairment), never doubted Jay's sincerity or determination. Yet despite Jay's lofty goals and ambitions, off and on between the ages of 8 and 17, there were strong feelings of loneliness, depression, insecurity, and confusion—feelings perhaps common to everyone during this age period, but stronger than in most youngsters and all too real and distressing.

Jay's college days, when she was away from home for the first time, proved exciting and challenging—a period of great personal growth and pain. New friends and responsibilities gave Jay increased self-confidence and zeal for pursuing a medical career. Several unsuccessful romantic involvements proved disheartening, though, and led her to increase her study efforts. Interpersonal relationships would always be threatening, even disastrous for Jay. This aspect of life—the failure to achieve a stable and long-lasting relationship with that "special someone"—bitterly gnawed at Jay's inner being. "After all," she would muse, "aren't people supposed to fall in love and marry? What is wrong, why can't I ever maintain a serious relationship for any length of time?"

Thanks to her excellent work during college, Jay was easily admitted to medical school. After the initial excitement, however, the hard realities took hold—more years of difficult work, intense competition, and, naturally, possible failure. The severe pressures and work load forced Jay to ignore potential romantic involvements, though she had many casual friends she could always contact for brief diversions. While she tried not to dwell on personal feelings and conflicts during this period of her life, they crept through periodically: "I don't deserve to be a doctor"; "I won't pass my exams"; "Who am I and what do I want from life?"; "Why can't I meet that special person?"; "Will I ever be truly happy?"

At the medical school graduation ceremonies Dr. and Mrs. Smith were as proud as they could possibly be. After all, their daughter was now, officially, Dr. Jaylene Elizabeth Smith, and she had graduated at the top of her class! (adapted from Lazarus & Monat, 1979, pp. 23–25).

How can we describe and understand Jaylene Smith's personality? How did she become what she is? Was she affected by being the oldest child in her family and by having only brothers with whom to grow up? In what ways is she like her father and in what ways like her mother? Why does Jay feel insecure and uncertain despite her obvious success? Why do her friends see her as charming and attractive, while she describes herself as introverted and overweight? These are the kinds of questions that personality psychologists would be likely to ask about Jay, and they are the kinds of questions we will try to answer in this chapter.

What do we mean when we speak of "personality"? Even psychologists have a hard time agreeing on a single definition of personality. One current definition, and the one that we will use, is that **personality** is the "pattern of characteristic thoughts, feelings, and behaviors that persists over time and situations and distinguishes one person from another" (Phares, 1984, p. 673). That's quite a mouthful, but notice two important parts of this definition. First, personality persists over time and across situations. We expect people to feel, think, and behave in certain consistent ways from day to day and situation to situation. Thus personality lends a degree of predictability and stability to an individual. Second, personality refers to those aspects that distinguish a person from everyone else. In a sense, personality is a person's "psychological signature," since it is both characteristic of and unique to that person.

We will begin our exploration of human personality by discussing several kinds of personality theory. We'll conclude by examining some of the ways in which psychologists measure different aspects of personality. These methods include interviews and various kinds of tests.

Trait theory Maintains that characteristic patterns of behavior, thought, and feeling are the result of a person's traits.

Traits Enduring dispositions within the individual that cause that person to think, feel, and act in characteristic ways.

Trait Theories

One approach to understanding personality is known as **trait theory.** According to this point of view, the thoughts, feelings, and behaviors that distinguish one person from another are due to enduring dispositions or **traits** within each person. These traits predispose people to think, feel, and act in certain characteristic ways. A person with the trait of introversion, for example, is likely to be introspective, self-controlled, and quiet, while a person with the trait of extroversion is likely to be outgoing, lively, and sociable.

We cannot observe traits directly—that is, we cannot see a trait such as "introversion" in the same way that we can see a person has blue eyes and brown hair. But we can infer the existence of traits from the person's behavior over a period of time and across a variety of situations. When we observe that Jay chose at an early age to pursue medicine, did well academically year after year, elected the necessary courses to qualify for medical school, persisted through four difficult years of medical study, and graduated first in her class, it seems reasonable to infer a trait of "determination" or "persistence" to account for her behavior. Similarly, you might reasonably conclude from the previous description of Jay that she also has traits of sincerity, motivation, and intelligence, as well as insecurity, introversion, shyness, and anxiety. These relatively few traits account for a great deal of Jay's behavior and they also provide a relatively brief summary of "what Jay is like."

Although trait theorists generally agree that traits are an important aspect of personality, they disagree on how many different personality traits there might be. Allport and Odbert (1936) searched through a dictionary and discovered about 18,000 English words that seem to refer in some way to personality. Though only about 4,500 of these words concern stable or enduring traits, that is still a massive list with which to work! But Raymond Cattell (1965) pointed out that many of those 4,500 words are actually synonyms or near-synonyms; if these are eliminated, the number of possible personality traits drops to around 200. Cattell went further and demonstrated that when people are rated on those 200 characteristics, various traits tend to cluster in groups. Thus, if a person is described as "persevering" or "determined," he or she is also likely to be thought of as responsible, ordered, attentive, and stable. Moreover, it is unlikely the person will be described as frivolous, neglectful, and

Table 12-1   Major Source Traits Identified by Cattell

Trait Label	High Scorers (+)	Low Scorers (−)
A	OUTGOING, warmhearted, cooperative, easygoing (Affectothymia)*	RESERVED, detached, critical, aloof, cold (Sizothymia)
B	MORE INTELLIGENT, bright, alert, thoughtful, abstract	LESS INTELLIGENT, dull, concrete thinking, unimaginative
C	STABLE, calm, mature, patient, persistent, steady (High ego strength)	EMOTIONALLY CHANGEABLE, easily upset, anxious, impulsive (Low ego strength)
E	ASSERTIVE, aggressive, competitive, conceited, confident (Dominance)	HUMBLE, mild, meek, obedient, conforming, modest (Submissiveness)
F	HAPPY-GO-LUCKY, lively, enthusiastic, cheerful, witty, talkative (Surgency)	SOBER, serious, pessimistic, subdued, depressed, worrying (Desurgency)
G	CONSCIENTIOUS, persevering, responsible (High super-ego)	EXPEDIENT, frivolous, immature, undependable, fickle (Low super-ego)
H	VENTURESOME, bold, uninhibited, spontaneous, genial (Parmia)	SHY, timid, withdrawn, aloof (Threctia)
I	TENDER-MINDED, immature, sentimental, dependent, demanding, impatient (Premsia)	TOUGH-MINDED, realistic, mature, self-sufficient, hard (Harria)
L	SUSPICIOUS, skeptical, wary, hard to fool, jealous (Protension)	TRUSTING, understanding, composed, gullible, credulous (Alaxia)
M	IMAGINATIVE, eccentric, absorbed, absent-minded (Autia)	PRACTICAL, careful, conventional, conscientious, logical (Praxernia)
N	SHREWD, calculating, worldly, expedient, astute (Shrewdness)	FORTHRIGHT, unpretentious, natural, naive, spontaneous (Artlessness)
O	APPREHENSIVE, worrying, troubled, moody, depressed (Guilt-proneness)	PLACID, self-assured, confident, serene, cheerful, resilient (Assurance)
Q1	EXPERIMENTING, liberal, freethinking (Radicalism)	CONSERVATIVE, traditional, conventional (Conservatism)
Q2	SELF-SUFFICIENT, resourceful, self-reliant, independent (Self-sufficiency)	GROUP-TIED, joiner, follower, dependent (Group adherence)
Q3	CONTROLLED, compulsive, self-disciplined (High self-concept)	CASUAL, lax, impulsive, careless (Low integration)
Q4	TENSE, frustrated, driven, overwrought (Ergic tension)	RELAXED, tranquil, composed, unworried (Low ergic tension)

*Labels in parentheses are the technical labels for the traits.
Source: Based in part on Cattell, 1965.

changeable. On the basis of extensive research of this kind, Cattell concluded that just 16 traits account for the complexity of human personality (see Table 12-1). However, not all trait theorists would agree with Cattell's list. In fact, Cattell himself later suggested it might be necessary to add 7 more traits to the original list of 16 (Cattell & Kline, 1977).

Hans Eysenck, a British psychologist, has proposed that all these traits can be collapsed into just two major dimensions of personality: introverted-extroverted and stable-unstable (Eysenck, 1970). Extroverts tend to be sociable, like parties, have many friends, and act impulsively, while introverts are quiet, introspective, shy, self-controlled, and careful. Stable people tend to be calm, steady, and relatively unresponsive to stimulation; unstable people are anxious, emotional, and tend to react strongly to stimulation.

Despite the apparent differences between Cattell and Eysenck, their views of personality are in many ways similar. For example, Eysenck's dimension of introverted-extroverted seems to include a number of Cattell's traits such as reserved, shy, self-sufficient, and controlled. Moreover, both Cattell and Eysenck believe that these traits lead to relatively consistent behavior patterns that the person is likely to show in a wide range of situations.

Using the trait perspective, we can gain some insight into Jaylene's personality. In terms of Eysenck's model, Jay would be described as somewhat introverted and unstable. Using Cattell's trait list for greater detail, we might conclude that Jay is intelligent (B+), assertive (E+), conscientious (G+), tough-minded (I−), and self-sufficient (Q2+). But she also seems somewhat emotionally unstable (C−), apprehensive (O+), and shy (H−). You can find evidence for these traits in the following additional material from Jay's profile:

According to Hans Eysenck, extroverts tend to be sociable, like parties, have many friends, and act impulsively.

Jay's first brother, born when she was 2 years old, was for some time a threat and a source of irritation to Jay, though she does not remember too clearly the details of their early relationship. Her parents recall that Jay would become angry and have temper tantrums when the new infant demanded and received much attention (especially from Mrs. Smith), while she herself now received relatively little—except on those occasions when, to her parents' dismay, she stubbornly refused to cooperate in her bowel training. The temper tantrums intensified when Jay's second brother was born just 1 year after the first. As time went on, the brothers seemed to form an alliance to undermine Jay's supreme position with their father. Jay, in turn, frequently fought with her brothers, usually verbally, though sometimes physically, to keep her status and to protect herself. In the process, she became closer to her father. Besides the mutual feelings of tenderness that bond most siblings, greater than average jealousy and rivalry characterized Jay's relationship with her younger brothers from early childhood to the present.

Jay's father is a rather quiet and gentle person who married when he was 35 years old. Although an excellent diagnostician, he decided to pursue medical research rather than enter private practice. Since his work often allowed him to study at home, he had extensive contact with his children, especially when they were young. His ambitions and goals for Jay were extremely high, and as she matured, he responded to her every need and demand almost immediately and with full conviction. Mrs.

Smith, who was 30 years old when she married, worked long hours away from home as a store manager and consequently saw her children primarily at nights and on an occasionally free weekend. Tired when she was with her family, she had little energy for "nonessential" interactions and devoted what efforts she could to feeding the children (especially the younger ones) and to making certain the house was in order. Because Dr. Smith was home frequently, he helped with these chores, but the major responsibility fell on Mrs. Smith's shoulders. Dr. and Mrs. Smith have had a "comfortable" relationship, though their interactions have occasionally been marred by intense stormy outbursts over seemingly trivial matters. These episodes are always followed by periods of mutual silence lasting for days at a time.

Two representative incidents regarding Jay and various boyfriends are worth noting. She often has an explosive fit of anger that terminates an important relationship. Her disposition in most other circumstances, though, is even-tempered, some would say inhibited. Interestingly, too, her relationships with other women, although more stable than those with men, are usually casual, uncommitted, and of short duration.

When Jay was 13, she became good friends with a male classmate, Mark. They had many hours of conversation, though Jay never was able "to be herself" and really express her feelings. The relationship continued to blossom until one fatal day when a low-keyed disagreement about the next weekend's activities suddenly erupted into a major altercation. After labeling Mark with a few choice epithets of the kind usually reserved for locker-room encounters, Jay ran away and tearfully professed that she did not want to see him again. Despite Mark's persistent efforts to talk with her and despite sharing some classes in school, Jay refused ever to have anything to do with her former friend.

Much later, while finishing her undergraduate education, Jay met Ted, a graduate student some 15 years older than herself. At 21, Jay felt she was falling in love again, but this time it was the "real" thing. Unfortunately, their relationship had existed for only about 2 months when disaster struck. Although Jay and Ted were close and trusted one another (though, again, Jay was inhibited in the relationship), an innocent conversation between Ted and a female classmate triggered Jay's rage. As Jay was walking across the campus, she spotted Ted and his acquaintance having a lively conversation and enjoying a laugh or two. As Ted turned his head, he caught a glimpse of Jay. He immediately called to her and asked her to come over and meet his friend. Jay turned quickly and hurried away. When Ted finally caught up with her, she screamed angrily in his face that she never wanted to see him again. And she never did. (adapted from Lazarus & Monat, 1979, pp. 216–218).

At this point we have a fairly good idea of "what Jay is like as a person"—her personality. But how did she get that way? How did Jay come to be so emotionally unstable in her relationships with men? And why is she so reserved around people in general? Trait theorists have been criticized for paying relatively little attention to this question of how personality traits develop (Phares, 1984; Pervin, 1984). Some would suggest that Jay inherited her traits from her parents. Others would look for ways in which she modeled herself after other people, or was rewarded for thinking and acting in certain ways. Let's look at these possibilities.

Does heredity have a hand in the development of personality? A growing body of research suggests that indeed it does. Comparative studies of identical and fraternal twins have shown that identical twins, who share exactly the same genetic material, are much more similar to one another than are fraternal twins on such personality characteristics as emotionality, activity, sociability, and impulsiveness. Thus, if one twin cries easily (a sign of emotionality), his identical twin brother is five times more likely than a fraternal twin to cry easily too. Similarly, if one twin

Androgyny

The concept of *androgyny,* meaning the fusion of male and female sides in one nature, is popular today largely because the women's movement has focused attention on what it means to be feminine—and thus also masculine—in our society.

Psychologists, too, have become interested in sex typing and androgyny. To measure how masculine, feminine, or androgynous a person is, Sandra Lipsitz Bem (1974, 1977) designed the Bem Sex Role Inventory (BSRI), which is made up of a list of 60 personality characteristics. It includes 20 traits that our society considers "masculine" (ambition, self-reliance, assertiveness); 20 traits that are considered "feminine" (affection, gentleness, understanding); and 20 traits that are neutral (honesty, friendliness, amiability). Bem arrived at this list after studying how a group of undergraduates rated the desirability of various traits for each sex. On the test, people describe themselves on each of these traits using a scale of 1 (never or almost never true) to 7 (always or almost always true). The difference between the total points assigned to masculine and feminine adjectives tells us how sex-typed a person is. If someone has approximately equal masculine and feminine scores, that person is considered to be androgynous.

Bem and her colleagues tested more than 1,500 undergraduates and found that half of them stuck with the "appropriate" sex role, 15 percent identified with the opposite sex, and about 30 percent were androgynous. Bem then went on to see whether androgynous people are actually more adaptable. She tested students for independence—a typically "masculine" trait—and conformity—a typically "feminine" trait. Students came to a lab for what they thought was an experiment on humor. Each person sat in a booth equipped with earphones and a microphone and

watched cartoons that had already been rated according to how funny they were. As each cartoon appeared on the screen, students heard the experimenter ask each student in turn to rate the film. Actually, what the students were hearing was a preprogrammed tape on which people claimed that funny cartoons were not funny, and vice versa. "Feminine" women found it much harder to be assertive and to resist conforming to these opinions than "masculine" men or androgynous students.

Other researchers have found connections between androgyny and personal adjustment. Androgynous people tend to feel happier and to tolerate stress better than subjects who conform to traditional sex roles (Shaw, 1982). Androgynous people also tend to be seen by others as well adjusted (Major, Carnevale, & Deaux, 1981). Finally, Heilbrun (1981) found that among women, androgyny is associated with higher self-esteem.

Despite the groundswell of enthusiasm for androgyny, the concept has encountered some pointed criticism. First, not all research shows that androgynous people are better adjusted. In one study in which subjects were given the BSRI and a battery of other tests, the better-adjusted individuals of both sexes had high masculinity scores (Jones, Chernovertz, & Hansson, 1978). Moreover, in every society in the world the behavioral patterns prescribed for women differ from those ordained for men. Critics have argued that the ideal of androgyny ignores a fundamental principle of social organization. We are born with a sex, and this biological status inevitably affects the way others behave toward us and the way we see ourselves and the world. According to these critics, to believe that a lifetime of socialization can be shed and androgyny adopted at will is naive (Locksley & Colten, 1979).

cannot sit still long (a sign of activity), an identical twin brother is three times more likely than a fraternal twin brother to act in the same way (Buss, Plomin, & Willerman, 1973).

Since emotionality and activity are part of Eysenck's dimension of stable-unstable, it should come as no surprise that Eysenck also concludes that more than half of the variation among people in emotional stability can be explained genetically. Moreover, whether a person is more introverted or extroverted also seems to be powerfully influenced by genetics (Henderson, 1982). However, there is no firm evidence that specific traits such as assertiveness or reliability or optimism are inherited. A person who inherits a tendency to be extroverted may be inclined to be impulsive, active, sociable, and talkative, but experience plays an important role in the development of these specific personality characteristics. Similarly, a person who inherits a tendency to be emotionally reactive may or may not be anxious or moody or restless or aggressive, depending on his or her experiences.

In Jaylene's case, for example, it is possible that she inherited tendencies toward introversion and emotional instability. But her experience in dealing with other people, including her brothers and her parents, probably had a great deal to do with making her less stable in her relationships with men than with women, more insecure and anxious than restless or excitable, and more self-sufficient and suspicious than reserved and aloof. At this point we turn to a discussion of how specific personality traits such as these can be shaped by experience.

Acquiring Personality Traits

As you may recall from Chapter 6, the frequency with which a behavior occurs can be increased by using *reinforcement*. For example, if someone is rewarded for doing well on a test, or if doing well removes the threat of punishment, that person is more likely to try to do well on tests in the future. On the other hand, *punishment* will reduce the likelihood that a behavior will occur again in the future. If a behavior is followed by neither reinforcement nor punishment, it is also likely to disappear (this process is called *extinction*).

Some personality theorists believe that these basic learning processes account for the development of personality characteristics. For instance, if a child's outgoing behavior is reinforced, the child will be more likely to act in an outgoing way in the future. If, in addition, shy, unsociable behavior is punished or at least ignored, the child will be even more likely to become outgoing. A large number of personality characteristics might be learned in this fashion.

Lazarus and Monat (1979) suggested, for example, that Jaylene may have learned to be shy and somewhat introverted because she was rewarded for spending time by herself studying. It is possible that her father rewarded her for devoting herself to her studies. Certainly she earned the respect of her teachers, and long hours of studying helped her avoid the somewhat uncomfortable feelings she experienced when she was around other people. Reinforcement may have shaped other parts of Jay's personality as well. It seems likely that her father and her teachers helped form her trait of self-discipline and her need to achieve in school through a

Some personality theorists feel this girl may learn to behave aggressively if she finds it is a successful response to her brother's teasing.

Trait Theory Versus the Situationist Perspective

A central assumption of trait theory is that in a given situation a person will consistently act the same way. What accounts for this predictability, say the trait theorists, is the presence of stable personality traits.

Since the late 1960s this view has come in for some forceful criticism. In 1968 psychologist Walter Mischel determined that studies showed some, but not much, stability of behavior from one situation to the next. His conclusion, therefore, was that personality traits do not exist. Environmental factors, Mischel proposed, are generally much stronger influences on behavior than personality variables. To the extent that behavior is consistent, it is because familiar features of a situation consistently elicit the same behavior (Phares, 1984). This opposing view to trait theory has come to be called the *situationist perspective.*

Suppose, for example, we found that Jaylene, the young doctor whose profile is presented in this chapter, consistently keeps herself apart from others or seems ill at ease during social situations of all kinds. Trait theorists would have little hesitation in describing her as shy. Situationists, however, would argue that the consistency in her be-havior is in fact minimal. They would say that Jay only seems shy to observers because we all tend to overestimate the consistency of other people's behavior and to ignore actions that do not square with our image of a person. Moreover, it is possible that Jay seems shy because she interacts with others in a limited number of settings, each of which reinforces her awkwardness and insecurity. In fact, according to situationists, most people are shy in some situations (e.g., parties where most of the guests are strangers, or with people one doesn't know well) and not in others (Lazarus & Monat, 1979).

A resolution of the trait/situationist conflict is gradually evolving. Most psychologists would agree that situations obviously make a difference in how people behave; nonetheless there is a certain amount of continuity in individual behavior. Even Mischel (1979) now concludes that there are consistencies in people's cognitive styles—in such things as their intelligence, approach to problems, expectancies, and value systems. While he does not refer to such cognitive styles as traits, he does feel that they lend a certain stability to the way people behave in various situations.

---

series of reinforcements. Even her aggression toward men may have been learned as a successful response to her brothers' teasing. If her hostility put an end to their taunts and was also rewarded by her father's affection, she may have learned to react with aggression to threats not only from her brothers but also from men in general.

In Chapter 6 we saw that people can also learn simply by observing what other people do and how they are rewarded or punished for that behavior. In order to learn to do something, the observer need not be reinforced. Simply watching is enough. The more rewarding or nurturing the model, the more powerful it is; and the more similar the model is to the observer, the more likely it is that learning will occur (Bandura, 1977). For children, it is their parents who generally best fit these criteria. For this reason, parents are the models who most influence their children's personalities.

In Jaylene's case, it is likely that at least some aspects of her personality were learned by observing her parents and brothers. Her aggressive behavior with boyfriends, for example, may have grown out of watching her parents fight. As a young child she may have observed that some people effectively deal with conflict by means of outbursts. Moreover, Jay surely noticed that her father, a "successful medical researcher," enjoyed and prospered in both his career and his family life, while her mother's two jobs as housewife and store manager left her somewhat frustrated and overtired. This contrast may have contributed in part to Jay's own inter-

Unconscious In Freud's theory, all the ideas, thoughts, and feelings of which we are not and cannot normally become aware.

Psychoanalysis Both Freud's personality theory and his form of therapy.

est in medicine and to her mixed feelings about the desirability of having a close relationship that might result in marriage.

We have seen how Jay could have learned to think and act in certain ways rather than others. But not all personality psychologists would agree that genes, operant conditioning, and social learning are the whole story. Jay herself cannot fully understand why she feels and acts as she does. Remember, she said, "What is wrong? Why can't I ever maintain a serious relationship for any length of time?" You too may suspect that there are "deeper" reasons for her insecurity, her explosive fits of anger, and her fear of people. These kinds of concerns are the mark of psychodynamic personality theorists, to whom we now turn.

Psychodynamic Theories

Life instincts In Freud's theory of personality, all those instincts involved in the survival of the individual and the species, including hunger, self-preservation, and sex.

Death instincts In Freud's theory of personality, the group of instincts that lead toward aggression, destruction, and death.

Id In Freud's theory of personality, the collection of unconscious urges and desires that continually seek expression.

Sigmund Freud

To this day, Sigmund Freud is the best known and most influential personality theorist. Freud opened up a whole new route for the study of human behavior. Up to his time, psychology had focused on consciousness, that is, those thoughts and feelings of which we are aware. Freud, however, stressed the **unconscious**—all the ideas, thoughts, and feelings of which we are not normally aware. Although many of his views were modified by later research (actually, Freud himself revised and expanded his theories throughout his life), his ideas are still the basis of **psychoanalysis** and they influence our language, literature, customs, and child-rearing practices.

BASIC CONCEPTS. According to Freud, the basis of human behavior is to be found in various unconscious instincts, or drives. He distinguished two classes of instincts: **life instincts** and **death instincts.** Relatively little is known about the death instincts, which show up as self-destructive or suicidal tendencies when directed toward the self, and as aggression or war when directed toward others. Under life instincts Freud included all those instincts involved in the survival of the individual and of the species: hunger, thirst, self-preservation, and especially sex. It is important to note that Freud used the term *sexual instinct* to refer not just to erotic sexuality but also to a desire for virtually any form of pleasure. In this broad sense, Freud regarded the sexual instinct as the most critical factor in the development of personality.

The life and death instincts are part of what Freud called the **id** (see

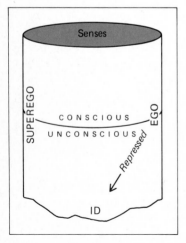

Figure 12-1

Diagram of the structural relationship formed by the id, ego, and superego. The ego is partly unconscious, partly conscious, and derives knowledge of the external world through the senses. The superego is also partly conscious and partly unconscious. But the id is entirely unconscious. The open space beneath the id indicates the limitlessness of the unconscious id. (After Freud, 1966)

Figure 12-1). The id is like a "seething cauldron" of unconscious urges and desires that are continually seeking expression. The id operates according to the **pleasure principle:** It tries to obtain immediate gratification and thus to pursue pleasure and avoid pain. Just as soon as an instinct arises, the id seeks to gratify it. But since the id is not in contact with the real world, it has just two ways of obtaining gratification. One is by reflex actions, such as coughing, which relieves an unpleasant sensation at once. Another is by what Freud termed *wish fulfillment*, or **primary-process thinking:** A person forms a mental image of an object or situation that partially satisfies the instinct and relieves the uncomfortable feeling. Primary-process thought is most clearly evident in dreams and daydreams, but it can occur in other ways. If you are angered by someone and spend the next half hour imagining all the brilliant things you might have said or done to get even, then you are engaging in a form of primary-process thinking.

Mental images of this kind can provide fleeting relief; however, they are not very effective in fully satisfying most needs. Just thinking about being with someone you love can be gratifying, but it is a poor substitute for actually being with that person! Therefore the id by itself is not very effective in gratifying instincts. It must ultimately have contact with reality if it is to relieve its discomfort. The id's link to reality is the ego.

Freud thought that the **ego** controls all thinking and reasoning activities. Through the senses, the ego learns about the external world. The ego also controls the ways of satisfying the id's drives in the external world. We noted earlier that in seeking to replace discomfort with comfort, the id acts according to the pleasure principle. In contrast, the ego operates by the **reality principle.** That is, it protects the person against dangers that might result from the indiscriminate satisfaction of the cravings of the id. By intelligent reasoning, the ego tries to delay appeasing the id's desires until it can satisfy those desires safely and successfully. For example, if you are thirsty, your ego will attempt to determine how best to obtain something to quench your thirst effectively and safely. Freud called this type of realistic thinking **secondary-process thinking.**

A personality consisting only of ego and id would be completely selfish. It would behave effectively, but unsocially. Fully adult behavior is governed by reality but also by morality, that is, by one's conscience or the moral standards people develop through interacting with their parents and society. Freud called this moral guardian the **superego.**

The superego is not present in a child at birth. As young children we are amoral and do whatever is pleasurable. As we mature, we assimilate, or adopt as our own, the judgments of our parents about what is "good" and "bad." In time, the external restraint applied by our parents is replaced by our own internal self-restraint. The superego, then, acting as conscience, takes over the task of observing and guiding the ego, just as the parents observe and guide the child.

According to Freud, the superego also compares the ego's actions with an **ego ideal** of perfection and then rewards or punishes the ego accordingly. Unfortunately, the superego may be too harsh in its judgments. Dominated by such a punishing superego, an artist, for example, realizing the impossibility of equaling Rembrandt or Michelangelo, may just give up painting.

Ideally, the id, ego, and superego work in harmony. The ego satisfies

Pleasure principle According to Freud, the way in which the id seeks immediate gratification of an instinct.

Primary-process thinking In Freud's theory, the process by which the id achieves immediate partial satisfaction of an instinct through mental images such as dreams and daydreams.

Ego According to Freud, the part of the personality that mediates between environmental demands (reality), conscience (superego), and instinctual needs (id); now often used as a synonym for "self."

Reality principle According to Freud, satisfaction of instincts safely and effectively in the real world; characteristic of the ego.

Secondary-process thinking In Freud's theory, the process by which the ego uses intelligent reasoning to find safe and effective ways to gratify id instincts in the real world.

Superego According to Freud, the social and parental standards the individual has internalized; the conscience and the ego ideal.

Ego ideal That part of the superego that consists of standards of what one would like to be.

"All right, deep down it's a cry for psychiatric help—but at one level it's a stick-up."

Libido According to Freud, the energy generated by the sexual instinct.

Fixation According to Freud, a partial or complete halt at some point in a person's psychosexual development.

Oral stage First stage in Freud's theory of personality development, in which the infant's erotic feelings center on the mouth, lips, and tongue.

Anal stage Second stage in Freud's theory of personality development, when a child's erotic feelings center on the anus and on elimination.

"Who needs a superego with 'Him' around?"

the demands of the id in a reasonable, moral manner approved by the superego. We are then free to love and to hate, and to express our emotions sensibly without guilt. When our id is dominant, our instincts are unbridled and we are apt to be a danger to ourselves and to society. When our superego dominates, our behavior is checked too tightly and we cannot enjoy a normal life.

PSYCHOSEXUAL STAGES. Freud's theory of personality development gives center stage to the way in which the sexual instinct is satisfied during the course of life. Recall that Freud thought of the sexual instinct not just as a desire for sexual activity, but in broader terms as a craving for sensual pleasure of all kinds. The energy from the sexual instinct he termed **libido.** As infants mature, their libido becomes focused on different sensitive parts of the body. During the first 1½ years of life, the dominant source of sensual pleasure for the child is the mouth. At about 18 months sensuality shifts to the anus, and at about age 3 it shifts again, this time to the genitals. The child's experience at each stage stamps his or her personality with tendencies that endure into adulthood. If for some reason the child is deprived of pleasure from the part of the body that dominates a stage, or if the child is allowed too much gratification, then it is possible that some sexual energy will remain tied to that part of the body more or less permanently. This is called **fixation,** and as we will see, it can lead to immature forms of sexuality and to certain characteristic personality traits. Let's look more closely at the psychosexual stages that Freud identified and their relationship to personality development.

During the **oral stage** (birth to 18 months) the infant derives most of its sensual pleasure from its mouth, lips, and tongue. Moreover, the child depends completely on other people to satisfy its needs. According to Freud, in the early portion of the oral stage the child relieves sexual tension by sucking and swallowing, and feels frustrated when it cannot do so. By about 8 months of age, when most children have developed some baby teeth, oral pleasure can also be obtained by chewing and biting.

According to Freud, a child's experience during the oral stage can have a profound effect on later personality. Infants given too much oral gratification may become both overly optimistic and extremely dependent on other people to meet their needs. However, if infants receive too little oral gratification, they may become pessimistic and respond with hostility when frustrated in later life. Lack of confidence, gullibility, sarcasm, and argumentativeness are also personality traits that Freud attributed to fixation at the oral stage.

With the onset of the **anal stage** (roughly 18 months to 3½ years), the primary source of sexual pleasure shifts from the mouth to the anus, although oral stimulation continues to provide some pleasure. Just about the time children begin to derive pleasure from holding in and excreting feces, toilet training takes place, and they must learn to regulate the new pleasure. Here again, if the parents are too strict or too lenient, the child may become fixated at the anal stage. For example, if parents are too rigid about toilet training, some children will show temper tantrums and later in life be messy and destructive. Other children will respond by retaining feces even to the point of constipation; later in life these children are likely to be obstinate, stingy, overly precise, and excessively orderly.

During the **phallic stage** (after the age of 3 or so) children discover their genitals and the pleasure of masturbation. It is at this time that the child develops a marked attachment for the parent of the opposite sex and becomes jealous of the parent of the same sex. Freud called this the **Oedipal conflict.** In Greek mythology, Oedipus killed his father and married his mother; he is thus a model for boys, who, Freud believed, sexually desire their mothers and would like to kill their fathers for blocking their goal. Because our society prevents children from killing their fathers, the boy has no choice but to repress these unacceptable impulses. Moreover, he is afraid that his father knows what he is thinking and is going to punish him. The result is that the boy is attracted to but repelled by his mother, and afraid of but violently jealous of his father. Freud believed that girls go through a corresponding conflict involving love for their fathers and jealousy toward their mothers.

Most children eventually resolve the Oedipal conflict by identifying with the parent of the same sex. But once again, excessive frustration or gratification at this stage can result in fixation at the phallic stage. According to Freud, one possible result of fixation at this stage is vanity and egotism. Men often express these characteristics by taking great pride in their sexual prowess and treating women with contempt. Women are more likely to become flirtatious and promiscuous. However, Freud suggested that phallic fixation can also lead to low self-esteem, a feeling of worthlessness, shyness, and an avoidance of heterosexual relationships.

At the end of the phallic period, Freud believed, children lose interest in sexual behavior and enter a **latency period.** Beginning around the age of 5 or 6 and lasting until children are 12 or 13, boys play with boys, girls play with girls, and neither sex takes much interest in the other.

At puberty we enter the last psychosexual stage, which Freud called the **genital stage.** At this time our sexual impulses reawaken. Now, however, they are directed toward members of the opposite sex. In lovemaking, the adolescent and the adult can satisfy unfulfilled desires from infancy and childhood. Ideally, immediate gratification of these desires is replaced by mature sexuality, in which postponed gratification, responsibility, and caring for others all play a part.

Unfortunately, many of Freud's concepts are difficult to translate into experimental terms, but his theory has received some limited confirmation from research. For example, people who eat and drink too much tend to mention oral images when interpreting inkblot tests (Masling, Robie, & Blondheim, 1967; Bertrand & Masling, 1969). Orally fixated subjects also seem to depend heavily on others, as Freud predicted (Fisher & Greenberg, 1977). Some evidence suggests that a few of the traits of the anally fixated personality also tend to appear together. For instance, individuals who are stingy are also likely to be neat (Fisher & Greenberg, 1977). However, there is no strong research evidence that these various personality characteristics stem from the kinds of early-childhood experiences described by Freud.

Returning to the case of Jaylene Smith, it is not possible in a brief space to delve into all the aspects of her personality that would be of interest to a Freudian psychologist. However, had Freud been Jay's therapist, one of the first things he would have noticed is the close correspondence between her description of herself and the set of phallic personality traits. Words such as "insecure, introverted, inadequate, dull,

Phallic stage Third stage in Freud's theory of personality development, when erotic feelings center on the genitals.

Oedipal conflict According to Freud, a child's sexual attachment to the parent of the opposite sex and jealousy toward the parent of the same sex.

Latency period In Freud's theory of personality, a period after the phallic stage in which the child appears to have no interest in the opposite sex.

Genital stage In Freud's theory of personality development, the final stage of normal adult sexual development.

unhappy, lonely, depressed" correspond closely to traits associated with the phallic personality. Working from this start, Freud would have expected to find corresponding difficulty in dealing with heterosexuality, perhaps avoidance of heterosexual relationships altogether. Jay, of course, is very much aware that she has problems relating to men, at least when these relationships get "serious," though she has not attributed her problems to conflicts over sexuality.

Freud would also have expected to find that Jay's relationship to her father was either very distant and unsatisfying, or unusually close and gratifying. We know that it was, in fact, the latter. But if Freud is correct, at around age 5 or 6 Jay undoubtedly became aware that she could not actually marry her father and do away with her mother, as Freud would say she wished to do. We have no information about this, but it is interesting that the arguments and fights between Jay and her mother subsided when Jay was "about 6 or 7 years of age." Moreover, we know that shortly thereafter, Jay began to experience "strong feelings of loneliness, depression, insecurity, and confusion." Clearly something important happened in Jay's life when she was 6 or 7, though we can only speculate about what it was.

The continued coolness in Jay's relationship with her mother and the closeness with her father also suggest that Jay has not satisfactorily resolved the Oedipal conflict, that she is still working it through at an unconscious level, and that as a result she is unable to make the progression into mature sexuality. In short, while Jay has given up her father as a prospective sexual partner, she has been unable to break free of the rest of her Oedipal feelings toward him and move on to mature relationships with other men.

Freud's beliefs, particularly his emphasis on sexuality, were not fully accepted even by some of his students. Carl Jung and Alfred Adler were two early followers of Freud who later broke with him and formulated their own psychodynamic theories of personality. But in recent years the most prominent of the neo-Freudians has been Erik Erikson.

Erik Erikson

Erik Erikson, who studied with Freud in Vienna, takes a more social view of personality development and stresses the workings of the ego more than Freud did. While he agrees with many aspects of Freud's theory of sexual development, Erikson believes that this is only part of the story. For Erikson, the quality of parent-child relationships is what counts. A child can be disciplined in a way that leaves a feeling of being loved or in a way that leaves the child feeling hated. The difference is largely in the atmosphere of the home. The important point is that children should feel that their own needs and desires are compatible with those of society. Only if children feel competent and valuable, in their own and society's eyes, will they develop a sense of identity. This, in Erikson's view, is crucial.

In contrast to Freud's emphasis on childhood years, Erikson feels that personality continues to develop throughout life. He outlined "eight ages of man," and suggested that success in each stage depends on a person's adjustments in previous stages (Erikson, 1963) (see Figure 12-2).

1. *Trust versus mistrust.* During the first year of life babies are torn between trusting and not trusting their parents. If needs are generally met, the infant comes to trust the environment and himself or herself. The result is faith in the predictability of the environment and optimism about the future. The frustrated infant becomes suspicious, fearful, and overly concerned with security.

2. *Autonomy versus shame and doubt.* During their first 3 years children's growing physical development allows them increasing autonomy and greater contact with their surroundings. They learn to walk, hold on to things, and control their excretory functions. If the child repeatedly fails in trying to master these skills, self-doubt may grow. One response to self-doubt is the practice of abiding compulsively by fixed routines. At the other extreme is hostile rejection of all controls, both internal and external. If parents and other adults belittle a child's efforts, he or she may also begin to feel shame and acquire a lasting sense of inferiority.

3. *Initiative versus guilt.* Between the ages of 3 and 6 children continue to develop their motor skills; efforts at autonomy become more efficient and goal-directed. If the child is unable to acquire a sense of initiative, strong feelings of guilt, unworthiness, and resentment may persist.

4. *Industry versus inferiority.* During the next 6 or 7 years children encounter a new set of expectations at home and at school. Children must learn the skills needed to become fully functioning adults, including personal care, productive work, and independent social living. If children are stifled in their efforts to become a part of the adult world, they may conclude that they are inadequate, mediocre, or inferior and lose faith in their power to become industrious.

Erik Erikson

5. *Identity versus role confusion.* At puberty, childhood ends and the responsibilities of adulthood loom large. The critical problem of this stage is to find one's identity. In Erikson's view, identity is achieved by integrating a number of roles—student, sister or brother, friend, and so on—into a coherent pattern that provides a sense of inner continuity or identity. Failure to forge an identity leads to role confusion and despair.

6. *Intimacy versus isolation.* During young adulthood men and women must resolve a new critical issue—becoming intimate with a member of the opposite sex. Marriage is usually the form this attempt ultimately takes. To love someone else, Erikson argues, we must have resolved our earlier crises successfully and feel secure in our identities. To form an intimate relationship, lovers must be trusting, autonomous, capable of initiative, and show other marks of maturity. Failure at intimacy carries with it painful loneliness and a sense of being incomplete.

7. *Generativity versus stagnation.* During middle adulthood, roughly between ages 25 and 60, the challenge is to remain productive and creative in all parts of one's life. People who have successfully navigated the six earlier stages are likely to find meaning and joy in all the activities of life—career, family, community participation. For others, life becomes a drab routine, and they feel dulled and resentful.

8. *Integrity versus despair.* With the onset of old age, everyone must try to come to terms with the approach of death. For some, this is a period of despair at the loss of former roles, such as employee, parent, Little League coach, den mother, and so forth. Yet, according to Erikson, this stage also represents an opportunity to attain full selfhood. By this Erickson means acceptance of one's life, a sense that it is complete and satisfactory. People who have gained full maturity by resolving earlier stages successfully possess the integrity to face death with a minimum of fear.

Relatively little of Erikson's theory has been verified by research. Nevertheless, some aspects of Erikson's theory have been studied. The concept of identity resolution has probably attracted the most attention. Waterman, Beubel, and Waterman (1970) investigated whether people who were successful in handling the crises of the first four stages were more likely to achieve a stable source of identity in the fifth stage. Their data suggest that this is indeed the case. While resolution of earlier crises may not be essential for ego identity, it does seem to be important.

Other research has examined the link between the formation of identity in Stage 5 and the achievement of intimacy in Stage 6. Is it necessary to achieve identity in order to achieve intimacy? The answer, again, seems to be yes. Orlofsky, Marcia, and Lesser (1973) found that the college men who were the least isolated socially were also those with the clearest sense of self. In a follow-up study of the same group of college men, Marcia (1976) observed that identity was still related to intimacy: Achieving a sense of personal identity apparently does make it possible

Figure 12-2

Erikson's 8 stages of personality development. Each stage involves its own developmental crisis, whose resolution is important to adjustment in successive stages. (Adapted from Erikson, 1950)

Stage	1	2	3	4	5	6	7	8
Oral	Basic trust vs. mistrust							
Anal		Autonomy vs. shame, doubt						
Genital			Initiative vs. guilt					
Latency				Industry vs. inferiority				
Puberty and adolescence					Identity vs. role confusion			
Young adulthood						Intimacy vs. isolation		
Adulthood							Generativity vs. stagnation	
Maturity								Ego integrity vs. despair

to have successful personal relationships. A more recent study also found that the relationships between identity and intimacy are quite similar for both sexes. Both men and women believe that a positive sense of identity is the basis for satisfying personal relationships (Orlofsky, 1978).

What does Erikson's theory tell us about Jaylene Smith's personality? Recall that one's success in dealing with later developmental crises depends on how effectively one has resolved earlier crises. The fact that Jay is having great difficulty in dealing with intimacy (Stage 6) suggests that she is still struggling with problems from earlier developmental stages. A loving relationship requires trust, autonomy, initiative, a sense of industry, and a sense of identity (Stages 1–5). But Jay is somewhat suspicious and insecure, she expresses a good deal of self-doubt, to some extent she feels unworthy ("I don't deserve to be a doctor"), she describes herself as "inadequate" and "dull," and she is still trying to work out a clear sense of her own identity: "Who am I and what do I want from life?"

Erikson would look for the source of these problems in the quality of Jay's relationships with others. We know that her mother "subtly" communicated her own frustration and dissatisfaction to her children and spent little time on "nonessential" interactions with them. These feelings and behavior patterns would be unlikely to result in the kind of basic trust and sense of security that Erikson believes are essential to the first stage of development. In turn, Jay's failure to establish basic trust would be expected to make future development more difficult. In addition, her relationship with her mother and brothers continued to be less than fully satisfactory. It is not surprising, then, that Jay had some difficulty working through subsequent developmental crises. Though her father certainly provided a close and caring relationship, Jay was surely aware that in part his affection depended on her fulfilling the dreams, ambitions, and goals he had for her. As we will see in the next section, this kind of "conditional love" can have significant effects on the development of personality.

A Humanistic Personality Theory

Thus far we have looked at two important viewpoints that psychologists have on personality. On the one hand, personality may reflect a person's traits, both inherited and learned; on the other, it may reflect the resolution of unconscious conflicts and developmental crises. Humanistic psychologists find neither of these viewpoints fully satisfactory. As we saw in Chapter 1, humanistic psychologists believe that life is a continuing process of striving to realize our potential, of opening ourselves to the world around us and experiencing joy in living. One influential theorist who represents this point of view is Carl Rogers.

According to Rogers, every organism is born with certain capacities, capabilities, or potentialities. Maddi (1980) has described these capacities as a "sort of genetic blueprint, to which form and substance [are] added as life progresses" (p. 93). The goal of life, according to Rogers, is to fulfill this genetic blueprint, to become whatever it is each of us is

Actualizing tendency According to Rogers, the drive of every organism to fulfill its biological potential and become what it is inherently capable of becoming.

Self-actualizing tendency According to Rogers, the drive of human beings to fulfill their self-concepts, or the images they have formed of themselves.

Fully functioning persons According to Rogers, individuals whose self-concepts closely resemble their inborn capacities or potentialities.

Unconditional positive regard The acceptance and love for another person regardless of that person's behavior.

Conditional positive regard The. acceptance and love for another person that depends upon that person's behavior.

inherently capable of becoming. Rogers calls this biological push toward fulfillment the **actualizing tendency.** It is worth noting that Rogers believes that the actualizing tendency characterizes all organisms—plants, animals, and humans. But in the course of life, human beings also form images of themselves, or self-concepts. Just as we try to fulfill our inborn biological potential, so, too, do we attempt to fulfill our self-concepts, our conscious sense of who we are and what we want to do. Rogers calls this striving the **self-actualizing tendency.** If you think of yourself as "intelligent," for example, you will strive to live up to that particular image of yourself. If another of your self-concepts is "athlete," you will attempt to fulfill that image as well.

When an individual's self-concept is relatively closely matched with his or her inborn capacities, then that person is likely to become what Rogers calls a **fully functioning person.** Such people are self-directed; they decide for themselves what it is they wish to do and to become, even though their choices may not always be sound ones. They are not unduly swayed by what other people think they ought to be or expect them to become. Fully functioning people are also open to experience—their own feelings as well as the world and other people around them—and thus find themselves "increasingly willing to be, with greater accuracy and depth, that self which [they] most truly [are]" (Rogers, 1961, pp. 175–176).

According to Rogers, people are likely to become more fully functioning if they are brought up with **unconditional positive regard.** This means that they feel themselves valued by others regardless of their feelings, attitudes, and behaviors. The warmth, respect, acceptance, and love they receive from others is "unconditional."

But oftentimes parents and others offer what Rogers calls **conditional positive regard.** This means that only certain aspects of an individual are valued and accepted. The acceptance, warmth, and love a person receives from others depends upon behaving in certain ways and fulfilling certain conditions. This can be very blatant, such as "Daddy won't love you if . . ." or "Mommy doesn't love girls who . . ." But it can also be expressed subtly; for example: "That's a nice idea, but wouldn't you really rather do . . .?" The message here is twofold: The other person finds your feelings or behaviors questionable and proposes alternatives he or she believes are better for you. Not surprisingly, the response to conditional positive regard is a tendency to change your self-concept to include those things that you "ought to be," to become more like the person you are expected to be. In the process your self-concept becomes more and more disassociated from your inborn capacity, and your life begins to deviate from your "genetic blueprint."

When people lose sight of their inborn potential, they tend to become constricted, rigid, and defensive, to feel threatened and anxious, and to experience considerable discomfort and uneasiness. Also, because their lives have been directed toward what other people value and want, they are unlikely to find much real satisfaction in what they do. At least some of these people are aware that they don't really know who they are or what they want. In Chapter 15 we will see how Rogers helps people rediscover their self-concepts through his client-centered therapy.

What does this humanistic personality theory tell us about Jaylene Smith? Jay's self-concepts would likely include "intelligent," "high achiever," and "physician." Yet she still wonders "Who am I and what do I want from life?" Rogers would suspect that Jay is reacting to some kind of discrepancy between her self-concepts and her inborn capacities. This is further borne out by her feeling that she doesn't "deserve to be a doctor," by worries about whether she will ever be "truly happy," and by the fact that when she was 13 she "never was able 'to be herself' and really express her feelings," even with a good friend. Her unhappiness, fearfulness, loneliness, insecurity, and other dissatisfactions similarly reflect the fact that Jay has not been able to become what she "most truly is." As a humanist, incidentally, Rogers would be quick to add that he does not know what Jay's real potentialities are, but that this is something she is capable of discovering for herself, perhaps with the support of a client-centered therapist.

Rogers would also certainly expect to find that in Jay's life acceptance and love were conditional on her living up to other people's ideas of what she should become. We know that throughout most of her life, Jay's father appears to have been her primary source of positive regard. They have a close, affectionate relationship in which he has tried to respond "to her every need and demand." Yet we also know that right from the start he had "ambitions and goals for Jay," which included her becoming "successful, wealthy, and most of all, independent" and a source of pride to him. Indeed, when Jay graduated from medical school, "Dr. and Mrs. Smith were as proud as they could possibly be. After all, their daughter was now, officially, Dr. Jaylene Elizabeth Smith, and she had graduated at the top of her class." We don't know with certainty that Dr. Smith made his love for Jay conditional on her living up to his dreams, but it seems probable that he unintentionally did so.

The personality theories we have discussed represent the efforts of various psychologists to explain, in an orderly and coherent manner, the characteristic behavior of people. But interest in personality centers not only on how and why people behave as they do, but also on how to evaluate and measure personality. And as you might expect, the different personality theories lead to very different techniques for assessing personality.

Personality Assessment

In some ways, testing personality is a lot like assessing intelligence (see Chapter 9). In fact, Cattell included intelligence as one of his 16 personality traits. In both cases, we are trying to measure something that we cannot touch or see. And in both cases, a "good test" has to be both reliable and valid. But there are special difficulties in measuring some aspects of personality that are not found in measuring intelligence and academic ability. As we mentioned earlier, personality reflects *characteristic* behavior—how a person consistently reacts to his or her environment. In assessing personality, then, we are not interested in someone's *best* behavior. We want to find out what that person's *typical* behavior is—how that person usually behaves in ordinary situations.

Another problem lies in the subject matter of personality testing. To get an accurate picture of a person's personality, the psychologist must often ask questions about sensitive areas, such as the person's emotional adjustment, relationships with other people, intimate family history, and attitudes. The question of privacy arises. How far may a psychologist delve into the personal life of another person? The privacy of the person being evaluated must be respected and protected.

In the intricate task of measuring personality, psychologists use four basic tools: the personal interview, the direct observation of behavior, objective tests, and projective tests.

The Personal Interview

Essentially, an interview is a conversation with a purpose—to get information from the person being interviewed. Interviews are often used in a clinical setting, to find out why someone is seeking treatment and to help in diagnosing the problem. They can also be used to check on a client's progress in therapy. Such interviews are likely to be unstructured. That is, the interviewer is free to ask the client questions about material that comes up and to ask follow-up questions whenever appropriate. Ideally, the interviewer should try to direct the conversation over a wide range of subjects, encouraging the person to freely discuss his or her experiences, feelings, and attitudes. The interviewer also watches the other person's behavior, such as his or her way of speaking, poise, or tenseness about certain topics. Quite often interviews of this kind are used in combination with a number of other more objective tests of personality.

When conducting systematic research on personality, investigators more often rely on the structured interview. Here, the order and content of the questions are fixed ahead of time, and the interviewer tries not to deviate from the format. This kind of interview is less personal, but it assures that the interviewer will obtain comparable information from everyone interviewed. It also is more likely to be effective in eliciting information about sensitive topics that might not be fully discussed in an unstructured interview.

For both kinds of interviewing, the skill and the behavior of the interviewer are important. He or she should build a sympathetic relationship with the person being interviewed, but not become too emotionally involved. The most effective interviewers are warm, interested in what the respondent has to say, calm, relaxed, and confident (Saccuzzo, 1975; Feshbach & Weiner, 1982). But because the behavior of the interviewer can make such a difference in the outcome of an interview, the results of interviews are often unreliable. Structured interviews tend to be better in this respect, because there is less chance that the behavior of the interviewer will significantly affect what the respondent says.

The personal interview is a basic tool of personality assessment. The structured interview follows a fixed order and content of questioning.

Observation

Another way to find out how a person usually behaves is to *observe* his or her actions in everyday situations over a long period. Behaviorists and other personality theorists who question the concept of traits prefer this method. Observing behavior in different situations gives a much better view of the effect that situation and environment have on behavior and the range of behaviors a person might show. Since most people tend to be self-conscious if they suspect they are being watched, observation works best with young children or with people who have problems with language. But observation can be used successfully with people of almost any age and in many settings: a company cafeteria, an assembly line, or wherever people work or socialize together.

Direct observation lets the observer see the person's behavior first-hand. It does not have to rely on how a person says he or she acts. And if several careful observers give unbiased and factual accounts of a person's behavior over time, the composite picture of that person's behavior can be quite accurate. However, there are drawbacks to direct observation. An observer may misinterpret the true meaning of some act. For example, he or she may think a child is being hostile when actually the child is merely protecting himself against the class bully. In addition, observation is an expensive, time-consuming method of research and therefore must be used selectively. Finally, as we have said, the mere presence of an observer can affect the behavior of the subject and interfere with the results.

In recent years the techniques of observation have been refined somewhat. For one thing, observations are now usually quantified. If, for example, aggression is being studied, the investigator typically determines in advance exactly what behaviors will be considered aggressive, and then counts the frequency with which the subject displays those behaviors. Moreover, it is now typical for experimenters to videotape behavior. This allows an entire research team to view the person's behavior repeatedly and at various speeds. Quite recently, with the introduction of small, inexpensive radio "beepers," a number of researchers have begun using people's observations of themselves as a source of data. At various times during the day the psychologist activates the beeper; the subject then stops what he or she is doing and either makes an entry in a notebook or fills out a brief questionnaire describing his or her behavior or thoughts or feelings at the moment the beeper went off.

Objective Tests

In an attempt to devise measuring instruments that do not depend on the skill of an interviewer or the interpretive abilities of an observer, psychologists have created **objective tests,** or personality inventories. Generally these are written tests that are given and scored according to a standard procedure. The tests are usually constructed so that the person merely chooses between a "yes" and "no" response or selects one answer among many choices.

Because of their efforts to create a way of accurately measuring personality traits, trait theorists in particular have favored objective tests. Cattell, for example, developed a 374-question personality test called the **Sixteen Personality Factor Questionnaire.** Not surprisingly, the **16PF** (as it is usually called) provides scores on each of the 16 traits identified by Cattell. The questions on the 16PF include the following:

Objective test Self-report personality test that is administered and scored in a standard way, such as the Minnesota Multiphasic Personality Inventory.

Sixteen Personality Factor Questionnaire (16PF) Objective test designed by Cattell to provide scores on his 16 basic personality traits.

Videotaped observations permit an entire research team to view the same behavior repeatedly and at different speeds.

**Eysenck Personality Inventory
(EPI)** Objective test developed
by Eysenck to measure his two
personality dimensions of
introverted-extroverted and
stable-unstable.

**Minnesota Multiphasic Person-
ality Inventory (MMPI)** The most
widely used objective personality
test, originally intended for
psychiatric diagnosis.

I prefer to marry someone who:
   (a) Commands general admiration
   (b) In between
   (c) Has artistic and literary gifts
My friends consider me a highly practical, realistic person.
   (a) Yes
   (b) In between
   (c) No
I think I am better described as:
   (a) Polite and quiet
   (b) In between
   (c) Lively and active

Research on the 16PF has gone on for more than 30 years and one recent reviewer concluded, "No other personality measuring instrument has a more substantial scientific foundation. Nor has any instrument undergone a more thorough examination by critics. . . . When evaluated by reasonable standards, the 16PF compares favorably with any other inventory that purports to measure variations in normal personality functioning" (Bolton, 1978, p. 1080). Other recent reviews are more critical, although they agree that the 16PF can be useful for some research purposes if used with care (Anastasi, 1982; Graham & Lilly, 1984).

Eysenck has also developed a test to measure his two personality dimensions: introversion-extroversion and stable-unstable. The **Eysenck Personality Inventory (EPI)** contains such items as "Do you usually take the initiative in making new friends?" and "Are you inclined to keep in the background on social occasions?" Extroverts tend to answer yes to the first question and no to the second. Other questions are intended to measure stability. For example, "Do you get attacks of shaking or trembling?" and "Are you sometimes bubbling over with energy and sometimes very sluggish?" would both be answered yes by an emotionally unstable person. Recent reviews of the EPI indicate that it is a reliable and valid measure of both introversion-extroversion and emotional stability, as claimed by Eysenck (Tellegen, 1978; Graham & Lilly, 1984).

The most widely used objective personality test is the **Minnesota Multiphasic Personality Inventory (MMPI).** Published in 1942 by Hathaway and McKinley, the MMPI was originally developed to help diagnose psychiatric disorders (see Figure 12-3). The test consists of 550 items to which the person answers "true," "false," or "cannot say." Some typical items are: "Once in a while I put off until tomorrow what I ought to do today"; "At times I feel like swearing"; "There are persons who are trying to steal my thoughts and ideas." Some of the items repeat almost the same question in different words: "I tire easily"; "I feel weak all over much of the time." This is done for ease of scoring and to check on the possibility of false or inconsistent answers.

The MMPI also has several scales that check on the validity of the responses. For example, if the person has answered too many items "cannot say," the test is considered invalid. The _L_, or lie, scale is scored on 15 items scattered throughout the test. Sample items rated on this scale are: "I do not always tell the truth" and "I gossip a little at times." Most of us would have to admit that despite our best intentions, our answers to these two questions would have to be "true." People who mark these and many other similar items "false" are probably consciously or

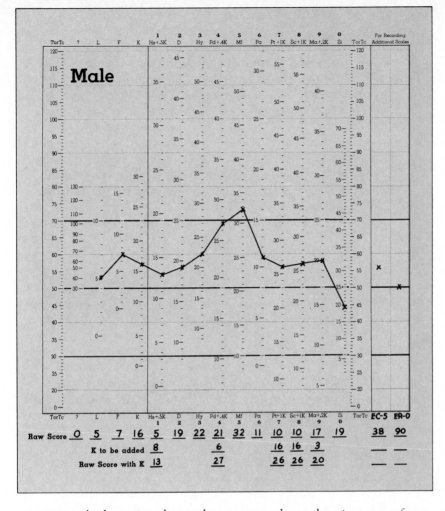

Raw Score: 0, 5, 7, 16, 5, 19, 22, 21, 32, 11, 10, 10, 17, 19 | EC-5 38, ER-0 90

K to be added: 8, 6, 16, 16, 3

Raw Score with K: 13, 27, 26, 26, 20

Figure 12-3
An MMPI profile.

unconsciously distorting the truth to present themselves in a more favorable light. The MMPI is generally highly regarded as a useful test for assessing some of the more clinically relevant dimensions of personality (Anastasi, 1982; Graham & Lilly, 1984).

Objective tests of personality offer a number of advantages over other methods of personality assessment. They are cheap to use, scoring is simple, and it is relatively easy for the testers to reach agreement about a person's performance on the test. This is not to say that such tests are without defects. All objective tests rely on self-report, and undoubtedly some people are more aware of their thoughts, feelings, and typical behavior than other people are (Buss, 1980). Moreover, because it is not hard to see the intent behind many of the questions on objective tests, it is often easy to mislead the test giver. Finally, the either-or format of many objective tests prevents people from explaining themselves more fully or qualifying their statements (Phares, 1984).

Projective Tests

As we saw earlier, psychodynamic theorists believe that to a great degree people are not aware of the unconscious determinants of their

Projective test Personality test consisting of ambiguous or unstructured material that does not limit the response to be given, such as the Rorschach inkblot test.

Rorschach test A projective test composed of ambiguous inkblots; the way a person interprets the blots is thought to reveal aspects of his or her personality.

Thematic Apperception Test (TAT) A projective test composed of ambiguous pictures about which a person writes stories.

Some psychologists feel that projective tests of personality such as the Rorschach test can uncover unconscious thoughts and fantasies.

behavior. Therefore these psychologists put very little faith in objective personality tests that rely on self-report. Instead they often prefer to use **projective tests** of personality. Most projective tests of personality consist of simple ambiguous stimuli that can elicit an unlimited number of responses. People may be shown some essentially meaningless material or a vague picture and be asked to tell what the material means to them. Or they may be given two or three words, such as "My brother is . . .," and be asked to complete the statement. They are given no clues as to the "best way" to interpret the material or finish the sentence. It is believed that in devising their own answers, they will "project" their personality into the test materials.

Projective tests have several advantages in testing personality. Since these tests are flexible and can be treated as a game or puzzle, they can be given in a relaxed atmosphere, without the tension and self-consciousness that sometimes accompany objective tests. Often the true purpose of the test can be hidden, so that responses are less likely to be faked. Some psychologists believe that the projective test can uncover unconscious thoughts and fantasies, such as latent sexual or family problems. In any event, the accuracy and usefulness of projective tests depend greatly on the skill and the bias of the examiner.

The **Rorschach test** is probably the best known of the projective personality tests. It is named for the Swiss psychiatrist who in 1921 published the results of his research on interpreting inkblots as a key to personality. Much work on the inkblot technique had already been done when Rorschach began to practice, but he was the first to use the technique to evaluate a person's total personality. After 10 years of testing thousands of blots, he finally chose 10 that seemed to arouse the most emotional response in people.

Each inkblot design is printed on a separate card and is unique in its form, color, shading, and white space. Five of the blots are black and gray; two have red splotches; three blots have patches of several colors. The cards are given to the subject one at a time and in a specific order. The subject is asked to tell what he or she sees in each blot. The test instructions are kept to a minimum, so that the subject's responses will be completely his or her own. Although no specific permission is given, the subject may turn the card and look at the blot from any angle and may make as many interpretations of each blot as he or she wants. After interpreting all the blots, the subject goes over the cards again with the examiner and tells which part of each blot determined each response.

Many psychologists simply interpret Rorschach responses intuitively. That is, they draw inferences from the responses just as they would from anything else the person says or does. But it is also possible to score Rorschach responses systematically and in great detail, though this is extremely complex and requires extensive training (Exner & Weiner, 1982). In formal scoring, attention is paid to such things as the part of each inkblot that the person used and how those portions were used to create the response. For example, was the person greatly influenced by the shape of the blot or by its color or shading? Did the person see movement in the inkblot (e.g., "This is a man running up a hill")? What kind of content did the person create (e.g., animals, people)?

Somewhat more demanding is the **Thematic Apperception Test (TAT)**, developed at Harvard by H. A. Murray and his associates. It consists of 20 cards picturing one or more human figures in various poses. Some of the pictures suggest a basic story; others give few plot hints. A person is shown the cards one by one. He or she has to make up a complete story for each picture, including what led up to the scene depicted, what the characters are doing at that moment, what their thoughts and feelings are, and what the outcome will be.

Although various scoring systems have been devised for the TAT, the examiner usually interprets the stories in the light of his or her personal knowledge of the subject. An important part of the evaluation is to determine if the subject seems to identify with the hero or heroine of the story or with one of the minor characters. Then the examiner must determine what the attitudes and feelings of the character reveal about the storyteller. The examiner also assesses each story for content, language, originality, organization, and consistency. Certain themes, such as the need for affection, repeated failure, or parental domination, may recur in several plots.

Both the Rorschach and the TAT are controversial personality tests. They are often not administered in a standard fashion, despite the fact that how the test is administered can have a significant effect on the results obtained (Anastasi, 1982). To make matters worse, they are seldom scored objectively and often the final interpretation of the results differs greatly from one examiner to another. It is not difficult to understand, therefore, why they are not well regarded as tests (Peterson, 1978; Swartz, 1978; Anastasi, 1982; Graham & Lilly, 1984). However, they do seem to have value as a form of supplementary interview that, when interpreted by a skilled examiner, can provide insight into a person (Dana, 1978; Anastasi, 1982).

"Rorschach! What's to become of you?"

Application

Locus of Control: Who Runs Your Life?

Suppose you have made plans to watch a late-night movie on TV. You walk around the corner to the convenience store to buy some beer and pretzels—only to find that the storekeeper has just locked up for the night. Would you be more likely to say to yourself, "Just my rotten luck!" or "It's my own fault: I should have left the house a few minutes earlier"?

People differ in the extent to which they believe what happens to them is due to external forces ("Just my luck!") or internal ones ("It's my own fault"). Recently psychologists have studied this personality disposition, which they call *locus of control.* Externally oriented people feel that their behavior is generally rewarded or punished by forces beyond their control, such as fate, other people who are powerful, and luck. At the opposite extreme are the individuals who believe that they are the source of their own reinforcements and rewards.

Many "externals," for example, believe that success depends on "being in the right place at the right time." They also tend to have faith in chance or fate. They are the buyers of lottery tickets, the readers of horoscopes, the owners of lucky charms. In the extreme, they see promotions as going to whomever the boss happens to like, marriage as depending on who chances to fall in love with whom, and life itself as a case of "whatever will be, will be."

Those with an "internal" orientation tend to see themselves as masters of their own fate. Rather than lottery tickets, they buy self-improvement books. They believe that promotion depends on hard work, on what you know rather than whom you know.

Rotter (1966) developed a test of internal versus external control that has been widely used by experimenters. The test consists of 17 questions that require the subject to choose between two alternatives. For example:

(a) In the long run, people get the respect they deserve in this world.
(b) Unfortunately, an individual's worth often passes unrecognized no matter how hard he tries.

People with an external locus of control tend to have faith in chance or fate.

Internals would be likely to choose (a), while externals would be likely to choose (b).

People who answer many of these questions in the external direction are usually more likely to conform to the views and wishes of others. Because they feel that they cannot control what happens to them, they tend to be more willing to rely on others for direction. People who answer mostly in the internal direction, by contrast, are much more independent and resist attempts by others to influence them (Phares, 1984). For example, one study (Ritchie & Phares, 1969) found that externals tended to adopt the opinions of people they regarded as authorities. Internals, by contrast, paid more attention to the content of the opinion than they did to the reputation of its source.

Internals differ from externals in a number of other ways as well. They tend to be more intelligent, possibly because brighter people can in fact control what happens to them more certainly than can those who are less talented (Mischel, 1981). Internals are also more success-oriented and tend to take more reasonable risks (Strickland, 1977). If internals tend to be more intelligent and success-oriented than externals, do they also fare better in school and in college? Prociuk and Breen (1975) found that internals outperformed externals in academic subjects. Phares (1978) observed that internal elementary-school students received higher grades than their external classmates, but he found no comparable differences among college students.

Locus of control may also be related to how people respond to the threat of disaster. Sims and Baumann (1972) arrived at this conclusion after investigating a curious fact. They noticed that over the course of a number of years fewer people in Illinois were killed by tornadoes than in Alabama although both states had about equal numbers of such storms. Sims and Baumann hypothesized that a larger proportion of the people living in Alabama were externals, who reacted to tornado watches with resignation rather than preparation. Research bore out their hunch: A significantly higher proportion of Alabamians endorsed external locus-of-control statements (Lazarus & Monat, 1979).

It is one thing to react passively to the threat of tornadoes, which are to a certain extent out of our control. But what about health care, which *is* under our control? The evidence is that here, too, externals tend to be more passive: They take fewer precautions to protect their health, participate less in physical activities, and seek less information about health maintenance (Strickland, 1979). All in all, people with an internal locus of control try harder for good health. This suggests that if physicians could determine which of their patients are external and which internal, they could better tailor the treatment to the individual. For example, since externals prefer structure imposed by others and tend not to take the initiative, they might require more active supervision by the doctor (Phares, 1984).

Summary

1. *Personality* refers to the pattern of characteristic thoughts, feelings, and behaviors that persists over time and situations and distinguishes one person from another.

2. *Trait theorists* maintain that a unique pattern of traits existing within each person determine that person's behavior. They define *traits* as relatively permanent and consistent dispositions to behave in characteristic ways. Trait theorists disagree on how many personality traits there might be. Cattell, for example, has identified 16 basic traits of personality. Eysenck has proposed just two major dimensions of personality: introverted-extroverted and stable-unstable.

3. Evidence suggests that such basic personality characteristics as introverted-extroverted and emotionally stable-unstable are greatly influenced by genetic factors. But specific personality traits such as assertiveness, optimism, and rigidity are largely the result of learning and experience.

4. Personality traits can be learned not only through direct reinforcement and punishment, but also by observing other people as models, especially those who are close to us. Parents are the models who most influence their children's personalities.

5. Sigmund Freud proposed the first major *psychodynamic theory* of personality. This theory and the related therapy are both known as *psychoanalysis*. Freud believed that personality reflects the interraction of the id, the ego, and the superego.

6. The *id* is the storehouse of energy from which the ego and superego develop. The id relieves the discomfort of instinctual drives by reflex actions or by wish fulfillment, which Freud called *primary-process thinking*. The id acts according to the *pleasure principle*. The *ego* operates on the *reality principle*. It controls thinking and reasoning and directs id energy into effective, realistic channels, a process known as *secondary-process thinking*. The *superego*, the moral guardian of behavior, compares the ego's actions with an *ego ideal* and a conscience and then rewards or punishes the ego accordingly.

7. As part of his theory of personality development, Freud identified several *psychosexual stages* through which children must pass and which correspond to changes in their attempts to satisfy their sexual instincts. During the first or *oral stage*, a child's dominant source of sensual pleasure is the mouth, lips, and tongue. In the second or *anal stage*, the focus of pleasure shifts to the anus and the pleasures of elimination. This is followed by the *phallic stage*, during which the focus switches to the genitals and an interest in masturbation. It is also during the phallic stage that children form a strong attachment to the parent of the opposite sex and feel jealousy toward the parent of the same sex. This is known as the *Oedipal conflict*. At the end of the phallic stage children lose interest in sexual behavior and enter a *latency period*. The sexual instinct reawakens at puberty, when children enter the *genital stage* and become erotically interested in members of the opposite sex.

8. According to Freud, a child's experience at each of the psychosexual stages stamps his or her personality with tendencies that endure into adulthood. If there is either too much or too little gratification of sensual pleasure at any one stage, it is possible that some sexual energy will remain fixated at that stage. *Fix-*

ation can lead to immature forms of sexuality and to certain characteristic personality traits.

9. In contrast to Freud, Erikson feels that personality continues to develop during the life span. He describes eight stages of personality development, each of which involves the resolution of a crisis: *trust versus mistrust; autonomy versus shame and doubt; initiative versus guilt; industry versus inferiority; identity versus role confusion; intimacy versus isolation; generativity versus stagnation;* and *integrity versus despair.* According to Erikson, success in each stage depends on a person's adjustment in the previous stages. Erikson strongly believes in the necessity of achieving a positive personal identity (Stage 5) if one is to be able to form successful personal relationships.

10. Humanistic psychologists look upon life as a process of striving to realize our potential, and thus view personality as one aspect of our efforts to develop and fulfill ourselves. According to Carl Rogers, all organisms are born with biological capacities and have the *actualizing tendency* to fulfill their inborn potential. In addition, human beings form self-concepts; the *self-actualizing tendency* drives them to live up to their images of themselves. Individuals whose self-concepts form a close match with their inborn capacities are more likely to realize their potential and become *fully functioning persons.* Fully functioning persons have been brought up with *unconditional positive regard* from others and are directed toward their own goals and ambitions. People who have been brought up with *conditional positive regard* deviate from their inborn potential and attempt to fulfill the goals that others have set for them. People who are not fully functioning are likely to feel threatened and anxious in general and dissatisfied with what they do.

11. Psychologists use four basic tools to assess personality: personal interviews, direct observation of behavior, objective tests, and projective tests.

12. During an *interview* the interviewer seeks to evaluate another person by listening to what the person says and by observing his or her behavior. In an unstructured interview the conversation may range over a number of subjects and the person is encouraged to freely discuss experiences, feelings, and attitudes. In a structured interview the content of questions is fixed beforehand and the interviewer tries not to deviate from the format. The skill and behavior of the interviewer are important factors in both kinds of interviews. Because the behavior of the interviewer can make a difference in the outcome of an interview, structured interviews are considered more reliable in doing systematic personality testing.

13. *Observation* is done to find out how a person behaves in everyday situations over a period of time and to determine the influence that situations and environments have on the range of behaviors a person might show. An advantage of direct observation is that the observer does not have to rely on a subject's own description of his or her behavior. Some disadvantages are the possibility of misinterpreting a behavior and the fact that the mere presence of an observer can affect the behavior of a subject. Modern observational techniques include videotaping and systematic forms of self-observation.

14. *Objective tests* of personality, or personality inventories, are given and scored according to a standardized procedure. Such tests are usually constructed as questionnaires requiring yes-or-no responses or the selection of one answer among multiple choices. Because all objective tests rely on self-report, their effectiveness depends on the honesty with which the questions are answered. The advantages of objective tests are that they are inexpensive to use, easy to score, and do not depend on the interpretive skills of an observer or interviewer. Three well-known personality inventories are the *Sixteen Personality Factor Questionnaire* (16PF), the *Eysenck Personality Inventory* (EPI), and the *Minnesota Multiphasic Personality Inventory* (MMPI).

15. *Projective tests* of personality use ambiguous stimuli that can elicit an unlimited number of responses. It is believed that a person will project his or her personality into the test material. Two well-known projective tests are the *Rorschach test,* consisting of 10 inkblot designs that subjects are asked to interpret; and the *Thematic Apperception Test* (TAT), consisting of 20 pictures about which subjects are asked to make up stories.

1. The pattern of characteristic thoughts, feelings, and behaviors that distinguishes one person from another is known as _____.

2. Cattell/Eysenck has identified 16 basic traits of personality; Cattell/Eysenck has proposed just two major personality dimensions.

3. According to _____ theory, unique and enduring dispositions within each person determine that person's behavior.

4. Freud's personality theory and his form of therapy are both known as _____.

5. The id/ego operates according to the reality principle; the id/ego acts according to the pleasure principle.

6. Primary process thinking/secondary-process thinking is the means by which the id partially relieves the discomfort of instinctual drives through forming mental images.

7. Match the following of Freud's terms with their appropriate definitions;

____ unconscious
____ id
____ superego
____ ego
____ ego ideal
____ libido

A. energy that comes from the sexual instinct
B. mediator between reality, the superego, and the id
C. unconscious urges that are always seeking expression
D. that part of the superego concerned with standards
E. ideas and feelings of which we are normally not aware
F. moral guardian of the ego

8. Freud proposed that children pass through a series of psychosexual stages. Arrange them in the correct order: anal, phallic, oral, genital, latency period.

9. Rogers believes that a person strives to live up to and fulfill a self-image; he calls this a person's _____ tendency.

10. According to Rogers, a person brought up with _____ _____ _____ feels worthy and accepted by others only if he or she live up to what others expect, desire, or demand.

11. In the structured/unstructured interview, the person being interviewed directs the flow of the interview; in the structured/unstructured interview, a predetermined set of questions directs the interview.

12. The mere presence of an observer can affect the behavior of the person being observed.   T/F

13. _____ tests require people to fill out questionnaires, which are then scored according to a standardized procedure.

14. In _____ tests of personality, people are shown ambiguous stimuli and asked to describe them or make up a story about them.

Outline

Adjustment

13

Let's begin the study of adjustment with several true stories.

In 1979 Iranian militants stormed the United States embassy in Teheran and took 52 Americans hostage. For 444 days the hostages lived in fear of their lives and endured the humiliations of captivity. To feel less like a prisoner and more like a person in charge of his life, one hostage saved food from meals and then played gracious host by offering it to other hostages who visited him in his cell. A diary kept by one American records other strategies: "Al's working on his painting . . . Dick's walking his daily 3 miles back and forth across the room, and Jerry's lying on his mattress reading."

When Eric de Wilde, an orphan, found a bag of jewels worth $350,000 on a Florida railroad track in 1983, it seemed like a fairy tale come true. But salesmen and reporters hounded him, and schoolmates and others kept calling him up with demands and threats. "Life is very difficult for the young man—a lot of things have happened to him in a hurry," said the lawyer de Wilde was forced to retain. But when the boy arrived in New York to sell his jewels at a public auction, he conducted himself with such dignified restraint that he managed to maintain his privacy and self-possession.

Janet Lodge had her first baby in 1984. She was filled with special joy, because at age 34 she had feared she would never become pregnant. But she found taking care of the baby, along with her other responsibilities, exhausting. Her husband, Michael, resented her constant fatigue and the fact that he didn't seem to come first in her life anymore. In an effort to solve these problems, Janet and Michael used some of their savings to pay for household help. Michael also took a more active role in looking after the baby, playing with her, and watching her development. This relieved some of Janet's burden and left her with more time and energy for her other responsibilities and for her life with Michael.

These three brief stories seem very different, but they have much in common. All the people involved were faced with significant new demands from their environment, they had to find ways of coping with the new event, and they all seemed to adjust about as well as could be expected under the circumstances. Like these people, each of us must adjust to a life that is less perfect than we would like, a life in which even

Adjustment Any effort to cope with stress.

Stress Emotional and physiological reactions to threatening situations and the pressure, frustration, conflict, and anxiety experienced in those situations.

pleasures seem to come with built-in complications. We need to adapt not just to great crises or to unexpected strokes of good fortune but also to the constant minor demands of everyday life.

Every **adjustment** is an attempt—successful or not—to deal with stress, to balance our desires against the demands of the environment, to weigh our needs against realistic possibilities, and to cope as well as we can within the limits of the situation. The student who fails to get the lead in the school play may quit the production in a huff, accept a smaller role, serve as theater critic for the school paper, or perhaps join the debating team. Each response is an adjustment to the stress of failure, although some may be less constructive in the long run than others.

This chapter will discuss the kinds of problems that people face in the course of living and the various ways in which they try to cope with these problems. Along the way we will see that most people's problems are numerous and complex, and that coping with stress is rarely easy. Finally, we will examine what psychologists mean when they refer to someone as "well adjusted."

What Do We Have to Adjust to?

"As we feared, Harkness was stunned by the news."

When we feel unable to cope with the demands of our environment, when we are threatened with physical or psychological harm, we begin to feel tense and uncomfortable. We are experiencing **stress.** This term describes our emotional and physiological reactions to situations in which we feel in conflict or threatened beyond our capacity to cope or endure.

Some things, of course, are inherently stressful, such as wars and natural disasters. Here the danger is very real: Lives are threatened, and often there is little or nothing people can do to save themselves. But even in naturally stressful situations the time of greatest stress is not necessarily the time when danger is at its height, as Seymour Epstein (1962) demonstrated when he studied the effects of anticipating stress on a group of 28 parachutists. Each man was asked to describe his feelings before, during, and after his jump. All reported an increase of fear and of desire to escape as the time for the jump approached. Once the men were in line and realized they could not turn back, however, they began to calm down. By the time they reached the most dangerous part of the jump—when they were in free-fall and waiting for their chutes to open—their fears had subsided. The time of greatest stress thus proved to be the period when the parachutists were *anticipating* danger.

But stress is not limited to life-and-death situations, nor, as two of our introductory anecdotes show, to unpleasant ones. The good things that happen to us, as well as the bad ones, cause stress because they carry with them "adjustive demands that must be dealt with if we are to meet our needs" (Coleman, 1979, p. 108). A wedding is exciting, but it is also a stressful event—most weddings are very complicated affairs, and in addition they mark a profound change in one's relationships with one's parents, friends, old boy- or girlfriends, and of course one's new spouse. A promotion at work is satisfying—but it brings with it the need to relate to new people in new ways, to learn to do new things, perhaps to dress differently and keep different working hours.

Notice that all the stressful events we have considered so far involve change. But most people have a strong preference for a sense of order, continuity, and predictability in their lives (Butler, 1975). Therefore any event, whether good or bad, that causes change and discontinuity in people's lives will be experienced as stressful. Put the opposite way, the stressfulness of various situations can be determined by the amount of change they require. In 1967 Holmes and Rahe devised a Social Readjustment Rating Scale (SRRS) to measure how much stress a person has undergone in any given period. The two researchers began by compiling a list of several dozen events deemed stressful because they create change, for better or worse, in the pattern of a person's life and therefore require adjustment. Each event was assigned a point value—depending on the amount of change it required. The most stressful event on the list is the death of a spouse. It has a rating of 100. At the bottom of the scale, a minor brush with the law is rated 11. Some of the other items on the SRRS are:

Divorce	73	Change in responsibilities	
Death of a close relative	63	at work	29
Personal injury or illness	53	Son or daughter leaving home	29
Marriage	50	Outstanding personal	
Marital reconciliation	45	achievement	28
Pregnancy	40	Change in living conditions	25
Gain of a new family		Change in schools	20
member	39	Change in social activities	18
A new mortgage	31	Vacation	13

Note that the stressfulness of these events has nothing to do with whether they are desirable or undesirable. "Change in responsibilities at work" carries 29 "stress units" whether it is due to a promotion to more interesting work, or being assigned a much bigger volume of boring detail work. "Change in living conditions" carries 25 "stress units" whether it means moving into a wonderful new house, or leaving an attractive large apartment that costs too much for a dreary, cramped one with a more affordable rent.

Using the SRRS scale, you simply add up the stress ratings of all the events people have lived through in a given period of time to determine the amount of stress they have experienced. In general, a total score of 150 or less is considered normal; 150–199 corresponds to mild stress; 200–299 suggests a moderate crisis; and 300 or higher indicates a major life crisis. For example, marital reconciliation (45) together with pregnancy (40), a new mortgage (31), a change in living conditions (25), and a change in social activities (18) total 159 points or "mild stress."

Holmes and Rahe emphasize stress that arises from fairly dramatic, one-time life events. But Lazarus (1981, 1983) points out that much stress arises from nonevents, that is, from "chronic or repeated conditions of living—boredom, continuing tension in a family relationship, lack of occupational progress, isolation and loneliness, absence of meaning and commitment" (1981, p. 60).

The heart of Lazarus' thinking is the concept of "hassles," which he

The good things that happen to us, as well as the bad, can cause stress. Marriage carries 50 "stress units" on the Social Readjustment Rating Scale.

Pressure A feeling that one must speed up, intensify, or change the direction of behavior or live up to a higher standard of performance.

Frustration Emotional reaction that occurs when a person is prevented from reaching a goal.

defines as petty annoyances, irritations, and frustrations. Such seemingly minor matters as being stuck in traffic, misplacing the car keys, or getting into a trivial argument may be as stressful, he holds, as major life events like those on the Holmes-Rahe scale. This does not mean that Lazarus discounts big events. Rather, he believes that big events matter so much not because they create stress directly, but because they trigger little hassles that give rise to stress. "Divorce," for example, "might force a man inexperienced at such tasks to make his own meals, do the laundry, or clean the house; it might force a woman to handle household finances or repair a leaky faucet for the first time" (1981, p. 62). Thus a major event creates a ripple effect. "In sum," Lazarus says, "it is not the large dramatic events that make the difference, but what happens day in and day out, whether provoked by major events or not" (1981, p. 62).

We have been speaking of external events and situations, both major and minor, as sources of stress. The reason these events are stressful is that they give rise to feelings of pressure, frustration, conflict, and anxiety. Each of these emotional experiences contributes to our overall feeling of stress. Let us take a look at each of them before we consider the differences in the way people perceive and adjust to stress.

Pressure

Pressure occurs when we feel forced to speed up, intensify, or shift the direction of our behavior, or to meet a higher standard of performance (Coleman et al., 1984). In part, our feelings of pressure arise from within us, from very personal goals and ideals. Because of our concern about our intelligence, appearance, popularity, or talents, we may push ourselves to reach ever higher standards of excellence. This kind of pressure can be constructive. It may lead, for example, to a serious effort to learn to play a musical instrument, which can ultimately bring us great pleasure. On the other hand, internal pressure can be destructive if our aims are impossible to achieve.

Pressure to compete affects nearly all relationships in American life. The combination of internal and external pressure in a job like sales can be intense.

A sense of pressure may also derive from outside influences. Among the most significant and consistent of these are seemingly relentless demands that we compete, that we adapt to the rapid rate of change in our society, and that we live up to what our family and close friends expect of us. The forces that push us to compete affect nearly all relationships in American life. We compete for grades, for popularity, for sexual and marital partners, and for jobs. We are taught to see failure as shameful. Hence the pressure to win can be intense.

Frustration

Frustration also contributes to feelings of stress. Frustration occurs when a person is prevented from reaching a goal because something or someone is in the way (see Figure 13-1). A teenager madly in love with a popular singer may learn that she is happily married. A high school student who does poorly on his College Boards may not get into his father's alma mater. These people must either give up their goals as unattainable or find some way to overcome the obstacles blocking them.

The teenager with a crush will probably recover quickly. The student faces a more complex problem. Most likely, his first reaction will be to get angry—at himself for not having studied harder, at his father for pushing him to apply to that college, at the admissions board for not taking into account the bad cold he had the day he took the College Boards. He may not be able to express his anger directly. He may not even realize or admit how disappointed he is. Nevertheless, he must either find a new way to reach his goal, or change it and be satisfied with another school.

Coleman (1979) identifies five basic sources of frustration. *Delays* are hard for us to accept because our culture stresses the value of time. Anyone who has been caught in a traffic jam is familiar with the frustration of delay. Also, because advertising makes consumer goods so attractive, we may become frustrated if something we would like to own is out of our immediate economic reach. *Lack of resources* is especially frustrating to low-income Americans, who cannot afford the new cars or vacations that TV programs and magazine articles would have us believe that everyone must have. *Losses*, such as the end of a love affair or a cherished friendship, are frustrating because they often make us feel helpless, unimportant, and worthless.

Failure is a frequent source of frustration in our competitive society. The aspect of failure that is hardest to cope with is guilt: We imagine that if we had done certain things differently, we might have succeeded, and so we feel responsible for our own or someone else's pain and disappointment. Finally, some people feel that life is *lonely* and *meaningless*. That can cause frustration, particularly if we blame society and feel unable to change the situation. Our sense of powerlessness may in turn lead to alienation, despair, and a feeling that nothing we do is really important.

Conflict

Of all life's troubles, **conflict** is probably the most common. A student finds that both of the required courses she wanted to take this year meet at the same time. In an election the views of one candidate on foreign policy reflect our own, but we prefer the domestic programs proposed by his opponent. A boy does not want to go to his aunt's for dinner, but neither does he want to listen to his mother complain if he stays at home.

Conflict arises when we face two incompatible demands, opportunities, needs, or goals. There is never any way to resolve conflict completely. We must either give up one of our goals, modify one or both of them, delay our pursuit of one, or learn to accept the fact that neither goal can be fully attained. Whatever we do, we are bound to experience some frustration; knowing this adds to the stressfulness of conflicts.

In the 1930s Kurt Lewin described conflict in terms of two opposite tendencies: *approach* and *avoidance*. When something attracts us, we want to approach it; when something frightens us, we try to avoid it. Lewin (1935) showed how different combinations of these tendencies characterize three basic types of conflict.

The first, diagrammed in Figure 13-2, he called **approach/approach conflict.** A person (the circle) is simultaneously attracted (the arrows) to two appealing goals (the plus signs). For example, a woman may want to

Conflict Tension caused by incompatible demands, opportunities, needs, or goals.

Approach/approach conflict Result of simultaneous attraction to two appealing possibilities.

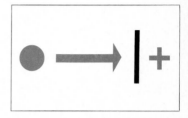

Figure 13-1

A diagram of frustration. The person (represented by a circle) is prevented by a barrier (the vertical line) from reaching a goal (+).

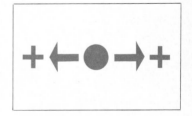

Figure 13-2

A diagram of approach/approach conflict. The person is attracted to two incompatible goals at the same time.

Avoidance/avoidance conflict
Result of facing a choice between
two undesirable possibilities.

Approach/avoidance conflict
Result of being simultaneously
attracted to and repelled by the
same thing.

pursue a career and also to raise a family. As a rational person, she
considers the alternatives. She could accept a job now and delay having
children, or she could have children now and look for work later on.
Alternatively, she could modify both goals by hiring a housekeeper and
working part time. Or she and her husband could share child-care duties.
Here the solutions are numerous, but this is not always the case. Suppose
the same woman wanted a career that required frequent, often prolonged
travel, say in international sales. She might conclude that a career would
necessitate neglecting her family. If she is right, it might in fact be
impossible for her to attain both goals simultaneously.

The reverse of this kind of dilemma is **avoidance/avoidance conflict,**
when a person is confronted with two undesired or threatening possibilities (Figure 13-3). When faced with an avoidance/avoidance conflict,
people usually try to escape. If escape is impossible, they cope in one of
a number of ways, depending on how threatening each alternative is.
Students who must choose between failing an exam or studying something they find terribly boring will probably decide to study, at least for
a time. Otherwise they may have to repeat the course, an even less
pleasant alternative. Making that kind of choice is not very stressful.
Consider, in contrast, the situation of a police officer assigned to a
high-crime area. There is risk involved in answering every radio call; but
since a police officer risks job, self-esteem, and the lives of fellow officers
by failing to respond, he or she will almost surely respond—but the cost
in stress will be high.

People caught in avoidance/avoidance conflicts often vacillate between one threat and another, like the baseball player caught between
first and second base. He starts to run toward second, then realizes he will
be tagged and turns around, only to realize he will be tagged on first if he
tries to go back there. In no-exit situations like this many people simply
wait for events to resolve their conflict for them.

Approach/avoidance conflicts (see Figure 13-4), in which a person is
both attracted to and repelled by the same goal, are also difficult to
resolve. A football player recovering from an operation may want to

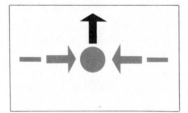

Figure 13-3
A diagram of avoidance/
avoidance conflict. Repelled
by two undesirable alter-
natives at the same time, the
person is inclined to try to
escape (the black arrow), but
often other factors prevent
such an excape.

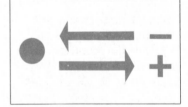

Figure 13-4
A diagram of approach/
avoidance conflict. The person
is both repelled by and
attracted to the same goal.

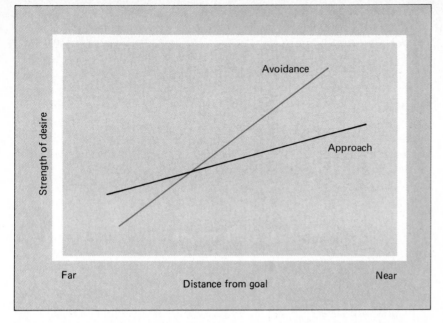

Anxiety Feeling of fear or fright, but without an identifiable source.

Figure 13-5
Both approach and avoidance increase as the distance to the goal decreases. At the point where the two lines cross, the person will begin to waver, unless he or she is forced to decide or the situation changes.

return to his team, but he knows he may limp for the rest of his life if he is injured again. A woman knows she will hurt a man she really likes if she goes out with others, but she realizes she will feel resentful toward him if she lets him stand in her way. Those whose parents taught them that sex is dirty and sinful may find themselves in adulthood simultaneously attracted to and repelled by members of the opposite sex.

The desire to approach a goal grows stronger as we get nearer to it, but so does the desire to avoid it. The avoidance tendency usually increases in strength faster than the approach tendency. In an approach/avoidance conflict, therefore, we approach the goal until we reach the point where the tendency to approach equals the tendency to avoid the goal (see Figure 13-5). Afraid to go any closer, we stop, fall back, approach again, vacillating until we have to make a decision or until the situation changes.

Often approach/avoidance conflicts are combined in complex patterns. A mother who loves classical music may dream that her son will be a great pianist. His father might want him to be an athlete. If the child practices the piano, he pleases his mother but upsets his father; if he stays after school for football practice, he disappoints his mother but pleases his father. *Double approach/avoidance conflict*, as Lewin called this, is diagrammed in Figure 13-6.

Figure 13-6
A diagram of double approach/avoidance conflict. We are caught between two goals, each of which has good and bad features.

Anxiety

Anxiety is a very complex and puzzling contributor to stress. In the examples we have discussed so far, the people under stress knew *why* they were frustrated or upset. Anxious people, by contrast, do not know why they feel this way. They experience all the symptoms of fear—"butterflies" in the stomach, shallow breathing, muscle tension, inability to think clearly, and so on—but they do not know why. Many psychologists use psychoanalytic theory to explain anxiety. According to this view, anxiety is a sign of internal, unconscious conflict. Some wish or desire that conflicts with the person's conscious values threatens to surface. A girl is furious with her mother, but firmly believes it is wrong to feel angry with one's parents. If her inhibitions against anger are particularly strong, she may use all her energy to keep from realizing just how furious she is. But the anger persists beneath the surface. Anytime it threatens to break through into her conscious awareness, she feels anxious and nervous; however, since the anger is still unconscious, she cannot understand what is causing her nervousness. All she knows is that *something* terrible is about to happen and she is afraid. We will look much more closely at anxiety, its causes and its effects, in the next chapter.

Stress and Individual Differences

Some people seem to cope with major life changes without experiencing great stress, while others have great difficulty with even minor problems. What accounts for the difference? The answer seems to be individual differences in perceiving and reacting to potentially stressful events.

An obstacle that looks like a molehill to one person strikes another as a mountain. An experienced construction worker thinks nothing of sitting on a girder hundreds of feet above the ground to drive a rivet or eat his lunch; but just watching him may be enough to make a passerby anxious. One patient facing a serious operation may feel less anxious than someone else going to a doctor for a routine physical exam. The person who gets fired from a job and the soldier who gets caught behind enemy lines may actually feel equally threatened. In short, how much stress we experience depends partly on the way we interpret the situation.

Several factors determine whether or not we find a particular situation stressful. Someone who is self-confident, who feels adequate to cope with life events, is less likely to find a given situation stressful than someone who lacks such self-assurance. For example, students who know they can study when they have to and have done well in the past are likely to be calmer the night before an exam than those who have done poorly on previous exams. People who have handled job changes well in the past are likely to find the next change less stressful than those who have had great difficulty adjusting to previous job changes.

Kobasa (1979) studied closely a group of people who either tolerated stress exceptionally well or actually thrived on it. What these stress-resistant people had in common was a trait Kobasa called *hardiness*: They felt very much in control of their lives, were deeply committed to their work and their own values, and experienced difficult demands from the environment as challenging rather than frightening. Kobasa's study suggests that people's response to stress depends partly on whether they believe they have some control over events or whether they feel helpless. Research cited by Seligman (1975) shows that people in seemingly hopeless situations not only become apathetic but, when the situation changes, fail to recognize that it is now possible to cope more effectively. They remain passive even when there are opportunities for improving the situation.

An obstacle that looks like a molehill to one person may strike another as a mountain. The mere sight of this construction worker may be enough to make a passerby anxious.

So much for individual differences in the susceptibility to stress. What about behavior under stress once it does occur? Here, too, there are differences among people. In natural disasters, for example, some people at once mobilize their forces to save themselves. Others fall apart. Still others are shaken but regain their composure—and ability to respond— almost immediately. And then there are those who simply refuse to admit that there is any danger. In the next section we will consider in detail what people choose to do—or not to do—when they are under stress.

How People Cope with Stress

Whatever its source, stress calls for adjustment. Psychologists distinguish between two general types of adjustment: direct coping and defensive coping. *Direct coping* refers to any action we take to change an uncomfortable situation. When our needs or desires are frustrated, we attempt to remove the obstacles between ourselves and our goal, or we give up. Similarly, when we are threatened, we try to eliminate the source of the threat, either by attacking it or by escaping from it.

Defensive coping refers to the different ways people convince themselves that they are not really threatened or that they do not really want something they cannot get. A form of self-deception, defensive coping is characteristic of internal, often unconscious conflicts. We are emotionally unable to bring a problem to the surface and deal with it directly because it is too threatening. In self-defense, we avoid the conflict.

Direct Coping

When we are threatened, frustrated, or in conflict, we have three basic choices for coping directly: confrontation, compromise, or withdrawal. We can meet a situation head-on and intensify our efforts to get what we want (confrontation). We can give up some of what we want and perhaps persuade others to give up part of what they want (compromise). Or we can admit defeat and stop fighting (withdrawal).

Take the case of a woman who has worked hard at her job for years but is not promoted. She learns that the reason is her stated unwillingness to move temporarily from the company's main office to a branch office in another part of the country in order to get more experience. Her unwillingness to move is an obstacle between her and her goal of advancing in her career. She has several choices. Let's look at each in turn.

CONFRONTATION. Confrontation means facing a stressful situation forthrightly, acknowledging to oneself that there is a problem for which a solution must be found, attacking the problem head-on, and pushing resolutely toward one's goal. The hallmark of the "confrontational style" (Golden, 1982) is making intense efforts to cope with stress and to accomplish one's aims. This may involve learning new skills, enlisting other people's help, or just trying harder. Or it may require trying to

Confrontation may require trying to change a stressful situation itself through such means as discussion, persuasion, and controlled anger.

change either oneself or the situation. The woman we have been describing might decide that if she wants very much to move up in the company, she will have to do an about-face and tell her boss that she is now willing to relocate. But she might, instead, try to change the situation itself in one of several ways. She could challenge the assumption that the branch office would give her the kind of experience her supervisor thinks she needs. She could try to persuade the boss that although she has never worked in a branch office, she nevertheless has enough experience to handle a better job in the main office. Or she could remind the supervisor of the company's need to promote more women to top-level positions.

Confrontation may also include expressions of anger. Anger can be effective, especially if we have really been unfairly treated and if we express our anger with restraint instead of exploding in rage. A national magazine once reported an amusing, and effective, example of controlled anger in response to an annoying little hassle. As a motorist came to an intersection, he had to stop for a frail old lady crossing the street. The driver of the car behind honked his horn impatiently, whereupon the first driver shut off the ignition, removed the key, walked back to the other car, and handed the key to the second driver. "Here," he said. "*You* run over her. I can't stand to do it. She reminds me of my grandmother."

"This toy is designed to hasten the child's adjustment to the world around him. No matter how carefully he puts it together, it won't work."
(Drawing by Mirachi; © 1964 *The New Yorker Magazine, Inc.*)

COMPROMISE. Compromise is one of the most common, and effective, ways of coping directly with conflict or frustration. We often recognize that we cannot have everything we want and that we cannot expect others to do just what we would like them to do. In such cases we may decide to settle for less than we originally wanted. A young person who has loved animals all her life and has long cherished the desire to become a veterinarian may discover in college that she has less aptitude for biology than she had hoped and that she finds dissecting specimens in the lab so distasteful that she could never bring herself to operate on animals. By way of compromise, she may decide to become an animal technician, a person who works as an assistant to a veterinarian.

WITHDRAWAL. In some circumstances the most effective way of coping with stress may be to withdraw from the situation. A person at an amusement park who is overcome by anxiety just looking at a roller coaster can move on to a less threatening ride or even leave the park entirely. The woman whose promotion seems to depend on temporarily relocating might simply quit her job and join another company. Or she might withdraw figuratively from the stressful situation by deciding that promotion no longer matters to her and that she has already advanced in her career as far as she wants to go.

We often equate withdrawal with simply refusing to face problems. But when we realize that our adversary is more powerful than we are, or that there is no way we can effectively change ourselves, alter the situation, or reach a compromise, and that any form of aggression would be self-destructive, withdrawal is a positive and realistic adjustment. In seemingly hopeless situations, such as submarine and mining disasters, few people panic (Mintz, 1951). Believing that there is nothing they can do to save themselves, they give up. If the situation is in fact hopeless, resignation may be the most effective way of coping.

Social Class and Stress

Abnormal behavior—as seen in crime, delinquency, family violence, and neurosis—is often linked to low socioeconomic status. Why should there be such a link?

Several studies point to a one-word answer: stress. People who belong to the lower socioeconomic class are both more exposed to stress and more vulnerable to it. Pearlin and Schooler (1978) put it this way: "The less educated and the poorer are more exposed to hardships and, at the same time, are less likely to have the means to fend off the stresses resulting from the hardships. Not only are life problems distributed unequally among social groups and collectivities, but it is apparent that the ability to deal with the problems is similarly unequal" (p. 17).

Kessler (1979) reached similar conclusions. He analyzed interviews done in 1967 and 1969 with 720 people, and also collected information about specific events that had occurred in the lives of those people in the same 2 years. In addition, he reviewed data on his subjects' physical and financial status, and on how much emotional distress they felt roughly 10 years after the events. When he compared members of the upper and lower classes, he found that the latter had had to face more stressful experiences (e.g., poor housing, dangerously crime-ridden neighborhoods, and long-term joblessness) than the former. His data also suggested that those in the lower classes had not coped with their difficulties as well as those in the upper class. And he found that stressful events of the same severity had had more impact on the emotional lives of lower-class subjects.

Several studies indicate that not only do people from lower socioeconomic classes have more diffi-

cult experiences to cope with than members of other classes but they are also more likely to suffer as a result. There are several possible reasons for this. Liem and Liem (1978) concluded that lower-class members have fewer people and fewer community resources to turn to for help in getting through hard times. Wills and Langer (1980) propose that low income and lack of education are associated with ineffective coping styles. Perhaps lower-class members tend to believe in an external locus of control (see Chapter 12)—that is, that external factors are responsible for what happens to them and they themselves have little personal control over their lives. Furthermore, there is evidence that lower-class members often doubt their ability to master difficult situations and have poor self-esteem.

None of this proves that social class itself is the direct cause of all the difficulties its members experience. It may be that lower-class membership offers few opportunities to learn effective methods of coping with stress. Alternatively, it may be that poor coping skills (which can be seen in any class) cause people to drift downward into the lower classes.

One final study deserves mention. Dohrenwend (1973) found a high incidence of stressful events (and resulting psychological disturbance) not only in lower-class members but also in women of all social classes. It is widely recognized that the social status of women (their worth in the eyes of others) is low, whether they belong to the lower, middle, or upper classes. The implication of Dohrenwend's study is that high vulnerability to stress, although common in the lower classes, is most closely associated with low social status, of which low social class is just one example.

Perhaps the greatest danger is that withdrawal will turn into avoidance of all similar situations. We may refuse to go to any amusement park or carnival again. The woman who did not want to move to a branch office may quit her job without even looking for a new one. In such cases, coping by withdrawal becomes maladaptive avoidance, and we begin to suspect that the adjustment is not really effective. Moreover, people who have given up are in a poor position to take advantage of a more effective solution if one comes along. For example, one group of fifth-grade students was given unsolvable problems by one teacher and solvable problems by another. When the "unsolvable" teacher later presented the students with problems that could be solved, the students were unable to

Defense mechanisms Self-deceptive techniques for reducing stress, including denial, repression, projection, identification, intellectualization, reaction formation, displacement, and sublimation.

Denial Refusing to acknowledge a painful or threatening reality.

solve them, even though they had solved nearly identical problems given by the other teacher (Dweck & Repucci, 1973).

Withdrawal, in whatever form, is a mixed blessing. Though it can be an effective method of coping, it has built-in dangers. The same tends to be true of defensive coping, to which we now turn.

Defensive Coping

Thus far we have been speaking of coping with stress that arises from recognizable sources. But there are times when we either cannot identify or cannot deal directly with the source of our stress. For example, you return to a parking lot to discover that someone has damaged your new car and then left the scene. Or your vacation trip must be delayed because the airport is buried under 3 feet of new snow. In other cases, a problem is so emotionally threatening that it simply cannot be faced directly. Perhaps you find out that someone you are close to is terminally ill. Or you learn that after 4 years of hard study you have failed to be admitted to any medical school and you may have to abandon your lifelong ambition of becoming a physician.

In all these cases you are under stress and there is little or nothing you can do to cope with the stress directly. In such situations people are likely to turn to **defense mechanisms** as a way of coping. Defense mechanisms are ways of deceiving oneself about the causes of a stressful situation that help to reduce pressure, frustration, conflict, and anxiety. The self-deceptive nature of such adjustments led Freud to conclude that they are entirely unconscious. Freud was particularly interested in distortions of memory and in irrational feelings and behavior, all of which he considered symptoms of a struggle against unconscious impulses. Therefore he believed that defensive ways of coping always spring from unconscious conflicts, and that we have little or no control over them. Not all psychologists accept this interpretation. Often we realize that we are pushing something out of our memory or otherwise deceiving ourselves. All of us have blown up at one person when we knew we were really angry with someone else.

Whether or not defense mechanisms operate unconsciously, they do provide a means of coping with stress that might otherwise be unbearable. Let's look more closely at some of the major defense mechanisms.

DENIAL. One common defense mechanism is **denial,** or the refusal to acknowledge a painful or threatening reality. As we saw in Chapter 11, the first reaction of most people when they learn that they are dying is denial. Lazarus (1969) cites the example of a woman who was near death from severe burns. At first she was depressed and frightened, but after a few days she began to feel sure she would soon be able to return home and care for her children, although all medical indications were to the contrary. By denying the extent of her injuries, this woman was able to stay calm and cheerful. She was not merely putting on an act for her relatives and friends: She *believed* she would recover. In a similar situation C.T. Wolff and his colleagues (1964) interviewed the parents of children who were dying of leukemia. Some parents denied their children's condition; others accepted it. Physical examinations revealed that those who were denying the illness did not have the physiological symptoms of stress, such as excessive stomach acid, found in those who accepted their children's illness.

Many psychologists would suggest that in these situations denial is a positive solution. But in other situations it clearly is not. Students who deny their need to study and instead spend most nights at the movies may well fail their exams. Heroin addicts who insist that they are merely experimenting with drugs are also deluding themselves.

REPRESSION. Perhaps the most common mechanism for blocking out painful feelings and memories is **repression.** Repression, a form of forgetting, means excluding painful thoughts from consciousness. The most extreme form of this defense is *amnesia*—total inability to recall the past. Soldiers who break down in the field often block out the memory of experiences that led to their collapse (Grinker & Spiegel, 1945). But forgetting that you are supposed to go for a job interview Thursday morning or forgetting the embarrassing things you said at a party last night may also be instances of repression.

Many psychologists believe that repression is a sign of struggle against impulses that conflict with conscious values. A teenage girl who has been taught that "nice" girls do not have sexual desires may flirt with a boy and then be shocked when he becomes sexually aroused. She may not be conscious of the conflict between her values and her actions.

Denial and repression are the most basic defense mechanisms. In denial, we block out situations that we cannot cope with. In repression, we block our unacceptable impulses or thoughts. These mechanisms form the bases for other defensive ways of coping.

PROJECTION. If a problem cannot be denied or repressed completely, it may be possible to distort its nature so that it can be more easily handled. One example of this is **projection,** the attribution of one's own repressed motives, ideas, or feelings to others. We ascribe feelings we do not want to someone else, thus locating the source of our conflict outside of ourselves. A corporation executive who feels guilty about the way he rose to power may project his own ruthless ambition onto his colleagues. He is simply doing his job, he believes, while his associates are all overly ambitious and preoccupied with power. A high school student talks his girlfriend into sneaking away with him for the weekend. It is a bad experience for both of them. Days later he insists that it was she who pushed him into it. He is not lying—he really believes that she did. Perhaps he feels guilty for insisting that they sneak away together, angry with her for not talking him out of it, disturbed by what he felt during the experience. To pull himself together, he locates the responsibility outside of himself. In both cases, the stressful problem has been repressed and then translated into a form that is less stressful and easier to handle.

Dana Bramel (1962) demonstrated projection with an experiment in which heterosexual male subjects were assigned a partner, and some were led to believe that they had measurable homosexual tendencies. Others were not so deceived. Bramel then studied the ways in which the deceived subjects tried to cope with the presumably disturbing "evidence" that they had homosexual tendencies. Many subjects used projection: In interviews after the experiment many more experimental than control

Repression Excluding uncomfortable thoughts from consciousness.

Projection Attributing one's own repressed motives, feelings, or wishes to others.

Identification Taking on the characteristics of someone else to avoid feeling incompetent.

subjects attributed homosexual tendencies to their *partners*. In other words, they dealt with the stress by locating the problem outside of themselves.*

IDENTIFICATION. The reverse of projection is **identification.** Through projection, we rid ourselves of undesirable characteristics that we have repressed by attributing them to someone else. Through identification, we take on the characteristics of someone else to share in that person's triumphs and to avoid feeling incompetent. The admired person's actions become a substitute for our own. Identification is sometimes considered a form of defensive coping because it enables people to resolve

*This study provoked considerable ethical controversy. The ethics of psychological research are discussed in Chapter 1 and in the box below.

The Ethics of Stress Research

A group of students who have assembled for a seminar suddenly notice that smoke is seeping under the door of the room where they are meeting. When they try to flee, they discover that the door is locked. This is not the prelude to a campus tragedy, but rather a psychology experiment (with a simulated fire to make it seem like real life) designed to investigate the effects of prior organization on group behavior under stress.

In the scientific community such experiments are highly controversial, and some psychologists believe they should be banned. No one doubts that such research has yielded important insights into stress. But many people fear that the new knowledge has been gained at a high price. As they see it, some research on stress is unethical because it can harm participants emotionally. The unwitting subjects in the simulated fire might have been badly frightened and, under stress, might have behaved in ways that would later give them cause for self-reproach. (There might have been physical harm inflicted as well in a panicky effort to escape.) In other experiments, they argue, researchers have led subjects to believe that they have failed important tests, that they have latent homosexual tendencies, or that they have caused pain or injury to others. Subjects have sometimes been deceived about the true nature of a study, coerced into participating, or even allowed to remain unaware that they were taking part in research (Cook, 1976).

At one extreme are the scientists who rank the obligation to protect subjects above all other considerations. They argue that researchers must never mislead subjects, must rule out research situations that subjects might find physically or emotionally stressful, and must brief potential participants thoroughly before seeking their consent to serve as subjects.

At the other extreme are those scientists who say that these restrictions cannot really minimize distress or prevent outright harm, but they will hamper research. When the obligation of scientists to protect human dignity is mentioned, this group cites the right of scientists to investigate and of society to profit from fruitful studies.

Many people on both sides of the controversy do not take such extreme positions. They hold, instead, that resourceful researchers can find ways to safeguard subjects without abandoning important research topics. In designing stress research, for example, psychologists can take advantage of situations in which stress occurs naturally. One way of doing this is to interview people in a dentist's waiting room, hospital patients about to undergo surgery, or students preparing for examinations.

As we saw in Chapter 1, the American Psychological Association recently adopted a set of "Ethical Principles in the Conduct of Research with Human Participants" (APA, 1982). Three of these principles are especially important to stress research. First, investigators must tell potential subjects in advance about any aspect of a study that could make them reluctant to take part if they knew about it. Then they must inform subjects about possible risks and protect them from "physical and mental discomfort, harm, and danger." Lastly, if any harmful consequences occur inadvertently, the investigators must assume responsibility "to detect and remove or correct" them.

conflicts vicariously. A parent with unfulfilled career ambitions may share emotionally in a child's professional success. When the child is promoted, the parent may feel as if he or she has triumphed.

Identification is often used as a form of self-defense in situations where a person feels utterly helpless. Psychoanalyst Bruno Bettelheim, once a prisoner in a Nazi concentration camp, described how some prisoners gradually came to identify with the Nazi guards. Over the years they began to copy the speech and mannerisms of the guards, and sometimes even their values. Bettelheim explains that the prisoners were completely dependent on the guards, who could treat them however they liked. The relationship between prisoner and guard was similar to that between child and parent. Bettelheim suggests that the guards may have consciously been trying to make the prisoners feel like children. For example, prisoners had to ask permission to go to the bathroom. Sometimes permission was denied, forcing on grown men the indignity of wetting their pants. Reduced to a childlike, helpless condition, prisoners reverted to a pattern developed in childhood: They identified with the aggressor (Bettelheim, 1943, 1960). Like children in conflict with a powerful and threatening adult, they admired their enemy and became like him as a way of defensively coping with unbearable and inescapable stress.

REGRESSION. People under severe stress, like the concentration camp victims described by Bettelheim, may revert to other kinds of childlike behavior as well. This is called **regression**. In Chapter 12, for example, we noted that people who become fixated at one of the early Freudian stages (oral, anal, or phallic) are especially likely to display the immature childlike traits associated with those stages whenever they come under stress.

Why do people regress? Some psychologists say it is because an adult cannot stand feeling helpless. Children, on the other hand, are made to feel helpless and dependent every day. Becoming more childlike can make total dependency or helplessness more bearable.

But regression is not always the result of imposed dependency. Adults who cry when their arguments fail may expect those around them to react sympathetically, as their parents did when they were children. Other adults may use temper tantrums in a similar way. In both examples people are drawing on childish behaviors to solve current problems, in the hope that someone will respond to them the way adults did when they were children. Inappropriate as it may seem, such immature and manipulative behavior often works—at least for a while.

INTELLECTUALIZATION. This defense mechanism is a subtle form of denial. We realize that we are threatened but detach ourselves from our problems by analyzing and intellectualizing them, almost as if they concerned other people and did not bother us emotionally. Parents who sit down to discuss their child's difficulties in a new school and hours later find themselves engaged in a sophisticated discussion of educational philosophy may be intellectualizing. They appear to be dealing with their problems but may, in fact, have cut themselves off from their emotions.

Like denial, **intellectualization** can be a useful defense under some circumstances. Doctors and nurses see pain and suffering every day of their working lives. They must keep some degree of detachment if they

Regression Reverting to childlike behavior and defenses.

Intellectualization Thinking abstractly about stressful problems as a way of detaching oneself from them.

Reaction formation Expression of exaggerated ideas and emotions that are the opposite of one's repressed beliefs or feelings.

Displacement Shifting repressed motives and emotions from an original object to a substitute object.

Sublimation Redirecting repressed motives and feelings into more socially acceptable channels.

are to remain objective. Bettelheim reports that he felt completely detached on his journey to a concentration camp. He simply did not feel that the experience was happening to him (Bettelheim, 1943).

REACTION FORMATION. The term **reaction formation** refers to a behavioral form of denial in which people express with exaggerated intensity ideas and emotions that are the opposite of their own. *Exaggeration* is the clue to this behavior. The man who praises a rival extravagantly may be covering up jealousy about his opponent's success. The woman who is overly cordial and claims, "I've never had an angry moment in my life," may be coping defensively with repressed hostile feelings that she finds intolerable. Reaction formation may also be a way of convincing oneself that one's motives are pure. The woman who feels ambivalent about being a mother may devote all her time to her children in an attempt to prove to *herself* that she is a good mother.

DISPLACEMENT. **Displacement** is the redirection of repressed motives and emotions from their original objects to substitute objects. Displacement permits repressed motives and feelings to find a new outlet. The man who has always wanted to be a father and learns that he cannot have children may feel inadequate. As a result, he may become extremely attached to a pet or to a brother or sister's child. The man who must smile and agree with his boss all day may come home and yell at his wife or children. The new object may not be a fully satisfactory substitute, but it probably provides at least some relief and perhaps allows the person to cope more effectively than would otherwise be possible.

SUBLIMATION. **Sublimation** involves transforming repressed motives or feelings into socially more acceptable forms. Aggressiveness might be transformed into competitiveness in business or sports. A strong and persistent desire for attention might be shaped into an interest in acting or politics. Curiosity about the human body might be transformed into an interest in painting or photographing nudes.

From the Freudian perspective, sublimation is not only necessary but desirable. If people can transform their sexual and aggressive drives into more socially acceptable forms, they are clearly better off. The instinctual drives are at least partially gratified with relatively little anxiety and guilt. Moreover, society benefits from the energy and effort channeled into the arts, literature, science, and other socially useful activities.

We have seen that there are many different ways of coping defensively with stress. Is defensive coping a sign that a person is immature, unstable, on the edge of a "breakdown"? The answer is no. The effects of prolonged stress can be so severe, as we will see in the next section, that in some cases defensive coping not only becomes essential to survival but even contributes to our overall ability to adapt and adjust. But even in less extreme situations people can profitably use defense mechanisms to cope with problems and stress. As Coleman (1979) points out, defenses are "essential for softening failure, alleviating tension and anxiety, and protecting one's feelings of adequacy and worth" (p. 153). But when a defense mechanism interferes with a person's ability to function, or creates more problems than it solves, psychologists consider the defense maladaptive.

What Stress Does to People

In 1976 the Canadian physiologist Hans Selye proposed that we react to physical and psychological stress in three stages that he called the "General Adaptation Syndrome." These three stages are the alarm reaction, resistance, and a final stage of exhaustion. The sequence may be repeated several times in a single day as new demands arise.

Stage 1, the alarm reaction, is the first response to stress. It begins when the body recognizes that it must fight off some physical or psychological danger. Emotions run high. We become more sensitive and alert. Respiration and heartbeat quicken, muscles tense, and other physiological changes occur. These changes help us to mobilize our coping resources in order to regain self-control. At this stage we might use either direct or defensive coping strategies. If neither of these approaches reduces the stress, we eventually enter Selye's second stage of adaptation.

During Stage 2, that of resistance, psychosomatic symptoms and other signs of strain appear as we struggle against increasing psychological disorganization. We intensify our use of both direct and defensive coping techniques. If our efforts succeed in reducing the stress, we return to a more normal state. But if the stress is extreme or prolonged, we may turn in desperation to coping techniques that are inappropriate to the present situation, and cling rigidly to those strategies despite evidence that they are not helping very much. If that happens, physical and emotional resources are further depleted and signs of wear and tear become even more apparent.

In the third stage the person is likely to make massive use of increasingly ineffective defense mechanisms in a desperate attempt to bring the stress under control. It is not unusual for some people to lose touch with reality and to show clear signs of emotional disorder or mental illness in this stage of adaptation. Other people may show signs of "burnout," such as inability to concentrate, irritability, procrastination, and a cynical belief that nothing is worthwhile (Freudenberger, 1983). At times, psychosomatic symptoms such as skin or stomach problems occur and some victims of burnout turn to alcohol or drugs in an effort to cope with stress. If stress continues, irreparable physical or psychological damage may occur—even death.

One of the most startling implications of Seyle's theory is the possibility that psychological stress may cause disease or at least make certain diseases worse. This idea is controversial, but recent studies strongly support the belief that psychological factors lie at the root of some of humanity's worst afflictions, including heart disease.

Some investigators have been able to measure physiological changes connected with stress. In a study of young Norwegian soldiers who were training to be parachutists, blood tests done in the early stages of training (when the recruits were most fearful) showed an increase in the amount of the hormone cortisol in their blood and a drop in the amount of testosterone. As the men became more accustomed to jumping, and therefore less fearful, hormone levels returned to normal (Ursin, Baade, & Levine, 1978). Similar hormone changes have been found in people experiencing such stressful conditions as riding a crowded commuter train, taking an oral exam for the PhD, and doing factory work

Coping with a highly stressful situation can cause physiological reactions such as quickened respiration and heartbeat, muscle tension, and even changes in hormonal levels.

that required many repetitions of the same operation in a short time (Frankenhauser, 1979).

Other research has demonstrated a connection between stress and the body's immune system, which protects against disease. Animal experiments have shown a relationship between psychological factors and the immune system. Immune-system activity in rats can be increased or decreased through conditioning, a kind of learning process that we studied in Chapter 6. Moreover, when mice are subjected to loud noises, their immune systems do not work as well as usual. The effect is similar when bighorn sheep undergo the stress of capture (Anderson, 1982).

Animal studies also demonstrate a connection between stress and cancer. In one study a group of mice known to be vulnerable to cancer was kept for 400 days in standard housing, in which they heard noise made by people and other animals. By the end of this period 92 percent of the mice had developed cancer. In contrast, when a comparable group of mice was kept in quiet, low-stress conditions, only 7 percent developed cancer. In other experiments cancer was diagnosed earlier and death occurred sooner in mice that got frequent shocks with no escape possible than in mice that were allowed to cope with the stress of shocks by escaping (Anderson, 1982).

Such studies, it must be emphasized, do not prove that stress *causes* cancer; rather they suggest that stress may weaken the body's capacity to fight cancer as well as other diseases. Of course, no one knows whether or not people react like laboratory animals. Still, researchers have found evidence of reduced effectiveness in the immune systems of Skylab astronauts just after they went through the stress of splashdown. And at least one psychologist has found a correlation between certain personality characteristics, including difficulty in handling stress, and cancer and other major diseases (Ader, cited in Anderson, 1982).

Moreover, it is common knowledge that stress on the job or in personal life seems to increase the risk of coronary disease. The connection between stress and illness is especially marked when a person can do nothing directly to control the source of stress, as in the loss of a job or the death of a relative (Glass, 1977). Also, "Type A" people are especially prone to heart disease. Extreme Type A people are obsessed by a sense of urgency of time and constantly try to do several things at once. They are often hostile and impatient, speak in staccato, tend to finish other people's sentences for them, and are competitive and difficult to get along with. At work they usually drive themselves harder than they do their subordinates (Friedman & Rosenman, 1974). "Type B" people, by contrast, are rarely driven to increase the quantity of work they do. They care, instead, about its quality and about the quality of their lives in general. Although they are often as intelligent, ambitious, and successful as their Type A counterparts, they are less aggressive.

Friedman and Rosenman (1974) found that the Type A men first studied in 1960 were nearly three times as likely to get heart disease within the next 10 years as the Type B men. Glass (1977) has suggested that Type A people are especially sensitive to negative sources of stress that threaten their control over their environment, and it appears to be their response to such stressful life events that increases their likelihood of heart disease.

Cancer and Stress

To many psychotherapists *illusion* is a bad word. In their view, staying in touch with reality is the hallmark of mental health, and people who cherish too many illusions, especially about important things, are not truly well adjusted.

Shelley E. Taylor (1983) takes a strikingly different view. "Far from impeding adjustment," she says, "illusion may be essential for adequate coping" (p. 1171).

Taylor reached this conclusion after a 2-year study of women with breast cancer. The women who coped best with the stress of disfiguring surgery, painful follow-up treatment, and fear of death proved to be those who constructed comforting illusions about themselves and their illness. Taylor defined illusions as beliefs that were based on an overly optimistic view of the facts or that had no factual basis at all.

The helpful illusions grew out of the women's attempts to do three things: to understand the causes of their cancer and its significance in their lives; to gain a sense of mastery over the disease in particular and their lives in general; and to restore their self-esteem in the face of a devastating experience.

Here are some of Taylor's findings on each of these points.

1. Although the causes of cancer are not fully understood, 95 percent of the women nevertheless believed that they knew why their cancer had occurred. Some blamed the stress of an unhappy marriage. Others mentioned birth control pills, heredity, or diet. The women's erroneous belief that they had pinpointed the reason for their illness seemed to make them feel better psychologically. It may have helped them to feel that they were not at the mercy of a capricious fate. Whatever the reason, even highly improbable explanations, like having been hit in the breast with a Frisbee, seemed useful.

   Moreover, many women took comfort from the belief that having cancer had in some ways made their lives better. "I have much more enjoyment of each day," said one. "You find out that things like relationships are really the most important things you have—the people you know and your family—everything else is just way down the line," said another (Taylor, 1983, p. 1163).

2. Having cancer is a very sobering experience that can make people feel powerless. To counter that feeling, two-thirds of the women expressed the conviction that if they thought the right thoughts and did the right things, they could prevent the recurrence of cancer. As one woman put it, "I think that if you feel you are in control of it, you can control it up to a point. I absolutely refuse to have any more cancer" (Taylor, 1983, p. 1163).

3. Numerous studies show that undergoing a major stressful experience often lowers self-esteem, even if the victim is blameless. That may explain why the women tried to feel better about themselves by drawing comparisons with others whom they chose to regard as less fortunate. "I think I did extremely well under the circumstances," said one woman, remarking that there are "some women who aren't strong enough, who fall apart and become psychologically disturbed" (Taylor, 1983, p. 1165).

It is clear that illusions promoted the adjustment of the women in Taylor's study. But relying on illusions would seem to be a very risky way of adjusting: If the illusion is shattered, then the person's sense of well-being should collapse as well. For example, imagine that a woman suffers a recurrence of cancer despite following a rigorous diet, or practicing positive thinking in the firm belief that it would keep her well. What happens to this woman's ability to cope?

Oddly enough, the women in Taylor's study did not seem to be too troubled when their theories turned out to be wrong, their self-protective measures useless. Of course, they were disheartened by their failing health. But their adjustment seemed none the worse because they had embraced an illusion and seen it fall to pieces. What they usually did then was simply take a new approach to coping, try to control another aspect of their lives, or seek to bolster their self-esteem in a new way.

To remain continuously in close touch with unrelieved reality is sometimes too much to bear. At such times, Taylor suggests, the well-adjusted people may be those who allow themselves to nurture their illusions and "are ultimately restored by those illusions" (p. 1168).

Sources of Extreme Stress

Outside the laboratory stress comes from a variety of sources, ranging from unemployment to wartime combat, from violent natural disaster to rape. In this section we will look briefly at some of these major stressors, the effects they have on people, and how people try to cope with them.

1. *Unemployment.* Joblessness is a major source of stress. One researcher found that when the jobless rate rises, so do first admissions to psychiatric hospitals, infant mortality, deaths from heart disease, alcohol-related diseases, and suicide (Brenner, 1973, 1976). In a study of aircraft workers who lost their jobs, Rayman and Bluestone (1982) found that many of the workers reported suffering from high blood pressure and from alcoholism, heavy smoking, and anxiety. Other studies have found signs of family strain. "Things just fell apart," one worker said after he and his wife both lost their jobs.

People seem to react to the stress of unemployment in several stages (Powell & Driscoll, 1973). First comes a period of relaxation and relief, in which they take a vacation of sorts, confident they will find another job. Stage 2, marked by continued optimism, is a time of concentrated job hunting. In Stage 3, a period of vacillation and doubt, people become moody, their relationships with family and friends deteriorate, and they scarcely bother to look for work. By the time they reach Stage 4, a period of malaise and cynicism, people have simply given up.

It is important to note that these effects are not universal, though they may be quite frequent. Moreover, there are some indications that joblessness may not so much create new psychological difficulties as bring to the surface previously hidden ones. Finally, two studies have shown that death rates go up and psychiatric symptoms get worse not just during periods of high unemployment but also during short, rapid upturns in the economy (Eyer, 1977; Brenner, 1979). This finding lends support to the idea we discussed earlier—that change (whether good or bad) causes stress. Unemployment is simply one source of major life change.

2. *Divorce and separation.* As Coleman (1984) observes, "the deterioration or ending of an intimate relationship is one of the more potent of stressors and one of the more frequent reasons why people seek psychotherapy" (p. 160). The partners may feel they have failed at one of life's most important endeavors. Strong emotional ties frequently continue to bind the pair. If only one spouse wanted to end the marriage, that one may feel sadness and guilt at hurting a once-loved partner; the rejected spouse may suffer from anger, feelings of humiliation, and self-recriminations over his (or her) role in the failure. Even if the decision to separate was shared, ambivalent feelings of love and hate can make life confusing. Under these circumstances it is common to find a great deal of defensive coping; denial and projection in particular are often used to cushion the impact of divorce or separation.

3. *Bereavement.* "But O the heavy change, now thou art gone, /Now thou art gone, and never must return." So John Milton wrote of the death of the young Lycidas, and few people who have lost someone to death would take issue with the poet's sentiments.

Most people come through the experience of bereavement without suffering permanent harm, but usually not without going through a long process that Freud called the "work of mourning." Janis and his colleagues (1969) have described normal grief as beginning with numbness and progressing through months of distress in which anger, despair, intense grief and yearning, depression, and apathy may all appear.

In a book based on his classic study of widows in London, Parkes (1972) offers poignant glimpses of typical grief. "It's like a dream," one widow said. "I feel I'm going to wake up and it'll be all right. He'll be back again." Several widows recognized in themselves an irrational need to try to find their dead husband. "Everywhere I go I am searching for him," one widow said. "In crowds, in church, in the supermarket. I keep scanning faces. People must think I'm odd." In the same vein, another widow said, "I go to the grave . . . but he's not there." Most of the women spoke of being angry. At the height of their grief, they sometimes blamed doctors for not doing more, God for taking the husband away, or even the husband himself, as if he had deserted them on purpose. "Why did he do this to me?" one woman said.

All these reactions are attempts to cope defensively with an inescapable and extremely painful reality. In most cases, they allow the survivor to gather strength for more direct coping efforts later on—such as selling belongings and moving out of the home they shared with the dead person.

4. *Combat.* In all wars, it is safe to say, some find it impossible to hold up under the extreme stress of battle. Disabling reaction to combat stress was called "shell shock" in World War I, "operational fatigue" or "war neurosis" in World War II, "combat exhaustion" in the Korean and Vietnam wars. In each war the symptoms were the same. The first sign of disintegrating self-control might be crying over small frustrations or bursting into rage in response to a harmless remark. The initial reaction later gave way to inability to sleep, cringing at sudden noises, psychological confusion, crying without being able to stop, or sitting silently and staring into space. In World War II about 5 percent of the combat soldiers were discharged for psychiatric reasons, and some of these veterans are still hospitalized as a result of the stress that was experienced.

Even soldiers who are able to cope relatively effectively with stress during combat often find that they have a great deal of difficulty coping after they leave the battlefield. This has come to be known as "post-traumatic stress disorder," a topic that is examined more closely in the box on page 424.

5. *Natural and manmade catastrophes.* These include floods, earthquakes, violent storms, fires, and plane crashes. Psychological reactions to all such stressors have much in common. At first, in the *shock* stage, "the victim is stunned, dazed, and apathetic," and sometimes even "stuporous, disoriented, and amnesic for the traumatic event." Then, in the *suggestible* stage, victims are passive and quite ready to do what rescuers tell them to do. In the third phase, the *recovery* stage, emotional balance is regained, but anxiety often persists, and victims may need to describe their experiences over and over again (Colemen et al., 1984). And some investigators report that in later stages survivors may feel irrationally guilty because they lived while others died. Said a stewardess who survived a plane crash, "It's not fair. Everyone else is hurt. Why aren't I?" (*Time*, Jan. 15, 1973, p. 53).

Psychological reactions to natural and manmade disasters have much in common. Victims progress from the initial shock stage to a suggestible stage to a final recovery stage.

Posttraumatic Stress Disorders

If all human behavior followed simple, strict rules of logic, then the symptoms of stress would disappear when the stressful events that caused them came to an end. But psychologists recognize that some stress disorders—those known as *posttraumatic stress disorders*—can arise *after* a person has suffered a severe trauma or crisis.

The kinds of events that can lead to posttraumatic stress disorders are usually outside the realm of ordinary grief and loss (APA, 1980). They are experiences that even the best adjusted among us would find terrifying and anxiety provoking: rape, for example, or military combat, or a devastating flood.

In some cases, posttraumatic disorders set in either right after a traumatic event or within a short time. But in other cases, months may go by, during which the victim appears to have recovered from the experience; then, without warning, psychological symptoms suddenly develop. In some instances, the symptoms disappear quickly, though they may recur repeatedly; in others, they continue for weeks or months.

Symptoms are often striking. To take one example, after a flood in which 125 people perished,

Recovery from any posttraumatic stress disorder depends a great deal on how much emotional support victims get from family, friends, and community.

a man whose wife and children were among the dead could not sleep unless he left a light burning in his room. Darkness reminded him of the awful moment when the power had failed just before the flood waters engulfed his house and killed his wife and children. Dramatic nightmares in which the victim seems to reexperience the terrifying event exactly as it happened, are common. So are daytime flashbacks, in which there is also a feeling of reliving the trauma. Generally, the victims of posttraumatic disorders cannot function well in their day-to-day existence, and they may withdraw from social life and from job and family responsibilities.

Combat veterans appear to be especially vulnerable to such problems. The Center for Policy Research in New York found that more than a third of the men who took part in heavy combat in Vietnam showed signs of serious posttraumatic distress. Certainly many Vietnam veterans have had unusual difficulty in readjusting to civilian life. Indeed, their symptoms tend to be so serious that the posttraumatic stress disorder in Vietnam returnees has been given its own name: the Vietnam syndrome.

Some of its manifestations are the same as in any posttraumatic disorder, but many Vietnam veterans have experienced additional problems, among them paranoia, inability to love or trust others, alienation from their own emotions, feelings of guilt about their combat experiences, and, most notably, feelings of uncontrollable anger that sometimes erupt in violence. Rates of drug and alcohol abuse have been higher than average in Vietnam returnees, and some of the veterans have been arrested for crimes they attribute to their emotional difficulties.

Many Vietnam veterans have sought psychiatric treatment. Psychiatrists and psychologists who work with them cite two factors that perhaps contribute to the severity of the symptoms. For one thing, civilian casualties in the Vietnam War were higher than in most wars, which may give rise to feelings of guilt. Another presumably important factor is the unpopularity of the war. Instead of being welcomed home as heroes, returning Vietnam soldiers were often cold-shouldered, as if some people blamed them for the war and for what many Americans view as its excesses. These critical attitudes are significant, for recovery from any posttraumatic disorder depends a great deal on how much emotional support victims get from family, friends, and community.

Psychologists hold different opinions about what constitutes good adjustment. Some base their evaluation on a person's ability to live according to social norms. Everyone has hostile and selfish wishes; everyone dreams impossible dreams. People who learn to control forbidden impulses and to limit their goals to those society allows are, by this definition, "well adjusted." A woman who grows up in a small town, attends her state university, teaches for a year or two, then settles down to a peaceful family life might be considered "well adjusted" to the extent that she is living by the predominant values of her community.

Other psychologists disagree strongly with this conformist viewpoint. Barron (1963) argues that "refusal to adjust . . . is very often the mark of a healthy character." Society is not always right. To accept its standards blindly—to say, for example, "My country, right or wrong"—is to renounce the right to make independent judgments. Barron suggests that well-adjusted people *enjoy* the difficulties and ambiguities of life; they do not sidestep them by unthinking conformity. They accept challenges and are willing to experience pain and confusion. Confident of their ability to deal with problems in a realistic and mature way, they can admit primitive or childish impulses into consciousness. Temporary regression does not frighten them. Barron sees flexibility, spontaneity, and creativity as signs of healthy adjustment.

Still other psychologists suggest that well-adjusted people have learned to balance conformity and nonconformity, self-control and spontaneity. They can let themselves go at times, but can control themselves in situations where acting on their impulses would be damaging. They can change themselves when society so demands, but they try to change society when this seems the better course. Such flexibility is often considered a sign that these people can realistically judge both the world around them and their own needs and capabilities. They both know their strengths and admit their weaknesses. As a result, they have chosen an approach to life that is in harmony with their inner selves. They do not feel they must act against their values in order to be successful. Their self-trust enables them to face conflicts and threats without excessive anxiety and, perhaps more important, lets them risk their feelings and self-esteem in intimate relationships.

Another means of evaluating adjustment is to use specific criteria, such as the following (Coleman & Hammen, 1974):

1. *Does the person's behavior really meet the stress, or does it simply postpone resolving the problem?* Various forms of escapism—drugs, alcohol, and even endless fantasizing through books, movies, and television—may divert us from our pain. But they do not eliminate the causes of our difficulties. Thus completely relying on escapism can never make for truly effective adjustment to a stressful situation.

2. *Does the action satisfy the person's own needs?* Often we act to reduce external pressures without considering our personal needs. People may abandon their own career goals because of the goals of a spouse. In the short run, external pressure on them may be reduced, but they may be

The Self-Actualizing Person

Another view of the well-adjusted person was provided by Abraham Maslow. People who are well adjusted attempt to "actualize" themselves. That is, they live in a way that they believe is best for their own growth and fulfillment regardless of what others may think. After studying a number of famous people and a group of college students, Maslow (1954) compiled a list of 15 traits that he believed were characteristic of self-actualizing people:

1. *More efficient perception of reality.* They judge people and events realistically and are better able than others to accept uncertainty and ambiguity.
2. *Acceptance of self and others.* They take others for what they are and are not guilty or defensive about themselves.
3. *Spontaneity.* This quality is shown more in thinking than in action. As a matter of fact, self-actualizing people are frequently quite conventional in behavior.
4. *Problem centering.* They are more concerned with problems than with themselves and are likely to have what they consider important goals.
5. *Detachment.* They need privacy and do not mind being alone.
6. *Autonomy.* They are able to be independent of their environment.
7. *Continued freshness of appreciation,* even of often-repeated experiences.
8. *Mystical experiences, or the oceanic feeling.*

This feeling, which Maslow includes under the heading of "peak experiences," frequently involves wonder, awe, a feeling of oneness with the universe, and a loss of self.
9. *Gemeinschaftsgefuhl,* or social interest. This is a feeling of unity with humanity in general.
10. *Interpersonal relationships.* Deep, close relationships with a chosen few characterize self-actualizing people.
11. *Democratic character structure.* Self-actualizing people are relatively indifferent to such matters as sex, birth, race, color, and religion in judging other people.
12. *Discrimination between means and ends.* They enjoy activities for their own sake, but also appreciate the difference between means and goals.
13. *Sense of humor.* Their sense of humor is philosophical rather than hostile.
14. *Creativeness.* Their creativity in any field consists mostly of the ability to generate new ideas.
15. *Resistance to enculturation.* They are not rebellious, but they are generally independent of any given culture.

Maslow did not consider self-actualizing people perfect—disregard of others is one of their possible faults. Moreover, having the characteristics on this list does not mean that you are self-actualizing, only that self-actualization is important to you and that you are the type of person who tries to achieve it.

frustrated and disappointed for the rest of their lives. A solution that creates such inner conflict is often not really an effective adjustment.

3. *Is the action in harmony with the person's environment?* Some people satisfy their needs in a way that hurts others. A young executive who uses people and manipulates co-workers may "get ahead" through such actions. But even if he does succeed in becoming vice president of his company, he may find himself without friends. He may become afraid that others will treat him as he treated them. Ultimately this situation can become seriously stressful and frustrating. Good adjustment must take into consideration both individual needs and the well-being of others.

We have seen that there are many different standards for deciding if a person is well-adjusted. It is apparent that a person considered well adjusted according to one standard may or may not be considered well adjusted by other criteria. As you might expect, the same holds true when we try to decide what behaviors are "abnormal"—the topic of the next chapter.

Application

The Stockholm Syndrome

One of the clearest illustrations of adaptation to extraordinary stress is the reaction of hostages to their captors. The stress of being taken hostage is sudden, unexpected, and intense. Hostages, captors, and outside authorities often have little control over events as they unfold. What kinds of adjustment mechanisms do people use in such situations?

One particularly striking pattern of coping has come to be known as the "Stockholm Syndrome." The most remarkable feature of this pattern is that hostages actually side with their captors—and the captors come to sympathize with their captives. The term "Stockholm Syndrome" derives from a 1973 bank robbery in Stockholm, Sweden, where robbers held four hostages captive for 6 days. By the end of the ordeal the hostages found themselves more loyal to the bank robbers than to the police. They ultimately refused to testify against their former captors. One woman hostage became so emotionally attached to one of the robbers that she broke her engagement to another man after the incident.

Psychologists define three stages of the syndrome:

1. The hostages begin to feel warm toward their captors.
2. The hostages develop negative feelings toward the authorities who are trying to rescue them.
3. The captors develop positive feelings toward their victims. Both groups are isolated and terrorized, and therefore come to believe, "We are in this together."

Why would a hostage come to like or even love a captor? Dr. Frank Ochberg, director of the Michigan Department of Mental Health, explains,

"When someone captures you and places you in an infantile position, he sets the stage for love as a response to infantile terror—he could kill you but he does not and you are grateful" (*Time*, 1979).

Dr. Robert Jay Lifton of Yale University writes of the "psychology of the pawn" (1961). Manipulated through constant fear of injury or death to act as instructed, pawns adapt to events beyond their control. They adopt certain behaviors for coping, such as submissiveness. Like other human beings, pawns are deeply sensitive to their limitations and unfulfilled potential. They are vulnerable to any feelings of guilt the captors may try to induce.

Lorraine Berzins, an officer with the Canadian Penitentiary Service, offers other insights into why a hostage develops a positive feeling toward a captor. In 1970 she was taken hostage at knifepoint by an inmate. She had been professionally trained to deal with violent behavior, and eventually she got

The effects of captivity on a hostage continue after liberation.

her captor to trust her. She observes:

There may be a clash between our different perceptions of a person's "good" qualities alongside his criminal behavior. . . . If a person is not trained or experienced enough to be able to accommodate the seeming contradiction of the two, he may need to deny one in order to preserve the other. The hostage, to preserve the trust that his survival depends on, may need to see his captor as "all good" to resolve the dissonance and maintain harmony between them. (Schreiber, 1978)

Why do the hostages develop negative feelings toward the authorities who are trying to rescue them?

For the authorities the desired outcome is the capture of the kidnappers and the recovery of persons and property. Having been on the outside and indulged in some of those same calculations himself as he followed other kidnap episodes in the news, the hostage is deeply distrustful of the negotiators. Suppose they overreact. . . . "I had this very strong feeling that my life wasn't as important to the negotiators as it was to me," says Berzins. (Schreiber, 1978)

Berzins also states, "If your way of coping with anxiety is to project blame onto other people, you're obviously not going to project it onto the hostage-taker because it's too dangerous. . . . The easiest target is the outside authorities."

The prisoner sometimes feels that he (or she) and the hostage-taker constitute a small group facing a hostile world. Isolated from outside information, Patty Hearst was told that her parents and society no longer cared about her. This lie was seemingly confirmed when police raided the Los Angeles hideout of her six captors and they burned to death (Conway & Siegelman, 1980).

A hostage may be unclear as to exactly what principles of the outside authorities he or she is defending. Lifton says that one of the ex-hostages in Iran viewed resistance to his captors partly as a matter of suffering for the sake of the Shah, whom he did not wholeheartedly support. The Iranians led him to focus on a questionable cause and to overlook the fact that he was being held illegally (*U.S. News & World Report*, 1979).

Why would captors develop positive attitudes toward their victims? Confronted by authorities who want to demonstrate that hostage-taking cannot succeed, captors know they may very well die. Concern about the pain and discomfort of their victims helps keep their minds off the stress that they themselves are feeling. Also, despite their proclamations of willingness to die for their cause, they often compromise their ideals. To survive themselves, they often refrain from harming their hostages.

The Stockholm Syndrome does not always occur. According to Lifton, if hostages have a "relatively strong belief system" or a "varied knowledge and a fluid kind of identity," they can withstand shocking challenges to their viewpoints (*U.S. News & World Report*, 1979). Moreover, captors may overmanipulate their victims, causing captives who were initially fearful to become angered by their humiliating treatment. These manipulations may be heavy-handed, easily perceived, and countered by hostages who reflect upon them and discuss them with one another.

Resentment at overmanipulation led the American hostages in Iran to develop strategies that maintained their pride. Resourceful secret communication systems and humorous cartoons mocking the Iranians enabled the Americans to enjoy outwitting their captors. Other strategies used by these hostages to preserve their individuality included demanding better food, maintaining a neat appearance, observing a busy daily schedule, and attempting to escape.

The effects of captivity on a hostage continue after liberation. They can include:

1. Feelings of guilt about hostages who have died or about people who are still hostages.
2. Lack of any feelings, which gives way periodically to an intense need to talk.
3. Suspicions that they are being deceived, especially by established authorities.
4. Hostility, in particular toward employers who expect ex-hostages to return to normal quickly.
5. Loss of confidence in the world, requiring continual reassurances from family and friends that the ex-hostage's life will not be violently interrupted again.
6. Need to find meaning in the ordeal, which leads some hostages to feel a sense of rebirth or a resolve to "turn over a new leaf."

If you have understood this chapter, you will recognize that all these after-effects are normal responses to extreme stress and that all of them are attempts to cope effectively with overwhelming pressure. Thus they illustrate, in exaggerated form, the same coping processes we all use in extraordinary situations.

1. *Adjustment* refers to any attempt to deal with stress; to adapt to your physical and social environment; and to achieve harmony between your desires and the demands and constraints imposed on you by the environment.

2. *Stress* refers to people's reactions to situations in which they feel threatened, pressured, frustrated, anxious, or in conflict. Pleasant and unpleasant situations can be stressful if they cause change and discontinuity in one's life. The Social Readjustment Rating Scale is used to measure how much stress a person has undergone within any given period. The scale classifies stress as normal, mild, moderate, or severe.

3. While significant life changes are obviously stressful, it is possible that little daily frustrations—"hassles"—cause at least as much stress. Both major and minor events are stressful in that they give rise to feelings of pressure, frustration, conflict, and anxiety. Minor frustrations may be triggered by major life events such as death or divorce.

4. *Pressure* occurs when we feel forced to speed up, intensify, or redirect our behavior, or to meet a higher standard of performance. We may pressure ourselves to live up to some internal standard of excellence. External sources of pressure include competition, change, and the expectations of family and friends.

5. *Frustration* occurs when people are prevented from achieving a goal. They must either give up the goal, find some new way to achieve it, or adjust to living with their disappointment. The five leading sources of frustration are delays, lack of resources, losses, failure, and the feeling that life is lonely and meaningless.

6. *Conflict* is probably the most common problem to which people must adjust. Conflict occurs when a person is faced with two incompatible demands, opportunities, needs, or goals.

7. One way of describing conflict is in terms of two opposite tendencies: approach and avoidance. We want to approach things that attract us and avoid things that repel us. These contradictory feelings produce three basic types of conflict.

8. In an *approach/approach conflict* we are attracted to two goals at the same time and must either make a choice between them or modify one or both of them in some way.

9. In an *avoidance/avoidance conflict* we face two undesired or threatening, yet unavoidable, alternatives and must either choose the one that causes the least discomfort or, in certain extreme instances, sit the situation out and wait for the inevitable.

10. In an *approach/avoidance conflict* we are both attracted to and repelled by the same goal. Both the desire to approach and the desire to avoid a goal grow stronger as we near it, with the avoidance tendency growing at a faster rate. In double approach/avoidance conflict there are good and bad features associated with both goals.

11. *Anxiety* is a form of stress in which people experience all the symptoms of fear but cannot identify what is frightening or upsetting them. Many psychologists consider anxiety a sign of internal, unconscious conflict.

12. People differ in their perception of stress. The same obstacle looks like a mountain to one person, like a molehill to another. Someone who is self-confident and has successfully handled similar situations in the past is less likely to find a given situation stressful than someone who lacks self-assurance. Highly stress-resistant people are inclined to feel committed, challenged, and in control of events in their lives.

13. There are two general types of coping with stress: direct coping and defensive coping. Direct coping refers to any action people take to change an uncomfortable situation: either by confronting problems directly, compromising, or withdrawing from the situation entirely. Withdrawal can sometimes be the most realistic form of adjustment; the danger of withdrawal, however, is that it may turn into avoidance of all similar situations.

14. Defensive coping is a means of coping with situations that people feel unable to resolve. Defensive coping involves the use of *defense mechanisms*. In using defense mech-

anisms, people deceive themselves about reality in order to reduce stress. The most common defense mechanisms are denial, repression, projection, identification, regression, intellectualization, reaction formation, displacement, and sublimation.

15. *Denial* is the refusal to acknowledge that a painful or threatening situation exists. *Repression,* a form of forgetting, is probably the most common means of blocking out unacceptable impulses or thoughts. *Projection* involves attributing one's own motives, feelings, or wishes to others. The reverse is *identification* — taking on the characteristics of someone else in order to share that person's successes and avoid feelings of personal incompetence.

16. *Regression* refers to the reversion to childlike, even infantile behavior in situations where no form of adult behavior will work. *Intellectualization* is a subtle form of denial in which we detach ourselves emotionally from our problems by analyzing them in purely rational terms. *Reaction formation* is exhibited when we exaggeratedly express emotions of ideas that are the opposite of what we really feel or believe.

17. *Displacement* is the redirection of repressed motives or emotions from original objects to substitute objects.

18. *Sublimation* is the redirection of repressed motives or emotions into more socially acceptable forms.

19. Defense mechanisms can be an adaptive means of coping with stress, particularly prolonged stress. They are considered maladaptive only when they interfere with a person's ability to function or when they create more problems than they solve.

20. Hans Selye believes that people react to stress in three stages that he calls the General Adaptation Syndrome: alarm, resistance, and exhaustion. In stage 1 the body mobilizes itself against the physiological effects of stress, and people begin to employ either direct or defensive coping strategies. Psychosomatic symptoms tend to appear in the second stage, and the use of coping strategies intensifies. The third stage is characterized by the application of increasingly ineffective defense mechanisms that can result in mental and physical exhaustion. If stress continues, irreparable physical and psychological damage may follow, including death.

21. A growing body of research points to a connection between prolonged stress and the weakening of the body's immune system. Some investigators have found a correlation between the ability to tolerate stress and such major diseases as cancer.

22. Stress is commonly known to increase the risk of heart disease. "Type A" people, who are especially prone to heart disease, tend to be unusually driven and aggressive. "Type B" people, who are less at risk for heart disease, are less driven and aggressive.

23. The major stressors—including unemployment, divorce and separation, bereavement, combat, and natural and manmade disasters—create major difficulties in adjustment and may produce disabling symptoms a long time after the events themselves are over.

24. The psychological reaction to unemployment typically follows a pattern that ends in physical illness, strained relationships, and total apathy and resignation. Divorce and separation are stressful because they bring about the end of an intimate relationship, and also because they induce feelings of sadness, guilt, rejection, failure, and ambivalence. The adjustment to loss requires working through an extended period of mourning. Combat stress may result in immediate disabling reactions such as loss of self-control or withdrawal from reality. This form of stress may also manifest itself later on as posttraumatic stress disorder. People's psychological reactions to natural and manmade catastrophes generally progress from a shock stage, to a passive and suggestible stage, and finally to a recovery stage. Anxiety may persist through the recovery stage, with victims continuing to relive their experience and to feel guilty for having survived.

25. Psychologists differ in their opinions about what makes a "well-adjusted person." Some believe that good adjustment depends on people's ability to conform to social norms, to control their drives, and to strive for goals of which society approves. Others feel that people are well adjusted when they are able to

face the difficulties and ambiguities of life with flexibility, spontaneity, and creativity. Still others suggest that the well-adjusted person is able to balance conformity and non-conformity, self-control and spontaneity. Finally, some psychologists evaluate a person's adjustment according to specific criteria, such as how well the adjustment actually solves the problem and satisfies both personal needs and the needs of others.

Review Questions

1. _____ refers to any attempt to deal with stress; to adapt to your physical and social environment; and to achieve harmony between your desires and the demands and constraints imposed by the environment.

2. People's reactions to situations in which they feel threatened, pressured, frustrated, anxious, or in conflict are known collectively as _____.

3. Both pleasant and unpleasant situations can be stressful.   T/F

4. Pressure/frustration occurs when we feel forced to speed up, intensify, or redirect our behavior, or to meet a higher standard of performance.

5. Frustration/conflict occurs when people are prevented from achieving a goal.

6. Probably the most common problem to which people must adjust is anxiety/conflict.

7. Match each type of conflict with its definition:
___ approach/approach
___ avoidance/avoidance
___ approach/avoidance
___ double approach/ avoidance

    A. We must choose between two undesired, yet unavoidable alternatives.
    B. We are both attracted and repelled by the same goal.
    C. We are attracted to two goals at the same time.
    D. Realization of one goal conflicts with the realization of a second.

8. _____ is a form of stress in which people experience all the symptoms of fear but cannot identify what is frightening them.

9. There are two general types of coping, _____ and _____ .

10. Confronting problems, compromising, or withdrawing from the situation entirely are all forms of _____ coping.

11. Defensive coping is a means of coping with situations that people feel unable to resolve/can exercise control over.

12. Match each of the following defense mechanisms with its definition.
___ Denial
___ Repression
___ Projection
___ Identification
___ Regression
___ Intellectualization
___ Reaction formation
___ Displacement
___ Sublimation

    A. a form of forgetting
    B. detachment from problems through rational analysis
    C. reversion to childlike, even childlike behavior
    D. expression of emotions or ideas that are the opposite of what we really feel or believe
    E. redirection of motives or emotions to other objects
    F. refusal to acknowledge that a painful or threatening situation exists
    G. attributing one's own motives and feelings to others
    H. redirection of motives or emotions into more socially acceptable forms
    I. taking on the characteristics of someone else in order to share that person's successes and avoid feelings of personal incompetence

13. The General Adaptation syndrome consists of three stages of reaction stress: _____ , _____ , and exhaustion.

14. Research so far has been unable to find a connection between stress and the strength of the body's immune system.   T/F

Outline

Abnormal Behavior

14

When does behavior become abnormal? The answer to this question is harder than it may seem. There is no doubt that the man on a street corner who claims to be George Washington or the woman who insists that elevators are trying to kill her is behaving abnormally, but what about the 20 students who cram themselves into a telephone booth, or the business executive who has three martinis every day for lunch? Whether these behaviors are classified as abnormal depends upon whose standards and system of values are being used: society's, the individual's, or the mental health professional's.

Table 14-1 presents three different views on mental health; each uses different standards to judge normal and abnormal behavior. Society's main concern is whether behavior conforms to the existing social order. The individual is concerned with his or her own sense of well-being. The mental health professional is concerned with characteristics of personality. Because these views are often at odds, it is difficult for psychologists to derive a single definition of normal and abnormal behavior that includes them all.

To some extent psychologists use *intrapersonal standards* of normality, that is, they try to evaluate people in terms of their own lives. Consider the following examples:

> A bookkeeper falls behind in her work because no matter how often she erases stray pencil marks on her ledger, she cannot get the page clean enough. Her employer does not understand. Finally, one morning, she cannot get up to go to work.

> The adolescent son of a wealthy suburbanite has a substantial allowance of his own, yet one night he is arrested for trying to hold up a gas station. He insists that there is nothing wrong with his actions.

> A quiet, well-behaved child suddenly covers the living room walls with paint. When questioned, she explains that "Johnny" did it. Within a few weeks the child is spending all her time alone in her room talking with her imaginary friend.

Each of these people is acting in an impaired, self-defeating manner. The bookkeeper has set herself an impossible task. Her need for neatness is so exaggerated that she cannot possibly succeed. The young man is

Table 14-1 Viewpoints on Mental Health

	Standards/Values	Measures
Society	Orderly world in which people assume responsibility for their assigned social roles (e.g., bread-winner, parent), conform to prevailing mores, and meet situational requirements.	Observations of behavior, extent to which a person fulfills society's expectations and measures up to prevailing standards.
Individual	Happiness, gratification of needs.	Subjective perceptions of self-esteem, acceptance, and well-being.
Mental Health Professional	Sound personality structure characterized by growth, development, autonomy, environmental mastery, ability to cope with stress, adaptation.	Clinical judgment, aided by behavioral observations and psychological tests of such variables as self-concept, sense of identity, balance of psychic forces, unified outlook on life, resistance to stress, self-regulation, ability to cope with reality, absence of mental and behavioral symptoms, adequacy in love, work, and play, adequacy in interpersonal relationships.

Source: Adapted from Strupp and Hadley, 1977.

surprised at the reactions of people to his robbery attempt. "Why all the fuss?" he asks. "So I got caught." His failure to accept certain basic social values is a psychological problem. All children use their imaginations—they invent people when they play and make excuses for unacceptable behavior. But the girl in the third example is unable—or unwilling—to turn her imagination off. Perhaps Johnny protects her from punishment, loss of love, loneliness. Johnny does all the things she cannot.

The behavior of these people is considered abnormal because their perception of reality is distorted and their ability to cope with life's demands is impaired. The bookkeeper is struggling to reach an impossible goal: perfection. The young man grasps neither the effects of his action on his intended victim nor the basic immorality of his behavior. The child, on the other hand, perceives her own normal impulses as terribly wrong, but since she cannot control them, she invents a second self. In each case, the important point about abnormal behavior is that the person's *interpretation of reality* makes adjustment impossible. Within that interpretation of reality, the person is trying to cope effectively. But each person's behavior creates more problems than it solves. Distorted perception, inappropriate behavior, and discomfort are three criteria of abnormal behavior.

A fourth criterion is danger—to oneself or to others. The person who is likely to attempt suicide or to harm someone else in a sudden outburst is an obvious threat. So, in a more general—though usually less dangerous—way, is the person who behaves irrationally. We all depend on being able to predict how people will act. We expect drivers to stop for red lights, grocers to give us food in exchange for money, friends to respect our feelings and be sympathetic. When people violate these written and unwritten rules, they create problems for themselves and for those around them. When these violations are extreme, we think such people need help. But this has not always been so.

What Is Abnormal Behavior?

Historical Views of Abnormal Behavior

No one knows for sure what was considered abnormal behavior thousands of years ago. On the basis of studies of contemporary primitive tribes, however, we can hazard a general description: In such cultures nearly everything was attributed to supernatural powers. Madness was a sign that spirits had possessed a person. Sometimes people who were "possessed" were seen as sacred, and their visions were considered messages from the gods. At other times the tribal wise men diagnosed the presence of evil spirits. Presumably this supernatural view of abnormal behavior dominated early societies.

The ancient Greeks viewed strange behavior differently. Hippocrates (c. 450–c. 377 B.C.), for example, maintained that madness was like any other sickness, a natural event arising from natural causes. Epilepsy, he reasoned, was caused by the brain melting down into the body, resulting in fits and foaming at the mouth. Melancholia, an imbalance in the body fluids, was cured with abstinence and quiet. Although Hippocrates' ideas may seem fanciful to us, they had a positive influence on the treatment of disturbed people, who as a result received care and sympathy like that offered to others suffering from physical ailments.

In the Middle Ages disturbed behavior, like almost every aspect of life, was seen in a spiritual context. The people of the time sought supernatural explanations for melancholy, incoherence, self-abusive, or violent behavior, or mere eccentricity. Abnormal behavior was often considered the work of demons; the disturbed person was often believed to be a witch or possessed by the devil. Exorcisms, from mild to hair-raising, were performed, and a number of unfortunate people endured horrifying torture. Some were burned at the stake.

Not all disturbed people were persecuted or tortured. Beginning in the late Middle Ages, and continuing throughout the 15th and 16th centuries, there were public and private asylums where mentally ill people could be confined (if not well cared for). Although some of these institutions were founded with good intentions, most were little more than prisons. In the worst cases, inmates might be chained down and given little food, light, or air. Although the idea of offering disturbed people some kind of "asylum" was an advance over treating them as witches, little was done to make sure that humane standards prevailed in these institutions until the late 18th century.

The year 1793 may be considered something of a turning point in the history of the treatment of the mentally ill. In that year Philippe Pinel became director of the Bicêtre Hospital in Paris. Under his direction, the hospital was drastically reorganized: Patients were removed from their chains and allowed to move about the hospital grounds, rooms were made more comfortable and sanitary, and dubious and violent medical treatments such as bleeding were abandoned. Pinel's reforms were soon followed by similar efforts in England and, somewhat later, in America. The most notable American reformer was Dorothea Dix (1802–1887), a schoolteacher from Boston who led a nationwide campaign for humane

A "witch" trial in Salem, Massachusetts. A supernatural view of abnormal behavior tended to prevail before the 18th century.

Philippe Pinel removing the chains from patients in the Bicêtre Hospital in Paris.

Biological model of abnormal behavior View that abnormal behavior has a biochemical or physiological basis.

Medical model of abnormal behavior View that people who behave abnormally are sick and in need of treatment by physicians.

Psychoanalytic model of abnormal behavior View that abnormal behavior is the result of unconscious internal conflicts.

Charcot demonstrating hypnotism to his students. This picture hung in Freud's study. Freud trained under Charcot, and much of his early work was based on the effects of hypnosis on his patients.

treatment of mentally ill people. The very concept of "mental illness" dates back to Dix; under her influence, the country's asylums were gradually turned into hospitals staffed by doctors, nurses, and attendants.

At about the same time that institutional reforms were beginning, Franz Anton Mesmer was achieving considerable fame for his success in curing everything from melancholy to blindness through hypnosis. Though Mesmer was something of a showman, a number of doctors took him seriously, among them the neurologist Jean-Martin Charcot. Charcot sought connections between the workings of the brain and the miraculous effects of hypnosis. Sigmund Freud, who studied under Charcot, based much of his early psychoanalytic work on the effects of hypnosis on disturbed people. Thus Mesmer's experiments had a lasting indirect influence on our understanding of abnormal behavior.

Although the idea that disturbed behavior might have an organic or physiological basis dates back to Hippocrates, this notion had little experimental support until 1894. In that year Fournier published an explanation of *paresis*—an overall breakdown of the mind and the body that was common among 19th century merchants and soldiers. He found that most of them had at some point contracted syphilis. Fournier concluded that syphilis caused the massive mental deterioration that characterized paresis. Thus began the search for medical cures for all forms of madness.

Current Views of Abnormal Behavior

Today there are several different viewpoints on abnormal behavior, each of which has a substantial following. Here, in brief, are some of the explanations psychology has offered for abnormal behavior:

The **biological model** holds that abnormal behavior has a biochemical or physiological basis. According to this view, a person who experiences severe depression, for example, probably has some imbalance in his or her brain chemistry. In part, the biological model rests on the evidence that a tendency toward some forms of abnormal behavior can be inherited (see Chapter 2). Moreover, some intriguing differences in brain chemistry between normal and disturbed people have been found. The fact that some drugs have striking effects on some kinds of abnormal behavior (as we shall see in the next chapter) gives further support to the biological model (Buchsbaum & Haier, 1983). Closely related to this viewpoint is the **medical model,** which suggests that people who behave abnormally are sick and are appropriately treated by physicians, often in hospitals. This approach has led to the classification of psychological symptoms and the naming of mental "disorders"—a procedure that enables doctors to compare cases and methods for treating them.

A very different viewpoint is the **psychoanalytic model** that was developed by Freud and his followers. According to this model, behavior disorders are symbolic expressions of unconscious internal conflicts. For example, a man who behaves toward women in a violent way may be unconsciously expressing rage at his mother for being unaffectionate toward him during his childhood. The psychoanalytic model argues that people must become aware that the source of their problems lies in their childhood and infancy, so they can resolve those problems more effectively.

More recently the **behavioral model** has begun to attract attention. According to this view, abnormal behavior, like all behavior, is the result of learning. Fear, anxiety, frigidity, and similar behaviors are learned according to the principles we discussed in Chapter 6. And they can be unlearned using those same principles, without the probing of an analyst or the use of drugs.

Two new views on abnormality have emerged quite recently, largely as reactions to one or more of the above points of view. Thomas Szasz (1974) has attacked the medical model, claiming that the idea of mental illness is a myth equivalent to the demonic myth of the Middle Ages. He notes that most of us find it difficult to deal with deviant people. When people behave in socially unacceptable ways, society simply disposes of them by labeling them sick and putting them in an institution. R. D. Laing (1967) takes an even more radical view. According to Laing, most of us refuse to admit our own craziness, preferring to live in an artificial world of logic, neat explanations, and happy endings. The so-called mentally ill, Laing says, have dared to step over the boundaries of this world into their own minds. Laing sees their journey into the unknown and chaotic parts of the self as an act of heroism (Laing, 1967). As the criticisms by Szasz and Laing suggest, the explanation for most kinds of abnormal behavior is still being debated. None of the competing points of view can claim to be the only "correct" theory. Each has shed light on certain types of abnormality, and each is likely to continue to do so. Given the many ways in which abnormal behavior is manifested and the difficulty of studying abnormality in humans (brains of living people can't be put under the microscope, for example), it is not surprising that no single theory has yet been proved right in every respect.

As you read about the various disorders in this chapter, you may feel an uncomfortable twinge of recognition. This is only natural and is nothing to worry about. Much abnormal behavior is simply normal behavior that is greatly exaggerated or displayed in inappropriate situations. Moreover, the similarities between yourself and a person with psychological problems are likely to be as instructive as the differences.

Behavioral model of abnormal behavior View that abnormal behavior is the result of faulty learning.

Anxiety disorders Disorders in which anxiety is a characteristic feature or the avoidance of anxiety seems to motivate abnormal behavior.

Anxiety Disorders

In some disorders, people experience "persistent feelings of threat and anxiety in facing the everyday problems of living" (Coleman et al., 1984, p. 187), or they experience severe anxiety when they try to change various behavior patterns that they find troublesome. Although all of us are afraid from time to time, we usually know why we are fearful, our fear is caused by something appropriate and identifiable, and it passes with time. But in the case of **anxiety disorders,** the person does not know why he or she is afraid, and the anxiety either persists in the absence of any obvious cause or it becomes overwhelming when the person tries to change his or her behavior. In short, the person's fear and anxiety don't seem to "make sense."

Panic attack A sudden unpredictable feeling of intense fear or terror.

Posttraumatic stress disorder A condition in which episodes of anxiety, sleeplessness, and nightmares are the result of some disturbing event in the past.

Obsessive-compulsive disorder A disorder in which a person feels compelled to think disturbing thoughts and perform senseless rituals.

Edvard Munch's *The Shriek.* Some see in this painting the fear and terror produced by a panic attack.

Until recently these disorders were part of the broader category of neurosis, and people experiencing them were called neurotic. But psychologists and psychiatrists have found it difficult to agree on precisely what "neurosis" means, and the term *neurotic* has become so widely used in everyday language ("I cleaned my room three times today—I guess that's pretty neurotic!") that it has little clinical usefulness. Therefore the most recent system for classifying abnormal behavior, the *DSM-III* (see box), has essentially dropped the term *neurosis.* Although some psychologists believe that the abandonment of the idea of neurosis is premature (Schumer, 1983; Coleman et al., 1984), we will follow *DSM-III* and treat the various neurotic disorders separately in this chapter.

The clearest examples of anxiety disorders are **panic attacks,** which are sudden, unpredictable attacks of intense fear or terror. During a panic attack a person may also have feelings of impending doom, chest pain, dizziness or fainting, and a fear of losing control or dying. A panic attack usually lasts only a few minutes, but such attacks recur for no apparent reason. For example:

> A 31-year-old stewardess . . . had suddenly begun to feel panicky, dizzy, had trouble breathing, started to sweat, and trembled uncontrollably. She excused herself and sat in the back of the plane and within ten minutes the symptoms had subsided. Two similar episodes had occurred in the past: the first, four years previously, when the plane had encountered mild turbulence; the second, two years earlier, during an otherwise uneventful flight, as in this episode. (Spitzer et al., 1981, p. 219)

In contrast to panic attacks, which seem to occur without any obvious cause or triggering event, **posttraumatic stress disorder,** as its name implies, is clearly related to some original stressful event. People who have lived through fires, floods, tornadoes, or the horrors of combat may experience episodes of fear and terror years afterward; sometimes these involve "reliving" the traumatic event. We discussed this disorder at some length in Chapter 13.

Another form of anxiety disorder is **obsessive-compulsive disorder.** *Obsessions* are involuntary thoughts or ideas that keep recurring despite the person's attempt to stop them. *Compulsions* are repetitive, ritualistic behaviors that a person feels compelled to perform. Obsessive thoughts are often of a horrible nature. One patient, for example, reported that "when she thought of her boyfriend she wished he were dead; when her mother went down the stairs, she 'wished she'd fall and break her neck'; when her sister spoke of going to the beach with her infant daughter . . . she 'hoped that they would both drown'" (Coleman et al., 1984, p. 199). Truly compulsive behaviors may be equally dismaying to the person who feels a need to perform them. They often take the form of washing or cleaning, as if the compulsive behavior were the person's attempt to "wash away" the contaminating thoughts. One patient reported that her efforts to keep her clothes and body clean eventually took up 6 hours of her day, and even then, "washing my hands wasn't enough, and I started to use rubbing alcohol" (Spitzer et al., 1981, p. 137).

At times anyone can experience mild obsessions or compulsions. Most of us have occasionally been unable to get a particular song lyric or chain of thought out of our head, or have felt that we *had* to walk so as to avoid stepping on cracks in the sidewalk. But in obsessive-compulsive disorder the obsessive thoughts and compulsive behavior are of a more serious nature. For example, a man who checks his watch every 5 minutes when his wife is late coming home is merely being normally anxious. But a man who feels that he must go through his house every hour checking every clock for accuracy, even though he knows there is no reason to do this, is showing signs of an obsessive-compulsive disorder.

Since people who experience obsessions and compulsions often do not seem particularly anxious, you may wonder why this disorder is considered an anxiety disorder. The answer is that if such people try to *stop* their irrational behavior, or if someone tries to stop them, they experience severe anxiety. In other words, it seems that the obsessive-compulsive behavior acts in some way to keep their anxiety down to a tolerable level.

Finally, **phobic disorders** are also closely linked to feelings of anxiety. A **phobia** is an intense, paralyzing fear of something in the absence of any

Phobic disorder A condition characterized by intense phobias and compulsive avoidance behavior.

Phobia Excessive, unreasonable fear attached to an apparently harmless stimulus.

Classifying Abnormal Behavior

For the past three decades the American Psychiatric Association (APA) has issued an official manual describing and classifying the various kinds of abnormal behavior. This publication, the *Diagnostic and Statistical Manual of Mental Disorders (DSM)*, has gone through three editions: The first appeared in 1952, the second in 1968, and the third in 1980. The manual currently in use, which is known as *DSM-III*, differs from its predecessors in being far more detailed and comprehensive.

The preparation of *DSM-III* took more than 5 years and was aimed at producing a diagnostic manual that would give a complete list of mental disorders, with each category painstakingly defined in terms of significant behavior patterns so that diagnoses would be both valid and reliable. For example, a person diagnosed as schizophrenic should indeed be suffering from schizophrenia and not some other disorder, and most professionals using the *DSM* criteria should arrive at the same diagnosis for that person. The manual is silent as to the causes of disorders (still a matter of dispute in most cases, even for familiar disorders). The committee that compiled *DSM-III* hoped that the volume would stand up well to professional scrutiny and be acceptable as a working tool to psychologists and psychiatrists of many theoretical persuasions.

But even before its official publication *DSM-III* was attacked. Some experts object to the very notion of classifying behavioral abnormalities as if they were diseases and publishing the classification in a medically oriented handbook. Other critics argued that there were no data to support the fine distinctions among the various disorders mady by *DSM-III*. Still others charged that *DSM-III* included too many kinds of behavior that have nothing to do with mental illness. As one group of commentators wrote:

> DSM-III includes many behaviors which have little or no medical relevance and belong properly in the province of the psychologist, e.g., gambling, malingering, antisocial behavior, academic and occupational problems, parent-child problems, marital problems, and the curious "substance use disorders," which apparently would bring almost any kind of behavior within the compass of psychiatry—drinking coffee, having sex, eating wiener schnitzel. (Eysenck, Wakefield, & Friedman, 1983, p. 189)

In addition to these and other criticisms, psychologists have objected that *DSM-III* is inappropriately biased toward *psychiatry* as opposed to psychology. (Psychiatrists are medical doctors; psychologists are not.) To many psychologists, *DSM-III* represents an attempt by medical doctors to define all mental problems, whatever their nature and severity, as diseases—when at least some might more appropriately be treated as "problems in living" (Smith & Kraft, 1983). Accordingly, the American Psychological Association is currently contemplating an alternative manual of classifications more appropriate to psychology.

Despite the many criticisms aimed at *DSM-III*, the manual is still widely used in diagnosing abnormal behavior, and probably will continue to be the standard manual for some time to come.

Displacement Conversion of a vague anxiety resulting from threatening unconscious impulses into a fear of something specific.

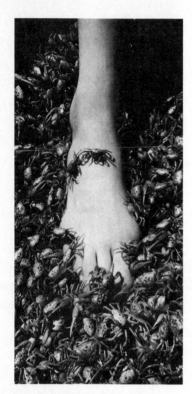

Most people would recoil from being covered with crabs. But an uncontrollable fear of these animals could be a phobia.

real danger—a fear of something that most other people find bearable. This fear is often recognized by the person suffering from it as unreasonable, but it remains nonetheless.

Of course, many people have irrational fears. Fears of heights, water, closed rooms, and cats are all common phobias. But when people are so afraid of snakes that they cannot go to a zoo, walk through a field, or even look at pictures of snakes without trembling, they may be said to have a phobic disorder. For example, one woman was so afraid of thunderstorms that she became anxious and would stay inside whenever the sky became overcast or the weather forecast predicted rain (Spitzer et al., 1981). Perhaps the most common phobic disorder is *agoraphobia*, "a marked fear of being alone, or being in public places from which escape might be difficult" (APA, 1980, p. 226). Sufferers avoid such things as elevators, tunnels, and crowds, especially crowded stores or busy streets.

What causes anxiety disorders? Most psychoanalytic theorists believe that they are the result of unconscious conflict. Unacceptable impulses or thought (usually sexual or aggressive) threaten to overwhelm the ego and break through into full consciousness. The person is still unaware of the unconscious impulses or thoughts, but he or she experiences the "early warning signal" of anxiety nonetheless, perhaps in the form of a panic attack. One way to minimize or avoid the anxiety is to concentrate intensely on other thoughts or on ritualistic behavior. For example, a young man who is about to finish his medical internship is repeatedly tortured by the thought that he has made a mistake. He cannot help thinking about the life he might have had if he had not gone to medical school and had not married early. Hostility toward his wife begins to surface. Then he discovers that if he concentrates on a list of symptoms of an illness that he memorized years ago in school, he can escape his worries about his life. Reciting lists becomes more and more frequent. Later he realizes that his wife is hinting that they should start a family. Every time the topic comes up, he becomes tense and anxious and goes to the bathroom to wash his hands. This, too, may reduce his anxiety, and he increasingly responds with this kind of behavior as a means of escaping tension and worry. Soon these trivial rituals—reciting lists, washing his hands—hold his life together, and also eat up more and more of his time and energy. In other words, repeated thoughts and actions—obsessive-compulsive behavior—that once helped control the tension and anxiety have now become problems themselves.

According to the psychoanalytic view, phobias are a result of **displacement.** People feel threatened by unconscious impulses, and by converting their vague anxiety into a fear of something specific like elevators or spiders, they gain at least the temporary illusion of controlling their fears. After all, you can avoid elevators, but how can you avoid the real source of your anxiety if you don't even know what it is?

Behavior theorists, on the other hand, believe that people who suffer from anxiety disorders have learned to associate fear and anxiety with an apparently harmless situation. It may be that the fear has generalized from some other, similar situation that really *was* harmful. Or the person may have had a terrifying experience in the past and been unable to unlearn that terror. For example, a young boy is savagely attacked by a large dog. Because of this experience, he is now terribly afraid of all large dogs. Even other children who saw the attack or heard about it may also come to fear dogs. As we saw in Chapter 6, because phobias are often learned after only one such event and are extremely hard to change, some learning theorists see them as *prepared responses*—responses built into us biologically through evolution. Seligman (1972) suggests that this is why there is a relatively limited range of phobic objects.

Obsessive-compulsive behavior may also be learned. In some cases, the learning may occur by trial and error, as when the intern in our example discovered that reciting lists reduced his anxiety. It can also be an exaggerated version of behavior that succeeded when we were children—washing our hands is a "good" action that parents praise (Dollard & Miller, 1950). If the behavior reduces anxiety, it is reinforced and is more likely to recur. Whatever the source of the behavior, if it succeeds in reducing anxiety, it will be more likely to occur again in the future when anxiety reappears.

From the biological point of view, there is some evidence that a tendency to experience anxiety and fearfulness may be in part inherited (Eysenck, 1970; Cattell, 1965; Sarason & Sarason, 1980). However, there is no evidence that specific kinds of anxiety disorders are inherited. In addition, as we will see in the next chapter, tranquilizer drugs such as Valium can markedly reduce anxiety, though this does not mean that the anxiety was *caused* by a biological problem of some kind.

Somatoform disorders Disorders in which there is an apparent physical disorder for which there is no organic basis.

Somatization disorder Disorder characterized by recurrent vague somatic complaints without a physical cause.

Conversion disorder Disorder in which a dramatic specific disability has no physical cause and instead seems related to psychological problems.

Somatoform Disorders

Somatoform disorders involve physical symptoms of serious bodily disorders without any physical evidence of organic causes for them. Sufferers from these disorders do not consciously seek to mislead people about their physical condition: The symptoms are real and not under voluntary control (APA, 1980).

In cases of **somatization disorder,** the person feels vague, recurring, physical symptoms for which medical attention has been repeatedly sought but no organic cause found. Complaints often involve back pains, dizziness, partial paralysis, abdominal pains, and sometimes anxiety and depression. One such patient, for example, had exploratory surgery for abdominal pain and nausea, and had also had episodes of fainting, dizziness, blurred vision, intolerance of food, difficulty in urinating, and pain in the extremities (Spitzer et al., 1981).

Less often people complain of more bizarre symptoms such as paralysis, blindness, deafness, seizures, loss of feeling, or false pregnancy. Sufferers from such **conversion disorders** have intact muscles and nerves, yet their symptoms are very real. (For example, a person with such a "paralyzed" limb has no feeling in it, even if stuck with a pin.) Although these extreme symptoms are relatively rare today, they used to be more common. They were noted by the ancient Greeks and Romans and referred to in the Middle Ages and the Renaissance. In the late 19th century a few hypnotists gained recognition for curing what was then called "hysteria." In fact, Freud began to develop his "talking cure" on cases of hysteria.

Sometimes it is easy to determine that there is no organic cause for a

Hypochondriasis A condition in which a person interprets small and insignificant symptoms as signs of serious illness in the absence of any organic symptoms of such illness.

conversion disorder. Some symptoms are anatomically impossible, as in "glove anesthesia," which is a lack of feeling in the hand from the wrist down. There is no way that damage to the nerves running into the hand could cause such a localized pattern of anesthesia. Another clue that the disorder has psychological causes is that the person sometimes may be quite cheerful about it! Psychologists call this attitude *la belle indifference,* or "beautiful indifference": The person seems blithely unconcerned about a serious medical condition. Psychologists also look for evidence that the "illness" resolves a difficult conflict for the person or relieves him or her of having to confront a difficult situation. For example, a housewife reported that she had serious attacks of dizziness, nausea, and visual disturbances that came on in the late afternoon and cleared up at about 8:00 P.M. After ruling out any physical cause for her problems, a therapist discovered that she was married to an extremely tyrannical man, who shortly after coming home from work in the evening would abuse her and her children verbally, criticizing her housekeeping, the meal she had prepared, and so on. Her attacks, while very real to her, served to remove her from this painful situation: Her psychological distress was unconsciously converted to physical symptoms (Spitzer et al., 1981).

A related somatoform disorder is **hypochondriasis.** Here the person interprets some small sign or symptom—perhaps a cough, bruise, or perspiration—as a sign of a serious disease. Although the symptom may exist, there is no evidence that it reflects a serious illness, though repeated assurances of this sort have little effect. As a result, the person is likely to visit one doctor after another looking for one who will share his or her conviction. For example, a middle-aged doctor went to a famous medical clinic convinced that he had cancer of the colon, even though he had been tested repeatedly and found in perfect health. Even after the

Psychosomatic Disorders

Psychosomatic disorders are real physical disorders that seem to have psychological causes. Many cases of ulcers, migraine headaches, asthma, high blood pressure, and other disorders are thought to be psychosomatic. In each case, the complaints have a valid *physical* basis but they are thought to stem originally from stress, anxiety, and other psychological causes. Indeed, modern medicine is beginning to accept the idea that many physical ailments are to some extent psychosomatic, since stress, anxiety, and various states of emotional arousal alter body chemistry and the functioning of bodily organs.

It is important to distinguish between psychosomatic disorders and *hypochondriasis* (commonly known as "hypochondria"). A person with a psychosomatic disorder is really sick; a hypochondriac is not. In hypochondriasis the person believes he or she is seriously ill *despite the absence of any substantial symptoms.* The hypochondriac might almost be said to be suffering from "disease phobia"—fear that he or she has a serious disease.

"Hypochondriacs get sick too, you know!"

Drawing by Dedini; © 1958 The New Yorker Magazine, Inc.

clinic's evaluation, he constantly examined his abdomen for signs of a tumor and performed diagnostic tests on himself weekly. Finally he was referred to a psychiatrist (Spitzer et al., 1981).

Psychoanalysts see all somatoform disorders as a displacement—or conversion—of emotional problems to physical problems. Freud concluded that the physical symptoms were always related to traumatic experiences buried in a patient's past: A woman who, years earlier, saw her mother physically abused by her father suddenly loses her sight; a man who was punished for masturbating later loses the use of his hand. By unconsciously developing a handicap, people punish themselves for forbidden desires or behavior, prevent themselves from acting out those desires or repeating that forbidden behavior, and regress to an earlier stage when others took care of them. Moreover, constant worry over physical symptoms can serve, as in the case of an obsession, to keep an unconscious impulse from rising to awareness.

Behaviorists, on the other hand, look for ways that the symptomatic behavior could have been learned and for signs that it might still be rewarding. They would suggest that the person learned in the past that sickly behavior, aches, pains, and so on can be used to avoid unpleasant situations. (Timely headaches and stomachaches have "solved" a lot of problems over the years.) In addition, a person who is ill often gets a good deal of attention, support, and care, which can be indirectly rewarding to at least some people some of the time.

Dissociative disorders Disorders in which some aspect of the personality seems fragmented from the rest, as in amnesia or multiple personality.

Amnesia Loss of memory for past events.

Dissociative Disorders

Dissociative disorders are among the most puzzling forms of mental disorders, both to the observer and to the sufferer. Dissociation means that part of a person's personality is separated or dissociated from the rest, and for some reason the person cannot reassemble the pieces. It usually takes the form of memory loss, a complete—but usually temporary—change in identity, or even the presence of several distinct personalities in one person.

Loss of memory without an organic cause may be a reaction to intolerable experiences. People may block out an event or a period of their lives if it had been extremely stressful. During World War II some hospitalized soldiers could not recall their names, where they lived, when they were born, or how they came to be in battle. But war and its horrors are not the only causes of **amnesia.** The person who betrays a friend to complete a business deal, or the unhappily married man who reserves a single ticket to Tahiti, may also forget—selectively—what they have

"Jane Doe" was near death when discovered by a Florida park ranger in 1980. She was also suffering from amnesia and could not remember her name, her past, or her ability to read or write. Despite later renewed ties to the past, Jane Doe never regained her memory.

Multiple personality Condition in which more than one personality seems present in a single person.

done. They may even assume an entirely new identity, although this is unusual.

Total amnesia, in which people forget everything, is quite rare, despite its popularity in novels and films. In one unusual case, the police picked up a 42-year-old man after he became involved in a fight with a customer at the diner where he worked. The man reported that he had no memory of his life before he had drifted into town a few weeks earlier. Eventually he was found to match the description of a missing person who had wandered from his home 200 miles away. Just before he disappeared, he had been passed over for promotion at work and had had a violent argument with his teenage son (Spitzer et al., 1981).

Even rarer and more bizarre than amnesia is the disorder known as **multiple personality,** in which a person has several distinct personalities that emerge at different times. This dramatic disorder, which has been the subject of popular fiction and films, is actually extremely rare. In the true multiple personality, the various personalities are distinct people, with their own names, identities, memories, mannerisms, speaking voices, and even IQs. Sometimes the personalities are so separate that they don't know that they inhabit a body with other "people"; sometimes personalities do know of the existence of others, and will even make disparaging remarks about them. Consider the following case of Maud and Sara K., two personalities that coexisted in one woman:

> In general demeanor, Maud was quite different from Sara. She walked with a swinging, bouncing gait that contrasted to Sara's sedate one. While Sara was depressed, Maud was ebullient and happy . . . in so far as she could, Maud dressed differently from Sara. . . . Sara used no make-up. Maud used a lot of rouge and lipstick, and painted her toenails deep red. . . . Sara was

Multiple Personality Disorder: Is It Real?

Multiple personality disorder is surely one of the most mysterious of all psychological abnormalities. How can a person have more than one distinct personality? How is it possible that some people have seemed to have more than *20* distinct personalities?

Throughout the history of psychology there have been psychologists who have doubted that true multiple personalities exist. According to these critics, famous cases in the literature like "the three faces of Eve" and "Sybil" (both subjects of popular books) are fraudulent. Either these people were clever enough to fool the therapists, or the therapists themselves accidentally planted the multiple personalities in their patients' heads. And once the person shows "evidence" of having an additional personality, this argument runs, the avid interest of the therapist in an exotic and rare disorder serves to reinforce the abnormal behavior and make it more likely to recur.

Some intriguing recent research, however, supports the existence of multiple personality disorder. A team of investigators at the National Institute of Mental Health has discovered that each of a person's different personalities has a distinct pattern of brain waves (Putnam, 1982). When normal people were trained to create "multiple personalities" through elaborate rehearsal, their brainwave patterns were the same, no matter which "personality" was tested. But people with real multiple personalities showed markedly different patterns of brain waves as they switched from one personality to another. In fact, the brain waves were as different as if they had actually come from completely different people. This finding not only seems to show that multiple personality disorder is real; it seems to offer one way in which real cases of multiple personality disorder can be distinguished from fakes.

It is typical for multiple personalities to contrast sharply with each other. It is as if the two (and sometimes more) personalities represent different aspects of a single person—one the more socially acceptable, "nice" personality, the other the darker, more uninhibited or "evil" side.

A far less dramatic (and much more common) dissociative disorder is **depersonalization disorder.** Its essential feature is that the person suddenly feels changed or different in a strange way. Some people feel they have left their bodies, others that their actions are mechanical or dreamlike. A sense of losing control of one's own behavior is common, and it is not unusual to imagine changes in one's environment. This kind of feeling is especially common during adolescence and young adulthood, when our sense of ourselves changes rapidly. Only when the sense of depersonalization becomes a long-term or chronic problem, or when the alienation impairs normal social functioning, can this be classified as a dissociative disorder (APA, 1980). For example, a 20-year-old college student sought professional help after experiencing episodes of feeling "outside" himself for 2 years. At these times he felt groggy, dizzy, and preoccupied. Since he had had several episodes while driving, he had stopped driving alone. Although he was able to keep up with his studies, his friends began to notice that he seemed "spacy" and self-preoccupied (Spitzer et al., 1981).

Psychoanalytic theorists believe that some dissociative disorders, like amnesia, are the result of a person's completely blocking out thoughts or impulses that arouse anxiety (or any associated thoughts that might possibly trigger anxiety). Multiple personality, on the other hand, involves a kind of projection, in which each personality can say of the others, in effect, "It's not *me* who's thinking or saying these terrible things." Depersonalization works in much the same way, though much less dramatically.

Behaviorists would not agree that dissociative disorders arise from unconscious conflicts, but they would agree that these behaviors can, under some circumstances, be rewarding, which is why they are learned and maintained.

Depersonalization disorder Condition in which a person feels unreal and unconnected to his or her body.

Affective disorders Conditions in which there is a disturbance of affect or emotional state.

Depression Disorder in which a person is overwhelmed by feelings of sadness, apathy, guilt, and self-reproach.

Affective Disorders

As their name suggests, **affective disorders** are characterized by disturbances in *affect,* or emotional state. Most people have a wide affective range—that is, they are capable of being happy or sad, animated or quiet, cheerful or discouraged, overjoyed or miserable, depending on the circumstances. In people with affective disorders this range is greatly restricted. These people seem stuck at one or the other end of the emotional spectrum, either consistently happy or consistently sad, with little regard for the circumstances of their lives. In other cases, they alternate between extremes of happiness and sadness.

The most common affective disorder is **depression,** a state in which a person feels overwhelmed with sadness, grief, and guilt. Depressed people are unable to experience pleasure from activities they once enjoyed, and are tired and apathetic—sometimes even to the point of being unable to make the simplest everyday decisions. They may feel as if they have failed utterly in life, and they tend to blame themselves for their problems. Seriously depressed people often have disturbed patterns of sleeping and eating (insomnia is common, and the person may lose interest in food). In very serious cases, depressed people may be plagued by suicidal thoughts or may even attempt suicide.

Suicide

In the United States more than 200,000 people attempt suicide each year (Rosenhan & Seligman, 1984). More women than men attempt suicide, but more men actually succeed at it, in part because men often choose more violent lethal methods such as shooting. Recent increases in the number of adolescents and young adults committing suicide have attracted public concern, but no convincing explanation has been offered for the increase. The stresses of leaving home, meeting the demands of college or career, and surviving loneliness or broken romantic attachments are particularly great at this time, however. It may be that in recent years problems from the "outside world"—unemployment, inflation, the emotional and financial costs of attending a prestigious college, the feeling that one's personal future may be threatened by a nuclear war—are adding to people's personal problems.

Several myths have grown up around the subject of suicide. These include the idea that the person who talks of committing suicide will never do it. In fact, most people who kill themselves have mentioned their intent beforehand. Such comments should *always* be taken seriously by the person's friends and family. A related misconception is that a person who has attempted suicide and failed is not "serious" about it. Often a failed suicide will try again, picking a more deadly method the second or third time. (And any suicide attempt is a sign that a person is deeply troubled and in need of help.) Another erroneous idea is that those who commit suicide are life's "losers"—people who have failed vocationally and socially. In fact, many people who kill themselves seem to have "every reason to live"—prestigious jobs, families, and so on. Doctors, for example, have a suicide rate several times that of the general population—which is probably related to the stresses of their work.

People considering suicide are overwhelmed with hopelessness.

People considering suicide are overwhelmed with hopelessness. They feel that things *cannot* get better, that there is no way out of their difficulties. This is depression in the extreme, and it is not a state of mind that someone is easily talked out of. It will do little good to tell such a person that things aren't really so bad. The person will only take this as further evidence that no one understands his or her suffering. But most suicidal people *do* want help, however much they may despair of obtaining it. If a friend or family member seems at all suicidal, make sure that person is not left alone, and seek professional help for him or her as soon as possible. Your local community mental health center is a good starting place, or you can call one of the national suicide hotlines (see telephone numbers in Chapter 15).

It is important to distinguish between the clinical disorder known as depression and the "normal" kind of depression that all people experience from time to time. It is entirely normal to become depressed when a loved one has died, when you've come to the end of a romantic relationship, when you have problems on the job or at school—even when the weather's bad or you don't have a date for Saturday night. Most psychologically healthy people get "the blues" occasionally for no apparent reason. But in all these instances, the depression either is related to a "real world" problem or passes quickly. Only when depression is serious, lasting, and seemingly unrelated to any stressful life event can it be classified as an affective disorder (APA, 1980). For example:

> A 50-year-old widow was transferred to a medical center from her community mental health center, to which she had been admitted three weeks previously with severe agitation, pacing, and handwringing, depressed mood accompanied by severe self-reproach, insomnia, and a 6–8 kg [15-pound] weight loss. She believed that her neighbors were against her, had poisoned her coffee, and had bewitched her to punish her because of her wickedness. Seven years previously, after the death of her husband, she had required hospitalization for a similar depression, with extreme guilt, agitation, insomnia, accusatory hallucinations of voices calling her a worthless person, and preoccupation with thoughts of suicide. (Spitzer et al., 1981, pp. 28–29)

But affective disorders do not always involve depression. Less commonly, people experience a state of **mania,** in which they become hyperactive and excessively talkative, are easily distracted, are euphoric or "high," and seem extremely flamboyant. People in a manic state have unlimited hopes and schemes, but often have little interest in carrying them out. They sometimes become aggressive and hostile toward others, as their self-confidence becomes more and more unrealistic. In an extreme case, people going through a manic episode may become wild, incomprehensible, or violent, until they collapse from exhaustion.

Oddly enough, manic episodes rarely appear by themselves; rather, they usually alternate with depression. The reason appears to be that manic behavior is a defense against depression. Manics sense deep despair just below the surface and do everything to deny their feelings. Such an affective disorder, in which both mania and depression are present, is known as **bipolar disorder** (the person alternates between two "poles" of mania and depression). Occasionally bipolar disorder is seen in a mild form: The person has alternating moods of unrealistically high spirits followed by moderate depression.

If manic disorders are, as believed, a defense against impending depression, the key to understanding affective disorders lies in understanding depression. Psychoanalysts believe that as children, depressed persons were never sure that they were loved and wanted. They felt angry about the lack of warmth in their family, but were afraid that if they expressed their hostility, they would only drive their parents further away. They grew up doubting that they were lovable and mistrusting the affection and confidence others offered them. In later life a sudden loss or a slow accumulation of disappointments taps this well of need and anger, and depression follows. According to this view, depression expresses mixed feelings. Depressed persons want love, but they never believe that anyone loves them, and they resent those on whom they depend for affection and attention.

Mania Disorder in which a person is overly excited and hyperactive.

Bipolar disorder Affective disorder in which a person experiences periods of both depression and mania.

Psychoanalysts stress the self-punishing side of depression. This may be payment for fantasies and behavior considered sinful. Depressed persons may also feel that if they punish themselves, then no one else will hurt them. In effect, they internalize and act out the parental role. As children, they knew that they would be punished for certain acts. If they sent themselves to their rooms without waiting for their parents to do so, they felt more in control. This combination of self-assertion and self-punishment continues into adulthood. Other theorists believe that depression is displaced aggression. Depressed persons, they feel, are furious at someone, but cannot express their anger. By turning their hostility against themselves, they eliminate the possibility of punishment.

Behaviorists view depression differently. The helplessness and hopelessness of depressed persons seem to derive primarily from inadequate or insufficient reinforcement (Lazarus, 1968). It may be that the person has never received much satisfaction in life, or it may be that the gratification to which the person has become accustomed is no longer forthcoming. In this regard, it is interesting to note that extreme depression is often associated with a real loss of some kind—a death, loss of job, failure to meet one's responsibilities or expectations (Paykel, 1982). It is also possible that depression is a form of *learned helplessness* (Rosenhan & Seligman, 1984). It has been found in animal studies that if an animal cannot escape from an unpleasant event (such as an electric shock) no matter what it does, it seems to give up and become apathetic. Some researchers have theorized that people may react in a similar way when they are confronted with unpleasant life events that are beyond their control (such as being fired from a job). However, since the behavior of depressed people differs significantly from that of "apathetic" lab animals, it is doubtful that this theory adequately explains all aspects of depression (Coleman et al., 1984).

Other researchers have looked to biological factors to explain depression and bipolar mood swings. This line of research has been encouraged by a growing consensus that at least in some cases, a susceptibility to affective disorders can be inherited. If you have relatives who have suffered from serious depression, for example, you are more likely to do so yourself. If some degree of heritability exists, what exactly is inherited? Presumably some biological defect that makes people more likely to become depressed, especially when they are under stress. Some promising research has linked depression and mania to certain chemical imbalances within the brain—principally, to high or low levels of certain neurotransmitters, which are chemicals that are involved in the transmission of nerve impulses from one cell to another (see Chapter 2). The fact that several effective antidepressant drugs are known to act on these neurotransmitters seems to support the idea that chemical imbalances within the brain are related in some way to depression (Carlson, 1980), though researchers have not yet identified precisely what mechanism is involved.

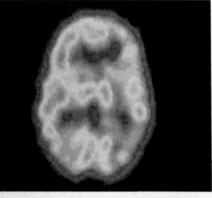

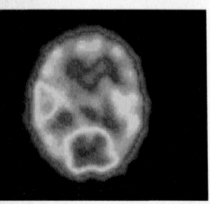

Some research has begun to link affective disorders with chemical imbalances in the brain. PET (positron emission tomography) scans can reveal the rates at which glucose is consumed in the brain. The normal brain in the top photo, suggests moderate levels of consumption (here indicated by yellow and blue). The brain in the bottom photo is of someone diagnosed as bipolar, and suggests higher levels of consumption (indicated by red).

Psychosexual Disorders

Ideas about what is normal and what is abnormal in sex vary with the times—and with the individual. As Kinsey showed years ago, most Americans enjoy sexual activities forbidden by laws that do not recognize current sexual mores. Among psychologists today there are two main schools of thought about what is normal and abnormal in sex. On the one hand are those who regard any activity not associated with heterosexual intercourse as deviant. On the other hand are those who prefer not to judge specific activities. Instead they focus on people's feelings about what they do. According to this view, if people are compulsive or guilty about their sex life, or if they cannot enjoy sex fully, then—and only then—are they sexually maladjusted.

Sexual dysfunction Inability to function effectively during sex.

Impotence In men, the inability to achieve or keep an erection.

Frigidity In women, the inability to become sexually aroused or reach orgasm.

Paraphilias Unconventional objects or situations that cause sexual arousal in some people.

Dysfunction

Sexual dysfunction consists of an inability to function effectively during sex. In men this may take the form of **impotence,** the inability to achieve or keep an erection. In women it is often **frigidity,** the inability to become sexually excited or to reach orgasm. These dysfunctions are common, especially in their milder forms. Most people undergo periods of sexual dysfunction caused by a lack of interest in their partner, or overexcitement, or anxiety about their sexual "performance." Only when such dysfunction becomes typical, when enjoyment of sexual relationships becomes impaired, should it be considered serious. Most truly impotent men and frigid women, for example, cannot have satisfying sexual relations, even after repeated attempts with a partner whom they desire.

Many psychologists feel that sexual dysfunction is based on fear of heterosexual intimacy. The impotent man may have been warned as a child about venereal disease or domineering females, and may feel threatened by women. Frigidity may result from a fear of pregnancy, fear of male domination, an overall fear of letting go, or a lingering sense—left over from childhood—that sex is somehow dirty or disgusting. For example:

> Mr. and Ms. B. have been married for 14 years and have 3 children. . . . Ms. B. has been able to participate passively in sex "as a duty" but has never enjoyed it since they have been married. . . . Whenever Ms. B. comes close to having a feeling of sexual arousal, numerous negative thoughts come into her mind, such as "What would my mother say about this?"; "What am I, a tramp?" . . . or "How could I look myself in the mirror after something like this?" These thoughts almost inevitably are accompanied by a cold feeling and an insensitivity to sensual pleasure. As a result, sex is invariably an unhappy experience. (Spitzer et al., 1981, pp. 96–97)

Sexual dysfunction in men often takes the form of impotency.

Paraphilias

A second group of psychosexual disorders involves the use of unconventional sex objects or situations known as **paraphilias.** Most people have unconventional sexual fantasies at some time, and this fantasizing

Fetishism The reliance on non-human objects to obtain sexual gratification.

Pedophilia Desire to have sexual relations with children.

Zoophilia Desire to have sexual relations with animals.

Voyeurism The desire to watch others having sexual relations or to spy on nude people.

Exhibitionism The compulsion to expose one's genitals in public.

Transvestism Dressing in the clothing of the opposite sex to achieve sexual gratification.

Sadomasochism Obtaining sexual gratification from aggression.

Homosexuality A preference for sexual relations with a partner of the same sex.

is often a healthy outlet that stimulates normal sexual enjoyment. The repeated use of nonhuman objects, however—a shoe, for instance, or a belt—as the preferred or exclusive method of achieving sexual excitement is considered a psychosexual disorder. It is known as **fetishism.** Fetishes often involve articles of clothing, and the fetish is frequently associated with someone a person was close to in childhood. Other deviations in the choice of sex objects include **pedophilia**—sexual relations with children—and **zoophilia**—sexual relations with animals. Other unconventional patterns of sexual behavior are **voyeurism,** watching other people have sex or spying on people who are nude instead of having sex oneself; **exhibitionism,** the compulsion to expose one's genitals in inappropriate situations; and **transvestism,** wearing clothes of the opposite sex. **Sadomasochism** ties sexual pleasure to aggression. To attain sexual gratification, sadists humiliate or physically harm their sex partners. Masochists cannot enjoy sex without accompanying emotional or physical pain. As with sexual dysfunction, most psychologists see the choice of unconventional sexual objects as indicating fear of heterosexual intimacy. For example:

> A 25-year-old male business executive requested psychiatric consultation because of his repeated need to peep at women undressing or engaging in sexual activity. The patient had been apprehended for this activity in the past, and the personnel office at his place of work had found out about it. . . . Once he had been chased from a "lovers' lane" by an irate man wielding a tire iron; another time he was discovered peeping into a bedroom window in a rural area and barely escaped being shot. . . . [The patient] had never been in love, nor had he experienced a durable, deep attachment to a woman. (Spitzer et al., 1981, pp. 44–45)

Homosexuality

Our society has traditionally considered **homosexuality** a mental disorder. Recent studies, however, indicate that homosexuals are no more maladjusted than heterosexuals, and the view of homosexuality as a mental disorder has increasingly been challenged (Coleman et al., 1984; Rosenhan & Seligman, 1984).

The controversy over whether to include homosexuality as a mental disorder in *DSM-III* was so heated that it generated over 180 pages of correspondence among members of the various committees involved in the American Psychiatric Association's efforts to classify mental disorders. The compromise was to list homosexuality in *DSM-III* as a disorder *only* when a person has persistent distress or anxiety because of his or her sexual orientation, has negative feelings about homosexuality, and wishes to be more heterosexual. For example:

> A 23-year-old unmarried male schoolteacher requests help with his distress about his preoccupation with homosexuality. He has felt "unmasculine" since childhood and "different from most boys" as he was growing up. . . . Since puberty he has felt fearful of girls, expecting to be rejected. . . . Now, although he has not yet had any overt homosexual experience, he is constantly preoccupied with a physical desire for homosexual contact. Yet, in a social sense, he is repulsed by the idea, finds it totally shameful and un-

Homosexuality is considered a disorder only if it causes a person undue, persistent stress and anxiety.

acceptable to his social and cultural goals. He wants to rid himself of these homosexual ideas and be able to make love to a woman. . . . He chronically has low self-esteem and is often depressed. (Spitzer et al., 1981, p. 82)

The prevalence of homosexual behavior—documented by Kinsey—is one of the reasons for the change in classification. His studies showed that 37 percent of white males had a homosexual experience resulting in orgasm sometime between adolescence and old age. The frequency of homosexual behavior in women was about half that found in men (Kinsey et al., 1948).

Many children and adolescents have homosexual experiences, often because intimate physical contact with the opposite sex is forbidden. This is also true in prisons and mental institutions, where the sexes are segregated. Some people who engage in homosexual activity enjoy relations with both sexes. Others are exclusively attracted to their own sex.

ORIGINS OF HOMOSEXUALITY. There are many conflicting theories about the origins of homosexuality. Psychoanalysts consider homosexuality the result of unresolved Oedipal conflicts. They say that the young boy who wants exclusive rights to his mother fears retribution from his father in the form of castration. To win his father's affection and to convince his father that he is not a rival, he begins imitating his mother. His sexual identity becomes confused, and in adulthood he seeks to restore his self-image through a "magical unity" with other men. The dynamics are somewhat different with girls. Psychoanalysts explain homosexuality in women as fixation in the mother-attached stage, as an inability to transfer love for the mother to love for the father. In both sexes, psychoanalysts say, homosexuality seems to develop most often in homes where one parent seems domineering, the other passive.

Many psychologists do not fully accept the psychoanalytic explanation; and there are differing interpretations of the data even among those who place the roots of homosexuality in early parent-child relationships. Evans (1969) studied a group of homosexuals who were not in therapy and compared them with a control group of heterosexuals, using a questionnaire devised by Bieber et al. (1962). The homosexual males reported more often that they had been fearful of physical injury, had avoided physical conflicts, and had been loners who did not engage in competitive sports. The mothers of the homosexuals had encouraged "feminine" rather than "masculine" attitudes, allied with the son against the father, and behaved seductively toward the son. The homosexuals had spent less time with their fathers, were more hostile toward and more fearful of them, and felt less accepted by and less accepting of their fathers than did the heterosexuals.

Evans, however, cautioned against concluding that the father was the cause of homosexuality. He pointed out that the father of a son who ultimately becomes homosexual may withdraw from and develop hostile feelings toward his son because of childhood signs of the son's homosexual tendency. He also noted that some homosexuals were raised without a father.

Gundlach (1969) found that the behavior of female homosexuals often had an emotional content quite different from that of male homosexuals. Homosexual women tend to seek warmth and affection from their partners, whereas homosexual men often search for domination and power. This significant difference, as well as the early family origins of female homosexuality, is hard to fit into the Bieber theory.

Hooker, a psychiatrist who has conducted many studies of homosexuals, concludes that "it can no longer be questioned that faulty, disturbed, or pathological parental relationships in early childhood are more commonly reported by male homosexual patients than by a comparable group of male heterosexuals" (Hooker, 1969, p. 141). She goes on, however, to warn that the origins of homosexuality cannot be established from psychiatric samples alone and that no conclusive pattern of causal relationships between early-childhood relationships with parents and subsequent homosexuality has been determined.

Behaviorists tend to see homosexuality as a learned behavior. In some cases, pleasant and rewarding homosexual experiences are cited by homosexuals as the reason for their sexual preference (Coleman et al., 1984). In addition, homosexuals frequently report negative experiences with heterosexuality. For example, White and Watt (1973) suggest that the most important factor in homosexual preferences may be the mother's attitude that sex is ugly, nasty, and degrading. This is generalized by children to mean that all intimate heterosexual relationships are likewise ugly, nasty, and degrading. But as children grow up, their sexual needs must be satisfied. Because they have learned to avoid the opposite sex, they may become homosexual.

While we have several hypotheses, we do not yet have a firmly established set of conclusions about the origins of either male or female homosexual behavior. It is worth repeating, however, that only when homosexuality is unwanted and causes great distress is it considered a psychological disorder, regardless of its cause.

In Chapter 12 we saw that a person's personality is his or her unique and enduring pattern of thoughts, feelings, and behaviors. And we also saw that people normally have the ability to adjust their behavior to fit the needs of different situations, despite certain characteristic views of the world and ways of doing things. But some people develop inflexible and maladaptive ways of thinking and behaving that are so exaggerated and rigid that they cause serious distress and social problems. People with such **personality disorders** may range from the harmless eccentric to the cold-blooded killer. Recently it has been estimated that at least half of those who seek help for a psychological problem show some evidence of a personality disorder (Turkat & Alpher, 1983).

One group of personality disorders is characterized by odd or eccentric behavior. For example, people who exhibit **schizoid personality disorder** lack the ability or desire to form social relationships and have no warm or tender feelings for others. Such "loners" cannot express their feelings and are perceived by others as cold, distant, and unfeeling. Moreoever, they often appear vague, absentminded, indecisive, or "in a fog." Because their withdrawal is so complete, schizoids seldom marry and may have trouble holding a job that requires them to work with or relate to others (APA, 1980). For example:

> A 36-year-old electrical engineer was "dragged" to a marital therapist by his wife because of his unwillingness to join in family activities, failure to take an interest in his children, lack of affection, and disinterest in sex. . . . The patient's history revealed long-standing social indifference, with only an occasional and brief friendship here and there. (Spitzer et al., 1981. p. 66)

People with **paranoid personality disorder** also appear to be odd. They are suspicious and mistrustful even when there is no reason to be, and are hypersensitive to any possible threat or trick. They refuse to accept blame or criticism even when it is deserved. They are guarded, secretive, devious, scheming, and argumentative, though they often see themselves as rational and objective. In one case, for example, a construction worker began to get into disputes with his co-workers because he was afraid that they might let his scaffolding slip in order to kill or injure him. Upon examination by a psychologist, he thought that his examiner was "taking their side" against him (Spitzer et al., 1981, p. 37).

A second cluster of personality disorders is characterized by dramatic, emotional, or erratic behavior. For example, people with **narcissistic personality disorder** display nearly total self-absorption, a grandiose sense of self-importance, a preoccupation with fantasies of unlimited success, a need for constant attention and admiration, and an inability to love or really care for anyone else (APA, 1980). The word *narcissism* comes from a character in Greek mythology named Narcissus, who fell in love with his own reflection in a pool and pined away because he could not reach the beautiful face he saw before him. For example, a male graduate student sought help because he was having difficulty completing his PhD dissertation. He bragged that his dissertation would revolutionize his field and make him famous—but he had not been able to write much

Personality disorders Disorders in which inflexible and maladaptive ways of thinking and behaving cause distress and conflicts.

Schizoid personality disorder Disorder in which a person is withdrawn and lacks feelings for others.

Paranoid personality disorder Disorder in which a person is inappropriately suspicious and mistrustful of others.

Narcissistic personality disorder Disorder in which a person has an exaggerated sense of self-importance and needs constant admiration.

Antisocial personality disorder
Disorder that involves a pattern of violent, criminal, or unethical and exploitative behavior and an inability to feel affection for others.

of it yet. He blamed his academic adviser for his lack of progress, called his fellow students "drones," and stated that everyone was jealous of his brilliance. He had frequent brief relationships with women, but few lasting friendships (Spitzer et al., 1981). Although excess self-esteem would seem to be the prominent problem here, this may not be the case. Otto Kernberg observes that the self-esteem of the narcissistic person is really very fragile: "The pathological narcissist cannot sustain his or her self-regard without having it fed constantly by the attentions of others" (Wolfe, 1978, p. 55).

Many psychologists believe that narcissism begins early in life. While all infants tend to be narcissistic, most grow out of it. But for reasons that we do not yet understand, the narcissistic person never makes the change. Some social critics assert that certain tendencies in modern American society—such as our worship of youth and beauty, and our disregard for old age—have contributed to an apparent "boom" in narcissistic personality disorders (Lasch, 1979). Clinical data, however, do not support this speculation. While acknowledging that our society stimulates narcissism, Kernberg argues that this cannot be the root of the disorder: "The most I would be willing to say is that society can make serious psychological abnormalities, which already exist in some percentage of the population, seem to be at least superficially appropriate" (Wolfe, 1978, p. 59).

One of the most widely studied personality disorders is **antisocial personality disorder.** People who exhibit this disorder used to be called "sociopaths" or "psychopaths." They lie, steal, cheat, and show little or no sense of responsibility, although often they are intelligent and charming on first acquaintance. The "con man" exemplifies many of the features of the antisocial personality. Other examples are the man who compulsively cheats his business partners because he knows their weak points; the impostors who appear in the papers after their deceit is discovered; and various criminals who show no guilt. The antisocial personality rarely shows the slightest trace of anxiety or guilt over his or her behavior. Indeed, these people blame society or their victims for the antisocial actions that they themselves commit. For example:

> A 21-year-old male was interviewed by a psychiatrist while he was being detained in jail awaiting trial for attempted robbery. The patient had a history of multiple arrests for drug charges, robbery, and assault and battery. Past history revealed that he had been expelled from junior high school for truancy, fighting, and generally poor performance in school. . . . He spent brief periods in a variety of institutions, from which he usually ran away. At times his parents attempted to let him live at home, but he was disruptive and threatened them with physical harm. . . . The patient has never formed close personal relationships with his parents, his two older brothers, or friends of either sex. He is a loner and a drifter, and has not worked for more than two months at any one job in his life. (Spitzer et al., 1981, p. 34)

Some psychologists feel that antisocial behavior is the result of emotional deprivation in early childhood. Respect for others is the basis of our social code, but if you cannot see things from the other person's perspective, rules about what you can and cannot do will seem to be only an assertion of adult power, to be broken as soon as possible. The child for whom no one cares, say psychologists, cares for no one. The child whose problems no one identifies with can identify with no one else's problems. Other psychologists feel that inconsistent parental behavior may explain many antisocial personality disorders. Sometimes the parents of these people punished them for being bad, sometimes they did not. Sometimes the parents worried over them and lavished attention on them, sometimes they ignored them and forced them to be prematurely independent. Thus these children felt that their actions had no influence on how others behaved toward them.

An entirely different body of research has sought the roots of antisocial personality disorder in biology. Although none of this research is definitive, it does suggest that some antisocial personalities may be victims of their nervous systems as much as of their upbringings. Some of the explanations that have been suggested are a malfunction in that region of the brain that seems to be responsible for inhibiting behavior; deficient emotional arousal resulting in a lack of "normal" fear responses; and a tendency to seek stimulation from the environment—in short, a need for thrills (Coleman et al., 1984).

Substance use disorders Disorders in which a person uses some substance, such as alcohol or drugs, in a way that is injurious to self or to others.

Substance abuse Pathological use of a substance resulting in disturbed functioning of at least a month's duration.

Substance dependence Severe form of substance-use disorder characterized by physiological dependence on the substance.

Substance Use Disorders

In our society, the use of some substances to alter mood or behavior is, under certain circumstances, regarded as normal behavior. This includes moderate intake of alcohol and of the caffeine in coffee, tea, or cola. It also includes the use of tobacco and, in various subcultures, such illegal substances as marijuana, cocaine, and amphetamines. We discussed each of these and their effects in Chapter 4. Here we shall focus on their abuse by some people.

According to *DSM-III*, when more or less regular use of a substance results in undesirable behavior changes that impair social or occupational functioning, the user is suffering from a **substance use disorder.** In some cases this may simply involve **substance abuse,** which is defined by three conditions: (1) a pattern of pathological use such as intoxication throughout the day, an inability to cut down or stop, a need for its daily use in order to function adequately, and the continuing use of the substance even if it makes a physical disorder worse; (2) disturbance in social relationships or deterioration of occupational functioning; and (3) signs of disturbance lasting for at least one month. The person who regularly goes on drinking binges, for example, that are severe enough to cause him or her ill health and problems within the family or on the job is involved in alcohol abuse.

For most drugs, including alcohol, continued abuse over a period of time can lead to **substance dependence.** (Although *DSM-III* does not use the term *addiction,* many professionals consider addiction and substance dependence to be one and the same thing.) Interestingly, many potent drugs, such as cocaine, LSD, and PCP, do not seem to produce physical dependence, even after prolonged and heavy use. In any event, substance dependence is much more serious than substance abuse and is marked by evidence of either *tolerance*—increasing amounts of the drug needed to achieve the same effect—or *withdrawal* symptoms—physical and psychological problems that appear if a person reduces or stops using the substance (APA, 1980). Both these conditions are present in the following case:

> A 42-year-old executive in a public relations firm was referred for psychiatric treatment by his surgeon, who discovered him sneaking large quantities of a codeine-containing cough medicine into the hospital. . . . An operation on his back five years previously had led his doctor to prescribe codeine to help relieve the incisional pain at that time. Over the intervening five years, however, he had continued to use codeine-containing tablets and had increased his intake to 60-90 5-mg tablets daily. He stated that he often "just took them by the handful—not to feel good, you understand, just to get by." He had tried several times to stop using codeine, but had failed. During this period he lost two jobs because of lax work habits and was divorced by his wife of 11 years. (Spitzer et al., 1981, p. 255)

Considering the difficulties that substance abuse and dependence cause for the abuser, we may wonder why some people come to abuse drugs and alcohol at all. The various schools of thought within psychology each provide somewhat different answers to this question. The psychoanalytic thinkers, for example, consider abuse to be an expression of an unconscious emotional problem. In particular, they believe that people who abuse drugs have an exaggerated need to feel dependent and to be taken care of. Behaviorist thinkers are more likely to point to the role of learning. Many addicts, for example, learn drug use as part of a deviant subculture. And some abusers accidentally learn that some drug relieves their anxiety or distress and then find themselves turning to it more and more often to solve their problems. Physiological psychologists see abusers as to some extent victims of their body chemistry: some people, they believe, metabolize drugs and alcohol differently and become addicted much more quickly—and powerfully—than others. Whatever the initial cause, however, frequent, heavy abuse can turn into actual dependence, at which point the person is physically "hooked" on continued use of the drug, as in the case of the codeine addict above. The body needs the substance just to function "normally."

Alcohol abuse and dependence, as the most serious substance abuse problem in our society, has been an area of particular challenge for researchers. Although we have no definitive answer yet to the question of what causes alcoholism, we do have some suggestive evidence. First, we know that people turn to alcohol to relieve stress from life problems. As a depressant, alcohol does exert a calming effect on the nervous system. The problem, of course, is that too-frequent use of this calming agent can produce more life stress (criticism from spouse, loss of job). Some researchers have tried to identify an "alcoholic personality," in the belief that alcoholics are often emotionally immature and needy, have low self-esteem, and do not tolerate frustration well (Coleman et al., 1984). On the other hand, many people who have these characteristics do not become alcoholics, so this cannot be the whole answer.

Going beyond the individual, some researchers have suggested that culture can be an important influence. Sometimes spouses and parents are powerful models in introducing people to a pattern of heavy drinking. And in some ethnic cultures, alcohol is more acceptable than in others. Orthodox Jews, who frown on the use of alcohol, and Muslims, who

There are no definitive answers to the question of what causes alcoholism, the most serious substance abuse problem in our society.

prohibit it, have low rates of alcoholism.

Another line of research has sought to find biological factors in alcoholism. Some investigators have suggested that alcoholics may be born with a genetic vulnerability to alcoholism. Since some groups of people are known to metabolize alcohol differently from others (Asians and American Indians, for example, react more strongly to alcohol than do Europeans), it is possible that there are inborn individual differences in alcohol tolerance as well (Coleman et al., 1984).

Finally, no discussion of substance abuse and dependence can be complete without a mention of several social factors that play a role in these disorders. In our society, alcohol and many drugs are widely available—perhaps more so now than at any time in our history. Moreover, we have come to expect that drugs solve problems, having learned this lesson from the prescriptions so readily dispensed by physicians and from a constant barrage of advertising for "medicine" to cure every conceivable ailment, to help us sleep or take off weight, to make us feel young and vigorous, and so on. Under the circumstances, it is hardly surprising that some people turn to alcohol and drugs to make them feel better. For most of us, use does not become abuse. But in those people who are psychologically troubled or physiologically vulnerable—or both—abuse or dependence are both very real possibilities.

Schizophrenic disorders Disorders in which there are disturbances of thought, communication, and emotions, including delusions and hallucinations.

Hallucinations Sensory experiences in the absence of external stimulation.

Delusions False beliefs about reality with no basis in fact.

Schizophrenic Disorders

It is a common misconception that schizophrenia means "split personality." This is not the case at all. The disorder commonly meant by the term *split personality* is actually multiple personality disorder, which, as we have seen, is a dissociative disorder. The misunderstanding comes from the fact that the root *schizo-* comes from the Greek verb meaning "to split." But what is split in schizophrenia is not so much the personality as the mind itself.

Schizophrenic disorders are marked by disordered thought and communication, inappropriate emotions, and bizarre behavior that lasts for months. Schizophrenics are out of touch with reality. They often suffer from **hallucinations** (false sensory perceptions), which most often take the form of hearing voices—although some schizophrenics experience visual, tactile, or olfactory hallucinations. Schizophrenics usually have **delusions** (false beliefs about reality with no factual basis), which distort their relationships with their surroundings and with other people. They may think that a doctor wishes to kill them or that they are receiving radio messages from outer space. They often regard their own bodies—as well as the outside world—as hostile and alien. Because their world is utterly different from the one most people live in, they usually cannot live anything like a normal life. Often they are unable to communicate with others, for when they speak, their words are a total confusion. The following case illustrates some of schizophrenia's characteristic features:

[The patient is a 35-year-old widow.] For many years she has heard voices, which insult her and cast suspicion on her chastity. . . . The voices are very distinct, and in her opinion, they must be carried by a telescope or a machine

Disorganized schizophrenia Type of schizophrenia in which bizarre and childlike behaviors are common.

Catatonic schizophrenia Type of schizophrenia in which disturbed motor behavior is prominent.

Paranoid schizophrenia Type of schizophrenia characterized by extreme suspiciousness and complex, bizarre delusions.

Undifferentiated schizophrenia Type of schizophrenia in which there are clear schizophrenic symptoms that don't meet the criteria for another type.

Estimated prevalance of major maladaptive behavior patterns in the United States in 1984

1,672,000 cases of schizophrenia
946,000 cases of major affective disorder
13,090,000 cases of anxiety-based disorders
9,218,000 cases of personality disorder
31,020,000 cases of "functional" mental disorder
60,500,000 cases of uncomplicated "demoralization"

Data from Coleman, 1984

from her home. Her thoughts are dictated to her; she is obliged to think them, and hears them repeated after her. She . . . has all kinds of uncomfortable sensations in her body, to which something is "done." In particular, her "mother parts" are turned inside out, and people send a pain through her back, lay ice-water on her heart, squeeze her neck, injure her spine, and violate her. There are also hallucinations of sight—black figures and the altered appearance of people—but these are far less frequent. . . . (Spitzer et al., 1981, pp. 308–309)

There are actually several kinds of schizophrenic disorders, which differ from one another in terms of characteristic symptoms.

Disorganized schizophrenia includes some of the more bizarre symptoms such as giggling, grimacing, and frantic gesturing. These people show a childish disregard for social conventions, and may urinate or defecate at inappropriate times. They are active, but aimless, and are often given to incoherent conversations.

The primary feature of **catatonic schizophrenia** is a severe disturbance of motor activity. People in this state may remain immobile, mute, and impassive. At the opposite extreme they become excessively excited, talking and shouting continuously. They may behave in a robotlike fashion when ordered to move, and some have even let doctors mold their arms and legs into strange and uncomfortable positions, which they then can maintain for hours.

Paranoid schizophrenia is marked by extreme suspiciousness and quite complex delusions. Paranoid schizophrenics may believe themselves to be Napoleon or the Virgin Mary, or may insist that Russian spies with laser guns are constantly on their trail because they have learned some great secret. These people may actually appear more "normal" than other schizophrenics if their delusions are compatible with everyday life; they are less likely to be incoherent or to look or act "crazy." However, they may become hostile or aggressive toward anyone who questions their thinking or tries to contradict their delusions (Sarason & Sarason, 1980).

Finally, **undifferentiated schizophrenia** refers to those people who have several of the characteristic symptoms of schizophrenia, such as delusions, hallucinations, or incoherence, yet do not show the typical symptoms of any other subtype.

Since schizophrenia is both a common mental disorder and a very serious one, considerable research has been directed at trying to discover its causes. As we saw in Chapter 2, it is now clear from a wide range of studies that there is some genetic component to schizophrenia. People who are schizophrenic are more likely than other people to have schizophrenic children, even when those children have lived with foster parents since birth (Heston, 1966). And if an identical twin becomes schizophrenic, the chances are about 50 percent that the other twin will also become schizophrenic; but if a fraternal twin becomes schizophrenic, the chances are only about 10 percent that the other twin will also become schizophrenic (Rosenthal, 1970). But note that even with identical twins, who are genetically exactly the same, half of the twins of schizophrenics do not themselves become schizophrenic.

These studies and others indicate that some kind of biological vulnerability to schizophrenia is inherited (Carlson, 1980; Rosenhan & Seligman, 1984). Recent research suggests that the problem may lie in excess amounts of *dopamine* in the central nervous system. Drugs that alleviate schizophrenic symptoms also decrease the amount of dopamine in the brain and block dopamine receptors. On the other hand, amphetamines increase the amount of dopamine in the brain, increase the severity of schizophrenic symptoms, and if taken in excess lead to what is called "amphetamine psychosis," which is very similar to schizophrenia (Coleman et al., 1984; Rosenhan & Seligman, 1984). However, research indicates that many people who are genetically vulnerable to schizophrenia do not become schizophrenic. Environmental factors—in particular, disturbed family relations—are also involved in determining whether a person will become schizophrenic. For example, according to the double-bind theory (Bateson et al., 1956), schizophrenics as children were taught to act in ways that contradicted their perception of reality and their own feelings. Because a little boy's mother resents him, she is stiff and remote when she holds him. Since she cannot accept her feelings of resentment, however, she demands that he react as if she were warm and loving. The boy knows that if he hugs her, she will pull away, but that if he does not, she will reproach him for not showing affection. This is the double-bind. He is damned if he does and damned if he doesn't. The child grows up mistrusting others and distorting the expressions of his own feelings.

Although quite different in emphasis, the various views of schizophrenic disorders are by no means mutually exclusive. Many theorists believe that a combination of some or all of these factors produces schizophrenia, and in practice, many psychologists use a combination of drugs and therapy to treat schizophrenia, as we shall see in the next chapter.

Application

Mental Illness and the Law

When David Berkowitz, better known as "Son of Sam," was arrested in New York in August 1977, he was taken into custody by a cordon of some 30 police officers wearing bullet-proof vests and carrying shotguns. Public emotions were running high. Berkowitz was suspected of murdering six young people and wounding seven others in a killing spree that had attracted headlines around the world. Berkowitz explained that he was part of an army led by someone he called General Jack Cosmo. The army was made up largely of "demon dogs" that roamed the world telling people to kill. Periodically, when Berkowitz was out driving around at night, he would hear orders to kill, and when he followed those orders, the demon dogs would "move in and feast."

Two court-appointed psychiatrists decided that Berkowitz was not fit to stand trial. But the psychiatrist appointed by the prosecutor's office later declared that Berkowitz could understand the proceedings against him and assist in his own defense, and the judge agreed with him. Within 2 weeks of being found competent to stand trial, Berkowitz entered a plea of guilty over the strong objections of his attorneys. Thus the question of his insanity at the time of the murders was never considered by the courts, and he is now serving a 365-year sentence in Attica prison in New York State.

Two quite separate questions were raised in the Berkowitz case: Was he competent to stand trial? And was he insane at the time of the killings? "Competence to stand trial" means that at the time of the trial (often months or years after the crime was committed), the defendant has a reasonable understanding of the proceedings, can make decisions and offer testimony, and understands the charges, pleas, and penalties. If an accused person is found unfit to stand trial, he or she is usually sent to a mental hospital until psychiatrists and the judge agree that the defendant is competent to return to the courtroom. In some cases, this means never. It is possible in fact for an accused person to be sentenced (in effect) to spend the rest of his or her life in an institution without ever being found guilty of a crime!

If at some point the person is declared competent to stand trial, then the court must determine whether he or she was insane at the time of the crime. The following rule is used by most courts to determine insanity: A person is not responsible for criminal conduct if, at the time of such conduct, as a result of mental disease or defect, he lacks substantial capacity either to appreciate the criminality (wrongfulness) of his conduct or to conform his conduct to the requirements of law.

The court ruled that Berkowitz was in fact competent to stand trial, but in order to rule on his insanity, the court would have had to decide whether at the time of the killings Berkowitz understood that what he was doing was wrong and that he was "substantially in control" of his behavior. If the answer to *either* of these questions had been no, then he would have been declared legally insane at the time he committed the crimes and been hospitalized until he no longer represented a threat to society, at which point he would have been released as a free man.

The insanity plea is quite rare: it arises in less than 1 percent of serious criminal cases according to most estimates (U.S. News & World Report, May 7, 1979, p. 42). But it is extremely controversial for many different reasons. Since criminals who are declared legally insane are not subject to punishment for their actions, the court system relies heavily on the advice and testimony of forensic psychologists and psychiatrists, who help determine the mental state of suspects both at the time of the crime and at the time of the trial. These experts also help in deciding questions about rehabilitation, parole, or fitness to stand trial at a later date (Robitscher & Williams, 1977). The influence of these experts on the outcome of court cases is increasingly controversial.

How large a part, if any, should these mental health experts play in deciding the fate of people who have violated the law? Some, like the well-known psychiatrist Thomas Szasz, feel that psychiatrists and psychologists should stay out of the legal arena altogether. He points to the danger of a "therapeutic state," in which dependence on psychiatric opinion might lead to a massive loss of personal liberties. Other critics are concerned that psychiatrists and psychologists are under pressure to testify as defense or prosecution attorneys want them to. At the other extreme, psychiatrist Bernard Diamond feels that psychiatry and psychology should play a larger role in the judicial process and in some cases even determine guilt. He believes that forensic psychiatry is an important way to educate the public, reform the law, and change social attitudes toward mental illness. In the middle of this dispute lies a skeptical public, which may distrust psychological jargon and feel that psychiatrists and psychologists "let off" dangerous criminals who pose a continuing threat to the community. In fact, the evidence suggests that forensic experts have compiled a poor record on being able to predict who will be dangerous in the future (Tierney, 1982). Trial lawyer F. Lee Bailey claims that jurors often say, "I know this guy is nuts, but we're not going to put him in some institution where some psychiatrist can let him out" (*Newsweek*, August 29, 1977, p. 28). And still other mental health experts, like Karl Menninger, believe that psychiatrists should stay out of the courtroom, but should be consulted after the trial on such matters as length of sentence, rehabilitation methods, and parole (Robitscher & Williams, 1977).

Other critics claim that clever defendants can fool the experts and, in some cases, be set free to commit additional crimes. Thomas Vanda, a Chicago man acquitted in 1975 after stabbing a teenage girl, later advised a fellow inmate to "act crazy" in front of psychiatrists. When Vanda offered this advice, it was 1979, and he was back in jail, charged with stabbing another young woman. And once again, he was pleading insanity.

Other critics of forensic psychiatry argue from the opposite point of view—the defendant's. It is almost impossible for someone to get a fair trial, they say, once he or she has been hospitalized as "incompetent." And, according to these critics, confinement in a mental hospital is in many respects more punitive and restrictive than being sent to prison (Brooks, 1974).

1. The distinctions between normal and abnormal behavior are unclear. Four criteria that are widely used to distinguish normal from abnormal behavior are: a distorted perception of reality, inappropriate behavior, discomfort, and danger to oneself or to others.

2. Various approaches have been taken to explaining and treating abnormal behavior over the centuries. Primitive societies probably attributed it to supernatural causes. The ancient Greeks looked for natural causes and treated disturbed people, like those with physical illnesses, with care and sympathy. In the Middle Ages abnormal behavior was considered a sign of possession by the devil, punishable by exorcism and even physical torture. This period also saw the rise of asylums for the confinement of the mentally ill. Reform efforts began in the late 18th century, in both Europe and America, to turn asylums into appropriately staffed hospitals for the mentally ill. The pioneering efforts of Fournier in the late 19th century redirected attention to the search for medical cures for all forms of abnormal behavior.

3. Today several models of mental disorder coexist. Most important among these are the *biological model,* which holds that disorders have a basis in a person's physiology; the closely related *medical model,* which suggests that behaviorial abnormalities are the result of disease; the *psychoanalytic model,* which sees abnormal behavior as the result of unconscious conflict left over from childhood; and the *behaviorial model,* which holds that abnormal behaviors are due to faulty learning. Each point of view sheds light on certain types of behavior disorders.

4. *Anxiety disorders* are those in which anxiety is either a prominent feature or in which abnormal behavior seems prompted by a need to avoid anxiety. These include *panic attacks,* abrupt feelings of intense fear or terror for no apparent reason; *posttraumatic stress disorder,* in which spells of anxiety are related to a disturbing event in the past; *obsessive-compulsive disorder,* in which a person feels compelled to

think disturbing thoughts and/or perform irrational actions to avoid anxiety; and *phobic disorder,* in which anxiety is provoked by a definite (and apparently harmless) stimulus. Psychoanalytic theorists think that anxiety disorders are largely the result of threatening unconscious conflicts. A person attempts to avoid anxiety by engaging in behavior that creates the temporary illusion of being in control. Behavior theorists, on the other hand, believe that anxiety results from the learned association of fear with earlier situations that may or may not have been harmful.

5. *Somatoform disorders* involve physical symptoms of disease with no apparent organic cause. These include *somatization disorders,* which are characterized by recurring vague physical symptoms such as aches, pains, and dizziness; *conversion disorders* (once known as hysteria), in which a dramatic physical disability, such as blindness or paralysis, seems related to psychological needs; and *hypochondriasis,* in which a person who has no real disease symptoms nevertheless feels certain that he or she is ill.

6. *Dissociative disorders* are those in which a person's personality seems fragmented. These disorders include *amnesia,* or loss of memory; *multiple personality disorder,* in which more than a single personality seems present in one person; and *depersonalization disorder,* in which a person experiences feelings of unreality and loss of control over the body.

7. *Affective disorders* are those characterized by disturbances in *affect,* or emotional state. The most common is *depression,* in which a person feels sad, apathetic, and self-reproachful. Its apparent opposite is *mania,* in which a person feels overly excited and hyperactive. Mania may actually be a defense against the depressed state. In *bipolar disorder* the person alternates between periods of mania and periods of depression.

8. *Sexual dysfunction* consists of an inability to

function effectively during sex. In men this may mean *impotence,* the inability to achieve or keep an erection. In women it may mean *frigidity,* the inability to become sexually excited or reach orgasm. Other sexual disorders include *paraphilias,* which involve the use of unconventional sex objects. Among these are *fetishism,* the use of nonhuman objects; *pedophilia,* sexual relations with children; *zoophilia,* sexual relations with animals; *voyeurism,* gratification from watching the sexual activities of others; *exhibitionism,* the compulsion to expose one's genitals to others inappropriately; *transvestism,* the urge to wear the clothes of the opposite sex; and *sadomasochism,* the linking of sexual pleasure and pain.

9. *Homosexuality* is not considered abnormal behavior unless the person is unhappy with his or her condition and is desirous of becoming heterosexual. There are conflicting views on the origins of homosexuality. Psychoanalysts believe it is the result of unresolved Oedipal conflicts. Behaviorists tend to see homosexuality as learned behavior resulting from rewarding homosexual experiences.

10. *Personality disorders* involve certain inflexible and maladaptive patterns of behavior that cause a person distress and conflict with society. Among them are *schizoid personality disorder,* in which a person is withdrawn and distant from any social relationships; *paranoid personality disorder,* in which a person is unrealistically suspicious and mistrustful of others; and *narcissistic personality disorder,* in which a person is self-absorbed and unable to form normal emotional ties to others. The most serious personality disorder—at least in its effects on society—is *antisocial personality disorder,* which involves a pattern of violent, criminal, or unethical and exploitative behavior together with no affectionate feelings for other people. Some psychologists feel that antisocial behavior results from emotional deprivation in childhood. Others seek its basis in physiological impairment, such as a malfunction in the brain region that inhibits behavior.

11. *Substance use disorders* are disorders in which undesirable or impaired behavior centers around the regular use of some substance, such as alcohol or drugs. *Substance abuse* is characterized by pathological use of a substance, resulting in self-injurious behavior, for at least one month's time. Continued abuse can lead to *substance dependence,* marked by physiological evidence of either toleration or withdrawal symptoms. Psychoanalytic thinkers consider substance abuse and dependence an expression of unconscious emotional problems. Behaviorists stress the role of learning—that drugs help relieve anxiety, for example. Physiological psychologists believe that body chemistry causes some people to become dependent more readily than others.

12. Alcohol abuse and dependence are the most serious substance use problems in our society. There are many theories about what causes alcoholism including personality, genetic, and cultural factors. Social factors are thought to play a role in all types of substance-use disorders. Society sanctions a certain amount of substance use, such as social drinking, and mood-altering substances tend to be widely available.

13. *Schizophrenic disorders* are the most serious mental disturbances, involving a disintegration of the personality and disturbances in thought, communication, and emotions. *Delusions* (mistaken beliefs about reality) and *hallucinations* (false sense perceptions) are characteristic features. There are several subtypes of schizophrenia. These include *disorganized schizophrenia,* in which bizarre and childlike behaviors are common; *catatonic schizophrenia,* in which disturbed motor behavior is most characteristic and prominent; *paranoid schizophrenia,* in which there are extreme suspiciousness and bizarre delusions, especially delusions of grandeur; and *undifferentiated schizophrenia,* in which a person shows several schizophrenic symptoms without fitting into one of the above categories. Schizophrenic disorders are serious and disabling, although they can sometimes be controlled by drugs so that the person can lead a more nearly normal life. Both biological and social factors seem to play a role in the development of schizophrenia; there seems to be a hereditary component to the disorder, but environmental stresses also seem to play a part.

Review Questions

1. Using four major criteria, psychologists can readily distinguish abnormal from normal behavior. T/F
2. According to the biological/medical model, behavioral abnormalities are the result of disease; the psychoanalytic/behavioral model associates behavioral abnormalities with faulty learning.
3. Panic attacks, phobias, and obsessive-compulsive disorder are three examples of _____ disorders.
4. A feeling of fear or losing control that happens without an obvious cause is characteristic of panic attacks/posttraumatic stress disorder.
5. In cases of somatization disorder/hypochondriosis, a person feels recurring, vague physical symptoms that cannot be linked to any organic cause.
6. Multiple personality and depersonalization disorder are two types of personality/dissociative disorders, characterized by signs of fragmented personality.
7. Affective/dissociative disorders are those characterized by disturbances in emotional state.
8. One theory about depression is that it is a form of self-punishment. T/F
9. An affective disorder involving swings between mania and depression is known as _____ disorder.
10. Match the following terms with their correct definitions:
    ____ sexual dysfunction
    ____ paraphilias
    ____ fetishism
    ____ pedophilia
    ____ zoophilia
    ____ voyeurism
    ____ exhibitionism
    ____ sadomasichism

    A. inappropriate exposure of one's genitals in public
    B. sexual gratification derived from inanimate objects
    C. desire for sexual relations with animals
    D. inability to function effectively during sex
    E. disorders involving the use of unconventional sex objects or situations
    F. sexual pleasure tied to aggression
    G. desire for sexual relations with children
    H. interest in watching the sexual activities of others

11. Match the following personality disorders with their correct definition:
    ____ schizoid personality disorder
    ____ paranoid personality disorder
    ____ narcissistic personality disorder
    ____ antisocial personality disorder

    A. characterized by extreme suspicion and mistrust of others
    B. marked by a pattern of criminal or exploitative behavior
    C. characterized by withdrawal from social contact and lack of feeling for others
    D. marked by extreme self-absorption and need for admiration

12. Maladaptive behavior that results in serious distress and social conflict is characteristic of schizophrenic/personality disorders.
13. The more severe form of substance use disorder is substance abuse/substance dependence, and requires evidence of tolerance or withdrawal.
14. Delusions, hallucinations, and disordered thought are symptomatic of _____ disorders.

Outline

Therapies

15

To many people, the term **psychotherapy** still evokes an image of a bearded man with a pipe sitting silently in a chair while a client, reclining on a nearby couch, recounts traumatic events in his or her life. As the anxious client reveals dreams, fantasies, fears, and obsessions, the therapist nods and scribbles a few words in a notebook, and perhaps asks a question or two. The therapist rarely offers the client advice and never reveals details of his or her own personal life.

This cliché of psychotherapy has some truth to it: Scenes like this one do occur. But there are many other forms of psychotherapy. And while some therapies have much in common, others bear little or no resemblance to one another.

Despite its prevalence in our society relatively few people know what psychotherapy is or what to think about it. Some consider it a disgrace to be in therapy. Others see it as self-indulgent because they believe that people should work out their problems on their own. Asking for help—and paying for it—seem to them signs of a weak character. Surprisingly too, psychotherapy is as controversial among psychologists as it is among laypeople. Many experimentally oriented psychologists look upon therapy as a vague and poorly defined art. They maintain that it is practically impossible to measure the effectiveness of one treatment over another. Other psychologists feel differently, and suggest that particular therapies may be better suited to certain kinds of people and problems.

Although there are many forms of psychotherapy to choose from, most therapists today do not strictly adhere to one technique but borrow from several to meet the needs of their clients. In this chapter we will survey the various therapies used in private practice and in institutions and describe some recent developments. We will explore the effectiveness of different psychotherapies in treating psychological disorders. Finally, we will look at the traditional treatment of severe emotional disturbance and consider some alternatives.

Psychotherapy Treatment of behavioral and emotional disorders using psychological techniques.

465

Insight Therapies

Insight therapy Type of psychotherapy aimed at having the client achieve greater self-understanding of his or her motives, expectations, means of coping, and so on.

Psychoanalysis Therapeutic technique created by Freud, based on uncovering people's unconscious motives, feelings, and desires.

A variety of therapies used in both private practice and institutions fall under the heading of **insight therapy.** While insight therapies differ from one another in orientation and technique, their main goal is to give people a better understanding of their feelings, motivations, and actions. In this section we will consider the major insight therapies as well as some recent developments.

Psychoanalysis

Psychoanalysis, the classic approach to psychotherapy, is based on the belief that the anxiety and problems that cause a person to seek help

Psychoanalytic Therapy: An Illustration

The interview that follows is one that would take place during the early stages of psychoanalysis and demonstrates free association. The analyst remains fairly quiet while the client, a 32-year-old male teacher with recurring headaches, talks about whatever occurs to him:

Client: This is like my last resort. I've been to so many doctors for this headache. But I tell you . . . I don't want . . . I know that there's something wrong with me though. I've known it since I was a kid. Like I started to tell you, when I was 17, I knew there was something wrong with me, that . . . and I told my father that I needed to see a doctor, and he laughed at me and said it was just foolishness, but he agreed to take me to his doctor, Dr. _____ on 125th Street, and I never went in; I chickened out.

Therapist: You chickened out, then. How'd you feel about that chickening out?

Client: I don't know. I don't feel *proud* that I wasn't able to talk over these . . . this feeling I had. . . . I wouldn't have wanted my father to know about my . . . some of my problems. 'Cause my father, he just . . . you know, I told him, my father, that there was something wrong, that I needed help, and he'd laugh at me and, you know, just to pacify me, you know, he took me to Dr. _____, but I didn't know Dr. _____. He was a friend of my father's, yeah, I don't know if . . . I don't remember thinking about it, but if I had talked to Dr. _____ about my problems like the problems I

talk about in here, and my father found out, he might get pretty mad. Yeah.

Therapist: Well, this would be insulting to him? He'd feel it would be a bad reflection on his upbringing of you, if you went to a doctor like this? Would this humiliate him?

Client: Yeah. I've got . . . My father and I didn't get along too well, and to tell the truth, I was ashamed of my father. He was born in Poland, and he was a self-made man. He went to the University of Warsaw and then Fordham. He was a pharmacist, but he was . . . he didn't care how he dressed. He was all sloppy and dirty, and he was short. He's about five foot one and stoop-shouldered. . . . We used to go to restaurants, my mother and him and me, and he would never leave a tip, never leave a tip, never leave a tip. I used to sneak back and I'd throw a few cents that I might have on the table, but he was so stingy, so tight. When we went on a train, when we went somewhere, I would try to pretend I wasn't with them. I'd want . . . I'd go in another . . . I do need some help, and I know I've got to do the talking. That's the hardest part for me, that you won't give me any guidelines, that I have to do everything myself, and you'll analyze me. . . . I didn't ever think I'd . . . I didn't want to think I was gonna end up here. I hate to think that this is the problem, but . . . (Hersher, 1970, pp. 135–139)

Somewhat later in therapy the analyst takes a more active role, as shown in this excerpt from a are symptoms of repressed problems from childhood. Usually these problems concern aggressive or sexual drives that the child thought were dangerous or forbidden. Psychoanalysis reverses this process and brings these repressed feelings to consciousness, so that the person can more effectively deal with them.

Successful psychoanalysis depends on two conditions: First, the person must not inhibit or control thoughts and fantasies. Slips-of-the-tongue and associations between seemingly unrelated thoughts are clues to underlying problems. This procedure is called **free association** (see Figure 15-1). Second, the analyst must remain completely neutral and mostly silent. Usually the client lies on a couch, and the analyst sits behind him or her, so that the analyst cannot be easily seen. The analyst's silence becomes a blank screen on which the client projects feelings that might otherwise be suppressed.

Analysis typically proceeds in stages. After the initial awkwardness

Free association In psychoanalysis, the uninhibited disclosure of thoughts and fantasies as they occur to the client.

---

session with a different client:

Therapist (summarizing and restating): It sounds as if you would like to let loose with me, but you are afraid of what my response would be.

Client: I get so excited by what is happening here. I feel I'm being held back by needing to be nice. I'd like to blast loose sometimes, but I don't dare.

Therapist: Because you fear my reaction?

Client: The worst thing would be that you wouldn't like me. You wouldn't speak to me friendly; you wouldn't smile; you'd feel you can't treat me and discharge me from treatment. But I know this isn't so; I know it.

Therapist: Where do you think these attitudes come from?

Client: When I was 9 years old, I read a lot about great men in history. I'd quote them and be dramatic. I'd want a sword at my side; I'd dress like an Indian. Mother would scold me: Don't frown; don't talk so much. Sit on your hands, over and over again. I did all kinds of things. I was a naughty child. She told me I'd be hurt. Then, at 14, I fell off a horse and broke my back. I had to be in bed. Mother then told me on the day I went riding not to, I'd get hurt because the ground was frozen. I was a stubborn, self-willed child. Then I went against her will and suffered an accident that changed my life, a fractured back. Her attitude was, "I told you so." I was put in a cast and kept in bed for months.

Therapist: You were punished, so to speak, by this accident.

Client: But I gained attention and love from Mother for the first time. I felt so good. I'm ashamed to tell you this: Before I healed, I opened the cast and tried to walk, to make myself sick again so I could stay in bed longer.

Therapist: How does that connect up with your impulse to be sick now and stay in bed so much? (*The client has these tendencies, of which she is ashamed.*)

Client: Oh . . . (*pause*)

Therapist: What do you think?

Client: Oh, my God, how infantile, how un-grown-up (*pause*). It must be so. I want people to love me and be sorry for me. Oh, my God. How completely childish. It is, *is* that. My mother must have ignored me when I was little, and I wanted so to be loved.

Therapist: So that it may have been threatening to go back to being self-willed and unloved after you got out of the cast (*interpretation*).

Client: It did. My life changed. I became meek and controlled. I couldn't get angry or stubborn afterward.

Therapist: Perhaps if you go back to being stubborn with *me,* you would be returning to how you were before, that is, active, stubborn, but unloved.

Client (excitedly): And, therefore, losing your love. I need you, but after all, you aren't going to reject me. But the pattern is so established now that the threat of the loss of love is too overwhelming with everybody, and I've got to keep myself from acting selfish or angry. (Wolberg, 1977, pp. 560–561)

Positive transference Development of warm feelings toward one's therapist.

Negative transference Displacement of hostility felt for a parent or other authority figure to one's therapist.

Insight An awareness of how and why we feel and act as we do.

Figure 15-1

An artist's conception of free association. You can see how each figure seems to grow out of the one before it.

wears off, most people enjoy the chance to talk without interruption and like having someone interested in their problems. After a few sessions they may test their analysts by talking about desires and fantasies they have never revealed before. When they discover their analysts are not shocked or disgusted, clients are reassured and see their analysts as warm and accepting. At this point many people feel they are getting better and express confidence in their analysts' ability to help them. Good feelings for one's analyst, which psychoanalysts see as reflecting positive feelings toward one's parents, are called **positive transference.**

This euphoria gradually wears off. As people expose their innermost feelings, they experience a terrible vulnerability. They want reassurance and affection, but their analysts remain silent. Their anxiety builds. Threatened by their analysts' silence and by their own thoughts, clients may feel cheated and accuse their analysts of being money-grabbers. Or they may feel that their analysts are really disgusted by their disclosures or are laughing about them behind their backs. This **negative transference** is a crucial step, for it reveals people's negative feelings about authority figures and their resistance to uncovering repressed emotions.

At this point in therapy analysts begin to interpret their clients' feelings. The goal of interpretation is **insight:** People must see why they feel and act as they do and how their present state of mind relates to childhood experiences. Analysts encourage clients to confront events they have only mentioned briefly and to recall them fully. In this way they help their clients to relive their childhood traumas and to resolve conflicts they could not resolve in the past. *Working through* old conflicts provides people with a second chance to review and revise the feelings and beliefs that underlie their problems.

This description applies to traditional, or orthodox, psychoanalysis. But only a handful of people who seek therapy go into traditional analysis. For one thing, as Freud himself recognized, analysis depends on people's motivation to change and on their ability to deal rationally with whatever analysis uncovers. Schizophrenics freely talk about their fantasies and unconscious wishes, but they often cannot use the analyst's interpretations effectively. Psychoanalysis is best suited to "potentially autonomous" people (Hersher, 1970)—not to severely disturbed people. Moreover, orthodox analysis may take 5 years or more, and most traditional analysts feel that at least 3 and sometimes 5 sessions a week are essential. Thus few people can afford psychoanalysis, and many others need immediate help for immediate problems.

Furthermore, some psychologists believe that orthodox psychoanalysis is outdated. Freud invented this technique in the late 19th century. He worked primarily with upper-class people who were struggling with the strict moral and social codes of a Victorian society. But society has changed. Today it may be harder for people to *find* rules for behavior than to break them.

Finally, and perhaps most importantly, psychodynamic personality theory has changed since the turn of the century (see Chapter 12), and these changes are reflected in different approaches to therapy. For example, although Freud felt that to understand the present one had first to understand the past, most neo-Freudians try to get their clients to cope with current problems, rather than with unresolved conflicts from the past. Also, neo-Freudians favor face-to-face discussions, and most take an active role—they interpret clients' statements freely, suggest topics for discussion, illustrate comments by role playing, and so on.

Client-Centered Therapy

Carl Rogers, the founder of **client-centered** or **person-centered therapy,** took bits and pieces of the neo-Freudians' views and revised and rearranged them into a radically different approach to therapy. Interestingly, in a recent survey of clinical and counseling psychologists, Rogers was rated the most influential psychotherapist today, well above Freud (Smith, 1982).

The goal of therapy, in Rogers' view, is to help clients become fully functioning, to open them up to all of their experiences and to all of themselves. Rogers calls his approach to therapy "client-centered" because he does not feel that the image of a patient seeking advice from an expert, the doctor, is appropriate. The best experts on individual people are the individuals themselves.

Rogers' ideas about therapy are quite specific. As we saw in Chapter 12, Rogers believes that defensiveness, rigidity, anxiety, and other signs

Client-centered or person-centered therapy A nondirective form of therapy developed by Carl Rogers that calls for unconditional positive regard on the part of the therapist; the aim of treatment is to help clients become fully functioning.

Client-Centered Therapy: An Illustration

Client: I guess I do have problems at school. . . . You see, I'm chairman of the Science Department, so you can imagine what kind of a department it is.

Therapist: You sort of feel that if you're in something that it can't be too good. Is that . . .

Client: Well, it's not that I . . . It's just that I'm . . . I don't think that I could run it.

Therapist: You don't have any confidence in yourself?

Client: No confidence, no confidence in myself. I never had any confidence in myself. I—like I told you that—like when even when I was a kid I didn't feel I was capable and I always wanted to get back with the intellectual group.

Therapist: This has been a long-term thing, then, it's gone on a long time.

Client: Yeah, the *feeling* is—even though I know it isn't, it's the feeling that I have that—that I haven't got it, that—that—that—people will find out that I'm dumb or—or . . .

Therapist: Masquerade . . .

Client: Superficial, I'm just superficial. There's nothing below the surface. Just superficial generalities, that . . .

Therapist: There's nothing really deep and meaningful to you.

Client: No—they don't know it, and . . .

Therapist: And you're terrified they're going to find out.

Client: My wife has a friend, and—and she and the friend got together so we could go out together with her and my wife and her husband. . . . And the guy, he's an engineer and he's, you know—he's got it, you know; and I don't want to go, I don't want to go because—because if—if we get together he's liable to start to—to talk about something I don't know, and I'll—I won't know about that.

Therapist: You'll show up very poorly in this kind of situation.

Client: That I—I'll show up poorly, that I'll—that I'll just clam up, that I . . .

Therapist: You're terribly frightened in this sort of thing.

Client: I—I'm afraid to be around people who—who I feel are my peers. Even in pool—now I—I play pool very well and—if I'm playing with some guy that I—I know I can beat, *psychologically,* I can run 50, but—but if I start playing with somebody that's my level, I'm done. I'm done. I—I—I'll miss a ball every time.

Therapist: So the . . . the fear of what's going on just immobilizes you, keeps you from doing a good job. (Hersher, 1970, pp. 29–32)

Rational-emotive therapy (RET) A highly directive therapeutic approach based on the idea that an individual's problems have been caused by his or her misinterpretations of events and goals.

Carl Rogers

of discomfort arise because people have experienced conditional positive regard. They have learned that love and acceptance are conditional on becoming what other people want them to be. Therefore, the cardinal rule in person-centered therapy is for the therapist to express *unconditional positive regard.* That is, therapists must show that they truly accept and value their clients—no matter what clients may say or do. Rogers feels that this is a crucial first step toward getting clients to accept themselves. Rather than taking an objective approach, Rogerian therapists try to understand things from the clients' point of view. They are also emphatically *nondirective.* They do not suggest reasons why clients feel as they do, or how they might better handle a difficult situation. Instead, they try to reflect clients' statements, sometimes asking questions and sometimes hinting at feelings clients have not put into words. Rogers feels that when therapists provide an atmosphere of openness and genuine respect, clients can find themselves.

Rational-Emotive Therapy

Unlike Rogerians, *rational-emotive therapists* look upon themselves as experts and upon their clients as people who do not know how to help themselves. According to Ellis (1973), most people compare themselves to other people and then rate themselves. This prevents them from accepting their natural faults and usually results either in self-contempt or in a pose of defensive superiority. Regardless of what might have happened in the past, rational-emotive therapists insist that people are solely responsible in the present for how they feel about themselves and for their happiness. The goal of **rational-emotive therapy** (RET) is to show clients that their own misinterpretations of events are causing their problems and to teach clients to see themselves more rationally.

RET therapists believe that people seek help when they find themselves acting in self-defeating ways. For example, some people feel that something is wrong with them if everyone they meet does not immediately love and admire them. Others "beat their brains out" trying to solve problems beyond their control. Still others simply refuse to examine obvious evidence and persist in thinking they are weak, sinful, or stupid. To correct these illogical and self-defeating beliefs, RET therapists use a variety of techniques, including persuasion, confrontation, challenge, commands, and even theoretical arguments. They do not "baby" their clients, and some people find their toughness hard to accept. They may go as far as to give "homework" assignments, encouraging clients to argue with their bosses, to ask the girl down the hall for a date, to pat the dog that frightens them. In short, RET therapists are very directive.

Recent Developments

Recent years have seen an explosion of insight-type therapies, possibly as many as several hundred, each gaining a degree of popularity and prominence for a time (Coleman et al., 1984). Bookstores are filled with books on how to change oneself, and self-help has been one of the major fads of the 1970s and 1980s. Even among the mainstream insight therapies, there has been considerable divergence from the traditional form of "couch" psychotherapy.

Rational-Emotive Therapy: An Illustration

Client: . . . I always doubt that I have what it takes intellectually. . . .

Therapist: Well, let's suppose you haven't. Let's just suppose for the sake of discussion that you really are inferior to some degree, and you're not up to your fellows—your old peers from childhood or your present peers. Now what's so catastrophic about that, if it were true?

Client: Well, this is a fear, I'm not . . . if they found out, then . . . if I can't keep my job teaching, then I . . . I couldn't support my family.

Therapist: How long have you been teaching?

Client: Seven years.

Therapist: So, being inferior, you've done pretty well in keeping your job. You're not that concerned about your job.

Client: I know my wife says this. She says that somebody would find me out, but I . . . still feel that I . . . I'm kidding everybody, that I have to be very careful what I say and what I do, because if they should find out that I haven't got it, then I don't know what I would do. If I don't feel that I'm capable of being a teacher, then I shouldn't be a teacher.

Therapist: Who said so?

Client: I don't know.

Therapist: I know. You said so. Don't you think there are lots of teachers in the school system who are not very good teachers?

Client: Yes, I know there are a lot of them, and I don't respect them. I don't feel they should be teachers if they aren't qualified.

Therapist: So you're saying you don't respect yourself, if you act ineffectively as a teacher. Right?

Client: Yes, I wouldn't respect myself.

Therapist: Why not?

Client: Because if . . . well, it wouldn't be right to say that I'm teaching when . . . if I haven't got the qualifications, if I'm not capable to do the job.

Therapist: Let's assume you're a lousy teacher. Now why are you tying up your performance? Lousy teacher, we're assuming now. You are a lousy teacher and may always be a lousy teacher. Why are you tying that aspect of you up with your total self? I am a slob because my teaching is slobbish. Now do you see any inconsistency with that conclusion?

Client: No, but I agree that I would be . . . it would be a terrible thing if I were to teach, and it wouldn't . . . and I wouldn't be capable. That it wouldn't be right. That would be like I was a fraud.

Therapist: But the terrible thing is that you would be a slob, a no-goodnik, a louse who couldn't respect you.

Client: It would be dishonest of me.

Therapist: Well, yeah. What's terrible about that?

Client: Well, it's terrible.

Therapist: But according to you, about half or more of the teachers in the school system are not-so-hot teachers. Right?

Client: Yes, and if I were the administrator, I would have to do something about that.

Therapist: Meaning fire them?

Client: Fire them.

Therapist: And then who would teach the kids?

Client: You mean, if I was the administrator I'd have to . . .

Therapist: Tolerate.

Client: To tolerate it . . . (Hersher, 1970, pp. 64–66)

One general trend is toward shorter-term "dynamic therapy" for most people—usually once a week for a fixed duration. Because they now operate within such a time-limited framework, insight therapies have become more problem- or symptom-oriented. Instead of slowly and patiently trying to construct a "narrative of the psyche"—the aim of traditional Freudian analysis—contemporary therapists are more likely to try to help their clients correct the immediate problems in their lives. Unlike Freudians, they see the individual as more in control and less at the mercy of early-childhood events. Although childhood is not discounted as a source of formative experiences, the focus is on the client's current life situation and relationships. In addition, therapists give clients more direct guidance and feedback, commenting on what

Does a therapist have to be a person? The increasing popularity of microcomputers has led inevitably to the development of software packages that focus on many of the same problems and strategies encountered in person-to-person therapy. Programs now exist to help with a wide variety of psychological concerns: making friends, losing weight, staying in school, changing jobs, managing stress, stopping smoking, and becoming more assertive. The value of such programs is still under debate.

Ironically, one of the first and most widely known therapy programs, ELIZA, was written as a joke—and then taken very seriously. Developed in 1964 by Dr. Joseph Weizenbaum to illustrate the absurdity of artificial intelligence, ELIZA simulates a traditional conversation between therapist and client. The client types in any message, and ELIZA types out its response. The resulting "dialogue" has many of the properties of spoken conversation:

Program: Was there much friction between you and him [your father] when you were growing up?
Person: Yes, we fought all the time.
Program: Perhaps you were afraid of him.
Person: I certainly was. He used to really blow up.
Program: Perhaps you are still a little fearful of older men.
Person: Let's talk about something else.
Program: Okay. Go ahead. I will try to follow what you have to say about it. (Hilgard et al., 1971, p. 514)

When it became clear that people *liked* ELIZA and were often more honest talking to a computer than they would be talking to a human therapist, the stage was set for the development of more therapeutic software.

Psychotherapists were quick to point out, however, that emotions such as empathy, sympathy, and understanding lie outside the realm of any machine. The therapeutic significance of pauses, silences, and confrontations may also be missed by a computer. Moreover, computers cannot deal effectively with bizarre conversation, as is illustrated by the following "dialogue":

Program: Do you say that because no one else will listen to you for some special reason?

Person: Etcetera.
Program: I'm not sure I fully understand you.
Person: Abracadabra. Heresahellofafunnybobo.
Program: Earlier you said your brother beats you up all the time. . . . (Spero, 1978, p. 282)

In the 1970s Lang developed a computerized Device for Automated Desensitization (DAD) to treat phobias. The device intructs patients to relax while showing them a program of pictures related to the things they are afraid of. Comparisons indicate that DAD is about as effective as a human therapist in administering this type of treatment (Arieti, 1975). In other cases, computerized devices teach children to speak. The children "play" with the computer, which is programmed to reward their success in speaking.

Advocates of electronic therapy observe that computers are uniquely suited to fostering psychological development. For one thing, programs can be self-modifying to fit the information supplied by the client. Any suggestions offered can then be specifically tailored to dealing with the problem at hand. For another, programs are interactive: Clients can make choices and then see their immediate consequences. Clients can also rate their own performance. And the computer can provide many possible outcomes for a given behavior, depending on circumstances. This shows the client that more than one "suitable" pattern exists.

Even family therapy is now available "on-line." There are computer services offering narratives and short courses on such subjects as "Fitting Together as a Family" and "Developing Babies' Thinking from Birth to Two." Users of one of these services can communicate with others who share the same concerns or with a professional counselor.

Some psychologists are now automating their offices and using therapeutic programs both for testing and as adjuncts to one-on-one therapy. Programs especially targeted to the needs of people who never receive professional attention could be a boon as well. However, the standards for *effective* software still remain to be worked out.

they are told, rather than just eliciting responses in a neutral manner.

One of the most notable trends in therapies in the past quarter century has been the proliferation of behavior therapies. Like the new insight therapies, they contrast in several respects with the traditional approach to therapy: Therapists are active rather than neutral; they concentrate on overt behavior rather than on its rationale; the therapy is brief rather than open-ended; and research evaluation is considered important (Garfield, 1981). In the next section we will examine several types of behavior therapies.

Behavior therapy Therapeutic approach aimed at teaching new behavior and based primarily on application of the principles of conditioning.

Behavior Therapies

Behaviorists do not consider disorders symptoms of hidden emotional conflicts that need to be uncovered and resolved. Rather, they argue that the behavior disorder *is* the problem. They feel that if they as therapists can teach people to respond with more appropriate behavior, they have in effect "cured" them.

Behavior therapies are based on the belief that all behavior, normal and abnormal, is learned. Hypochondriacs learn that they get attention when they are sick; schizophrenics learn that they are safe when they withdraw from reality. Therapists do not need to know how or why people learned to behave as they do; their job is to teach people more satisfying ways of behaving. Behaviorists use several techniques to build new habits.

Behavioral contracting A form of operant conditioning therapy in which client and therapist set reinforcements for reaching behavioral goals.

Aversive conditioning Behavior therapy technique that aims at eliminating undesirable behavior patterns by teaching the person to associate them with pain and discomfort.

Operant Conditioning

As we saw in Chapter 6, *operant conditioning* techniques are based on the idea that a person learns to behave in different ways if new behaviors are rewarded and old ones are ignored or punished. In one form of operant conditioning called **behavioral contracting,** the therapist—or anyone trying to help someone change a behavior pattern—and client agree on behavioral goals and on the reinforcement the client will receive when the goals are reached. These goals and reinforcements are often written down in a contract that binds both the client and the therapist as if by legal agreement. The contract specifies the behaviors to be followed, the penalties for not following them, and any privileges to be earned (Harmatz, 1978). One such contract might be: "For each day that I smoke fewer than 20 cigarettes, I will earn 30 minutes of time to go bowling. For each day that I exceed the goal, I will lose 30 minutes from the time I have accumulated."

Aversive Conditioning

Aversive conditioning is aimed at eliminating undesirable behavior patterns. Therapists teach clients to associate pain and discomfort with the behavior they want to unlearn. This form of behavior therapy has been used successfully to treat alcoholism, obesity, and smoking.

Cigarette smoking can be reduced or eliminated through aversive conditioning.

Desensitization Behavior therapy technique designed to gradually reduce anxiety about a particular object or situation.

"Leave us alone! I am a behavior therapist! I am helping my patient overcome a fear of heights!"

Sometimes the therapist uses real physical pain. Dent (1954) treated alcoholics by giving them a drug that produces extreme nausea when it mixes with alcohol in the stomach. Those being treated were encouraged—in fact, instructed—to drink. Each time they did, they became violently sick. Soon they felt sick just seeing a bottle of whiskey. Convicted child molesters have been cured by showing them pictures of naked children and then giving them electric shocks (Knight, 1974). The use of electric shock as an aversive stimulus has declined in recent years. In addition to the substantial ethical questions it raises—and the fact that less dangerous techniques exist—its effectiveness has been questioned: Although it can create avoidance in the presence of the certainty of punishment, unwanted behaviors may well continue in real-life situations when no such threat exists. In other words, new behaviors that generalize to other settings are not created. More recently, people have been taught to block behavior with unpleasant fantasies. For example, without undergoing shock treatment, the child molesters could learn to associate things they feared with pictures of children, and to associate things they enjoyed with pictures of adults.

Desensitization

In some cases, aversive conditioning may be harmful. For example, if a little boy who is afraid of dogs is taken by the hand and urged to approach the dog that bit him, he might well be terrified the next time someone takes his hand. In such cases, **desensitization,*** a method for gradually reducing irrational fear, would be a more useful technique. A therapist might, for example, give the child cookies and milk if he sits by a window and watches a chained dog outside. Once he seems calm in this situation, the therapist might give him cookies only if he goes out into the yard and plays some distance away from the chained dog. Waiting at each stage until the child seems relaxed, the therapist gradually moves the child closer to the dog. Behaviorists have used desensitization to cure phobias about snakes, heights, closed rooms, and sex. These examples indicate that behaviorists can successfully treat specific problems and fears, from psychotic behavior to a child's fear of dogs. But many of the people who consult psychotherapists are vague about their problems—they feel anxious and unhappy most of the time. Can behaviorists treat such diffuse anxiety?

Wolpe (1973) believes they can. Chronically anxious people may not know why they feel tense, but they can distinguish among different levels of anxiety. For example, in his first session a politician tells the therapist that he is very anxious about speaking to crowds. The therapist looks for more details. She asks if the man is more threatened by an audience of 500 than by an audience of 50, more tense when he is addressing men than when he is speaking to both men and women, and so on. Perhaps this politician feels more anxious talking to adolescents than to small children. Thus the therapist establishes a *hierarchy*, from the least to the most anxiety-provoking situations.

After establishing a hierarchy, therapists teach clients to clear their minds, to release tense muscles, and to relax. In some cases, drugs or mild

*Desensitization was also discussed in Chapter 6.

hypnosis help the client to relax. Once clients have mastered the technique of deep relaxation, they begin to work at the bottom of their anxiety hierarchy. Therapists ask the clients to imagine the least threatening situation and to signal when they begin to feel tense. At the signal, the therapists tell the clients to forget the scene and to concentrate on relaxing. After a short time they instruct them to return to the scene. This process is repeated until the clients feel completely relaxed about that scene. Then they advance up the hierarchy this way until they can imagine the situation they are most afraid of without anxiety. Wolpe reports that most clients transfer what they learn in his office to real-life situations.

Countertransference A therapist's projecting of his or her own emotions onto the patient.

Group therapy Form of psychotherapy in which clients meet regularly in a group.

Family therapy A therapeutic approach that sees the family as a unit and as part of the problem in an individual's treatment.

Group Therapies

Both insight and behavioral therapies are limited to the interaction of a client with a therapist. Many psychologists think this less than ideal. People may attach great importance to their therapists' real and imagined reactions. Therapists are human, so there is always some degree of **countertransference** (therapists' projecting their own emotions onto clients). Furthermore, therapy sessions are unlike everyday life. People seldom find the psychoanalyst's neutrality or the Rogerian therapist's unconditional positive regard among their friends and family. It may be hard to transfer the insight and confidence gained in therapy to other situations.

    Group therapies allow both therapist and client to see how the person acts with others. They also let people shed inhibitions and express themselves in a safe setting. Finally, groups are a source of reinforcement. Traditional therapy groups are an extension of individual psychotherapy. The participants may also be seeing the therapist individually. Such groups meet once or twice weekly, for about 1½ hours.

Traditional therapy groups are an extension of individual psychotherapy. They allow both therapist and client to see how a person acts with others.

Family Therapy

    A special form of group therapy is **family therapy.** This therapy is based on the theory that if one person in the family is having problems, it is often a signal that the entire family unit needs assistance. Family therapists feel that most psychotherapists treat people in a vacuum. There is no attempt to meet the person's parents, spouse, and children. The primary goals of family therapy are improving family communication, encouraging family members to become more empathic, getting members to share responsibilities, and reducing conflict. To achieve these goals, all family members must see that they will benefit from changes in their behavior. Family therapists concentrate on changing how family members satisfy their needs rather than trying to change those needs or the individual members' personalities (Horn, 1975).

    Family therapy is indicated when problems exist between husband and wife, parents and children, or other family members. It is also indicated when a client's progress in individual therapy seems to be slowed by his or her family, or when a family member has trouble adjusting to a client's improvement. Goldenberg (1973) notes, however, that all families may

Family therapy works toward improving communication among family members. All members need to see that they will benefit from changes in their behavior.

Gestalt therapy Form of therapy, either individual or group, that emphasizes the wholeness of the personality and attempts to re-awaken people to their emotions and sensations in the here-and-now.

not benefit from family therapy. Some problems are too entrenched. Important family members may be absent or unwilling to cooperate; or one family member may monopolize the session, so that the therapy becomes unworkable. In such cases, a different therapeutic approach might work better.

Gestalt, Sensitivity, and Encounter Groups

Gestalt therapy is largely an outgrowth of the work of Frederick (Fritz) Perls at the Esalen Institute in California. Perls began his career as a psychoanalyst, but later turned vehemently against Freud and psychoanalytic techniques. He felt "Freud invented the couch because he could not look people in the eye" (1974, p. 118). Gestalt therapy emphasizes the here-and-now and encourages face-to-face confrontations.

Gestalt Therapy: An Illustration

Therapist: Try to describe just what you are aware of at each moment as fully as possible. For instance, what are you aware of now?

Client: I'm aware of wanting to tell you about my problem, and also a sense of shame—yes, I feel very ashamed right now.

Therapist: Okay. I would like you to develop a dialogue with your feeling of shame. Put your shame in the empty chair over here *(indicates chair)*, and talk to it.

Client: Are you serious? I haven't even told you about my problem yet.

Therapist: That can wait—I'm perfectly serious, and I want to know what you have to say to your shame.

Client: *(awkward and hesitant at first, but then becoming looser and more involved):* Shame, I hate you. I wish you would leave me—you drive me crazy, always reminding me that I have a problem, that I'm perverse, different, shameful—even ugly. Why don't you leave me alone?

Therapist: Okay, now go to the empty chair, take the role of shame, and answer yourself back.

Client: *(moves to the empty chair):* I am your constant companion—and I don't *want* to leave you. I would feel lonely without you, and I don't hate you. I pity you, and I pity your attempts to shake me loose, because you are doomed to failure.

Therapist: Okay, now go back to your original chair and answer back.

Client: *(once again as himself):* How do you know I'm doomed to failure? *(Spontaneously shifts*

chairs now, no longer needing direction from the therapist; answers himself back, once again in the role of shame.) I know that you're doomed to failure because *I* want you to fail and because I control your life. You can't make a single move without me. For all you know, you were *born* with me. You can hardly remember a single moment when you were without me, totally unafraid that I would spring up and suddenly remind you of your loathsomeness.

Client: You're right; so far you *have* controlled my life—I feel constantly embarrassed and awkward. *(His voice grows stronger.)* But that doesn't mean that you'll continue to control my life. That's why I've come here—to find some way of destroying you. *(Shifts to the "shame" chair.)* Do you think *he* can help you? *(Bill, as shame, points to the therapist.)* What can he do? He hardly knows you as I know you. Besides, he's only going to see you once or twice each week. I am with you every single moment of every day!

Therapist: Bill, look how one hand keeps rubbing the other when you speak for shame. Could you exaggerate that motion? Who does that remind you of?

Client: *(rubbing his hands together harder and harder):* My mother would do this—yes, whenever she was nervous she would rub her hands harder and harder.

Therapist: Okay, now speak for your mother. (Shaffer, 1978, pp. 92–93)

Gestalt therapy is designed to make people self-supporting. It can be done with individuals, but it is more frequently done in a group setting. The therapist is active and directive and usually concentrates on one person at a time. The emphasis in Gestalt therapy is on the *whole* person, and the therapist's role, as Perls describes it, is to "fill in the holes in the personality to make the person whole and complete again" (Perls, 1969, p. 2). Gestalt therapists try to make people aware of their feelings, to awaken them to sensory information they may be ignoring. Many techniques may be used—people are told to talk about themselves in the first person ("I keep looking away" instead of "My eyes keep looking away"). In this way, therapists remind clients that they alone are responsible for everything they do. If clients want to discuss a third person, they must speak directly to that person or act out a conversation if that person is absent. Gestalt therapy, like psychoanalysis, uses people's dreams to help uncover information. Often clients are asked to act out all parts in their dreams—both people and objects.

Sensitivity groups, like the group sessions conducted at the Esalen Institute, seek to enhance *awareness* by focusing on nonverbal communication and the senses. Often the participants are well-adjusted—in their own minds, too well-adjusted. They feel they have lost touch with simple things. How many people rush around and never pause to look into a stranger's eyes or smell the air on a spring day? How many people never touch anyone except for their lover, spouse, or children? Sensitivity groups use exercises to reawaken the senses.

Encounter groups take this process one step further. They demand that participants *respond* to the immediate situation and express themselves directly. By stripping away the social pretenses of everyday life, encounter groups force people to give up their inhibitions and stop acting in ways they think others expect them to act. For example, Susan attacks John and he responds by saying, "You're projecting." This may be correct, but John is avoiding his own feelings about being attacked. How does he feel? Threatened? Hurt? Angry? By coming to grips with such feelings, participants feel better and less anxious. Sometimes encounter groups have *marathon sessions* in which participants meet all day, every day, for a weekend or more, either in the therapist's office or at a vacation retreat.

Large-Group Awareness Training

In the past decade encounter groups appear to have been eclipsed in popularity by various schools of large-group awareness training, the best known of which is **est** (Erhard Seminar Training). By 1980 more than 250,000 people had participated in est training—as many as several hundred at a time in a single training seminar.

Est begins with a pretraining session at which trainees agree to certain conditions, such as staying seated and silent unless called upon, and using the bathroom, eating, and smoking only during breaks. The training itself occurs over the following two weekends; it is conducted by an authoritarian trainer who derides trainees and their accomplishments. Trainees must raise their hands if they wish to stand and speak, and must remain standing until they are thanked by the trainer and applauded by

Sensitivity group Group that meets over a period of time to share feelings and help members gain insight into their own emotional reactions.

Encounter group Therapy group emphasizing sensory experiences and interpersonal communication.

est A form of large-group awareness training that emphasizes the direct experience of reality.

Est training seminars are conducted by a group leader in a highly authoritarian manner. Est seminars can be highly emotional, as trainees express anger or criticism and examine images from the past.

Nonprofessional "Therapists"

If you suffer from a physical ailment that doesn't clear up, the chances are you'll soon see a doctor. If you're emotionally troubled, however, statistics show that you're much less likely to visit a mental health professional. Instead, you are more likely to talk things over with someone you already know, such as your supervisor, hairdresser, bartender, or lawyer. According to Emory L. Cowen (1982), "For the most part, people do *not* bring their personal troubles to mental health professionals at *any* point in their unfolding, least of all in response to early, sometimes keenly important, signs of distress" (p. 385). Among the reasons for this reluctance are the high cost of such services, their geographic or practical inaccessibility, and their ideological unacceptability to some people. "Even when such barriers do not exist," Cowen says, "many troubled individuals prefer to talk with people who are known and trusted in more natural contexts—people who are willing to listen when they are ready to talk" (p. 385). And there is some evidence that at least some of these nonprofessional "therapists" are as effective as trained therapists in helping people (Strupp & Hadley, 1979).

Cowen (1982) surveyed 325 of these nonprofessional "therapists" such as bartenders and hairdressers. He found that discussions of personal problems do indeed arise with "substantial frequency," and that the sorts of problems raised—children, health, marriage, depression, anxiety, jobs, money, and sex—were not different from those raised with mental health professionals. And the amateur therapists perceived themselves as being somewhat helpful. On the whole,

they rated themselves in the "moderately effective" range, with hairdressers rating themselves a bit higher and bartenders a bit lower than lawyers and supervisors. When the groups were asked about their effectiveness, Cowen says, the general response was, "We're coping and doing a decent job, but there are gaps and we could use help" (Cowen, 1982, p. 393).

Among the tactics most frequently cited by the amateurs were "offering support and sympathy," "trying to be lighthearted," and "just listening." Lawyers, however, emphasized asking questions, giving advice, and pointing out the consequences of bad ideas in addition to giving support and sympathy. Cowen notes that women were called on to deal with personal problems more often than men, that they felt more at home in this role and performed it more patiently and sympathetically, and that they used more engaging, task-oriented handling strategies than their male counterparts.

Interestingly, the amateurs said they saw helping others with their problems as a normal and sometimes very important part of their jobs. As one hairdresser put it, "To be perfectly truthful, I regard myself as a B− hairdresser. But my business is booming. Mostly that's because I listen to people, care about their personal concerns, and try to be helpful. The guy down the street is really an A+ hairdresser—one of the best in town. But he's going to go out of business because he can't stand people and is incapable of listening sympathetically to *anyone's* problems" (Cowen, 1982, p. 390).

the audience. If trainees express criticism or anger, they are met with studied indifference by the trainer, who reminds them that they themselves chose to take est training.

Est trainees learn that their lives can be made to work only if they experience reality directly—and that their belief systems, understanding, and reasonableness are isolating them from such an experience (Finkelstein, Wenegrat, & Yalom, 1982). Powerful feelings are released as trainees examine images from their past, including their childhood. Trainees subsequently learn that though they may not have voluntarily caused their misfortunes, they are totally responsible for their present experience of them.

In the final sessions trainees learn that the emotional upsets of life result from machinelike, illogical associations that link the experiences of the present with past threats or losses. In other words, they are mechanical, illogical "feeding tubes."

Est graduates seem to indicate a general satisfaction with est training—about the same as that found among people who have participated in encounter groups. One unpublished study (Hosford et al., 1980) shows that compared with control groups awaiting est training, est graduates show changes on psychological tests that indicate improved mental health. Another unpublished study that was more effectively designed (Hoepfner, 1975) shows no effect of est training. Though severely disturbed clients are least likely to benefit from est training, research has shown that they are not likely to be permanently harmed by it either (Finkelstein et al., 1982).

Effectiveness of Psychotherapies

Though insight therapy, behavior therapy, and group therapy represent different approaches to the goal of improved mental health, they share one characteristic: All are *psycho*therapies—that is, they deal with disorders by using psychological methods. But is psychotherapy *effective*? Is it any better than no treatment at all? And if it is, how much better is it?

One of the first studies to consider these questions was done by H. J. Eysenck (1952), who surveyed 19 published reports covering more than 7,000 cases. Eysenck concluded that individual psychotherapy was no more effective against neurotic disorders than no therapy at all: "Roughly two-thirds of a group of neurotic patients will recover or improve to a marked extent within about two years of the onset of their illness whether they are treated by means of psychotherapy or not" (p. 322).

Although Eysenck's conclusions caused a storm in the psychological community, his study immediately stimulated more research. A later review of the literature done by Meltzoff and Kornreich (1971) found more "good" or acceptable results than did Eysenck, and therefore concluded that psychotherapy is effective and is superior to no treatment. Bergin (1971) also found evidence of treatment-related improvement. Bergin questioned the "spontaneous recovery" of the control subjects in the studies Eysenck surveyed, noting that even though they received no formal therapy, many of them did get help from friends, clergy, physicians, and teachers. He concluded that the improvement rate among people in psychotherapy was greater than that of untreated control subjects. Sloane et al. (1975), who compared people who had received psychoanalytic psychotherapy, those who had had behavior therapy, and a control group of people who were on a waiting list for therapy, found that both therapies were superior to the control condition in reducing major symptoms.

In 1977 a dramatically new approach was taken to the efficacy question. Smith and Glass (1977) reported an averaging of the results of a large number of studies, from which they concluded that the typical therapy client is better off than 75 percent of untreated controls. But is this result due simply to the fact that the therapy patients believed they would be helped, or is it due to the actual treatment itself? Landman and Dawes (1982) conclude that while initiating *any* treatment will create a small improvement, actually receiving therapy leads to a much greater improvement. In other words, the effects of receiving therapy appear to be due to more than just *believing* that you are going to get better.

Is any particular form of psychotherapy better than the others? Is group therapy or behavior therapy, for example, more effective than insight therapy? In general, the answer seems to be no—but each kind of psychotherapy may be particularly appropriate for certain kinds of people and problems. Insight therapy, for example, is best suited to people seeking extensive scrutiny of themselves or profound self-understanding, relief of inner conflict and anxiety, or better relationships with others. On the other hand, behavior therapy is probably most appropriate in cases where there is a specific behavioral problem. Desensitization, for example, is most effective with conditioned avoidance responses such as phobias and anxiety disorders. Aversive techniques are successful in producing impulse control, and modeling combined with positive reinforcement has helped in learning more complex responses. Behavioral approaches have also been successful with sexual dysfunctions such as frigidity and impotence.

Some psychologists think that behavior therapies oversimplify the treatment of disorders. The chief opposition to behavior therapies comes from traditional psychoanalysts. Analysts, as we noted earlier, believe that disturbed behavior is a symptom of unconscious problems. They argue that if you teach people to give up their symptoms without resolving the underlying conflicts, new symptoms—perhaps even less desirable ones—will appear. But Wolpe (1969) says this is not so: Of 249 people he treated for neurotic problems using behavior therapy, only 4 developed new symptoms.

Is behavior therapy more effective than insight therapy in bringing about positive changes in people? Sloane and his colleagues (1975) studied 94 people with anxiety or personality disorders. They randomly divided these people into three groups: 31 people were assigned to behavior therapy, 30 to insight therapy, and 33 to a waiting list.

Clients in behavior therapy were treated with several behavior techniques, including systematic desensitization, assertiveness training, and avoidance conditioning. Those in insight therapy were treated with short-term therapy. And those on the waiting list received no specific therapy; they were told that they would have to wait 4 months before their therapy would begin.

After 4 months the researchers found that all three groups had improved, but those in the two groups receiving therapy had improved the most. When the subjects were asked if they felt better, those who had received behavior therapy reported more improvement than either of the other groups. The researchers concluded, however, that despite people's feelings of well-being, "there is no clear evidence for the superiority of behavior therapy" (Sloane et al., 1975, p. 376). Many therapists believe that combining these two forms of treatment may be the best form of therapy for many clients (Gomes-Schwartz et al., 1978).

What about group therapy? Therapy groups allow psychologists to reach more people at lower costs and in less time. But are such groups therapeutic? Encounter and sensitivity groups have been severely criticized. Goldenberg (1973) points out that their benefits appear to be only short-term. After the "high" feeling passes, people are generally no better off than they were before. Moreover, sensitivity and encounter groups

Insight therapy seems best suited to those seeking a greater degree of self-understanding or better relationships with others.

emphasize emotions and play down the intellect. "Gut-level feelings are in, while head trips are out . . . . Yet lasting change probably requires some integration of the intellect with the senses" (Goldenberg, 1973, p. 407).

Hartley, Roback, and Abramowitz (1976) share this pessimistic view of sensitivity and encounter groups. But they suggest that many objections to encounter groups could be overcome and the number of "casualties" reduced if effective screening methods excluded severely disturbed people and people in crisis; if potential group members were adequately informed about group goals and behavior; if leaders were specifically trained to deal with recurring problems; and if leaders were certified by a regulatory body.

Meyer and Smith (1977) take a more positive stance on the effectiveness of group therapy. In their view, group therapy gives participants immediate realistic feedback, a range of behavioral models, and group validation of decisions and future plans. Moreover, they contend that group therapy helps clients with a range of disorders.

It should be noted that the trend in psychotherapy is toward eclecticism; that is, toward a recognition of the value of a broad treatment package rather than commitment to a single form of therapy. Although an eclectic model doesn't guarantee greater effectiveness—an inconsistent hodgepodge of techniques and concepts could result instead—the majority of therapists now identify with this approach (Smith, 1982).

Physical treatment Treatment of behavior disorders with such methods as electroconvulsive therapy, insulin shock treatment, psychosurgery and drug therapy.

Electroconvulsive therapy (ECT) A physical therapy in which a mild electrical current is passed through the brain for a short period, often producing convulsions and temporary coma; used to alleviate sudden and severe depression.

Physical Treatment

Sometimes therapists find they cannot "reach" people with any of the therapies we have described because they are extremely agitated, disoriented, or totally unresponsive. In these cases, therapists may decide to use **physical treatment** to change clients' behavior so that they can benefit from therapy. Physical treatment is also used both to restrain clients who are dangerous to themselves and to others and in institutions where there are only a few therapists for many patients.

Shock Therapies

Shock therapies are most often used for sudden and severe depression. In **electroconvulsive therapy** (ECT) one electrode is placed on each side of the person's head, and a mild current is turned on for a very short time. This produces a brief convulsion, followed by a temporary coma. Muscle relaxants administered in advance prevent dangerously violent contractions. When patients awake several minutes later, they normally have amnesia for the period immediately preceding the procedure and remain confused for the next hour or so. With repeated treatments, people often become generally disoriented, but this clears after treatment concludes. Treatment normally consists of fewer than a dozen sessions of ECT.

No one knows exactly why shock treatment works, but most researchers believe that convulsions produce both physiological and psychological changes (Sarason & Sarason, 1980).

While ECT appears to be effective in alleviating certain severe depressions, it has many critics and its use is extremely controversial. For example, the procedure is clearly capable of damaging the brain. Such damage has been found in animals sacrificed immediately after ECT treatment, and it is possible that each treatment destroys a number of central nervous system neurons. Nevertheless, defenders of ECT insist that it is highly effective and works relatively quickly, which is important when dealing with suicidally depressed people. In any case, ECT is used much less frequently now than it was a decade ago.

In **insulin shock treatment** the patient is given an intramuscular injection of insulin, which lowers the level of glucose (sugar) in the blood and produces a coma that the patient comes out of when glucose is administered. This treatment places great stress on the body, especially the cardiovascular and nervous systems. In addition, the therapeutic results of insulin shock treatment and the relapse rate have been disappointing. As a result, insulin shock is seldom used today.

Psychosurgery

As we saw in Chapter 2, changing a person's behavior and emotional state by brain surgery is a drastic step, especially since the effects of **psychosurgery** are difficult to predict. In a prefrontal lobotomy the frontal lobes of the brain are severed from the deeper centers beneath them, on the assumption that in extremely disturbed patients the frontal lobes intensify emotional impulses from the lower brain centers (chiefly the thalamus and hypothalamus). Unfortunately lobotomies can work with one person and fail completely with another—possibly producing permanent undesirable side effects, such as an inability to inhibit impulses or a virtually total absence of feeling.

Prefrontal lobotomies are rarely performed today. In fact, no psychosurgical procedures are used except as desperate measures to control such conditions as intractable psychoses, severe and debilitating disorders, and occasionally for pain control in a terminal illness.

Drug Therapies

Most psychiatrists prefer drugs to either shock treatment or psychosurgery. Two major advantages of drugs are that they produce only temporary changes in body chemistry, and the side effects are easier to predict. Moreover, the dosage can be varied from one person to another.

Before the mid-1950s drugs were not widely used in therapy because the only available sedatives induced sleep as well as calm. Then the major tranquilizers *reserpine* and the *phenothiazines* were introduced. In addition to alleviating anxiety and aggressive behavior, both of these drugs reduce psychotic symptoms, such as hallucinations and delusions. Thus they are called *antipsychotic drugs*. The first of the phenothiazines was *chlorpromazine* (Thorazine), and it became the treatment of choice for schizophrenia.

Valium

Valium, known in scientific circles as diazepam, is an antianxiety drug or minor tranquilizer. After its introduction in 1963, Valium rapidly became the most widely prescribed drug in the United States. In 1978 about 68 million prescriptions were written for Valium, Librium, and other related tranquilizers at a wholesale market value of $360 million (Clark & Hager, 1979).

The benefits of Valium do not come without substantial costs. Side effects of drowsiness and motor impairment are sometimes responsible for car accidents. It can cause negative effects when taken with other drugs, including alcohol. Valium may also interfere with serotonin, a natural brain chemical that is an antidepressant and aids in normal sleep. Dr. E. H. Uhlenhuth of the University of Chicago warns that "if a doctor does not recognize a depressed patient and pulls out Valium, he may make the patient more depressed and even suicidal" (*Newsweek,* November 12, 1979, p. 101). Valium, with its anxiety-easing properties, may also mask clinically significant symptoms and could prevent a person from seeking needed psychotherapy (Coleman et al., 1984).

But perhaps the most serious worry is that Valium users will become dependent on the drug. The drug does have addictive potential and critics are concerned that it is too freely prescribed. More-over, an abrupt discontinuation of the drug can cause serious withdrawal symptoms such as tremors, nervousness, weakness, weight loss, nausea, retching, abdominal pain and cramping, insomnia, muscle twitches, facial numbness, and muscle cramps (Pevnick et al., 1978).

Defenders of Valium, however, argue that its negative effects are exaggerated. According to them, those who have trouble with the drug are people who disregard the doctor's orders. Valium proponents view the large percentage of people using the drug as "reasonable evidence of consumer satisfaction" rather than as a sign of overprescription or increased dependence (Cole & Davis, 1975).

Despite the arguments against it, Valium's value should not be overlooked. Although side effects and dependency may develop—even with the prescribed dosage—Valium is relatively safe and helps people deal with profound anxiety. Caution and restraint, however, should be exercised by physicians in prescribing the drug. It should be reserved for those seriously affected by anxiety and not be regarded as a cure for all the stresses and strains of everyday life. Also, Valium is not a cure in itself. Whenever possible, it should be used in combination with psychotherapy to help people deal with the causes of their problems.

How do antipsychotics work? Research with animals indicates that in part phenothiazines inhibit the functioning of the hypothalamus, which controls arousal. Brain-wave studies further suggest that this prevents internal arousal signals from reaching the higher portions of the brain (Sarason & Sarason, 1980). In addition, it appears that virtually all the antipsychotics block dopamine receptors in the brain.

Antipsychotic drugs are not without side effects, however. They can cause dryness in the mouth and throat, muscle stiffness, jaundice, and tremors of the extremities, as well as a stiffness of the face that resembles Parkinson's disease. A particularly serious side effect of long-term treatment with antipsychotics is *tardive dyskinesia,* a disturbance of motor control, particularly in the muscles of the face, for which no effective treatment has been developed. Moreover, although the antipsychotics alleviate the most critical symptoms of schizophrenia, patients are not restored to fully alert and functioning status, and symptoms often reappear after drug treatment is withdrawn. Still, as the following case study shows, the antipsychotics can sometimes have dramatic effects (Grinspoon, Ewalt, & Shader, 1972).

Ms. W. was a 19-year-old, white, married woman who was admitted to the treatment unit as a result of gradually increasing agitation and hallucinations

Barbiturates A class of sedative drugs with high addictive potential.

over a three-month period. Her symptoms had markedly intensified during the four days prior to admission. . . . She had had a deprived childhood, but had managed to function reasonably well up to the point of her breakdown.

At the outset of her hospitalization, Ms. W. continued to have auditory and visual hallucinations and appeared frightened, angry, and confused. . . . Her condition continued to deteriorate for more than two weeks, at which point medication was begun. . . .

She responded [to thioridazine (Mellaril)] quite dramatically during the first week of treatment. Her behavior became, for the most part, quiet and appropriate, and she made some attempts at socialization. She continued to improve, but by the fourth week of treatment began to show signs of mild depression. Her medication was increased, and she resumed her favorable course. By the sixth week she was dealing with various reality issues in her life in a reasonably effective manner, and by the ninth week she was spending considerable time at home, returning to the hospital in a pleasant and cheerful mood. She was discharged exactly 100 days after her admission, being then completely free of symptoms.

A second group of drugs—the monoamine oxidase (MAO) inhibitors and the tricyclics—is used to combat depression. These drugs seem to work by increasing the amounts of serotonin and norepinephrine in the brain (Berger, 1978). The fact that these drugs often completely eliminate depression with few side effects has led some researchers to predict that in the near future specific types of depression will be fully treatable with specific antidepressant drugs (Akiskal, 1979; Maugh, 1981).

A third group of drugs—antianxiety drugs, or minor tranquilizers—is prescribed in great quantities to the American public to relieve anxiety and tension. One class of sedatives, the **barbiturates,** are highly addictive and have a low threshold of dosage safety. The more commonly prescribed antianxiety drugs are Miltown, Equamil, Librium, Valium, and Dalmant. Some of these drugs diminish generalized anxiety without decreasing adaptive functioning, although their effect is basically sedative. A few are also potentially addictive.

Finally, the simple salts of *lithium* are effective in relieving about 70 percent of manic disorders. Lithium is also sometimes successful in alleviating the depression episodes of manic-depressives, and recent research suggests that some depressives may be helped by this drug as well (Coppen, Metcalfe, & Wood, 1982).

Institutionalization

For the severely mentally ill, hospitalization has been the "treatment of choice" in the United States for the past 150 years. Of all the money spent on mental health in this country, 70 percent goes to hospital care (Kiesler, 1982a), and the direct cost of inpatient services is estimated to exceed $6 billion a year. More than 1.8 million people are admitted to mental hospitals annually.

However, mental hospitals are often large, isolated, state-run institutions in which patients face rather bleak prospects. Most such institutions are severely understaffed and cannot afford intensive therapy for all

On Being Sane in Insane Places

D. L. Rosenhan (1973) wanted to study the quality of care in mental hospitals. Eight sane people—Rosenhan himself, three psychologists, a pediatrician, a psychiatrist, a painter, and a housewife—applied for admission at 12 different psychiatric hospitals. The hospitals were a mixed group—old and new, public and private, understaffed and adequately staffed. The "pseudopatients" told the admitting doctor that they heard voices that said "empty," "hollow," and "thud." (These words were chosen because they suggest *existential psychosis*—a feeling that life is meaningless—no cases of which have ever been reported.) The voices were the only problem the pseudopatients said they had, and all gave their authentic life histories to the doctor. They all "passed" and were admitted. Seven of them were diagnosed as schizophrenic, and the eighth was labeled manic-depressive.

Once admitted, all the pseudopatients behaved normally. They talked to the other patients and openly took notes about what they saw on the wards. They told the staff they no longer heard voices and tried to get discharged. Many of the real patients knew at once that the pseudopatients were sane. One said, "You're not crazy. You're a journalist, or professor [referring to the constant note taking]. You're checking up on the hospital." The staff, on the other hand, "knew" the pseudo-patients were psychotic because the admitting diagnosis said so. One staff nurse described the note taking—recognized by the patients as a sign of sanity—as "Patient engages in writing behavior."

The pseudopatients found the hospitals highly dehumanizing. They had no privacy, their direct questions were ignored, and they were treated as though they did not exist. On a men's ward, one nurse showed just how little regard she had for patients by unbuttoning her blouse to adjust her bra. In over 3 months of hospitalization, six of the pseudopatients estimated that they talked with a doctor for about 7 minutes a day. They also noted that the doctors did not respond openly to their direct questions and avoided looking them in the eyes. Rosenhan concluded that "the consequences to patients hospitalized in such an environment—the powerlessness, depersonalization, segregation, mortification, and self-labeling—seem undoubtedly countertherapeutic" (p. 252).

This study caused a lot of controversy among the psychiatric community. Rosenhan's critics said that his sample was too small, and that his judgment should not be generalized to all mental hospitals. Most doctors did agree, however, that hospital care could be improved if hospitals were staffed with more qualified people, and if more money were available.

---

patients, so only the patients who seem to have the best chance of being cured, or at least of improving, are given therapy. Others receive only custodial care—the staff looks after them and sees that they are washed, dressed, fed, and that they take their medicine, but these patients may see a psychologist or psychiatrist for only a few minutes a week. Some hospitals have good recreational and vocational facilities; others have only a television set. Not surprisingly, the patients on many wards are apathetic and seem to accept a permanent "sick role."

Contrary to popular belief, (1) mental hospitalization is increasing far faster than the population rate; (2) mental hospitals—both state and private—account for only 25 percent of admissions for mental illness (most admissions for mental illness are to general hospitals without psychiatric units); (3) lengths of stay have decreased only at state and Veterans Administration psychiatric hospitals (where they still average 6 and 5 months, respectively); (4) several more effective alternatives to hospitalization exist; (5) mental hospitalization accounts for 25 percent of total hospital days in the United States (Kiesler, 1982b).

Hospitalization as a treatment for mental illness is no bargain. What are the more effective—and more cost-effective—alternatives?

Contrary to popular belief, mental hospitalization is increasing far faster than the population rate. More than 1,800,000 people are admitted to mental hospitals annually.

Therapies **485**

Deinstitutionalization The practice of providing patients with continued mental health care in the local community rather than keeping them in institutions.

Deinstitutionalization

The advent of antipsychotic drugs in the 1950s created a favorable climate of opinion for the policy of **deinstitutionalization**—releasing patients back into the community. The idea of deinstitutionalization was further strengthened in 1963, when Congress passed legislation that established a network of community mental health centers around the nation.

The practice of placing patients in more humane facilities or returning them under medication to care within the community intensified during the 1960s and 1970s. The many community-based mental health centers that were starting up at the time made deinstitutionalization appear quite feasible. In fact, by 1975 there were 600 regional mental health centers, which accounted for 1.6 million instances of outpatient care.

However, deinstitutionalization has run into serious problems. Discharged patients are often confronted with poorly funded community mental health centers and a related lack of adequate follow-up care. Moreover, they are often poorly prepared to live in the community and receive little guidance in coping with the mechanics of daily life. Patients who return home can become a burden to their families, especially if they don't get close follow-up care. Residential centers, such as halfway houses, vary in quality, but many provide inadequate medical and psychological care and minimal contact with the outside world. In any case, the dearth of sheltered housing forces many former patients into non-psychiatric facilities often located in dirty, unsafe, and isolated neighborhoods. And former patients are further burdened by a social stigma, which is perhaps the largest single obstacle to their rehabilitation (Bassuk & Gerson, 1978). Moreover, although deinstitutionalization and outpatient care are presumed to be well-established national policy objectives in mental health, Medicare, Medicaid, Blue Cross–Blue Shield, and other large insurers typically cover inpatient care completely but discourage outpatient care by requiring copayments and limiting the number of treatment visits.

The full effects of deinstitutionalization are not entirely known because the number of follow-up studies on discharged patients has been inadequate—in part because patients are transient and difficult to follow for long periods. Some argue that deinstitutionalization should be discouraged until more research is done on the practice and its alternatives. They fear that the potential cost to society of burgeoning numbers of vagrants and mentally disabled people living in lonely hotels and dangerous streets could be vast—much greater than supporting the hospitals that would otherwise accommodate them. Others say that despite all the problems, deinstitutionalization is an essential part of mental health treatment.

The success or failure of deinstitutionalization appears to hinge on the quality of continuing care available in the community. To succeed, the process requires better planning, more funding, and greater community support than it generally receives at present. "Full-spectrum" services are required, including psychotherapy and social services such as case management and crisis intervention. Staff trained to cope with the problems of the mentally ill living in the community are also needed. In addition, short-term rehospitalization arrangements should be available for those who need to return to the hospital.

Alternative Forms of Treatment

Deinstitutionalization assumes that institutionalization occurred in the first place. Recently, however, forms of treatment that avoid hospitalization altogether have received increasing attention. Kiesler (1982a) examined 10 controlled studies in which seriously disturbed patients were randomly assigned either to hospitals or to an alternative program. The alternative programs took many forms: patients living at home who were trained to cope with daily activities; a small homelike facility in which staff and residents shared responsibility for residential life; hostels offering therapy and crisis-intervention; family crisis therapy; day-care treatment; visits from public health nurses combined with medication; and intensive outpatient counseling combined with medication. Whatever the specific form of the alternatives, they all involved daily professional contact and skillful preparation of the community to receive the patients. On the other hand, the hospitals to which some people were assigned provided very good patient care, probably substantially above average for institutions in the United States. Nevertheless, in 9 out of 10 studies the outcome was more positive for alternative treatments than for hospitalization, even though hospitalization cost 40 percent more than the alternative programs. Moreover, patients given alternative care were less likely to undergo hospitalization later, which suggests that to a degree hospitalizing mental patients is a self-perpetuating process. Many such people "could be treated in alternative settings more effectively and less expensively," Kiesler concludes (1982a, p. 358).

Prevention

Yet another approach is to prevent the onset of mental illness in the first place. Although many preventive programs have been shown to be effective in eliminating or reducing disturbance, no more than 2 percent of the money spent on mental health goes for prevention (Albee, 1982). Practically all current efforts are targeted at treatment after mental illness develops. However, advocates of prevention observe that there are many more disturbed people in this country than could possibly be seen individually by mental health professionals. For example, Albee (1982) recently estimated that "the mental health community actually sees fewer than one in five of the seriously disturbed people" (p. 1043). Since treatment programs cannot begin to reach all those in need, the desirability of making greater effort at prevention becomes clear.

Prevention means reducing the incidence of emotional disturbance right from the start. In turn, this requires finding and eliminating the conditions that cause or contribute to behavior disorders and fostering well-being instead. Prevention can take several forms. Among the most

Crisis intervention helped in reducing the number of serious delayed reactions among victims of the 1981 Kansas City Hyatt Regency Hotel disaster and their families.

important preventive measures are those that identify and remove the organic factors that can cause problems. For example, when the number of prospective parents who receive genetic counseling increases, the number of infants born with brain damage decreases.

Reducing stress—which may require changes in the physical and social environment—is another important preventive measure, although the effects of stress on emotional disturbance are not as clear-cut as the effects of organic factors. Yet another preventive strategy is teaching young people the social and cognitive skills that increase their ability to deal with life's problems. Frustration and emotional disturbance later in life are thereby reduced (Albee, 1982).

A good example of prevention occurred after the Hyatt Regency Hotel disaster in Kansas City in 1981, when the sudden collapse of two aerial walkways in the midst of a crowded "tea dance" killed 111 people and injured more than 200. The disaster had a major emotional impact on the rescuers and survivors, as well as on hotel and media employees, medical personnel, hotel guests, and the family and friends of the dead and injured (Gist & Stolz, 1982). An estimated 5,000 people faced psychological consequences, and because virtually all the victims were local, the entire community felt the impact.

By the Monday after the Friday evening disaster, all the community mental health centers in the area had organized support group activities. Training was arranged for the professionals and natural caregivers, such as ministers, who would respond to Hyatt-related emotional problems. In addition, a major campaign was undertaken to publicize the availability of psychological services and to "legitimize the expression and acceptance of psychological reactions to the disaster" (Gist & Stolz, 1982, p. 1137). Press releases delivered a consistent message to the community, describing the reactions that were to be expected after a disaster, emphasizing that they were normal responses that needed to be shared and accepted, and reminding people that help was available. As a result of these preventive steps, the number of serious delayed reactions was far below what would otherwise have been expected.

The response of the local mental health community to the Hyatt disaster was one example of **crisis intervention,** an important preventive strategy. Crisis intervention means providing immediate help for individuals and families who are facing extremely stressful situations and who feel overwhelmed and unable to cope. "Hot lines" are one form of crisis intervention; short-term crisis therapy is another. Although crisis intervention is frustrating for the counselors involved because they rarely get to see how—or if—the problems are resolved, it is a crucial mental health service, providing thousands of desperately troubled people with a critical safety valve: a place to go for immediate counseling by someone who will listen and try to help.

Preventing behavior disorders rather than treating them afterward has been the ideal of the mental health community—if not the reality—since 1970 at least, when the final report of the Joint Commission on Mental Health of Children called for prevention as a new focus in mental health work. Ironically, because preventive programs are often long-range in scope and indirect in focus, they may be the first to be eliminated in times of economic hardship, when cuts are being made on the basis of "cost-effectiveness."

How to Find Help

As we have seen in this chapter, there is no such thing as *therapy* in a definitive sense; there are only *therapies*. There are probably as many approaches to therapy as there are practicing psychologists. While we have referred to a number of them in this chapter, there are others—many of them developed through a synthesis of various techniques and practices. Whole books could be (and have been) written to list the many people and organizations dedicated to helping those who feel they need some kind of counseling.

It should be clear by now that therapy and psychological counseling are not just intended to help "crazy" people. Unfortunately, the notion that seeking help for your problems is a sign of weakness or mental illness is hard to dispel. But the fact is that tens of thousands of people have been helped through psychological counseling and therapy. These people include business executives, artists, sports heroes, celebrities, and students. They are, in short, people like you and me. Therapy is a common, useful aid in coping with daily living.

College is a time of stress and anxiety for many students. The pressure of work, the competition for grades, the exposure to different people with different views, the tension of relating to your peers—these and other factors add up to considerable emotional and physical stress. These problems can be made worse because many students are away from home for the first time. Most colleges and universities have their own counseling services—many of them as sophisticated as the best clinics in the country. Most communities also have a community mental health program. As an aid to a potential search for the right counseling service, we are including a list of some of the other available resources for people seeking mental health professionals. Many of these services have national offices that, if contacted, will provide you with local branches and the appropriate people to contact in your area.

ALCOHOL AND DRUG ABUSE

Alcohol and Drug Problems Association
1130 17th St. NW
Washington, D.C 20036

National Clearinghouse for Alcohol Information
P.O. Box 2345
Rockville, Maryland 20852

National Clearinghouse for Drug Abuse Information
Room 110
1400 Rockville Pike
Rockville, Maryland 20852

Veterans Administration
Alcohol and Drug Dependency Services
810 Vermont Ave. NW
Washington, D.C. 20005

Association of Halfway Houses
Alcoholism Programs, Inc.
786 E. 7th St.
St. Paul, Minnesota 55106

General Service Board
Alcoholics Anonymous, Inc.
P.O. Box 459, Grand Central Station
New York, N.Y. 10017

For those with a friend or relative who has an alcohol problem:

Alanon Family Group Headquarters, Inc.
P.O. Box 182, Madison Square Station
New York, N.Y. 10010

SMOKING

The National Congress of Parents and Teachers
700 North Rush St.
Chicago, Illinois 60611

Weight and Smoking Counseling Service
400 E. 59th St.
New York, N.Y. 10022
212–755–4363

DEPRESSION AND SUICIDE

Rescue, Inc.
Room 25, Boston Fire Headquarters
115 Southampton St.
Boston, Massachusetts 02118
617–426–6600

International Association for Suicide
  Prevention
Suicide Prevention Center
1041 S. Menlo Ave.
Los Angeles, California 90006
213-381-5111

Payne Whitney Suicide Prevention Program
525 E. 68th St.
New York, N.Y. 10021
212-472-6162

National Save-A-Life League
815 Second Ave., Suite 409
New York, N.Y. 10017
212-736-6191

SEXUAL AND SEX-RELATED PROBLEMS

Community Sex Information, Inc.
P.O. Box 2858, Grand Central Station
New York, N.Y. 10017

Sex Information and Education Council
  of the United States (SIECUS)
137-158 N. Franklin St.
Hempstead, New York 11550
516-483-3033

Mary Ann Largen
National Rape Task Force Coordinator
National Organization for Women
  Legislative Office
1107 National Press Building
Washington, D.C. 20004
202-347-2279

Association of Women in Psychiatry
Women's Studies Dept., University of Delaware
34 W. Delaware
Newark, Delaware 19711

Association of Gay Psychiatrists
P.O. Box 29527
Atlanta, Georgia 30359
404-231-0751

Homosexual Community Counseling Center, Inc.
30 E. 60th St.
New York, N.Y. 10022
212-688-0628

STRESS

American Academy of Stress Disorders
8 S. Michigan Ave.
Chicago, Illinois 60603
312-263-7343

Neurotics Anonymous
1341 G St. NW, Room 426
Washington, D.C. 20005

National Commission Against Mental Illness
1101 17th St. NW
Washington D.C. 20036
202-296-4435

FOR HELP IN SELECTING A THERAPY

Psychiatric Service Section
American Hospital Association
840 N. Lake Shore Drive
Chicago, Illinois 60611

Mental Health Help Line
789 West End Ave.
New York, N.Y. 10024
212-663-4372

Psychotherapy Selection Service
3 E. 80th St.
New York, N.Y. 10021
212-861-6387

GENERAL INFORMATION ON MENTAL HEALTH AND COUNSELING

Mental Health Association
1800 N. Kent St.
Arlington, Virginia 22209
703-528-6405

The American Psychiatric Association
1700 18th St. NW
Washington, D.C. 20009

The American Psychological Association
1200 17th St. NW
Washington, D.C. 20036

The Mental Health Materials Center
419 Park Ave. South
New York, N.Y. 10016

The National Institute of Mental Health
1400 Rockville Pike
Rockwall Bldg. Room 505
Rockville, Maryland 20850

Community Psychology Division
The American Psychiatric Association
c/o Barbara Dohrenwend
CUNY Graduate Center
33 W. 42nd St.
New York, N.Y. 10036

Counseling Division
The American Psychiatric Association
c/o Norman I. Kagan
Department of Education
Michigan State University
East Lansing, Michigan 48823

Rehabilitation Psychiatry Division
The American Psychiatric Association
c/o Durand Jacobs
VA Hospital
10701 East Boulevard
Cleveland, Ohio 44106

There are, in addition, several comprehensive guides to therapists, services, and practitioners. They should be available at your school or local library:

Robert D. Allen, ed. *The Mental Health Almanac.* New York: Garland STPM Press, 1978.

Ellen Gay Detlefsen, ed. *The National Directory of Mental Health.* New York: Wiley, 1980.

Judith Norback, ed. *The Mental Health Yearbook Directory.* New York: Van Nostrand Reinhold, 1980.

Clara Claiborne Park, ed. *You Are Not Alone.* Boston: Little, Brown, 1976.

Summary

1. *Insight therapy* is a general term that comprises a variety of therapies used in private practice and institutions. Insight therapies try to give people a better understanding of their feelings, motivations, and actions.

2. *Psychoanalysis,* as developed by Freud, is based on the belief that the anxiety and problems that cause a person to seek help are symptoms of repressed problems from early childhood. Psychoanalysis brings these repressed problems to consciousness, so that the person can directly deal with them by working through them. This entails passing through stages of *positive* and *negative transference* toward the therapist. Successful analysis depends on the person's effort not to inhibit or control his or her thoughts and fantasies, but to express them in a process of *free association.* The goal of analysis is *insight.* The analyst remains neutral and, for the most part, silent.

3. Many psychologists disagree with Freud's approach to psychotherapy. Most neo-Freudians believe that therapists should take an active role in trying to get their clients to focus on coping with current problems rather than on resolving past conflicts.

4. According to Carl Rogers' *client-centered* or *person-centered therapy,* the goal is to help people become fully functioning, to open them up to all of their experiences and to all of themselves so that they have no reason to act defensively. The client-centered therapist is nondirective and tries only to reflect the client's statements.

5. *Rational-emotive therapy (RET)* assumes that people are solely responsible for their feelings about themselves and thus for their happiness. RET therapists directly show their clients how their misinterpretations of events cause their problems and teach their clients to see events more rationally.

6. Recently there has been an explosion of insight-type therapies that are generally of shorter duration than traditional psychotherapy and focus on the practical resolution of current problems.

7. Behaviorists reject the idea that behavior disorders are symptoms of hidden emotional conflicts and hold instead that the behavior disorder itself is the problem. *Behavior therapies* are based on the belief that all behavior is learned. The behavior therapist seeks to teach the client more satisfying behavior by applying principles of conditioning.

8. In *operant conditioning,* people learn to behave in different ways if new behaviors are rewarded and old behaviors ignored or pun-

ished. *Behavioral contracting* is a form of operant conditioning in which client and therapist
agree to preset goals and conditions.

9. *Aversive conditioning* is aimed at eliminating
undesirable behavior patterns by teaching clients to associate pain and discomfort with the
undesirable response.

10. Irrational fears and anxiety have been successfully treated using desensitization. Wolpe believes that chronically anxious people may not
know why they feel tense, but that they can
distinguish among different levels of anxiety.
The therapist establishes a *hierarchy* from the
least to the most anxiety-producing situations,
and then teaches the person to relax. The
therapist begins with the least threatening
scene and works up to the most threatening
one.

11. *Group therapies* allow both the therapist and
the client to see the client interacting with
others. They also give clients a chance to shed
inhibitions and express themselves in a safe
atmosphere, and provide them with a source
of reinforcement.

12. *Family therapy* is a special form of group therapy. It is based on the idea that when one
family member has problems, the whole family may need help. It aims to improve communication and empathy among family members
and to enable them to share leadership and
reduce conflict.

13. *Gestalt groups* emphasize the whole person and
attempt to reawaken a person to his or her
feelings. *Sensitivity groups* stress the here-and-
now and are designed to enhance awareness
by focusing on nonverbal communication and
reawakening the senses. *Encounter groups* also
stress the here-and-now. They demand that
participants respond to the immediate situation and try to strip away the social pretenses
of everyday life.

14. *Large-group awareness training* such as est has
become popular in recent years. Est teaches
people to experience reality directly, instead
of experiencing automatic associations with
the past.

15. The question of *effectiveness* of psychotherapy
has become an important one. Although the
original survey by Eysenck that initiated the

debate suggested that psychotherapy was no
more effective than no treatment, the majority of subsequent well-controlled surveys of
outcome indicate that the effectiveness of psychotherapy is moderately high. Although no
particular form of psychotherapy seems inherently superior to any other, different forms are
especially suited to different problems.

16. Among the *physical treatments* for mental illness, the use of *electroconvulsive therapy*
(ECT), which may be helpful with some
severe depressions, is decreasing in frequency.
Psychosurgery, such as lobotomy, which is irre-
versible, is even more rare.

17. *Drug therapy* has been a powerful tool in the
treatment of mental illness. The antipsychotic
drugs have been important in the treatment of
major disorders such as schizophrenia, reducing anxiety and aggression, and decreasing
hallucinations and delusions. *Tardive dyskinesia* is a serious side effect of long-term
treatment with antipsychotic drugs. Antidepressant drugs—namely, *monoamine oxidase
(MAO) inhibitors* and the *tricyclics*—can be
extremely effective in reversing depression.
Antianxiety drugs, or the major tranquilizers,
are widely prescribed to relieve tension. *Lithium* has been remarkably effective in com-
bating manic disorders.

18. Severe mental illness is most often treated by
the hospitalization of the patient. Many mental institutions are large, impersonal, state-run
facilities that have been criticized as mere
"warehouses" for the mentally ill, providing
little real treatment and little real expectation
of recovery. The rate of mental institutionalization has risen in spite of the growing popularity of the idea of deinstitutionalization.

19. *Deinstitutionalization*, or the release of mental
patients from large institutions to more humane facilities or back to the community, has
not been a great success. The process requires
more follow-up care, more funding, and more
community support than it has received. As a
result, many of the formerly institutionalized
now simply live as vagrants.

20. There are many alternatives to institu-
tionalizing the mentally ill, such as halfway
houses, and they have been shown to be at
least as effective as inpatient hospitalization—and often significantly cheaper. Until
the major insurers fund such alternatives as

fully as they fund hospitalization, however, the alternatives will not be significant factors in the health-care picture.

21. Preventing mental illness is even less costly than the most efficient methods of treating it.

Removing the organic factors that can create problems, reducing stress and increasing coping skills, and providing *crisis intervention* are all important forms of prevention.

Review Questions

1. Which of the following is the goal of working through problems in psychoanalysis:
   a. free association
   b. positive transference
   c. counter-transference
   d. insight

2. Match the terms at left with the appropriate descriptions at right:
   ___ psychoanalysis
   ___ client-centered therapy
   ___ dynamic therapy
   ___ rational-emotive therapy

   A. aimed at teaching clients to stop misinterpreting events and to see themselves more rationally
   B. based on the idea that anxiety stems from repressed problems from childhood
   C. goal is to help clients become more fully functioning
   D. trend in therapy toward operating within a time-limited framework

3. Rogerian therapists show that they value and accept their clients by providing _____ _____ .

4. In contrast with _____ therapies, which seek to increase clients' self-awareness, _____ therapies try to teach people more appropriate ways of acting.

5. A client begins therapy to get rid of an irrational fear of elevators. A technique the therapist is likely to employ is desensitization/behavior contracting.

6. The behavior therapy known as _____ _____ discourages undesired behaviors by associating them with pain and discomfort.

7. Match the therapies at left with their descriptions at right:
   ___ Gestalt
   ___ sensitivity groups
   ___ encounter groups
   ___ large-group awareness training

   A. seeks to enhance awareness by focusing on nonverbal communication and the senses
   B. teaches people to experience reality directly and to avoid illogical associations with past experiences
   C. emphasizes the whole person and awareness of feelings
   D. stresses the here-and-now and the stripping away of social pretenses

8. Family therapists concentrate on changing the needs and personalities of individual family members. T/F

9. Behavior therapy has been generally found to be more effective than insight therapy for most types of problems. T/F

10. Drugs that help to control schizophrenia are called _____ :
    a. barbituates
    b. tricyclics
    c. lithium
    d. antipsychotics

11. The practice of treating severely mentally ill people in large, state-run facilities is known as _____ .

12. The mentally ill who receive alternative care are less likely to undergo hospitalization later on. T/F

13. The establishment of halfway houses and similar facilities within the community is an example of the movement toward _____ .

14. Crisis intervention and hot lines are two example of _____ , that is, coping with mental illness before it occurs.

Outline

Social Psychology

We all spend much of our time alone thinking about our relations with other people. We try to explain to ourselves why we like one person and dislike another. We attempt to make sense of other people's behavior given the situations and our own behavior. We examine our attitudes and think about how they compare to those of the people around us. We meet with others in groups and wonder whether the group will be effective in solving problems.

Social psychologists address the same questions, only with more systematic methods than we use at home in our armchair. **Social psychology** is the scientific study of the way in which the thoughts, feelings, and behaviors of one individual are influenced by the real, imagined, or inferred behavior or characteristics of other people. We will start the chapter by examining the ways in which we perceive other people and the things that cause us to like some people and not others.

Social psychology The scientific study of the way in which the thoughts, feelings, and behaviors of one individual are influenced by the real, imagined, or implied behavior or characteristics of other people.

Social Perception

Before we meet someone, we want to know what kind of person he or she is so we can adjust our expectations and behavior accordingly. Unfortunately, such information is often difficult to acquire, so we are forced to form first impressions of people using only scanty evidence.

Impression Formation

How do we form our first impressions of people? What external cues do we use? And how accurate are we?

When we meet someone for the first time, we may notice a number of things about that person—clothes, gestures, manner of speaking, tone of voice, firmness of handshake, and so on. We then use these cues to fit the person into readymade *categories*. No matter how little information we may have or how contradictory it may be, no matter how many times

495

Schemas A unified set of characteristics stored in memory about a category of people.

In forming our first impressions of someone, we use external cues to fit the person into categories.

in the past our initial impressions of people have been wrong, we still classify and categorize people. And each of these categories carries with it a set of characteristics called **schemas** that we presume apply to all the people in the category.

Schemas serve a number of important functions. For one thing, they allow us to make inferences about other people. We assume, for example, that a friendly person is also likely to be good-natured, to accept a social invitation from us, or to do us a small favor. We may not know these things for sure, but our schema for "friendly person" allows us to infer them.

Schemas also play a crucial role in how we interpret and remember information. In fact, research shows that people have difficulty with information that does not fit an established schema. For example, in one study some subjects were told that they would be getting information about friendly, sociable men. Other subjects were informed that the men were achievement-oriented intellectuals. Both groups were then given the same information about 50 men, and then asked to say how many of the men were friendly and how many were intellectual. The subjects who had expected to hear about friendly men dramatically overestimated the number of friendly men, and those who had expected to hear about intellectual men greatly overestimated the number of intellectual men. Moreover, each group of subjects forgot many of the details that were inconsistent with their expectations (Rothbart, Evans, & Fulero, 1979). In short, the subjects tended to hear and remember what they expected to hear.

Schemas can also lure us into "remembering" things about people that we never actually observed. For most of us, shyness, quietness, and preoccupation with one's own thoughts, for example, are all traits associated with the schema "introvert." If we notice that Marjorie is shy, we are likely to categorize her as an introvert. Later we may "remember" that she also seemed preoccupied with her own thoughts. In other words, thinking of Marjorie as an introvert saves us the trouble of taking into account all the subtle shadings of her personality. But this can easily lead to errors if we attribute to Marjorie qualities that belong to the schema but not to her.

Now that you've had a chance to read about how impressions are formed, consider some information about a young man named Jim:

Jim left the house to get some stationery. He walked out into the sun-filled street with two of his friends. . . . Jim entered the stationery store, which was full of people. Jim talked with an acquaintance while he waited for the clerk to catch his eye. On his way out, he met the girl to whom he had been introduced the night before. They talked for a short while, and then Jim left for school.

After school, Jim left the classroom alone. . . . The street was brilliantly filled with sunshine. Jim walked down the street on the shady side. Coming down the street toward him, he saw the pretty girl whom he had met the previous evening. Jim crossed the street and entered a candy store. . . . Jim waited quietly until the counterman caught his eye and then gave his order. Taking his drink, he sat down at a side table. When he had finished his drink, he went home.

What do you think of Jim? Would you say he is introverted or extroverted? Luchins (1957b) used these two descriptions to study the **primacy effect** in impression formation: the extent to which the first information we receive about someone influences our impression of that person more heavily than later information. Ninety-five percent of the people who read only the first paragraph described Jim as an extrovert, while 86 percent of those who read only the second paragraph described him as an introvert. When people were asked to read both paragraphs in the order given above, 78 percent described Jim as an extrovert (as you probably did). When the order of the paragraphs was reversed, fully 63 percent called him introverted. Apparently in each case, the first paragraph "primed" a certain schema, a way of thinking about Jim. The subjects then reinterpreted, explained away, or ignored facts in the second paragraph that were inconsistent with the schema suggested by the first paragraph.

If people are specifically warned to beware of first impressions, or if they are encouraged to interpret information about others slowly and carefully, the primacy effect can be weakened or even nullified (Luchins, 1957a; Stewart, 1965). Generally, however, the first impression is the lasting impression, and it can affect our behavior even when it is not entirely accurate. In one study Snyder and Swann (1978) asked pairs of subjects to play a competitive game. They then told one member of each pair that the partner was either hostile or friendly. Players who were led to believe their partners were hostile behaved differently from players led to believe their partners were not hostile. In turn, the supposedly hostile partners actually began to display hostility. Later on, the partners con-

Primacy effect The extent to which early information about someone weighs more heavily than later information in influencing one's impression of that person.

To avoid the primacy effect, interviewers must take care to interpret information about others slowly and carefully.

tinued to show hostility, even though they were now paired with new partners who had no expectations about them at all. The expectation of hostility therefore produced actual aggressiveness in the other, and this behavior persisted with another partner. When we bring about expected behavior in another person in this way, our impression has become a **self-fulfilling prophecy.**

Self-fulfilling prophecy The process in which a person's expectation about another person elicits behavior from the second person that confirms the expectation.

Stereotype A set of characteristics presumed to be shared by all members of a social category.

STEREOTYPES. A **stereotype** is a set of characteristics believed to be shared by all members of a social category. In effect, a stereotype is a special kind of schema that is based on almost any distinguishing feature, including sex, race, occupation, physical appearance, place of residence, and membership in a group or organization (Hansen, 1984). When our first impressions of people are governed by a stereotype, we tend to infer things about them solely on the basis of their social category and to ignore facts that are inconsistent with the stereotype. As a result, we may remember things about them selectively or inaccurately, thereby perpetuating the initial stereotype.

Like schemas in general, stereotypes can easily become the basis for self-fulfilling prophecies. Snyder, Decker, Tanke, and Berscheid (1976) paired college-age men and women who were strangers to each other and arranged for each pair to talk by phone. Before the call, each male was given a snapshot, presumably of the woman he was about to call. In fact, the snapshot was a randomly selected photo of either an attractive or an unattractive woman. Attractiveness carries with it a stereotype of being sociable and socially adept (see box on p. 499). The males in the experiment therefore expected attractive partners to display these qualities and expected the unattractive females to be unsociable, awkward, and serious. These expectations produced radically different behavior. The men who believed they were talking to an attractive woman were warm, friendly, and animated; in response, the women acted in a friendly, animated way. The other men spoke to their partners in a cold, reserved

Snyder, Decker, Tanke, and Berscheid (1976) demonstrated experimentally how the favorable expectations we have of physically attractive people can become self-fulfilling prophecies.

People Do Judge Books—and People—by Their Covers

Appearance does make a difference. Physical attractiveness, clothing, hairstyle, and eyeglasses all can powerfully influence the conclusions that other people reach about your character. Moreover, you may not be able to buy groceries with your good looks, but your appearance can have a real impact on your chances for success in life.

Attractive people are generally given credit for more than their beauty. They are presumed to be more intelligent, interesting, happy, kind, sensitive, and successful than people who are not perceived as attractive. They are also thought to make better spouses and to be more sexually responsive (Dion, Berscheid, & Walster, 1972). People also tend to assume that handsome or beautiful strangers more closely resemble them in terms of personality traits than do less attractive individuals (Marks & Miller, 1980). If this weren't distressing enough, positive assumptions also attach themselve to the partner of an attractive woman: Subjects rate a male more positively if a woman described as his girlfriend is attractive than if she is not (Meiners & Sheposh, 1977). Being beautiful carries with it a few negative preconceptions, however. Attractive women are more likely to be seen as vain and apt to cheat on their husbands (Dermer & Thiel, 1975).

Aspects of appearance other than attractiveness also affect our judgments of others. People who wear glasses are thought at first to be more intelligent, reliable, and persevering than people who do not (Argyle & McHenry, 1971). And, as dress-for-success handbooks have been quick to point out, clothes make the man, or woman. A black raincoat, penny-loafers, or a shirt with a floral pattern does not reflect favorably on the credentials of a young man eager to enter banking.

Appearance can have material consequences. Attractive people are often more persuasive in attempts to communicate with others. In addition, other people try harder to please good-looking individuals (Sigall, Page, & Brown, 1971). Another study found that even in nursery school, children are more responsive to attractive than to less attractive peers. Moreover, teachers tend to be more lenient toward the bad behavior of an exceptionally attractive child, and to have higher expectations about his or her intelligence and grades. These reactions can eventually give attractive people substantial advantages in life.

This almost universal favorable attitude toward physical attractiveness can become a self-fulfilling prophecy. Physically attractive people may come to think of themselves as good or lovable because they are continually being treated that way. Conversely, unattractive people may begin to see themselves as bad or unlovable because they have always been regarded that way—even as children (Aronson, 1984).

manner. In response, the women reacted in a cool, distant manner. In other words, the stereotype took on a life of its own, subtly forcing the women to play appropriate roles.

So far we have seen how people form impressions of other people and how those impressions affect subsequent behavior. But social perception goes beyond simple impression formation. We also try to make sense out of people's behavior, to uncover the reasons why they act as they do. This is the subject of the next section.

Attribution

Suppose you run into a friend at the supermarket. You greet him warmly, but he barely acknowledges you, mumbles "Hi," and walks away. You feel snubbed and try to explain his behavior. Did he behave that way because of something in the situation? Perhaps you said something that offended him, or he was having no luck finding the groceries he wanted, or someone had just blocked his way by leaving his cart in the middle of

Attribution theory Theory that addresses the question of how people make judgments about the causes of behavior.

Distinctiveness The extent to which a behavior is present only when a particular stimulus is also present.

Consensus The extent to which everyone in a given situation is behaving in the same way.

Consistency The extent to which a particular event produces the same behavior each time it is present.

Fundamental attribution error The tendency of people to overemphasize personal causes for other people's behavior and to underemphasize those causes for their own behavior.

Just world hypothesis An attribution error based on the assumption that bad things happen to bad people and good things happen to good people.

an aisle. Or did something within him, some personal trait such as moodiness or arrogance, lead him to behave that way? Clearly it makes quite a difference which of these explanations is correct.

Social interaction is filled with occasions like this one that invite us to make judgments about the causes of behavior. And social psychologists have discovered that we go about this process of judgment in predictable ways, which are summarized under the heading **attribution theory.** One of the most influential of these attribution theories was developed by Harold Kelley (1967). According to Kelley, we rely on three kinds of information about behavior in an effort to draw conclusions about its cause.

The first piece of information is **distinctiveness.** If Joan laughs during a particular movie, but not very often at movies in general, we would tend to assume that the movie was funny, not that Joan has a tendency to laugh. To the extent that a behavior (laughing) occurs only when a particular event also occurs (the movie), we tend to attribute the behavior to that event.

Second, we consider **consensus:** the degree to which other people in the situation are behaving in the same way. If everyone in the theater is laughing, we tend to attribute Joan's laughter to the film. But if she alone is laughing, we would tend to attribute her behavior to some aspect of her personality, such as an unusual sense of humor. Thus high consensus points to the environment as a cause, while low consensus suggests a cause that is unique to the person.

Finally, we consider **consistency** of behavior or the extent to which the behavior is the same whenever the presumed cause is present. If behavior is inconsistent, it is probably due to some temporary feature of the environment. If Joan saw the movie last week but did not laugh then, we cannot confidently explain her mirth either in terms of her or the movie. Instead, we would tend to assume that a passing mood, a good day at work, or some other momentary circumstance is operating.

Research has generally confirmed the predictions of Kelley's model. However, it has become increasingly clear that his model does not take into account all aspects of the attribution process. In particular, our attributions appear open to a number of intriguing biases.

Probably the most important bias is our general tendency to attribute our own actions to situational factors and the behavior of others to internal or personal factors (Jones & Nisbett, 1972). In your view, the unforeseen bump and icy conditions caused your fall as you zoomed down the ski hill. A companion, however, might be more inclined to relate your mishap to your inexperience as a skier or to your carelessness or awkwardness. The tendency to give too much emphasis to personal factors when accounting for other people's actions is so common that one psychologist has termed it the **fundamental attribution error** (Ross, 1977).

Another kind of attribution error arises from the assumption that the world is just: Bad things happen to bad people and good things happen to good people. This is called the **just world hypothesis.** Thus when misfortune strikes someone, we often assume the person deserved it rather than give full weight to situational factors that may actually have been responsible. One explanation for this attribution error is that we defend ourselves against the implied possibility that such a thing could happen to us. For example, by relocating the cause of a major accident from a

By attributing the cause of a major accident to someone's negligence rather than to chance, we lessen the implication that something similar could happen to us.

chance event (something that could happen to us) to the victim's own negligence (a trait that we, of course, do not share), we defend against realizing that we could ever suffer such a misfortune (Chaikin & Darley, 1973).

Attraction and Liking

So far we have seen how people form impressions of one another and judge the causes of their behavior. When people meet, what determines if they will like each other? This is the subject of much speculation and not a little mystification, with popular explanations running the gamut from fate to compatible astrological signs. Romantics believe that irresistible forces propel them toward an inevitable meeting with their beloved, but social psychologists take a more hardheaded view of the matter. They have found that attraction and liking are closely linked to such things as *proximity, similarity of attitudes and interests, complementarity, attractiveness, rewardingness,* and *reciprocity.*

PROXIMITY. Proximity is probably the most important factor in determining attraction. The closer two people live to each other, the more they like each other.

Festinger, Schachter, and Back (1950) investigated the effects of proximity on friendship in Westgate West, a housing project for married students. The project consisted of two-story apartment complexes, with five apartments to a floor. The investigators found that 44 percent of the residents were most friendly with their next-door neighbors, while only 10 percent said their best friends lived down the hall. An even smaller number were best friends with an upstairs or downstairs neighbor (see Figure 16-1). Similarly, Nahemow and Lawton (1975) found that 93 percent of the residents of an inner-city housing project chose their best friends from the same building.

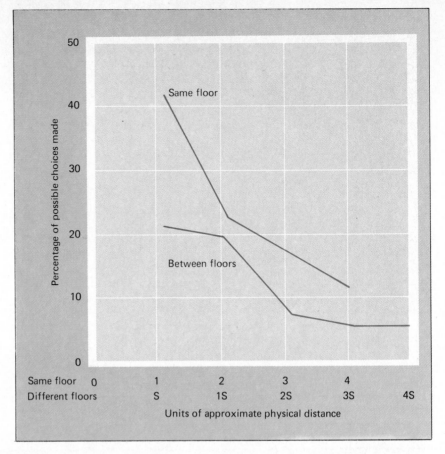

Figure 16-1

The relationship between proximity and liking. "Units of approximate physical distance" means how many doors apart the people lived—2S means 2 doors and a stairway apart. The closer together people lived, the more likely they were to become friends.

(Reprinted from Festinger, Schachter, and Back, 1950.)

How to Win Friends the Hard Way

You don't necessarily have to be a nice guy to get people to like you. Psychologists have discovered that insults and blunders can win friends too, under the right conditions (Worchel & Cooper, 1979).

Do your friends greet your compliments with cool smiles or unenthusiastic thanks? Well then, win them over with insults. In one study people who insulted other people before commencing a series of compliments were liked much more than those who delivered nothing but compliments. Apparently people who begin with insults establish their credibility by doing so. Their subsequent compliments are more rewarding than still another good word from a person who has nothing but good words (Aronson & Linder, 1965).

Blunders can also endear you to others if you are perceived generally as being highly competent. In an experiment some subjects listened to a taped interview with a highly competent person who was being interviewed for a chance to compete in a college quiz show. He answered 92 percent of the sample questions correctly and was described as an achiever in high school. Other subjects heard another tape of an interview with a candidate who sounded much less competent. For each tape, half of the subjects heard a version of the tape that also included the sound of the candidate spilling coffee all over his suit. The other half of the subjects did not hear this blunder. Afterward subjects were asked whether they liked the person being interviewed. Competent persons were more popular than less competent ones, but the most popular of all were the competent people who committed a clumsy blunder (Aronson, Willerman, & Floyd, 1966). The blunder seemed to reduce the distance between the average person and those who were perceived as highly competent, making the latter more attractive.

Thus, if similarity of interests, complementarity, and attractiveness fail to lay the groundwork for a desired relationship, do not despair. You may be able to make good use of some of your usually less than charming qualities to achieve your goal.

Attraction and liking are closely linked to such things as proximity, similar interests, complementary needs, attractiveness, rewardingness, and reciprocity.

SIMILARITY. Similarity of attitudes and interests is another important basis for attraction. When we know that a person shares our attitudes and interests, we tend to have more positive feelings toward that person (Byrne, 1961). The higher the proportion of attitudes that two people share, the stronger the attraction between them (Byrne & Nelson, 1965). This relationship between similarity and attraction holds only up to a point, however. Some bases of similarity clearly are more important than others. A shared taste for bran muffins is not as consequential for friendship as a common interest in sports or religion. And the true degree of similarity may not be as important as *perceived* similarity (Marsden, 1966). We often assume that we share attitudes with people who attract us in other ways. Some research indicates that marriage may rest in part on the illusion of similarity. Spouses tend to perceive more similarity in their partner's attitudes than in fact exists (Byrne & Blaylock, 1963).

COMPLEMENTARITY. Opposites do sometimes attract. Some relationships are based on complementarity rather than similarity. Winch (1958), for example, found a tendency for each partner in a marriage to possess needs or personality traits that the other lacked. For instance, women who displayed a need to take care of others were often married to men who needed to be nurtured.

ATTRACTIVENESS. Not only do we tend to credit attractive people with lots of positive qualities, but we also tend to like them more than less attractive people. In a classic experiment Walster and her colleagues (1966) randomly paired male with female subjects at a dance. During a break in the dance participants were asked how much they liked their partner. The only predictor of liking that the researchers could uncover was attractiveness. The better-looking the partner, the more he or she

Attitude A fairly stable organization of beliefs, feelings, and behavior tendencies directed toward some object such as a person or group.

was liked. This relationship has been found to hold among members of the same sex as well: The physically attractive are more popular than less attractive people (Byrne, London, & Reeves, 1968).

REWARDINGNESS. According to the *reward model of attraction*, we tend to like people we associate with rewards. But the relationship between attraction and rewardingness is complex. For example, Aronson's (1984) gain-loss theory of attraction suggests that *increases* in rewarding behavior influence attractiveness more than constant rewarding behavior does. In other words, if you were to meet and talk with the same person at three successive parties, and if, during these conversations, that person's behavior toward you changed from polite indifference to overt flattery, you would be inclined to like this person more than if he or she had immediately started to praise you during the first conversation and continued the praise each time you met. The reverse is also true: We tend to dislike people whose opinion of us changes from good to bad even more than we dislike those who consistently display a low opinion of us from the start.

RECIPROCITY. People tend to like others who like them. According to Gouldner (1960), once person A has expressed liking for person B, B feels a strong obligation to reciprocate. Thus it is not surprising that a number of studies have found that subjects are attracted to people they believe like them (e.g., Backman & Secord, 1959).

Attitudes

The phrase "I don't like his attitude" is a telling one. People are often told to "change your attitude." What does this mean? Just what are attitudes? How are they formed? How can they be changed?

The Nature of Attitudes

An **attitude** toward something has three major components: *beliefs* about the object, *feelings* about the object, and *behavior tendencies* toward the object. Beliefs include facts, opinions, and our general knowledge about the object. Feelings include love, hate, like, dislike, and similar sentiments. Behavior tendencies include our inclinations to act in certain ways toward the object—to approach it, avoid it, and so on. For example, our attitude toward a political candidate includes our beliefs about the candidate—his or her qualifications and positions on crucial issues, expectations about how the candidate will vote on those issues, etc. We also have feelings about the candidate—liking or disliking, trust or mistrust—and we are inclined to behave in certain ways toward the candidate—to vote for or against him or her, to contribute time or money to the person's campaign, to attend or avoid rallies for the candidate, etc.

Our attitude toward a political candidate includes our beliefs, feelings, and behavioral tendencies toward that person. These three factors tend to be consistent with one another.

As we will see shortly, there is a strong tendency for these three aspects of an attitude to be consistent with one another. For example, if we have positive feelings toward something, we tend to have positive beliefs about it and to behave positively toward it. This does not mean, however, that our *actual* behavior will accurately reflect our attitude. Let's look more closely at the relation between attitudes and behavior.

Attitudes and Behavior

The relationship between attitudes and behavior is not always straightforward. In one noted study done in the early 1930s, R. T. LaPiere (1934) traveled through the United States with an Oriental couple—at a time when prejudice against Orientals was still running high in this country. LaPiere discovered that they were refused service at only 1 of the 250 hotels and restaurants they visited. Six months later LaPiere sent a questionnaire to each of these establishments and asked if they would serve Chinese people. Most said they would not. LaPiere therefore concluded that attitudes are not reliable predictors of actual behavior. Subsequent research on the relationship between attitudes and behavior has often supported LaPiere's conclusion (Wicker, 1969).

But Fishbein and Ajzen (1975) point out that the weak relationship between attitudes and behavior may be due to improper measurement of either attitudes or behavior or both. For example, LaPiere measured attitudes toward Chinese people in general and then used that to predict specific behavior. If LaPiere had asked about attitudes toward the particular Chinese people who traveled with him rather than about Chinese people in general, the correlation between attitudes and behavior probably would have been higher.

Other researchers have pointed out that behavior is influenced by

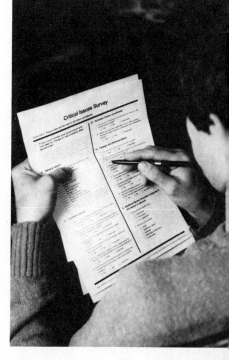

Attitudes do not predict actual behavior very well unless both are measured at the same level of specificity.

many factors besides attitudes. For instance, Ajzen and Fishbein (1980) have argued that behavior is closely linked to a person's intentions. Intentions, in turn, are only partly a product of the person's attitudes; they also reflect his or her acceptance of norms, including social pressures to perform or not to perform the behavior.

Personality traits are also important. Some people consistently match their actions to their attitudes (Norman, 1975). Others have a tendency to override their own attitudes in order to behave properly in the given situation. As a result, attitudes do not predict behavior as well among some people as among others (Snyder & Tanke, 1976).

Attitudes, then, can predict behavior, but psychologists have learned that many other variables affect the relationship between the two. Intentions, social norms, and willingness to override one's attitudes are just a few of these other factors.

The Development of Attitudes

How do we acquire our attitudes? Where do they come from? Many of our most basic attitudes derive from early, direct personal experience. Children are rewarded with positive encouragement when they please their parents, and they are punished through disapproval when they displease them. These early experiences give the child enduring positive and negative attitudes toward objects (Oskamp, 1977). Attitudes are also formed by imitation. Children mimic the behavior of their parents and peers, and thus acquire attitudes even when no one is trying to influence their beliefs.

But parents are not the only source of attitudes, and often they are not even the most lasting influence in our lives. Our teachers, friends, and even famous people can be more important. If a young man joins a fraternity, for example, he may model his behavior and attitudes on those of the members. If a young woman idolizes one of her teachers, she may adopt many of the teacher's attitudes toward controversial subjects, even if they run counter to attitudes expressed by her parents.

Television and newspapers also have a great impact on the formation of attitudes in our society. Television bombards us with messages—not merely through commercials, but in more subtle ways: Violence is a commonplace in life . . . women are dependent on men . . . without possessions your life is empty, and so on. Similarly, Hartmann and Husband (1971) have shown that without experience of their own, children, especially, rely on television to form their social attitudes. They found that white children in England who had little contact with nonwhites tended to associate race relations with conflicts and hostility more often than white children who lived in integrated neighborhoods. The first group of children was informed exclusively by TV news reports that focused on the problems caused by integration.

Attitudes can result from imitating other people. Children often adopt their parents' attitudes on issues, even when no attempt is made to influence their beliefs.

Attitude Change

A man watching TV on Sunday afternoon ignores scores of beer commercials, but makes a note of an overnight delivery service that he sees advertised. The same political speech convinces one woman to vote one way and her next door neighbor to vote another. What makes one attempt to change attitudes fail and another succeed? More generally, just how and why do attitudes change? When do we resist change? And how successful is our resistance likely to be?

The answers to these questions depend in part on the technique used to change our attitudes. We will look first at attempts to change attitudes with various kinds of persuasive messages.

THE INFORMATIONAL APPROACH. Although we are all bombarded with attempts to change our attitudes on subjects ranging from abortion to toothpaste, few of the methods used by interest groups and advertising agencies succeed. One of the major reasons for this is our ability to tune out what we do not want to hear. Brock and Balloun (1967) found that subjects were more likely to attend to *supportive* messages than *nonsupportive* ones. Kleinhessilink and Edwards (1975) took this a step further. They found that people listen to even nonsupportive messages as long as they are easy to refute. But they block out any nonsupportive messages that are hard to refute.

Even if we do attend to a message, several factors determine how likely it is to change our attitudes. In part, the effectiveness of the message depends upon its *source*. The *credibility* of the source is especially important. One source may have greater expertise or be more trustworthy than the other and thus be more credible (Hass, 1981). For example, we are less likely to change our attitude toward the oil industry's anti-pollution efforts if the president of a major refining company tells us about them than we are if we hear the same information from an impartial commission appointed to study the situation.

Recent research indicates that the credibility of the source is most important when we are not inclined to pay attention to the message itself (Petty & Cacioppo, 1981; Cooper & Croyle, 1984). In cases where we have some interest in the message, then the message itself plays a greater role in determining whether we change our attitudes. For example, the more arguments the message makes in favor of a position, the more effective the message (Calder, Insko, & Yandell, 1974). Also, audiences who are familiar with a subject seem to respond better to moderately novel arguments than to old standbys they have heard many times before.

Another important aspect of the message is *fear*. Research has found that fear is an effective persuader in efforts to convince people to get tetanus shots (Dabbs & Leventhal, 1966), to drive safely (Leventhal & Niles, 1965), and to take care of their teeth (Evans et al., 1970). But too much fear can scare the audience to such an extent that the message has little effect (Worchel & Cooper, 1984).

Whether to include both sides of an argument is another well-researched question. The data indicate that one-sided and two-sided arguments are equally persuasive. But a two-sided presentation generally makes the speaker seem less biased and thus adds to his or her credibility.

The organization of a message and the medium in which it is presented also affect its impact. In presenting two sides of a question, for example, it is generally better to put forth your own side first. But if a long time elapses between presentation of the first and second positions, the audience tends to recall best what it heard last. In this situation, present

Cognitive dissonance Perceived inconsistency between two cognitions.

your own view second (Miller & Campbell, 1959). As to the choice of medium, writing appears to be best suited to getting others to understand complex arguments. Videotaped or live media presentations are more effective in persuading an audience once it has understood an argument (Chaiken & Eagly, 1976).

Overall, the most important factors in changing attitudes are those that have to do with the audience, though these factors are often the most difficult to control.

Commitment of the audience to their present attitudes is critical. A person who has just gone on a speaking tour publicly advocating more liberal abortion laws is less likely to change his or her attitudes toward the subject than someone who has never openly expressed an opinion one way or the other. Likewise, a person whose attitudes are shared with other people is less susceptible to attitude change. Moreover, if the attitude has been instilled during early childhood by important groups such as the family, even massive assaults on the attitude can be ineffective.

Another audience factor is the *discrepancy* between the contents of the message and the present attitudes of the audience. Up to a point, the greater the difference between the two, the greater the likelihood of attitude change. However, if the discrepancy is too great, the audience may reject the new information altogether. The expertise of the communicator is important in this context, as well. Influence increases with the size of the discrepancy only when the speaker is considered an expert (Worchel & Cooper, 1984).

A number of personal characteristics, including aspects of personality, also tend to make some people more susceptible to attitude change than others. People with low self-esteem are more easily influenced, especially when the message is complex and hard to understand. Highly intelligent people tend to resist persuasion because they can think of counter-arguments more easily. When the message is complex, however, only highly intelligent people may be able to understand it and hence be influenced by it.

Traditionally, women have been considered easier to influence than men. A review of the relevant research, however, shows that this is only true when men conduct the research; otherwise there are no sex differences in persuasability (Eagly, 1978). Eagly accounts for this discrepancy by noting that male experimenters tend to use materials unfamiliar to women, making them seem more subject to attitude change in general.

In theory, then, attitudes are open to change. But in fact, they are very difficult to change. Fortunately for advertisers, politicians, and others, attitude change is often not as important as a change in behavior—buying Brand X, voting for Jim Smith. In fact, in many cases it is possible to change behavior directly and then obtain attitude change as a result. We will now look in more detail at how behavior can affect attitudes.

THE COGNITIVE CONSISTENCY APPROACH. One of the more fascinating approaches to understanding attitude change is the theory of **cognitive dissonance,** developed by Leon Festinger (1957). Cognitive dissonance exists whenever a person has two contradictory cognitions at the same time. In this theory, a cognition is a piece of knowledge about something. "I do not like gory movies" is a cognition. So is "Yesterday I went to see the *Texas Chainsaw Massacre.*" These two cognitions are dissonant—each one implies the opposite of the other. According to Festinger, cognitive dissonance creates unpleasant psychological tension, and this tension motivates the individual to try to resolve the dissonance in some way.

Sometimes changing one's attitude is the easiest way to reduce the discomfort of dissonance. I cannot easily change the fact that I have gone to a gory movie. Therefore it is easier to change my attitude about such movies. My new attitude now fits my behavior.

It is important to point out that discrepant behavior does not necessarily bring about attitude change. There are other ways a person can reduce cognitive dissonance. One alternative is to *increase the number of consonant elements,* or thoughts that support one or the other dissonant cognitions. For example, I might note that the movie was a bargain since it was "dollar night" at the theater, that I really needed to get out by myself for a while, and that the movie would probably teach me something about abnormal psychology. Now my action is less discrepant with my attitude toward gory films. Another option is to *reduce the importance of one or both cognitive elements.* "I just wanted to check and be sure that I really don't like that sort of movie. And I was right, I don't." By reducing the significance of my behavior, I reduce the dissonance I experience.

So far in the discussion we have ignored an important question: Why would someone engage in attitude-discrepant behavior in the first place? One answer is that cognitive dissonance is a part of everyday life. For example, simply choosing between two or more desirable alternatives leads inevitably to dissonance. Suppose you are in the market for a typewriter, but you can't decide between a Smith-Corona and an Underwood. If you choose the Smith-Corona, all of its bad features and all of the good aspects of the Underwood contribute to dissonance (Worchel & Cooper, 1979). After you have chosen the Smith-Corona, one way to reduce the dissonance is through attitude change: You might decide that the Underwood really didn't type as smoothly as you thought and that some of the "bad" features of the Smith-Corona are actually desirable. Another reason for engaging in attitude-discrepant behavior is that you are enticed to do so. Perhaps someone offers you a small bribe or reward: "I will pay you 25 cents just to try my product." Curiously, the larger the reward, the smaller the change in attitude that is likely to result. When rewards are large, dissonance is at a minimum, and attitude change is small, it if happens at all. Apparently, when people are convinced that there is a good reason to perform a discrepant act, they experience little dissonance and their attitudes are not likely to change, though their behavior may shift for a time. However, if the reward is small, just barely enough to induce behavior that conflicts with one's attitude, dissonance will be great, maximizing the changes for attitude change. The trick is to get the discrepant behavior to happen, yet leave people feeling personally responsible for the dissonant act. That way they are more likely to change their attitudes than if they feel they were forced to act in a way that contradicts their beliefs (Cooper, 1971; Kelman, 1974).

Social Influence

Social influence Any actions performed by one or more persons to change the attitudes, behavior, or feelings of one or more others.

Conformity Voluntarily yielding to social norms, even at the expense of one's own preferences.

To social psychologists, **social influence** refers to "any actions performed by one or more persons to change the attitudes, behavior, or feelings of one or more others" (Baron & Byrne, 1981, p. 229). In the previous section we studied one form of social influence: attitude change. In the discussion to follow, we'll focus on the direct control of behavior by others without regard to underlying attitudes.

Conformity

To conform is to choose to yield to social norms, which are shared ideas and expectations about how members of a group should behave. Some norms are written into law, while many more are unwritten expectations enforced by teasing, frowns, ostracism, and other informal means of punishment. Without norms, social life would be chaotic. With them, the behavior of other people becomes fairly predictable despite great differences in underlying attitudes and preferences.

Most cases of uniformity are not cases of **conformity.** For instance, millions of Americans drink coffee in the morning, but they do not do so to conform. They drink coffee because they have learned to like and desire it. Conformity implies a conflict between the individual and the group—a conflict that the individual resolves by yielding his or her own preferences or beliefs to the norms or expectations of a larger group.

Since the early 1950s, when Solomon Asch conducted the first careful study of the subject, conformity has been a major subject of research in social psychology. In a series of experiments Asch demonstrated that under some circumstances people conform to group pressures even when this results in the denial of physical evidence. His studies ostensibly tested visual judgment. People were asked to choose from a card with several lines of differing lengths the line most similar to the line on a comparison card (see Figure 16-2). The lines were deliberately drawn so that the comparison was obvious and the correct choice was clear. All but one of the subjects were planted by the experimenter. On certain trials these people deliberately gave the same wrong answer. This put the subject on the spot. Should he conform to what he knew to be a wrong decision and agree with the group, thereby denying the evidence of his own senses, or should he disagree with the group and not conform?

Most subjects chose to conform about 35 percent of the time. There were large individual differences, however, and in subsequent research experimenters discovered that two kinds of factors influence the likelihood that a person will conform: characteristics of the situation and characteristics of the individual. The size of the group is one situational variable that has been studied extensively. Asch (1951) found that the likelihood of conformity increased with group size until four confederates were present. After that point, the number of others made no difference in the subjects' tendency to ignore the evidence of his own eyes. Another important factor is the degree of unanimity in the group. If just one confederate broke the perfect agreements of the majority by giving the

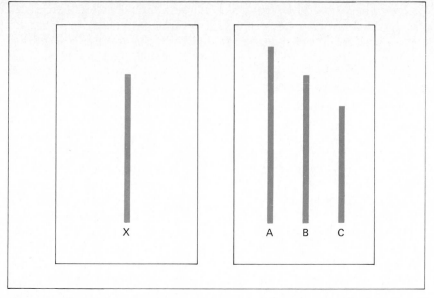

Figure 16-2

In Asch's experiment on conformity, subjects were shown a comparison card like the one on the left, and were asked to indicate which of the three lines on the card on the right was the most similar.

correct answers, conformity among the subjects in the Asch experiments fell from an average of 35 percent to about 25 percent (Asch, 1956). Apparently, having just one "ally" eases the pressure on the subject to conform. The ally need not even share the subject's viewpoint. Just breaking the unanimity of the majority is enough to reduce conformity (Allen & Levine, 1971).

The nature of the task is still another situational variable that affects conformity. For instance, conformity has been shown to vary with the difficulty and the ambiguity of a task. When the task is difficult or poorly defined, conformity tends to be higher (Blake, Helson, & Mouton, 1956). In an ambiguous situation, individuals are less sure of their own view and are more willing to conform to that of the majority.

Personal characteristics also influence conforming behavior. The more an individual is attracted to the group, expects to interact with it in the future, is of relatively low status in the group, and does not feel completely accepted by the group, the more he or she tends to conform (Worchel & Cooper, 1979). The fear of rejection apparently motivates conformity when a person scores high on one or more of these variables.

Compliance

Conformity is a response to pressure exerted by norms that are generally left unstated. In contrast, **compliance** is a change of behavior in response to the explicit request of someone else. The demand may reflect a social norm, as when a doorman of a nightclub informs a customer that proper attire is required. Or the request may be intended to satisfy the needs of the person making it: "Please help me fold the sheets."

Social psychologists have studied several techniques by which people can get others to comply with their request. One procedure is based on the so-called "foot-in-the-door effect." Any seller knows that the moment a person allows the sales pitch to begin, the chances of making a sale improve greatly. In general, once a person has granted a small request, he or she is more likely to comply with a larger one too.

In the most famous study of this phenomenon, Freedman and Fraser (1966) approached certain residents of Palo Alto, California, posing as members of a Committee for Safe Driving. Residents were asked to place a large, ugly sign reading "Drive Carefully" in their front yards. Only 17 percent agreed to do it. Then other residents were asked to sign a petition calling for more safe-driving laws. When these same people were later asked to place the ugly "Drive Carefully" sign in their yards, an amazing 55 percent agreed to do so. Compliance with the initial small request more than tripled the rate of compliance with the larger request.

Why this technique works so well is not clear. One possibility is that agreeing to the token act (signing the petition) changes the subject's self-perception slightly to that of a person favoring the cause. When presented with the larger request, the person then feels obligated to comply (Synder & Cunningham, 1975). Another explanation is that the subject becomes more comfortable in helping situations in general after being asked for a small commitment (Rittle, 1980).

Another trick from the salesperson's bag is the "lowball procedure" (Cialdini, Cacioppo, Bassett, & Miller, 1978). The first step of this procedure is to induce a person to agree to do something. The second step is to raise the cost of compliance after the commitment to the behavior has been made. Among new-car dealers, lowballing works as follows: The dealer persuades the customer to buy a new car by reducing the price well below that of competitors. Once the customer has agreed to buy the car, however, the terms of the sale shift abruptly, making the car even more costly than the market rate. One technique is to reduce the trade-in value promised by the used-car manager. Despite the added costs, many customers follow through on their commitment to buy.

Under certain circumstances a person who has refused to comply with one request may be more likely to comply with a second. This phenomenon has been labeled the "door-in-the-face" effect (Cialdini et al., 1975). In one study, researchers approached students and asked them to make an unreasonably large commitment: Would they counsel delinquent youths at a detention center for 2 years? Nearly everyone declined, thus effectively "slamming the door in the face" of the researcher making the request. Upon then being asked to make a much smaller commitment—supervising children during a trip to the zoo—many of the same subjects quickly agreed. The door-in-the-face effect may work because subjects interpret the smaller request as a concession by the experimenter, and they feel pressured to comply in return (Deaux & Wrightsman, 1984).

The door-to-door seller knows that once a person has complied with a small request, he or she is likely to comply with a larger one too.

Obedience

Compliance involves agreeing to change behavior in response to a request. **Obedience** is compliance with a command. Like compliance, it is a response to an explicit message, but in this case the message is a direct order, generally from a person in authority such as a police officer, principal, or parent, who can back up the command if necessary. Obedience is social influence in its most direct and powerful form.

Obedience A change of behavior in response to a command from another person, typically an authority figure.

Several studies by Stanley Milgram that were mentioned in Chapter 1 showed how far many people will go to obey someone in authority (Milgram, 1963). Milgram informed his subjects that they would be participating in an experiment designed to test the effects of punishment on learning. Their job was to administer an electric shock to another subject, actually a confederate, every time he made an error in a learning trial. The shocks were to be increased in voltage for each error, up to a potentially fatal 450 volts. In fact, the learner received no real shock whatsoever. Each time a subject balked, the experimenter pointed out that he was expected to continue. An astounding 65 percent of Milgram's subjects proceeded to administer the entire series of shocks, up to the maximum.

What factors influence the degree to which people will do what they are told? Studies in which people were asked to put a dime in a parking meter by people wearing uniforms showed that one important factor is the amount of power vested in the person giving the orders. A guard whose uniform looked like a policeman's was obeyed more often than either a man dressed as a milkman or a civilian. Another factor is surveillance. If we are ordered to do something and then left alone, we are less likely to obey than when we are being watched. This seems to be truer when the order involves an unethical act. Most of the subjects still put a dime in the meter when the policeman-impersonator was out of sight, but Milgram found that his "teachers" were less willing to give severe shocks when the experimenter left the room.

Milgram's experiments revealed other factors that influence a person's willingness to follow orders. When the victim was in the same room as the teacher, obedience dropped sharply. When another "teacher" was present who refused to give shocks, obedience also dropped. But when responsibility for an act was shared, so that the person was only one of many doing it, obedience was much greater. Executions by firing squads illustrate this principle.

What makes people willing to obey an authority figure, even if it means violating their own principles? Milgram (1974) thinks that people feel obligated to those in power: first, because they respect their credentials and assume they know what they are doing; and second, because often they have established trust with the people in authority by agreeing to do whatever they ask. Once this happens, subjects may feel conflict about what they are doing, but through rationalization can "forget" about it and thus minimize the conflict.

Helping Behavior

Attitude change, conformity, compliance, and obedience are not the only ways in which we are influenced by other people. Our willingness to help others is another behavior that is sensitive to social influence. Our treatment of others is often motivated by our own self-interest. We offer

Altruistic or **helping behavior**
Behavior or action on the part of
an individual that is not linked to
personal gain.

our boss a ride home from the office because we know that our next promotion depends on how much he or she likes us. We volunteer to water our neighbors' lawn while they are away because we want to use their pool. But if this kind of behavior is *not* linked to personal gain, it is called **altruistic** or **helping behavior.** A person who acts in an altruistic way does not expect any recognition or reward in return, except perhaps the good feeling that comes from helping the needy. Many altruistic acts, including many charitable contributions, are directed at strangers and are made anonymously (Hoffman, 1977).

Under what conditions is altruistic behavior most likely to occur? Like other social-psychological phenomena, altruism in influenced by two sets of variables, those pertaining to the situation and those relevant to the individual.

Probably the most important situational variable is the presence of other people. As the number of passive bystanders increases, the likelihood decreases that any one of them will help someone in trouble. In one experiment subjects completing a questionnaire heard a taped "emergency" in the next room, complete with a crash and screams. Of those who were alone, 70 percent offered help, but of those who were with an experimenter who did nothing, only 7 percent offered help (Latané & Rodin, 1969).

Another key aspect of the situation is its ambiguity. Any factors that make it harder for others to recognize a genuine emergency tend to reduce the probability of helping. Clark and Word (1974) had a "workman" carry a ladder and a venetian blind past a subjects' waiting room. A loud crash soon followed. In this ambiguous situation the fewer the bystanders, the more likely the workman was to receive help. When he clarified matters by calling out that he was hurt, however, all subjects without exception went to his aid.

The personal characteristics of bystanders also affect helping behavior. Not all bystanders are equally likely to help a stranger. According to Moriarty (1975), increasing the amount of personal responsibility one person feels for another increases the likelihood of altruistic support. In his experiment subjects were more likely to try to stop the theft of a stranger's property if they had promised to watch the property while the stranger was away than if they had had no contact with him or her. The amount of empathy we feel with another person also affects our willingness to act in an altruistic way. Krebs (1975) found that when subjects felt that their values and personalities were similar to a victim's, they were more likely to try to help, even if their own safety was jeopardized.

Mood also makes a difference. A person in a good mood is more likely to help another in need than is someone who is in a neutral or bad mood. Isen & Levin (1972) demonstrated this by leaving a dime in the scoop of a pay phone in order to put the finder in a good mood. These subjects were much more likely than other subjects to help a confederate who dropped a folder full of papers on the sidewalk near the phone booth. Other research suggests that individuals who fear embarrassment are less likely to help (McGovern, 1976). Mistakenly offering help to someone who does not really need it can be highly embarrassing. Finally, when others are watching, people who score high on the need for approval are more likely to behave altruistically than low scorers (Satow, 1975).

Deindividuation

We have seen several cases of social influence in which people act differently in the presence of others than they would by themselves. Perhaps the most striking and frightening instance of this is *mob behavior*. Some well-known violent examples are the beatings and lynchings of blacks, the looting that sometimes accompanies urban rioting, and the wanton destruction of property that occurs during otherwise peaceful protests and demonstrations. After a power blackout in New York City in 1977 during which considerable looting took place, some of the looters were interviewed. These interviews indicated that many people would never have thought of looting had they been alone, and that others were later shocked by their own behavior.

One reason for such behavior is that people lose their personal sense of responsibility in a group, especially in a group subjected to intense pressures and anxiety. This is called **deindividuation** because people respond not as individuals, but as anonymous parts of a larger group. In general, the more anonymous people feel in a group, the less responsible they feel as persons.

Groups of four women were recruited to take part in a study supposedly involving responses to strangers (Zimbardo, 1969). In one group, the women were greeted by name, wore name tags, and were easily identifiable. In another group, they wore oversized white lab coats and hoods over their heads; they resembled members of the Ku Klux Klan and were not identifiable at all. The groups were given an opportunity to deliver electric shocks to a woman not in the group. The subjects who were "deindividuated" gave almost twice as many electric shocks as did the subjects who were clearly identifiable. Apparently, being "deindividuated" produced more aggressive and more hostile behavior. This supports the idea that a loss of a feeling of individuality may be a major cause of the violent, antisocial behavior sometimes shown by groups.

Deindividuation partly explains mob behavior. Another factor is that, in a group, one strongly dominant and persuasive person can convince people to act through a "snowball effect": Convince a few, and they convince others. Moreover, large groups provide *protection*. Anonymity makes it difficult to press charges. If two, or even ten, people start smashing windows, they will probably be arrested. If a thousand people do it, very few of them could be caught or punished.

Deindividuation Loss of personal sense of responsibility in a group.

Group Processes

The various kinds of social influence that we have just discussed can take place between two people, in groups of three or more, or even when no one else is physically present. We refrain from walking our dog on our neighbor's lawn, comply with jury duty notices that we receive in the mail, and obey traffic signals even when no one else is present to enforce the social norms that dictate these actions. We now turn our attention

Risky shift Greater willingness to take risks in decision making in a group than as independent individuals.

Polarization A shift in attitudes by members of a group toward more extreme positions than the ones held before group discussion.

to processes that do depend on the presence of other people. Specifically, we will examine processes that tend to occur when people interact in small groups. One of the most studied group processes is decision making.

Group Decision Making

There is a tendency in our society to turn important decisions over to groups. In the business world most important decisions are made around a conference table rather than behind one person's desk. In politics major policy decisions are seldom vested in just one person. Groups of advisers, cabinet officers, committee members, or aides meet to deliberate and decide. In the courts a defendant may request a trial by jury, and for some serious crimes a jury trial is required by law. And of course the U.S Supreme Court renders group decisions on issues of major importance.

Why are so many decisions entrusted to groups rather than to individuals? One reason is that we tend to assume that individuals acting alone are more likely to take greater risks than a group considering the same issue. We assume that a corporate board, or a cabinet, or a jury will be more judicious and cautious than any single individual.

The assumption that groups make more conservative decisions than individuals remained unchallenged until the early 1960s. At that time James Stoner (1961) designed an experiment to test this idea. He asked subjects individually to counsel imaginary persons who had to choose between a risky but potentially rewarding course of action and a conservative and less rewarding alternative. Next, the advisers met in small groups to discuss each decision until they reached unanimous agreement. Stoner and many other social psychologists were surprised to find that the groups consistently proposed a riskier course of action than that counseled by the group members working alone. This phenomenon is known as the **risky shift.**

Subsequent research suggests that the risky shift is simply one aspect of a more general group phenomenon called **polarization**—the tendency

One of the most studied group processes is group decision making.

for individuals to become more extreme in their attitudes as a result of group discussion. Groups that start out fairly risky will become more so during discussion, but groups that tend to be cautious will grow even more cautious during their deliberations (Fraser, 1971).

What causes polarization in decision-making groups? In part, people discover during discussion that the other groups members share their views to a greater degree than they realized. In an effort to be seen positively by the others, at least some group members are likely to become strong advocates for what appears to be the dominant sentiment in the group. Thus the group discussion tends to shift to a more extreme position, as new and more persuasive arguments begin to emerge. As group participants listen to these arguments and find themselves in general agreement, their own positions tend to become more extreme. In other words, initially popular positions tend to attract the most persuasive arguments. In turn, these arguments not only reassure people that their initial attitudes are correct but also intensify those attitudes so that the group as a whole becomes more extreme in its position. Thus if you refer a problem to a group in order to ensure it will be resolved in a cautious, conservative direction, it is important to make sure that the members of the group are cautious and conservative in the first place.

The Effectiveness of the Group

Another reason for assigning so many important problems to groups is the assumption that the members of the group will pool their skills and expertise and therefore be more likely to solve the problem effectively than would any individual member working alone. "Two heads are better than one" reflects this way of thinking about groups.

In fact, groups are more effective than individuals only under some circumstances. According to Steiner (1972), the effectiveness of a groups depends on three factors: (1) the nature of the task, (2) the resources of the group members, and (3) the interaction among group members. There are many different kinds of tasks, each of which demands certain kinds of skills. If the requirements of the task match the skills of the group members, the group is likely to be more effective than any single individual. To build the first atom bomb, for example, the directors of the Manhattan Project assembled a team of specialists in various subfields of physics and engineering. For one scientist working alone, the task would have been impossible.

Even if the task and personnel are matched perfectly, the way in which the people interact in the group can always reduce its efficiency. For example, high-status individuals tend to exert more influence in groups, independent of their problem-solving ability. If high-status members are not the most qualified group members to solve the problem, the group may well settle upon the wrong answer, even though one or more of the participants could have found the right answer working alone. In one experiment with bomber crews, Torrance (1954) found that the low-status gunners who correctly solved a problem were about six times less likely than the high-status pilots to convince the group that their answer was correct.

Another factor is group *size*. The larger the group, the more likely it is to include someone who has the skills needed to solve a difficult problem. On the other hand, it is much harder to coordinate the activities of a large group than those of a small group.

Still another variable is *cohesiveness* of a group. When the people in the group like one another and feel committed to the goals of the group, cohesiveness is high. Under these conditions, members may work hard for the group, spurred on by high morale. But cohesiveness can also cause serious problems that undermine the quality of group decision making. Janis (1972) has called this phenomenon *groupthink*. Strong pressure to conform, he believes, prevents people from expressing critical ideas. In a group, amiability and morale take precedence over judgment. As group cohesiveness increases, self-criticism decreases, and members seem more willing to act at the expense of nonmembers. Members with doubts may hesitate to express them. The result may be bad decisions—such as the Bay of Pigs invasion or the Watergate coverup.

Leadership

A group may be formal or informal, task oriented or purely social, but it is sure to have a leader. The leader may be a formal leader—the chairman of the board, for instance—or merely the member who exerts the strongest influence on the group. Group leadership can be self-perpetuating, or it may change, as in a parliamentary system when a vote of "no confidence" causes the government to fall.

There are many theories about the emergence of group leaders. The dominant theory for many years was the *great man theory*. This theory states that leaders are extraordinary people who assume positions of influence and then shape events around them. In this view, Washington, Napoleon, and even Hitler were "born leaders" who would have led any nation at any time in history.

Most historians and psychologists now regard this theory as naive because it ignores social and economic factors. For instance, had Germany not lost World War I and suffered a crippling depression, its people might not have been open to the nationalistic fervor that Hitler preached. Moreover, had Hitler been born in America, his chances of becoming a world leader in the 1930s would have been significantly lower.

An alternative theory suggests that leadership is the result of the right person being in the right place at the right time. For instance, in the late 1950s and early 1960s, Dr. Martin Luther King, Jr. emerged as the leader of the black civil rights movement. Dr. King was clearly a "great man": intelligent, dynamic, eloquent, and highly motivated. Yet had the times not been right, according to this theory, it is doubtful that he would have been as successful as he was.

Recently social scientists have argued that there is more to leadership than either the great man theory or the right-place-at-the-right-time theory implies. According to the *transactional view*, a number of factors interact to determine who becomes the leader of a group. The leader's traits, certain aspects of the situation in which the group finds itself, and the response of the group and the leader to each other are all important considerations. Fred Fiedler's contingency model of leader effectiveness is based on such a transactional view of leadership (Fiedler, 1967, 1981). According to Fiedler, a number of factors affect the success of a leader. Personal characteristics are important, and Fiedler thinks of them in terms of two contrasting leadership styles. One kind of leader is task-oriented, concerned with doing the task well even at the expense of poor relationships among members of the group. Other leaders are just the reverse. Which style is most effective depends on three sets of factors. One is the nature of the task: Some problems are clearly structured, while others are ambiguous. The second consideration is the relationship between leader and group: whether the leader has good or bad personal relations with the group members. The third consideration is the leader's ability to exercise great or little power over the group. Fiedler has shown that if conditions are either very favorable (good leader-member relations, structured task, high leader power) or very unfavorable (poor leader-member relations, unstructured task, low leader power) for the leader, the most effective leader is the one who is task-oriented and concerned with completing the task successfully. However, when conditions within the group are only moderately favorable for the leader, the most effective leader is one who is concerned about maintaining good interpersonal relations. Fiedler's view of leadership, which has received a great deal of support from research conducted in the laboratory as well as in real-life settings, clearly indicates that there is no such thing as an ideal leader for all situations. "Except perhaps for the unusual case, it is simply not meaningful to speak of an effective or of an ineffective leader; we can only speak of a leader who tends to be effective in one situation and ineffective in another" (Fiedler, 1967, p. 261).

Environmental psychology The study of how the environment influences individuals and their relationships with others.

Personal space The amount of physical distance between one person and another.

Environmental Psychology

In recent years more attention has been paid to how our environment influences us and our relationships with others. Because we accept our environment as a given, we are often unaware of the effects of such factors as crowding, noise, isolation, and urban tension. **Environmental psychology** studies how these factors contribute to the complex ways in which we relate to our world.

Personal Space

Personal space is a phrase coined by the anthropologist Edward T. Hall (1959). It means, quite simply, the amount of physical space between people, how they relate to this space, and how they manipulate it in their relationships with others. In one experiment a student posed as a policeman and interviewed other students about the contents of their wallets. As the interview progressed, the "policeman" edged closer to the students. When the "policeman" moved as close as 8 inches to a student, the student usually grew tense, uncomfortable, and suspicious. When the

Without the built-in barriers, these people would probably feel an invasion of personal space.

distance was kept at about 2 feet, the interviews went smoothly, with no sign of discomfort from the students (Insel & Lindgren, 1978).

In general, the more intimate we are with people, the more likely we are to sit or stand closer to them. Similarly, the more friendly people are with one another, the less they notice how close to one another they are standing or sitting. Indeed, the distance you put between yourself and others is one way of showing interest or liking, especially with someone you have just met or want to get to know. If we do not want to meet people—for instance, while studying at the library—we are inclined to view any attempt to "enter" our space as an invasion. Robert Sommer (1959) tested this by having women approach other women who were studying alone at a library table. If the confederate sat down a few chairs away, she was ignored. But if she sat next to the subject, the subject often expressed discomfort, irritation, and even anger.

In follow-up studies, Fisher and Byrne (1975) discovered some interesting differences in the way men and women react to strangers who invade their personal space, again at library tables. The experimenters had confederates approach students sitting alone and sit either directly across the table or in the chair next to the student on the same side of the table. Regardless of the invader's sex, males were most disturbed by a person sitting across from them, while females were bothered more by someone sitting beside them. Another study revealed that even when no intruder was present, men tended to guard their personal space by placing books or other objects in front of them, while women built barriers on either side.

The circumstances in which we find ourselves also affect our perception of personal space. When a stranger has no other choice but to stand close to us, we tend to ignore the intrusion of our personal turf. At rush hour, for instance, buses and trains in some cities are so jammed that it is often impossible to preserve even a trace of personal space. Thus people who would otherwise be repelled by the closeness of strangers seem to pay no heed to their proximity during these hours. On the other hand, if we sense that some strange person is deliberately invading our personal space, even in a crowded setting, we are likely to be offended (Russell & Ward, 1982).

Environmental Stress

DENSITY AND CROWDING. In New York City as many as 70,000 people live and work within a single square mile. One of New York's larger apartment complexes could house the entire population of many small towns. Sidewalks are so jammed at certain hours of the day that even walking from one place to another becomes a challenge, and traffic maneuvers such as passing, weaving, and dodging become as important to people walking on the sidewalk as to the cars on the street. Although many suburban towns were originally built to avoid this sort of crowding, they, too, have become densely populated, and it is becoming increasingly rare—especially in the older, more developed areas of the country—for people to have the kind of "elbow room" that Americans have been brought up to value and expect.

Because of increased crowding in urban and suburban areas, more attention has been paid recently to how human beings react to crowding and to the invasion of their "personal space." Researchers in this area often distinguish between **density,** the number of people per square foot, and **crowding,** which is the subjective experience of being crowded (e.g., Stokols, 1972). It is possible to feel crowded even when density is low. If, for example, you go to a secluded beach to swim with a friend and discover that there are five or six other people there, you may *feel* crowded even though there is no lack of physical space.

Many studies have examined how animals react to high population density. Calhoun (1962) created rat colonies in which the population was far denser than normal. He found that rats developed "abnormal" traits under these conditions that had not been present before: Maternal behavior was disturbed; cannibalism and homosexuality developed. In general, the rats behaved as if their social bonds had been dissolved.

Although similar reactions to high population density were observed in mice, lemmings, and hares, it is not entirely clear how these findings relate to human behavior. Some studies have found strong positive correlations between density and various forms of social pathology such as juvenile delinquency, mental illness, and the infant death rate (Schmitt, 1966). Others have failed to find a link between density and pathology.

Among humans, the distinction between density and crowding seems to be critical—it's the *experience* of being crowded that produces psychological stress. In part, the stress may be due to sensory overload: Sights and sounds multiply so fast that they soon overload the sensory circuits of the people in the crowd (Stokols, 1978). In part, the stress of crowding may also be due to lack of privacy (Altman, 1975). When individuals cannot withdraw from contact with others or prevent them from intruding on their personal space, stress results. In addition, when many people surround us, it is more difficult to control our interactions with them. The loss of control over one's surroundings can be stressful. Baum and Valins (1977), for example, discovered that students living in long-

Density In environmental psychology, the number of people per unit of area.

Crowding In environmental psychology, the subjective experience of being crowded, regardless of actual population density.

corridor dorms felt more crowded than students living in short-corridor residences, even though actual density was the same. The reason appeared to be that the heavier traffic in the halls and lounges of long-corridor dorms led to feelings of greater crowding. Students who lived in the long-corridor dorms were also more likely to feel powerless about controlling their environment.

Not everyone reacts to crowding in the same way. Individualistic persons tend to experience more stress from crowding than those who work easily in cooperation with others. Compatibility is also important. Being enclosed in tight quarters with others whose company one does not enjoy is a perfect recipe for stress, as we have all learned. Some evidence suggests that men suffer more stress from high-density conditions than do women (Penrod, 1984).

NOISE. Noise can have a powerful impact on mental functioning. In a classroom in a large city several years ago, hundreds of students had just begun to work on a Graduate Record Examination when the sound of an electric guitar pierced the walls. A quarter of a mile away, in a park, a young man had set up a pair of loudspeakers so powerful that the examinees could hear every mistake he made on his guitar. Because it was impossible for most of the students to concentrate on the examination under these distracting conditions, the proctors had to collect the exam booklets and move everyone to a room on the other side of the building.

But noise affects more than concentration. It also affects interpersonal interaction, including the tendency to help others who are in need. In one study subjects exposed to different levels of noise saw a stranger drop a stack of books and magazines. The greater the noise, the less likely subjects were to help pick up the books (Matthews & Cannon, 1975). Noise also seems to impair the ability to notice cues in social situations and in the environment in general. In one experiment subjects watching a videotape while exposed to noise were less able to distinguish victims from harm-doers than were other subjects who were not exposed to noise (Siegel & Steele, 1979). Finally, noise facilitates aggressive responses. In one experiment a group of college students heard loud random bursts of noise and then were angered by a confederate. Next they had the chance to "shock" another person. These subjects delivered more intense shocks than students who had heard only soft noise (Donnerstein & Wilson, 1976). Noise, then, is more than a distraction. Under certain conditions, it can also reduce altruism, attention to social cues, and self-restraint in interaction with others.

Noise can be a major source of environmental stress.

Application

Prejudice and Discrimination

Although we often use the terms *prejudice* and *discrimination* interchangeably, they are, in fact, different. Prejudice is an unfair, intolerant, or unfavorable *attitude* toward another group of people.

Discrimination is an *act* or a series of acts taken toward another group—or toward people who belong to that group—that are unfair when compared with our behavior toward other groups. On the basis of your reading so far in this chapter, you should not be surprised to learn that prejudice (an attitude) and discrimination (a behavior) do not always occur together. A motel owner who is prejudiced against blacks may nonetheless manage to be polite as she rents a room to a black family. She is prejudiced but does not discriminate. Conversely, the personnel manager of a conservative bank may refuse to hire a woman he has interviewed for a management job, not because he is sexist himself, but because bank policy discourages the hiring of women managers. In this case, discrimination is present without prejudice.

PREJUDICE. Like attitudes in general, prejudice has three components: beliefs, feelings, and behavior tendencies. Prejudicial beliefs are virtually always stereotypes, and as we mentioned earlier in this chapter, the use of stereotypes leads to certain kinds of errors in thinking about other people. When a prejudiced employer interviews a black, for instance, the employer attributes to the job candidate before him or her all of the traits associated with the black stereotype. To make matters worse, qualities of the individual that are inconsistent with the stereotype are ignored or quickly forgotten. In his classic study *The Nature of Prejudice*, Gordon Allport (1954) recorded the following dialogue:

Mr. X: The trouble with the Jews is that they only take care of their own group.

Mr. Y: But the record of the Community Chest campaign shows that they gave more generously in proportion to their numbers to the general charities of the communities than did non-Jews.

Mr. X: That shows that they are always trying to buy favor and intrude into Christian affairs. They think of nothing but money; that is why there are so many Jewish bankers.

Mr. Y: But a recent study shows that the percentage of Jews in the banking business is negligible, far smaller than the percentage of non-Jews.

Mr. X: That's just it; they don't go in for respectable business; they are only in the movie business or run night clubs.

Along with stereotyped beliefs, prejudicial attitudes are usually marked by strong emotions such as dislike, fear, hatred, or loathing. Understandably, such attitudes also tend to lead the individual to discriminate against the group in question.

SOURCES OF PREJUDICE. There have been many studies of the sources of prejudice, and an extraordinary number of theories have been advanced about its causes.

Frustration-Aggression. One of the most popular theories explains prejudice in terms of the submerged frustrations of the prejudiced group. (Allport, 1954; Hovland & Sears, 1940). The *scapegoat theory* asserts that prejudice and discrimination result from displaced aggression. Historically, for example, violence against the Jews often followed periods of economic unrest or natural catastrophe. Similarly, blacks in this country have been scapegoats for the economic frustrations of lower-income white Americans who are essentially powerless. Poor whites who feel exploited and oppressed cannot vent their anger on the proper target, so they displace their hostility by directing it against those who are even "lower" on the social scale than they are—blacks.

Authoritarian Personality. Another theory explains prejudice in terms of the psychological characteristics of the bigot. Adorno and his colleagues (1950) linked prejudice to a complex cluster of personality traits termed *authoritarianism*. Authoritarians tend to be rigidly conventional, submissive to authority, hostile toward people who violate conventional values, inclined to think about the world according to rigid categories, preoccupied with power and toughness, and both destructive and cynical. Such individuals fear, suspect, and reject all groups other than the ones to which they belong.

Conformity. Conformity is also important in forming and sustaining prejudice and discrimination. If we want to associate with people who also have clearly expressed prejudices, we are more likely to go along with their prejudices than we are to resist them. During the 1960s in the South, for example, many restaurant owners maintained that they themselves did not mind serving blacks, but their customers would not tolerate it (Deaux & Wrightsman, 1984). Children are especially likely to conform to the attitudes of their peers, which is partly why it has often been so hard to integrate schools. Those white children who are willing to go to school with black children are subjected to immense peer-group pressure to conform to the hostile behavior—based on stereotypes—displayed by their friends and classmates.

REDUCING PREJUDICE. Earlier in this chapter we noted that people tend to like others who are similar to them. How important is racial similarity to people's liking for others? In a series of studies (Byrne & Wong, 1962; Rokeach & Mezei, 1966; Stein et al., 1965) some subjects were given a description of a person of another race whose attitudes were similar to their own, while other subjects received descriptions of a person of their own race whose attitudes were very different from their own. The results showed that, in general, similarity of attitudes was more important than belonging to the same racial group in determining who was liked.

It would indeed be pleasant to believe that these findings directly bear on real contacts between people. If this were so, it would indicate —as many educators and activists believed—that simply *educating* people about the similarities between themselves and others might reduce racial tensions. These studies, however, primarily apply to relatively nonintimate relationships—working or studying together, for example. Racial similarity is far more important in intimate relationships such as dating or marriage.

It is also wise to remember that the subjects in these studies were presented with hypothetical people and situations, and that there was a subtle pressure to be objective and nonbiased. In real life, biases are often more important. Silverman (1974) described various people as roommates to incoming college students. Some subjects were told that these choices would actually *be* their assigned roommates. Other subjects were told that these were merely hypothetical roommates. Racial discrimination was far more important to the choice of *actual* roommates than to the choice of *imagined* roommates. But similarity in attitude and belief was important in both groups. Thus, although it is somewhat discouraging to see the difference between our "lip service" to racial equality and our

practice of it, these studies offer some hope that people will weigh attitude similarity fairly under the right conditions.

During the late 1950s, when school desegregation was given massive attention, many people believed that it too would change prejudicial attitudes. This belief has proved to be only partly true. Moreover, the attempt to educate the public with films and literature designed to explode racial myths has been a dismal failure (Aronson, 1984). As we have seen, people are quite adept at ignoring what clashes with their own deep-seated beliefs.

There has, however, been some progress. We now know that when blacks and whites share the same goals and cooperate to reach them, prejudice lessens. The important point here is that mere *contact* between groups is not enough to lessen prejudice. The contact must be *interdependent* and *cooperative*, not competitive. Interracial groups organized to solve specific problems cooperatively—a student council, a working team, a study group—can reduce prejudice. Unfortunately, these situations are rare in society, although studies among residents of housing projects, department store workers, and police officers all show the same thing: When racial groups work or live together in noncompetitive, nonthreatening situations, racial animosities decrease (Clore et al., 1978).

One interesting series of studies by Elliot Aronson and his colleagues (Aronson et al., 1978) seems to point the way for future efforts at reducing racial prejudice. Each student in a class was given a different section of material to learn and report on to his or her fellow students—it was called the *jigsaw method* because the pieces fit together to form a whole. The students were left on their own, but were told that they would be tested on the material. Thus it was to their advantage to learn from one another, to coax those who needed it, and to cooperate in assembling the "whole picture." The results were remarkable. While it took some students longer than others to realize the value of cooperation, most of the groups adapted well, and children of all races found themselves cooperating and learning from one another.

This method, however, works best with young children. It is also hard to implement such a program on any but a small scale. Still, it offers some hope for those who believe that education is the best way to change people's preconceived racial prejudices.

1. *Social psychology* is the scientific study of the way in which the thoughts, feelings, and behaviors of one individual are influenced by the real, imagined, or implied behavior or characteristics of other people.

2. Social perception involves forming impressions of other people. When we first meet someone, we use cues to fit him or her into pre-existing categories called *schemas.* Schemas allow us to make inferences about other people and to recall facts about them. They can also lead to selective or inaccurate recall.

3. A *primacy effect* exists when the first information that we receive about someone weighs more heavily than later information in the formation of impressions. Under certain conditions, the primacy effect can be overcome.

4. When our expectations about a person elicit behavior from that person that fits the expectation, a *self-fulfilling prophecy* is said to have occurred.

5. A *stereotype* is a special kind of schema in which we believe a set of characteristics is shared by all the people who belong to a particular social group. As with all schemas, stereotypes can affect what we remember about people and become self-fulfilling prophecies.

6. The study of the inferences we make about the behavior of other people is called *attribution theory.* An attribution is an inference that one draws about the actions of another—or oneself—on the basis of observing overt behavior. In making attributions we tend to consider such things as *distinctiveness, consensus,* and *consistency* of behavior.

7. The attribution process is subject to a number of biases, of which the most important is the *fundamental attribution error:* the tendency to overemphasize personal causes for the behavior of others and to underemphasize those causes for our own behavior. Another attribution bias is the tendency to attribute catastrophes to personal rather than situational factors; to assume that if people behave differently from us in a situation, it is because of personal factors; and to take personal credit for good events and deny responsibility for bad things (the *just world hypothesis*).

8. Many factors propel us toward liking another person. Some of the major factors are: proximity, similarity of attitudes and interests, complementary needs, attractiveness, rewardingness, and reciprocity.

9. An *attitude* is a fairly stable organization of beliefs, feelings, and behavior tendencies directed toward some object such as a person or group.

10. Attitudes do not predict behavior very well unless both attitudes and behavior are measured at the same level of specificity. Moreover, behavior is also affected by the person's intentions, social norms, and willingness to override his or her attitudes.

11. Some attitudes derive from our personal experience and from the information we received from our parents when we were children. Admired individuals, as well as social groups, may also have a lasting influence on attitudes. Studies also show that television is a major source of societal attitudes. Children, especially, rely on television to form their social attitudes.

12. Various factors contribute to the success of an attempt to change an attitude by providing information. Credibility of the source, the content of the message (number of arguments presented, use of fear), and the organization of the message all affect the amount of attitude change. Also important are characteristics of the audience, such as its commitment to its present attitudes, the discrepancy between the message and present attitudes, and personality characteristics.

13. Changes of behavior sometimes lead to changes of attitude. *Cognitive dissonance* theory maintains that a state of unpleasant tension follows from the clashing of two incompatible cognitions. We are motivated to try to reduce dissonance in one way or another. When the discrepancy is between behavior and attitude, it is often easiest to reduce dissonance by changing the attitude.

14. Attitude change is a common result of cog-

nitive dissonance because changing one's attituee is an easier means of reducing dissonance than the other two alternatives, which are 1) increasing the number of consonant elements, and 2) reducing the importance of one or both cognitive elements.

15. *Social influence* refers to any actions performed by one or more persons to change the attitudes, behavior, or feelings of one or more others. Attitude change is one form of social influence. Conformity, compliance, and obedience are the results of successful attempts to exert social influence on behavior.

16. *Conformity* is the voluntary yielding to social norms, even at the expense of one's own preferences. *Compliance* is a change of behavior in response to an explicit request from another person. Like compliance, *obedience* is a change in behavior in response to an explicit statement by another person, in this case a command from an authority figure.

17. *Altruistic* or *helping behavior* is unselfish helping behavior. The likelihood of altruism is determined by situational variables and variables related to the bystander. The greater the number of bystanders and the greater the ambiguity of the situation, the less likely bystanders are to help a stranger in need. In addition, the mood of the bystander and other personal qualities affect the likelihood of helping behavior.

18. *Deindividuation* may partly account for the antisocial, even violent, behavior sometimes shown by groups. Large groups provide protection and anonymity to individuals.

19. The assumption that groups make more conservative decisions than individuals turn out to be true only if group members are somewhat conservative at the start. The reason is that group discussion tends to *polarize* the attitudes of members. If members are inclined to take risks, then the group decision is likely to be riskier than individual decisions (the so-called *risky shift*).

20. The effectiveness of a group depends on three factors: (1) the nature of the task, (2) the resources of the group members, and (3) the interaction among group members. If the requirements of the task match the skills of group members, groups are likely to be more effective than the same number of individuals working alone. However, the social status of group members, group size, and cohesiveness also determine how effective a group will actually be.

21. All groups have a leader, whether a formal one or an informal one. Some theorists argue that leaders are great men who could lead no matter what the historical conditions. Another theory stresses that leaders happen to appear in the right place at the right time. The transactional viewpoint argues that both personal traits and situational factors are important. Also important is the relation between the leader and the group.

22. *Environmental psychology* studies the way in which such things as personal space, crowding, and noise affect the way we relate to the world around us and to other people. *Personal space* denotes the amount of physical distance between one person and another. There are differences in the way national groups, ethnic and cultural groups, and even the two sexes relate to personal space. In general, the degree of intimacy or liking of other people determines our willingness to stand or be seated close to them. Circumstances also dictate perception of personal space. Forced proximity is more readily tolerated than what is perceived as a deliberate invasion of personal space.

23. Several sources of environmental stress are high population *density, crowding,* and noise. *Density* refers to the number of persons per unit of area. While animals appear to be greatly affected by high density, in humans it seems that the experience of feeling crowded is more important. Noise also affects people profoundly, especially when it is unpredictable and uncontrollable. Noise not only distracts, it also affects interpersonal interaction, ability to notice social cues, and self-restraint.

1. The scientific study of the way in which the thoughts, feelings, and behaviors of one individual are influenced by the real, imagined, or implied behavior or characteristics of other people is _____ _____.

2. When we first meet someone, we use cues to fit that person into pre-existing categories called _____. Sometimes we think and behave in accordance with a _____, a set of characteristics thought to be shared by all of the people who belong to a particular social group.

3. A _____ effect exists to the extent that the first information that we receive about someone weighs more heavily than later information in the formation of impressions.

4. The study of the inferences we make about the behavior of other people is
   a. psychology
   b. social psychology
   c. attribution theory
   d. cognitive dissonance

5. Which of the following has NOT been established as a factor that promotes liking between two persons?
   a. proximity
   b. complementary needs
   c. complemenary attitudes and interests
   d. rewardingness

6. A/an _____ is a fairly stable organization of beliefs, feelings, and behavioral tendencies directed toward some object such as a person or group.

7. The best way to predict behavior is to measure attitudes. T/F

8. Which of the following decreases the likelihood that a message will change the attitude of an audience?
   a. credible sources
   b. attitudes shared with other people
   c. inclusion of numerous arguments for the desired attitude
   d. moderate appeal to fear

9. _____ _____ theory maintains that a state of unpleasant tension follows the clashing of two incompatible cognitions.

10. According to cognitive dissonance theory, when a discrepancy between behavior and attitudes exists, it is often easiest to change _____ to reduce the dissonance.
    a. attitudes
    b. behavior
    c. neither attitudes nor beheavior
    d. intentions

11. Match each of the following terms with its definition:
    ___ social influence
    ___ compliance
    ___ obedience
    ___ conformity

    A. Voluntarily yielding to social norms, even at the expense of one's own preferences.
    B. A change of behavior in response to a command from another person.
    C. A change of behavior in response to an explicit request from another person or from a group.
    D. Any actions performed by one or more persons to change the attitudes, behavior, or feelings of others.

12. If group members are inclined to take risks, then the group decision is likely to be riskier than individual decisions. This phenomenon is termed the _____ _____.

13. A shift in attitudes by members of a group toward more extreme positions than the one held before group discussion is termed _____.

14. The effectiveness of a group depends on three factors: 1) the nature of the _____, 2) the resources of the group members, and 3) the _____ among group members.

15. All groups have a leader, whether a formal one or an informal one. T/F

16. _____ _____ studies the way in which such things as personal space, crowding, and noise affect the way we relate to the world around us and to other people.

17. Density, crowding, and noise are all sources of environmental _____.

18. The way in which different kinds of people—men and women, national groups, and ethnic groups—relate to personal space does not vary much. T/F

Appendix:
Measurement and
Statistical Methods

Statistics A branch of mathematics used by psychologists to organize and analyze data.

Nominal scale A set of categories for classifying objects.

Ordinal scale Scale indicating order or relative position of items according to some criterion.

Most of the experiments described in this book involve measuring one or more variables and then analyzing the data statistically. The design and scoring of all the tests we have discussed are also based on statistical methods. **Statistics** is a branch of mathematics. It provides techniques for sorting out quantitative facts and ways of drawing conclusions from them. Statistics let us organize and describe data quickly, guide the conclusions we draw, and help us make inferences.

Statistical analysis is essential to conducting an experiment or designing a test, but statistics can only handle numbers—groups of them. To use statistics, the psychologist first must measure things—count and express them in quantities.

Scales of Measurement

No matter what we are measuring—height, noise, intelligence, attitudes, and so on—we have to use a scale. The data we want to collect determine the scale we will use and, in turn, the scale we use helps determine the conclusions we can draw from our data.

NOMINAL SCALES. If we decide to classify a group of people by the color of their eyes, we are using a **nominal scale.** We can count how many people have blue eyes, how many have green eyes, how many have brown eyes, and so on, but we cannot say that one group has more or less eye color than the other. The colors are simply different.

A nominal scale is a set of arbitrarily named or numbered categories. If we look up how many Republican, Democratic, and Independent voters registered in a certain congressional district in the last election year, we are using a nominal scale. Since a nominal scale is more of a way of classifying than of measuring, it is the least informative kind of scale. If we want to compare our data more precisely, we will have to use a scale that tells us more.

ORDINAL SCALES. If we list horses in the order in which they finish a race, we are using an **ordinal scale.** On an ordinal scale, data are ranked from first to last according to some criterion. An ordinal scale tells the order, but nothing about the distances between what is ranked first and second or ninth and tenth. It does not tell us how much faster the winning horse ran than the horses that placed or showed. If a person ranks her preferences for various kinds of soup—pea soup first, then tomato, then onion, and so on—we know what soup she likes most and what soup she likes least, but we have no idea how much better she likes tomato than onion, or if pea soup is far more favored than either one of them.

Since we do not know the distances between the items ranked on an ordinal scale, we cannot add or subtract ordinal data. If mathematical operations are necessary, we need a still more informative scale.

INTERVAL SCALES. An **interval scale** is often compared to a ruler that has been broken off at the bottom—it only goes from, say, 5½ to 12. The intervals between 6 and 7, 7 and 8, 8 and 9, and so forth are equal, but there is no zero. A thermometer is an interval scale—even though a certain degree registered on a Fahrenheit or centigrade thermometer specifies a certain state of cold or heat, there is no such thing as no temperature at all. One day is never twice as hot as another; it is only so many equal degrees hotter.

An interval scale tells us how many equal-size units one thing lies above or below another thing of the same kind, but it does not tell us how many times bigger, smaller, taller, or fatter one thing is than another. An intelligence test cannot tell us that one person is three times as intelligent as another, only that he or she scored so many points above or below someone else.

RATIO SCALES. We can only say that a measurement is 2 times as long as another or 3 times as high when we use a **ratio scale,** one that has a true zero. For instance, if we measure the snowfall in a certain area over several winters, we can say that 6 times as much snow fell during a winter in which we measured a total of 12 feet as during a winter in which only 2 feet fell. This scale has a zero—there may be no snow.

Interval scale Scale with equal distances between the points or values, but without a true zero.

Ratio scale Scale with equal distances between the points or values and with a true zero.

Central tendency Tendency of scores to congregate around some middle value.

Measurements of Central Tendency

Usually when we measure a number of instances of anything—from the popularity of TV shows to the weights of 8-year-old boys to the number of times a person's optic nerve fires in response to electrical stimulation—we get a distribution of measurements that range from smallest to largest or lowest to highest. The measurements will usually cluster around some value near the middle. This value is the **central tendency** of the distribution of the measurements.

Suppose, for example, you want to keep 10 children busy tossing rings around a bottle. You give them 3 rings to toss each turn, the game has 6 rounds, and each player scores 1 point every time he or she gets the ring around the neck of the bottle. The highest possible score is 18. The distribution of scores might end up like this: 11, 8, 13, 6, 12, 10, 16, 9, 12, 3.

Mean Arithmetical average calcu-
lated by dividing a sum of values
by the total number of cases.

Median Point that divides a set of
scores in half.

Mode Point at which the largest
number of scores occurs.

Frequency distribution A count
of the number of scores that
fall within each of a series of
intervals.

What could you quickly say about the ring-tossing talent of the group? First, you could arrange the scores from lowest to highest: 3, 6, 8, 9, 10, 11, 12, 12, 13, 16. In this order, the central tendency of the distribution of scores becomes clear. Many of the scores cluster around the values between 8 and 12. There are three ways to describe the central tendency of a distribution. We usually refer to all three as the *average*.

The arithmetical average is called the **mean**—the sum of all the scores in the group, divided by the number of scores. If you add up all the scores and divide by 10, the total number of scores in this group of ring tossers, you find that the mean for the group is 10.

The **median** is the point that divides a distribution in half—50 percent of the scores fall above the median and 50 percent fall below. In the ring-tossing scores, 5 scores fall at 10 or below, 5 at 11 or above. The median is thus halfway between 10 and 11—10.5.

The point at which the largest number of scores occurs is called the **mode.** In our example, the mode is 12. More people scored 12 than any other.

Differences Between the Median and Mode

If we take many measurements of anything, we are likely to get a distribution of scores in which the mean, median, and mode are all about the same—the score that occurs most often (the mode) will also be the point that half the scores are below and half above (the median). And the same point will be the arithmetical average (the mean). This is not always true, of course, and small samples rarely come out so symmetrically. In these cases, we often have to decide which of the three measures of central tendency—the mean, the median, or mode—will tell us what we want to know.

For example, a shopkeeper wants to know the general incomes of passersby so he can stock the right merchandise. He might conduct a rough survey by standing outside his store for a few days from 12:00 to 2:00 and asking every 10th person who walks by to check a card showing the general range of his or her income. Suppose most of the people checked the ranges between $8,000 and $10,000 a year. However, a couple of the people made a lot of money—one checked $100,000–$150,000, one checked the $200,000-or-above box. The mean for the set of income figures would be pushed higher by those two large figures and would not really tell the shopkeeper what he wants to know about his potential customers. In this case, he would be wiser to use the median or the mode.

Suppose instead of meeting two people whose incomes were so great, he noticed that people from two distinct income groups walked by his store—several people checked the box for $9,000–$10,000, several others checked $14,000–$15,000. The shopkeeper would find that his distribution was bimodal. It has two modes—$9,500 and $14,500. This might be more useful to him than the mean, which could lead him to think his customers were a unit with an average income of about $12,000.

Another way of approaching a set of scores is to arrange them into a **frequency distribution**—i.e., to select a set of intervals and count how many scores fall into each interval. A frequency distribution is useful for large groups of numbers; it puts the number of individual scores into more manageable groups.

Frequency histogram Type of bar graph that shows frequency distributions.

Frequency polygon Type of line graph that shows frequency distributions.

Suppose a psychologist tests memory. She asks 50 college students to learn 18 nonsense syllables, then records how many syllables each student can recall 2 hours later. She arranges her raw scores from lowest to highest in a rank distribution:

2	6	8	10	11	14
3	7	9	10	12	14
4	7	9	10	12	15
4	7	9	10	12	16
5	7	9	10	13	17
5	7	9	11	13	
6	8	9	11	13	
6	8	9	11	13	
6	8	10	11	13	

The scores range from 2 to 17, but 50 individual scores are too cumbersome to work with. So she chooses a set of 2-point intervals and tallies the number of scores in each interval:

Interval	Tally	Frequency (f)
1–2			1
3–4	|||	3
5–6	⑪		6
7–8	⑪ ||||	9
9–10	⑪ ⑪ |||	13
11–12	⑪ |||	8
13–14	⑪ ||	7
15–16	||	2
17–18			1

Now she can tell at a glance what the results of her experiment were. Most of the students had scores near the middle of the range, and very few had scores in the high or low intervals. She can see these results even better if she uses the frequency distribution to construct a bar graph—a **frequency histogram.** Marking the intervals along the horizontal axis and the frequencies along the vertical axis would give her the graph shown in Figure A-1. Another way is to construct a **frequency polygon,** a line graph. A frequency polygon drawn from the same set of data is shown in Figure A-2. Note that the figure is not a smooth curve, since the points are connected by straight lines. With many scores, however, and with small intervals, the angles would smooth out and the figure would resemble a rounded curve.

The Normal Curve

Ordinarily, if we take enough measurements of almost anything, we get a *normal distribution.* Tossing coins is a favorite example of statisticians. If you tossed 10 coins into the air 1,000 times, and recorded the heads and tails on each toss, your tabulations would reveal a normal

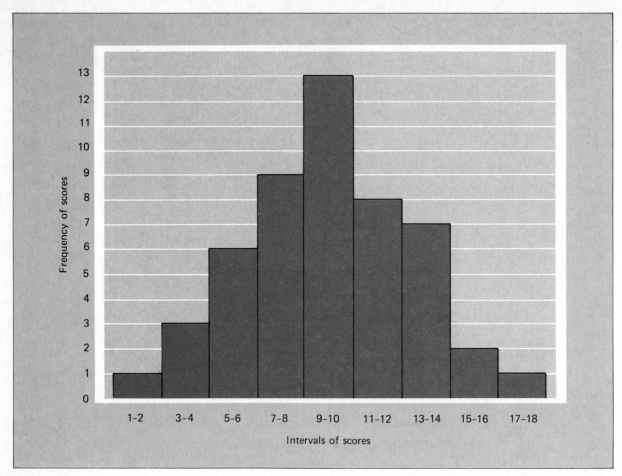

Figure A-1

A frequency histogram for a memory experiment. The bars indicate the frequency of scores within each interval.

Figure A-2

A frequency polygon drawn from data used in Figure A-1. The dots, representing the frequency of scores in each interval, are connected by straight lines.

distribution. 5 heads and 5 tails would occur most often, 6 heads/4 tails and 4 heads/6 tails would be the next most frequent, and so on down to the rare all heads or all tails.

Plotting a normal distribution on a graph yields a particular kind of frequency polygon called a **normal curve.** Figure A-3 shows data on the heights of 1,000 men. Superimposed over the gray bars that reflect the actual data is an "ideal" normal curve for the same data. Note that the curve is absolutely symmetrical—the left slope parallels the right slope exactly. Moreover, the mean, median, and mode all fall on the highest point on the curve.

The normal curve is a hypothetical entity. No set of real measurements shows such a smooth gradation from one interval to the next, or so purely symmetrical a shape. But because so many things do approximate the normal curve so closely, the curve is a useful model for much that we measure.

Normal curve Hypothetical, bell-shaped distribution curve that occurs when a normal distribution is plotted as a frequency polygon.

Skewed Distributions

If a frequency distribution is asymmetrical—if most of the scores are gathered at either the high end or the low end—the frequency polygon will be *skewed.* The hump will sit to one side or the other and one of the curve's tails will be disproportionately long.

If a high-school mathematics instructor, for example, gives his students a sixth-grade arithmetic test, we would expect nearly all the scores

Figure A-3

A normal curve, based on measurements of the heights of 1,000 adult males.

(From A. B. Hill, *Principles of Medical Statistics*, 8th ed. London: Oxford University Press, 1966.)

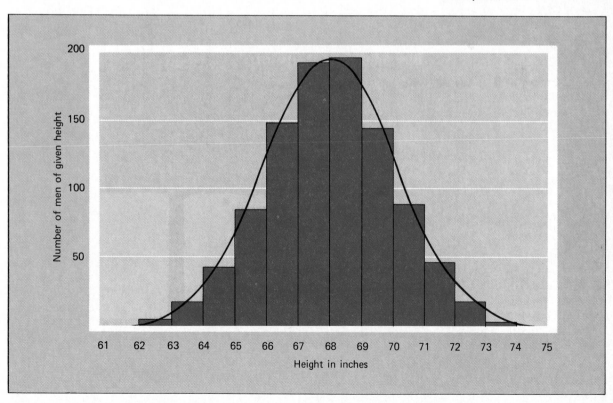

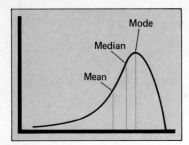

Figure A-4

A skewed distribution. Most of the scores are gathered at the high end of the distribution, causing the hump to shift to the right. Since the tail on the left is longer, we say that the curve is skewed to the left. Note that the mean, median, and mode are different.

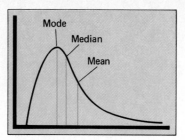

Figure A-5

In this distribution most of the scores are gathered at the low end, so the curve is skewed to the right. The mean, median, and mode do not coincide.

to be quite high. The frequency polygon would probably look like the one in Figure A-4. But if a sixth-grade class is asked to do advanced algebra, the scores would probably be quite low. The frequency polygon would be very similar to the one shown in Figure A-5.

Note, too, that the mean, median, and mode fall at different points in a skewed distribution, unlike in the normal curve, where they coincide. Usually, if you know that the mean is greater than the median of a distribution, you can predict that the frequency polygon will be skewed to the right. If the median is greater than the mean, the curve will be skewed to the left.

Bimodal Distributions

We have already mentioned a bimodal distribution in our description of the shopkeeper's survey of his customers' incomes. The frequency polygon for a bimodal distribution has two humps—one for each mode. The mean and the median may be the same, as in Figure A-6, or different, as in Figure A-7.

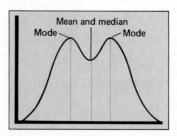

Figure A-6

A bimodal distribution in which the mean and the median are the same.

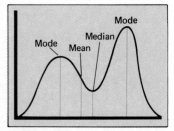

Figure A-7

In this bimodal distribution the mean and median are different.

Sometimes it is not enough to know the distribution of a set of data and what their mean, median, and mode are. Suppose an automotive safety expert feels that too much damage occurs in tail-end accidents because automobile bumpers are not all the same height. It is not enough for him to know what the average height of an automobile bumper is. He also wants to know about the variation in bumper heights: How much higher is the highest bumper than the mean? How do bumpers of all cars vary from the mean? Are the latest bumpers closer to the same height?

Range Difference between the largest and smallest measurements in a distribution.

Range

The simplest measure of variation is the **range**—the difference between the largest and smallest measurements. Perhaps the safety expert measured the bumpers of 1,000 cars 2 years ago and found that the highest bumper was 18 inches from the ground, the lowest only 12 inches from the ground. The range was thus 6 inches—18 minus 12. This year the highest bumper is still 18 inches high, the lowest still 12 inches from the ground. The range is still 6 inches. Moreover, he finds that the means of the two distributions are the same—15 inches off the ground. But look at the two frequency polygons in Figure A-8—there is still something he needs to know, since how the measurements cluster around the mean is drastically different. To find out how the measurements are distributed

Figure A-8

Frequency polygons for two sets of measurements of automobile bumper heights. Both are normal curves and in each distribution the mean, median, and mode are 15. But the variation from the mean is different, causing one curve to be flattened, the other to be much more sharply peaked.

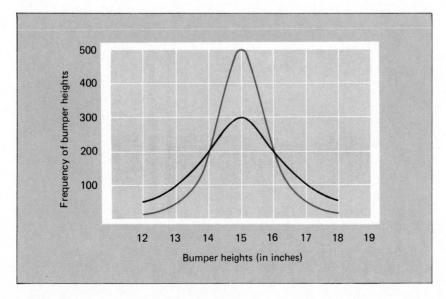

around the mean, our safety expert has to turn to a slightly more complicated measure of variation—the standard deviation.

Standard deviation Statistical measure of variability in a group of scores or other values.

The Standard Deviation

The **standard deviation,** in a single number, tells us much about how the scores in any frequency distribution are dispersed around the mean. Calculating the standard deviation is one of the most useful and widely used statistical tools.

To find the standard deviation of a set of scores, we first find the mean. Then we take the first score in the distribution, subtract it from the mean, square the difference, and jot it down in a column to be added up later. We do the same for all the scores in the distribution. Then we add up the

Figure A-9

Step-by-step calculation of the standard deviation for a group of 10 scores with a mean of 7.

Number of scores = 10		Mean = 7
Scores	*Difference from mean*	*Difference squared*
4	7 – 4 = 3	$3^2 = 9$
5	7 – 5 = 2	$2^2 = 4$
6	7 – 6 = 1	$1^2 = 1$
6	7 – 6 = 1	$1^2 = 1$
7	7 – 7 = 0	$0^2 = 0$
7	7 – 7 = 0	$0^2 = 0$
8	7 – 8 = – 1	$- 1^2 = 1$
8	7 – 8 = – 1	$- 1^2 = 1$
9	7 – 9 = – 2	$- 2^2 = 4$
10	7 – 10 = – 3	$- 3^2 = 9$

Sum of squares = 30
÷
Number of scores = 10
Variance = 3
Standard deviation = $\sqrt{3}$ = 1.73

Figure A-10

A normal curve, divided to show the percentage of scores that fall within each standard deviation from the mean.

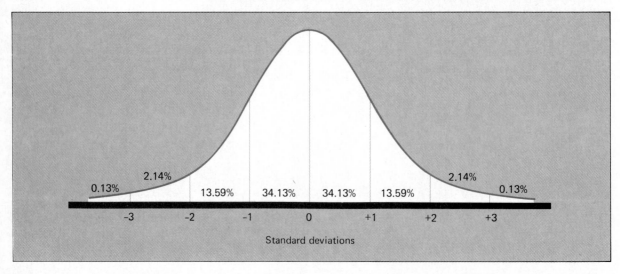

column of squared differences, divide the total by the number of scores in the distribution, and find the square root of that number. Figure A-9 shows the calculation of the standard deviation for a small distribution of scores.

In a normal distribution, however peaked or flattened the curve, about 68 percent of the scores fall between 1 standard deviation above the mean and 1 standard deviation below the mean (see Figure A-10). Another 27 percent fall between 1 standard deviation and 2 standard deviations on either side of the mean, 4 percent more between the 2nd and 3rd standard deviations on either side. More than 99 percent of the scores fall between 3 standard deviations above and 3 standard deviations below the mean. This makes the standard deviation useful for comparing two different normal distributions.

Now let us see what the standard deviation can tell our automotive safety expert about the variations from the mean in his two sets of data. The standard deviation for the cars he measured 2 years ago, he finds, is about 1.4. A car with a bumper height of 16.4 is 1 standard deviation above the mean of 15; one with a bumper height of 13.6 is 1 standard deviation below the mean. Since he knows that his data fall into a normal distribution, he can figure that about 68 percent of the 1,000 cars he measured will fall somewhere between these two heights: 680 cars will have bumpers between 13.6 and 16.4 inches high. For his more recent set of data, the standard deviation is just slightly less than 1. A car with a bumper height of about 14 inches is 1 standard deviation below the mean; a car with a bumper height of about 16 is 1 standard deviation above the mean. Thus in this distribution 680 cars have bumpers between 14 and 16 inches high. This tells the safety expert that car bumpers are becoming more similar, although the range of heights is still the same (6 inches) and the mean height of bumpers is still 15.

Scatter plot Diagram showing the association between scores on two variables.

Measures of Correlation

Measures of central tendency and measures of variation are used to describe a single set of measurements—like the children's ring-tossing scores—or to compare two or more sets of measurements—like the two sets of bumper heights. Sometimes, however, we need to know if two sets of measurements are in any way associated with one another—if they are correlated. Is parental IQ related to children's IQ? Does the need for achievement relate to the need for power? Is watching violence on TV related to aggressive behavior?

One fast way to determine if two variable are correlated is to draw a **scatter plot.** We assign one variable (X) to the horizontal axis of a graph, the other (Y) to the vertical axis. Then we plot a person's score on one characteristic along the horizontal axis and his or her score on the second characteristic along the vertical axis. Where the two scores intersect we draw a dot. When several scores have been plotted in this way, the pattern of dots tells if the two characteristics are in any way correlated with each other.

Correlation coefficient Statistical measure of the strength of association between two variables.

If the dots on a scatter plot form a straight line running between the lower left-hand corner and the upper right-hand corner, as they do in Figure A-11a, we have a perfect *positive correlation*—a high score on one of the characteristics is always associated with a high score on the other one. A straight line running between the upper left-hand corner and the lower right-hand corner, as in Figure A-11b, is the sign of a perfect *negative correlation*—a high score on one of the characteristics is always associated with a low score on the other one. If the pattern formed by the dots is cigar-shaped in either of these directions, as in Figure A-11c, we have a modest correlation—the two characteristics are related, but not highly correlated. If the dots spread out over the whole graph, forming a circle or a random pattern, as they do in Figure A-11d, there is no correlation between the two characteristics.

A scatter plot can give us a general idea if a correlation exists and how strong it is. To describe the relation between two variable more precisely, we need a **correlation coefficient**—a statistical measure of the degree to which two variables are associated. The correlation coefficient tells us the degree of association between two sets of matched scores—that is, to what extent high or low scores on one variable tend to be associated with high or low scores on another variable. It also provides an estimate of how well we would be able to predict from a person's score on one characteristic how high he or she will score on another characteristic. If we know, for example, that a test of mechanical ability is highly correlated with success in engineering courses, we could predict that success on the test would also mean success as an engineering major.

Correlation coefficients can run from $+1.0$ to -1.0. The highest possible value ($+1.0$) indicates a perfect positive correlation—high

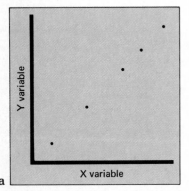

Figure A-11

Scatter plots can be used to give a rough idea of the strength and direction of correlation. Plot *a* shows a perfect positive correlation, plot *b* shows a perfect negative correlation. Plot *c* shows a moderate positive correlation, but in plot *d* there is no correlation at all.

a

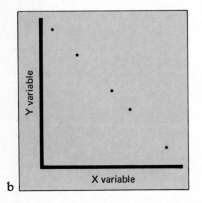

b

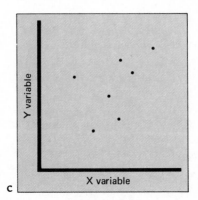

c

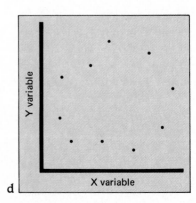

d

scores on one variable are always and systematically related to high scores on a second variable. The lowest possible value (-1.0) means a perfect negative correlation—high scores on one variable are always and regularly related to low scores on the second variable. In life most things are far from perfect, of course, so most correlation coefficients fall somewhere between $+1.0$ and -1.0. A correlation below $\pm.20$ is considered insignificant, from $\pm.20$ to $\pm.40$ is low, from $\pm.40$ to $\pm.60$ is moderate, from $\pm.60$ to $\pm.80$ is high, and from $\pm.80$ to ±1.0 is very high. A correlation of zero indicates that there is no correlation between two sets of scores—no regular relation between them at all.

Correlation tells us nothing about causality. If we found a high positive correlation between participation in elections and income levels, for example, we still could not say that being wealthy made people vote or that voting made people wealthy. We would still not know which came first, or if some third variable explained both income levels and voting behavior. Correlation only tells us that we have found some association between scores on two specified characteristics.

Sample Selection of cases from a larger population.

Random sample Sample in which each potential subject has an equal chance of being selected.

Using Statistics to Make Predictions

Behind the use of statistics is the hope that we can generalize from our results and use them to predict behavior. We hope, for example, that we can use the record of how well a group of rats run through a maze today to predict how another group of rats will do tomorrow, that we can use a man's scores on a sales aptitude test to predict how well he will sell life insurance, that we can measure the attitudes of a relatively small group of people about pollution control to indicate what the attitudes of the whole country are. But first we have to determine if our measurements are representative and if we can have confidence in them.

Sampling

It is often impossible, or at least impractical, to measure every single occurrence of a characteristic. No one could expect to measure the memory of every human being, or test all the rats or pigeons in the world in Skinner boxes, or record the maternal behavior of all female monkeys.

In a large population we usually study a **sample** of cases of some reasonable, practical size and then generalize our results to the population as a whole. One way to guarantee that the results of our measurements are accurate for the whole population is to make sure that the sample is truly a random one.

Suppose, for example, that each household in a neighborhood is sold one chance on door prizes at a local raffle. After all the stubs are put into a big drum and churned around, a blindfolded person is asked to reach into the drum and pull out the winning numbers. The prizewinners would then constitute a **random sample** from that neighborhood because, in

"Young man, I am no random sample."
(©Punch/Rothco)

Biased sample Sample that does not truly represent a whole population.

Significance Probability that results obtained were due to chance.

theory, every single household is likely to win a prize—chance determines which households are selected.

A **biased sample** does not truly represent the population in question. If we want to find out if a town's garbage is being collected adequately, we could not just stand outside the best department store in town at 3:00 in the afternoon and ask everyone who happened by how many times his or her garbage had been collected that week and at what time. The people who shop at that department store in the middle of the afternoon on a workday are unlikely to represent the town's population. We would have to figure out how to make sure that all the town's neighborhoods will be presented proportionally in our sample.

Generalizations based on biased samples can lead to erroneous conclusions. If the advertising manager of a bank wanted to test a few potential campaigns designed to persuade all middle-aged people with incomes over $100,000 to set up trust funds for their children, she would be unwise to base her decisions on interviews with migrant workers. The classic sampling story involves a national magazine that predicted the election of a certain candidate, who then lost the election. The magazine had based its prediction on a telephone survey. The editors forgot, however, that many voters did not have telephones at that time, and it turned out that many people without phones voted for the other candidate.

Probability

Errors based on inadequate sampling procedures are somebody's fault. Other kinds of errors occur randomly. In the simplest kind of experiment a psychologist will gather a representative sample, split it randomly into two groups, and then apply some experimental manipulation to one of the groups. Afterward he will measure both groups and determine if the experimental group's score is now different from the score of the control group. But even if there is a large difference between the scores of the two groups, the psychologist may still be wrong to attribute the difference to his manipulation. Random effects might influence his results and introduce error.

Statistics give the psychologist many ways to determine precisely if the difference between the two groups is really significant, if something other than chance produced the results, and if he would get the same results if he repeated the experiment with different subjects. These probabilities are expressed as measures of **significance.** If the psychologist computes the significance level for his results as .05, he knows that there are 19 chances out of 20 that the results are not due to chance. But there is still 1 chance in 20—or a .05 likelihood—that the results are due to chance. A .01 significance level would mean that there is only 1 chance in 100 that the results are due to chance.

Glossary Index

Answers to Questions

Chapter 1
1. scientific   2. structuralism, E; functionalism, A; behaviorism, D; psychoanalysis, H; existential psychology, C; humanist psychology, F; Gestalt psychology, B; cognitive psychology, G   3. b
4. Galton   5. reinforcement
6. behavior; mental processes
7. describe; explain; predict; control   8. naturalistic observation   9. laboratory
10. independent; dependent
11. c   12. correlational   13. pure; applied   14. d   15. b

Chapter 2
1. neuron, D; nerve, A; axon, C; dendrite, B   2. positive; negative
3. relative refractory   4. F
5. neurotransmitters   6. peripheral nervous system   7. d   8. cerebral cortex   9. sensory projection areas, B; association areas, C; motor projection areas, A.   10. reticular formation   11. F   12. pancreas, C; gonads, D; thyroid, B; anterior pituitary, A   13. hormones   14. c

Chapter 3
1. F   2. difference   3. cornea, D; pupil, H; iris, A; lens, F; fovea, B; retina, E; rod, G; cone, C
4. dark   5. b   6. hue; saturation; brightness   7. subtractive
8. trichromatic   9. trichromats
10. oval window, 2; anvil, 1; cochlea, 4; auditory nerve, 5; round window, 3   11. frequency

theory, B; volley principle, A ; place theory, C   12. vestibular senses   13. b   14. taste buds; sweet; sour; salty; bitter

Chapter 4
1. perception   2. c   3. figure; ground   4. similarity, D; continuity, C; common fate, B; proximity, E; closure, a
5. perceptual constancy
6. distance; depth   7. retinal disparity, B; texture gradient, M; shadowing, M; convergence, B; motion parallax, M; accommodation, M; stereoscopic vision, B; linear perspective M; superposition, M   8. monaural
9. apparent movement   10. visual illusions   11. b   12. altered state of consciousness   13. insomnia; apnea; narcolepsy   14. delta
15. F   16. alcohol, D; amphetamines, A; barbiturates, F; opiates, B; cocaine, C; hallucinogens, E

Chapter 5
1. motives; emotions   2. c   3. F
4. hunger center; satiety center
5. d   6. testosterone   7. stimulus motives   8. sex, U; curiosity, U; affiliation, L; activity, U; power, L; aggression, L; manipulation, U; achievement, L; contact, U; avoidance of success, L
9. aggression   10. achievement
11. affiliation   12. T   13. Yerkes Dodson   14. intensity

15. Cannon-Bard, B; cognitive theory, C; James-Lange, A
16. expressive behavior   17. facial expressions; body language

Chapter 6
1. conditioning   2. before   3. c
4. spontaneous recovery
5. stimulus generalization
6. operant conditioning
7. shaping   8. primary   9. fixed-ratio schedule, B ; variable-ratio schedule, C; fixed-interval schedule, A; variable-interval schedule, D   10. increase   11. F
12. discrimination   13. d
14. observational   15. contingency

Chapter 7
1. sensory registers   2. attention
3. cocktail-party   4. short-term memory   5. decay; interference
6. proactive   7. elaborative rehearsal   8. rote rehearsal
9. semantic; episodic   10. retrieval cues   11. eidetic   12. c
13. survey, question, read, recite, review   14. T

Chapter 8
1. cognition   2. images; concepts
3. A   4. T   5. language
6. phonemes; morphemes; sentences   7. linguistic relativity
8. top-down; bottom-up   9. T
10. C; A; B; E; D   11. D
12. compensatory   13. set
14. functional fixedness   15. F
16. noncompensatory   17. B

Chapter 9

1. Cattell, C; Spearman, B; Thurstone, A; Guilford, D
2. operations, contents, products
3. IQ, 100, Binet-Simon Scale
4. T   5. Wechsler Adult Intelligence Scale (WAIS)
6. group tests, C   7. performance; culture-fair   8. d   9. reliable
10. a   11. validity   12. F   13. c
14. F   15. a

Chapter 10

1. cross-sectional   2. prenatal
3. F   4. rooting reflex, c; grasping reflex, a; sucking reflex, b
5. maturation   6. developmental norms   7. perceptual ability, b; depth perception, d; visual acuity, a; object permanence, c   8. visual cliff   9. remember   10. T
11. sensory-motor stage, d; preoperational thought, a; concrete operations, b; formal operations, c
12. schemes   13. attachment
14. social cognition

Chapter 11

1. puberty   2. menarche   3. c
4. concrete; formal
5. preconventional level, b; conventional level, a; postconventional level, c
6. identity   7. performance; verbal   8. F   9. F   10. money
11. denial, anger, bargaining, depression, acceptance   12. death denying

Chapter 12

1. personality   2. Cattell; Eysenck   3. trait
4. psychoanalysis   5. ego; id
6. primary-process thinking
7. unconscious, e; id, c; superego, f; ego, b; ego ideal, d; libido, a
8. oral, anal, phallic, latency period genital   9. self-actualizing
10. conditional positive regard
11. unstructured; structured
12. T   13. objective
14. projective

Chapter 13

1. adjustment   2. stress   3. true
4. pressure   5. frustration
6. conflict   7. approach/approach, c; avoidance/avoidance, a; approach/avoidance, b; double approach/avoidance, d   8. anxiety
9. direct; defensive   10. direct
11. feel unable to resolve
12. denial, f; repression, a; projection, g; identification, i; regression, c; intellectualization, b; reaction formation, d; displacement, e; sublimation, h
13. alarm; resistance   14. F

Chapter 14

1. F   2. medical; behavioral
3. anxiety   4. panic attacks
5. somatization disorder
6. dissociative   7. affective   8. T
9. bipolar   10. sexual dysfunction, D; paraphilias, E; fetishism, B; pedophilia, G; zoophilia, C; voyeurism, H; exhibitionism, A; sadomasochism, F   11. schizoid personality disorder, C; paranoid personality disorder, A; narcissistic personality disorder, D; antisocial personality disorder, B
12. personality   13. substance dependence   14. schizophrenic

Chapter 15

1. d   2. psychoanalysis, b; client-centered therapy, c; dynamic therapy, d; rational-emotive therapy, A   3. unconditional positive regard   4. insight; behavior   5. desensitization
6. aversive conditioning
7. Gestalt, C; sensitivity groups, A; encounter groups, D; large-group awareness training, B   8. F
9. F   10. d
11. institutionalization   12. T
13. deinstitutionalization
14. prevention

Chapter 16

1. social psychology   2. schemas, stereotype   3. primacy   4. c   5. c
6. attitude   7. F   8. b
9. cognitive dissonance   10. a
11. social influence, D; compliance, C; obedience, B; conformity, A   12. risky shift
13. polarization   14. task, interaction   15. T
16. environmental psychology
17. stress   18. F

References

Acredolo, L. P., & Hake, J. L. (1982). Infant perception. In B. B. Wolman, (Ed.), *Handbook of developmental psychology*. Englewood Cliffs, N.J.: Prentice-Hall.

Adams, J. L. (1976). *Conceptual blockbusting: A pleasureable guide to better problem solving*. San Francisco: San Francisco Book Co.

Adams, P. R., & Adams, G. R. (1984, March). Mount Saint Helen's ashfall: Evidence for a disaster stress reaction. *American Psychologist, 30*, 252–260.

Ahishal, H. S. (1979). A behavioral approach to depression. In R. A. Depue (Ed), *The psychobiology of depressive disorders: Implications for the effects of stress*. New York: Academic Press.

Adorno, T. W. et al. (1950). *The authoritarian personality*. New York: Norton.

Ajzen, I., & Fishbein, M. (1980). *Understanding attitudes and predicting behavior*. Englewood Cliffs, N.J.: Prentice-Hall.

Albee, G. W. (1982, September). Preventing psychopathology and promoting human potential. *American Psychologist, September, 37*, 1043–1050.

Allen, V. L., & Levine, J. M. (1971). Social support and conformity: The role of independent assessment of reality. *Journal of Experimental Social Psychology, 7*, 48-58.

Allport, G. W. (1954). *The nature of prejudice*. New York: Anchor.

Allport, G. W., & Odbert, H. S. (1936). Trait-names: A psycholexical study. *Psychological Monographs, 47* (1, Whole No. 211).

Alpern, D. M., & Agrest, S. (1977, August 29). Crime: Will he stand trial? *Newsweek*, p. 28.

Altman, I. (1975). *The environment and social behavior*. Monterey, CA: Brooks/Cole.

American Psychiatric Association (1980). *Diagnostic and statistical manual of mental disorders* (3rd ed.). Washington, D.C.: American Psychiatric Association.

American Psychological Association (1953). *Ethical standards of psychologists*. Washington, D.C.

American Psychological Society (1973, 1982). *Ethical principles in the conduct of research with human participants*. Washington, D.C.

Amoore, J. E., Johnston, J. W., Jr., & Rubin, M. (1961, February). The stereo-chemical theory of odor. *Scientific American*, pp. 42–49.

Anastasi, A. (1976). *Psychological testing*. New York: Macmillan.

Anastasi, A. (1981). Coaching, test sophistication, and developed abilities. *American Psychologist, 36* (10), 1086–1093.

Anastasi, A. (1982). *Psychological testing* (5th ed). New York: Macmillan.

Anderson, A. (1982, December). How the mind heals. *Psychology Today*, pp. 51–56.

Anderson, N. H., & Hubert, S. (1963). Effects of concomitant recall on order effects in personality impression formation. *Journal of Verbal Learning and Verbal Behavior, 2*, 379–391.

Archer, W. (1935). *On dreams*. London: Methuen.

Arieti, S. (Ed.), (1975). *American handbook of psychiatry* (Vol. VI, chap. 36). New York: Basic Books.

Arlin, P. K. (1975). Cognitive development in adulthood: A fifth stage? *Developmental Psychology, 11*, 602–606.

Argyle, M., & McHenry, R. (1971). Do spectacles really affect judgments of intelligence? *British Journal of Social and Clinical Psychology, 10*, 27–29.

Arnheim, R. (1969). *Visual thinking*. Berkeley: University of California Press.

Arnold, M. B. (1960). *Emotion and personality* (2 Vols.). New York: Columbia University Press.

Aronson, E. (1980). *The social animal*. San Francisco: Freeman.

Aronson, E. (1984). *The social animal* (4th ed.). New York: W. H. Freeman.

Aronson, E., Cookie, S., Sikes, J., Blaney, N., & Snapp, M. (1978). *The jigsaw classroom*. Beverly Hills, Ca: Sage.

Aronson, E., & Cope, V. (1968). My enemy's enemy is my friend. *Journal of Personality and Social Psychology, 8*, 8–12.

Aronson, E., & Lindner, D. E. (1965). Gain and loss of esteem as determinants of interpersonal attractiveness. *Journal of Experimental Social Psychology, 1*, 156–171.

Aronson, E., Willerman, B., & Floyd, J. (1966). The effect of a pratfall on increasing interpersonal attractiveness. *Psychonomic Science, 4*, 227–228.

Asch, S. (1946). Forming impressions of personality. *Journal of Abnormal and Social Psychology, 41*, 258–290.

Asch, S. (1956). Studies of independence and conformity: I. A minority of one against a unanimous majority. *Psychological Monographs, 70*, No. 9.

Asch, S. E. (1951). Effects of group pressure upon the modification and distortion of judgments. In H. Guetzkow (Ed.), *Groups, leadership, and men*. Pittsburgh: Carnegie Press.

Atchley, R. C. (1975). Dimensions of widowhood in later life. *Gerontologist, 15,* 176–178.

Atchley, R. C. (1976). *The sociology of retirement.* Cambridge, Mass.: Schenkman.

Atkinson, J. W., & Birch, D. (1970). *The dynamics of action.* New York: Wiley.

Atkinson, J. W., & Raynor, J. O. (1975). *Motivation and achievement.* Washington, D.C.: Winston.

Atwood, M. E., and Polson, P. G. (1976). A process model for water jug problems. *Cognitive Psychology, 8,* 191–216.

Averill, J. R., & Boothroyd, P. (1977). On falling in love in conformance with the romantic ideal. *Motivation and Emotion, 1,* 235–247.

Azzi, R., Fix, D. S. R., Keller, R. S., & Rocha e Silva, M. I. (1964). Exteroceptive control of response under delayed reinforcement. *Journal of the Experimental Analysis of Behavior, 7,* 159–162.

Bachtold, L. M., & Werner, E. E. (1973). Personality characteristics of creative women. *Percept. Mot. Skills, 36,,* 311–319.

Backman, C. W., & Secord, P. F. (1959). The effect of perceived liking on interpersonal attraction. *Human Relations, 12,* 379–384.

Bager, N., & Schurr, C. (1976), *Sexual assault.* New York: Grosset & Dunlop.

Balagura, S. (1973). *Hunger: A biopsychological analysis.* New York: Basic Books.

Bandura, A. (1962). Social learning through imitation. In M. R. Jones (Ed.), *Nebraska symposium on motivation.* Lincoln: University of Nebraska Press.

Bandura, A. (1965). Influence of models' reinforcement contingencies on the acquisition of imitative responses. *Journal of Personality and Social Psychology, 1,* 6, 589–595.

Bandura, A. (1973). *Aggression: A social learning analysis.* Englewood Cliffs, N.J.: Prentice-Hall.

Bandura, A. (1977). *Social learning theory.* Englewood Cliffs, N.J.: Prentice-Hall.

Bandura, A., Ross, D., & Ross, S. A. (1963). Transmission of aggression through imitation of aggressive models. *Journal of Abnormal and Social Psychology, 63,* 575–582.

Bargh, J. A. (1983). Automatic and conscious processing of social information. In R. S. Wyer & T. K. Srull (Eds.), *The handbook of social cognition.* Hillsdale, N.J.: Erlbaum.

Baron, R. A., & Byrne, D. (1981). *Social psychology: Understanding human interaction* (3rd ed.). Boston: Allyn & Bacon.

Barron, F. (1963). *Creativity and psychological health.* Princeton, N.J.: Van Nostrand.

Barron, F., & Harrington, D. M. (1981). Creativity, intelligence, and personality. *Annual Review of Psychology, 32,* 439–76.

Barron, F., Jarvik, M., & Bunnell, S., Jr. (1964, April). The hallucinogenic drugs. *Scientific American.*

Bassuk, E. L., & Gerson, S. (1978, February). Deinstitutionalization and mental health services. *Scientific American,* pp. 46–53.

Bateson, G., Jackson, D. D., Haley, J., & Weakland, J. H. (1956). Toward a theory of schizophrenia. *Behavioral Science, 1,* 251–264.

Baum, A., & Valins, S. (1977). *Architecture and social behavior: Psychological studies of social density.* Hillsdale, N.J.: Erlbaum.

Baumrind, D. (1972). Socialization and instrumental competence in young children. In W. W. Hartup (Ed.), *The young child: Reviews of research,* (Vol. 2). Washington, D.C.: National Association for the Education of Young Children, pp. 202–224.

Baumrind, D. (1978). A dialectical materialist's perspective on knowing social reality. *New Directions for Child Development, 2.*

Baxter, D. W., & Olszewski, J. (1960). Congenital insensitivity to pain. *Brain, 1960, 83,* 381.

Bazelon, D. L. (1982, February). Veils, values, and social responsibility. *American Psychologist,* pp. 115–121.

Beaubier, J. (1980). Biological factors in aging. In C. L. Fry (Ed.), *Aging in culture and society.* Brooklyn, N.Y.: J. F. Bergin.

Beck, R. C. (1978). *Motivation: theories and principles.* Englewood Cliffs, N.J.: Prentice-Hall.

Beier, E. G. (1974, October). Nonverbal communication: how we send emotional messages. *Psychology Today,* pp. 53–56.

Belmont, L., & Marolla, F. A. (1973, December 14). Birth order, family size, and intelligence. *Science, 182*(4117), pp. 1096–1101.

Benderly, B. L. (1981, March). The multilingual mind. *Psychology Today,* pp. 9–12.

Benson, H. (1975). *The relaxation response.* New York: William Morrow.

Benson, H., Alexander, S., & Feldman, E. L. (1975). Decreased premature ventricular contractions through use of the relaxation response in patients with stable ischemic heart disease. *Lancet, 2,* 380–382.

Benson, H., Kotch, J. B., Crassweller, K. D., & Greenwood, M. M. (1979). The relaxation response. In D. Goleman & R. Davidson (Eds.), *Consciousness: Brain, states of awareness and mysticism.* New York: Harper & Row.

Benson, H., & Wallace, R. K. (1972). Decreased drug abuse with transcendental meditation—a study of 1,862 subjects. In C. J. D. Zarafonetis (Ed.), *Drug abuse proceedings of the international conference.* Philadelphia: Lea and Febiger.

Berger, R. J. (1969). The sleep and dream cycle. In A. Kales (Ed.), *Sleep: physiology and pathology.* Philadelphia: Lippincott.

Bergin, A. E. (1966). Some implications of psychotherapy research for therapeutic practice. *Journal of Abnormal Psychology, 71,* 235–246.

Bergman, J. (1974). Are little girls being harmed by Sesame Street? In J. Stacey, S. Bereaud, & J. Daniels (Eds.), *And Jill came tumbling after: Sexism in American education.* New York: Dell.

Berkowitz, L. (1973, July). The case for bottling up rage. *Psychology Today,* pp. 24–32.

Berkowitz, L. (1983, November). Aversively stimulated aggression. *American psychologist,* 1135–1144.

Berkowitz, L., & Donnerstein, E. (1982, March). External validity is more than skin deep. *American Psychologist,* pp. 245–257.

Bernstein, I. L. (1978). Learned taste aversions in children receiving chemotherapy. *Science, 200*, pp. 1302–1303.

Berscheid, E., & Walster, E. (1974). A little bit about love. In T. L. Huston (Ed.) *Foundations of interpersonal attraction.* N.Y.: Academic Press.

Berscheid, E., & Walster, E. (1978). *Interpersonal attraction.* Reading, Mass.: Addison-Wesley.

Bersoff, D. N. (1981). Testing and the law. *American Psychologist, 36* (10), pp. 1047–1056.

Bertrand, S., & Masling, J. (1969). Oral imagery and alcoholism. *Journal of Abnormal Psychology, 74*(1), 50–53.

Bettelheim, B. (1943). Individual and mass behavior in extreme situations. *Journal of Abnormal and Social Psychology, 38*, 417–452.

Bettelheim, B. (1960). *The informed heart.* New York: Free Press.

Bieber, I., et al. (1962). *Homosexuality: A psychoanalytic study.* New York: Basic Books.

Birdwhistell, R. L. (1952). *Introduction to kinesics.* Louisville, Ky.: University of Louisville Press.

Birdwhistell, R. L. (1974). Toward analyzing American movement. In S. Weitz (Ed.), *Nonverbal communication: Readings with commentary.* New York: Oxford University Press.

Birnbaum, I. M., Parker, E. S., Hartley, J. T., & Noble, E. P. (1978). Alcohol and memory: Retrieval process. *Journal of Verbal Learning and Verbal Behavior, 17*, 325–335.

Birnbaum, M. H. & Bellers, B. A. (1979). Stimulus recognition may mediate exposure effects. *Journal of Personality and Social Psychology, 37*, 391–394.

Birren, J. E. (1983, March). Aging in America: Role for psychology. *American Psychologist*, pp. 298–299.

Blake, R. R., Helson, H., & Mouton, J. (1956). The generality of conformity behavior as a function of factual anchorage, difficulty of task and amount of social pressure. *Journal of Personality, 25*, 294–305.

Blakemore, C., & Cooper, G. F. (1970). Development of the brain depends on the visual environment. *Nature, 228*, pp. 477–478.

Blasi, A. (1980). Bridging moral cognition and moral action: A critical review of the literature. *Psychological Bulletin, 88*(1), 1–45.

Block, H. H., Block, J., & Harrington, D. M. (1974). *The relationship of parental teaching strategies to ego-resiliency in preschool children.* Paper presented at the meeting of the Western Psychological Association, San Francisco.

Block, J. H. (1979). Another look at sex differentiation in the socialization behaviors of mothers and fathers. In F. Denmark & J. Sherman (Eds.), *Psychology of women: future directions of research.* New York: Psychological Dimensions, Inc.

Blum, J. M. (1979). *Pseudoscience and mental ability: The origins and fallacies of the IQ controversy.* New York: Monthly Review Press.

Bolles, R., & Fanselow, M. (1982). Endorphins and behavior. *Annual Review Psychology, 33*, 87–101.

Bolton, B. F. (1978). Sixteen personality factor questionnaire. In O. K. Burios (Ed.) *The eighth mental measurements yearbook.* Highland Park, N.J.: Gryphan, 1078–80.

Booth, A. & Welch, S. (1973). The Effects of Crowding: A cross-national study. Unpublished manuscript, Ministry of State for Urban Affairs, Ottawa, Canada, 1973.

Boring, E. G., Langfeld, H. S., Weld, H. P. (1976). *Foundations of psychology.* New York: Wiley

Bornstein, M. H., & Marks, L. E. (1982, January). Color revisionism. *Psychology Today*, pp. 64–71.

Botwinick, J. (1967). *Cognitive processes in maturity and old age.* New York: Springer.

Bowd, A. D. (1980, February). Ethics and animal experimentation. *American Psychologist*, pp. 224–225.

Bower, T. G. R. (1971, October). The object in the world of the infant. *Scientific American*, pp. 20–38.

Bower, T. G. R. (1972). Object perception in infants. *Perception, 1*, 15–30.

Bower, T. G. R. (1976). Repetitive processes in child development. *Scientific American, 235*(5), 38–47.

Bower, T. G. R. (1977). Comment on Yonas et al., Development of sensivity to information for impending collision. *Perception and Psychophysics, 21*, 281–282.

Bower. T. G. R. (1982). *Development in infancy,* **(2nd ed.)** San Francisco: Freeman.

Brady, J. V., et al. (1958). Avoidance behavior and the development of gastroduodenal ulcers, *Journal of the Experimental Analysis of Behavior, 1*, 69–72.

Bramel, D. (1962). A dissonance theory approach to defensive projection. *Journal of Abnormal and Social Psychology, 64*, 121–129.

Brazelton, 1983.

Breland, K., & Breland, M. The misbehavior of organisms. In M. E. P. Seligman & J. L. Hager (Eds.) (1972). *Biological boundaries of learning.* Englewood Cliffs, N.J.: Prentice-Hall.

Brenner, M. H. (1973). *Mental illness and the economy.* Cambridge, Mass.: Harvard University Press.

Brenner, M. H. (1979). Influence of the social environment on psychopathology: The historic perspective. In J. E. Barrett (Ed.), *Stress and mental disorder.* N.Y.: Raven Press.

Brock, T. C., & Balloun, J. L. (1967). Behavioral receptivity to dissonant information. *Journal of Personality and Social Psychology, 6*, 413–428.

Broderick, C. B. (1982). Adult sexual development. In B. B. Wolman (Ed.), *Handbook of developmental psychology.* Englewood Cliffs, N.J.: Prentice-Hall.

Brody, N. (1980). Social motivation. *Annual Reveiw of Psychology, 31*, 143–168.

Bronfenbrenner, U. (1977). Toward an experimental ecology of human development. *American Psychologist, 32*(7), pp. 513–531.

Brooks, A. D. (1974). *Law, psychiatry, and the mental health system.* Boston: Little, Brown.

Broughton, R. J. (1975). Biorhythmic variations in consciousness and psychological functions. *Canadian Psychological Review, 16*, 217–239.

Brown, B., & Grotberg, (1980). "Heat start: A successful experiment." *Courrier* (Paris: International Children's Centre.)

Bourne, L. E. Jr., Dominowski, R. L., & Loftus, E. F. (1979). *Cognitive processes.* Englewood Cliffs, N.J.: Prentice-Hall.

Brown, P. L., & Jenkins, H. M. (1968). Autoshaping of the pigeon's key peck. *Journal of Experimental and Analytical Behavior, 11*, 1–8.

Brown, R., & Kulik, J. (1982; orig. pub. 1877). *Cognition, 5*, 73–99. Reprinted in U. Neisser (Ed.), *Memory observed: Remembering in natural contexts.* San Francisco: W. H. Freeman.

Brown, R. W., & Berko, J. (1960). Word association and the acquisition of grammar. *Child Development, 31,* 1–14.

Brown, R. W., & Lenneberg, E. H. (1954). A study in language and cognition. *Journal of Abnormal Social Psychology, 49,* 454–462.

Browning, D. (1982, February). Waiting for mommy. *Texas monthly,* pp. 124–131, 183–192, 197.

Brownmiller, S. (1975). *Against our will: men, women and rape,* N.Y.: Simon and Schuster.

Bruch, C. B. (1971). Modification of procedures for identification of the disadvantaged gifted. *Gifted Child Quarterly, 15,* 267–272.

Bruner, J. S., & Koslowski, B. (1972). Visually preadapted constituents of manipulatory action. *Perception, 1,* 3–14.

Buchsbaum, M. S. (1983, July). "The Mind Readers: An Action Portfolio of the Working Brain." *Psychology Today,* pp. 58–62.

Buchsbaum, M. S., & Haier, R. J. (1983). Psychopathology: Biological approaches. *Annual Review Psychology, 34,* 401–30.

Bucher, R., & Lovaas, O. I. (1968). Use of aversive stimulation in behavior modification. In M. R. Jones (Ed.) *Miami Symposium on the prediction of behavior: Aversive Stimulation.* Coral Gables, Fla.: University of Miami Press.

Budzynski, T., Stoyva, J., & Adler, C. (1970). Feedback-induced muscle relaxation: Application to tension headache. *Journal of Behavior Therapy and Experimental Psychiatry, 1,* 205–211.

Buss, A. H., Plomin, R., & Willerman, L. (1973). The inheritance of temperaments. *Journal of Personality, 41.*

Buss, A. H. (1980). *Self-consciousness and social anxiety.* San Francisco: Freeman.

Butler, R. N. (1963). The life review: An interpretation of reminiscence in the aged. *Psychiatry, 26,* 63–76.

Butter, M. (1982), Social-emotional consequences of day care for preschool children. In E. F. Zigler & E. W. Gordon (Eds.) *Day care: scientific and social policy issues.* Boston: Auburn House.

Byrne, D. (1961). Interpersonal attraction and attitude similarity. *Journal of Abnormal and Social Psychology, 62,* 713–715.

Byrne, D. (1977). The imagery of sex. In Money, J. and Masaph, H. (eds.), Handbook of sexology, pp. 327–350. N.Y.: Elsevier/North Holland.

Byrne, D., & Blaylock, B. (1963). Similarity and assumed similarity of attitudes between husbands and wives. *Journal of Abnormal and Social Psychology, 67,* 636–640.

Byrne, D., London, O., & Reeves, K. (1968). The effects of physical attractiveness, sex, and attitude similarity on interpersonal attracton. *Journal of Personality, 36,* 259–271.

Byrne, D., & Nelson, D. (1964). Attraction as a function of attitude similarity-dissimilarity: The effect of topic importance. *Psychonomic Science, 1,* 93–94.

Byrne, D., & Nelson, D. (1965). Attraction as a linear function of properties of positive reinforcements. *Journal of Personality and Social Psychology, 1,* 659–663.

Byrne, D., & Wong, T. J. (1962). Racial prejudice, interpersonal attraction, and assumed dissimilarity of attitudes. *Journal of Abnormal and Social Psychology, 65,* 246–253.

Cain. W. S. (1981, July). Educating your nose. *Psychology Today,* pp. 48–56.

Calder, B. J., Insko, C. A., & Yandell, B. (1974). The relation of cognitive and memorial processes to persuasion in simulated jury trial. *Journal of Applied Social Psychology, 4,* 62–92.

Calhoun, J. B. (1962). Population density and social pathology. *Scientific American, 206,* pp. 139–148.

Campbell, A. (1975, May). The American way of mating: marriage si, children only maybe. *Psychology Today,* pp. 39–42.

Campbell, A. (1976). Subjective measures of well-being. *American Psychologist, 31,* pp. 117–124.

Campos, J. L., Langer, A., & Krowitz, A. (1970). Cardiac responses on the visual cliff in prelocomotor human infants. *Science, 170,* 196–197.

Carlson, N. R. (1980). *Physiology of Behavior* (2nd ed.). Boston: Allyn & Bacon.

Carlson, R. (1980). Studies of Jungian typology: II. Representations of the personal world. *Journal of Personality and Social Psychology, 38,* 801–810.

Carlson, R. & Levy, N. (1973). Studies of Jungian typology: I. Memory, social perception, and social action. *Journal of Personality, 41,* 559–576.

Carroll, J. B., & Horn, J. L. (1981). On the scientific basis of ability testing. *American Psychologist, 36*(10), pp. 1012–1020.

Carroll, J. L. & Rest, J. R. (1982). Moral development. In B. Wolmar (Ed.) *Handbook of developmental psychology.* Englewood Cliffs: Prentice-Hall.

Carroll, J. M., Thomas, J. C., & Malhotra, A. (1980). Presentation and representation in design problem solving. *British Journal of Psychology, 71,* 143–153.

Cartwright, D. S. (1956). Self-consistency as a factor affecting immediate recall. *Journal of Abnormal and Social Psychology, 52,* 212–218.

Carver, C. S., DeGregorio, E., & Gillis, R. (1980). Ego-defensive bias in attribution among two categories of observers. *Personality and Social Psychology Bulletin, 6,* 44–50.

Catania, A. C., & Cutts, D. (1963). Experimental control of superstitious responding in humans. *Journal of the Experimental Analysis of Behavior, 6,* 203–208.

Cattell, R. B. (1965). *The scientific analysis of personality.* Baltimore: Penguin.

Cattell, R. B. (1971). *Abilities; Their structure, growth, and action.* Boston: Houghton-Mifflin.

Cattell, R. B. & P. Kline (1977). *The scientific analysis of personality and motivation.* New York: Academic Press.

Chaikin, A. L., & Darley, J. M. (1973). Victim or perpetrator?: Defensive attribution of responsibility and the need for order and justice. *Journal of Personality and Social Psychology, 25,* 268–275.

Chaiken, S., & Eagly, A. H. (1976). Communication modality as a determinant of message persuasiveness and message comprehensibility. *Journal of Personality and Social Psychology, 34,* 605–614.

Chase, W. G., & Simon, H. A. (1973). Perception in chess. *Cognitive Psychology, 4,* 55–81.

Chavis, D. M., Stucky, P. E., & Wandersman, A. (1983, April). Returning basic research to the community. *American Psychologist,* pp. 424–434.

Chiriboga, D. A. (1978). Evaluated time: A life course perspective. *Journal of Gerontology, 33,* 388–393.

Chodorkoff, B. (1954). Self perception, perceptual defense,

and adjustment. *Journal of Abnormal and Social Psychology, 49,* 508–512.

Chomsky, N. (1965). *Aspects of the theory of syntax.* Cambridge, Mass.: M.I.T. Press.

Christian, J. J., Flyger, V., & Davis, D. (1960). Factors in the mass mortality of a herd of sika deer. *Carvus Nippon. Chesapeake Science, 1,* 79–95.

Chu, G. C. (1967). Prior familiarity, perceived bias, and one-sided versus two-sided communications. *Journal of Experimental Social Psychology, 3,* 243–254.

Chumlea, W. C. (1982). Physical growth in adolescence. In B. B. Wolman (ed.), *Handbook of developmental psychology.* Englewood Cliffs, N.J.: Prentice-Hall.

Cialdini, R. B., Cacioppo, J. T., Bassett, R., & Miller, J. A. (1978). Lowball procedure for producing compliance: Commitment then cost. *Journal of Personality and Social Psychology, 36,* 463–476.

Cialdini, R. B., Vincent, J. E., Lewis, S. K., Catalan, J., Wheeler, D., & Darby, B. L. (1975). A reciprocal concessions procedure for inducing compliance: The door-in-the-face technique. *Journal of Personality and Social Psychology, 21,* 206–215.

Clark, H. H., & Clark, E. V. (1977). *Psychology and language: An introduction to psycholinguistics.* New York: Harcourt Brace Jovanovich.

Clark, M., Gosnell, M., Shapiro, D., Huck, J., & Marbach, W. D. (1979, November 12). Drugs and psychiatry: A new era. *Newsweek.* pp. 101.

Clark, M., & Hager, M. (1979, September) 24. Valium abuse: The yellow peril. *Newsweek,* p. 66.

Clark, R. D., & Word, L. E. (1974). Where is the apathetic bystander? Situational characteristics of the emergency. *Journal of Personality and Social Psychology, 29,* 279–287.

Clarren, S. K., & Smith, D. (1978). The fetal alcohol syndrome. *New England Journal of Medicine, 298,* 1063–1067.

Clausen, J. A. (1975). The social meaning of differential physical and sexual maturation. In S. E. Dragstin & G. H. Elder (Eds.), *Life cycle: psychological and social context.* New York: Wiley.

Clore, G. L. & Baldridge, B. (1968). Interpersonal attraction: the role of agreement and topic interest. *Journal of Personality and Social Psychology, 9,* 340–346.

Clore, G. L., Bray, R. B., Atkin, S. M., & Murphy, P. (1978). Interracial attitudes and behavior at a summer camp. *Journal of personality and Social Psychology, 36,* 107–116.

Cohen, D. B. (1976). Dreaming: Experimental investigation of representation and adaptive properties. In G. Schwartz & D. Shapiro (Eds)., *Consciousness and self-regulation.* New York: Plenum.

Cohen, L. B. (1979). Our developing knowledge of infant perception and cognition. *American Psychologist, 34,* 894–899.

Cohen, R. A. (1969). Conceptual styles, culture conflict, and nonverbal tests. *American Anthropologist, 71,* 828–856.

Cole, J., & Davis, J. M. (1975) Anti-anxiety drugs. In S. Arieti (Ed.), *American handbook of psychiatry* (Vol. V). New York: Basic Books.

Cole, N. S. (1981). Bias in testing. *American Psychologist, 36*(10), pp. 1067–1077.

Colegrove, F. W. (1982; orig. pub. 1899). Individual memories, *American Journal of Psychology, 10,* 228–255. Reprinted in U. Neisser, (Ed.), *Memory observed: Remem-*

bering in natural contexts. San Francisco: W. H. Freeman.

Coleman, J. C. (1979). Contemporary psychology and effective behavior (4th ed.). Glenview, Ill.: Scott, Foresman.

Coleman, J. C., Butcher, J. N., & Carson, R. C. (1984) *Abnormal psychology and modern life.* (7th ed.). Glenview, Ill.: Scott, Foresman.

Coleman, J. C., & Hammen, C. L. (1974). *Contemporary psychology and effective behavior.* Glenview, Ill.: Scott, Foresman.

Coleman, J. S. (1974). *Youth: Transition to adulthood* (Report of the President's Science Advisory Committee). Chicago: University of Chicago Press.

Collings, V. B. (1974). Human taste response as a function of locus of stimulation on the tongue and soft palate. *Perception and Psychophysics, 16,* 169–197.

Comfort, A. (1976). *A good age.* New York: Crown.

Commons, M. L., Richards, F. A. & Armon, S., (1982). *Beyond formal operations: Late adolescent and adult cognitive development.* New York: Praeger.

Conger, J. J. (1977). *Adolescence and youth: Psychological development in a changing world* (2nd ed.). New York: Harper & Row.

Conger, J. J., & Peterson, A. C. (1984). *Adolescence and youth,* 3rd ed. New York: Harper & Row.

Conway, F., & Siegelman, J. (1980). *Snapping.* New York: Dell.

Cook. S. W. (1976). Ethical issues in the conduct of research in social relations. In P. Nejelski (Ed.), *Social research in conflict with law and ethics.* Cambridge, Mass.: Ballinger.

Coombs, C. H., Coombs, L. C., & McClelland, G. H. (1975). Preference scales for number and sex of children. *Population Studies, 29,* 273–298.

Cooper, J. (1971). Personal responsibility and dissonance. *Journal of Personality and Social Psychology, 18,* 354–363.

Cooper, J., & Croyle, R. T. (1984). Attitudes and attitude change. *Annual Review of Psychology, 35,* 395–426.

Cooper, R., & Zubek, J. (1958). Effects of enriched and restricted early environments on the learning ability of bright and dull rats. *Canadian Journal of Psychology, 12,* 159–164.

Coopersmith, S. (1967). *The antecedents of self-esteem.* San Francisco: W. H. Freeman.

Coppen, A., Metcalfe, M., & Wood, K. (1982). Lithium. In E. S. Payhel (Ed.), *Handbook of affective disorders.* New York: Guilford Press.

Cornell, J. C. (1984, March) vs. the paranormal. *Psychology Today,* 28–34.

Cotter, L. H. (1967). Operant conditioning in a Vietnamese mental hospital. *American Journal of Psychiatry, 124,* 23–28.

Cowen, E. L. (1982). Help is where you find it: Four informal helping groups. *American Psychologist, 37,* 385–395.

Cowen, E. L., Pederson, A., Babijian, H., Izzo, L. D., & Trost, M. A. Long-term follow-up of early detected vulnerable children. *Journal of Clinical and Consulting Psychology, 41,* 438–446.

Craig, G. J. (1980). *Human development.* Englewood Cliffs, N.J.: Prentice-Hall.

Craig, G. J. (1980). *Human development* (2nd ed.). Englewood Cliffs, N.J.: Prentice-Hall.

Craig, G. (1983). *Human development.* (3rd ed.). Englewood Cliffs, N.J.: Prentice-Hall.

Craik, F.I.M., & Watkins, M. J. The role of rehearsal in short-term memory. *Journal of Verbal Learning and Verbal Behavior, 12,* 599–607.

Crockenberg, S. B. (1980). Creativity tests: A boon or boondoggle for education? *Review of Educational Research, 42,* 27–44.

Cronbach, L. J. (1970). *Essentials of psychological testing.* New York: Harper & Row.

Cumming, E., & Henry, W. E. (1961). *Growing old: The process of disengagement.* New York: Basic Books.

Cunningham, S. (1983, June). Animal activists rally in streets, urge Congress to tighten laws. *APA Monitor,* pp. 1, 27.

Curtis, H. J. (1965). The somatic mutation theory. In R. Kastenbaum (ed.), *Contributions.*

Cutrona, C. E., (1982). Transition to college: Loneliness and the process of social adjustment. In L. A. Peplau & D. Perlman (eds.), *Loneliness: A sourcebook of current theory, research, and therapy.* New York: Wiley.

Dabbs, J. M., & Leventhal, H. (1966). Effects of varying the recommendations in a fear-arousing communication. *Journal of Personality and Social Psychology, 4,* 525–531.

Dalal, A. S., & Barber, T. X. (1970). Yoga and hypnotism. In T. X. Barber (Ed.), *LSD, marijuana, yoga and hypnosis.* Chicago: Aldine.

D'Amato, M.R. (1974). Derived motives. *Annual Review of Psychology, 25,* 83–106.

Darley, J. M. & Latané, B. (1968). Bystander intervention in emergencies: Diffusion of responsibility. *Journal of Personality and Social Psychology, 8,* 377–383.

Darwin, Charles. (1872). *The expression of the emotions in man and animals.* London: John Murray.

Davison, G. C., & Stuart, R. B. (1975). Behavior therapy and civil liberties. *American Psychologist, 30,* 755–763.

Davitz, J. (1952). The effects of previous training on postfrustration behavior. *Journal of Abnormal and Social Psychology, 47,* 309–315.

Dean, S. R. (1970). Is there an ultraconscious? *Canadian Psychiatric Association Journal, 15,* 57–61.

Deaux, K., & Wrightsman, L. (1984). *Social psychology in the 80s* (4th ed.). Monterey, CA: Brooks/Cole.

de Beauvoir, S. (1972). *The coming of age* (Patrick O'Brian, trans.). New York: Putnam.

de Charms, R. (1968). *Review of theories of motivation: From mechanism to cognition* by B. Weiner. *Contemporary Psychology, 19,* 4–6.

de Charms, R., & Muir, M. S. (1978). Motivation: Social approaches. *Annual Review of Psychology,* 91–113.

de Groot, A. D. (1966). Perception and memory versus thought: Some old ideas and recent findings. In B. Kleinmuntz (Ed.), *Problem Solving: Research, Method and Theory,* Wiley.

de Groot, A. D. (1981, May 4). A drug to make people smarter? *Newsweek.*

Deikman, A.J. (1973). Deautomatization and the mystic experience. In R. E. Ornstein (Ed.), *The nature of human consciousness.* San Francisco: Freeman.

Dekker, E., Pelser, H. E., & Groen, J. (1957). Conditioning as a cause of asthmatic attacks. *Journal of Psychosomatic Research, 2,* 97–108.

Delgado, J.M.R. (1969). *Physical control of the mind: Toward a psycho-civilized society.* New York: Harper & Row.

Dember, W. N. (1965). The new look in motivation. *American Scientist, 53,* 409–427.

Dember, W. N., Earl, R. W., & Paradise, N. (1957). Response by rats to differential stimulus complexity. *Journal of Comparative and Physiological Psychology, 50,* 514–518.

Dement, W. C., (1965). An essay on dreams: The role of physiology in understanding their nature. In F. Barron et al. (Eds.), *New directions in psychology* (Vol. 2). New York: Holt, Rinehart and Winston.

Dement, W. C. (1974). *Some must watch while some must sleep.* San Francisco: Freeman.

Dement, W. C., Cohen, H., Ferguson, J., & Zarcone, V. (1970). A sleep researcher's odyssey: The function and clinical significance of REM sleep. In L. Madow and L. H. Snow (Eds.), *The psychodynamic implications of the physiological studies on dreams.* Springfield, Ill.: Charles C. Thomas.

Dement, W. C., & Wolpert, E. (1958). Relation of eye movements, body motility, and external stimuli to dream content. *Journal of Experimental Psychology, 55,* 543–553.

Denney, N. W. (1982). Aging and cognitive changes. In B. B. Wolman (Ed.), *Handbook of developmental psychology.* Englewood Cliffs, N.J.: Prentice-Hall.

Dennis, W. (1966). Creative productivity between the ages of 20 and 80 years. *Journal of Gerontology, 21,* 1–8.

Dennis, W., & Dennis, M. G. (1940). The effect of cradling practices upon the onset of walking in Hopi children. *Journal of Genetic Psychology, 56,* 77–86.

Dent, J. Y. (1954). Dealing with the alcoholic at home. *Medical World of London, 81,* 245.

Dermer, M., & Thiel, D. J. (1975). When beauty may fail. *Journal of Personality and Social Psychology, 31,* 1168–1176.

DeValois, R. L., & DeValois, K. K. (1975). Neural coding of color. In E. C. Carterette & M. P. Friedman (Eds.), *Handbook of perception: Seeing* (Vol. 5). New York: Academic Press, pp. 117–166.

DeVries, H., & Stuiver, M. (1961). The absolute sensitivity of the human sense of smell. In W. A. Rosenblith (Ed.), *Sensory communication.* Cambridge, Mass.: MIT Press.

DiCaprio, N. S. (1983). *Personality Theories: A guide to human nature* (2nd ed.) New York: Holt.

Dickinson, A., & Mackintosh, N. J. (1978). Classical conditioning in animals. *Annual Review of Psychology, 29,* 587–612.

DiFranco, D., Muir, D. W., & Dodwell, P. C. (1978). Reaching in very young infants. *Perception, 7,* 385–392.

Dimond, E. G. (1971). Acupuncture anaesthesia. *Journal of the American Medical Association, 218,* 1558.

Dion, K. K., Berscheid, E., & Walster, E. (1972). What is beautiful is good. *Journal of Personality and Social Psychology, 24,* 285–290.

Dirks, J., & Gibson, E. (1977). Infants' perception of similarity between live people and their photographs. *Child Development, 48,* 124–130.

Dobzhansky, T. (1973, December). Differences are not deficits. *Psychology Today,* pp. 97–101.

Dollard, J., & Miller, N.E. (1950). *Personality and psychotherapy.* New York: McGraw-Hill.

Donahue, W., Orbach, H. L., & Pollack, O. (1960). Retirement: The emerging social pattern. In C. Tibbets (Ed.), *Handbook of social gerontology*. Chicago: University of Chicago Press.

Doherty, W., & Jacobson, N. (1982). Marriage and the family. In B. Wolman (Ed.) *Handbook of developmental Psychology*. Englewood Cliffs, N.J.: Prentice-Hall.

Dohrenwend, B. S. (1973). Social status and stressful life events. *J. Pers. Soc. Psychol.* 28:225–35.

Donnerstein, E., & Wilson, D. W. (1976). The effects of noise and perceived control upon ongoing and subsequent aggressive behavior. *Journal of Personality and Social Psychology, 34,* 774–781.

Doob, A. N., & Wood, L. (1972). Catharsis and aggression: The effects of annoyance and retaliation on aggressive behavior. *Journal of Personality and Social Psychology, 22,* 156–162.

Dreyer, P. H. (1982). Sexuality during adolescence. In B. B. Wolman (Ed.), *Handbook of developmental psychology*. Englewood Cliffs, N.J.: Prentice-Hall.

Dubois, P. M. (1981). *The hospice way of death.* New York: Human Sciences Press.

Dunkle, T. (1982, April). The sound of silence. *Science '82,* pp. 30–33.

Dweck, C. S., & Reppucci, N. D. (1973). Learned helplessness and reinforcement responsibility in children. *Journal of Personality and Social Psychology, 25,* 109–116.

Eagly, A. H. (1978). Sex differences in influenceability. *Psychological Bulletin, 85,* 86–116.

Eagly, A. H. (1983, September). Gender and social influence: A social psychological analysis. *American Psychologist,* pp. 971–981.

Eimas, P. D., & Tartter, V. C. (1979). The development of speech perception. In H. W. Reese & L. P . Lipsitt (Eds.), *Advances in child development and behavior,* (Vol. 13). New York: Academic Press.

Eisdorfer, C. (1983, February). Conceptual models of aging: The challenge of a new frontier. *American Psychologist,* pp. 197–202.

Ekman, P. (1980). *The face of man.* Garland STPM Press.

Ekman, P., & Oster, H. (1979). Facial expressions of emotion. *Annual Review of Psychology, 30,* 527–554.

Elder, G. H. (1963). Parental power legitimation and its effect on the adolescent. *Sociometry, 26,* 50–65.

Elkind, D. (1968). Cognitive development in adolescence. In J. F. Adams (Ed.), *Understanding adolescence.* Boston: Allyn and Bacon.

Elkind, D. (1969). Egocentrism in adolescence. In R. E. Grinder (Ed.), *Studies in adolescence* (2nd ed.). New York: Macmillan.

Ellis, A. (1973). *Humanistic psychotherapy: The rational emotive approach.* New York: Julian Press.

Ellsworth, P. C. (1977). From abstract ideas to concrete instances: Some guidelines for choosing natural research settings. *American Psychologist, 32*(8), pp. 604–615.

Elstein, A. A., Shulman, L. S., & Sprafka, S. A. (1978). *Medical problem solving.* Cambridge, MA: Harvard University Press.

Engen, T. (1973). The sense of smell. *Annual Review of Psychology, 24,* 187–206.

Entwisle, D. R., & Hayduk, L. A. (1978). *Too great expectations.* Baltimore: Johns Hopkin's Unversity Press.

Epstein, A. N., Fitzsimmons, J. T. & Simons, B. (1969). Drinking caused by the intracranial injection of angiotensin into the rat. *Journal of Physiology,* London, *200,* 98–100.

Epstein, S. (1962). The measurement of drive and conflict in humans: Theory and experiment. In M. R. Jones (Ed.), *Nebraska symposium on motivation.* Lincoln: University of Nebraska Press.

Eran, L. E., & Peterson, R. A. (1982). Abnormal behavior: Social approaches. *Annual Review of Psychology, 33,* 231–264.

Ericsson, K. A., & Chase, W. G. (1982, November-December). Exceptional memory. *American Scientist,* pp. 607–615.

Erikson, E. H. (1963). *Childhood and society* (2nd ed.). New York: Norton.

Erikson, E. H. (1968). *Identity: Youth in crisis.* New York: Norton.

Eron, L. D. (1982). Parent-child interaction, television violence, and aggression of children. *American Psychologist, 37,* 2, pp. 197–211.

Evans, D. R., Newcombe, R. G., & Campbell, H. (1979). Maternal smoking habits and congenital malformations: A population study. *British Medical Journal, 2,* 171–173.

Evans. L. I., Rozelle, R. M., Lasater, T. M., Dembroski, R. M., & Allen, B. P. (1970). Fear arousal, persuasion and actual vs. implied behavioral change: New perspective utilizing a real-life dental hygiene program. *Journal of Personality and Social Psychology, 16,* 220–227.

Evans, R. B. (1969). Childhood parental relationships of homosexual men. *Journal of Consulting and Clinical Psychology, 33,* 129–135.

Exner, J. E., & Weiner, I. B. (1982). *The Rorschach: A comprehensive system.* New York: Wiley.

Eyer, J. (1977). Prosperity as a cause of death. *International Journal of Health Services, 7,* 125–150.

Eysenck, H. J. (1952). The effects of psychotherapy: An evaluation. *Journal of Consulting and Clinical Psychology, 16,* 319–324.

Eysenck, H. J. (1967). The biological basis of personality. Springfield, Ill.: Charles C. Thomas.

Eysenck, H. J. (1970). *The structure of human personality* (3rd ed.). London: Methuen.

Eysenck, H. J. (1973). *Eysenck on extraversion.* New York: Wiley.

Eysenck, H. J., Wakefield, J. A., Jr., & Friedman, A. F. (1983). Diagnosis and clinical assessment: The DSM-III. *Annual Review of Psychology, 34,* 167–93.

Fagan, J. F., III (1973). Infant's delayed recognition: Memory and forgetting. *Journal of Experimental Child Psychology, 16,* 424–450.

Fagot, B. I. (1974). Sex differences in toddlers' behavior and parental reactions. *Developmental Psychology, 10,* 554–558.

Fantz, R. L. (1961, May). The origin of form perception. *Scientific American,* pp. 450–463.

Fantz, R. L. (1965). Visual perception from birth as shown by pattern selectivity. *Annals of the New York Academy of Sciences, 118,* 793–814.

Farber, Susan. (1981, January). "Telltale Behavior of Twins." *Psychology Today,* pp. 58–62; 79–80.

Fast, J. (1970). *Body language.* New York: M. Evans.

Feshback, S. (1976). The use of behavior modification procedures: a comment on Stoltz et al. *American Psychologist, 31,* 538–541.

Feshback & B. Weiner (1982). *Personality.* Lexington, MA.: D. C. Heath.

Festinger, L. (1954). A theory of social comparison processes. *Human Relations, 2*(2), 117–140.

Festinger, L. (1957). *A theory of cognitive dissonance.* Evanston, Ill.: Row, Peterson.

Festinger, L., Schachter, S., & Back, K. (1950). *Social pressures in informal groups: A study of human factors in housing.* New York: Harper & Row.

Fiedler, F. E. (1967). *A theory of leadership effectiveness.* New York: McGraw-Hill.

Fiedler, F. E. (1981). Leadership effectiveness. *Behavioral Scientist, 24,* 619–623.

Fiedler, F. E. & Chemers, M. H. (1974). *Leadership and Effective Management.* Glenview, Ill.: Scott, Foresman.

Field, T., & Widmayor, S. (1982). Motherhood. In B. Wolman (Ed.). *Handbook of developmental psychology.* Englewood Cliffs, N.J.: Prentice-Hall.

Figis, E. (1970). *Patriarchal attitudes.* London: Faber & Faber.

Finkelstein, P., Wenegrat, B., & Yalom, I. (1982). Large group awareness training. *Annual Review Psychology, 33,* 515–539.

Fishbein, M., & Ajzen, I. (1975). *Belief, attitude, intention and behavior: An introduction to theory and research.* Reading, Mass.: Addison-Wesley.

Fisher, J. D., & Byrne, D. (1975). Too close for comfort: Sex differences in response to invasions of personal space. *Journal of Personality and Social Psychology, 32,* 15–21.

Fisher, S., & Greenberg, R. P. (1977). *The scientific credibility of Freud's theories and therapy.* New York: Basic Books.

Fishman, D. B. & Neigher, W. D. (1982, May). American psychology in the eighties. *American Psychologist,* pp. 533–546.

Fliegler, L. A., & Bish, C. E. (1959). The gifted and talented. *Review of Educational Research, 29,* 408–450.

Foulkes, D. (1966). *The psychology of sleep.* New York: Scribner's.

Fox, L. H. (1981). Identification of the academically gifted. *American Psychologist, 36,* (10), pp. 1103–1111.

Frankenhauser, M. (1979), Psychoneuroendocrine endocrine approaches to the study of emotion as related to stress and coping. Nebraska Symposium on Motivation, The University of Nebraska Press.

Fraser, C. (1971). Group risk-taking and group polarization. *European Journal of Social Psychology, 1,* 7–30.

Freedman, J. L., & Fraser, S. C. (1966). Compliance without pressure: The foot-in-the-door technique. *Journal of Personality and Social Psychology, 4,* 195–202.

Freudenberger, H. (1983). The public lectures. *The Monitor* (APA). p. 24.

Friedan, B. (1963) *The feminine mystique.* New York: Norton.

Friedman, M., & Rosenman, R. H. (1974). *Type A behavior and your heart.* New York: Knopf.

Friedrich, O. (1983, August 15). What do babies know? *Time,* pp. 52–60.

Freize, I., Parsons, J., Johnson, P., Ruble, D., & Zellman, G. (1978). *Women and sex roles: A social-psychological perspective.* New York: W. W. Norton.

Freudenberger (1983). Cited in *The Monitor,* October, p. 24.

Funkenstein, D. H., King, S. H., & Drolette, M. (1953). The experimental evocation of stress. In *Symposium on stress.* Division of Medical Sciences of the National Research Council and Army Medical Services Graduate School of Walter Reed Army Medical Center. Washington, D. C.: Government Printing Office.

Gallistel, C. R. (1981, April). Bell, Magendie, and the proposals to restrict the use of animals in neurobehavioral research. *American Psychologist,* pp. 357–360.

Garcia, J., Hankins, W. G., & Rusiniak, K. W. (1974). Behavioral regulation of the milieu interne in man and rat. *Science, 185,* pp. 824–831.

Garcia, J., & Koelling, R. A. (1966). Relation of cue to consequence in avoidance learning. *Psychonomic Science, 4* 123–124.

Gardner, H. (1981, February). "How the split brain gets a joke." *Psychology Today,* pp. 74–78.

Gardner, H. (1981, May). Prodigies' progress. *Psychology Today,* pp. 75–79.

Garfield, S. (1981, February). Psychotherapy: A 40-year appraisal. *American Psychologist, 36,* 174–183.

Gazzaniga, M. S. (1983, May). "Right hemisphere language following brain bisection." *American Psychologist* pp. 525–537.

Geer, J.; Heiman, J. R.; & Leitenberg, H. (1984). *Human sexuality.* Englewood Cliffs, N.J.: Prentice-Hall.

Gelman, David et al (1981, May 18). "Just how the sexes differ." *Newsweek:* pp. 72–83.

Gelman, R. (1979). Preschool thought. *American Psychologist, 34,* 900–905.

Gerbner, G., & Gross, L. (1974). *Trends in network television drama and viewer conceptions of social reality, 1967-1973: violence profile number 6.* Philadelphia: Annenberg School of Communications, University of Pennsylvania (ERIC Document Reproduction Service No. ED 101682).

Gergen, K. J. (1973). The codification of research ethics—views of a Doubting Thomas. *American Psychologist, 28,* pp. 907–912.

Getzels, J. W., & Jackson, P. (1962). *Creativity and intelligence.* New York: Wiley.

Giambra, L. (1974, December). Daydreams: The backburner of the mind. *Psychology Today,* pp. 66–68.

Ginsburg, H. (1972). *The myth of the deprived child.* Englewood Cliffs, N.J.: Prentice-Hall.

Gist, R., & Stolz, S. (1982, October). Mental health promotion and the media. *American Psychologist, 37,* 1136–1139.

Glass, D. C. (1977) *Behavior patterns, stress and coronary disease.* New York: Wiley.

Glick, I. O., Weiss, R. S., & Parkes, C. M. (1974). *The first year of bereavement.* New York: Wiley.

Gold, P. E., & Delanoy, R. L. (1981). ACTH modulation of memory storage processing. In J. L. Martinez, Jr., R. A. Jensen, R. B. Messing, H. Rigter, & J. L. McGaugh (Eds.), *Endogenous peptides and learning and memory processes.* New York: Academic Press.

Golden, G. (1982). Coping with aging: Denial and avoidance in middle-aged care-givers. Unpublished doctoral dissertation, University of California, Berkeley.

Goldenberg, H. (1973). *Contemporary clinical psychology.* Monterey, Ca.: Brooks/Cole.

Goleman, D. (1981, February). The 7000 faces of Dr.

Ekman. *Psychology Today*, pp. 43–49.

Goleman, D. (1981, October). Forgetfulness of things past. *Psychology Today*, pp. 17–20.

Gomes-Schwartz, B., Hadley, S. W., & Strupp, H. H. (1978). Individual psychotherapy and behavior therapy. *Annual Review of Psychology, 29*, 435–471.

Gottesman, I. I. & Shields, J. (1982). *The Schizophrenic Puzzle* N.Y.: Cambridge University Press.

Gould, J. L., & Gould, C. G. (1981, May). The instinct to learn. *Science '81*, pp. 44–50.

Gouldner, A. (1960). The norm of reciprocity: A preliminary statement. *American Sociological Review, 25*, 161–178.

Grady, D. (1983, October). Sounds instead of silence. *Discover*, pp. 54–57.

Graham, J. R., & Lilly, R. S. (1984). *Psychological testing*. Englewood Cliffs: Prentice-Hall.

Graziadei, P. P. C., Levine, R. R., & Graziadei, G. A. M. (1979). Plasticity of connections of the olfactory sensory neuron: Regeneration into the forebrain following bulbectomy in the neonatal mouse. *Neuroscience, 4*, 713–728.

Greenberg, C. & Firestone, I. (1977). Compensatory responses to crowding: Effects of personal space intrusion and privacy reduction. *Journal of Personality and Social Psychology, 35*, 637–644.

Greenberg, R., & Pearlman, C. (1967). Delirium tremens and dreaming. *American Journal of Psychiatry, 124*, 133–42.

Greenberger, E. (1983, January). The case of child labor. *American Psychologist*, pp. 104–111.

Gregory. R. L. (1970). *The intelligent eye*. New York: McGraw-Hill Book Company.

Gregory, R. L. (1966, 1978). *Eye and brain: The psychology of seeing*. 3rd ed. New York: McGraw-Hill Book Company.

Griffitt, W., & Gray, P. (1969). Object evaluation and conditioned affect. *Journal of Experimental Research in Personality, 4*, 1–8.

Grinker, R. R., & Spiegel, J. P. (1945). *War neurosis*. Philadelphia: Blakiston.

Grinspoon, L. (1969, December). Marihuana. *Scientific American*.

Grinspoon, L., Ewalt, J. R., & Shader, R. I. (1972). *Schizophrenic: Pharmacotherapy and psychotherapy*. Baltimore: Williams & Wilkins Co.

Grossman, H. J. (Ed.) (1973). Manual on terminology and classification in mental retardation. Washington, D.C.: Am. Assoc. Ment. Defic., rev. ed.

Groves, P. M., & Rebec, F. V. (1976). Biochemistry and behavior: Some central actions of amphetamine and antipsychotic drugs. *Annual Review of Psychology, 27*, 91–127.

Guilford, J. P. (1961). Factorial angles to psychology. *Psychological Reveiw, 68*, 1–20.

Gundlach, R. H. (1969). Childhood parental relationships and the establishment of gender roles of homosexuals. *Journals of Consulting and Clinical Psychology, 33*, 136–139.

Haan, N., & Day, D. (1974). A longitudinal study of change and sameness in personality development: Adolescence to later adulthood. *International Journal of Aging and Human Development, 5*, 11–39.

Haan, N., Smith, M. B., & Block, J. (1968). Moral reason of young adults: Political-social behavior, family background and personality correlates. *Journal of Personality and Social Psychology, 10*, 183.

Haier, Richard J. et al. "Naxolone alters pain perception after jogging." *Psychiatry Research*, in press.

Haith, M. M., & Campos, J. J. (1977). Human infancy. *Annual Review of Psychology, 28*, 251–293.

Hall, E. T. (1959). *The silent language*. Garden City, N.Y.: Doubleday.

Hansen, R. D. (1984). Person perception. In A. S. Kahn (ed.), *Social Psychology*. Dubuque, Iowa: Wm. C. Brown.

Harlow, H. F. (1958). The nature of love. *American Psychologist, 13*, pp. 673–685.

Harlow, H. F. (1959, June). Love in infant monkeys. *Scientific American*, pp. 68–74.

Harlow, H. F., & Zimmerman, R. R. (1959). Affectional responses in the infant monkey. *Science, 130*, 421–432.

Harmatz, M. G. (1978). *Abnormal psychology*. Englewood Cliffs, N.J.: Prentice-Hall.

Harrell, R. F., Woodyard, E., & Gates, A. I. (1955). *The effect of mother's diet on the intelligence of the offspring*. New York: Teacher's College, Columbia Bureau of Publications.

Harris, J. R. & Liebert, R. M. (1984). *The child*. Englewood Cliffs, N.J.: Prentice-Hall.

Harrison, A. A., & Saeed, L. (1977). Let's make a deal: An analysis of revelations and stipulations in lonely hearts advertisements. *Journal of Personality and Social Psychology, 35*, 257–264.

Hartley, D., Roback, H. B., & Abramowlitz, S. I. (1976). Deterioration effects in encounter groups. *American Psychologist, 31*, pp. 247–255.

Hartman, E. L. (1973). The functions of sleep. New Haven: Yale University Press.

Hartmann, P., & Husband, C. (1971). The mass media and racial conflict. *Race, 12*, 267–282.

Harvey, J. H., Town, J. P., Yarkin, K. L., (1981). How fundamental is "The fundamental attribution error"? *Journal of Personality and Social Psychology, 40*, 346–349.

Harvey, J. H. & Weary, G. (1984). Current Issues in attribution theory and research. *Annual Review of Psychology, 35*, 427–59.

Hass, R. G. (1981). Effects of source characteristics on cognitive responses in persuasion. In R. E. Petty and J. T. Cacioppo (Eds.), *Attitudes and persuasion: Classic and contemporary approaches*. Dubuque, Iowa: Wm. C. Brown, pp. 141–172.

Hastie, R. (1981). Schematic principles in human memory. In E. T. Higgins, C. P. Herman, & M. P. Zanna (Eds.), *Social cognition: The Ontario symposium* (Vol. 1). Hillsdale, N.J.: Erlbaum.

Hatch, O. G. (1982, September). Psychology, society, and politics. *American Psychologist*, pp. 1031–1037.

Hearst, E. (1975). The classical-instrumental distinction: reflexes, voluntary behavior, and categories of associative learning. In W. K. Estes (Ed.), *Handbook of learning and cognitive processes* (Vol. 2). *Conditioning and behavior theory*. Hillsdale, N.J.: Lawrence Erlbaum.

Heath, R. C. (1972). Pleasure and brain activity in man. *Journal of nervous and mental disease, 154*, 3–18.

Heider, E. R. (1972). Universals in color naming and memory. *Journal of Experimental Psychology, 93*, 10–20.

Heider, E. R., & Oliver, D. C. (1972). The structure of the color space in naming and memory in two languages. *Cognitive Psychology, 3*, 337–354.

Hodapp, R., & Mueller, E. (1982). Early social development.

In B. Wolman (Ed.). *Handbook of developmental psychology.* Prentice-Hall, pp. 284–300.

Hoepfner, R. (1975). Castro Valley Unified School District Title III: *Parents as partners summative evaluation report.* Castro Valley Unified Sch. Dist., Castro Valley, Calif.

Hoffman, H. S., & DePaulo, P. (1977). Behavioral control by an imprinting stimulus. *American Scientist, 65,* 58–66.

Hoffman, L. (1983). The study of employed mothers over half a century. In M. Lewis (Ed.). *In the shadow of the past: Psychology portrays the sexes.* New York: Columbia University Press.

Hoffman, L. W. (1974). Fear of success in males and females. *Journal of Consulting and Clinical Psychology, 42,* 353–358.

Hoffman, L. W. (1977). Changes in family roles, socialization, and sex differences. *American Psychologist, 32*(8), 644–657.

Hoffman, M. L. (1977). Personality and social development. *Annual Review of Psychology, 28,* 295–321.

Hohmann, G. W. (1966). Some effects of spinal cord lesions on experienced emotional feelings. *Psychophysiology, 3,* 143–156.

Holmes, D. S. (October, 1974). Investigations of repression. *Psychological Bulletin, 81,* 632–653.

Holmes, D. S. (1976a). Debriefing after psychological experiments: I. Effectiveness of postdeception dehoaxing. *American Psychologist, 31*(12), 858–867.

Holmes, D. S. (1976b). Debriefing after psychological experiments: II. Effectiveness of postexperiment desensitizing. *American Psychologist, 31*(12), 868–875.

Holmes, D. S. (1984, January). Meditation and somatic arousal reduction: A review of the experimental evidence *American Psychologist,* pp. 1–10.

Holmes, T. H., & Rahe, R. H. (1967). The social readjustment rating scale. *Journal of Psychosomatic Research, 11,* 213.

Hooker, E. (1969). Parental relations and male homosexuality in patient and nonpatient samples. *Journal of Consulting and Clinical Psychology, 33* 140–142.

Horn, J. (1975, March). Family therapy—a quick fix for juvenile delinquency. *Psychology Today,* pp. 80–81.

Horn, J. L. (1976). Human abilities: A review of research and theory in the early 1970s. *Annual Review of Psychology, 27,* 437–485.

Horn, J. L., & Donaldson, G. (1976). On the myth of the intellectual decline in adulthood. *American Psychologist, 31,* 701–719.

Horn, J. L. (1982). The aging of human abilities. In B. B. Wolman (Ed.), *Handbook of developmental psychology* Englewood Cliffs, N.J.: Prentice-Hall.

Horner, M. (1969, November). A bright woman is caught in a double bind. *Psychology Today,* pp. 36–38, 62.

Horvath, F. S. (1977). The effect of selected variables on interpretation of polygraph records. *Journal of Applied Psychology, 62,* 127–136.

Hosford, R. E., Moss, C. S., Cavior, H., & Kevish, B. (1980). *Research on erhard seminar training in a correctional institution.* Fed. Correct. Inst., Lompoc, Calif.

Hovland, C. I., & Sears, R. R. (1940). Minor studies in aggression: VI. Correlation of lynchings with economic indices. *Journal of Abnormal and Social Psychology, 9,* 301–310.

Hudspeth, A. J. (1983, January). The hair cells of the inner ear. *Scientific American,* pp. 54–64.

Hunt, M. (1974). *Sexual behavior in the 1970s.* Chicago: Playboy Press.

Hunt, M. (1982, January 24). How the mind works. *The New York Times Magazine,* pp. 31–33, 47–52, 64–65.

Hyde, J. S. (1981). How large are cognitive gender differences? *American Psychologist, 36*(8), pp. 892–901.

Hyde, J. S. (1982). *Understanding human sexuality,* (2nd ed.) N.Y.: McGraw-Hill.

Inhelder, B., & Piaget, J. (1958). *The growth of logical thinking from childhood to adolescence* (A. Parson & S. Milgram, trans.). New York: Basic Books.

Insel, P. M., & Lindgren. H. C. (1978). *Too close for comfort: The psychology of crowding behavior.* Englewood Cliffs, N.J.: Prentice-Hall.

Isen, A. M., & Levin, P. F. (1972). The effect of feeling good on helping: Cookies and kindness. *Journal of Personality and Social Psychology, 21,* 384–388.

Izard, C. E. (1971). *The face of emotion.* N.Y.: Appleton-Century-Crofts.

Heilbrun, A. B. Jr. (1981). Gender differences in the functional linkage between androgyny, social cognition, and competence. *Journal of Personality and Social Psychology, 41,* 1106–1118.

Heiman, J. R. (1977). A psychophysiological exploration of sexual arousal patterns in females and males. *Psychophysiology, 14,* 266–274.

Held, R., & Hein, A. (1963). Movement-produced stimulation in the development of visually guided behavior. *Journal of Comparative and Physiological Psychology, 56,* 872–876.

Helson, R. (1971). Women mathematicians and the creative personality. *Journal of Consulting and Clinical Psychology, 36,* (2), 210–220.

Henderson, N. D. (1982). Human behavior genetics. *Annual Review of Psychology, 33,* 403–440.

Hendricks, J., & Hendricks, C. D. (1977). *Aging in mass society: myths and realities.* Cambridge, Mass.: Winthrop.

Henry, W. E. (1956). *The analysis of fantasy.* New York: Wiley.

Heron, W. (1957, January.) The pathology of boredom. *Scientific American.*

Hersher, L. (Ed.) (1970) *Four psychotherapies.* New York: Appleton-Century-Crofts.

Hess, B. (1971). *Amicability.* Unpublished doctoral dissertation, Rutgers University.

Heston, L. L. (1966). Psychiatric disorders in foster-home-reared children of schizophrenic mothers. *British Journal of Psychiatry, 112,* 819–825.

Hilgard, E. R. (1969). Pain as a muzzle for psychology and physiology. *American Psychologist, 24,* 103–113.

Hilgard, E. R. (1974, November). Hypnosis is no mirage. *Psychology Today,* pp. 121–128.

Hilgard, E. R. (1975). Hypnosis. *Annual Review of Psychology, 26,* 19–44.

Hilgard, E. R. (1977). *Divided consciousness: Multiple controls in human thought and action.* New York: Wiley-Interscience.

Hill, C. T., Rubin, Z., & Peplau, L. A. (1976). Breakups before marriage: The end of 103 affairs. *Journal of Social Issues, 32* 147–168.

Hill, R., Foote, N., Aldous, J., Carlson, R., & McDonald, R. (1970). *Family development in three generations.*

Cambridge, Mass.: Schenkman.

Hill, W. F. (1956). Activity as an autonomous drive. *Journal of Comparative and Physiological Psychology, 49,* 15–19.

Hobbs, N., & Robinson, S. (1982). Adolescent development and public policy. *American Psychologist, 37,* (2), pp. 212–223.

Hochberg, J. E. (1978). *Perception.* Englewood Cliffs, N.J.: Prentice-Hall.

Hodgkin, A. L., & Huxley, A. F. (1952). A quantitative description of current and its application to conduction and excitation in nerves. *Journal of Physiology, 117,* 500–544.

Jacobs, B. L., & Trulson, M. E. (1979). Mechanism of action of LSD. *American Scientist, 67,* 396–404.

Janis, I. L. (1972). *Victims of groupthink: A psychological study of foreign-policy decisions and fiascos.* Boston: Houghton Mifflin.

Jensen, A. R. (1969). How much can we boost IQ and scholastic achievement? *Harvard Educational Review, 39,* 1–123.

Jones, E. E., & Nisbett, R. E. (1972). The actor and the observer: Divergent perceptions of the causes of behavior. *Attribution: Perceiving the causes of behavior.* Morristown, N.J.: General Learning Press.

Jones, M. C. (1924). Elimination of children's fears. *Journal of Experimental Psychology, 7,* 381–390.

Jones, M. C. (1958). A study of socialization patterns at the high school level. *Journal of Genetic Psychology, 93,* 87–111.

Jones, M. C. (1965). Psychological correlates of somatic development. *Child Development, 36,* 899–911.

Jones, M. C., & Bayley, N. (1950). Physical maturing among boys as related to behavior. *Journal of Educational Psychology, 41,* 129–148.

Jones, W., Chernovertz, M. E., & Hansson, R. O. (1978). The enigma of androgyny: Differential implications for males and females? *Journal of Consulting and Clinical Psychology, 46,* 298–313.

Jorgensen, B. W., & Cervone J. C. (1978). Affect enhancement in the pseudorecognition task. *Personality and Social Psychology Bulletin, 4,* 285–288.

Kagan, J. (1976). Emergent themes in human development. *American Scientist, 64,* 186–196.

Kahana, B. (1982). Social behavior and aging. In B. B. Wolman, (Ed.), *Handbook of developmental psychology* Englewood Cliffs, N.J.: Prentice-Hall.

Kaplan, H. S. (1974). *The new sex therapy.* N.Y.: Brunner/Mazel.

Kaplan, H. S. (1979). *Disorders of sexual desire.* N.Y.: Simon and Schuster.

Kastenbaum, R. (1977). *Death, society, and human behavior.* St. Louis: Mosby.

Kastenbaum, R., & Costa, P. T., Jr. (1977). Psychological perspectives on death. *Annual Review of Psychology, 28,* 225–249.

Kaufman, L. (1979). *Perception: The world transformed.* N. Y.: Oxford University Press.

Kaufman, L., & Rock, I. (1962, July). The moon illusion. *Scientific American,* pp. 120–130.

Kelley, H. H. (1967). Attribution theory in social psychology. In D. Levine (Ed.), *Nebraska symposium on motivation.* Lincoln: University of Nebraska Press.

Kelly, J. B. (1982). Divorce: The adult perspective. In B. B.

Wolman, (Ed.), *Handbook of developmental psychology,* Englewood Cliffs, N.J.: Prentice-Hall.

Kelman, H. C. (1974, May). Attitudes are alive and well and gainfully employed in the sphere of action. *American Psychologist,* pp. 310–324.

Kempe, R. S., & Kempe, C. H. (1978). *Child abuse.* Cambridge, Mass.: Harvard University Press.

Kennedy, G. C. (1953). The role of depot fat in the hypothalmic control of food intake in the rat. *Proceedings of the Royal Society, B140,* 578–592.

Kennedy, J. M. (1983, January-February). What can we learn about pictures from the blind? *American Scientist,* pp. 19–26.

Kennedy, T. (1964). Treatment of chronic schizophrenia by behavior therapy: case reports. *Behavior Research Therapy, 2,* 1–7.

Kessler, R. C. (1979). Stress, social status, and psychological distress. *J. Health Soc. Behav.* 20:259–72.

Kety, S. S. (1979). Disorders of the human brain. *Scientific American, 241,* 202–214.

Kiesler, C. A. (1982, December). Public and professional myths about mental hospitalization, *American Psychologist, 37,* 1323–1339.

Kiesler, C. A. (1982a, April). Mental hospitals and alternative care: Noninstitutionalization as potential public policy for mental patients. *American Psychologist, 37,* 349–360.

Kimmel, D. C. (1974). *Adulthood and aging.* N.Y.: Wiley.

Klatzky, R. L. (1980). *Human memory: Structures and processes* (2nd ed.). San Francisco: W. H. Freeman.

Kleemeier, R. W. (1962). Intellectual changes in the senium. *Proceedings of the Social Statistics Section of the American Statistical Association.* Washington, D.C.: American Statistical Association.

Klein, G. S. (1951). The personal world through perception. In R. R. Blake & G. V. Ramsey (Eds.), *Perception: An approach to personality.* N.Y.: Ronald Press.

Kleinhesselink, R. R., & Edwards, R. E. (1975). Seeking and avoiding belief-discrepant information as a function of its perceived refutability. *Journal of Personality and Social Psychology, 31,* 787–790.

Kleitman, N. (1963). *Sleep and wakefulness* (rev. ed.). Chicago: University of Chicago Press.

Klineberg, O. (1938). Emotional expression in Chinese literature. *Journal of Abnormal and Social Psychology, 33,* 517–520.

Knight, M. (1974, May 21). Child molesters try "shock" cure. *New York Times,* pp. 43, 83.

Kobasa, S. C. (1979). Stressful life events, personality, and health: An inquiry into hardiness. *Journal of Personality and Social Psychology, 37,* 1–11.

Koestler, A. (1964). The act of creation. N.Y.: Macmillan.

Kohlberg, L. (1976). Moral stages and moralization: The cognitive-developmental approach. In T. Lickona (Ed.), *Moral Development and Behavior* N.Y.: Holt, Rinehart, Winston.

Kohlberg, L. (1979). *The meaning and measurement of moral development.* Clark Lectures, Clark University.

Kohlberg, L. (1981). *The philosophy of moral development.* Vol. I. San Francisco: Harper & Row.

Kolodny, R. C., Masters, W. H., & Johnson, V. E. (1979). *Textbook of sexual medicine.* Boston: Little, Brown.

Koner, M. (1982). *The tangled wing.* N.Y.: Holt, Rinehart & Winston.

Konner, Melvin. (1982, September). "She & he." *Science* pp. 54–61.

Knox, R. E. & Safford, R. K. (1976). Group caution at the race track. *Journal of Experimental Social Psychology, 12,* 317–324.

Krebs, D. (1975). Empathy and altruism. *Journal of Personality and Social Psychology, 32,* 1134–1140.

Kübler-Ross, E. (1969). *On death and dying.* N.Y.: Macmillan.

Kübler-Ross, E. (1975). *Death: the final stage of growth.* Englewood Cliffs, N.J.: Prentice-Hall.

Laing, R. D. (1967). *The politics of experience.* New York: Ballantine.

Lamb, M. E. (1979). Paternal influences and the father's role. *American Psychologist, 34,* 938–943.

Lambert, W. W., Solomon, R. L., & Watson, P. D. (1949). Reinforcement and extinction as factors in size estimation. *Journal of Experimental Psychology, 39,* 637–641.

Landman, J. C., & Dawes, R. M. (1982, May). Psychotherapy outcome: Smith and Glass' conclusions stand up under scrutiny. *American Psychologist, 37* (5), pp. 504–516.

LaPiere, R. T. (1934). Attitudes versus actions. *Social Forces, 13,* 230–237.

LaRue, A., & Jarvik, L. (1982). Old age and biobehavioral changes. In B. Wolman (Ed.). *Handbook of developmental psychology.* Englewood Cliffs, Prentice-Hall.

Lasch, C. (1979). *The culture of narcissism.* New York: Norton.

Latané, B., & Rodin, J. (1969). A lady in distress: Inhibiting effects of friends and strangers on bystander intervention. *Journal of Experimental Social Psychology, 5,* 189–202.

Laughlin, H. P. (1963). *Mental mechanisms.* New York: Appleton-Century-Crofts.

Lazarus, A. P. (1968). Learning theory in the treatment of depression. *Behavior Research and Therapy, 8,* 83–89.

Lazarus, R. S. (1966). *Psychological stress and the coping process.* New York: McGraw-Hill.

Lazarus, R. S. (1969). *Patterns of adjustment and human effectiveness.* New York: McGraw-Hill.

Lazarus, R. S. (1974). *The riddle of man.* Englewood Cliffs, N.J.: Prentice-Hall.

Lazarus, R. S. (1981, July). Little hassles can be hazardous to health. *Psychology Today,* pp. 58–62.

Lazarus, R. S. (1982). Thoughts on the relations between emotion and cognition. *American psychologist, 37,* 1019–1024.

Lazarus, R. S. & Monat, A. (1979). *Personality* (3rd ed.). Englewood Cliffs, N.J.: Prentice-Hall, Inc.

Leeper, R. W. (1935). A study of a neglected portion of the field of learning: The development of sensory organization. *Pedagogical Seminary and Journal of Genetic Psychology, 46,* 41–75.

Leeper, R. W. (1948). A motivational theory of emotion to replace "emotion as disorganized response." *Psychological Review, 55,* 5–21.

Lefcourt, H. M. (1973, May). The function of the illusions of control and freedom. *American Psychologist,* pp. 417–425.

Lehman, H. C. (1953). *Age and achievement.* Princeton, N.J.: Princeton University Press.

LeMagnen, J. (1952). Les pheromones olfactosexuals chez le rat blanc. *Archives des Sciences Physiologiques, 6,* 295–332.

Lenneberg, E. (1967). *Biological foundations of language.* New York: Wiley.

Leonard, R. L. (1975). Self-concept and attraction for similar and dissimilar others. *Journal of Personality and Social Psychology, 31,* 926–929.

Lerner, R. M., & Karabenick, S. A. (1974). Physical attractiveness, body attitudes, and self-concept in late adolescents. *Journal of Youth and Adolescence, 3,* 307–316.

Lerner, R. M., & Shea, J. A. (1982). Social behavior in adolescence. In B. Wolman (Ed.). *Handbook of developmental psychology.* Englewood Cliffs, N.J.: Prentice-Hall.

Lerner, R. M., & Spanier, G. B. (1980). *Adolescent development: A life-span perspective.* New York: McGraw-Hill.

Leventhal, H., & Niles, P. (1965). Persistence of influence for varying duration of exposure to threat stimuli. *Psychological Reports, 16,* 223–233.

Levinger, G., Senn, D. J., & Jorgensen, B. W. (1970). Progress toward permanence in courtship: A test of the Kerckhoff-Davis hypothesis. *Sociometry, 33,* 427–443.

Levinson, B. M. (1959). Traditional Jewish cultural values and performance on the Wechsler tests. *Journal of Educational Psychology, 50,* 177–181.

Levinson, D. J. (1978). *The seasons of a man's life.* New York: Knopf.

Levinthal, C. (1979). *The physiological approach in psychology.* Englewood Cliffs, N.J.: Prentice-Hall.

Levy, B. A. (1978). Speech processing during reading. In A. M. Lesgold, J. W. Pellegrino, S. D. Fckhema, & R. Glaser (Eds.). *Cognitive psychology and instruction.* New York: Plenum.

Lewin, K. A. (1935). *A dynamic theory of personality* (K. E. Zener & D. K. Adams, trans.). New York: Mc-Graw-Hill.

Liben, L. (1974). Operative understanding of horizontality and its relation to long-term memory. *Child Development, 45,* 416–424.

Lieberman, M. A. (1965). Psychological correlates of impending death: Some preliminary observations. *Journal of Gerontology, 20,* 181–190.

Lieberman, M. A., & Coplan, A. S. (1969). Distance from death as a variable in the study of aging. *Developmental Psychology, 2,* 71–84.

Liebert, R. M., & Baron, R. A. (1972). Short-term effects of televised aggression on children's aggressive behavior. In J. P. Murray, E. A. Rubinstein, & G. A. Comstock (Eds.), *Television and social behavior* (Vol. 2). *Television and social learning.* Washington, D.C.: U.S. Government Printing Office.

Liebert, R. M., & Spiegler, M. D. (1982). *Personality: Strategies and issues,* (4th ed.) Dorsey Press.

Liebeskind, J. C., & Paul, L. A. (1977). Psychological and physiological mechanisms of pain. *Annual Review of Psychology, 28,* 41–60.

Liem, R., Liem, J. V. (1978). Social class and mental illness reconsidered: The role of economic stress and social support. *J. Health Soc. Behav.* 19:139–56.

Lifton, R. L. (1961). *Thought reform and the psychology of totalism.* New York: Norton.

Lindsay, P. H., & Norman, D. A. (1977). *Human information*

processing (2nd ed.). New York: Academic Press.

Linn, R. L. (1982). Admissions testing on trial. *American Psychologist, 37* (3), pp. 279–291.

Lipsey, M. W. (1974, July). Research and relevance. *American Psychologist,* pp. 541–553.

Lipsitt, L. P. (1971, December). Babies: They're a lot smarter than they look. *Psychology Today,* pp. 70–72, 88–89.

Locke, S., et al. (1983). Life change stress and human natural killer cell activity. In Locke, S. E., & Hornig-Rohan, M. (Eds.), *Mind and immunity: Behavioral immunology.* New York: Institute for the Advancement of Health.

Locksley, A., & Colten, M. E. (1979). Psychological androgyny: A case of mistaken identity? *Journal of Personality and Social Psychology, 37,* 1017–1031.

Loehlin, J. C., & Nichols, R. C. (1976). *Heredity, environment, and personality.* Austin: University of Texas Press.

Loftus, E. F., Miller, D. G., & Burns, H. J. 1978). Semantic integration of verbal information into a visual memory. *Journal of Experimental Psychology: Human Learning and Memory, 4,* 19–31.

Loftus, E. (1980). *Memory.* Reading, Mass: Addison-Wesley.

Loftus, E. (1983, May). Silence is not golden. *American Psychologist,* pp. 564–572.

Lopata, H. Z. (1973). *Widowhood in an American city.* Cambridge, Mass.: Schenkman.

Lorenz, K. (1935). Der Kumpan in der Umwelt des Vobels. *Journal of Ornithology, 83,* 137–213, 289–413.

Lorenz, K. (1968). *On aggression.* New York: Harcourt.

Lowenthal, M. F., & Chiriboga, D. (1972). Transition to the empty nest: Crisis, change, or relief. *Archives of General Psychiatry, 26,* 8–14.

Luchins, A. (1957b). Primacy-recency in impression formation. In C. Hovland, W. Mandell, E. Campbell, T. Brock, A. Luchins, A. Cohen, W. McGuire, I. Janis, R. Feierbend, & N. Anderson (Eds.), *The order of presentation in persuasion.* New Haven: Conn.: Yale University Press.

Luce, G., & Segal, J. (1966). *Sleep.* New York: Coward, McCann, & Geoghegan.

Ludwig, A. M. (1969). Altered states of consciousness. In C. T. Tart (Ed.), *Altered states of consciousness.* New York: Wiley.

Lykken, D. T. (1960). The validity of the guilty knowledge technique: The effects of faking. *Journal of Applied Psychology, 44,* 258–262.

Lykken, D. T. (1975, March). Guilty knowledge test: The right way to use a lie detector. *Psychology Today,* pp. 56–60.

Lykken, D. T. (1960). The validity of the guilty knowledge technique: The effects of faking. *Journal of Applied Psychology, 44,* 258–262.

Lykken, D. T. (1975, March). Guilty knowledge test: The right way to use a lie detector. *Psychology Today,* pp. 56–60.

Maccoby, E., & Jachlin, C. N. (1984). *The psychology of sex differences.* Stanford, CA: Stanford University Press.

MacKinnon, D. W. (1962). The nature and nurture of creative talent. *American Psychologist, 1*(7), pp. 484–495.

MacLeod, D.I.A. (1978). Visual sensitivity. *Annual Review of Psychology, 29,* 613–645.

Maddi, S. R. (1980). *Personality theories: A comparative evaluation* (4th ed.). Homewood: IL: Dorsey.

Major, B., Carnevale, P.J.D., & Deaux, K. (1981). A different perspective on androgyny: Evaluations of masculine and feminine personality characteristics. *Journal of Personality and Social Psychology, 41,* 988–1001.

Manz, W. & Lueck, H. (1968). Influence of wearing glasses on personality ratings: Cross-cultural validation of an old experiment. *Perceptual and Motor Skills, 27,* 704.

Maratsos, M. P. (1973). Nonegocentric communication abilities in preschool children. *Child Development, 44,* 697–700.

Marcia, J.E. (1976). Identity six years after: A follow-up study. *Journal of Youth and Adolescence, 5,* 145–160.

Marek, G. R. (1982; orig. pub. 1975). *Toscanini.* London: Vision Press. Reprinted in U. Neisser (Ed.), *Memory observed: Remembering in natural contexts.* San Francisco: W. H. Freeman.

Marlatt, G. A., & Rohsenow, D. J (1981, December). The think-drink effect. *Psychology Today,* pp. 60–69, 93.

Marks, G., & Miller, N. (1980). The effect of physical attractivenes on perception of similarity. Unpublished manuscript, University of Southern California.

Marsden, E. N. (1966). Values as determinants of friendship choice. *Connecticut College Psychological Journal. 3.* 3–13.

Marvin, R. S. (1975). Aspects of the pre-school child's changing conception of his mother. Unpublished.

Masling, J., Rabie, L., & Blondheim, S. H. (1967). Obesity, level of aspiration, and Rorshach and TAT measures of oral dependence. *Journal of Consulting Psychology, 31*(3), pp. 233–239.

Maslow, A. H. (1954). Motivation and personality. New York: Harper & Row.

Mason, W. A., & Lott, D. F. (1976). Ethnology and comparative psychology. *Annual Review of Psychology, 27,* 129–154.

Masters, W. H., & Johnson, V. E. (1970). *Human sexual inadequacy.* Boston: Little, Brown.

Masters, W. H., & Johnson, V. E. (1979). *Homosexuality in perspective.* Boston: Little, Brown.

Masters, W. H., Johnson, V. E., & Kolodny, R. C. (1982). *Human sexuality.* Boston: Little, Brown.

Mathews, K. E., & Cannon, L. K. (1975). Environmental noise level as a determinant of helping behavior. *Journal of Personality and Social Psychology, 32,* 571–577.

Matsunaga, S. (1983, October). The federal role in research, treatment, and prevention of alcoholism. *American Psychologist,* pp. 1111–1115.

Maugh, T. M. (1981). Biochemical markers identify mental states. *Science, 214,* 39–41.

Mayer, R. E. (1983). *Thinking, problem solving, cognition.* San Francisco: W. H. Freeman.

Mayer, W. (1983, October). Alcohol abuse and alcoholism: The psychologist's role in prevention, research, and treatment. *American Psychologist,* pp. 1116–1121.

McBurney, D., & Collings, V. (1977). *Introduction to sensation/perception.* Englewood Cliffs, N.J.: Prentice-Hall.

McCarthy, A. (1980). Voices of their captors: When the hostages come home. *Commonweal.*

McClelland, D. C. (1958). Methods of measuring human motivation. In J. W. Atkinson (Ed.), *Motives in fantasy, action and society: A method of assessment and study.* New York: Van Nostrand.

McClelland, D. C. (1965). Achievement and entrepreneurship: A longitudinal study. *Journal of Personality and Social Psychology, 1,* 389–392.

McClelland, D. C. (1973). Testing for competence rather than for "intelligence." *American Psychologist, 28,* pp. 1–4.

McClelland, D. C., & Atkinson, J. W. (1948). The projective expression of needs: I. The effect of different intensities of the hunger drive on perception. *Journal of Psychology, 25,* 205–222.

McClelland, D. C., et al. (1953). *The achievement motive.* New York: Appleton-Century-Crofts.

McCloskey, M., & Egeth, H. E. (1983, May). Eyewitness identification: What can a psychologist tell a jury? *American Psychologist,* pp. 550–563.

McConnell, R. A. (1969). ESP and credibility in science. *American Psychologist, 24,* 531–538.

McFadden, D., & Wightman, F. L. (1983). Audition: Some relations between normal and pathological hearing. *Annual review of Psychology, 34,* 95–128.

McGough, J. L. (1983, February). Preserving the presence of the past. *American Psychologist,* pp. 161–174.

McGovern, L. P. (1976). Dispositional social anxiety and helping behavior under three conditions of threat. *Journal of Personality, 44,* 84–97.

McGeer, P. L., & McGeer, E. G. (1980). Chemistry of mood and emotion. *Annual Review of Psychology, 31,* 273–307.

McGrath, M. J., & Cohen, D. B. (1978). REM sleep facilitation of adaptive waking behavior: A review of the literature. *Psychological Bulletin, 85,* 24–57.

McKellar, P. (1957). *Imagination and thinking.* New York: Basic Books.

McMurray, G. A. (1950). Experimental study of a case of insensitivity to pain. *Archives of Neurology and Psychiatry. 64,* 650.

Mednick, S.A. (1962). The associative basis of creativity. *Psychological Review, 69*(3), 220–232.

Meiners, M. L., & Sheposh, J. P. (1977). Beauty or brains: Which image for your mate? *Personality and Social Psychology Bulletin, 3,* 262–265.

Meltzoff, J., & Kornreich, M. (1971, July). It works. *Psychology Today,* pp. 57–61.

Mercer, J. R. (1972, September). The lethal label. *Psychology Today,* pp. 45–97.

Mercer, T. B., & Lewis, J. G. (1978). Using the system of multicultural assessment (SOMPA) to identify the gifted minority child. In A. Y. Baldwin, G. H. Gear, & L. J. Lucito (Eds.). Educational planning for the gifted: Overcoming cultural, geographic, and socioeconomic barriers. Reston, Va.: Council for Exceptional Children.

Meyer, A. (1982, June). Do lie detectors lie? *Science 82,* pp. 24–27.

Meyer, R. G., & Smith, S. R. (1977). A crisis in group therapy. *American Psychologist, 32,* 638–643.

Michael, R. P., Bonsall, R. W., & Warner, P. (1974). Human vaginal secretions: Volatile fatty acid content. *Science, 186,* 1217–1219.

Milgram, S. (1963). Behavioral study of obedience. *Journal of Abnormal and Social Psychology, 67,* 371–378.

Milgram, S. (1974). *Obedience to authority.* New York: Harper & Row.

Miller, B.C. (1976). A multivariate developmental model of marital satisfaction. *Journal of Marriage and the Family, 38,* 643–657.

Miller, J. A. (1984, April 21). Looking out for animal research. *Science News,* p. 247.

Miller, N., & Campbell, D. (1959). Recency and primacy in persuasion as a function of the timing of speeches and measurements. *Journal of Abnormal and Social Psychology, 59,* 1–9.

Minton, H. L., & Schneider, F. W. (1980). *Differential Psychology.* Monterey, CA: Brooks/Cole.

Mintz, A. (1951). Nonadaptive group behavior. *Journal of Abnormal and Social Psychology, 46,* 150–159.

Mischel, W. (1968). *Personality and assessment.* New York: Wiley.

Mischel, W. (1979). On the interface of cognition and personality: Beyond the person-situation debate. *American Psychologist, 34,* 740–754.

Mischel, W. (1981). *Introduction to personality.* N.Y.: Holt, Rinehart & Winston.

Mitchell, J. (1974). *Psychoanalysis and feminism.* New York: Pantheon.

Mollon, J. D. (1982). Color vision. *Annual Review of Psychology, 33,* 41–85.

Moncrieff, R. W. (1951). *The chemical senses.* London: Leonard Hill.

Moray, N. (1959). Attention in dichotic listening: Affective cues and the influence of instructions. *Quarterly Journal of Experimental Psychology, 11,* 56–60.

Moriarty, T. (1975). Crime, commitment and the responsive bystander: Two field experiments. *Journal of Personality and Social Psychology, 31,* 370–376.

Morrison, A. (1983, April). A window on the sleeping brain. *Scientific American,* pp. 94–102.

Moskowitz, B. A. (1978). The acquisition of language. *Scientific American, 239,* 92–108.

Munsinger, H. (1975). The adopted child's IQ: A critical view. *Psychological Bulletin, 82,* 623–659.

Murray, H. A. (1938). *Explorations in personality.* New York: Oxford U. Press.

Murray, H. G. & Denny, J. P. (1969). Interaction of ability level and interpolated activity in human problem solving. *Psychological Reports, 24,* 271–276.

Mussen, P. H., & Jones, M. C. (1957). Self-conceptions, motivations, and interpersonal attitude of late and early maturing boys. *Child Development, 28,* 243–256.

Mussen, P. H., & Jones, M. C. (1958). The behavior-inferred motivations of late and early maturing boys. *Child Development, 29,* 61–67.

Nahemow, L., & Lawton, M. P. (1975). Similarity and propinquity in friendship formation. *Journal of Personality and Social Psychology, 32,* 205–213.

National Commission on Marijuana and Drug Abuse. (1973a). *Drug use in America: Problem in perspective.* Washington, D.C.: U.S. Government Printing Office.

National Commission on Marijuana and Drug Abuse. (1973b). *Drug use in America: Problem in perspective. Technical papers—appendix.* Washington, D. C.: U.S. Government Printing Office.

Nauta, W. J. H., & Feirtag, M. (1979). The organization of the brain. *Scientific American, 241,* 88–111.

Neisser, U. (1967). *Cognitive psychology.* New York: Appleton-Century-Crofts.

Neisser, U. (1982). *Memory observed: Remembering in natural contexts*. San Francisco: W. H. Freeman.

Neugarten, B. L. (1976). *The psychology of aging: An overview*. APA Master Lecturer. Washington, D. C.: American Psychological Association.

Neugarten, B. L., & Hagestad, G. O. (1977). Age and the life course. In R. H. Binstock & E. Shanas (Eds.), *Handbook of aging and the social sciences*. New York: Van Nostrand Reinhold.

Newman, B. M. (1982). Mid-life development. In B B. Wolman (Ed.), *Handbook of developmental psychology*. Englewood Cliffs, N.J.: Prentice-Hall.

Nichenson, R. S., & Adams, M. J. (1979). Long-term memory for a common object. *Cognitive Psychology, 11,* 287–307.

Nielsen, G. D. & Smith, E. E. (1973). Imaginal and verbal representations in short-term recognition of visual forms. *Journal of Experimental Psychology, 101,* 375–378.

Nisbett, R. E., & Borgida, E. (1975). Attribution and the psychology of prediction. *Journal of Personality and Social Psychology, 32,* (5), 932–943.

Norman, R. (1975). Affective-cognitive consistency, attitudes, conformity, and behavior. *Journal of Personality and Social Psychology, 32* (1), 83–91.

Norman, W. T. (1963). Toward an adequate taxonomy of personality attributes: Replicated factor structure in peer nomination personality ratings. *Journal of Abnormal and Social Psychology, 66,* 574–583.

Olendorf, D. (1982, November 28). Old notions, false notions, about aging. *Detroit Free Press*, pp. 26–32.

Olson, G., Olson, R., Kastin, A., & Coy, D. (1979). Endogenous opiates: Through 1978. *Neuroscience and Biobehavioral Reviews, 3,* 285–299.

Olton, D. S., & Noonberg, A. R. (1980). *Biofeedback: Clinical applications in behavioral science*. Englewood Cliffs, N.J.: Prentice-Hall.

Orlofsky, J. L. (1978). Identity formation, N achievement, and fear of success in college men and women. *Journal of Youth and Adolescence, 7,* 49–62.

Orlofsky, J. L., Marcia, J. E., & Lesser, I. M. (1973, February). Ego identity status and the intimacy versus isolation crisis of young adulthood. *Journal of Personality and Social Psychology, 27*(2), 211–219.

Ortar, G. (1963). Is a verbal test cross-cultural? *Scripta Hierosolymitana, 13,* 219–235.

Oskamp, S. (1977). *Attitudes and opinions*. Englewood Cliffs, N.J.: Prentice-Hall.

Page, E. B., & Grandon, G. M. (1979). Family configuration and mental ability. Two theories contrasted with U. S. data. *American Educational Research Journal, 16,* 257–272.

Pahnke, W. N., & Richards, W. A. (1969). Implications of LSD and experimental mysticism. In C. T. Tart (Ed.), *Altered states of consciousness*. New York: Wiley.

Paivio, A. (1975). Coding distinctions and repetition effects in memory. In G. H. Bower (Ed.), *Psychology of learning and motivation* (Vol. 9). New York: Academic Press.

Pallak, M. S. (1982, May). Psychology in the public forum. *American Psychologist*, p. 475.

Palmer, J. O. (1979). *The psychological assessment of children*. New York: Wiley.

Parke, R. D., & Asher, S. R. (1983). Social and personality development. *Annual Review of Psychology, 34,* 465–509.

Parkes, C. M. (1976). Components of the reaction to loss of limb, spouse, a home. *Journal of Psychosomatic Research, 16,* 343–349.

Pattison, E. M. (1977). *The experience of dying*. Englewood Cliffs, N.J.: Prentice-Hall.

Pavlov, I. P. (1927). *Conditioned reflexes* (G. V. Anrep, trans.). London: Oxford University Press.

Paykel, E. S. (1982). Life events and early environment. In E. S. Paykel (Ed.), *Handbook of affective disorders*. N.Y.: Guilford Press.

Pearlin, L. I., Schooler, C. (1978). The structure of coping. *J. Health Soc. Behav.* 19:2–21.

Pendleton, M. G., & Batson, C. D. (1979). Self-presentation and the door-in-the face technique for inducing compliance. *Personality and Social Psychology Bulletin, 5,* 77–81.

Penrod, S., (1983). *Social Psychology*. Englewood Cliffs, N.J.: Prentice-Hall.

Perlin, M. (1976). On behavior therapy and civil liberties, *American Psychologist, 31,* pp. 534–536.

Perls, F. S. (1969). *Gestalt theory verbatim*. Moab, Ut.: Real People Press.

Personal Computing. (1983, December). The wide, wide world of personal computing. pp. 13–14.

Pervin, L. A. (1984). *Personality: Theory and research, (4th Ed.)*. New York: John Wiley & Sons.

Peskin, H. (1967). Pubertal onset and ego functioning. *Journal of Abnormal Psychology, 72,* 1–15.

Peskin, H. (1973). Influence of the developmental schedule of puberty on learning and ego functioning. *Journal of Youth and Adolescence, 2,* 273–290.

Peterson, R. A. (1978). Rorschach. In O. K. Buros (Ed.). *The eighth mental measurements yearbook*. Highland Park, N.J.: Gryphon, p. 1042.

Petty, R. E., & Cacioppo, J. T. (1981). *Attitudes and persuasion: Classic and contemporary approaches*. Dubuque, Iowa: Wm. C. Brown.

Pevnick, J., Jasinski, D. R., & Haertzen, C. A. (1978). Abrupt withdrawal from therapeutically administered diazepam. *Archives of General Psychiatry, 35,* 995–998.

Phares, E. J. (1976). *Locus of control in personality*. Morristown, N.J.: General Learning Press.

Phares, E. J. (1978). Locus of control. In H. London & J. E. Exner, Jr. (Eds.), *Dimensions of personality*. New York: Wiley.

Phares, E. J. (1984). *Introduction to Personality*. Columbus, Ohio: Charles E. Merrill.

Phillips, J. L., Jr. (1969). *The origins of the intellect: Piaget's theory*. San Francisco: Freeman.

Piaget, J. (1932). *The moral development of the child*. New York: Harcourt Brace.

Piaget, J. (1969). The intellectual development of the adolescent. In G. Caplan & S. Lebovici (Eds.), *Adolescence: Psychosocial perspectives*. New York: Basic Books.

Piaget, J., & Szeminska, A. (1952; orig. French ed. 1941). *The child's conception of number* (C. Gattegno & F. M. Hodgson, trans.). New York: Humanities Press.

Pineo, P. C. (1961). Disenchantment in the later years of marriage. *Marriage and Family Living, 23,* 3–11.

Pines, Maya. (1983, September). "The human difference." *Psychology Today* pp. 62–68.

Plomin, R., DeFries, J. C., & McClearn, G. E. (1980). *Behavioral genetics: A primer*. San Francisco: W. H. Freeman.

Plutchik, R. (1980). *Emotion: a psychoevolutionary synthesis.* N.Y.: Harper & Row.

Poincaré, H. (1924). *The foundations of science* (G. B. Halstead, trans.). London: Science Press.

Porter, R. H., & Moore, J. D. (1982). Human kin recognition by olfactory cues. *Physiology and Behavior, 27.*

Porter, R. W., et al. (1958). Some experimental observations on gastrointestinal ulcers in behaviorally conditioned monkeys. *Psychosomatic Medicine, 20,* 379–394.

Powell, D. H., & Driscoll, P. F. (1973). Middle class professionals face unemployment. *Society, 10* (2), 18–26.

Power, C., & Reimer, J. (1978). Moral atmosphere: An educational bridge between moral judgment and action. *New Directions for Child Development, 2.*

Prociuk, T. J., & Breen, L. J. (1975). Defensive externality and its relation to academic performance. *Journal of Personality and Social Psychology, 31,* 549–556.

Prociuk, T. J., & Breen, L. J. (1977). Internal-External locus of control and information-seeking in a college academic situation. *Journal of Social Psychology, 101,* 309–310.

Pruitt, D. G. (1971). Conclusions: Toward an understanding of choice shifts in group discussion. *Journal of Personality and Social Psychology, 20,* 495–510.

Pryor, K. (1981, April). The rhino likes violets. *Psychology Today,* pp. 92–98.

Pulaski, M.A.S. (1974, January). The rich rewards of make believe. *Psychology Today,* pp. 68–74.

Putnam, F. W. (1982, October). Traces of Eve's faces. *Psychology Today,* p. 88.

Quimme, P. (1977). *The Signet book of American wine.* New York: New American Library.

Rao, D. C., N. E. Gottesman, and I. I. Lew. (1981). "Path analysis of qualitative data on pairs of relatives: Application to schizophrenia." *Human Heredity.*

Rayman, P. & Bluestone, B. (1982). The private and social response to job loss: A metropolitan study. Final Report of Research sponsored by the Center for Work and Mental Health, National Institute of Mental Health.

Reed, S. F., Ernst, G. W., & Banerji, R. (1974). The role of analogy in transfer between similar problem states. *Cognitive Psychology, 6,* 435–450.

Reed, S. K. (1982). *Cognition: Theory and applications.* Monterey, CA: Brooks/Cole.

Renzulli, J. S. (1978). What makes giftedness? Reexamining a definition. *Phi Delta Kappar, 60,* 180–184; 216.

Reschly, D. J. (1981). Psychology testing in educational classification and placement. *American Psychologist, 36* (10), pp.1094–1102.

Rescorla, R. A. (1967). Pavlovian conditioning and its proper control procedures. *Psychological Review, 74,* 71–80.

Rescorla, R. A., & Holland, P. C. (1982). Behavioral studies of associative learning in animals. *Annual Review of Psychology, 33,* 265–308.

Restak, R. (1982, May). Islands of genius. *Science 82,* pp. 62–67.

Rice, B. (1979, September). Brave new world of intelligence testing. *Psychology Today,* pp. 27–38.

Riegel, K. F. (1973). Dialectical operations: The final period of cognitive development. *Human Development, 16,* 346–370.

Riegel, K. F., Riegel, R. M. & Meyer, G. (1967). A study of the dropout rates of longitudinal research on aging and the prediction of death. *Journal of Personality and Social Psychology, 5,* 342–348.

Riesen, A. H. (1950, July). Arrested vision. *Scientific American,* pp. 16–19.

Ritchie, E., & Phares, E. J. (1969). Attitude change as a function of internal-external control and communication status. *Journal of Personality, 37,* 429–443.

Rittle, R. H. (1980). Changes inself vs. situational perceptions as mediators of the foot-in-the-door effect. *Personality and Social Psychology Bulletin.*

Robitscher, J., & Williams, R. (1977, December). Should psychiatrists get out of the courtroom? *Psychology Today,* p. 85.

Rodgers, J. E. (1982, June). The malleable memory of eyewitnesses. *Science '82,* pp. 32–36.

Rodgers, J. E. (1982, July/August). Roots of madness. *Science '82,* pp. 85 –91.

Rodin, J. (1981, April). Current status of the internal-external hypothesis for obesity. *American Psychologist,* pp. 361–371.

Rogers, C. R. (1959). A theory of therapy, personality, and interpersonal relationships as developed in the client-centered framework. In S. Koch (Ed.) *Psychology: A study of science.* New York: McGraw Hill, pp. 184–256.

Rogers, C. R. (1961). *On becoming a person: A therapist's view of psychotherapy.* Boston: Houghton-Mifflin.

Rogers, D. (1980). *The adult years: An introduction to aging.* Englewood Cliffs, N.J.: Prentice-Hall.

Rokeach, M., & Mezei, L. (1966). Race and shared belief as factors in social choice. *Science, 151,* 167–172.

Rollins, B. C., & Feldman, H. (1970). Marital satisfaction over the life cycle. *Journal of Marriage and the Family, 32,* 20–28.

Rolls, B. J., Wood, R. J., & Rolls, E. T. (1980). The initiation, maintenance and termination of drinking. In J. M. Sprague & A. N. Epstein (Eds.). *Progress in psychobiology and physiological psychology, 9.* New York: Academic Press.

Rosch, E. H. (1973). Natural categories. *Cognitive Psychology, 4,* 328–350.

Rosenberg, S. D., & Farrell, M. P. (1976). Identity and crisis in middle-aged men. *International Journal of Aging and Human Development, 7,* 153–170.

Rosenhan, D. L. (1973). On being sane in insane places. *Science, 179,* 250–258.

Rosenhan, D. L., & Seligman, M E.P. (1984). *Abnormal psychology.* New York: Norton.

Rosenthal, D. (1970). *Genetic theory and abnormal behavior.* New York: McGraw-Hill.

Rosenthal, R., et al. (1974, September). Body talk and tone of voice: The language without words. *Psychology Today,* pp. 64–68.

Rosenzweig, M. R., & Leiman, A. L. (1982). Physiological Psychology. Lexington, Mass.: D. C. Heath.

Rosenzweig, S. (1983). Mental health deinstitutionalization: Reservations. *American Psychologist,* p. 349.

Ross, D. (1966). Relationship between dependency, intentional learning, and incidental learning in preschool children. *Journal of Personality and Social Psychology, 4,* 374–381.

Ross, L. (1977). The intuitive psychologist and his shortcomings: Distortions in the attribution process. In L. Berkowitz

(Ed.), *Advances in experimental social psychology*, Vol. 10, New York: Academic Press.

Rothbart, M., Evans, M., & Fulero, S. (1979). Recall for confirming events: Memory processes and the maintenance of social stereotypes. *Journal of Experimental Social Psychology, 15*, 343–355.

Rotter, J. B. (1966). Generalized expectancies for internal versus external control of reinforcement. *Psychological Monographs, 80* (Whole No. 609).

Rubenstein, C., & Shaver, P. (1982). The experience of loneliness. In L. A. Peplau & D. Perlman (Eds.), *Loneliness: A sourcebook of current theory, research, and therapy.* N.Y.: Wiley.

Rubin, J. A., Provenzano, F. J., & Luria, A. (1974). The eye of the beholder: Parents' views on sex of newborns. *American Journal of Orthopsychiatry, 44*, 512–519.

Rubin, Z. (1981, May). Does personality really change after 20? *Psychology Today*, pp. 18–27.

Rubin, Z. (1983, March). Taking deception for granted. *Psychology Today*, pp. 74–75.

Rubinstein, C. (1982). Psychologists learn the darnedest things. *Psychology Today*, p. 17.

Rubinstein, E. (1983, July). Television and behavior: Research conclusions of the 1982 NIMH report and their policy implications. *American Psychologist*, pp. 820–825.

Rusbult, C. E. (1980). Commitment and satisfaction in romantic associations: A test of the investment model. *Journal of Experimental Social Psychology, 16*, 172–136.

Russell, J. A., & Ward, L. M. (1982). Environmental psychology. *Annual Review of Psychology, 83*, 651–88.

Rutter, M. (1982). Social-emotional consequences of day care for preschool children. In E. F. Zigler, & E. W. Gordon, (Eds.) *Day care: Scientific and social policy issues.* Boston: Auburn House.

Ryan, S. (1974). *A report on longitudinal evaluations of preschool programs: Vol. 1: Longitudinal evaluations* (DHEW Publications No. OHD 74–24). Washington, D.C.: Office of Human Development.

Ryckman, R. M. (1982). *Theories of Personality* (2nd ed.) Monterey, Ca.: Brooks/Cole.

Saccuzzo, D. P. (1975). What patients want from counseling and psychotherapy. *Journal of Clinical Psychology, 31*(3), 471–475.

Sameroff, A. J. (1975). Early influences on development: Fact or fancy? *Merrill-Palmer Quarterly of Behavior Development, 21.*

Samuels, M. T. (1974). *Children's long-term memory for events.* Unpublished doctoral thesis, Cornell University.

Sanford, N. (1956). The approach of the authoritarian personality. In L. L. McCary (Ed.) *Psychology of personality.* Grove Press.

Sanford, R. N. (1937). The effects of abstinence from food upon imaginal processes: A further experiment. *Journal of Psychology, 3*, 145–159.

Sarason, I. G., & Sarason, B. R. (1980). *Abnormal psychology: The problem of maladaptive behavior.* Englewood Cliffs, N.J.: Prentice-Hall.

Sarnoff, I., & Zimbardo, P. G. (1961). Anxiety, fear, and social affiliation. *Journal of Abnormal and Social Psychology, 62*, 356–363.

Satow, K. L. (1975). Social approval and helping. *Journal of Experimental Social Psychology, 11*, 501–509.

Sattler, J. M. (1975). *Assessment of children's intelligence.*

N.Y.: Holt, Rinehart & Winston.

Scarr, S., & Weinberg, R. A. (1976). IQ test performance of black children adopted by white families. *American Psychologist, 31*, 726–739.

Schachter, D. L. (1976). The hypnagogic state: A critical review of the literature. *Psychological Bulletin, 83*, 452–481.

Schachter, S. (1959). *The psychology of affiliation: Experimental studies of the sources of gregariousness.* Stanford, Ca.: Stanford University Press.

Schachter, S. (1971a, February). Some extraordinary facts about obese humans and rats. *American Psychologist*, 129–144.

Schachter, S. (1971b, April) Eat, eat. *Psychology Today* pp. 44–47, 78–79.

Schachter, S., & Singer, J. E. (1962). Cognitive, social, and physiological determinants of emotional state. *Psychological Review, 69*, 379–399.

Schiffman, H. R. (1976). *Sensation and perception: An integrated approach.* N. Y.: Wiley.

Schmitt, R. C. (1966). Density, health and social disorganization. *Journal of the American Institute of Planners, 32*, 39–40.

Schreiber, J. (1978). *The ultimate weapon: Terrorists and world order.* N. Y.: Morrow.

Schwartz, B. (1978). *Psychology of learning and behavior.* N. Y.: Norton.

Schwartz, G. E. (1974, April). TM relaxes some people and makes them feel better. *Psychology Today*, pp. 39–44.

Schwartz, J. H. (1980, April). The transport of substances in nerve cells. *Scientific American*, pp. 152–171.

Schweinhart, L. J., & Weikart, D. P. (1980). Young children grow up: The effects of the Perry Preschool Program on youths through age 15. *Monographs of the High/Scope Educational Research Foundation* (Series No. 7).

Scott, J. P., and Fuller, J. L. (1965). *Genetics and the social behavior of the dog.* Chicago: University of Chicago Press.

Sears, R. R., Maccoby, E. E., & Levin, H. (1957). *Patterns of child rearing.* N. Y.: Harper & Row.

Segal, M. W. (1974). Alphabet and attraction: An unobtrusive measure of the effect of propinquity in a field setting. *Journal of Personality and Social Psychology, 30*, 654–657.

Seligman, M.E.P. (1972). Phobias and preparedness. in M.E.P. Seligman & J. L. Hager (Eds.), *Biological boundaries of learning.* Englewood Cliffs, N.J.: Prentice-Hall.

Seligman, M.E.P. (1975). *Helplessness.* San Francisco: Freeman.

Selman, R. L. (1981). The child as a friendship philosopher. In S. Asher & J. Gottman (Eds.), *The development of children's friendships.* Cambridge: Cambridge University Press.

Shanas, E. (1972). Adjustment to retirement. In F. M. Carp (Ed.), *Retirement.* N. Y.: Behavioral Publications.

Shaw, J. S. (1982). Psychological androgyny and stressful life events. *Journal of Personality and Social Psychology, 43*, 145–153.

Shepard, R. N., & Metzler, J. (1971). Mental rotation of three-dimensional objects. *Science, 171*, 701–703.

Shibles, W. (1974). *Death: An interdisciplinary analysis.* Whitewater, Wis.: Language Press.

Siegal, J. M., & Steele, C. M. (1979). Noise level and social discrimination. *Personality and Social Psychology Bulletin, 5,* 95–99.

Siegel, O. (1982). Personality development in adolescence. In B. B. Wolman (Ed.), *Handbook of developmental psychology.* Englewood Cliffs, N.J.: Prentice-Hall.

Sigall, H., Page, R., & Brown, A. C. (1971). Effect of expenditure as a function of evaluation and evaluator attractiveness. *Representative Research in Social Psychology, 2,* 19–25.

Siipola, E. M. (1935). A study of some effects of preparatory set. *Psychological Monographs, 46*(210).

Silverman, B. I. (1974). Consequences, racial discrimination, and the principle of belief congruence. *Journal of Personality and Social Psychology, 29,* 497–508.

Sims, J. H ., & Baumann, D. D. (1972). The tornado threat: Coping styles of the north and south. *Science, 176,* 1386–1391.

Singer, J. L. (1969). Drives, affects, and daydreams: The adaptive role of spontaneous imagery of stimulus-independent meditation. In J. Antrobus (Ed.), *Cognition and Affect: The City University of New York Symposium.* Boston: Little, Brown, pp. 131–158.

Singer, J. L. (1974). Daydreaming and the stream of thought. *American Scientist, 41,* pp. 417–425.

Singer, J. L. (1975). *The inner world of daydreaming.* New York: Harper Colaphan.

Singer, J. L., & Singer, D. G. (1976). Fostering creativity in children: Can TV stimulate imaginative play? *Journal of Communications, 26,* 74–80.

Singer, J. L., & Singer, D. G. (1983, July). Psychologists look at television: Cognitive, developmental, personality, and social policy implications. *American Psychologist,* pp. 826–834.

Singular, S. (1982, October). A memory for all seasonings. *Psychology Today,* pp. 54–63.

Sistrunk, F., & McDavid, J. W. (1971). Sex variable in conforming behavior. *Journal of Personality and Social Psychology, 17,* 200–207.

Skeels, H. M. (1938). Mental development of children in foster homes. *Journal of Consulting Psychology, 2,* 33–43.

Skeels, H. M. (1942). The study of the effects of differential stimulation on mentally retarded children: A follow-up report. *American Journal of Mental Deficiencies, 46,* 340–350.

Skeels, H. M. (1966). Adult status of children with contrasting early life experiences. *Monographs of the Society for Research in Child Development, 31*(3), 1–65.

Skinner, B. F. (1948). "Superstition" in pigeons. *Journal of Experimental Psychology, 38,* 168–172.

Skinner, B. F. (1957). *Verbal behavior.* Englewood Cliffs, N.J.: Prentice-Hall.

Sloane, R. B., et al. (1975). Short-term analytically oriented psychotherapy versus behavior therapy. *American Journal of Psychiatry, 132,* 373–377.

Smith, D. (1982, July). Trends in counseling and psychotherapy. *American Psychologist, 37,* 802–809.

Smith, D., & Kraft, W. A. (1983, July). DSM-III: Do psychologists really want an alternative? *American Psychologist,* pp. 777–784.

Smith, G. P., & Gibbs, J. (1976). Cholecystokinan and sati-

ety: Theoretic and therapeutic implications. In D. Novin, W. Wyrwicka, & G. Bray (Eds.), *Hunger: Basic mechanics and clinical implications.* New York: Raven.

Smith, M. L., & Glass, G. V. (1977). Meta-analysis of psychotherapy outcome studies. *American Psychologist, 32,* 752–760.

Smyser, A. A. (1982, November). Hospices: Their humanistic and economic value. *American Psychologist,* pp. 1260–1262.

Snyder, M., & Cunningham, M. R. (1975). To comply or not comply: Testing the self-perception explanation of the "foot-in-the-door" phenomenon. *Journal of Personality and Social Psychology, 31,* 64–67.

Snyder, M., & Swann, W. B., Jr. (1978). Behavioral confirmation in social interaction: From social perception to social reality. *Journal of Experimental Social Psychology, 14,* 148–162.

Snyder, M., & Tanke, E. D. (1976). Behavior and attitude: Some people are more consistent than others. *Journal of Personality, 44,* 501–517.

Snyder, M., Tanke, E. D., & Berscheid, E. (1977). Social perception and interpersonal behavior: On the self-fulfilling nature of social stereotypes. *Journal of Personality and Social Psychology, 35,* 656–666.

Snyder, S. H. (1977). Opiate receptors and internal opiates. *Scientific American, 236,* 44–56.

Sommer, R. (1959). Studies in personal space. *Sociometry, 22,* 247–260.

Sontag, L. W. (1964). Implications of fetal behavior and environment for adult personalities. *Annals of the New York Academy of Science, 134,* 782–786.

Speigel, T. A. (1973). Caloric regulation of food intake in man. *Journal of Comparative and Physiological Psychology, 84,* 24–37.

Spero, M. (1978) Thoughts on computerized psychotherapy. *Psychiatry, 41,* 279–288.

Spezzano, C. (1981, May). Prenatal psychology: Pregnant with questions. *Psychology Today,* pp. 49–57.

Spiesman, J. C. (1965). Autonomic monitoring of ego defense process. In N. S. Greenfield & W. C. Lewis (Eds.), *Psychoanalysis and current biological thought.* Madison: University of Wisconsin Press.

Spitzer, R. L., Skodol, A. E., Gibbon, M., & Williams, J.B.W. (1981). *DSM-III case book.* Washington, D.C.: American Psychiatric Association.

Stapp, J. & Fulcher, R. (1982, November). The employment of 1979 and 1980 doctorate recipients in psychology. *American Psychologist 37*(41) 1159–1185.

Stechler, G., & Halton, A. (1982). Prenatal influences on human development. In B. B. Wolman, (Ed.), *Handbook of developmental psychology.* Englewood Cliffs, N.J.: Prentice-Hall.

Stein, D. D., Hardyck, J. A., & Smith, M. B. (1965). Race and belief: An open and shut case. *Journal of Personality and Social Psychology, 1,* 281–289.

Steiner, J. A. (1972). A questionnaire study of risk-taking in psychiatric patients. *British Journal of Medical Psychology, 45,* 365–374.

Steiner, J. E. (1979). Facial expressions in response to taste and smell stimulation. In H. W. Reese & L. P. Lipsitt (Eds.), *Advances in child development and behavior,* (Vol. 13). New York: Academic Press, pp. 257–296.

Stern, R. M., Breen, J. P. Watanabe, T., & Perry, B. S.

(1981). Effect of feedback of physiological information on responses to innocent associations and guilty knowledge. *Journal of Applied Psychology, 66,* 677–681.

Sternberg, R. J. (1981). Testing and cognitive psychology. *American Psychologist, 36* (10), 1081–1089.

Sternberg, R. J. (1982, April). Who's intelligent? *Psychology Today,* pp. 30–39.

Sternberg, R. J., & Davidson, J. E. (1982, June). The mind of the puzzler. *Psychology Today,* pp. 37–44.

Sternberg, R. J., Conway, B. E., Ketron, J. L. & Bernstein, M. (1981). People's conceptions of intelligence. *Journal of Personal and Social Psychology, 41*(1), 37–55.

Stevens, C. F. (1979). The neuron. *Scientific American, 241,* 54–65.

Stevens-Lang, J. (1984). *Adult life* (2nd ed.). Palo Alto, CA.: Mayfield.

Stewart, R. H. (1965). Effect of continuous responding on the order effect in personality impression formation. *Journal of Personality and Social Psychology, 1,* 161–165.

Stinnett, M., Carter, L. M., & Montgomery, J. E. (1972). Older persons' perceptions of their marriages. *Journal of Marriage and the Family, 34,* 665–670.

Stock, M. B., & Smythe, P. M. (1963). Does undernutrition during infancy inhibit brain growth and subsequent intellectual development? *Archives of Disorders in Childhood, 38,* 546–552.

Stokols, D. (1972). On the distinction between density and crowding: Some implications for future research. *Psychological Review, 79,* 275–279.

Stokols, D. (1978). A typology of crowding experiences. In A. Baum & Y. Epstein (Eds.), *Human response to crowding.* Hillsdale, N.J.: Erlbaum.

Stolz, S. B., Wienckowski, L. A., & Brown, B. S. (1975). Behavior modification: A perspective on critical issues. *American Psychologist, 30,* pp. 1027–1048.

Stone, L. J., & Church, J. (1968). *Childhood and adolescence: A psychology of the growing person* (2nd ed.). New York: Random House.

Stone, R. A., & Deleo, J. (1976). Psychotherapeutic control of hypertension. *New England Journal of Medicine, 294,* 80–84.

Stoner, J.A.F. (1961). A comparison of individual and group decisions involving risk. Unpublished master's thesis, School of Industrial Management, MIT.

Straus, M. A. (1977, March). Normative and behavioral aspects of violence between spouses. Paper presented at the Symposium on Violence, Simon Fraser University.

Stickland, B. R. (1977). Internal-external control of reinforcement. In T. Blass (Ed.), *Personality variables in social behavior.* Hillsdale, N.J.: Lawrence Erlbaum.

Strickland, B. R. (1979). Internal-external expectancies and cardiovascular functioning. In L. C. Perlmutter & R. A. Monty (Eds.) *Choice and perceived control.* Hillsdale, N.J.: Erlbaum.

Streib, G. F., & Schneider, C. J. (1971). *Retirement in American society: Impact and progress.* Ithaca, N.Y.: Cornell University Press.

Strommen, E. A., Mckinney, J. P., & Fitzgerald, H. E. (1983). *Developmental psychology: The school-aged child,* new. ed. Homewood, Ill.: The Dorsey Press.

Strongman, K. T. (1978). *The psychology of emotion.* New York: Wiley.

Strouse, J. (Ed.) (1974). *Women in analysis: Dialogues on psychoanalytic views of femininity.* New York: Grossman.

Suedfeld, P. (1975, January-February). The benefits of boredom: Sensory deprivation reconsidered. *American Scientist,* pp. 60–69.

Suedfeld, P. E., & Borrie, R. A. (1978). Altering states of consciousness through sensory deprivation. In A. Sugerman & R. Tarter (Eds.), *Expanding dimensions of consciousness.* New York: Springer, pp. 226–252.

Suomi, S. J., & Harlow, H. F. (1977). Production and alleviation of depressive behaviors in monkeys. In J. D. Maser and M.E.P. Seligman (Eds.), *Psychopathology: Experimental models.*

Swartz, J. D. (1978). Thematic apperception test (Review). In O. K. Buros (Ed.), *The eighth mental measurements yearbook* (Vol. 1). Highland Park, N.J.: The Gryphon Press.

Swingle, P. (1970). Exploitative behavior in non-zero sum games. *Journal of Personality and Social Psychology, 16,* 121–132.

Szasz, T. (1974, December). Our despotic laws destroy the right to self-control. *Psychology Today,* pp. 20–29, 127.

Tanner, J. M. (1971). Sequence, tempo, and individual variation in growth and development of boys and girls aged twelve to sixteen. *Daedalus, 100,* 907–930.

Tavris, C. (1982). *Anger: the misunderstood emotion.* N.Y.: Simon & Schuster.

Taylor, S. & Mettee, D. (1971). When similarity breeds contempt. *Journal of Personality and Social Psychology, 20,* 75–81.

Taylor, S. E. (1983, November). Adjustment to threatening events. *American Psychologist,* pp. 1161–1173.

Tellegen, A. (1978). Eysench personality inventory. In O.K. Buros (Ed.) *The eighth mental measurements yearbook.* Highland Park, N.J.: Gryphon. pp. 802–804.

Thomas, A., Chess, S., & Birch, H. G. (1970, August). The origin of personality. *Scientific American,* pp. 102–109.

Thompson, D. F., & Meltzer, L. (1964). Communication of emotional intent by facial expression. *Journal of Abnormal and Social Psychology, 68,* 129–135.

Thompson, R. F. (1975). *Introduction to physiological psychology.* New York: Harper & Row.

Thurstone, L. L. (1938). Primary mental abilities. *Psychometric Monographs, 1.*

Tierney, J. (1982, June). Doctor, is this man dangerous? *Science '82,* pp. 28–31.

Time (1979, December 24). The trauma of captivity.

Timiras, P. S. (1972). *Developmental physiology and aging.* New York: Macmillan.

Timiras, P. S. (1978). Biological perspecitves on aging. *American Scientist, 66,* 605–613.

Tittle, R. H. (1980). Changes in self vs. situational perceptions as mediators of the foot-in-the-door effect. *Personality and Social Psychology Bulletin.*

Toffler, A. (1970). *Future shock.* New York: Random House.

Tomkins, S. S., & McCarter, R. (1964). What and where are the primary affects: Some evidence for a theory. *Percpetual and Motor Skills, 18,* 119–158.

Torrance, E. P. (1954). Leadership training to improve aircrew group performance. *USAF ATC Instructor's Journal, 5,* 25–35.

Tresemer, D. (1974, March). Fear of success: Popular, but

unpopular. *Psychology Today*, pp. 82–85.

Trotter, R. J. (1983, August). Baby face. *Psychology Today*, pp. 12–20.

Tversky, A., & Kahneman, D. (1973). Availability: A heuristic for judging frequency and probability. *Cognitive Psychology 5*, 207–232.

Tyron, R. C. (1940). Genetic differences in maze-learning abilities in rats. In *39th Yearbook, Part I*. National Society for the Study of Education. Chicago: University of Chicago Press.

Turkat, I. D., & Alpher, V. S. (1983, July). An investigation of personality disorder descriptions. *American Psychologist*, pp. 857–858.

Turnbull, C. M. (1961). Observations. *American Journal of Psychology, 1*, 304–308.

Turner, B. F. (1982). Sex-related differences in aging. In B. B. Wolman (Ed.), *Handbook of developmental psychology*. Englewood Cliffs, N.J.: Prentice-Hall.

Ullman, C. A. (1957). Teachers, peers, and tests as predictors of adjustment. *Journal of Educational Psychology, 48*, 257–267.

Ungerer, J. A., Brody, L. R., & Zelazo, P. R. (1978). Long-term memory for speech in 2- to 4-week-old infants. *Infant Behavior and Development, 1*, 177–186.

U.S. News & World Report (1979, December 31). An expert's view of the hostages' ordeal.

U.S. News and World Report (1979, May 7). Behind growing outrage over insanity pleas. p. 42.

Ursin, H. et al. (Eds.) (1978). Psychology of stress: A study of coping men. N.Y.: Academic Press.

Valenstein, E. S. (1973). *Brain control*. New York: Wiley.

Valenstein, E. S. (1977). The brain and behavior control. In *Master lectures on behavior control*. Washington, D.C.: American Psychological Association.

Vandenbos, G. R., DeLeon, P. H., & Pallak, M. S. (1982, November). An alternative to traditional medical care for the terminally ill: Humanitarian, policy, and political issues in hospice care. *American Psycholgist*, pp. 1245–1248.

Van Dyke, C. & Byck, R. (1982, March). Cocaine. *Scientific American*.

Vaughan, E. D. (1977). Misconceptions about psychology among introductory psychology students. *Teaching of Psychology, 4* (3), 138–140.

Verhave, T. (1966). The pigeon as a quality-control inspector. *American Psychologist, 21*, 109–115.

Vinokur, A., & Burnstein, (1974). Effects of partially shared persuasive arguments on group-induced shifts: A group problem-solving approach. *Journal of Personality and Social Psychology, 29*, 305–315.

Wahba, N. A., & Bridwell, L. G. (1976). Maslow reconsidered: A review of research on the need hierarchy theory. *Organizational Behavior and Human Performance, 15*, 212–240.

Waid, W. M., Orne, E. C., & Orne, M. T. (1981). Selective memory for social information, alertness, and physiological arousal in the detection of deception. *Journal of Applied Psychology, 66*, 224–232.

Waid, W. M., & Orne, M. T. (1981). Cognitive, social, and personality processes in the psysiological detection of deception. In L. Berkowitz (Ed.) *Advances in Experimental Social Psychology* (Vol. 14). New York: Academic Press.

Waid, W. M., & Orne, M. T. (1982). The physiological detection of deception. *American Scientist, 70*, 402–409.

Walk, R. D., & Gibson, E. J. (1961). A comparative and analytical study of visual depth perception. *Psychological Monographs*, No. 75.

Walker, J. (1981, May). The amateur scientist. *Scientific American*, pp. 176–184.

Walker, L. J., & Richards, B. S. (1979). Stimulating transitions in moral reasoning as a function of stage of cognitive development. *Developmental Psychology, 15*, 95–103.

Walker, P. C., & Johnson, R.F.Q. (1974). The influence of presleep suggestions on dream content: Evidence and methodological problems. *Psychological Bulletin, 81*(6), 362–370.

Wallace, R. K., & Benson, H. (1972, February). The physiology of meditation. *Scientific American*.

Wallach, M. A., & Wing, C. W., Jr. (1969). *The talented student*. New York: Holt, Rinehart & Winston.

Walster, E. (1966). Assignment of responsibility for an accident. *Journal of Personality and Social Psychology, 3*, 73–79.

Walster, E., Aronson, V., Abrahams, D., & Rottmann, L. (1966). Importance of physical attractiveness in dating behavior. *Journal of Personality and Social Psychology, 4*, 508–516.

Walster, E. & Walster, G. W. (1978). *Love*. Reading, Mass.: Addison-Wesley.

Wang, G. H. (1923). The relation between spontaneous activity and oestrous cycle in the white rat. *Comparative Psychology Monographs, 49*, 15–19.

Waterman, C. K., Buebel, M. E., & Waterman, A. S. (1970). Relationship between resolution of the identity crisis and outcomes of previous psychosocial crises. *Proceedings of the Annual Convention of the American Psychological Association, 5* (Pt. 1), 467–468.

Watson, D., & Tharp, R. (1977). *Self-directed behavior*, (2nd ed). Monterey, CA: Brooks/Cole.

Watson, D., & Tharp, R. (1981). *Self-directed behavior* (3rd ed.). Monterey, Ca: Brooks/Cole.

Watson, J. B. (1913). Psychology as the behaviorist views it. *Psychological Review, 20*, 158–177

Watson, J. B. (1930). *Behaviorism*. N.Y.: W. W. Norton.

Watson, J. B., & Rayner, R. (1920). Conditioned emotional reactions. *Journal of Experimental Psychology, 3*, 1–14.

Watson, J. S. (1971). Cognitive-perceptual development in infancy: Setting for the seventies. *Merrill-Palmer Quarterly, 12*, 139–152.

Webb, W. B., & Cartwright, R. D. (1978). Sleep and dreams. *Annual Review of Psychology, 29*, 223–252.

Weil, A. (1972, October). The open mind. *Psychology Today*, pp. 51–66.

Weintraub, W., & Aronson, H. (1968). A survey of patients in classical psychoanalysis: Some vital statistics. *Journal of Nervous and Mental Disorders, 146*, 98–102.

Weisenberg, M. (1977). Pain and pain control. *Psychological Bulletin, 84*, 1008–1044.

Weiss, R. S. (1973). *Loneliness: The experience of emotional and social isolation*. Cambridge, Mass.: MIT Press.

Weitzenhoffer, A. (1978). Hypnotism and altered states of consciousness. In A. Sugarman & R. Tarter (Eds.), *Expanding dimensions of consciousness*. New York: Springer.

Wess, J. M. (1971). Effects of coping behavior in different

warning signal conditions on stress pathology in rats. *Journal of Comparative and Physiological Psychology, 1*, 1–14.

Westoff, C. F. (1974). Coital frequency and conception. *Family Planning Perspectives, 3*, 136–141.

White, R. W., & Watt, N. F. (1973). *The abnormal personality* (4th ed.). New York: Ronald Press.

Whitehurst, G. J. (1982). Language development. In B. B. Wolman (Ed.), *Handbook of developmental psychology*, Englewood Cliffs, N.J.: Prentice-Hall.

Whorf, B. L. (1956). *Language, thought, and reality*. New York: M.I.T. Press-Wiley.

Wickelgren, W. A. (1974). *How to solve problems: Elements of a theory of problems and problem solving*. San Francisco: W. H. Freeman.

Wickelgren, W. A. (1979). *Cognitive psychology*. Englewood Cliffs, N.J.: Prentice-Hall.

Wicker, A. (1969). Attitudes versus actions: The relationship of verbal and overt behavioral responses to attitude objects. *The Journal of Social Issues, 25*, 1–78.

Wiesel, T. N., & Hubel, D. H. (1963). Effects of visual deprivation on morphology and physiology of cells in the cat's geniculate body. *Journal of Neurophysiology, 26*, 978–993.

Williams, H. K. (1977). *Psychology of women: Behavior in a biosocial context*. New York: Norton.

Williams, M. D. (1976). Retrieval from very long-term memory. Unpublished doctoral dissertation, University of California, San Diego.

Wills, T. A., Langner, T. S. (1980). Socioeconomic status and stress. See Minter & Kimball 1980, pp. 159–73.

Wilson, D. W., & Donnerstein, E. (1976). Legal and ethical aspects of nonreactive social psychological research: An excursion into the public mind. *American Psychologist, 31*,(11), 765–773.

Wilson, G. (1978). Introversion/extroversion. In H. London & J. E. Exner (Eds.) *Dimensions of Personality*. New York: Wiley, pp. 217–261.

Winch, R. F. (1958). *Mate selection: A study of complementary needs*. N.Y.: Harper & Row.

Winter, D. G. (1973). *The power motive*. N.Y.: Free Press.

Winter, D. G. (1976, July). What makes the candidates run? *Psychology Today*, pp. 45–49, 92.

Witkin, H. A., et al. (1962). *Psychological differentiation*. N.Y.: Wiley.

Wolberg, L. R. (1977). *The Technique of Psychotherapy* (3rd ed.). New York: Grune and Stratton.

Wolf, M., Mees, H., & Risley, T. (1964). Application of operant conditioning procedures to the behavior problems of an autistic child. *Behavior Research Therapy, 1*, 305–312.

Wolfe, L. (1978, June). Why some people can't love. *Psychology Today*, p. 55.

Wolff, C. T., Friedman, S. B., Hofer, M. A., & Mason, J. W. (1964). Relationship between psychological defenses and mean urinary 17-hydroxycorticosteroid excretion rates: I. A study of parents of fatally ill children. *Psychosomatic Medicine, 26*, 576–591.

Wolman, B. B. (Ed.) (1978). *Psychological aspects of gynecology and obstetrics*. Oradell, N.J.: Medical Economics.

Wolpe, J. (1969, June). For phobia: A hair of the hound. *Psychology Today*, pp. 34–37.

Wolpe, J. (1973). *The practice of behavior therapy* (2nd ed.). N.Y.: Pergamon Press.

Wolpe, J., & Rachman, S. (1960). Psycholanalytic evidence: A critique of Freud's case of little Hans. *Journal of Nervous and Mental Diseases, 130*, 198–220.

Woods, P. J. (ed.) (1979). *The psychology major*. American Psychological Association: Washington, D. C., Chapter 4, pp. 27–29, Chapters 12–15, pp. 103–125.

Wooley, O. (1971). Long-term food regulation in the obese and non-obese. *Psychosomatic Medicine, 33*, 436.

Worchel, S. (1974). The effect of those types of arbitrary thwarting on the instigation to aggression. *Journal of Personality, 42*, 301–318.

Worchel, S., & Cooper, J. (1979). *Understanding social psychology*. Homewood, Ill.: Dossey.

Yamamoto, K., & Chimbidis, M. E. (1966). Achievement, intelligence, and creative thinking in fifth grade children: A correlational study. *Merrill-Palmer Quarterly, 12*(3), 233–241.

Yellott, J. I. (1981, July). Binocular depth inversion. *Scientific American*.

Young, P. (1983, August). A conversation with Richard Jed Wyatt. *Psychology Today*. pp. 36–41.

Zaidel, E. (1983, May). "A response to Gazzaniga: Language in the right hemisphere, convergent perspectives." *American Psychologist*, pp. 542–546.

Zajonc, R. B. (1968). Attitudinal effects of mere exposure. *Journal of Personality and Social Psychology, 8*, 1–29.

Zajonc, R. B., & Markus, G. B. (1975). Birth order and intellectual development. *Psychological Review, 82*(1), 74–88.

Zelazo, P., Zelazo, N. A., & Kolb, S. (1972, April). "Walking" in the newborn. *Science, 176*, pp. 314–315.

Zigler, E., & Berman, W. (1983, August). Discerning the future of early childhood intervention. *American Psychologist*, pp. 894–901.

Zilbergeld, B., & Evans, M. (1980, August). The inadequacy of Masters and Johnson. *Psychology today*, pp. 28–43.

Zimbardo, P. G. (1969). The human choice: Individuation, reason, and order versus deindividuation, impulse, and chaos. In N. J. Arnold & D. Levine (Eds.), *Nebraska symposium on motivation*. Lincoln: University of Nebraska Press.

Zimmerman, A. M., Bruce, W. R., & Zimmerman, S. (1979). Effects of cannabinoids on sperm morphology. *Pharmacology, 18*, 143–148.

Zubek, J. P. (1973). Review of effects of prolonged deprivation. In J. E. Rasmussen (Ed.), *Man in isolation and confinement*. Chicago: Aldine.

Zuckerman, M., & Wheeler, L. (1975). To dispel fantasies about the fantasy-based measure of fear of success. *Psychological Bulletin, 82*, 932–946.

Zwislocki, J. J (1981, March-April). Sound analysis in the ear: A history of discoveries. *American Scientist*, pp. 184–192.

Acknowledgments

Figures, tables, text

Fig. 2-3 Carlson, Neil R., *Physiology of Behavior,* 2nd ed. Boston: Allyn & Bacon, 1981. **Fig. 2-10 Levinthal, C.,** *The Physiological Approach to Psychology,* Englewood Cliffs, N.J.: Prentice-Hall, 1979.

Fig. 3-6 Hubel, David H., "Visual Cortex of the Brain," *Scientific American* (1963) All rights reserved. **Fig. 3-18** Dunkle, T., "The Sound of Silence," *Science '82,* (April, 1982) pp. 30–33. **Fig. 3-21** Hudspeth, A.J., "The Hair Cells of the Inner Ear," *Scientific American,* (January, 1983). **P. 83** Boring E. G., Langfeld, H.S., and Weld, H. P., *Foundations of Psychology,* Wiley: New York, 1948, p. 338. In H. R. Schiffman (1976). Sensation and Perception. New York: John Wiley, p. 77. Reprinted by permission of John Wiley & Sons, Inc.

Fig. 4-4 Gregory, R. L., *The Intelligent Eye,* New York: McGraw-Hill, 1970, p. 14. **Fig. 4-13** Gibson, James T., *The Perception of the Visual World,* Houghton Mifflin, © 1950, 1977, Used with permission. **Figs. 4-13 & 4-18** Boring, E. G., Langfeld, H.S., Weld, H. P., *Foundations of Psychology,* New York: John Wiley & Sons, Inc., © 1948, 1976, pp. 77, 338. Reprinted by permission of John Wiley & Sons. **Fig. 4-14** From Leeper, R. W. A Motivational Theory of Emotion to Replace "Emotion as Disorganized Response." *Psychological Review.* 1948, 55, 5–21. **Fig. 4-20** Gregory, R. L., *Eye and Brain,* New York: McGraw-Hill, 1966. **Fig. 4-23** Heron, W. "Cognitive and Physiological Effect of Perceptual Isolation." In P. Solomon et al. (eds.), SENSORY DEPRIVATION. Cambridge, MA: Harvard University Press, 1961, p. 9, Figure 2.1. Reprinted by permission. **Fig. 4-24** Wallace, R. K., and Benson, H., "The Physiology of Meditation" *Scientific American,* (1972) All rights reserved. **Fig. 4-25** Luce, Guy Gaer, Segal, Julius, *Sleep,* "Brain Wave Patterns" (1966) Bill Berger, Assoc., Printed by permission. **P. 144** (top) Hechinger, Nancy, "Seeing Without Eyes," *Science 81,* March, p. 41. (bottom). Kennedy, J. M., "Papers in Language Use and Language Function" *Scientific American,* Haptic Pictures, (1983) Jan.-Feb., pp. 20–26 University of Toronto, 13.

Fig. 5-3 Dember, W. N., "The New Look in Motivation," *American Scientist,* 1965, 53, 409–427. **Fig. 5-4** Maslow, A. H., *Motivation and Personality,* New York: Harper & Row, 1954. **Fig. 5-5** Plutchick, Robert, *The Emotions: Facts, Theories and a New Model.* Random House (1962). Reprinted by permission of the publisher. **Fig. 5-6** Plutchick, Robert, "Primary and Mixed Emotions," *Psychology Today* (Feb. 1980), p. 75. **Fig. 5-7** Hebb, D. O. "Drives and the CNS (conceptual nervous system). *Psychological Review,* 1955, 62, 243–254.

Figs. 6-4 & 6-5 Skinner, B. F., "Teaching Machines." Copyright © 1961 by *Scientific American,* Inc. All rights reserved. **Fig. 6-6** Reprinted from *Psychology Today Magazine.* Copyright © 1980 American Psychology Association.

Table 9-1 Sternberg, R. J., "Who's Intelligent". *Psychology Today,* (April, 1982) pp. 30–39

Fig. 10-1 Bayley, 1956 **Fig. 10-2** Jackson, 1928. **Fig. 10-3** Fantz, R. L. "Visual perception from birth as shown by pattern selectivity" *Annals of the New York Academy of Sciences,* (1965) pp. 118, 793–814

Table 11-1 Stevens-Long, J. *Adult Life,* 2nd ed. Palo Alto, CA: Mayfield Publishing Co. (1984)

Fig. 12-1 Adapted from a diagram from *The Complete Introductory Lectures on Psychoanalysis* by Sigmund Freud. Translated and edited by James Strachey. With the permission of W. W., Norton & Co., Inc. Copyright 1966 by W. W. Norton and Co., Inc. Copyright © 1965, 1964, 1963 by James Strachey. Also permission of the Hogarth Press, Ltd. in *New Introductory Lectures on Psychoanalysis* by Sigmund Freud **Fig. 12-2** Erikson, Erik (1950) **Table 12-1** Cattell, R. B., *The Scientific Analysis of Personality,* Baltimore: Penguin (1965) **Table 12-2** Maddi, J. *Personality Theories: A Comparative Analysis,* (Rev. ed.) Homewood, IL: The Dorsey Press, (1972), pp. 271, 273, 276

Quote from Richard S. Lazarus & Alan Monat, PERSONAl ITY, 3rd ed., © 1979, pp. 23-25. Reprinted by permission of Prentice-Hall, Inc., Englewood Cliffs, N.J.

Table 14-1 Strupp H. H. & Hadley S. W., "A Tripartite Model of Mental Health and Therapeutic Outcomes:

With Special Reference to Negative Effects in Psychotherapy." AMERICAN PSYCHOLOGIST, 1977, 32, 190. Copyright © by the American Psychological Association. Reprinted by permission. **Cases:** R. L. Spitzer, A. E., Skodol, M. Gibbon, and J.B.W. Williams, *DSM-111 Case Book,* Washington, D.C.: American Psychiatric Association, (1981)

Fig. 16-1 Festinger, L., Schachter, S., and Bach, K. *Social Pressures in Informal Groups: A Study of Human Factors in Housing,* (New York: Harper and Row) 1950, Snyder, M., Tanke, E.D. & Berscheid, E., "Social Perception and Interpersonal Behavior" *Journal of Personality and Social Psychology* (1977)

Fig. A-3 Hill, A. B., *Principles of Medical Statistics* 8th ed., London: Oxford University Press, 1966.

Photographs and Cartoons

Chapter 1 opening Richard Laird, FPG **2** New York Public Library **3** (top) The Granger Collection; (bottom) The Bettmann Archive **4** Psychology Archives **5** Psychology Archives **6** Tony Mendoza, Archive Pictures **7** (top) WHO Photo; (bottom) © 1981 Jill Krementz **10** Ken Karp **11** © 1960 United Feature Syndicate, Inc. **12** Bohdan Hrynewych, Southern Light **13** Van Bucher, Photo Researchers, Inc. **16** Eric Kroll, Taurus Photo **21** Shell Oil Company **22** Katrina Thomas, Photo Researchers, Inc.

26 UCLA School of Medicine **28** Carolina Biological Supply Co. **33** E. R. Lewis, Y. Z. Zeevi, and T. E. Everhart, Dept. of Electrical Engineering & Computer Sciences, U. of California, Berkeley **39** AFIP Science Source, Photo Researchers, Inc. **40** (both) Dan McCoy, Rainbow **41** (left) Dan McCoy, Rainbow; (right) **43** Lester V. Bergman & Associates, Inc. **54** Taurus Photos, Inc. **55** Leonard Lessin, Photo Researchers, Inc. **57** John Running, Stock, Boston **69** Charles Mayer, Photo Researchers, Inc.

66 Michael Phillip Manheim, Photo Researchers, Inc. **72** Figure 3-2 Don Wong, Photo Researchers, Inc. **78** Figure 3-10 Inmont Corp. **80** Figure 3-11 Fritz Goro, *Life Magazine*, Time, Inc. **81** Figure 3-13 Fritz Goro, *Life Magazine*, Time, Inc. **84** Figure 3-14 Kaz Mori, Taurus Photos **91** Bob McNerling, Taurus Photos **94** Susan Johns, Photo Researchers, Inc. **98** Brian Blake, Photo Researchers, Inc.

104 Michael Phillip Manheim, Photo Researchers, Inc. **107** Figure 4-4 (bottom) J. N. Robinson, Photo Researchers, Inc. **108** Figure 4-5 Haags Gemeentemuseum, The Hague **113** (same as CO 104) **115** Taurus Photos **116** (left) Elizabeth Weiland, Photo Researchers, Inc.; (right) Tom McHugh, Photo Researchers, Inc. **118** (top) Bob Gruen, Star File; (bottom) The Museum of Modern Art **122** Figure 4-22 William Vandivert, Scientific American **125** James Hamilton **137** Detroit Institute of Art **141** Charles Gatewood **148** Tim Davis, Photo Researchers, Inc. **151** Bohdan Hrynewych, Southern Light **153** (left) Billy E. Barnes, Southern Light; (right) Joan Leboll Cohen, Photo Researchers, Inc. **157** University of Wisconsin Primate Laboratory **158** Carl Purcell, Photo Researchers, Inc. **159** Harry F. Harlow, University of Wisconsin Primate Laboratory **160** Michael Philip Manheim, Photo Researchers, Inc. **163** Hugh Rogers, Monkmeyer Press Photo **164** Michael Evans, The White House **165** AP/Wide World Photo **178** (left) Will McIntyre, Photo Researchers, Inc.; (right) Richard Hutchings, Photo Researchers, Inc. **179** Robert Goldstein, Photo Researchers, Inc. **180** Los Angeles Police Department

185 Jacque Charles, Stock, Boston **186** Bohdan Hrynewych, Southern Light **187** Howard Earl Oible, Photo Researchers, Inc. **195** Paul Conklin, Monkmeyer Press **197** (top) Eliot Elisopin, Life Magazine; (bottom) Ken Davis **199** Ray Ellis, Rapho/Photo Researchers, Inc. **201** Bill Belknap, Rapho/Photo Researchers, Inc. **204** Irene Springer **208** Ken Davis **211** Bohdan Hrynewych, Southern Light

218 F. B. Grunzweig, Photo Researchers, Inc. **220** Lynn Robinson Betts **223** Jan Halaska, Photo Researchers, Inc. **224** Margot S. Branitsas, Photo Researchers, Inc. **226** Ken Davis **230** Ken Davis **231** James Foote, Photo Researchers, Inc. **233** Larry Mulvehill, Photo Researchers, Inc. **234** Robert Perron, Photo Researchers, Inc. **235** Laimute E. Druskis **240** Christopher Morrow, Stock, Boston

246 Laimute E. Druskis **249** Roger Troy Peterson, Photo Researchers, Inc. **252** Bill Bachman, Photo Researchers, Inc. **258** Owen Franken, Stock, Boston **259** Charles Gatewood **265** Guy Gillette, Photo Researchers, Inc. **266** Susan Berkowitz, Taurus Photos **268** Larry Mulvehill, Photo Researchers, Inc.

272 Richard Hutchings, Photo Researchers, Inc. **277** Owen Franken, Stock, Boston **279** Sing-Si Schwartz **281** Stephen Collins, Photo Researchers, Inc. **286** Ken Karp **288** Frederick D. Bodin, Stock, Boston **290** Owen Franken, Stock, Boston **291** Charles Gatewood **293** Elizabeth Crews, Stock, Boston **294** Joseph Szabo, Photo Researchers, Inc. **295** Charles Gopton, Stock, Boston **296** Nick Sapieka, Stock, Boston **299** Franke Keating, Photo Researchers, Inc.

306 Mimi Forsyth, Monkmeyer Press **309** (top) Russ Kinne, Photo Researchers, Inc.; (bottom) Tom McHugh, Photo Researchers, Inc. **310** (top) Ken Karp; (bottom) Richard Frieman, Photo Researchers, Inc. **314** (all) Suzanne Szasz

319 William Vandivert **331** Will McIntyre, Photo Researchers, Inc. **333** Jeff Albertson, Stock, Boston **336** Freda Leinwand, Monkmeyer Press **337** Debbie Dean

346 Richard Hutchings, Photo Researchers, Inc. **348** Ken Karp **352** Suzanne Anderson, Photo Researchers, Inc. **353** Ed Lettau, Photo Researchers, Inc. **355** Arthur Glauberman, Photo Researchers, Inc. **359** Will McIntyre, Photo Researchers, Inc. **361** Richard Frieman, Photo Researchers, Inc. **364** Marilyn Stouffer, Photo

Researchers, Inc. **367** Ray Ellis, Photo Researchers, Inc.

372 Emile Toberfeld, Taurus Photos **375** © 1959 by the United Feature Syndicate, Inc. **377** Abigail Heyman, Archive Pictures **380** Suzanne Szasz, Photo Researchers, Inc.
383 PUNCH/Rothco **384** © 1978 S. Gross **387** Jill Krementz **392** Frank Siteman, Taurus Photos
393 Burgoyne, Inc. **396** University of Florida, Dept. of Clinical Psychology, Photo Researchers, Inc. **397** © 1976 by Sidney Harris, *Saturday Review.*
398 Ethan Hoffman, Archives Pictures

402 Richard Hutchings, Photo Researchers, Inc. **404** Reprinted with permission of Charles Scribner's Sons from *Good News/Bad News,* by Henry R. Martin, Copyright © 1977 Henry R. Martin. **405** Catherine Ursillo, Photo Researchers, Inc. **406** George E. Jones III, Photo Researchers, Inc. **410** Robert A. Isaacs, Photo

Researchers, Inc. **411** American Airlines **419** Catherine Ursillo, Photo Researchers, Inc. **423** UPI, Bettmann Archive **424** Thomas S. England, Photo Researchers, Inc. **425** United Feature Syndicate, Inc. **427** UPI/Bettmann Archive

432 Jack Sullivan, Photo Researchers, Inc. **434** (both) The Bettmann Archive **436** The Bettmann Archive **438** Editorial Photocolor Archives **440** Arthur Tress, Photo Researchers, Inc. **446** UPI/The Bettmann Archive **449** Ken Karp **450** Yan Lukas, Photo Researchers, Inc. **456** Owen Franken, Stock, Boston

464 Geoffrey Gove, Photo Researchers, Inc. **474** Zimbel, Monkmeyer **481** Zimbel, Monkmeyer **485** Michael O'Brien, Archive Pictures **488** AP/Wide World Photos **468** Fig. 15-1 Picture Collection, The Branch Libraries, New York Public Library **470** Courtesy of Carl Rogers **473** Stephen Green, Armytage Photo **474** © 1975 *Medical Tribune.* Reprinted by permission of Sidney Harris **475** (top) Ken Karp; (bottom) Joseph Nettis, Photo Researchers, Inc. **477** Sandy Solmon, Gibbe Photos

494 Eric Kroll, Taurus Photos **496** Jim Anderson, Woodfin Camp & Associates **497** Freda Leinwand, Monkmeyer **501** Miriam Reinhardt, Photo Researchers, Inc. **503**

505 (top) UPI/The Bettmann Archive (right) **506** Ken Karp **512** Richard Hutchings, Photo Researchers, Inc. **516** Eric Kroll, Taurus Photos **520** The University of Texas at Austin News and Information Service **522** Dana Hyde, Photo Researchers, Inc.

539 PUNCH/Rothco

Name Index

Subject Index

Beauty. *See* Appearance
Behavior. *See also* Abnormal
   behavior; Learning; Physiology, behavior and
   attitudes and, 504, 505–6
   attribution to kinds of, 499–50
   genetics and, 53, 57–61
   helping, 513–14
   mob, 515
   modification, 212
   reflex, 46–47, 311
   sex differences in, 11, 60,
      337–38
   therapies, 473–75, 480
Behavioral contracting, 473
Behavioral model of abnormal
   behavior, 437
Behavioral sciences, 11–12
Behaviorism, 5–7
Behavior therapy, 473–75, 480
Beliefs, 504, 522–24
Bem Sex Role Inventory (BSRI),
   379
Bereavement, 368, 422–23
Beta endorphin, 52
Beta waves, 38
Bias, 13, 14, 500. *See also* Preju-
   dice
Biased sample, 540
Bilinguals, brain of, 250
Bimodal distribution, 534
Binaural cues, 117–18
Binet-Simon Scale, 279
Binocular cues, 113, 116–17
Binocular depth inversion, 117
Binocular vision, 317
Biofeedback, 206, 213–15
Biological clocks, 131
Biological model of abnormal
   behavior, 436
Biology, sex roles and, 337–39
Bipolar disorder, 447, 448
Bipolar neurons, 74, 76, 77, 85
Birth order, 291, 335
Blindness:
   color, 82, 84
   location of sound and, 118
   perception and, 143–44
Blind spot, 77
Blunders, attraction and, 502
Body language, 177–78
Bottom-up processing, 251
Botulism, 34
Brain, 36–46
   of bilinguals, 250
   development, 315
   divisions of, 36–42

electrical stimulation of, 44
hemispheric specialization,
   42–45, 263
hunger control, 151–52
memory's location in, 241–42
neural connections:
   to ear, 88–89
   to eye, 77–79
   to nose, 92–93
reticular formation of, 45–46
sensory experience and, 68
sex drive and, 155
stem, 37
transplants, 61–62
waves, 38, 128, 444
Breeding, selective, 289
Brightness, 80
Brightness constancy, 111
British Cruelty of Animals Act,
   20
BSRI, 379
Burnout, stress and, 419
Bystanders, altruism of, 514

Caffeine, 35
California Institute of Technology,
   43
California Test of Mental Maturity
   (CTMM), 281
Camouflage, 107
Cancer, stress and, 420, 421
Cannon-Bard theory, 172, 173
Capacity:
   humanistic personality theory
      and, 389–91
   for language, 326
   of short-term memory, 224–25
Captivity, effects of, 427–28
Career, adulthood and, 362–65
Careers in psychology, 21–23
Catastrophe, extreme stress from,
   423
Catatonic schizophrenia, 458
Categorization:
   impression formation and,
      495–96
   of problem, 258–59
Category membership, degree of,
   250
CAT scanning, 40, 41
Cell body, 28
Central nervous system, 36–47,
   315
Central tendency, measures of,
   529–34
Cerebellum, 37

Cerebral cortex, 38–45. *See also*
   Brain
   areas of, 38–42, 79
   hemispheric specialization of,
      42–45, 263
Change:
   attitude, 506–9
   of life, 356
   stress from, 404–5
Characteristic behavior. *See* Per-
   sonality
Chicago, University of, 4–5
Child abuse, 160
Childhood. *See* Infancy and child-
   hood
Child psychologist, 9
Children:
   dreams of, 135
   marital happiness and, 360, 361
Chimpanzees, use of language by,
   253
Chlorpromazine, 482
Christensen-Guilford Test, 300
Chromosomes, 54–55
Chunking, 225
Circadian cycle, 131
Clairvoyance, 120
Class, social, 291, 293, 413
Classical conditioning, 186–95
   extinction and spontaneous
      recovery, 191–92
   generalization and discrimina-
      tion, 192–94
   higher-order, 194–95
   in human beings, 187–89
   necessary factors in, 189–91
   operant vs., 206–8
   Pavlov's experiments on, 186–87
Client-centered therapy, 469–70
Climacteric, 356
Clinical psychology, focus of, 10
Clocks, biological, 131
Closure, principle of, 107
Coaching, 301
Cocaine, 35, 141
Cochlea, 87, 88
Cochlear implant, 99–100
"Cocktail-party phenomenon,"
   222, 223
Coding:
   in long-term memory, 234–35
   in short-term memory, 225–26
Coefficient, correlation, 283, 285
Coefficient, correlation, 538–39

Internal-external theory of obesity, 152
Internal language acquisition theory, 324–26
Internal orientation, 397–99
Interneurons, 29, 77
Interpretation:
  in problem solving, 257–59
  of reality, 434
Interstimulus interval, 189
Interval scale, 529
Intervention:
  crisis, 488
  programs, IQ and, 301–2
Interview, personal, 392
Intimacy versus isolation stage, 387
Intrapersonal standards of normality, 433–34
Introspection, objective, 3
Introverted-extroverted personality dimensions, 377, 394
Inversion, binocular depth, 117
Ions, 29, 30
IQ. See Intelligence
Isolation vs. intimacy stage, 387

James-Lange theory, 171–72, 173, 175
Jensen controversy, 294-95
Jigsaw method of reducing prejudice, 524
Jobs in psychology, 21–23
Joint Commission on Mental Health of Children, 488
Juries, eyewitness testimony and, 242–43
Just noticeable difference (jnd), 70–71
Just world hypothesis, 500–501

Kinesics, 177
Korsakoff's psychosis, 227

Lab, sleep, 131–32
La belle indifference, 442
Lack of resources, frustration and, 407
Language:
  body, 177–78
  as building blocks of thought, 250–53
  chimpanzees' use of, 253
  development of, 323–26
  experience and, 252–53

memory development and, 323
perception and, 113
Large-group awareness training, 477–79
Late adulthood, 355
Latency period, 385
Law, mental illness and the, 459–60
Leadership, 518–19
Learned helplessness, 159, 210, 449
Learned motives, 160–66
  achievement, 162–63
  affiliation, 165–66
  aggression, 160–62
  avoidance of success, 163–64
  power, 164–65
Learning, 185–216
  acquiring personality traits, 380–82
  aggression, 160–62, 211–13
  classical conditioning, 186–95, 206–8
  cognitive, 208–13
  contemporary views of, 206–13
  curves, 190
  defined, 185–86
  dreams and, 137
  hunger and, 153
  observational, 211
  operant conditioning, 195–208, 213–15
  sex differences in, 60
  theory, social, 210–13
  vicarious, 211
  visual, 317–18
Leipzig, University of, 2
Lens, 71, 72
Levelers, 112
Libido, 384
Lie detector, 180–81
Life, change of, 356
Life instincts, 382–83
Light:
  adaptation, 76
  color vision and, 79
  intensity, vision and, 74–75
Liking, determinants of, 501–4. See also Attraction
Limbic system, 46, 47
Linear perspective, 114, 144
Linguistic relativity hypothesis, 251–53
Lithium, 484
Lobotomy, 492
Location of memory, 241–42
Location of sounds, 117–18

Locus of control, 397–99, 413
Loneliness, frustration and, 407
Longitudinal method, 15, 308
Long sleepers, 134
Long-term memory (LTM), 233–37
  organization of, 235
  coding in, 234–35
  storage and retrieval in, 235–37
Loom-zoom procedure, 320
Losses, frustration and, 407
Loudness, 87, 89, See also Hearing
Love, conditional, 389. See also Emotions
"Lowball procedure," 512
LTM. See Long-term memory
Lysergic acid diethylamide (LSD), 34, 142

McGill University, 123
Maladaptive avoidance, 413
Malnutrition, effect of, 292, 309
Mania, 447, 484
Manipulation as stimulus motivation, 158–59
Mantra, 126–27
Marijuana, 140, 227
Marriage, 359–61
Masking of tinnitus, 100
Mass media:
  attitude development and, 506
  sex role socialization by, 339
Master's degree, 21, 22
Maturation, 313. See also Adolescence; Adulthood; Development
Mbuti pygmies of Zaire, 113
Mean, 530
Meaninglessness, frustration and, 407
Means-end analysis, 261
Measurement, 528–39
  of central tendency, 529–34
  of correlation, 537–39
  for prediction, 539–40
  scales of, 528–29
  of variation, 535–37
Mechanisms, defense, 414–18
Media. See Mass media
Median, 530
Medical decision making, 268–69
Medical model of abnormal behavior, 436

Shame and doubt versus autonomy, 387
Shape constancy, 110–11
Shaping, 197
Sharpeners, 112
Shock therapies, 481–82
Short sleepers, 134
Short-term memory, 224–33
  capacity of, 224–25
  coding in, 225–26
  elaborative rehearsal, 231–33, 235
  retention and retrieval in, 226–29
  rote rehearsal, 229–31
Shriek, The (Munch), 438
Siblings, socialization by, 335
Sickness, motion, 91, 92
Significance, 540
Sign language, 253
Similarity:
  of attitudes, 524
  attraction and, 503
  principle of, 109
Situationist perspective, trait theory vs., 381
Sixteen Personality Factor Questionnaire (16PF), 393–94
Size constancy, 110
Skewed distributions, 533–34
Skin, tactile sensations of, 96–97
Skinner box, 196–97
Skin response, galvanic, 180
Sleep, 130–38
  lab, 131–32
  need for, 138
  stages of, 132–33, 134, 138
Smell, sense of, 92–93, 321–22
Smoking, counseling sources for, 489
"Snowball effect," 515
Social class:
  IQ tests and, 291, 293
  stress coping and, 413
Social cognition, 339–40
Social competence, 275
Social development, 331–40
  in adolescence, 352–54
  in adulthood, 359–65
  in childhood, 333–37
  in infancy, 331–33
  sex typing and sex roles, 337–39, 359, 379
Social influence, 510–15
  compliance, 511–12
  conformity, 510–11
  deindividuation, 515

helping behavior, 513–14
obedience, 16–71, 512–13
Socialization, 333–37
  by school, 335–37, 339
  sex roles and, 338–39
  social cognition and, 340
Social learning theory, 210-13
Social motives, 160, 162–66
Social psychology, 495-527
  attitudes, 504–9
    behavior and, 504, 505–6
    change in, 506–9
    toward death, 366
    development of, 506
    nature of, 504–5
    toward retirement, 364–65
    similarity of, 524
  environmental psychology, 519–22
  focus of, 10
  group processes, 515–19
  prejudice and discrimination, 505, 522–24
  social influence, 510–15
  social perception, 495–504
    attraction and liking, 501–4
    attribution, 499–501
    impression formation, 495–99
Social Readjustment Rating Scale (SRRS), 405
Sociologist's viewpoint, 11–12
Sociopaths, 454
Solution strategies, 264–65
Solutions, producing and evaluating, 259–62. *See also* Problem solving
Somatic nervous system, 48
Somatization disorder, 441
Somatoform disorders, 441–43
SOMPA, 287, 298
"Son of Sam," 459–60
Sound. *See also* Hearing
  localization, 117–18
  waves, 85–87
Space, personal, 519–21
Specialization, hemispheric, 42–45, 263
Specialization of receptor cells, 68
Species differences in color vision, 79
Speed-reading, 75, 225–26
Spinal cord, 46–47, 97, 99
Split-half reliability, 283
Split personality, 457
Spontaneous recovery, 191–92, 204–6
Spouse, death of, 362

SQ3R method, 340–41
SRRS, 405
Stable-unstable personality dimensions, 377, 394
Stage theory of cognitive development, 327–30
Stagnation stage, generativity versus, 387
Standard deviation, 536–37
Standards. *See also* Norms
  APA, 22
  of normality, intrapersonal, 433–34
  social learning theory and, 213
Stanford-Binet Intelligence Scale, 279–80, 283–85, 288
Statistics, 528, 539–40. *See also* Measurement
Status, 413, 517
Stem, brain, 37
Stereochemical theory of odors, 93
Stereoscopic vision, 116
Stereo sound, 117–18
Stereotypes, 498–99
  defined, 498
  sex role, 338–39
Stimulation:
  of brain, electrical, 44
  intelligence and, 292–93
  sensory deprivation of, 123–25
Stimulus:
  conditioned vs. unconditioned, 187–89, 190
  generalization, 192–94, 203
interstimulus interval, 189
  motives, 150, 157–59
  sensory thresholds and, 68–71
  sexual, 155–56
Stirrup, 87, 88
STM. *See* Short-term memory
Stockholm syndrome, 427–28
Storage. *See* Memory
Strain studies, 57
Stress, 404–24
  adjustment to, 404–24
    from anxiety, 409–10
    from conflict, 407–9
    defensive coping, 414–18
    direct coping, 411–14
    from frustration, 406–7
    individual differences and, 410–11
    from pressure, 406
    social class and, 413

Threshold:
for neural impulse, 30
sensory, 68–71
theory of intelligence and
creativity, 300
Thyroid gland, 50–51
Thyroxin, 50
Timbre, 87
Tinnitus, 100
TM, 126–27
Tolerance, substance, 455–56
Tomography:
computerized axial, 40, 41
positron emission, 41, 448
Tongue, sense of taste and, 94–95
Top-down processing, 251
Torrance Test of Creative Thinking,
300
Training:
avoidance, 202–3, 205
awareness, 477–79
Trait(s):
acquiring personality, 380–82
defined, 375
genetics and, 53–61
mental, 53
theories, 375–82
Tranquilizers, 482, 484. *See also*
Drug(s)
Transactional view of leadership,
518–19
Transcendental meditation (TM),
126–27
Transference, positive vs. negative,
468
Transplants, brain, 61–62
Transvestism, 450
Trauma, childhood, 331
Treatment. *See also* Therapies
alternative forms of mental
health, 487
physical, 481–84
Trial, competence to stand,
459–60
Trichromatic theory, 82–85
Trichromats, 82
Tricyclics, 484
Trust versus mistrust stage, 387
Twin studies:

genetics and, 58, 379–80
of IQ, 289–90
Type A and B people, 420
Typing, sex, 337–39

Unanimity, conformity and,
510–11
Unconditional positive regard,
390, 470
Unconditioned response, 187–89
Unconditioned stimulus, 187–89,
190
Unconscious, the, 382
Unconscious motives, 166
Undifferentiated schizophrenia,
458
Unemployment as source of
extreme stress, 442
Utricle, 90

Validity of intelligence tests,
284–85
Valium, 483
Values, influence on perceptions
of, 112. *See also* Moral
development; Norms
Variable-interval schedule, 199,
200
Variable-ratio schedule, 200, 201
Variables, 14
Variation, measures of, 535–37
Verbal ability, 44, 275
Verbal communication, 175
Verbal intelligence, 357
Vestibular sacs, 90
Vestibular senses, 90–92
Vicarious learning, 211
Vietnam War, posttraumatic stress,
disorder from, 424
Vineland Social Maturity Scale, 296
Violence, 160, 340–41. *See also*
Aggression
Vision, 71–85. *See also* Perception
binocular, 317
color, 78, 79–85
eye and, 69, 71–79, 116–17
motion sensations and, 92

stereoscopic, 116
Visual acuity, 75–76, 318–19
Visual cliff, 319–20
Visual coding, 226
Visual illusions, 106, 120–23
Visual learning, 317–18
Visual registers, 220–21
Volley principle, 90
Voyeurism, 450

WAIS-R, 280, 283–85
Walking ability, 316
Wallach and Kogan Creative Battery,
300
Washoe (chimp), 253
Waves:
brain, 38, 128, 444
sound, 85–87
Wechsler Adult Intelligence Scale-
Revised (WAIS-R), 280,
283–85
Well-adjusted person, 425–27. *See
also* Stress
Widows, widowers, 362
Wish fulfillment, 383
"Witch" trial, 435
Withdrawal:
as direct coping, 412–14
symptoms, 456, 483
Women, avoidance of success by,
163–64. *See also* Gender
Work, 159, 362–65. *See also*
Occupation
Working backward, 261
Working memory. *See* Short-term
memory
Working through conflict, 468

Yerkes-Dodson law, 169
Yoga, 126
Young adulthood, 355
Youth employment, 353. *See also*
Adolescence

Zen, 126
Zener cards, 120
Zoophilia, 450

Photograph by Andrew Sachs

About the Author

Charles (Tony) Morris is presently Associate Chairman of the Department of Psychology at the University of Michigan, Ann Arbor. He received his B.A. degree *cum laude* from Yale University in 1962 and his Ph.D. from the University of Illinois in 1965. His early research was in the area of group processes, leadership, and group effectiveness. More recently he has focussed on the study of personality, particularly shyness and social anxiety.

He is an award-winning teacher and counselor whose popular introductory psychology course enrolls more than 1,000 students a year. He is also a Fellow of the American Psychological Association. His interests, however, extend far beyond psychology. He is a composer and songwriter, rosarian, amateur astronomer, ham radio operator, airplane pilot, licensed ship captain, and the author of a monthly column in a popular microcomputer magazine.